INTERNATIONAL FINANCE
A Casebook

Mihir A. Desai

Harvard University
and
National Bureau of Economic Research

John Wiley & Sons, Inc.

ASSOCIATE PUBLISHER	Judy Joseph
ASSISTANT EDITOR	Brian Kamins
SENIOR PRODUCTION EDITOR	Lisa Wojcik
DESIGNER	Kevin Murphy
COVER PHOTO	©Comstock/Getty Images

This book was set in Quark by Matrix Publishing Services and printed and bound by Hamilton Printing. The cover was printed by Phoenix Color Corp.

This book is printed on acid free paper. ∞

ISBN-13   978-0-471-73768-1
ISBN-10   0-471-73768-2

Printed in the United States of America

10 9 8 7 6 5 4 3 2 1

Dedication

To Arvind and Sumi Desai

Acknowledgements

Anyone who has taught or participated in a case discussion knows that the case method pedagogy embodies a collaborative ethic. Teaching by the case method without motivated, thoughtful participants is a painful experience for all involved. Writing case studies similarly relies on a large body of enthusiastic and insightful collaborators. This experience would have been impossible if it weren't for the many remarkable people who have invested in me and the cases in it. Most directly, my collaborators in writing the cases that comprise this book deserve special recognition and they are noted at the beginning of each case. First and foremost, Mark Veblen contributed unstintingly as a partner in writing many of these cases and his influence is widespread in the book beyond the cases that he co-wrote with me. This book would not have been possible without his enthusiasm and hard work. Kathleen Luchs co-wrote a number of cases and has ushered many others through to completion. Her sunny disposition, prodigious effort and patience ensured that many of the cases in this book came to fruition. Finally, case protagonists, students and academics around the world have made this effort possible by volunteering their time for the case studies and by providing feedback on the cases themselves.

More indirect support came from my co-authors on other projects, particularly Fritz Foley and Jim Hines, who were more patient with me than I had a right to expect. Fritz and Jim have also influenced this book through innumerable discussions on many of the topics covered here. The generosity of Harvard Business School deserves special note. I learned what I know about case-writing from teaching groups led by Rick Ruback and Carl Kester. My department chairs during the creation of this case material—André Perold, Peter Tufano and Stu Gilson—and my director of research—Paul Gompers—were very generous in their support as were my finance area colleagues and Dean Kim Clark. John Owen has supported me in innumerable ways that go beyond the traditional job description. I also benefited from the international research offices of the school as many individuals, particularly Gustavo Herrero, were extremely helpful in drawing together the varied resources needed to complete a book like this. The team at John Wiley—Judith Joseph, Brian Kamins and Lisa Wojcik—provided just the right combination of gentle prods, helpful feedback and enthusiasm to drive this project from conception to completion.

By far, my largest debts are to my family. My parents, Arvind and Sumi Desai, have set an enduring example of hard work, kindness and humility to which I will always aspire. Deepa, Sumit and Avni have steadfastly provided a refuge and their enthusiasm and zest for life are guiding lights. Finally, Teena entered my life as this book came together. Her boundless affection, understanding and wise counsel at every turn are my inspiration.

About the Author

Mihir A. Desai is the Rock Center Associate Professor of Finance and Entrepreneurial Management and the MBA Class of 1961 Fellow at Harvard Business School (HBS) where he has taught since 1998. He is also a Faculty Research Fellow in the National Bureau of Economic Research's Public Economics and Corporate Finance Programs. His research on international finance and public economics has been published in leading academic journals such as the *Quarterly Journal of Economics*, the *Journal of Finance*, the *Journal of Financial Economics* and the *Journal of Public Economics* and has been cited widely in the business press. A fuller discussion of his research and publications can be found at www.people.hbs.edu/mdesai.

The cases in this book were developed for Professor Desai's second-year elective, entitled "International Financial Management," that he has taught at HBS since 2004. In addition, Professor Desai co-teaches Public Economics at Harvard College, is the Faculty Chair of the executive program on Cross-Border Financial Decision Making and has participated in numerous executive education programs at HBS. He received the Student Association Award for teaching excellence from the HBS Class of 2001.

Professor Desai received his Ph.D. in political economy from Harvard University; his MBA as a Baker Scholar from HBS; and a bachelors degree in history and economics from Brown University. In 1994, he was a Fulbright Scholar to India. His professional experiences include working at CS First Boston and advising a number of firms and governmental organizations.

Table of Contents

Introduction

Much of the finance that is taught in textbooks and classrooms implicitly assumes that borders do not exist. Yet, most real-world financial decision makers struggle with the realities of cross-border transactions. Managers are forced to consider the effects of different exchange rates, tax rules, country risk factors, and legal regimes as they undertake the basic financing and investment decisions of corporate finance in a cross-border setting. These cross-border factors are increasingly important as a growing share of corporate profits arise from international investments and transactions, as financing across borders becomes cheaper, as mergers increasingly take place across borders, and as differing legal and tax rules coexist and often clash. The cases in this book provide the foundations for learning how finance works in this richer, cross-border setting.

The cases in this book provide managers with a detailed and analytic look at major decisions undertaken by firms. This firm-centric emphasis sets this book apart from leading textbooks on international finance that emphasize macroeconomics and government influence on global markets. Here, the focus is on the issues that managers confront in an international setting: How do I value a firm with assets in multiple places around the world? What is the appropriate way to think about the cost of capital for the worldwide operations of a single firm? How should I hedge exposures arising from international operations? How should I finance my worldwide operations? How should I evaluate managers that are operating in very different economic and financial settings?

Many of the cases challenge managers to work through analytic exercises. The aim is to provide managers with the skills and insights they need to address the critical issues and questions in international finance—skills that cannot be acquired if these issues are only considered in abstract, theoretical terms. Nearly all of the cases are based on actual companies, real managers, and genuine issues they have faced. Much of the analysis is based on nonpublic data that allows readers to look inside different companies and consider how other firms and managers approach the challenges created by multinational operations and cross-border transactions. These cases constitute the bulk of the second-year elective in international finance at Harvard Business School.

STRUCTURE OF THE BOOK

The book is organized into four major parts. The parts have been sequenced so that more complexities are layered on with each module. Part 1, Exchange Rates, Markets, and Firms, focuses on what managers need to know about global markets in currencies and assets, and how changes in exchange rates impact firms. Part 2, Multinational Finance, provides cases that consider the many complex financial decisions that arise when firms have operations and investments outside a home country. Part 3, Cross-Border

Financing, features cases that emphasize the opportunities created by global financial markets and the financing mechanisms firms use to exploit these opportunities. Finally, the cases in Part 4, Institutions and Finance, examine the interactions among firms and legal and regulatory regimes and how institutional environments influence firm financial decisions.

The case studies included here are set in many different countries and across a variety of industries. Geographic settings for the cases include China, Singapore, South America, Eastern Europe, the European Union, and the United States. Both highly developed and emerging markets are featured, as well as international institutions and global markets. The cases are described in more detail below to provide readers with an overview of the book's range of issues, companies, and settings.

PART 1   EXCHANGE RATES, MARKETS, AND FIRMS

Module 1.1. Exchange Rates and Global Markets

The first cases in the book provide the foundation for understanding international finance. They cover the intricacies of the foreign exchange market, the basics of exchange rates, the interactions between currencies and global stock markets, and the benefits of international diversification.

Chapter 1. Foreign Exchange Markets and Transactions
This note describes the foreign exchange market and introduces different types of foreign exchange instruments. Examples are employed throughout to reinforce understanding. A brief problem set is included to provide practice in exchange rate calculations.

Chapter 2. Exchange Rate Policy at the Monetary Authority of Singapore
Focusing on the decisions of Singapore's central banker, this case demonstrates how monetary and exchange rate policy are formulated and implemented. The case provides a framework for understanding the economic determinants of exchange rates, real exchange rates, and exchange rate regime choice.

Chapter 3. Innocents Abroad: Currencies and International Stock Returns
This case explores the value of international diversification in asset allocation by examining interactions between currency movements and international stock returns. This case forces readers to calculate currency effects and create efficient portfolios based on raw data.

The cases in this module, particularly the first and third, are distinctive from those in the remainder of the book. These cases emphasize specific exercises and provide the reader with the foundations necessary to tackle the subsequent cases with their richer managerial settings.

Module 1.2. Exchange Rates and Firms

The cases in Module 1.2 explore how firms are affected by changes in foreign exchange rates and the strategies and tools managers use to manage exchange rate fluctuations.

Chapter 4. Hedging Currency Risks at AIFS
A company that sends students abroad must decide whether to hedge a euro-dollar exposure created by lags between the setting of prices and the incurring of

costs. The case provides an introduction to the basics of hedging, including why there is a demand for hedging and the instruments used in hedging.

Chapter 5. Foreign Exchange Hedging Strategies at General Motors: Transactional and Translational Exposures

In the context of two hedging strategy decisions at GM, this case reviews GM's foreign exchange management policy and introduces hedging practices and techniques in a complex multinational setting. The nature and consequences of transactional and translational exposures are worked through in detail.

Chapter 6. Foreign Exchange Hedging Strategies at General Motors: Competitive Exposures

The case examines how competitive exposures arise, how they differ from other types of currency exposures, and how they can be quantified in the context of GM's competitive exposure to the Japanese yen.

By emphasizing firm responses to exchange rate uncertainty, these cases highlight the motivations for risk management, the difficulties in implementing these strategies, and the many additional complexities introduced by accounting and managerial concerns in multinational firms.

PART 2 MULTINATIONAL FINANCE

Although managing a firm's exchange rate exposure is important to firms in global markets, numerous other challenges face financial managers in multinational firms. Specifically, managers must decide how to finance their operations around the world, how to allocate capital efficiently across subsidiaries, how to adapt cost of capital calculations and valuation to different environments, and how to evaluate managers consistently across worldwide operations. The cases in this section provide managers with practical insights into some of the key financial decisions multinational firms have to make *inside* their firm.

Module 2.1. Financing Decisions within the Firm

The cases in this module focus on the kinds of internal financial decisions and issues that commonly confront managers in multinational firms: how subsidiaries should be financed, how different tax regimes influence financial decisions, and how firms can measure and compare the performance of businesses and managers in different countries.

Chapter 7. The Refinancing of Shanghai General Motors

This case considers how a rapidly maturing subsidiary should refinance itself with particular attention to the ownership structure of a joint venture, the currency characteristics of its debt, the switch from project finance to multinational finance, the conflicts between parent and subsidiary concerns, and how the legal environment can constrain financial choices.

Chapter 8. Corporate Inversions: Stanley Works and the Lure of Tax Havens

The case examines the costs and benefits of a strategic reincorporation intended to avoid the U.S. worldwide income tax system. In the process, the case provides a primer on the incentives and complications of international taxation. This case also emphasizes the potential changes in shareholder value resulting from a corporate expatriation and the corporate tax avoidance strategies that firms use in global capital markets.

Chapter 9. The Continuing Transformation of Asahi Glass: Implementing EVA

Asahi Glass, the sixth largest corporation in Japan, was hit hard by the banking crisis in Japan in the 1990s and subsequently underwent a major restructuring in order to regain its economic strength. This case follows Asahi Glass's response to these economic pressures, focusing on the implementation of corporate governance standards and economic value added (EVA) calculations in a multinational setting. In the process, readers gain insights into how the main-bank relationships in Japan influenced firms and the opportunities and pitfalls in adapting EVA to a global setting.

Module 2.2. Valuing Cross-Border Investments

The cases in Module 2.2 focus on cross-border investments and valuation, with particular emphasis on how firms value foreign acquisitions or capital investment projects abroad. Basic finance courses and texts typically provide managers with the basics of valuation, but managers need to understand how to use valuation techniques in a cross-border setting. How can a manager value a business with operations in different countries and currencies? How should a firm value investments in countries that are politically or economically unstable? The cases provide managers with guidance on these issues.

Chapter 10. Valuing a Cross-Border LBO: Bidding on the Yell Group

This case addresses how a bidder should value a firm with operations in two different countries—the United States and the United Kingdom. The relative stability of the countries involved allows readers to focus on the basics of cross-border valuation where cash flows in different currencies need to be valued jointly. In addition to the valuation issues, methods of financing are also discussed and incorporated into the valuation of a leveraged buyout (LBO), and readers can gain insight into the fee structure of LBOs.

Chapter 11. Globalizing the Cost of Capital and Capital Budgeting at AES

AES, a U.S.-based power company, is forced to reevaluate its static capital budgeting procedures, especially in emerging markets. This case looks at the method for globalizing the cost of capital and the appropriateness of AES's model, and in doing so, provides a rich setting for thinking about cross-border valuation when country risk is involved. Readers can work through the cost of capital for 15 projects worldwide using the model developed by AES and assess its usefulness.

Chapter 12. Dow Chemical's Bid for the Privatization of PBB in Argentina

The privatization of a major petrochemical producer (PBB) in Argentina provided an opportunity for Dow Chemical to become the largest plastics producer in Latin America. Acquiring PBB would allow Dow to become an integrated producer of plastic goods, but Dow first had to decide how to value a newly privatized company in a volatile economy. Readers can work through a detailed valuation of three distinct projects with varying exchange rate exposures. In the process, readers can explore how country risk can be incorporated into cash flows rather than discount rates.

These cases show how the basics of valuation—projections of expected cash flow and discount rates—can be adapted to incorporate basic currency effects (the Yell LBO), country risk generally (AES), and specific, large devaluation risks (Dow).

Cross-Border Financing • xv

PART 3 CROSS-BORDER FINANCING

In each of the cases in Part 3, managers attempt to tailor financing decisions to the opportunities created by global financial markets. The cases examine how firms raise capital across borders, how firms decide where to list their shares, how political issues can influence these decisions, and how cross-border settings create arbitrage opportunities.

Chapter 13. Drilling South: Petrobras Evaluates Pecom

Petrobras is a partially state-owned entity that is trying to remove itself from the purview of the state by acquiring Pecom, an Argentine oil company severely affected by a national financial crisis. Petrobras must consider the governance implications of a cross-border listing, the effects of a currency crisis on a company, and the uncertainties inherent in valuing a distressed foreign company. The case also illustrates how a company's choice of currency for its financing can have a significant impact on its performance.

Chapter 14. Nestlé and Alcon—The Value of a Listing

Executives at Nestlé, a Swiss company, have to consider the effect of taking their successful Texas-based eye-care company, Alcon, public. This case chronicles the decisions faced by managers, primarily the effect of the listing on both Nestlé and Alcon's valuations and also the choice of potential stock exchanges on which to list Alcon. The varied motivations for cross-listing are discussed.

Chapter 15. Cross-Border Listings and Depositary Receipts

This note explains the intricacies and motivations for how companies can access investors outside their home countries including cross-listings, global listings, and depositary receipts. The note also provides a discussion of managerial motivations for such cross-lisitings and the academic research on the economic consequences of cross-listings.

Chapter 16. Tax-Motivated Film Financing at Rexford Studios

Many U.S. film studios seek financing abroad to take advantage of particularly favorable tax rules, and this case on Rexford Studios examines how overlapping tax jurisdictions create opportunities for tax arbitrage. The case illustrates the financing possibilities that arise in such situations, discusses their valuation, and requires readers to analyze a sale-leaseback transaction to understand the value of the opportunity.

Chapter 17. The Strategy and Sources of Motion Picture Finance

This note examines how the financing patterns of an entire industry have been shaped by tax strategies, opportunities for tax arbitrage, and the global financial markets.

The three cases of this section are most usefully paired with the two notes of this section. Rexford is best analyzed in conjunction with the note on motion picture finance. Similarly, Nestlé/Alcon and Petrobras/Pecom are usefully read in conjunction with the note on cross-border listings for more context.

PART 4 INSTITUTIONS AND FINANCE

A highly globalized world has increased the likelihood that firms and investors will find themselves operating in settings where basic rights (such as shareholder protections) and regulations (such as reporting requirements) are not what they are used to in the well-developed markets of the United States and Europe. These institutional differences challenge managers to rethink many standard financial practices. In addition, many legal issues span borders, forcing managers to consider how to navigate foreign and multilateral legal bodies.

Module 4.1. Finance in Weak Institutional Environments

If returns to investments can be secured less reliably, how should investors alter their decisions and managerial actions? When insiders steal money, what recourse do investors have? This section considers how finance changes when the institutional environment is less secure.

Chapter 18. Growing Up in China: The Financing of BabyCare Ltd.

BabyCare has developed a unique model to deal with the challenges of doing business in China but has found receiving third-round expansion capital a significant challenge. This case examines the specific strengths and weaknesses of BabyCare's unique business model for dealing with the difficulties of operating in an emerging market. Readers must work through a valuation of BabyCare, its financing needs, and the merits of a specific investment opportunity. The case provides insight into how entrepreneurial finance and venture capital practices adapt in emerging market settings.

Chapters 19–23. Czech Mate (A–E)

This case series details the expropriation of an investor and the mechanisms by which that investor recouped his investment. Ron Lauder has invested in a recently privatized Czech television station but does not realize that a key executive is in the process of expropriating the full value of his investment. The case provides an opportunity to examine the causes and consequences of expropriation, the contracting problems that can impact foreign investors, and the remedies available to foreign investors through bilateral investment treaties.

Module 4.2. Regulatory Regimes

The final section of this casebook deals with the multilateral regulatory regimes that influence finance. The cases demonstrate that the decisions faced by multilateral institutions are just as complex as those faced by the firms and countries which they interact with.

Chapter 24. Antitrust Regulations in a Global Setting: The EU Investigation of the GE–Honeywell Merger

In the final year of Jack Welch's tenure, General Electric clashed with the European Union (EU) Commission over a potential merger with Honeywell, an avionics manufacturer. Although the United States found no difficulties with the merger, the EU argued that the combination of GE and Honeywell would create a dominant firm in the aerospace industry that would impede business competition. The dispute between the EU and GE–Honeywell raises questions about how industries and competition should be defined for antitrust purposes, highlights differences between European and U.S. antitrust authorities, and provides a perspective on the antitrust issues raised by cross-border mergers.

Chapter 25. Redesigning Sovereign Debt Restructuring Mechanisms
Anne Krueger of the International Monetary Fund (IMF) must consider if the world needs a new method for resolving sovereign defaults. Historically, creditors have handled sovereign debt crises in an ad hoc manner. A potential solution is an international statutory debt-restructuring regime that is administered by a multi-lateral agency. This case examines three major debt crises and looks at the historical policies of the institutions involved and the possibilities for reform.

A READER'S ROADMAP

Although the case studies are the centerpiece of this volume, readers are also provided with several additional resources to make the most of the cases. Each section in the book starts with a brief introduction, followed by a detailed overview of the case studies and suggestions for additional reading.

Each case overview describes the setting of the case and the major issues that the case addresses. For each case, there is also a series of questions to help readers focus on the key issues and learning points. For many of the cases, the questions include a specific analytic exercise. Financial decisions almost always require analysis, and readers who sharpen their pencils and do the numbers will gain valuable practical experience in financial decision making in cross-border settings. Such analysis is the foundation for a broader understanding of the issues involved and should allow for a deeper evaluation of the more managerial considerations that the cases also emphasize.[1]

Finally, additional readings are also referenced at the end of section introductions. These readings are typically academic papers or overviews of major subjects that frame the issues of the case in a broader setting. Though not required to get through the cases, these readings are invaluable for those readers seeking deeper understanding of the major issues. More generally, two sites are particularly relevant for readers seeking more information on the topics discussed in this book. First, www.nber.org. provides access to leading economic research on a wide variety of topics. In addition, www.ssrn.com provides a broader array of legal, accounting, and managerial papers that may be helpful. Both websites feature helpful search engines.

[1]Executable spreadsheets with the exhibits are available through a website maintained by the publisher at www.wiley.com/college/desai.

PART 1

EXCHANGE RATES, MARKETS, AND FIRMS

The last half-century has brought about tremendous growth in international capital and product flows. In the process, the market for foreign exchange, colloquially known as the "Forex" or "FX" market, has grown into the world's largest financial market. With a daily trading volume of $1.9 *trillion,* it is more than four times the size of the market for U.S. Treasuries and more than thirty times the size of combined NASDAQ and NYSE markets.[1] The notional amount of outstanding currency derivatives market was nearly $27 trillion as of March 2005.[2] Aside from the magnitude of the overall market for currency instruments, the operations of firms create significant exposures to shifting exchange rates, forcing managers to understand the dynamics of exchange rates and how exchange rate movements impact their firms.

This section of the book aims to provide managers with the vocabulary and the macroeconomic framework they need to understand the foreign exchange market and to operate effectively in a multicurrency environment. The cases in the first module of this section, Exchange Rates and Global Markets, focus on how exchange rates work and how they are determined, and on the interactions between currencies and global markets. The cases in the second module, Exchange Rates and Firms, explore how exchange rates impact firms and how managers can design hedging strategies to manage the risks that arise from unexpected changes in exchange rates.

---

[1]For a summary of the survey see http://www.forex.com/04-10.07.html. The BIS survey noted an increase in average daily forex turnover to $1.9 trillion in April 2004. The complete survey is available at http://www.bis.org.

[2]http://www.bis.org/publ/qtrpdf/r_qa0503.pdf#page=99.

EXCHANGE RATES AND GLOBAL MARKETS

Currencies can be extremely confusing. Quoting conventions differ from country to country, and an entirely distinct vocabulary needs to be developed to ensure understanding of currencies. When an American watches the dollar/euro exchange rate go up (that is, more dollars per euro), that actually means the dollar is "going down" (that is, depreciating relative to the euro). This chapter builds the foundations that are needed to understand how exchange rates work and provides the tools needed to work through the cases in this book.

The module opens with Foreign Exchange Markets and Transactions, a note accompanied by a problem set that methodically builds the concepts needed to tackle the following cases in this book. This note describes the foreign exchange market and introduces different types of foreign exchange instruments. Examples are employed throughout to reinforce understanding. It is worthwhile to work through this note carefully because readers need to understand the foreign exchange market, as well as foreign exchange transactions and instruments, before tackling subsequent cases in this book. Although readers expert in exchange rates may want to skip this note, many students who felt similarly have found the note invaluable.

The second case, Exchange Rate Policy at the Monetary Authority of Singapore, is set in a central bank and examines how monetary and exchange rate policy are formulated and implemented. It provides a framework for understanding the economic determinants of exchange rates and explores exchange rate regime choice.

The third case in this chapter, Innocents Abroad: Currencies and International Stock Returns, emphasizes a second theoretical element necessary for understanding international finance: the implications of currency movements for global investment opportunities. The case examines the interactions between currency movements and international stock returns, and explores the value of international diversification. Readers are challenged to calculate stock returns, currency effects, and efficient portfolios.

This chapter covers an ambitious amount of material. The cases require time and effort in order to ensure that readers are comfortable with exchange rates and the associated economic issues. These first cases, problems, and exercises are aimed at providing readers with the essential tools they need to get the most out of the following cases in this book.

OVERVIEW OF THE CASES

Foreign Exchange Markets and Transactions

This note addresses the basic building-block questions most managers have about exchange rates. The purpose is to provide managers with an understanding of the mechanics of exchange rates, an introduction to the various instruments involved, and a grasp of the determinants of exchange rate movements. The note is very hands-on. It demonstrates the mechanical calculations and uses real-world data in the form one actually finds it—straight out of the back section of the *Wall Street Journal*. The note begins with exchange rates and measurement conventions and then covers actual transactions in the "spot" and "forward" markets. The section on derivative contracts includes a discussion of futures, swaps, and options. In short, the note is quite comprehensive and, as a result, requires some time to get through if the concepts are not already extremely familiar.

This note includes no assignment questions but instead presents a problem set. Working through the problem set will help readers become familiar and comfortable with the "vocabulary" of foreign exchange and currency transactions. Although it is tempting to skip over this part of the material, this understanding of currencies is fundamental to several cases that follow in the book.

Exchange Rate Policy at the Monetary Authority of Singapore

Dr. Khor, assistant managing director, Monetary Authority of Singapore (MAS), and his team of monetary policy experts weigh the merits of different exchange rate regimes. As a small economy in the world market, and in the wake of the Asian financial crisis, the team of economists looks carefully at the monetary policy reforms adopted by its Southeast Asian neighbors. They also observe the decline in foreign direct investment in Southeast Asia as a consequence of China's growing appetite for investment capital. The fundamental strengths of Singapore's economy have given the MAS time to consider its decision carefully, but now Dr. Khor and his team must finalize their recommendations for monetary policy over the next decade.

This case provides readers with a broader appreciation of how a major player in FX markets—a central bank—thinks about influencing exchange rates. After reading the case, consider the following questions:

- What are the advantages and disadvantages of a fixed versus floating exchange rate system?
- What is a real exchange rate?
- What do you think determines exchange rates in the short term (less than six months), medium term (six months to several years), and long term?
- How do exchange rates interact with trade balances, inflation rates, and fiscal policies?
- How do exchange rates impact firms?

Innocents Abroad: Currencies and International Stock Returns

Sandra Meyer, founder of the investment firm CapGlobal Advisors, LLC, has to present the case for international diversification to a skeptical client who is responsible for a state pension fund. Foreign equities have underperformed U.S. equities for some time, and the client wonders whether the pension fund is losing out on potential returns by investing in international stock markets that are underperforming the U.S. market. Meyer plans to use data on international stock returns and currency movements to convince her client that international diversification does add value to the pension fund's equity portfolio and to demonstrate how currency movements influence international stock returns.

This case allows readers to explore international investing by working with raw data. The only way to make sure one understands this material thoroughly is to "get messy with the numbers," using 23 years of data on stock market returns and exchange rates to complete specific analyses. The exercises allow readers to compare returns of different national stock markets; measure the impact of currency fluctuations on returns to U.S. investors; and construct globally diversified portfolios. In reading the case, readers should consider how they would use the data to develop a presentation for a client who is skeptical about the value of international diversification. The components of the presentation are clearly delineated at the end of the case.

ADDITIONAL READING

ADLER, MICHAEL, and DUMAS, BERNARD. 1983. "International Portfolio Choice and Corporation Finance: A Synthesis." *Journal of Finance,* 38: 925–985.

Bank for International Settlements, *Triennial Central Bank Survey of Foreign Exchange and Derivatives Market Activity*, Bank for International Settlement. Available at http://www.bis.org

BORDO, MICHAEL D. 2003. "Exchange Rate Regime Choice in Historical Perspective." NBER Working Paper No. 9645.

CROSS, SAM Y. 1998. *The Foreign Exchange Market in the United States*. Federal Reserve Bank of New York, 1998. Available at http://www.ny.frb.org/education/addpub/usfxm/forward.pdf

DESAI, MIHIR A., and C. FRITZ FOLEY. 2004. "The Comovement of Returns and Investment Within the Multinational Firm." NBER Working Paper No. 10785.

FRANKEL, JEFFREY A. 1997. "Recent Exchange Rate Experience, The Tobin Tax, and Other Proposals for Reform." Federal Reserve Bank of Dallas, September 14–15, 1995. Published in Part I, *Exchange Rates, Capital Flows and Monetary Policy in a Changing World Economy*, edited by W. Gruben, D. Gould and C. Zarazaga. Boston: Kluwer Academic Publishers.

STULZ, RENE. "International Portfolio Choice and Asset Pricing: An Integrative Survey." Chapter 6 of R. A. Jarrow, V. Maksimovic, W. T. Ziemba (eds.), *Handbooks in Operations Research and Management Science,* Volume 9: Finance. Amsterdam: Elsevier Science Publishers 1995.

1

Foreign Exchange Markets and Transactions

Among the 193 countries in the world, there are over 164 different types of currencies with which individuals, companies, and governments conduct trade and financial transactions. Globalization and economic expansion create a need for a mechanism to convert one currency into another. Without such a mechanism, it would be difficult for individuals to travel and spend money in other countries, for companies to purchase and import foreign goods, or for investors to participate in developing economies around the world. For example, vacationing in Thailand requires Thai bahts, importing German BMWs for resale in the U.S. requires euros, and investing in Mexican government bonds requires Mexican pesos. International trade requires individuals, companies, and institutions to negotiate and transact using foreign currencies.

The first section of this note, "The Foreign Exchange Market," provides an overview of the foreign exchange market and a brief outline of its development. The second section, "What is an Exchange Rate?" provides a definition of exchange rates and describes the different ways in which exchange rates are quoted and calculated. This section explains how to convert one currency into another currency, how to calculate cross-exchange rates, and the meaning of bid/ask quotes on the foreign exchange market. Readers who are already familiar with these foreign exchange calculations may skip this section. The third section, "Exchange Rate Movements," focuses on changes in exchange rates: what does it mean for a currency to appreciate or depreciate, how are these changes measured, and what do changes in exchange rates mean? The final section of the note, "Foreign Exchange Transactions," describes the different types of foreign exchange instruments, including spot transactions, forwards, swaps, futures, and options. The examples in this last section illustrate how different foreign exchange instruments work and how they are valued. Throughout the note, there are examples and formulas to assist the reader. Each section also includes references to exercises in the Appendix. These exer-

Professor Mihir A. Desai and Research Associates Christina B. Pham, Kathleen Luchs, and Yanjun Wang prepared this case.

cises test and reinforce the understanding of the various foreign exchange calculations and transactions covered in this note.

FOREIGN EXCHANGE MARKET

One currency is exchanged for another currency on the foreign exchange market. Until the 1970s, the foreign exchange market was small and specialized. The market changed fundamentally when the post-war Bretton Woods system broke down. Under the Bretton Woods system, the U.S. dollar was convertible to gold and other currencies were convertible to U.S. dollars at fixed exchange rates. In 1971, the U.S. suspended the convertibility of the dollar to gold, and by 1973 the U.S. and other nations had accepted floating exchange rates. The change to floating exchange rates, the growth in international trade, and the increase in capital flows around the world led to the rapid growth of the foreign exchange market. Today, it is the largest market in the world with $1.2 trillion average daily turnover in 2001. The U.S. dollar is involved in a majority of all transactions in the foreign exchange market, and in 2001 the most traded currency pair was the U.S. dollar/euro, accounting for 30% of average daily turnover.[1]

The market is an elaborate network of trading desks, banks, corporations, and individuals who buy and sell currencies all over the world. The largest trading center is the United Kingdom with 31% of foreign exchange turnover in 2001. The U.S. has a 16% share of foreign exchange trading, and Japan has a 9% share.[2] Australia, Hong Kong, Singapore, Switzerland, and Germany are also large centers for foreign exchange trading, and there are numerous smaller centers in other countries. These centers are highly integrated globally, 24 hours a day, with real-time price information gathered from numerous sources and distributed globally by firms such as Reuters and Moneyline Telerate.[3] Most trading is over-the-counter (OTC) and transactions include spot transactions, outright forwards and swaps. Other foreign exchange products—currency futures and currency options—are traded on organized exchanges. The major participants in the foreign exchange market are commercial and investment banks.

The foreign exchange market continues to evolve. The introduction of the euro eliminated the need for exchange among several European currencies and contributed to a 14% decline in foreign exchange market turnover between 1998 and 2001. Worldwide consolidation in the financial sector has also affected market turnover, because of less interbank trading. The number of banks participating in the foreign exchange market declined from 2,417 to 1,945 between 1995 and 2001, and there is a trend towards fewer banks with larger market shares in the foreign exchange market.[4] Another significant change has been the introduction of electronic brokering systems. Such systems account for an increasing share of turnover, especially in the spot market, and there are initiatives to expand such systems into other market segments.[5]

[1]Bank for International Settlements, *Triennial Central Bank Survey: Foreign Exchange and Derivatives Market Activity in 2001*, March 2002, pp. 3, 11 available at http://www.bis.org/publ/rpfx02.htm.

[2]Ibid., p. 12.

[3]For Reuters, see http://about.reuters.com/productinfo/data_treasury/; for Moneyline Telerate see http://www.moneyline.com/about/about_home.jsp.

[4]Bank for International Settlements, *Triennial Central Bank Survey: Foreign Exchange and Derivatives Market Activity in 2001*, March 2002, pp. 9-10 available at http://www.bis.org/publ/rpfx02.htm.

[5]Sam Y. Cross, *The Foreign Exchange Market in the United States*, Federal Reserve Bank of New York, 1998, pp. 121-2 available at http://www.ny.frb.org/education/addpub/usfxm/; also see European Central Bank, *Review of the Foreign Exchange Market Structure*, March 2003 available at http://www.ecb.int/pub/pdf/fxmarketstructure200303en.pdf.

WHAT IS AN EXCHANGE RATE?

This section of the note provides a definition of exchange rates and explains how exchange rates are quoted and calculated. Included in this section are examples of different kinds of exchange rate calculations using direct and indirect quotes, cross-exchange rates, and bid/ask quotes.

An exchange rate is the rate at which one currency can be exchanged for another. These rates are available from many print and electronic sources. *The Wall Street Journal,* for example, posts the exchange rates of the 48 most commonly traded currencies in its "Money & Investing" section every day. Table 1 is a snapshot of the listings for Tuesday April 15, 2003. Tuesday's listings use rates as quoted at 1 PM Eastern Time the previous Monday (as written in the small print at the top of the table). Most exchange rate tables list the latest quotes (in this case, Monday's quotes) as well as the quotes of the previous business day (in this case, Friday's quotes).

TABLE 1 Exchange Rates as Listed in *The Wall Street Journal*

Exchange Rates

The foreign exchange mid-range rates below apply to trading among banks in amounts of $1 million and more, as quoted at 1 p.m. Eastern time by Reuters and other sources. Retail transactions provide fewer units of foreign currency per dollar.

Country	U.S. $ Equivalent		Currency per U.S. $	
	Mon	Fri	Mon	Fri
Australia (Dollar)	0.6049	0.6052	1.6532	1.6523
Brazil (Real)	0.3164	0.3123	3.1606	3.2020
Chile (Peso)	0.001387	0.001387	720.98	720.98
Denmark (Krone)	0.1451	0.1448	6.8918	6.9061
Russia (Ruble)	0.03205	0.03197	31.201	31.279
Thailand (Baht)	0.02331	0.02326	42.9	42.992

Source: The Wall Street Journal, Tuesday April 15, 2003, p. C14.

Understanding Exchange Rates

An exchange rate is the price of a currency. Just as a product in a store has a price, a unit of currency has a price. For example, a book in a British airport can cost 12.75 British pounds or 20 U.S. dollars. Likewise, a euro can cost either £ 0.68 or $1.07.

£	12.75	£	0.68
$	20.00	$	1.07

Focusing on the U.S. dollar price for the book and the euro, there are two ways to look at a transaction—from the customer perspective and from the store perspective. In the case of the book, from the customer perspective, the customer gets a book in exchange for 20 dollars.

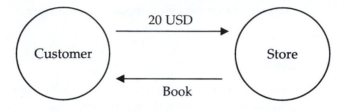

We can write this relationship in terms of an "exchange rate":

$$\frac{1 \text{ book}}{20 \text{ USD}} = \frac{1}{20} \text{ book/USD} = 0.05 \text{ book/USD}$$

This ratio says that the customer gets . . .

one book per 20 U.S. dollars

OR, put another way,

one-twentieth of a book per 1 U.S. dollar

From the store perspective, it gets 20 U.S. dollars per book, or:

$$\frac{20 \text{ USD}}{1 \text{ book}} = \frac{20}{1} \text{ USD/book} = 20 \text{ USD/book}$$

This ratio says that the store gets 20 U.S. dollars per one book.

Note that the exchange rates above—1/20 (or 0.05) book/USD and 20/1 (or 20) USD/book—are simply inverse ratios of one another.

In the case of the euro, from the customer perspective, the customer gets one euro in exchange for 1.07 U.S. dollars.

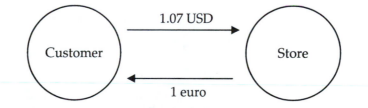

The "exchange rate" then, is:

$$\frac{1 \text{ euro}}{1.07 \text{ USD}} = \frac{1}{1.07} \text{ euros/USD} = 0.93 \text{ euros/USD}$$

This ratio, 0.93 euros/USD, says that the customer gets . . .

1 euro per 1.07 U.S. dollars

OR, put another way,

0.93 euros per 1 U.S. dollar

The inverse of that ratio gives the store perspective:

$$\frac{1.07 \text{ USD}}{1 \text{ euro}} = 1.07 \text{ USD/euro}$$

This ratio says that the store gets 1.07 U.S. dollars per 1 euro.

No matter which form the exchange rate takes—the ratio or inverse ratio—the relationship between the currencies is the same. Getting 1.07 U.S. dollars per 1 euro is the same as getting 1 U.S. dollar per 0.93 euro.

Calculating Exchange Rates

Exchange rates that are listed in the form of "U.S. $ Equivalent" are called direct quotes, and give the price of a unit of foreign currency in U.S. dollars, or how many U.S. dollars it costs to buy a unit of the foreign currency. Rates listed in the form of "Currency per U.S. $" are called indirect quotes, and give the price of one U.S. dollar in the foreign currency, or the number of units of foreign currency required to buy one U.S. dollar. Table 1 above lists both direct and indirect quotes.

EXAMPLE 1

CHANGING AN INDIRECT QUOTE INTO A DIRECT QUOTE

In Table 1, the indirect quote (Currency per U.S. $) on Monday for the Danish krone is 6.8918.

The rate, 6.8918, means that a trader on the foreign exchange market would get 6.8918 krone per 1 USD:

$$\frac{6.8918 \text{ krone}}{1 \text{ USD}}$$

To turn this into a direct quote, take the inverse of the ratio:

$$\frac{1 \text{ USD}}{6.8918 \text{ krone}} = \frac{1}{6.8919} \text{ USD/krone:} \quad 0.1451 \text{ USD/krone}$$

The answer, 0.1451 USD/krone, means that a trader on the foreign exchange market would get 0.1451 U.S. dollar per Danish krone. This rate is shown in Table 1 as the "U.S. $ Equivalent" for the krone, on Monday.

EXAMPLE 2

CALCULATING TRANSACTION AMOUNTS BASED ON EXCHANGE RATES

General Motors has a project in Brazil and needs to buy materials from Brazilian suppliers. The company will need 1,000,000 Brazilian reals to buy its materials. How many U.S. dollars does General Motors need in order to purchase the reals?

Using Table 1, the Monday indirect quote for Brazilian reals is 3.1606, meaning one USD will buy 3.1606 reals. To buy 1,000,000 reals, the company needs $316,395.62:

$$\frac{USD}{3.1606\ Reals} \times 1,000,000\ Reals = 316,395.62\ USD$$

The same calculation can be done using the direct quote for Brazilian reals. In Table 1, the direct quote is 0.3164, meaning one real costs 0.3164 USD. To buy 1,000,000 reals, the company will need:

$$\frac{0.3164\ USD}{Real} \times 1,000,000\ Reals = 316,400.00\ USD$$

(The two answers differ only because of a rounding error. If you use the indirect quote to calculate the direct quote (1/3.1606) the direct quote for the real is .316395, rounded to .3164 in Table 1.)

This example shows that no matter which quote is used - direct or indirect - the results are the same. Calculations simply need to be set up so that the correct units eliminate.

See Exercise 1 in the Appendix to calculate other direct and indirect exchange rates.

Cross Exchange Rates

Most quotations in exchange rate tables—like those provided in Table 1—are expressed in terms of the U.S. dollar. However, certain occasions require exchange rates expressed in terms of two non-U.S. dollar currencies. These rates are called **cross exchange rates**. For example, if a Japanese company and a Chinese company anticipate a business transaction, they would be interested in the yen-yuan renminbi exchange rate rather than either the yen-U.S. dollar or the yuan renminbi-U.S. dollar rate. Below is an example of a cross rates table provided in *The Wall Street Journal*.

TABLE 2 Key Currency Cross Rates (Late New York Trading Monday, April 14, 2003)

	Dollar	Euro	Pound	SFranc	Peso	Yen	CdnDlr
Canada	1.4537	1.5661	2.2873	1.0462	0.13659	0. 01208	. . .
Japan	120.38	129.69	189.41	86.638	11.311	. . .	82.810
Mexico	10.6428	11.4655	16.745	7.6596	. . .	0.08841	7.3212
Switzerland	1.3895	1.4969	2.1862	. . .	0.13055	0.01154	0.9558
U.K.	0.63560	0.6847	. . .	0.4574	0.05972	0.00528	0.43721
Euro	0.92820	. . .	1.4605	0.66806	0.08722	0.00771	0.63854
U.S.	. . .	1.0773	1.5734	0.71970	0.09396	0.00831	0.68790

Source: The Wall Street Journal, Tuesday April 15, 2003, p. C14.

In reading a cross rates table, each row represents the exchange rate from the perspective of the country in the far left column. For example, reading the top row for Canada from left to right: there are 1.4537 Canadian dollars per U.S. dollar, 1.5661 Canadian dollars per euro, 2.2873 Canadian dollars per British pound, and so on across the line.

In the absence of a published cross rate for a pair of currencies, cross exchange rates can be determined using USD-referenced exchange rates.

Exercises 2 and 3 in the Appendix provide practice in calculating cross exchange rates.

EXAMPLE 3

DETERMINING CROSS EXCHANGE RATES[6]

A Mexican traveler wants to go hiking in the Nepalese Himalayas and would like to change his pesos (MXN) for Nepalese rupees (NPR). Given the USD-MXN exchange rate (0.09760 USD = 1 MXN) and the USD-NPR exchange rate (0.01358 USD = 1 NPR), find the MXN-NPR cross rate.

With the rates available, set up the problem so that the USD terms cancel, giving the required rate of MXN/NPR:

$$\frac{1 \text{ MXN}}{0.09760 \text{ USD}} \times \frac{0.01358 \text{ USD}}{1 \text{ NPR}} = \frac{0.01358}{0.09760} \text{ MXN/NPR} \qquad 0.1391 \text{ MXN/NPR}$$

Once the MXN/NPR rate has been calculated, the inverse ratio (1/0.1391) provides the NPR/MXN exchange rate.

FORMULA 1

As a general rule, to find the cross rate of two USD-referenced exchange rates, set up the problem so that the correct terms cancel.

Given . . .

  X USD/Currency A and . . .

  Y USD/Currency B

Calculate the cross rate with the formula below:

$$\frac{Y \text{ USD/Currency B}}{X \text{ USD/Currency A}} = \text{Cross Rate in terms of Currency A/Currency B}$$

This formula can also be set up as a multiplication problem, like the one used above in Example 3:

$$\frac{\text{Currency A}}{X \text{ USD}} \times \frac{Y \text{ USD}}{\text{Currency B}} = \frac{Y}{X} \text{ Currency A/Currency B}$$

NOTE: These two formulas are different forms of the same equation.

Bid/Ask Spread

When banks or brokers facilitate currency transactions such as the ones discussed above, they charge a fee for their services. In many cases part of this fee comes from the difference

---

[6]The international currency codes (e.g., MXN) used here and in other examples are available at www.oanda.com.

between the bank's bid and ask quotes, called the **bid/ask spread**. A bid quote is a bank's "buy" price and an ask quote is a bank's "sell" price. The difference between the quotes—the bid/ask spread—constitutes the bank's brokerage fee or profit on the transaction.

Bank currency quotes are usually given in pairs, with the first rate being the bid quote and the second rate the ask quote. For example, the euro is quoted at $1.23–31, which means that the bid price is $1.23 per euro and the ask price is $1.31 per euro. Differences in bid and ask prices are inherent in all currency transactions when dealing with financial intermediaries, but, for simplicity's sake, they are ignored in most of the examples used in this note. Example 4 illustrates how the bid/ask spread affects foreign exchange transactions.

EXAMPLE 4

BID/ASK SPREADS AND THE COST OF CURRENCY CONVERSIONS

You plan to take a business trip to Europe and want to convert $1,000 to euros. The U.S. bank quote for the euro is $1.23–31, meaning the bank will buy euros at $1.23 and sell euros at $1.31. The bank sells you $1000 worth of euros at its sell price of $1.31 and you receive € 763.36:

$$\text{US } \$1,000 \times \frac{€}{\text{US } \$1.31} = € \; 763.36$$

On your trip, you complete all of your business in the U.K. and therefore use none of your euros. When you return to the U.S., you want to change your euros back to dollars. You note that the bank's quote for euros is unchanged at $1.23–31. The bank buys your euros at its bid price of $1.23, and for your euros you receive $938.93:

$$€ \; 763.36 \times \frac{\text{US } \$1.23}{€} = \text{US } \$938.93$$

Due to the bank's bid/ask spread, you have paid $61.07 for the two currency conversions, or 6.11% of the total amount ($61.07/$1000 = 6.11%).

FORMULA 2

CALCULATING BID/ASK SPREADS

To calculate the percentage spread use the following formula:

$$\frac{\text{Ask rate } - \text{ Bid rate}}{\text{Ask rate}} = \text{\% Bid/Ask Spread}$$

Using the numbers from Example 4 above, the spread of the euro is:

$$\frac{\text{US\$1.31 } - \text{ US\$1.23}}{\text{US\$1.31}} = 6.11\%$$

Exercise 4 in the Appendix provides practice in calculating bid/ask spreads.

EXCHANGE RATE MOVEMENTS

Prices of currencies can fluctuate just as prices of goods can fluctuate. This section examines currency appreciations and depreciations, how currency fluctuations are measured, and the meaning of changes in exchange rates.

Currency Appreciation and Depreciation

When a currency increases in value relative to other currencies, it is said to "appreciate;" when a currency decreases in value, it is said to "depreciate." The concept of currency appreciation and depreciation can be demonstrated with the book example used earlier. Assume that the value of the book has appreciated due to increased customer demand. We can look at this relationship again from the store perspective and from the customer perspective.

Store Perspective

Because the value of the book increased, the store can demand more of the customer's dollars per book sold. Instead of getting 20 USD per book, the store can now get 30 USD per book. If the store is using the book as currency to gain U.S. dollars, the book's "purchasing power" has increased because one book can "purchase" 10 more U.S. dollars than before.

                    Purchasing power of book
                                                    increases

USD 20.00   USD 30.00

Customer Perspective

Because the value of the book has appreciated, the customer gets less of a book per dollar spent. One dollar used to buy the customer 1/20th of a book (20 USD bought the whole book). Now, one dollar will only buy 1/30th of the book (now it takes 30 USD to buy the whole book). In essence, the purchasing power of the customer's money has decreased.

                    Purchasing power of USD
                                                    decreases

USD 1.00   USD 1.00

The increase in the value of the book means that the store gains more purchasing power while the customer's dollar loses purchasing power. If the value of the book depreciates, the inverse scenario occurs. The book's purchasing power lessens, lowering the price of the book, and the customer's purchasing power in U.S. dollars increases.

In the same way, the purchasing power of one currency relative to another currency can appreciate or depreciate. For example, if the British pound appreciates relative to the U.S. dollar, then the pound can buy more U.S. dollars and a U.S. dollar can buy fewer British pounds.

EXAMPLE 5

DETERMINING WHETHER A CURRENCY HAS APPRECIATED OR DEPRECIATED

Examine the euro-U.S. dollar exchange rate on two different dates:

Date	Exchange Rate
April 20, 2003	0.92109 EUR/USD
April 24, 2003	0.90570 EUR/USD

According to these rates, on April 20th, 100 U.S. dollars could buy 92.11 euros . . .

$$\frac{0.92109 \text{ EUR}}{\text{USD}} \times 100 \text{ USD} = 92.11 \text{ EUR}$$

. . . while on April 24th, 100 U.S. dollars could only buy 90.57 euros, 1.54 fewer euros than before.

Since the U.S. dollar buys less on April 24th, its purchasing power has decreased and the dollar is said to have depreciated. Because the euro now has more value relative to the U.S. dollar, the euro is said to have appreciated.

FORMULA 3

To determine whether a currency has appreciated or depreciated, follow these simple rules.

Given that . . .

Previous Exchange Rate: X Currency A/Currency B and . . .
Current Exchange Rate: Y Currency A/Currency B . . .

If $X > Y$ ($X - Y > 0$), Currency A has appreciated and Currency B has depreciated, relative to one another.

If $X < Y$ ($X - Y < 0$), Currency A has depreciated and Currency B has appreciated relative to one another.

Exercise 5 in the Appendix requires you to determine if currencies have appreciated or depreciated.

Measuring Fluctuations

Exchange rate fluctuations are often presented in percentage terms, relative to some reference currency. For example, the Mexican peso could depreciate 25% relative to the U.S. dollar or the euro could appreciate 10% relative to the British pound. Calculating these fluctuations correctly can be confusing, so it is important to set up the problem correctly.

EXAMPLE 6

CALCULATING THE PERCENTAGE FLUCTUATION OF AN EXCHANGE RATE

Consider the movement of the Mexican peso (MXN) - U.S. dollar (USD) exchange rate from 10 to 20:

Previous Exchange Rate	Current Exchange Rate
$\dfrac{10 \text{ MXN}}{1 \text{ USD}}$ —	$\dfrac{20 \text{ MXN}}{1 \text{ USD}}$

To calculate its percentage fluctuation, follow the steps below.

Step 1: Convert exchange rates into a standard form of:

$$\frac{\text{Benchmark Currency}}{\text{Fluctuating Currency}}$$

We are interested in the fluctuation of the Mexican peso, so we rearrange the exchange rates in terms of benchmark currency/fluctuating currency. The benchmark currency is the U.S. dollar and the fluctuating currency is the Mexican peso.

Previous Exchange Rate	$\rightarrow$	Current Exchange Rate
$\dfrac{1 \text{ USD}}{10 \text{ MXN}}$	$\rightarrow$	$\dfrac{1 \text{ USD}}{20 \text{ MXN}}$
0.10 USD/MXN	$\rightarrow$	0.05 USD/MXN

Step 2: Determine if the fluctuating currency has appreciated or depreciated, and by how much. In this case, the USD has appreciated (.10 > .05), and the MXN has depreciated by .05.

Step 3: Calculate the change as a percentage of the original exchange rate.

$$\frac{\text{Amount change}}{\text{Original exchange rate}} \times 100 = \% \text{ change}$$

$$\frac{0.05}{0.10} \times 100 = 50\% \text{ depreciation}$$

These calculations indicate that the Mexican peso depreciated 50% against the U.S. dollar. To measure the percentage appreciation of the U.S. dollar:

$$\frac{\text{Amount change}}{\text{Original exchange rate}} \times 100 = \% \text{ change}$$

$$\frac{10}{10} \times 100 = 100\% \text{ appreciation}$$

The U.S. dollar has appreciated 100% against the Mexican peso.

Exercises 6 and 7 in the Appendix provide practice in measuring currency fluctuations.

Why Exchange Rates Change

The determinants of exchange rates are complex, and a full discussion of this topic is beyond the scope of this note.[7] It is useful, nonetheless, to consider briefly why currencies appreciate and depreciate, and why currencies are sometimes described as overvalued or undervalued.

Purchasing Power Parity

A well-known (and controversial) theory about why exchange rates change is the theory of Purchasing Power Parity (PPP), which is derived from the law of one price. According to this theory, goods that are freely traded should cost the same everywhere, measured in the same currency. The exchange rates between currencies, therefore, should be such that the currencies have equivalent purchasing power. According to the theory of PPP, exchange rates change, over the long term, because the purchasing power of one currency increases (or decreases) relative to another currency.

Economists use complex 'baskets' of goods to assess how exchange rates reflect purchasing power parity across countries, but simpler approaches can also provide insights into exchange rates and currency fluctuations. *The Economist*, for example, compares the price of a McDonald's Big Mac hamburger in the U.S. and in various other countries in an annual survey.[8] In 2003, the average price of a Big Mac in the U.S. was $2.71 while in Denmark the burger cost the equivalent of $4.10 at the then-current exchange rate. According to the theory of PPP, the difference in the purchasing power of the dollar and the krone will, over time, result in changes in the exchange rate between the two currencies. In this case, the krone would be expected to depreciate against the dollar until its purchasing power was equivalent to that of the dollar.

EXAMPLE 7

THE ECONOMIST BIG MAC INDEX

	Big Mac Prices		Implied PPP of the dollar	Actual dollar exchange rates April 22, 2003	Under(−)/over(+) valuation against the dollar %
	In local currency	In dollars			
United States	$2.71	2.71			
China	Yuan 9.90	1.20	3.65	8.28	−56
Denmark	Krone 27.75	4.10	10.20	6.78	+51
Japan	Yen 262	2.19	96.7	120	−19

Source: "McCurrencies," *The Economist*, April 24, 2003, p. 80.

Taking Japan as an example, the table is read as follows: In the U.S., a Big Mac costs $2.71. The price of a Big Mac in Japan is ¥262. In dollars, the cost is $2.19, using the actual dollar exchange rate of 120 yen/dollar (262/120 = $2.19).

Since a Big Mac in Japan has a price of ¥262, the implied PPP of the dollar is 96.7 yen (262/2.71 = 96.7). The implied PPP is the exchange rate that would give the Big Mac the equivalent price in both currencies.

Comparing the implied PPP exchange rate and the actual exchange rate for the yen to the dollar suggests that the yen is undervalued by 19% relative to the dollar, calculated from the actual exchange rate and the implied PPP exchange rate (120-96.7/120).

---

[7]Textbooks on international finance and international economics address the question of the determinants of exchange rates; a recommended reference is Paul R. Krugman and Maurice Obstfeld, *International Economics: Theory and Policy*, 5th ed. (Reading, Mass.: Addison-Wesley, 2000).

[8]"McCurrencies," *The Economist*, April 24, 2003, p. 80.

In Exercise 8 in the Appendix you can use the Big Mac index to calculate exchange rates based on purchasing power parity and to evaluate the strength or weakness of the U.S. dollar relative to other currencies.

Interest Parity

Another theory on exchange rate movements is the theory of Interest Parity. This theory states that the foreign exchange market is in equilibrium when the expected rates of return on deposits of any two currencies measured in the same currency are equal. The argument is that if deposits in one currency offered higher expected returns than those in another, there would be excess demand for the former and excess supply of the latter, since investors would all demand deposits that give better returns. Expected exchange rate movements, therefore, can be inferred by differences in interest rates. Interest Parity implies that potential holders of foreign currency deposits should be indifferent between any two currencies as far as expected returns are concerned.

FOREIGN EXCHANGE TRANSACTIONS

Learning how to read, calculate and convert exchange rates will help in understanding the foreign exchange market and its transactions. Five main groups of transactions are covered in this note: spot transactions, forwards, swaps, futures, and options. Forwards, swaps, futures, and options belong to the class of financial instruments called **derivatives**. Derivatives are contracts that derive their value from some underlying asset—in this case, the asset is currency. They are used to manage foreign exchange risk or take speculative positions on currency movements. This section of the note explains the different types of foreign exchange transactions and how companies use financial instruments to hedge their currency exposures.

Spot Transactions

The daily exchange rates quoted in *The Wall Street Journal* and other news sources are called **spot rates**—market rates that hold for transactions that take place on the "spot." Foreign exchange transactions based on these rates are called **spot transactions**. For example, if you were to go to a foreign exchange window and convert U.S. dollars into British pounds, the exchange rate the teller would use is the spot rate, and the conversion would be called a spot transaction.

Forwards

Spot transactions are useful and commonly employed in the foreign exchange market, but there are times when organizations or individuals want to make trades, not today, but some time in the future. These types of transactions are called forward transactions, and the rate used is called the **forward rate**. The forward rate is greater or less than the spot rate, depending on whether the currency is expected to appreciate or depreciate. If the currency is expected to appreciate in the future, the forward rate is priced higher than the spot rate, and the rate is said to contain a **premium**. If the currency is expected to depreciate in the future, the forward rate is priced lower than the spot rate, and the rate is said to contain a **discount**. A premium or discount simply denotes the direction of the forward rate in relation to the spot rate.

The Wall Street Journal posts the forward rates of commonly traded currencies in its daily 'Exchange Rates' table. Below are the rates published on Tuesday April 15, 2003, recorded at close of business Monday April 14, 2003.

TABLE 3   Exchange Rates (with Forward Rates) as Listed in
The Wall Street Journal

Exchange Rates

The foreign exchange mid-range rates below apply to trading among banks in amounts of $1 million and more, as quoted at 1 p.m. Eastern time by Reuters and other sources. Retail transactions provide fewer units of foreign currency per dollar.

Country	U.S. $ Equivalent		Currency per U.S. $	
	Mon	Fri	Mon	Fri
Canada (Dollar)	0.6879	0.6879	1.4537	1.4537
1-month forward	0.6868	0.6869	1.4560	1.4558
3-months forward	0.6844	0.6845	1.4611	1.4609
6-months forward	0.6803	0.6804	1.4699	1.4697
Switzerland (franc)	0.7197	0.7179	1.3895	1.3930
1-month forward	0.7203	0.7183	1.3883	1.3922
3-months forward	0.7215	0.7192	1.3860	1.3904
6-months forward	0.7232	0.7213	1.3827	1.3864
U.K. (Pound)	1.5734	1.5715	0.6356	0.6363
1-month forward	1.5703	1.5783	0.6368	0.6376
3-months forward	1.5644	1.5624	0.6392	0.6400
6-months forward	1.5555	1.5536	0.6429	0.6437

Source: The Wall Street Journal, Tuesday April 15, 2003, p. C14.

Forward transactions are based on the buying and selling of **forward contracts**. A forward contract is an agreement between a buyer and seller to trade a particular currency on some date in the future for a fixed price, regardless of the currency's spot rate on the future date. The contracts are usually made for one, three, or six months into the future. Forward contracts are negotiated between two parties—usually a company and a bank—and are customized for the maturity date and transaction amount. Therefore, it is possible to create what are called "perfect hedges" with forwards. Perfect hedges are when companies or individuals completely eliminate their exposure in the market for the transaction amount and time frame they need.

EXAMPLE 8

A U.S. auto importer buys 4 Rolls Royces from a manufacturer in England at £ 250,000 per car. The U.S. firm puts in the order, but does not have to pay the British manufacturer until it receives the cars in 3 months. Upon receiving the cars, the U.S. importer will have to pay the British manufacturer £1,000,000 (4 × £ 250,000).

When dealing with such large sums of money, even the slightest movement in the exchange rate means that a company's obligations may fluctuate by thousands of dollars. If the company decides not to enter into a forward contract, it is "exposed" to the market and susceptible to exchange rate movement. A forward contract eliminates the company's exposure to exchange rate movements over the next three months because the company knows the exact rate at which it will exchange currencies. The U.S. importer decides to enter into a forward contract to lock in a rate for its currency transaction. Below is an outline of the importer's transaction:

EXAMPLE 8 (CONTINUED)

1. On April 15, 2003 the importer calls bank and requests a forward contract for:

- £ 1,000,000
- Settlement date: July 15, 2003 (three months later)
- At forward rate: 1.5644 USD/£ (see Table 3 above). The forward rate is lower than the spot rate (forward discount) because the pound is expected to depreciate

2. On July 15, 2003 the U.S. importer receives the car shipment in its warehouse

- Importer settles the contract with bank, using the agreed-upon rate of 1.5644 USD/£, regardless of the spot rate. Importer pays the bank $1,564,400 in return for £ 1,000,000.

$$\frac{\$1.5644}{£} \times £\,1,000,000 = \$1,564,400$$

- Importer pays British manufacturer in pounds

See Exercise 9 in the Appendix to calculate the cost of a forward contract.

Swaps

To hedge against the risk of exchange rate fluctuations, a company may use a forward contract, as described above, or it may set up a **swap**—essentially a series of forwards under one contract that hedges long-term, sustained foreign exchange exposure. For example, a U.S. firm that anticipates receiving annual payments in krona from a subsidiary in Sweden might enter a swap agreement with a Swedish firm that receives regular fees in U.S. dollars for work done in the U.S. Swaps are arranged by brokers and banks. There are many types of swap arrangements with different payment schedules and contract structures, but the basic idea is that a swap enables two parties who have complementary foreign exchange exposure/obligations to pair up and trade their currencies privately. Like forwards, swap contracts are customized for the needs of the signing parties, with a predetermined rate of exchange and a contract maturity date. Swaps and forwards differ in that a swap contract typically covers multiple future transactions and can have anywhere between five and ten years until maturity, whereas a forward contract is drawn for one transaction and usually has a shorter maturity.

Futures

Futures contracts are contracts that specify a *standard* volume of a currency to be exchanged on a settlement date some time in the future. Futures contracts are similar to forward contracts, except that forward contracts are customized between buyers and sellers who are genuinely interested in conducting the currency transactions, whereas futures contracts are standardized for trading on markets like the Chicago Mercantile Exchange. The following table shows currency futures prices published in *The Wall Street Journal* on Tuesday April 15, 2003. Current futures prices also appear online at http://www.prophetfinance.com/tradequest/futuresquotes.asp.

A typical futures contract will specify basic elements such as type of currency, amount of currency included in one contract, futures rate, and settlement date. As much as possible, these elements are standardized to facilitate fast trading on the exchange floor and a futures contract will specify a standardized volume of the currency being sold. For example, Table 4 notes that each Canadian dollar futures contract contains

100,000 CAD ("CAD 100,000"), each Swiss franc contract contains 125,000 CHF ("CHF 125,000") and each British pound contract contains 62,500 GBP ("£ 62,500"). Because futures can only be bought in these increments and cannot be tailored to specific transaction amounts, they are often used as a vehicle for currency speculation rather than as a hedging tool since it can be difficult to structure a "perfect hedge" with futures.

TABLE 4   Currency Futures Table

						LIFETIME		OPEN
	OPEN	HIGH	LOW	SETTLE	CHG	HIGH	LOW	INT
Canadian Dollar (CME)-CAD 100,000; $ per CAD								
June	.6857	.6866	.6828	.6854	—	.6876	.6197	88,699
Sept	.6816	.6827	.6797	.6816	—	.6840	.6185	3,602
Est vol 4,251; vol Fri 13,063; open int 95,922, −668.								
Swiss Franc (CME)-CHF 125,000; $ per CHF								
June	.7182	.7239	.7170	.7213	.0020	.7577	.5940	36,712
Sept	—	—	—	.7229	.0020	.7565	.6270	551
Est vol 2,570; vol Fri 12,408; open int 37,292, +1,721.								
British Pound (CME)-£ 62,500; $ per £								
June	1.5636	1.5704	1.5620	1.5672	.0024	1.6416	1.5000	23,138
Sept	1.5600	1.5600	1.5540	1.5572	.0024	1.6256	1.5100	464
Est vol 1,154; vol Fri 6,541; open int 23,671, +49.								

Source: The Wall Street Journal, Tuesday April 15, 2003, p. C12.

EXAMPLE 9

HOW TO READ THE LISTING FOR A FUTURES CONTRACT

The listing for the June Swiss franc contract in Table 4 can be read as:

On Friday, April 11, 2003 (Friday's rates published on Tuesday), a Swiss futures contract with an expiration on the third Wednesday of June 2003, opened at 0.7182 USD/CHF and settled at 0.7213 USD/CHF. The rate hit a high of 0.7239 and a low of 0.7170 for the day, compared to a lifetime high and low of 0.7577 and 0.5940, respectively. There was a 0.0020 USD/CHF increase from Thursday's settle price to Friday's settle price.

In the market for Swiss franc futures, there are approximately 2,570 contracts bought and sold per day, with 12,408 contracts bought and sold on Friday April 11, 2003. In the entire Chicago Mercantile exchange, there are 37,292 Swiss franc futures contracts open. Though there was activity in 12,408 contracts Friday, the net change in number of open contracts was only 1,721 (interest in Swiss franc futures increased by 1,721 contracts).

The notations, "$ per CAD," "$ per CHF," and "$ per £" mean that the rates listed under the "open," "high," "low," and "settle" columns are direct exchange rate quotes—

expressed as U.S. dollar amount per unit of foreign currency. The months in the left-most column represent the expiration month of the contract (futures have standardized settlement dates, which are the third Wednesdays of March, June, September, and December).

Other information about currency futures included in the table are price movements for futures during the day (shown in the "OPEN", "SETTLE", "HIGH", and "LOW" columns) and over the lifetime of the contract. The table also shows the number of open contracts for futures with a particular expiration date in the column headed "OPEN INT" (short for "open interest"). For example, as of Friday April 11, 2003, there were 88,699 Canadian futures contract (expiration third Wednesday of June 2003) open. This number is important to traders because it indicates how popular that particular contract is; the more demand there is for the contract in the market, the greater the open interest. "Est vol," or estimated volume, shows the average number of contracts bought and sold in one day; this value lets a trader know how much activity there is in the market for futures contracts in that particular currency. "vol <day>" gives the actual number of contracts bought and sold during the trading day. The "open int" value following "vol <day>" shows the number of contracts open for that currency in the entire exchange, and the negative or positive value at the end of the line shows the net change in open interest. That value indicates whether interest in futures for that currency is increasing or decreasing.

In comparing Tables 3 and 4, it becomes apparent that the rates of currency futures are similar to those of currency forwards. Like forwards, futures allow traders to lock in the prices at which they can purchase currencies some time in the future. Though futures do not allow perfect hedges, there are still some companies that use them for imperfect hedges because of their smaller sized contracts. While the typical size of a forward contract is in excess of $1 million, the size of a futures contract is usually only around $100,000.

While forward contracts usually end in the actual exchange of currencies, most futures contracts are "closed out"—or sold—before settlement since most traders have no interest in taking delivery of the actual currency. The gain or loss to the holder of a futures contract is determined by the difference between the buy and sell prices of the contract. The change in the price of a contract (with a given future rate and settlement date) depends on two things: 1) movement of the spot rate over time, and 2) changing expectations about the spot rate's value on the settlement date. For example, if the spot rate of a British pound rose over a one-month period, a British pound futures contract would also rise in value by approximately the same amount. In this case, the purchase and subsequent sale of the contract would be profitable. If the spot rate depreciated, the value of the contract would likewise decline, and the sale of the contract would be unprofitable. These price movements in futures contracts account for the gains and losses of the traders on the currency futures market.

Options

Understanding how forwards work helps in understanding how options work. Consider this first scenario: A U.S. construction company puts in a bid to build a 42-hectare software park for the Vietnamese government. If the company gets the bid, it will have to purchase materials and hire workers in Vietnam, which will require approximately 17 billion Vietnamese dong (VND). However, if the company does not get the bid, it will not need to purchase anything in Vietnam, and therefore will not need any Vietnamese currency. Since the dong is a highly volatile currency, the construction company does not want to risk having to pay higher prices on the currency in the future and would like to lock in at a set exchange rate. However, a forward obligates a currency purchase, whereas the company does not want to purchase the money if it does not get the contract. Ideally, the company would be able to lock in at a certain price, and then have the *option* of buying the currency if it wins the bid.

Now consider a second scenario: A French biotech company hires an American company to build its advanced science laboratories in Paris. At the request of the French company, the American company accepts payment in euros. The American company might have the opportunity to use its euros on a different project in the near future and therefore does not want to exchange its euros for dollars immediately. If the company does not use the euros it receives, it wants to insulate itself against the possible depreciation of the euro. Ideally, the American company would be able to lock in at a certain exchange rate, and then have the *option* of selling its euros within a specified period of time.

Both these companies' needs could be fulfilled with the use of currency **options**. Options are contracts that allow their owners to either buy or sell a currency at a designated price within a specific period of time. *The Wall Street Journal* lists currency options daily in the "Marketplace" section of the newspaper under the heading, "Futures Options Prices." Table 5 below is a snapshot of options prices published on Wednesday April 16, 2003 of rates recorded at close of business Tuesday April 15, 2003.

TABLE 5   Currency Options Prices as Listed in *The Wall Street Journal*

FUTURES OPTIONS PRICES

Tuesday, April 15, 2003

Final or settlement prices of selected contracts. Volume and open interest are totals in all contract months.

Currency

STRIKE	CALL-SETTLE			PUTS-SETTLE		

Japanese Yen (CME)

12,500,000 yen; cents per 100 yen

PRICE	MAY	JUN	JLY	MAY	JUN	JLY
8250	1.24	. . .	. . .	0.34	0.66	. . .
8300	0.92	1.26	1.69	0.52	0.86	1.04
8350	0.66	1.02	. . .	0.76	1.12	1.27
8400	0.46	0.81	1.19	1.06	1.41	. . .

Est vol 1,154 Mn 539 calls 1,017 puts
Op int. Mon 32,664 calls 45,759 puts

Euro Fx (CME)

125,000 euros; cents per euro

PRICE	MAY	JUN	JLY	MAY	JUN	JLY
10700	1.48	1.97	2.15	0.58	1.07	1.57
10750	1.17	1.69	. . .	0.77	1.29	. . .
10800	0.92	1.44	1.66	1.02	1.54	. . .
10850	0.70	1.21	. . .	1.30	1.81	. . .

Est vol 3,887 Mn 956 calls 1,420 puts
Op int. Mon 35,924 calls 24,257 puts

Source: The Wall Street Journal, Wednesday April 16, 2003, p. C11.

Definition and Nomenclature

A currency **call** option is a contract that grants its owner the right—not the obligation—to *buy* a specific currency, and a currency **put** option grants its owner the right to *sell*. Both call and put options have designated prices and volumes, as well as defined periods within which the options must be exercised. Exercising an option simply means acting upon your right to buy or sell the currency. An **American option** can be exercised anytime during the contract period. A **European option** can only be exercised on the date the contract expires.

Like futures, options are sold in standard volumes, which are specific to each currency. For example, the table above shows that there are 12,500,000 currency units per one Japanese yen option and 125,000 units per one euro option. Options traded on exchanges can only be purchased in increments of these standard volumes.

In order for the contract owner to exercise his call or put option, the spot rate of the currency must reach a certain threshold, called a **strike** price, before the option expires. For call options, the spot rate has to rise above the strike price, and for put options, the spot rate has to fall below the strike price before the owner can exercise. Table 5 lists four different strike prices for yen option contracts. The strike price of 8250 translates into $.00825 per yen. A call option at this strike price could be exercised if the spot rate for yen is higher than $.00825.

Call options are said to be "in the money" when the current spot rate is above the strike price. When the spot rate equals the strike price, the option is referred to as "at the money." When the spot rate is below the strike price, the call option is said to be "out of the money." For put options, the terms mean just the opposite; a put option is "in the money" when the spot rate is lower than the strike price (see Figure 1).

The fee paid to buy an option is called the premium. Regardless of whether you exercise the option, you still must pay the premium. Listed in Table 5 above, under the 'call-settle' and 'put-settle' columns, are the premiums for different option contracts. For Japanese yen options, the premium is listed as "cents per 100 yen." This means that at a strike price of 0.008250 US$/¥, the buyer must pay $0.0124 (1.24 cents) per 100 yen for a contract that settles in May. Since there are 12,500,000 yen in one option, each option costs $1,550.00.

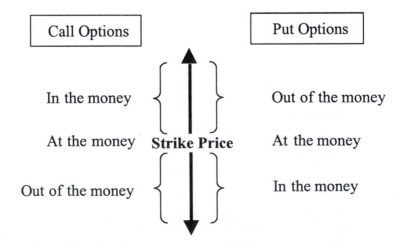

Figure 1 Call and Put Options Classifications

EXAMPLE 10

HOW MUCH IS THE PREMIUM ON A 3-MONTH PUT OPTION FOR EUROS AT A STRIKE PRICE OF $1.07?

From Table 5, the details of a 3-month option purchased in April and settled in July are:

Strike price: 10700, or $1.07

Premium: 1.57 cents/euro

Volume: 125,000 euros/option

Calculation:

$$\frac{1.57 \text{ cents}}{\text{euro}} \times \frac{125,000 \text{ euros}}{1 \text{ option}} \div \frac{\$1.00}{100 \text{ cents}} \quad \$1,962.50/\text{option}$$

The premium on the option contract is $1962.50.

Options premiums are based on many factors but, in general, the more likely it is that the contract owner will exercise the option, the higher the premium. Thus, premiums on call options with a strike price close to the current spot rate are higher than the premiums for call options with strike prices greater than the current spot rate. Options that are already "in the money" (meaning, for call options, that the strike price is lower than the current spot rate) have the highest premiums because they can be exercised immediately. Longer-term option contracts generally have higher premiums than short-term contracts. For example, in Table 5, the premiums for euro options expiring in July are higher than the premiums for euro call options expiring in May at the same strike price; this is because there is more time for the euro to reach the price for the option to be in the money—and therefore worth exercising—with the longer contract.

Corporations that conduct international trade can sometimes use currency options to cover their risk against unfavorable exchange rate movements. Companies with future foreign currency needs and wanting to hedge against exchange rate appreciation would purchase call options; companies holding large amounts of foreign currency and wanting to hedge against depreciation over time would purchase put options.

Evaluating Foreign Exchange Instruments

The availability of different foreign exchange instruments provides firms with choices for hedging their foreign exchange exposure. This section compares the benefits and risks of buying or selling foreign currency at spot rates, forward contracts, and options.

Consider a situation in which a firm anticipates a possible need for foreign currency, but is not yet certain of that need. For example, Thriller Driller Corporation (TDC) of Massachusetts places a bid on an oil drilling contract off the coast of Russia in March of 2003. If it wins the bid, it will need approximately 62,000,000 rubles to purchase Russian materials and services. However, it will not know if the bid is accepted until June of 2003 (3 months after placing the bid). The company considers four different strategies to obtain the rubles it might need, and considers the benefits and risks of each strategy.

1. Purchase rubles at today's spot rate. TDC could purchase rubles at the March 2003 spot rate before it knows the results of the bid. If the company's bid is successful in June and the spot rate goes up, it will have saved money because it bought the currency at a lower rate. If it wins the bid and the spot rate depreciates, TDC will have effectively lost money because it could have bought the currency at a lower rate in June. If TDC does not get the bid and the spot rate appreciates, the company can still sell the rubles at the June spot rate and make a profit. Conversely, if the company's bid fails and the exchange rate depreciates, TDC can either hold the currency and hope that the exchange rate rises, or sell the currency at a loss.

2. Purchase rubles at the June spot rate. The company could wait until it knows the results of the bid and only purchase the currency at the June 2003 spot rate if the bid is successful. If the bid is successful and the spot rate appreciates, the company will have effectively lost money because it now pays more for the currency than it would have had it bought at the March price. However, if the bid is successful and the spot rate depreciates, waiting will have saved the company money. If the bid is not successful, TDC simply does not buy.

3. Purchase a forward contract for rubles. The company could purchase a forward contract and lock in the March 2003 forward rate for purchase of the rubles in June 2003. If TDC's bid is successful, no matter what the movement of the spot rate, the difference was already taken into account in the premium or discount on the forward rate. If TDC's bid is not successful, the company would still be obligated to purchase the rubles at the forward rate. If the spot rate has appreciated by June 2003, TDC can resell the currency on the spot market and make a profit. If the spot rate has depreciated, TDC can either keep the currency or sell it at a loss.

4. Purchase a ruble call option. The company could purchase a call option contract in March 2003 that expires in June. If the company's bid is successful and the spot rate rises above the strike price, the company exercises and buys rubles at a lower rate than the June spot rate. If the bid is successful and the spot rate declines, the company does not exercise the option and simply buys rubles at the lower June spot rate. On the other hand, if the bid is unsuccessful and the spot rate rises above the strike price, the company can still exercise and sell the currency back to the spot market and make a profit. If the bid is unsuccessful and the spot rate declines, the company does nothing and experiences a net loss on the premium it paid for the contract. The call option locks the company into a strike price and caps the company's losses if it does not win the bid. All risk variables are hedged.

Table 6 summarizes the benefits and risks of the different foreign currency instruments for TDC.

TABLE 6   Analysis of TDC Purchase of Russian Rubles

	Bid successful; ruble ↑	Bid successful; ruble ↓	Bid unsuccessful; ruble ↑	Bid unsuccessful; ruble ↓	Unhedged risk
Scenario 1 Purchase rubles in March 2003 at spot rate	Effective gain; rubles bought at lower rate	Effective loss; rubles bought at higher rate	Sell rubles at profit	Sell rubles at loss	Bid result; spot rate movement
Scenario 2 Purchase rubles in June 2003 at spot rate	Effective loss; rubles bought at higher rate	Effective gain; rubles bought at lower rate	N/A	N/A	Spot rate movement
Scenario 3 Purchase forward contract for rubles	N/A	N/A	Settle forward contract; sell rubles at profit	Settle forward contract; sell rubles at loss	Bid result
Scenario 4[a] Purchase call option for rubles	Exercise or sell option and exchange currency on spot market	Lose premium; buy rubles at June spot rate	Exercise; sell rubles at profit	Lose premium	None

[a]Assume for "currency ↑" situations that the spot rate rises above the strike price.

Source: Created by casewriter.

CALCULATING AND USING EXCHANGE RATES

Exercise 1 Fill in the table using the direct and indirect quotes provided.

Currency	U.S.$ Equivalent	Currency per U.S.$	Equivalent of 100 U.S.$
China (Yuan Renminbi)	0.1208		
Japan (Yen)		120.38	
Mexico (Peso)			1064.28
Singapore (Dollar)		1.7803	
Taiwan (Dollar)	0.02878		
Turkey (Lira)			161,290,300
U.K. (Pound)	1.5734		
Venezuela (Bolivar)		1597.44	
Euro	1.0773		

CALCULATING CROSS EXCHANGE RATES

Exercise 2 Use these exchange rates to answer the questions below:

Country	Currency per U.S. $
China—yuan renminbi (CNY)	8.2871
Japan—yen (JPY)	119.040
Argentina—peso (ARS)	2.975
Vietnam—dong (VND)	16041

(a) A Japanese manufacturing firm, Japanohondapokemon, placed a purchase order with Beijing conglomerate, Maydinchina, to procure 10,000 tons of raw materials at a cost of 9,030,200 yuan renminbi. How many yen does the Japanese firm have to exchange in order to pay the bill in yuan renminbi?

(b) A trader at well-known investment banking firm, Silverman Pouches, has an Argentinean client who is interested in investing in emerging markets. The trader suggests the purchase of Vietnamese government-issued bonds, currently selling at 1,604,100 Vietnamese dong (VND) per bond. How many Argentine pesos (ARS) will it cost if the client wants to purchase 250 bonds?

Exercise 3 Fill in the cross rates table below. Derive the missing rates from the rates already provided.

	U.S. Dollar	Vietnam VNDong	Taiwan TDollar	Indonesia Rupiah	Egypt EPound
Egypt	5.97540				......
Indonesia			248.845	......	
Taiwan		0.002344	......		
Vietnam	16,041.0	......			
U.S.	......				

(Continued)

CALCULATING AND USING EXCHANGE RATES

(Hint: The Egypt EPound/U.S. dollar rate is given as 5.9754. The inverse of this—1/5.9754—is the U.S. dollar/EPound exchange rate, which can be inserted in the table. In the same way, use the other exchange rates given to calculate the inverse rates. To complete the table, use currency pairs referenced to the same currency to calculate cross exchange rates according to Formula 1.)

CALCULATING BID/ASK SPREADS

Exercise 4   You are planning a trip to Europe and Japan and want to change U.S. dollars into euros and yen. Your bank provides the following quotes:

	Bid	**Ask**
Euros	$1.194	$1.245
Yen	$.009245	$.00967

What are the bank's bid/ask spreads? How much would you lose if you converted $500 into euros and $500 into yen, and then back into dollars?

CURRENCY APPRECIATIONS AND DEPRECIATIONS

Exercise 5   You are given two different exchange rates per pair of currencies. Determine whether the currency in question appreciated or depreciated. Mark the correct column. NOTE: You are given a mixture of direct and indirect quotes.

Dates	Exchange Rate	Currency to Consider	Appreciated	Depreciated
4/24/2003	0.91130 EUR/USD	EUR		
4/28/2003	0.90630 EUR/USD			
6/17/1997	23.2 BHT/USD	BHT		
1/13/1998	55.8 BHT/USD			
4/25/2002	1.6430 CHF/USD	CHF		
4/26/2002	0.6140 USD/CHF			
6/26/2002	0.0008324 USD/KRW	KRW		
2/18/2003	0.0008286 USD/KRW			
1/30/1999	1.0038 ARS/USD	USD		
2/5/2001	1.00050 USD/ARS			
1/30/2000	2.3442 CAD/GBP	CAD		
9/20/2000	2.0927 CAD/GBP			
12/12/2002	0.01629 INR/IQD	INR		
2/2/2003	68.0289 IQD/INR			
12/27/2002	1.776 AUD/USD	USD		
12/28/2002	1.7831 AUD/USD			

(Continued)

CALCULATING AND USING EXCHANGE RATES

The international currency codes used above are as follows:

AUD	Australian Dollar	EUR	Euro	USD	U.S. Dollar
ARS	Argentine Peso	GBP	British Pound		
BHT	Thai Baht	INR	Indian Rupee		
CAD	Canadian Dollar	IQR	Iraqi Dinar		
CHF	Swiss Franc	KRW	Korean Won		

MEASURING CURRENCY FLUCTUATIONS

Exercise 6 If the Mexican peso depreciates 50% against the U.S. dollar, how much would the peso have to appreciate to return to its original level?

Exercise 7 The Brazilian real (BRL) exchange rate moved from 3.2020 BRL/USD to 3.1606 BRL/USD over two days. Calculate the real's percentage change and note whether it appreciated or depreciated.

CALCULATING ACTUAL AND IMPLIED PPP EXCHANGE RATES

Exercise 8 Below is an excerpt from the 2003 Big Mac Index. Using the values given, fill in the table with the missing values.

The Economist Big Mac Index

	Big Mac Prices		Implied PPP of the dollar	Actual dollar exchange rates April 22, 2003	Under(−)/ over(+) valuation against the dollar %
	In local currency	In dollars			
United States	$2.71	2.71	—	—	—
Australia	A$ 3.00	1.86	1.11	1.61	☐
Brazil	Real 4.55	1.48	1.68	☐	−45
China	Yuan 9.90	☐	3.65	8.28	−56
Denmark	Krone 27.75	4.10	☐	6.78	+51
Egypt	Pound 8.00	1.35	2.95	☐	−50
Hong Kong	HK$11.50	☐	4.24	7.80	−46
Malaysia	M$5.04	1.33	☐	3.80	−51
Russia	Ruble 41.00	1.32	15.1	31.1	☐
South Korea	Won 3,300	2.71	☐	1,220	nil
Switzerland	SFr 6.30	4.59	2.32	☐	☐

Source: "McCurrencies," *The Economist*, April 24, 2003, p. 80.

(Note: See Example 7 above for an explanation of the Big Mac Index.)

(Continued)

CALCULATING AND USING EXCHANGE RATES

CALCULATING THE COST OF A FORWARD CONTRACT

Exercise 9   A U.S. multinational, Hoola Hoopa, Inc., hired a Canadian IT consulting firm to upgrade its internal network. In 6 months when the contract is over, Hoola Hoopa will need 1.5 million Canadian dollars to pay the consultants. The company needs to decide whether or not it should enter into a forward contract to hedge its exchange rate risk. Fill in the answers below using the US $ Equivalent rates listed in the table below.

Country	U.S. $ Equivalent		Currency per U.S. $	
	Mon	Fri	Mon	Fri
Canada (Dollar)	0.6879	0.6879	1.4537	1.4537
1-month forward	0.6868	0.6869	1.4560	1.4558
3-months forward	0.6844	0.6845	1.4611	1.4609
6-months forward	0.6803	0.6804	1.4699	1.4697
Switzerland (franc)	0.7197	0.7179	1.3895	1.3930
1-month forward	0.7203	0.7183	1.3883	1.3922
3-months forward	0.7215	0.7192	1.3860	1.3904
6-months forward	0.7232	0.7213	1.3827	1.3864
U.K. (Pound)	1.5734	1.5715	0.6356	0.6363
1-month forward	1.5703	1.5783	0.6368	0.6376
3-months forward	1.5644	1.5624	0.6392	0.6400
6-months forward	1.5555	1.5536	0.6429	0.6437

Source: The Wall Street Journal, Tuesday April 15, 2003, p. C14.

    a.   Canadian dollar spot rate: _____

    b.   Canadian dollar 6-months forward rate: _____

    c.   What it would cost Hoola Hoopa if the company were to purchase the Canadian dollars spot on April 15, 2003: _____

    d.   What it would cost Hoola Hoopa if it hedged with a forward contract on April 15, 2003 to purchase 1.5 million Canadian dollars 6 months later on October 15, 2003: _____

Compare the cost of the forward contract, or the hedged position, with the cost of buying the Canadian dollars on the spot market on October 15, 2003. Fill in the table below to show the cost of buying C$1.5 million at different spot rates, and then calculate Hoola Hoopa's potential gains or losses from hedging with a futures contract.

(Continued)

CALCULATING AND USING EXCHANGE RATES

Spot Rate on Oct 15, 2003	Unhedged Position	Hedged Position	Potential Gains/Losses in US$ from Hedge
0.6521			
0.6700			
0.6803			
0.6850			
0.6900			

(Note: The Company's unhedged position is the cost in US$ of C$1.5 million at the various spot rates given for Oct. 15, 2003. The Company's hedged position is the cost of a forward contract on April 15, 2003 to purchase 1.5 million Canadian dollars 6 months later on October 15, 2003.)

2

Exchange Rate Policy at the Monetary Authority of Singapore

Dr. Khor Hoe Ee, Assistant Managing Director, Monetary Authority of Singapore (MAS), reviewed the year-end economic data for 2001. He had just met with a number of his colleagues and now paged through the statistics they had discussed. Dr. Khor wondered whether the monetary system that has served Singapore so well since the late 1970s—and had filled the void left by the collapse of the Bretton Woods currency system—was still the best model for Singapore to follow. Singapore's managed float, sometimes referred to by journalists as a "dirty float," stood in contrast to the systems used by some of its neighbors: Hong Kong had remained strongly committed to its peg against the U.S. dollar, and Australia had just recently shifted to a completely floating regime. A key item on the agenda for the Monetary Policy Committee meeting at the end of January was to review and set monetary policy in response to the changing economic environment. As head of the MAS's Economics Department, Dr. Khor knew that he was responsible for recommending a policy response that would be consistent with Singapore's strategy for sustainable economic growth with price stability as well as supporting Singapore's role as a major global financial center.

A great deal had happened in the domain of monetary policy in the last five years, much of which posed challenges for Singapore. Since the massive currency depreciations

Professor Mihir A. Desai and Research Associate Mark F. Veblen prepared this case. Authors would like to thank Dr. Khor Hoe Ee, Assistant Managing Director (Economic Research and Financial Stability), Mr. Wong Fot Chyi, Executive Director (Macroeconomic Surveillance), Mr. Edward Robinson, Principal Economist (Economic Policy Department) and Dr. Chow Hwee Kwan (Economic Policy Department) for the series of discussion meetings on which this case study was based and their comments on an earlier draft. However, the case study is meant to be pedagogic and any reference to specific individual, department or institution is meant to be purely illustrative. Any inaccuraccies or misrepresentations in the case study should not be attributed to the MAS. HBS cases are developed solely as the basis for class discussion. Cases are not intended to serve as endorsements, sources of primary data, or illustrations of effective or ineffective management.

of the Asian Financial Crisis, major reforms had been implemented or were being considered across Asia. Singapore was surrounded by neighbouring countries whose domestic economies were faltering. One commentator even quipped that Singapore's best hope of returning to the heady growth rates of the past was "If Singapore could just sail north and land near Hong Kong or Taiwan." Furthermore, Southeast Asia had watched its share of foreign direct investment decline as FDI increasingly shifted to China. To make matters worse, the frequency of economic shocks had increased dramatically after 1997, creating a much less stable environment than the one that accompanied Singapore's rapid growth years earlier.

Dr. Khor was confident that Singapore's economy—with its high savings rate, vast stock of foreign reserves, strong trading relationships, and sterling reputation in international markets—was fundamentally strong. At the same time, he was conscious of the rapidly changing economic environment, and he wanted Singapore to be seen as proactive in responding.

SINGAPORE'S UNIQUE SITUATION

Legacy as a Trading Center

Singapore was still heavily influenced by its legacy as a trading port established in the colonial days of the British Empire in connection with the British East India Company. For centuries, monetary considerations—such as maintaining a payment system that inspired confidence among its trading partners—were at the forefront of the minds of government planners. Singapore's small size and lack of abundant natural resources reinforced the importance of the trading sector. Before gaining its independence, Singapore anchored its currency to British sterling, which in turn was on the gold standard.

In 1965, however, Singapore became an independent state and took on the responsibilities of self-government. Leaders at the time formulated three developmental imperatives: (1) reduce unemployment, (2) promote industrialization, and (3) become a globally competitive off-shore financial center. The first two imperatives were ultimately met through an export-led[1] economic growth strategy. While such a strategy might have suggested holding the currency value down artificially, the third imperative required freedom from capital constraints and a stable currency that had the confidence of traders and investors.

The MAS was established in 1971, and at that time Singapore operated a currency board system. However, with the collapse of the Bretton Woods system in the early 1970s (ending the gold standard that had prevailed since the late nineteenth century), world currencies began to fluctuate against one another, and Singapore struggled to develop its own monetary policy framework. Nearly a decade later, a new framework centered on the management of the exchange rate was developed: in response to the oil

---

[1]Singapore determined that its position as a small economy prevented it from effectively pursuing an import substitution model, where the domestic economy would over time develop the ability to produce goods that otherwise needed to be imported. Its reasoning was that because of its small size, it would never have the ability to produce all of the goods it needed. Instead it focused on goods and services where it possessed a comparative advantage and became a strong exporter of those products.

shocks that rattled global markets in the mid- and late 1970s, Singapore developed a managed float system that one analyst dubbed an "inflation killer."

Government Guided Growth

Presiding over Singapore's robust economic growth after the Second World War was a government extensively involved in the economy. In addition to its ties to and ownership of local companies across many industries, the government stimulated high savings rates through a mandated social insurance system, the Central Provident Fund (funded through equal employee and employer contributions). This, combined with steady public savings through persistent budget surpluses (see Exhibit 1) since the mid-80s, supported a high savings rate (see Exhibit 2) and a large accumulation of foreign reserves (see Exhibit 3). As a result, Singapore became a net creditor to the rest of the world. The savings accumulation in excess of domestic investment demand helped to produce a long-term real appreciation of the Singapore dollar. (The large stock of savings also gave MAS a powerful incentive to maintain the value of the Singapore dollar in order to maintain the international purchasing power of the savings of Singaporean citizens.)

EXHIBIT 1

GOVERNMENT BUDGET SURPLUSES (BILLIONS OF SINGAPORE DOLLARS)

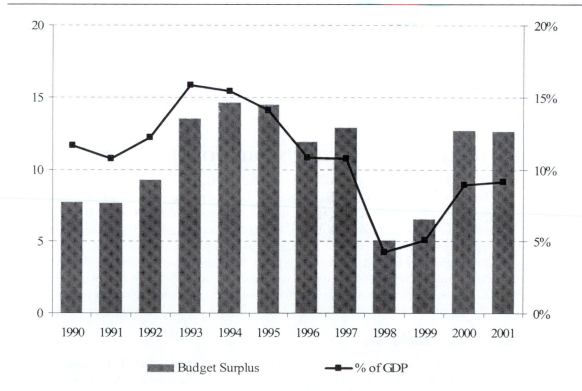

Budget Surplus   % of GDP

Source: Monetary Authority of Singapore and casewriter calculations.

EXHIBIT 2

GROSS NATIONAL SAVINGS RATE, SINGAPORE (AS % OF GDP)

Source: Monetary Authority of Singapore.

OVERVIEW OF THE MONETARY AUTHORITY OF SINGAPORE

The Monetary Authority of Singapore Act of 1970 consolidated the government branches and agencies that had previously been performing the functions normally associated with a central bank into a single entity. A Board of Directors is composed of nine members, including Chairman, Deputy Chairman, and a Managing Director, the last of whom was responsible for the day-to-day operations of the MAS (see organizational chart in Exhibit 4). Monetary policy functions were handled by the Economics Department and the Monetary Management Division, while the Financial Supervision & Promotion group was charged with overseeing the financial sector. On January 1, 1971 the Monetary Authority of Singapore officially took on the following responsibilities:

Monetary and Exchange Rate Policy

The central banking functions consolidated into the MAS included responsibility for formulating and implementing the appropriate monetary policies to achieve price stability. Over the years, the MAS built a reputation for rigorous economic analysis and a strong commitment to its stated policies. Historically, Singapore had kept inflation near or below 2% per year (see Exhibit 5).

EXHIBIT 3

FOREIGN RESERVES (BILLIONS OF SINGAPORE DOLLARS)

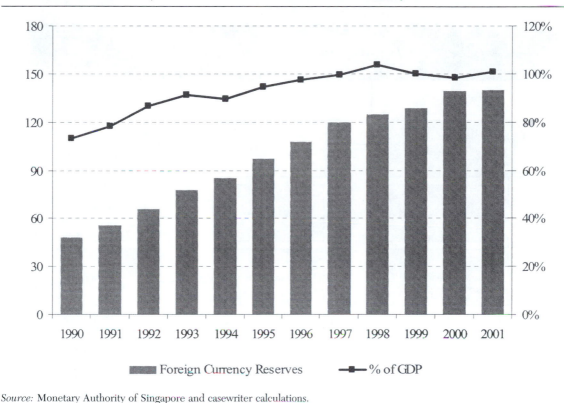

Foreign Currency Reserves   —■— % of GDP

Source: Monetary Authority of Singapore and casewriter calculations.

Financial Sector Supervision

The MAS had regulatory authority over the financial sector, determining such policies as banking capital requirements and other measures designed to prevent large-scale failures of financial institutions that might threaten the stability of the domestic financial system. In recent years, the MAS had sought to issue guidelines focusing on controlling systematic risk, while encouraging a flexible environment where banks could compete with other large financial centers.

Banker to Financial Institutions

The MAS maintained Singapore's centralized payment system, the conduit through which banks transferred funds amongst themselves on behalf of their customers. A sophisticated transaction-by-transaction settlement system reduced systemic credit risk in comparison to end-of-day netting systems, because banks no longer had to wait until the end of the business day to find out whether their counterparty would be able to make payment.

EXHIBIT 4

MAS ORGANIZATIONAL CHART

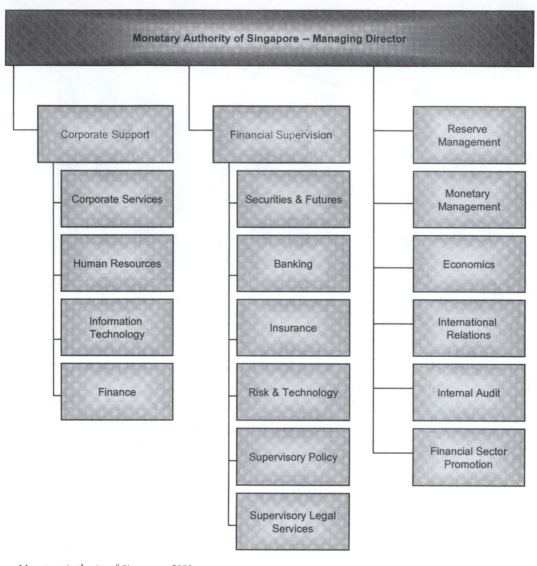

Source: Monetary Authority of Singapore, 2001.

Financial Agent of the Government

In the ordinary course of conducting its affairs, the government required the same sorts of deposit and capital raising facilities for which a corporation might turn to a commercial bank. The MAS provided these services for the government.

Financial Sector Development

Beyond regulating and supervising Singapore's financial institutions, the MAS played an active role in assuring that the business climate in Singapore was favorable to such

EXHIBIT 5

INFLATION IN SINGAPORE AS COMPARED TO AN INDEX OF INDUSTRIALIZED COUNTRIES

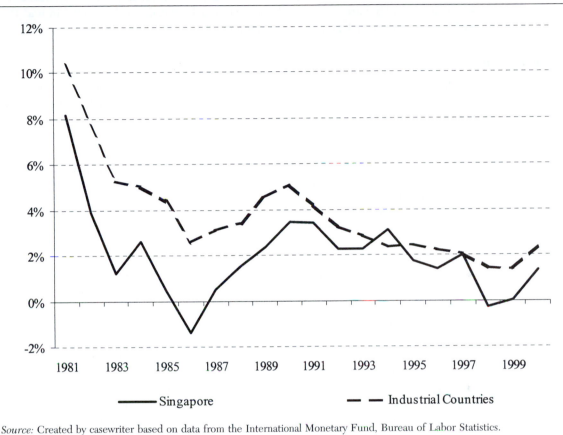

Source: Created by casewriter based on data from the International Monetary Fund, Bureau of Labor Statistics.

things as financial innovation in order to ensure that Singapore maintained its position as a major global money-center.

Procedure for Conducting Monetary Policy

The monetary policy process involved three distinct phases: formulation by the Economics Department, approval by the Monetary Policy Committee, and implementation by the Monetary Management Division.

Formulation

The Economics Department relied on a formal econometric model of the Singapore economy for different exchange rate policy scenarios. Crucial variables it considered in predicting possible developments in the Singapore economy included foreign GDP growth, foreign inflation, and commodity prices.[2]

[2]For a more comprehensive description of the methodology, see Monetary Authority of Singapore, *Economics Explorer #5: Implementation of Monetary Policy* (Singapore: February 2000), available at ⟨http://www.mas.gov.sg/⟩.

Approval

The Monetary and Investment Policy Committee, headed by the Chairman of the MAS, met twice a year in order to give Singapore's monetary policy a comprehensive review and decide on the monetary policy stance for the period ahead. The group also convened on a weekly basis to discuss economic and financial developments around the world that could impact Singapore's economy.

Implementation

The Monetary Management Division (MMD) handled the transactions designed to maintain the desired exchange rate band for the Singapore dollar. MMD monitored the movements in the exchange rate closely and ensured that it moved in an orderly fashion within the policy band specified by the monetary policy committee.

> MMD relies largely on intervention in the foreign exchange markets, as and when necessary, mainly through the purchase or sale of U.S. dollars against the Singapore dollar. By influencing the value of the S\$/US\$ exchange rate, the values of the bilateral exchange rate between the Singapore dollar and the other currencies in the trade-weighted basket will also be determined, given their independent movements against the U.S. dollar.
>
> —Senior MMD official

In order to increase the transparency of monetary policy formulation and conduct, the MAS released a Monetary Policy Statement (MPS) and the Macroeconomic Review semiannually. The MPS provided an assessment of the MAS's outlook on the economy and announced the monetary policy stance for the period ahead, while the Macroeconomic Review provided the analysis and assessments of the GDP growth and inflation developments in the Singapore economy, thereby presenting the basis for the policy decision. In addition, the MAS released various publications which articulated the framework of monetary policy to the market and provided information on the background analysis and on Singapore's economic outlook. This transparency was in line with the code of "good practices," which the International Monetary Fund (IMF) established in the wake of the Asian financial crisis of 1997/98.

MONETARY POLICY FORMULATION

Policy Tools

In achieving its goal of maintaining price stability, the MAS faced a decision as to what variable to use as its policy tool. It could, like central banks in larger economies, influence domestic interest rates by increasing or decreasing the domestic money supply or simply establish a benchmark policy interest rate. Alternatively, it could influence exchange rates by effecting an appreciation or depreciation in the currency. The MAS could not, however, simultaneously control interest rates, exchange rates, and maintain an open capital account (i.e., allow free and continuous conversion of the currency). This trilemma was commonly referred to among economists as the "unholy trinity."

Determining which variable would be most effective as a monetary policy tool required examining the structure of the underlying economy. Singapore was a price taker in international markets and maintained openness to both trade and capital flows. Trade was at the heart of nearly every aspect of the Singaporean economy: of every GDP dollar, 70 cents was based on external demand, and 57 cents stemmed from imports. Both import and export volumes consistently exceeded total GDP (see Exhibit 6). Further-more, although Singapore was a financial hub, the domestic banking market was quite small. As a consequence, interest rate impacts trickled slowly through the economy, and exchange rate changes immediately impacted expenditures.[3] This made the exchange rate the natural policy tool.

Rather than manage the Singapore dollar against the U.S. dollar—by far Singapore's largest direct and indirect currency exposure[4]—the MAS developed a synthetic

---

EXHIBIT 6

TRADING SECTOR COMPARED TO ECONOMY OVERALL

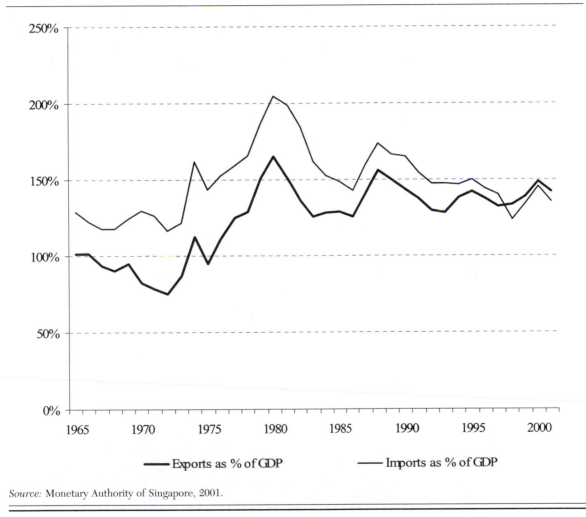

——— Exports as % of GDP   ——— Imports as % of GDP

Source: Monetary Authority of Singapore, 2001.

---

[3]Singapore dollar interest rates had long tracked U.S. dollar rates very closely. They had consistently re-mained slightly lower because of the constantly anticipated appreciation of the Singapore dollar. This an-ticipation reflected two decades of steady real appreciation of the Singapore dollar.

[4]Many of Singapore's trading partners either pegged their currencies directly to the U.S. dollar or ob-served significant correlations with the U.S. dollar. Exposures to these currencies magnified the effects of the U.S. dollar on the Singaporean economy.

currency, an index tracking a "trade-weighted" basket of currencies. This gave the MAS a more precise tool for measuring and controlling the relationship between exchange rates and the domestic price level. The basket was composed of the currencies of Singapore's major trading partners, and the currencies were weighted in the basket in proportion to the amounts of imports and exports that were sourced from or destined to a particular country.

Singapore was particularly susceptible to <u>import inflation</u>. Any slide in the value of the Singapore dollar meant that the prices of imported goods were effectively higher, thus raising the local CPI. Similarly, an increase in relative foreign prices, a rise in the price of Thai rice for example, reduced the purchasing power of local currency. At the same time, Singapore's labor market was extremely tight. Thus, any significant rise in external demand would require Singaporean factories to pay premiums to hire additional workers as they strove to increase output. Such increases in incomes with the domestic economy already at full employment could produce <u>wage inflation</u>. The effects could cause real misallocations of resources that the MAS wished to avoid through cushioning the economy from any misalignment in exchange rates.

The Current Policy: "Band-Basket-Crawl"

The band-basket-crawl characteristics in the managed float system in Singapore represented a middle ground between (i) a fixed regime pegged to a particular currency at a specific rate, and (ii) a floating exchange rate regime of freely convertible currency at rates determined on a continuous basis by the market. The band was centered around the target exchange rate. It was designed to "crawl" (historically upwards in Singapore's case) over time, allowing the band to reflect the long-term changes in economic fundamentals. Short-term stability was accomplished by enforcing the upper and lower bounds of the band within which the currency was allowed to float. As one analyst commented, "It is never a game between the central bank and speculators. It is a game between the central bank and the economy." For the two decades leading up to the Asian crisis, the MAS had successfully deterred speculators from attacking the currency by enforcing the band, and had accommodated long-term market trends by providing enough flexibility for real variables in the economy to impact the equilibrium level of the exchange rate.

Had the exchange rate been fixed at some historical level, over time pressures from the real economy—increasing productivity, high savings rates, and sustained economy growth—would have shifted the currency into a position of being undervalued in real terms. This would have led to higher increases in wages and prices given the openness of the economy. On the other hand, had the exchange rate been allowed to float freely against foreign currencies, short-term deviations from the MAS's chosen optimal exchange rate path would have been both more frequent and more pronounced. An increase in the volatility of the currency would certainly have hindered Singapore's efforts to develop into a financial hub for global markets and would also have made it more difficult for businesses that were inherently trade-dependent to plan for the future.

Understanding the Environment: Econometric Model of the Singaporean Economy

In order to project the optimal exchange rate path for Singapore, MAS economists needed a sophisticated model of both the Singaporean economy and of the linkages that govern exchange rate determination in the markets. This monetary policy model utilized econometric techniques to estimate likely outcomes based on empirical data. MAS economists forecasted both a "bottom up" aggregation of sectoral estimates from internal industry specialists over a three to five year horizon and economy-wide growth projections. (This "bottom up" aggregation served as an alternative short-term economy-wide growth forecast.) Using this as a framework for the structural elements of the Singaporean economy, the model then simulated possible outcomes for economic growth and the exchange rate based on fundamental parity relationships. These included two "no arbitrage" conditions which held in the long run: uncovered interest parity and purchasing power parity. The first held that spot rates (prices for immediately completed transactions) and prevailing interest rates would align themselves such that interest rate differentials compensated investors only for anticipated appreciations or depreciations in the respective currencies. The second held that in the long run, nominal exchange rates would reflect relative inflation rates and relative real economic growth rates across countries.

Based on these predictions and simulations, MAS economists chose the target exchange rate with the objective of balancing a number of goals:

- Inflation should not exceed a maximum threshold, implicitly around 2%
- Unemployment should remain in line with the "non-accelerating inflation rate of unemployment" (NAIRU)
- Wages should keep pace with productivity improvements
- Subject to these conditions, maximize economic growth while retaining the flexibility to absorb possible external shocks

Scenario Analysis

The Economics Department spent a great deal of time performing scenario analysis and asking "what if" questions for potential shocks that might impact the economy. Examples of shocks economists considered were "What if the high equity valuations and especially technology-related equity valuations in the United States collapse suddenly?" or "What if China devalues the renminbi?" or "What if our exchange rate appreciates x%?" In considering all these options, the MAS was searching for the exchange rate level that would best create the conditions for price stability over the medium term.

Effects of a Prolonged Real Appreciation

Singapore had experienced a 4% per year real appreciation in its currency from 1980 to 1997. The steady real exchange rate appreciation was consistent with two facts that reflected strong and improving fundamentals in the real economy:

- Singapore's average annual productivity growth, at around 5%, exceeded that of its trading partners by a factor of more than two
- Singapore's high savings and investment rates (current account surpluses were on the order of 20% of GDP beginning in 1986) led to a massive accumulation of net foreign assets

During the 1980s and 1990s, the MAS focused on inflation and not on using the exchange rate as a competitive tool—it did not keep the value of the currency low in order to spur exports. Singaporean industry, as a result, faced competitors from abroad whose costs *relative to Singaporean companies* fell every year simply because of the real appreciation in the Singapore dollar. This forced Singaporean companies to either become more efficient or constantly move up the value chain to focus on higher value-added goods and services where low-cost foreign producers were not able to compete directly. This process was normally unpopular in other countries because it frequently resulted in job losses. It proved sustainable in Singapore, however, because the labor market was very tight and the economy operated consistently at full employment.

Real vs. Nominal

The 4% annual real appreciation was not a measure of the exchange rate between currencies observed in the market (the nominal exchange rate), but rather a measure of the exchange rate between "goods" across countries (the real exchange rate). The nominal exchange rate measured the ratio at which Singapore dollars were traded for other currencies in the spot market. It fluctuated continuously. The real exchange rate measured the ratio at which Singapore dollars were equivalent to other currencies in purchasing power terms. In other words, the real exchange rate took into account relative inflation levels. For example, if Singapore experienced inflation of 2% more than one of its trading partners, and the Singapore dollar depreciated by 2% with respect to that trading partner's currency, the real exchange rate would not have changed.

By adjusting the observed nominal exchange rate changes for changes in relative price levels (e.g., the inflation level in Singapore as compared to the inflation level in

EXHIBIT 7A

REAL AND NOMINAL EXCHANGE RATE, SINGAPORE DOLLAR VS. U.S. DOLLAR

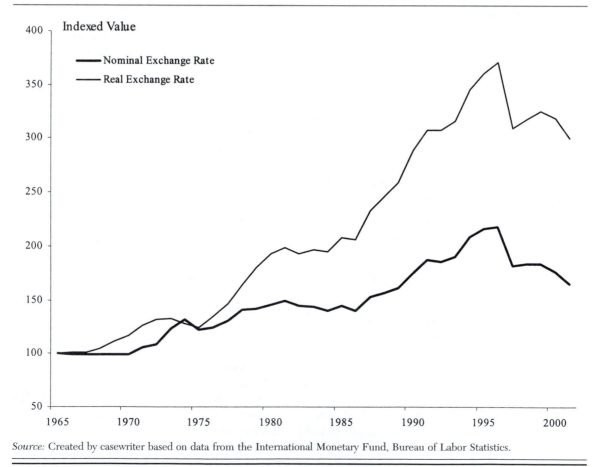

Source: Created by casewriter based on data from the International Monetary Fund, Bureau of Labor Statistics.

EXHIBIT 7B

TREASURY BILL RATE, SINGAPORE AND THE UNITED STATES (3-MONTH RATE)

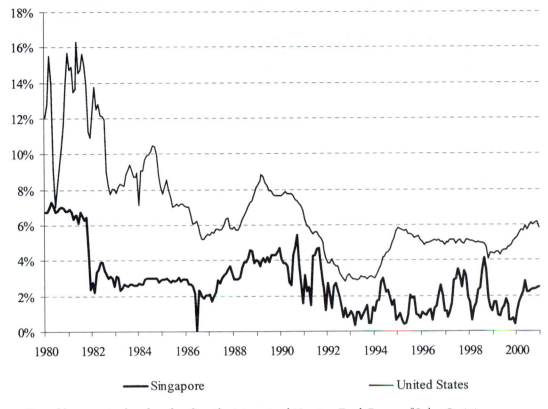

Singapore   United States

Source: Created by casewriter based on data from the International Monetary Fund, Bureau of Labor Statistics.

the U.S.), MAS economists could compute changes in the real exchange rate. Exhibit 7a reports the evolution of the real and nominal exchange rates for the Singapore dollar over time. Exhibit 7b highlights the corresponding interest rate differentials after 1980.

MAS OPERATIONS AND POLICY IMPLEMENTATION

After the Monetary Policy Committee had approved a policy stance proposed by the Economics Department, the Monetary Management Division was tasked with executing the strategy. The MMD was responsible for (1) implementing monetary policy, (2) conducting money market operations, (3) acting as the fiscal agent for the government (issuing Singapore Government Securities), and (4) providing ancillary banking services to the government.

Managing the Entire Basket . . .

The first task centered on intervening, if necessary, in the foreign exchange markets to influence the trade-weighted Singapore dollar exchange rate. Such interventions might occur while the exchange rate was within the band, with activity escalating as the exchange rate moved closer to the outer bounds of the band. Although the MAS did not publish either the list of currencies in the basket or the weightings of each currency in the basket, equity research analysts had come close to replicating the basket by backing into a model basket using published import and export data for Singapore with its major trading partners. (Exhibit 8a and Exhibit 8b provide past exchange rates and trade volume data that were helpful to analysts in replicating the MAS's calculations.)

Specifically, the trade-weighted index was computed as the product across each foreign currency of the number of units of foreign currency per Singapore dollar. The following is a stylized representation of the computation:

$$TWI_{SGD} = \prod_{i=1}^{n} \left(\frac{x_i}{SGD} \right)^{w_i}$$

The following stylized example proceeds on the simplifying assumption of a central bank contemplating a basket of only three currencies. This serves as a conceptual discussion of how intervention directed at bilateral rates can influence the outcome of the domestic currency on a trade-weighted basis.

. . . Through a Single Exchange Rate

One important aspect of this formula was that Singapore could accomplish all of its intervention activities by intervening only in the U.S. dollar/Singapore dollar foreign exchange market.[5] This principle used the following logic. Beginning with the trade-weighted index, it was possible to isolate a single currency (the U.S. dollar exchange market provided the most liquidity) in which to transact as outlined in Table 1.

TABLE 1 Managing the Entire Basket . . . through a Single Exchange Rate

(1.) $TWI = \left(\frac{USD}{SGD} \right)^{w_{USD}} \times \left(\frac{JPY}{SGD} \right)^{w_{JPY}} \times \left(\frac{EUR}{SGD} \right)^{w_{EUR}}$

(2.) $TWI = \left(\frac{USD}{SCD} \right)^{w_{USD}} \times \left(\frac{JPY}{USD} \times \frac{UWD}{SGD} \right)^{w_{JPY}} \times \left(\frac{EUR}{USD} \times \frac{USD}{SGD} \right)^{w_{EUR}}$

(3.) $TWI = \left(\frac{USD}{SCD} \right)^{w_{USD}+w_{JPY}+w_{EUR}} \times \left(\frac{JPY}{USD} \right)^{w_{JPY}} \times \left(\frac{EUR}{USD} \right)^{w_{EUR}}$

(4.) $TWI = \left(\frac{USD}{SGD} \right)^{w_{USD}} \times \left(\frac{JPY}{USD} \right)^{w_{JPY}} \times \left(\frac{EUR}{USD} \right)^{w_{EUR}}$

1. Hypothetically, the central bank identified three currency exposures (U.S. dollars, yen and euros) to manage and assigned each a weight depending on each currency's importance to Singapore's trading relationships. The weights summed to 1.

2. The central bank decomposed each foreign exchange rate into cross rates through the U.S. dollar.

3. The central bank extracted all of the USD exposure.

4. The central bank could now use a single variable (USD/SGD exchange rate), scaled by observable market levels, as a lever to control its target (the TWI).

Source: Casewriter.

[5]This assumed that Singapore was a small economy that did not impact the exchange rates of other foreign currencies vis-à-vis one another.

EXHIBIT 8A

EXCHANGE RATES AGAINST CURRENCIES OF MAJOR TRADING PARTNERS

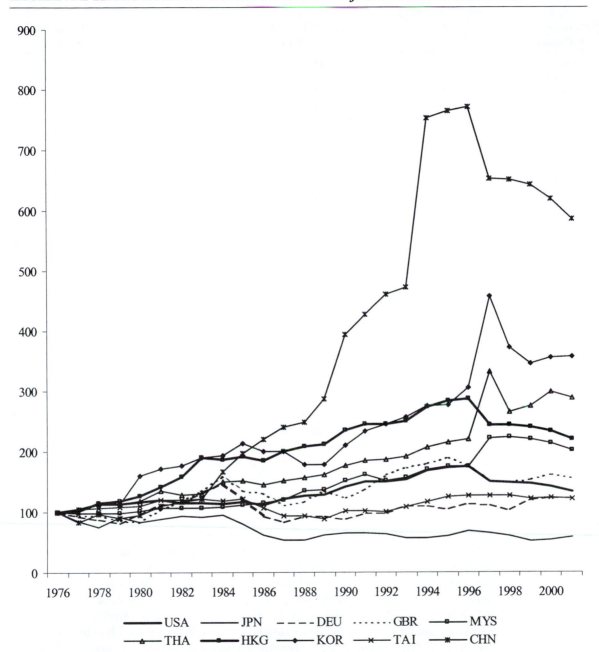

Source: Monetary Authority of Singapore, crossed rates based on data from the International Monetary Fund, International Financial Statistics.

EXHIBIT 8B

TRADE VOLUMES WITH RESPECT TO MAJOR TRADING PARTNERS

Country (billions of US$)	Singapore Exports to Country, 1998	Singapore Imports from Country, 1998
China	5.0	3.8
Germany	3.5	3.1
Hong Kong	8.9	4.3
Japan	7.0	16.0
Malaysia	15.2	13.8
South Korea	2.6	4.2
Taiwan	4.9	4.0
Thailand	4.3	4.9
United Kingdom	4.1	2.8
United States	22.0	17.0
Total	77.5	73.9

Source: Created by casewriter based on United Nations bilateral trade data available through Statistics Canada.

The actual transactions in the foreign exchange markets were conducted through eleven primary dealer banks, three of which were local financial institutions and the remaining eight of which were foreign banks. These eleven banks handled all of the MAS's transactions in Singapore Government Securities (SGS), and some subset of them might be used in the event of an intervention.

As the MAS built up its credibility in world markets, interventions became less frequent, because market players became mindful of the MAS's intentions. In effect, investor confidence instilled in the market a sort of self-imposed discipline. As the exchange rate moved toward the bounds of the band, traders anticipated interventions by the MAS and therefore stopped pushing the currency's value further away from the (perceived) center of the band.

Money Market Operations

The MAS needed assurance that at any given time there were sufficient funds in circulation in the domestic economy to keep the financial system functioning smoothly. All banks in Singapore maintained cash balances with MAS for the purpose of meeting their reserve requirements and settlement of interbank transactions. The cash balances with MAS—called the Minimum Cash Balance (MCB)—were set equivalent to 3% of the banks' liabilities bases. While MCB for banks was allowed to fluctuate between 2% and 4% of their liability bases on a day-to-day basis, they had to ensure that the average MCB ratio for any two-week maintenance period was not less than 3%. (The percentage did not vary with the duration of the deposit, e.g., checking accounts versus time deposits.) Every morning, the MAS received from the government agencies a summary of expected funds transfers for the day. Daily fluctuations in transfer payments for retirement benefits, for example, could significantly impact daily liquidity needs.

As monetary policy was centered on the management of the trade-weighted exchange rate, the MAS conducted money market operations to ensure sufficient liquidity in the banking system to meet banks' demand for reserve and settlement balances. The amount of liquidity to inject or withdraw from the banking system depended on the net liquidity impact of:

1. the MAS' foreign exchange operations, if any, and its maturing money market operations;

2. changes in banks' liabilities base and hence, their MCB requirements;

3. net changes in currency demand;

4. net issuance of government securities; and

5. the government's funds transfers.

Based on historical experience, banks maintained average cash balances with MAS of 3.1%–3.3% of their liability bases. Within this range, the overnight interbank rate would remain fairly stable, although its volatility might also depend on the distribution of funds in the banking system. If figures from the government suggested that the money supply might dip below 3% of bank liabilities, the MAS could step into the market and inject additional funds. Conversely, at levels above 3%, the MAS could withdraw funds from the economy. The instruments used for money market operations included (1) SGS repos/reverse repos (2) FX swaps and reverse swaps, and (3) direct borrowing and lending. (See Appendix A for a description of the transactions used in implementing money market operations.) The MAS dealt exclusively with the eleven primary dealers for money market operations.

Benchmark Yield Curve

In its capacity as the financial agent of the government, the MAS regularly issued SGS of varying maturities. As a matter of fiscal policy, the government had no need for public borrowing, but the MAS consciously wished to create a liquid market in domestic fixed income securities. In order to support such a market, a benchmark yield curve in government securities was required—this set pricing levels for corporate debt. This was partially motivated by a desire to encourage the use of bonds, a longer duration, and therefore more stable, source of capital as an alternative to bank debt. Furthermore, it created the possibility that foreign issuers would turn to Singapore to raise SGD-denominated debt. This market had, in fact, experienced significant growth over the course of the previous few years (see Exhibit 9).

RECENT DEVELOPMENTS

In 1997, heightened concern about Thailand's ability to service its foreign debt began a string of speculative attacks on regional currencies in East and Southeast Asia. For most of the countries impacted, the underlying concerns stemmed from a belief that (1) domestic debt denominated in foreign currency would no longer be serviceable if the currencies were allowed to float, and (2) the central banks could no longer artificially sustain then prevailing exchange rates. Countries such as Hong Kong and Singapore, however, had demonstrated foreign reserves that indicated that they would, in fact, be able to defend the currency against such a speculative attack. While both were

EXHIBIT 9

ISSUANCE OF SINGAPORE DOLLAR DENOMINATED BONDS BY NON-SINGAPOREAN COMPANIES (MILLIONS OF U.S. DOLLARS)

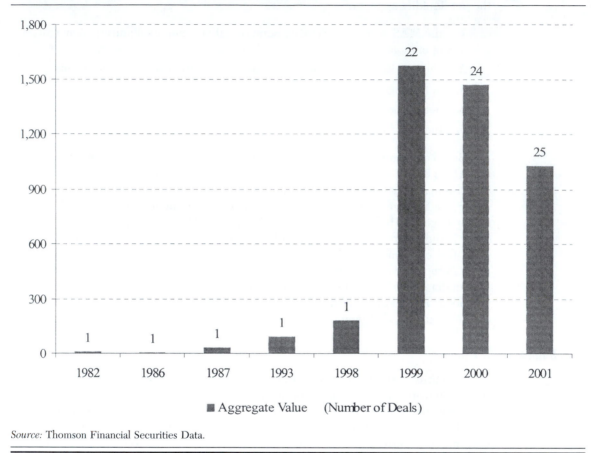

■ Aggregate Value   (Number of Deals)

Source: Thomson Financial Securities Data.

ultimately successful in averting the economic turmoil inflicted upon their neighbors, both were deeply impacted.

MAS economists realized that real exchange rates across the region would need to fall and that there were two ways in which this could be accomplished. Either the nominal exchange rate had to fall, or relative prices in the domestic economy had to adjust.[6] The MAS took the view that, in a market that was so influenced by expectations and where credibility was crucial, sending the right signals would be an important element to weathering the storm. In particular, the MAS signaled a willingness to allow the nominal exchange rate to depreciate somewhat, but in an orderly manner. In an unusual move, the MAS widened the band within which the exchange rate would be allowed to fluctuate. Contemporaneously, fiscal policy was adjusted, implementing significant cost-

[6]This corresponds perfectly to the mathematical relationship between real and nominal exchange rates: the product of changes in the price level (inflation) and changes in the real exchange rate determine the nominal exchange rate.

cutting budgetary measures. In particular, employer contribution rates to the Central Provident Fund were reduced, thus lowering the effective cost of labor. More subtle cost reduction methods took the form of altering pay schedules for civil servants, whose pay scales often served as a benchmark for the private sector. The government was also the largest landlord, and influenced property prices depending on the rate at which it built residential and commercial real estate and released land for sale into the market.

While the MAS was legally independent (separating monetary policy from fiscal policy), one consequence of Singapore being a small country was that the group of people making high-level policy decisions was quite small, so quick and coordinated fiscal and monetary actions were possible. In the aftermath of the Asian Financial Crisis, the fundamental cause of economic weakness was not so much one of monetary policy but rather a much lower level of external demand. While MAS policies could temporarily affect imbalances of these sorts, real economic problems required real economic solutions rather than tweaks to foreign exchange policies.

THE INTERSECTION OF FISCAL AND MONETARY POLICY

During the period of sustained exchange rate appreciation, it was economically accurate to attribute much of the strength in the Singapore dollar to improving economic fundamentals. In some sense, this created an association between a strong currency and a strong economy and similarly to strong politics. Under such a framework, periods of appreciation (to combat inflationary pressures) were much easier for the MAS to accommodate than periods when conditions called for a depreciation.

MAS economists contended that deflationary shocks were largely cyclical and did not need to be considered by a central bank that was concerned with intermediate- to long-term price stability. Some analysts responded that whether cyclical or not, the impact on a small open economy was the same, and as such, monetary policy could be used to accommodate some of the shock. However, there were limitations to the extent that domestic monetary policy could influence foreign demand, especially when Singapore's exports tended to be many times more income elastic than price elastic.

MAS economists also asserted that a monetary easing would have "pass through" effects. These longer term effects of allowing the currency to fall included increased exports, increased employment, increased income, increased money supply, and finally increased domestic prices. MAS believed that the "pass through" effects from an easing would eventually have appeared as inflation down the road.

THE "GAP" MODEL: CONSIDERING FISCAL EFFECTS

Singapore's rapid economic growth and industrialization played a key part in the sustained real appreciation of the Singapore dollar prior to the Asian Crisis. Dr. Khor was, however, aware of a theory recently endorsed by some of Singapore's academic community. The "Gap" model pointed to another underlying driver of the currency appreciation: persistent annual budget surpluses (on the order of 12% of GDP) beginning in 1985. Economically, this represented a net withdrawal of funds from the domestic economy that created a need for obtaining capital from abroad to make up for shrinking liquidity. This in turn bid up the value of the Singapore dollar, creating deflationary pressure. (As the purchasing power of the Singapore dollar in terms of traded goods rose, the corresponding prices of domestic, non-traded goods had to fall to maintain purchasing power parity.) This deflationary pressure risked significant detrimental effects on the domestic economy, and was seen in dropping property values, stock market values, and asset prices (so-called "triple deflation"). These falling values were important because many of the assets were pledged as collateral for loans.

According to the theory, however, it was not merely the budget surplus, but the gap between the budget surplus and foreign direct investment (FDI) that flowed into the country. FDI—while it was pouring in during the 1980s and 1990s—had the effect of offsetting the deflationary pressures created by the surpluses. Although the manufacturing sector continued to attract large foreign investments, levels of FDI did not mirror the previous growth trend. Unlike in the West, fiscal policy has not been regularly used as an activist tool for economic stimulus.

ALTERNATIVE APPROACHES: HONG KONG

In contrast to Singapore's policy of managing its exchange rate, Hong Kong had operated under a currency board since 1984, with its exchange rate fixed at HK$7.8 per US$1. Under this regime, Hong Kong's central bank stood ready to exchange U.S. dollars for Hong Kong dollars at this rate. The supply of outstanding Hong Kong dollars thus fluctuated in response to demand for its currency in world markets. The peg to the U.S. dollar was taken on largely for political reasons: an experiment with floating rates had proven quite volatile and, with the handover back to China in 1997 approaching, choosing a system that inspired investor confidence was crucial. A more discretionary system would have provided more flexibility in buffering shocks, but it would not have afforded any protection from the risk that Hong Kong would not be able to maintain a monetary policy truly independent of China.

This situation had led to very different inflation patterns since the mid-1980s, a period during which both Hong Kong and Singapore experienced rapid economic growth, and also to radically different reactions to the Asian financial crisis of 1997/98. Exhibit 10 provides data to compare the real exchange rate movements and inflation in Hong Kong and Singapore. While the real exchange rate appreciation in Hong Kong led to inflation in the 5–10% per year range, inflation in Singapore hovered between 0–3%. Where the exchange rate acted as a buffer for Singapore, Hong Kong absorbed the appreciation directly in terms of internal price appreciation (inflation and a property value bubble).

During the Asian financial crisis, when both currencies came under pressure, Hong Kong experienced a severe deflation as the money supply contracted. During the Asian financial crisis, investors feared that Hong Kong might devalue its currency—that the government's pledge to maintain the pegged exchange rate was not credible. Though the value of stocks in Hong Kong fell by nearly 25%, the government raised interest rates to entice foreign investors to hold Hong Kong dollars. Hong Kong ultimately succeeded at maintaining its peg to the U.S. dollar. The high interest rates, however, imposed a real cost to the economy as it slid into recession.

More generally, Singapore had cultivated extensive expertise among its central bankers and economists. This group actively reviewed and amended policies as appropriate. Hong Kong, on the other hand, was saddled with a system that was politically difficult to change. The comparison of these two different paths demonstrated how important such policy choices could be for the real economy.

EXHIBIT 10

REAL EXCHANGE RATE EVOLUTION, HONG KONG VS. SINGAPORE

Panel 1: Real Exchange Rates (vs. U.S. dollar)

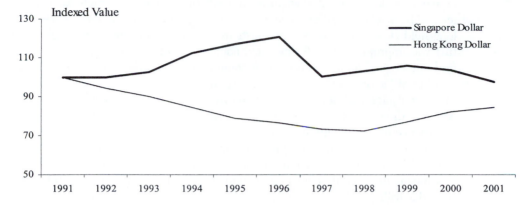

Panel 2: Inflation

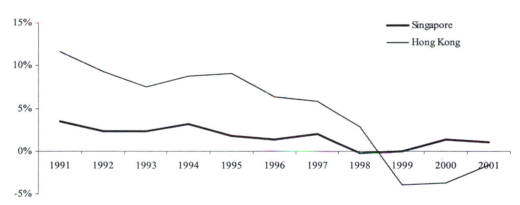

Panel 3: Money supply

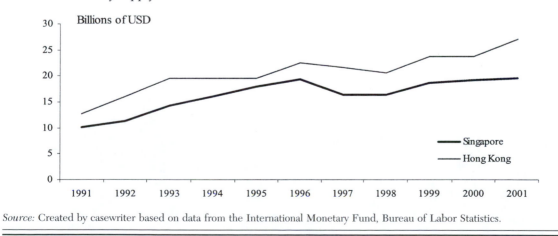

Source: Created by casewriter based on data from the International Monetary Fund, Bureau of Labor Statistics.

CONCLUSION

Dr. Khor had a wealth of information to review before making a recommendation to be considered by the Monetary Policy Committee. He was also a long-time MAS veteran who understood that Singapore's anti-inflation vigilance through exchange rate policy had been a large part of Singapore's monetary and economic success. He shared the long-held view among MAS economists that there was no single exchange rate system that was appropriate for all times and countries, and even individual countries might find one regime more appropriate at some times than others. Khor recognized that a number of factors—a deterioration in regional terms of trade, the cyclical downturn in the electronics and semiconductor industries, the reduced economic influence of ASEAN, the unemployment induced by allowing financial sector consolidation, and the emergence of China with its reforms—had made his policy decisions much more difficult. Knowing the limitations of having only monetary tools at his disposal, he nonetheless had high hopes for creating the conditions necessary for price stability. Whether this meant financial deregulation, a more flexible float, or something else, Khor expected a grilling at January's policy meeting about the significant risks involved in a major shift in monetary policy.

LIQUIDITY CONSIDERATIONS IN IMPLEMENTING MONETARY POLICY IN A SMALL OPEN ECONOMY

Trading foreign exchange directly involved buying and selling US$ for S$. When the MAS bought S$ using US$, that had the effect of lowering the supply of S$ in the economy and thus reducing domestic liquidity. The Monetary Management Division had a number of tools at its disposal to counteract the impact on domestic liquidity:

Foreign exchange (reverse) swaps—The MAS could simultaneously sell (purchase) a S$ for spot delivery and purchase (sell) S$ for forward delivery. In such a swap, the MAS lent S$ and borrowed US$ at the execution date by selling S$ in exchange for US$ on the spot market and simultaneously entered into a forward contract to buy (sell) the same amount of S$ for delivery in the future, effectively reversing the original lending (borrowing).[7]

Direct lending to or borrowing from banks—The MAS also had the option of lending (borrowing) funds at interbank interest rates directly to Singaporean banks to increase (decrease) liquidity.

Direct purchases and sales of Singapore Government Securities (SGS)—Similarly, the MAS could transact with banks for SGS. The purchase (sale) by the MAS of such securities had the effect of injecting funds into (withdrawing funds from) the financial system.

Repurchase or reverse repurchase agreements on SGS—In a "repo" transaction, a bank lent the MAS Singapore Government Securities in exchange for S$ and agreed to later repurchase those securities. This had the effect of temporarily injecting S$ into the financial system.

Two other policies influenced the MAS's liquidity interventions. As described earlier, contributions to the Central Provident Fund amounted to a withdrawal of funds from the economy. Additionally, conservative fiscal policies resulted in continued budget surpluses, providing a second contractionary pressure on domestic liquidity.

---

[7]For further detail, see Richard M Levich, *International Financial Markets: Prices and Policies*, Second Edition (New York: 1991).

3

Innocents Abroad: Currencies and International Stock Returns

February 2004 was a busy month for Sandra Meyer, founder of CapGlobal Advisors, LLC (CapGlobal). The local state pension fund was one of her largest clients, and its Chief Investment Officer, Henry Bosse, had expressed concern about the wisdom of allocating assets internationally. Bosse wasn't particularly concerned about Meyer's specific investment decisions—her returns compared quite favorably to international market indices—but rather questioned whether he should be allocating any of his portfolio to international investments in light of their recent underperformance vis-à-vis U.S. equities (see Exhibit 1). Specifically, in a recent phone conversation with Meyer, he had expressed skepticism that an international strategy might not really add much value to his overall portfolio and in fact might create unnecessary currency risks. Meyer knew that to keep Bosse as a client, she would have to explain the fundamentals of global markets and justify her strategy.

Meyer's firm conviction was that her approach to asset allocation added value to her clients' overall portfolios. Nonetheless, she understood the fundamental difficulty in sustaining attention in international stocks. In particular, when the domestic market performed well, internationally diversified investors questioned why they were not fully invested in the United States; when domestic markets were sinking, the gains of their foreign exposures were often not large enough to sustain attention. Meyer knew that her mission was to educate her clients on (i) the benefits of international diversification, (ii) the impact of currency movements on returns of global portfolios, and (iii) the drivers and consequences of correlations among global equity markets.

CapGlobal Advisors, LLC

Meyer had founded CapGlobal after nearly ten years working as an equity research analyst for a major investment bank. The firm had grown to seven professionals, all of

Professor Mihir A. Desai and Research Associates Kathleen Luchs and Mark F. Veblen prepared this case. This case was developed from published sources. HBS cases are developed solely as the basis for class discussion. Cases are not intended to serve as endorsements, sources of primary data, or illustrations of effective or ineffective management.

EXHIBIT 1

INDEX RETURNS FOR THE EAFE AND S&P 500 (IN NATIVE CURRENCY) FROM 1981 TO 2003

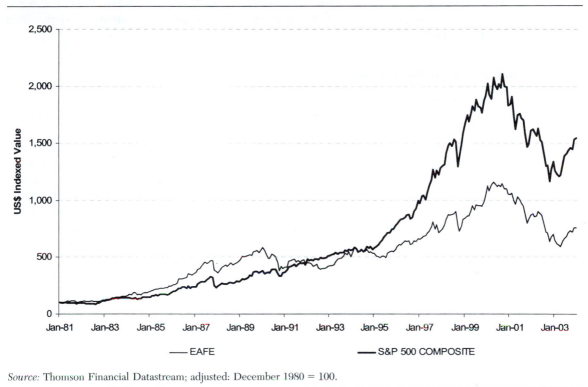

Source: Thomson Financial Datastream; adjusted: December 1980 = 100.

whom focused on different areas of international portfolio management, including equities, fixed income instruments, and currency. CapGlobal served a small number of large institutional clients by handling their international portfolio allocations. CapGlobal's methodology focused on quantitative modeling and extensive research on international markets.

QUANTITATIVE BUILDING BLOCKS

CapGlobal's models synthesized data from markets around the world both at the individual country level and across much broader regional areas. While Meyer didn't fool herself into thinking that the past would predict the future, she relied heavily on data on past returns to get a feel for the return and volatility characteristics of various markets. By examining individual foreign markets and measuring the returns and standard deviations of those markets in both local currency and U.S. dollars, she developed the foundations for her diversification strategies.

Meyer decided she had to examine the performance of international equities over a considerable period in her presentation to Bosse. While Bosse and some other clients were now questioning the value of international investments, Meyer recalled the advertisements fund managers had placed in major financial publications during the 1980s hyping the outperformance of foreign investments held by U.S. investors and extolling the virtues of international diversification. Fund managers had argued that foreign stock markets offered not only higher returns, but also less risk, suggesting that U.S. investors were missing out on a free lunch. Meyer therefore decided to analyze the performance of international and U.S. equities from 1981 to 2003 and also for shorter periods within that time frame.

Returns and Standard Deviations

For her upcoming meeting with Bosse, Meyer wanted to provide her client with information on the returns and standard deviations of various foreign equity markets, and to compare these markets with each other and with the U.S. equity market. Meyer included Australia, Canada, France, Germany, Hong Kong, Japan, and the United Kingdom as well as the U.S. in her analysis. Since she wanted to calculate the returns for each of these markets, Meyer used total return stock market indices which included dividends (see Appendix A). Meyer first calculated the monthly returns for the different markets. Then, she calculated the average monthly return and standard deviation of each stock market from 1981 to 2003. To compare the returns over different periods, Myer split the data into two shorter periods, 1981–1991 and 1992–2003, and calculated average monthly returns and standard deviations for each of the equity markets for these shorter periods as well.

Meyer also wanted to measure the returns of the various markets in terms of U.S. dollars, so her next step was to convert each of the indices to U.S. dollars using the exchange rates in Appendix A. Then, she calculated the average monthly return and standard deviation for each market in terms of U.S. dollars for the entire period 1981–2003, and for the two shorter periods, 1981–1991 and 1992–2003.

Meyer herself used the data to calculate average monthly returns, but she knew from experience that most clients found it easier to understand annual returns. Consequently, she needed to annualize the average monthly returns and the standard deviations in order to demonstrate the differences across markets and over different time periods to Bosse.[1]

Market Correlations

In addition to charting the risk and return characteristics of the various markets, Meyer wanted to show her client the correlations of the different country markets with each other. First, she calculated the correlations of the returns based on local currency and then she repeated the exercise using the U.S. dollar based returns. Meyer used returns for the same time periods as above: 1981–2003, and the sub-periods 1981–1991 and 1992–2003. She spent some time reviewing how market correlations changed over time, and how the correlations based on U.S. dollar returns varied from those based on local currency returns. She found this one of the more interesting parts of the analysis and she wanted to be prepared for possible questions about the causes for convergences and divergences between markets.

---

[1]The standard deviation of the monthly returns can be annualized by multiplying the monthly standard deviation by the square root of 12.

DISENTANGLING CURRENCY EFFECTS AND EQUITY RETURNS ON INTERNATIONAL PORTFOLIO RETURNS

Meyer recognized that U.S. equity investors might ultimately care about their total U.S. dollar return and therefore she had to clarify the impact of currency movements on those returns. For example, in December 1987, when the Nikkei fell 6.97% in a single month, U.S. equity investors were cushioned by the yen's 8.17% appreciation against the dollar. In effect, U.S. investors netted a 1.3% return that month. The reverse occurred in March of 2001, when the yen fell 6.8% against the dollar, more than wiping out the 3.8% Nikkei equity return. Meyer wanted to show her client, year by year, what portion of international market returns was accounted for by equity performance and what portion resulted from currency movements.

Meyer also understood that many of her clients were mainly interested in whether international equities performed better or worse than U.S. equities over a given period. In other words, it was the performance of international stocks relative to U.S. stocks that was important to many clients. Meyer therefore spent some time thinking about how she could best demonstrate the performance of international equities relative to U.S. equities, and also about how to clarify the impact of currency movements on returns to U.S. investors. She decided to analyze the historical data on the performance of a domestic index, the S&P 500, and an international index, Morgan Stanley Capital Inc.'s Europe, Australasia, and Far East (EAFE) index.[2] (See Appendix B for annual returns for the S&P 500 and for both the U.S. dollar based and the native currency EAFE indices.)

To show the performance of foreign equities relative to U.S. equities, Meyer simply compared the returns on the dollar based EAFE index with those of the S&P 500 index. In 1983, for example, the dollar based EAFE had a return of 24.6% and the S&P 500 had a return of 22.6%, so the EAFE outperformed the S&P 500 by 2% that year.

While Meyer knew that Bosse would be interested in the performance of the EAFE index relative to the S&P 500 index from year to year, she wanted to take the analysis a step further. Meyer wanted to demonstrate how local equity returns and currency movements each contributed to the returns to U.S. investors. In 1983, when the EAFE outperformed the S&P 500 by 2%, foreign equities had actually gained 10% relative to the S&P 500. U.S. investors might not have realized the same gain because foreign currencies declined almost 8% against the dollar, meaning that the return of the EAFE index relative to the S&P 500 index was about 2% that year.

To demonstrate these effects, Meyer calculated the return on foreign equities relative to the S&P 500, using the native currency-based EAFE index and the S&P 500. In 1983, this EAFE index rose 32.6% and the S&P 500 rose 22.6%, meaning that local equities outperformed the S&P 500 by 10%. Since she had already calculated that the dollar based EAFE index outperformed the S&P 500 by 2% that year, Meyer could show that currency movements contributed −8% to the overall return of international equities to U.S. investors relative to the S&P 500. Table A shows the approach Meyer used to decompose the foreign equity return and the foreign currency return from the EAFE return for 1983.

[2]The MSCI EAFE® Index (Europe, Australasia, Far East) is a free float-adjusted market capitalization index that is designed to measure developed market equity performance, excluding the U.S. & Canada. As of April 2002 the MSCI EAFE Index consisted of the following 21 developed market country indices: Australia, Austria, Belgium, Denmark, Finland, France, Germany, Greece, Hong Kong, Ireland, Italy, Japan, the Netherlands, New Zealand, Norway, Portugal, Singapore, Spain, Sweden, Switzerland and the United Kingdom. Source: ⟨http://www.msci.com/methodology/index.html⟩.

TABLE A   EAFE Returns to U.S. Investors Relative to the S&P 500: Contribution by Foreign Equity Returns and Foreign Currency Returns in 1983

EAFE Return (native currency based index)	32.6%	
EAFE Return (dollar based index)	24.6%	
S&P 500 Return	22.6%	
	EAFE Return to U.S. Investor relative to S&P 500:	24.6% − 22.6% = 2.0%
	Contribution of foreign equity return: Return on foreign equities relative to the S&P 500:	32.6% − 22.6% = 10.0%
	Contribution of foreign currency return: EAFE Return to U.S. Investor less foreign equity return:	2.0% − 10.0% = −8.0%

Source: Casewriter.

SYNTHESIZING THE RESULTS

Meyer wanted to synthesize the data she had analyzed in a risk-return framework so she could show how international diversification enhanced the returns that were possible for a domestic investor. Using this framework she could explain why the benefits existed and what could cause them to wax and wane.

Using the monthly index values for the S&P 500 and the EAFE indices in Appendix C, Meyer calculated the monthly returns on the indices. She used this data to construct a series of portfolios, starting with a 100% allocation in the S&P 500, then calculating the returns of a portfolio with a 90% allocation to the S&P 500 and 10% to EAFE. She worked through different portfolio mixes, ending with a 100% allocation to EAFE. Again, she wanted to get a sense of these figures over time, particularly looking at the 1981 to 2003 time period, then the sub-periods of 1981–1991 and 1992–2003. She was, of course, also curious to see whether the results were robust to the choice of currency and wanted to compare the results using the U.S. dollar based EAFE and the native currency based EAFE.

For this part of her analysis, Meyer used monthly returns because she judged this approach provided a better measurement of the standard deviation of the returns. For her client presentation, however, she again planned to annualize the average monthly returns and the standard deviations. She also planned to use the results to map the efficient frontiers in a typical mean-variance graph to demonstrate how different international allocations in a portfolio affected the portfolio's risk-return characteristics.

BUILDING THE CLIENT PRESENTATION

Meyer knew she faced a serious marketing problem: she needed to convince Bosse—and possibly other clients—of the financial rewards of internationally diversified portfolios. She therefore carefully reviewed the arguments she wanted to make, and the analyses she would need to support those arguments. Meyer decided to include the following information in her presentation:

- The annualized returns and standard deviations for the equity markets of Australia, Canada, France, Germany, Hong Kong, Japan, the United Kingdom, and the U.S. from 1981–2003, and over two sub-periods, 1981–1991 and 1992–2003, using both native currency based returns and U.S. dollar based returns.

- The correlations between the different markets over the entire period and over the same sub-periods using first the returns data based on local currencies and then the U.S. dollar based data.

- The annual performance of foreign equities (as measured by the EAFE index) relative to U.S. equities (as measured by the S&P 500 index) from 1981–2003 and the decomposition of that relative performance into local equity returns and currency returns.

- The returns and standard deviations of a series of portfolios based on different mixes of foreign and U.S. equities, using the returns on the S&P 500 and EAFE indices (both native currency and dollar based) to construct these portfolios. Again, Meyers planned to present the results for different time periods: 1981–2003, 1981–1991, and 1992–2003, and wanted to use the data to map efficient frontiers for each of the different time periods.

Meyer knew she had a struggle ahead to convince her clients of the continued value of international diversification after their prolonged experience of U.S. indices outperforming those abroad. Nonetheless, she was confident she could demonstrate the benefits and she set to work on the presentation she had outlined.

APPENDIX A

EXCHANGE RATES AND STOCK MARKET INDEX VALUES FROM 1981 TO 2003

	Exchange Rate (Foreign per USD)							Index Values							
	Australia	Canada	France[a]	Germany[a]	Hong Kong	Japan	U.K.	Australia	Canada	France	Germany	Hong Kong	Japan	U.K.	U.S.
12/31/80	0.8465	1.1945	4.5475	1.9735	5.1100	203.1000	0.4186	312.14	229.7	250.83	129.27	328.28	152.53	820.03	147.28
01/30/81	0.8486	1.1943	4.9075	2.1320	5.2880	206.7000	0.4227	281.74	227.26	237.53	125.87	361.29	158.03	813.14	142.61
02/27/81	0.8658	1.2013	5.0150	2.1310	5.3370	209.7000	0.4537	272.12	221.64	245.98	126.09	340.37	158.26	851.22	145.56
03/31/81	0.8570	1.1873	4.9975	2.1105	5.2870	211.2500	0.4479	298.26	238.45	251.81	128.94	314.97	166.93	859.16	149.85
04/30/81	0.8702	1.1962	5.2550	2.2105	5.3710	215.7800	0.4674	292.9	237.39	237.56	134.44	323.2	178.84	924.04	149.17
05/29/81	0.8782	1.2037	5.5625	2.3300	5.4705	223.9000	0.4831	294.85	241.05	194.39	130.66	378.14	179.33	888.79	149.55
06/30/81	0.8712	1.2006	5.7180	2.3940	5.5500	226.8500	0.5181	286.25	232.47	181.9	137.04	402.15	188.49	904.89	148.44
07/31/81	0.8809	1.2339	5.8710	2.4710	5.7870	240.4000	0.5435	255.94	224.31	212.29	138.51	402.89	191.11	914.58	147.58
08/31/81	0.8699	1.2020	5.8650	2.4475	5.9300	230.5000	0.5420	254.84	217.36	215.91	133.87	394.85	190.6	959.03	139.24
09/30/81	0.8750	1.2069	5.5625	2.3250	6.1200	232.3000	0.5546	229.2	193.17	209.79	129.07	301.59	176.15	799.93	133.63
10/30/81	0.8795	1.2030	5.6550	2.2435	5.8620	232.8000	0.5371	216.51	190.43	202.09	128.53	303.19	176.63	834.55	140.35
11/30/81	0.8682	1.1766	5.6040	2.2138	5.6125	214.2000	0.5115	233.87	207.02	210.77	132.92	338.63	178.41	925.01	146.17
12/31/81	0.8865	1.1863	5.6850	2.2380	5.6875	219.8000	0.5222	233.78	202.98	208.78	130.14	327.21	184.15	921.97	143.22
01/29/82	0.9149	1.1967	5.8940	2.3165	5.7900	228.3000	0.5322	213.12	188.33	223.08	133.17	329.91	188.24	970.63	142.78
02/26/82	0.9315	1.2290	6.0890	2.3880	5.8950	237.2500	0.5495	192.65	182.7	232.64	135.19	298.48	180.37	929.97	136.34
03/31/82	0.9529	1.2305	6.2820	2.4175	5.8430	248.2500	0.5615	181.3	176.78	215.33	139.85	277.17	171.42	965.27	136.24
04/30/82	0.9422	1.2197	6.0960	2.3310	5.8170	235.8500	0.5573	204.69	173.67	231.21	139.74	315.44	176.58	987.08	141.81
05/28/82	0.9521	1.2440	6.1250	2.3475	5.7475	243.3000	0.5583	203.62	173.49	230.38	137.33	333.09	177.03	1025.47	137.33
06/30/82	0.9784	1.2929	6.8300	2.4595	5.9025	255.0000	0.5762	189.44	161.48	212.82	133.45	303.01	174	982.56	136.05
07/30/82	1.0111	1.2556	6.8550	2.4660	5.9405	258.1000	0.5754	189.44	169.68	205.69	133.19	280.03	170.16	1014.66	134.62
08/31/82	1.0371	1.2392	7.0120	2.4970	6.0475	261.1000	0.5812	201.12	195.36	216.47	132.04	241.16	171.84	1050.74	151.16
09/30/82	1.0532	1.2363	7.1380	2.5290	6.2850	268.3000	0.5901	210.32	193.15	209.28	138.4	216.87	170.64	1105.22	153.13
10/29/82	1.0686	1.2261	7.2400	2.5600	6.8700	277.1000	0.5963	210.06	216.98	212.96	137.73	180.15	176.59	1131.23	170.55
11/30/82	1.0440	1.2373	6.9730	2.4650	6.6700	249.2000	0.6127	202.58	224.62	215.23	139.34	167.61	190.87	1146.47	178.89
12/31/82	1.0204	1.2297	6.7400	2.3780	6.4800	234.7000	0.6180	205.08	240.1	211.44	149.01	185.77	196.98	1172.63	182.58

(Continued)

EXCHANGE RATES AND STOCK MARKET INDEX VALUES FROM 1981 TO 2003

| | Exchange Rate (Foreign per USD) | | | | | | | Index Values | | | | | | | |
	Australia	Canada	France[a]	Germany[a]	Hong Kong	Japan	U.K.	Australia	Canada	France	Germany	Hong Kong	Japan	U.K.	U.S.
01/31/83	1.0334	1.2367	6.9940	2.4650	6.5675	239.8500	0.6578	227.91	242.85	227.59	147.97	217.69	194.06	1218.76	189.48
02/28/83	1.0477	1.2290	6.9000	2.4340	6.6160	237.8500	0.6616	213.61	258.03	234.27	158.5	252.74	195.71	1233.17	193.84
03/31/83	1.1571	1.2341	7.2810	2.4310	6.7225	239.0000	0.6745	222.76	264.87	257.01	175.67	250.18	205.52	1279.04	199.91
04/29/83	1.1533	1.2262	7.3960	2.4665	6.9050	238.3000	0.6421	259.64	291.13	274.32	187.14	256.79	209.49	1377.33	215.58
05/31/83	1.1349	1.2300	7.5730	2.5245	7.1450	238.8500	0.6248	273.83	298.13	289.91	177.21	230.98	213.85	1378.32	213.23
06/30/83	1.1425	1.2276	7.6250	2.5410	7.1500	239.2800	0.6523	266.93	303.37	288.25	185.26	244.47	221.26	1448.87	220.39
07/29/83	1.1362	1.2340	7.9600	2.6485	7.2400	241.7500	0.6579	300.11	306.8	299.85	190.41	273.22	227.2	1413.32	215.36
08/31/83	1.1387	1.2340	8.1150	2.6970	7.5450	246.4500	0.6693	312.88	310.57	319.32	181.26	246.16	230.93	1435.5	217.49
09/30/83	1.1147	1.2330	7.9950	2.6315	8.1500	235.6500	0.6677	322.16	319.72	331.09	184.21	196.07	235.65	1419.27	221.9
10/31/83	1.0947	1.2326	8.0130	2.6315	7.8025	234.0500	0.6688	308.03	301.51	331.18	197.86	221.57	233.66	1399.99	220.18
11/30/83	1.0933	1.2392	8.2040	2.6990	7.8085	232.5000	0.6835	334.36	328.18	350.98	201.34	219.98	234.88	1476.5	223.81
12/30/83	1.1154	1.2445	8.3350	2.7250	7.7805	231.7000	0.6889	344.86	327.06	364.6	202.95	227.07	251.12	1498.48	221.97
01/31/84	1.0903	1.2493	8.6160	2.8165	7.8005	234.6700	0.7137	337.57	314.79	400.12	213.68	285.29	266.99	1615.22	219.59
02/29/84	1.0599	1.2519	7.9950	2.5983	7.7870	233.4300	0.6709	323.5	308.63	382.38	205.08	278.8	266.26	1585.49	210.79
03/30/84	1.0681	1.2766	7.9900	2.5940	7.8170	224.7500	0.6957	334.41	306.34	390.29	205.96	270.92	299.75	1696.02	214.04
04/30/84	1.0881	1.2845	8.3450	2.7215	7.8185	227.0000	0.7153	336.78	302.54	430.03	207.84	275.11	296.43	1736.62	216.58
05/31/84	1.1123	1.2946	8.3850	2.7318	7.8135	231.5800	0.7218	285.48	291.88	424.56	201.56	247.78	264.83	1571.2	204.48
06/29/84	1.1608	1.3199	8.5360	2.7815	7.8200	237.3000	0.7366	289.79	290.82	418.14	207.02	244.2	271.58	1612.47	208.99
07/31/84	1.2099	1.3115	8.9150	2.9063	7.8400	245.3000	0.7649	297.62	285.49	384.34	193.78	218.25	260.88	1577.57	207.83
08/31/84	1.1781	1.2974	8.8670	2.8895	7.8430	241.9000	0.7648	321.87	319.63	427.5	205.82	254.86	281.07	1739.76	230.76
09/28/84	1.2063	1.3183	9.4200	3.0720	7.8100	246.9000	0.8104	322.61	321.32	444.86	219.04	277.33	285.26	1799.56	230.7
10/31/84	1.1762	1.3150	9.2950	3.0305	7.8220	245.7000	0.8207	325.62	318.22	447.66	222.41	287.63	298.36	1835.51	232.53
11/30/84	1.1666	1.3242	9.5250	3.1100	7.8265	247.5000	0.8354	322.17	320.56	447.76	225.52	320.27	302.91	1902.59	230.6
12/31/84	1.2121	1.3217	9.6525	3.1550	7.8250	251.6000	0.8636	312.29	327.03	449.48	229.74	345.03	316.88	2035.25	236.6
01/31/85	1.2288	1.3272	9.6750	3.1630	7.7980	254.8000	0.8846	334.63	352.38	479.56	240.96	393.11	321.83	2144.03	255.33

(Continued)

APPENDIX A   (*Continued*)

EXCHANGE RATES AND STOCK MARKET INDEX VALUES FROM 1981 TO 2003

	Exchange Rate (Foreign per USD)							Index Values							
	Australia	Canada	France[a]	Germany[a]	Hong Kong	Japan	U.K.	Australia	Canada	France	Germany	Hong Kong	Japan	U.K.	U.S.
02/28/85	1.4085	1.3835	10.2200	3.3440	7.8000	259.4500	0.9268	342.87	352.26	495.85	244.63	390	337.09	2129.8	258.8
03/29/85	1.4286	1.3675	9.4050	3.0830	7.7970	251.0000	0.8091	357.38	354.65	512.86	249.18	393.49	342.39	2149.88	258.43
04/30/85	1.5516	1.3670	9.4500	3.0980	7.7795	251.5000	0.8058	386.02	361.33	532.09	258.19	429.08	331.86	2178.34	258.96
05/31/85	1.5078	1.3745	9.3350	3.0590	7.7730	251.2000	0.7776	380.55	377.35	571.89	276.79	456.28	342.2	2227.74	274.24
06/28/85	1.4959	1.3592	9.2400	3.0290	7.7620	248.4000	0.7637	372.4	371.98	548.14	294.88	441.61	352.02	2099.69	279.08
07/31/85	1.3839	1.3540	8.5425	2.7995	7.7490	236.4500	0.7087	402.99	381.36	517.23	281.3	465.38	337.03	2155.13	277.99
08/30/85	1.4255	1.3659	8.5875	2.8110	7.8045	239.0000	0.7189	396.35	388.63	539.1	301.23	465.41	347.87	2308.67	275.38
09/30/85	1.4245	1.3710	8.1725	2.6790	7.7625	216.5000	0.7100	423.86	364.87	508.91	321.56	426.41	351.36	2218.98	265.66
10/31/85	1.4306	1.3668	7.9750	2.6190	7.7925	211.5500	0.6942	438.18	369.98	534.7	359.99	473.61	353.18	2374.59	278.19
11/29/85	1.4579	1.3840	7.6650	2.5125	7.8015	202.1000	0.6716	420.95	393.9	602.78	351.94	487.55	346	2471.9	298.11
12/31/85	1.4667	1.3985	7.5075	2.4470	7.8075	200.2500	0.6920	432.99	401.22	642.66	398.81	497.32	363.12	2434.58	312.69
01/31/86	1.4010	1.4233	7.3200	2.3880	7.8070	192.3000	0.7082	460.01	390.46	667.68	391.88	481.29	360.48	2490.57	316.34
02/28/86	1.4300	1.4230	6.8655	2.2308	7.8050	180.5500	0.6916	448.74	394.06	725.78	388.13	486.88	377.38	2676.03	339.62
03/31/86	1.4053	1.3970	7.2050	2.3450	7.8165	177.6000	0.6787	486.84	423.48	831.19	418.23	471.78	442.4	2902.58	358.85
04/30/86	1.3501	1.3738	6.8955	2.1650	7.7920	167.6000	0.6447	517.07	426.89	921.34	435.98	531.18	437.29	2925.05	355.17
05/30/86	1.3990	1.3797	7.4060	2.3250	7.8110	174.5000	0.6792	535.86	435.86	861.53	399.78	515.08	453.41	2841.93	372.09
06/30/86	1.4848	1.3870	7.0230	2.2010	7.8090	163.8000	0.6527	502.08	431.06	852.24	390.25	487.9	472.65	2936.59	379.02
07/31/86	1.6781	1.3795	6.8100	2.0935	7.8080	153.8500	0.6705	476.81	410.28	914.31	370.07	516.95	499.95	2800.99	359.5
08/29/86	1.6420	1.3881	6.6700	2.0355	7.8035	154.5500	0.6720	498.66	424.4	1005.53	419.82	532.9	537.18	2989.74	384.79
09/30/86	1.5926	1.3888	6.6410	2.0272	7.8020	154.3500	0.6912	527.61	419.49	932.15	397.94	579.54	538.96	2822.52	351.83
10/31/86	1.5605	1.3905	6.7175	2.0610	7.7995	163.4000	0.7115	584.18	431.43	949.02	400.45	642	498.84	2974.1	371.06
11/28/86	1.5375	1.3840	6.4550	1.9730	7.7845	162.0500	0.6976	587.96	432.93	976.09	412.21	673.37	528.09	3001.89	379.17
12/31/86	1.5031	1.3831	6.3770	1.9235	7.7915	158.3000	0.6745	624.84	437.98	989.08	407.41	724.62	554.35	3108.61	369.46
01/30/87	1.5110	1.3420	6.1075	1.8330	7.7650	153.6500	0.6605	625.32	481.57	1037.65	365.05	727.22	616.96	3367.15	418.91
02/27/87	1.4771	1.3324	6.0830	1.8275	7.7955	153.2700	0.6468	687.82	502.31	1067.33	348.51	823.72	641.62	3670.76	434.81

(*Continued*)

EXCHANGE RATES AND STOCK MARKET INDEX VALUES FROM 1981 TO 2003

	Exchange Rate (Foreign per USD)							Index Values							
	Australia	Canada	France[a]	Germany[a]	Hong Kong	Japan	U.K.	Australia	Canada	France	Germany	Hong Kong	Japan	U.K.	U.S.
03/31/87	1.4194	1.3087	6.0000	1.8020	7.7990	145.6800	0.6223	721.15	541.98	1126.22	358.92	789.5	704.42	3742.34	444.29
04/30/87	1.4245	1.3363	6.0020	1.7985	7.8040	140.6700	0.6022	748.64	534.4	1136.56	360.86	779.42	776.12	3844.8	438.98
05/29/87	1.4041	1.3440	6.0900	1.8240	7.8085	144.1000	0.6137	767.99	536.39	1098.11	354.15	853.52	793.74	4159.64	440.86
06/30/87	1.3872	1.3337	6.0915	1.8262	7.8105	146.8000	0.6200	779.43	548.46	1039	375.58	943.75	743.97	4391.22	463.9
07/31/87	1.4323	1.3326	6.1860	1.8590	7.8077	149.9000	0.6285	896.69	589.82	1084.1	400.95	1040.97	748.25	4556.24	483.7
08/31/87	1.3996	1.3183	6.0520	1.8108	7.8075	141.7500	0.6124	957.92	584.67	1113.35	409.37	1085.3	787.74	4369.08	504.22
09/30/87	1.4108	1.3100	6.1650	1.8428	7.8075	146.5000	0.6155	990.75	569.42	1059.67	401.49	1189.68	788.49	4598.2	492.25
10/30/87	1.4925	1.3180	5.8680	1.7283	7.8040	138.4000	0.5809	592.05	443.12	833.79	314.49	645.15	696.83	3418.96	390.11
11/30/87	1.4184	1.3091	5.5790	1.6405	7.7700	132.4200	0.5478	613.02	428.24	781.33	277.84	623.59	682.59	3059.8	358.2
12/31/87	1.3850	1.3033	5.3280	1.5708	7.7620	121.2500	0.5302	623.62	458.23	750.9	277.05	672.04	638.24	3324.18	383.78
01/29/88	1.4124	1.2768	5.6550	1.6785	7.7750	127.7500	0.5653	594.19	447.33	674.86	261.75	694.59	699.73	3501.96	400.81
02/29/88	1.3916	1.2634	5.7180	1.6883	7.8010	128.4500	0.5639	603.42	467.5	817.7	295.41	701.14	755.82	3472.8	418.14
03/31/88	1.3492	1.2364	5.6125	1.6558	7.8020	124.1000	0.5301	692.75	478.01	758.64	294.97	744.71	778.57	3443.32	405.66
04/29/88	1.3200	1.2315	5.6910	1.6746	7.8180	124.9200	0.5323	712.86	481.45	838.22	295.28	760.31	795.93	3561.64	410.5
05/31/88	1.2467	1.2339	5.7540	1.7015	7.8160	124.5500	0.5350	783.69	470.53	909.87	300.03	741.38	767.75	3533.05	412.7
06/30/88	1.2587	1.2130	6.1275	1.8170	7.8035	133.5300	0.5853	765.78	496.48	979.78	314.93	801.01	787.55	3698.17	432.74
07/29/88	1.2461	1.2107	6.3190	1.8750	7.8070	133.0500	0.5848	800.23	488.59	986.05	323.6	798.72	806.88	3713.53	430.71
08/31/88	1.2441	1.2400	6.3785	1.8787	7.8055	136.5200	0.5944	786.95	476.47	970.2	323.82	725.89	770.26	3521.79	417.67
09/30/88	1.2771	1.2173	6.3715	1.8730	7.8110	133.9000	0.5914	787.8	477.02	1066.76	346.32	724.14	776.21	3671.02	435.64
10/31/88	1.2195	1.2197	6.0830	1.7820	7.8105	125.5000	0.5653	803.44	492.56	1117.17	357.64	784.06	770.78	3765.7	442.82
11/30/88	1.1429	1.1878	5.9290	1.7360	7.8050	121.9000	0.5407	747.79	478.85	1119.83	352.36	795.52	817	3660	435.25
12/30/88	1.1716	1.1928	6.0600	1.7735	7.8090	125.0500	0.5529	762.04	491.49	1196.53	368.31	805.79	843.05	3670.73	443.92
01/31/89	1.1269	1.1835	6.3860	1.8785	7.7985	130.5000	0.5714	798.75	525.82	1270.65	376.28	918.59	878.93	4222.48	474.16
02/28/89	1.2519	1.1990	6.2060	1.8230	7.8015	126.8700	0.5734	759.26	519.65	1216.17	369.58	902.28	869.52	4179.06	461.89
03/31/89	1.2210	1.1936	6.3970	1.8965	7.7880	132.7700	0.5934	751.5	525.52	1269.97	378.63	903.88	872.18	4358.59	472.25

(Continued)

APPENDIX A   (Continued)

EXCHANGE RATES AND STOCK MARKET INDEX VALUES FROM 1981 TO 2003

	Exchange Rate (Foreign per USD)							Index Values							
	Australia	Canada	France[a]	Germany[a]	Hong Kong	Japan	U.K.	Australia	Canada	France	Germany	Hong Kong	Japan	U.K.	U.S.
04/28/89	1.2594	1.1865	6.3550	1.8802	7.7800	132.8500	0.5921	786.43	534.83	1307.58	392.84	931.39	878.07	4441.23	497.64
05/31/89	1.3294	1.2062	6.6990	1.9760	7.7760	142.3300	0.6363	817.29	553.38	1365.14	401.99	814.62	894.5	4486.64	518.28
06/30/89	1.3233	1.1985	6.6360	1.9545	7.7980	144.0000	0.6456	818.48	562.47	1373.18	424.9	673.86	865.02	4544.35	515.73
07/31/89	1.3222	1.1809	6.3170	1.8658	7.8070	136.9500	0.6002	892.2	596.03	1423.2	447.37	767.92	932.59	4849.07	560.84
08/31/89	1.3077	1.1763	6.6050	1.9582	7.8110	144.6000	0.6357	962.12	602.6	1456.44	461.68	749.89	919.55	4982.85	570.47
09/29/89	1.2907	1.1789	6.3500	1.8725	7.8030	139.6000	0.6194	950.8	594.49	1493.81	468.2	827.13	951.84	4842.77	569.47
10/31/89	1.2778	1.1741	6.2460	1.8413	7.8110	142.7300	0.6339	906.08	591.53	1387.71	440.57	818.48	943.96	4493.02	558.51
11/30/89	1.2780	1.1633	6.0650	1.7800	7.8165	142.9100	0.6371	885.81	590.99	1439.87	473.37	828.19	990.66	4764.76	570.81
12/29/89	1.2669	1.1580	5.7740	1.6895	7.8070	143.8000	0.6194	927.17	600.37	1534.61	520.52	853.31	1007.32	5082.68	582.78
01/31/90	1.3012	1.1858	5.7300	1.6880	7.8120	144.5500	0.5955	947.12	560.98	1448.84	532.68	832.9	958.47	4942.17	544.05
02/28/90	1.3156	1.1923	5.7350	1.6965	7.8090	148.8200	0.5920	894.65	563.45	1426.47	525.95	895.42	894.37	4795.79	551.19
03/30/90	1.3249	1.1705	5.6850	1.6883	7.8095	157.8200	0.6068	886.48	560.39	1506.47	573.08	914.71	779.75	4776.54	566.5
04/30/90	1.3333	1.1654	5.6340	1.6790	7.7940	158.8500	0.6102	829.3	518.84	1573.85	535.77	905.08	777.05	4496.53	554.33
05/31/90	1.3024	1.1745	5.7310	1.6990	7.7820	152.6400	0.5965	884.44	557.17	1623.49	546.6	951.82	853.3	5017.59	607.34
06/29/90	1.2633	1.1665	5.5945	1.6658	7.7885	152.3500	0.5731	889.84	554.9	1575.4	557.9	1020.74	822.26	5107.63	606
07/31/90	1.2598	1.1530	5.3220	1.5875	7.7645	146.1300	0.5376	945.99	561.85	1536.44	578.23	1078.11	790.34	5032.8	604.28
08/31/90	1.2255	1.1545	5.2850	1.5760	7.7630	143.9300	0.5285	907.71	534.67	1339.93	495.43	952.74	694.1	4676.67	549.08
09/28/90	1.2115	1.1565	5.2430	1.5665	7.7635	138.2700	0.5338	845.39	510.95	1200.47	412.51	850.02	553.03	4321.21	522.12
10/31/90	1.2742	1.1678	5.0760	1.5157	7.7965	129.9500	0.5144	819.32	499.36	1289.72	448.04	923.66	660.39	4496.88	522.9
11/30/90	1.2920	1.1658	5.0650	1.5000	7.8005	133.1000	0.5157	828.75	512.58	1265.64	452.63	917.12	588.6	4697.91	559.2
12/31/90	1.2953	1.1605	5.1000	1.4970	7.8010	135.7500	0.5185	813.12	530.64	1228.47	441.93	942.61	619.59	4698.62	574.64
01/31/91	1.2778	1.1629	5.0285	1.4785	7.7955	131.4500	0.5089	852.42	536.62	1263.16	442.55	1021.42	614.97	4764.2	603.93
02/28/91	1.2734	1.1499	5.1955	1.5260	7.7920	132.9500	0.5236	911.27	567.85	1418.95	479.1	1128.95	699.44	5294.06	647.47
03/29/91	1.2937	1.1595	5.7550	1.6975	7.7940	140.6000	0.5719	941.41	578.05	1456.96	473.07	1187.21	705.33	5527.88	667.62
04/30/91	1.2798	1.1520	5.8130	1.7185	7.7955	136.3800	0.5806	1012.01	581.96	1446.2	493.16	1147.42	703.61	5596.26	668.94

(Continued)

APPENDIX A (*Continued*)

EXCHANGE RATES AND STOCK MARKET INDEX VALUES FROM 1981 TO 2003

	Exchange Rate (Foreign per USD)							Index Values							
	Australia	Canada	France[a]	Germany[a]	Hong Kong	Japan	U.K.	Australia	Canada	France	Germany	Hong Kong	Japan	U.K.	U.S.
05/31/91	1.3168	1.1453	5.9000	1.7397	7.7380	138.4500	0.5889	1011.86	596.53	1496.72	515.32	1189.53	705.03	5637.42	697.06
06/28/91	1.3038	1.1424	6.1480	1.8138	7.7650	137.9000	0.6180	1019.57	584.36	1418.81	492.85	1178.96	655.77	5478.78	666.34
07/31/91	1.2853	1.1519	5.9360	1.7465	7.7600	137.4200	0.5936	1073.02	596.75	1433.59	489.25	1305.3	670.14	5867.31	700.33
08/30/91	1.2736	1.1422	5.9390	1.7485	7.7610	136.8500	0.5952	1059.94	598.85	1516.67	495.5	1317.08	626.42	6031.9	719.77
09/30/91	1.2508	1.1318	5.6625	1.6625	7.7430	132.8500	0.5708	1082.11	582.55	1549.78	483.2	1305.67	660.55	6040.41	711.52
10/31/91	1.2835	1.1230	5.6985	1.6680	7.7690	130.6000	0.5739	1168.36	605.35	1536.63	477.12	1345.77	678.28	5932.88	723.95
11/29/91	1.2749	1.1350	5.5580	1.6270	7.7620	130.0800	0.5664	1119.97	595.54	1462.88	470.32	1381.49	622.55	5637.88	697.82
12/31/91	1.3170	1.1558	5.1950	1.5200	7.7800	124.9000	0.5359	1161.41	608.67	1481.47	468.85	1433.59	616.09	5750.75	779.75
01/31/92	1.3296	1.1752	5.4800	1.6075	7.7620	125.5500	0.5590	1141.03	626.66	1570.97	500.01	1527.05	588.27	5978.11	768.4
02/28/92	1.3266	1.1820	5.5670	1.6373	7.7570	129.1500	0.5695	1142.52	627.3	1661.58	519.51	1643.81	563.61	6023.41	776.27
03/31/92	1.2987	1.1902	5.5815	1.6465	7.7390	132.9200	0.5759	1124.54	602	1649.76	511.56	1659.36	514.05	5775.25	762.04
04/30/92	1.3219	1.1960	5.5780	1.6525	7.7590	133.3000	0.5634	1185.22	595.61	1723.36	512.44	1814.58	481.5	6328.67	781.43
05/29/92	1.3214	1.2048	5.3980	1.6065	7.7445	127.7500	0.5467	1206.49	602.29	1736.73	525.15	2055.51	501.08	6513.09	787.98
06/30/92	1.3374	1.1972	5.1260	1.5240	7.7305	125.8700	0.5253	1180.67	599.36	1639.71	508.93	2065.93	451.7	6066.63	775.18
07/31/92	1.3435	1.1845	5.0005	1.4807	7.7348	127.3500	0.5208	1162.51	606.67	1532.84	471.18	1983.91	446.45	5788.47	809.99
08/31/92	1.3974	1.1952	4.7790	1.4018	7.7287	122.9500	0.5027	1116.22	602.39	1490.37	449.25	1903.43	504.51	5594.34	794.26
09/30/92	1.4008	1.2480	4.7895	1.4147	7.7237	120.0000	0.5621	1074.26	587.89	1513.42	436.96	1868.38	476.78	6193.82	804.5
10/30/92	1.4384	1.2405	5.2350	1.5430	7.7315	123.3000	0.6400	1035.85	598.08	1506.83	446.98	2098.68	467.33	6458.3	812.91
11/30/92	1.4658	1.2561	5.4135	1.5935	7.7410	124.4200	0.6607	1061.63	594.65	1537.51	458.48	1989.63	483.92	6775.25	843.6
12/31/92	1.4514	1.2714	5.5270	1.6197	7.7430	124.8500	0.6609	1143.61	607.64	1599.14	458.61	1908.13	480.79	7049.6	856.04
01/29/93	1.4721	1.2700	5.4510	1.6110	7.7330	124.9700	0.6732	1128.82	602.34	1557.79	466.14	1992.53	479.35	7072.14	861.66
02/26/93	1.4378	1.2498	5.5790	1.6423	7.7340	118.1000	0.7035	1191.63	626.95	1733.1	501.89	2203.49	475.54	7282.8	869.43
03/31/93	1.4196	1.2573	5.4680	1.6105	7.7310	114.9000	0.6627	1232.95	653.21	1795.75	504.93	2253.42	534.21	7378.5	890.29
04/30/93	1.4194	1.2702	5.3555	1.5876	7.7310	111.1270	0.6371	1239.16	689.54	1738.46	494.33	2421.89	603.93	7288.84	868.87
05/31/93	1.4573	1.2707	5.3615	1.5880	7.7242	107.1700	0.6408	1266.52	701.58	1711.33	495.95	2611.61	606.4	7392.27	892.48

(*Continued*)

APPENDIX A (*Continued*)

EXCHANGE RATES AND STOCK MARKET INDEX VALUES FROM 1981 TO 2003

	Exchange Rate (Foreign per USD)							Index Values							
	Australia	Canada	France[a]	Germany[a]	Hong Kong	Japan	U.K.	Australia	Canada	France	Germany	Hong Kong	Japan	U.K.	U.S.
06/30/93	1.5008	1.2823	5.7450	1.7060	7.7440	106.8000	0.6698	1271.78	715.57	1769.96	506.48	2512.75	585.39	7559.58	897
07/30/93	1.4535	1.2844	5.9630	1.7405	7.7560	105.0500	0.6734	1345.18	713.67	1869.88	536.1	2472.96	616.13	7674.82	894.53
08/31/93	1.4903	1.3208	5.8650	1.6780	7.7485	104.7300	0.6726	1443.35	752.55	2002.93	572.75	2650.45	629.36	8183.38	927.89
09/30/93	1.5504	1.3360	5.7050	1.6340	7.7345	106.0500	0.6684	1459.84	729.49	1950.57	567.08	2711.3	606.95	8056.25	923.89
10/29/93	1.5026	1.3220	5.9000	1.6771	7.7280	108.3500	0.6720	1578.05	784.18	2019.69	617.44	3324	609.7	8442.82	940.99
11/30/93	1.5188	1.3372	5.9040	1.7175	7.7255	109.0800	0.6733	1502.33	773.2	1977.98	618.61	3343.86	516.92	8457.69	927.73
12/31/93	1.4743	1.3255	5.8975	1.7395	7.7280	111.7000	0.6768	1613.86	799.83	2149.24	661.23	4306.68	542.83	9177.14	942.43
01/31/94	1.4114	1.3270	5.9070	1.7399	7.7237	108.7200	0.6664	1719.97	849.14	2250.75	644.39	4150.11	615.81	9498.97	971.25
02/28/94	1.4045	1.3522	5.7890	1.7038	7.7270	104.2200	0.6723	1634.03	823.59	2159.8	624.3	3759.66	618.52	9144.21	948.19
03/31/94	1.4255	1.3838	5.7000	1.6680	7.7280	102.4000	0.6720	1538.72	808.35	2040.27	630.42	3325.22	591.42	8530.73	907.16
04/29/94	1.4015	1.3818	5.6800	1.6610	7.7253	102.0500	0.6615	1558.73	802.25	2104.6	659.06	3303.91	604.59	8665.87	919.52
05/31/94	1.3541	1.3845	5.6235	1.6448	7.7263	104.7400	0.6614	1571.88	810.52	1984.78	627.68	3504.12	632.54	8244.56	928.53
06/30/94	1.3680	1.3825	5.4355	1.5850	7.7300	98.5100	0.6459	1506.69	755.26	1863.02	605.66	3229.28	630.23	8077.43	904.42
07/29/94	1.3534	1.3835	5.4195	1.5875	7.7255	100.0500	0.6487	1565.05	786.1	2032.44	632.16	3505.67	616.51	8583.96	934.07
08/31/94	1.3434	1.3712	5.4080	1.5795	7.7280	100.1100	0.6510	1618.32	820.4	2030.72	648.57	3660.55	619.75	9022.89	972.64
09/30/94	1.3514	1.3410	5.2915	1.5508	7.7273	99.0500	0.6341	1552.5	820.01	1876.82	603.47	3557.17	596.28	8444.37	950.8
10/31/94	1.3477	1.3527	5.1500	1.5043	7.7275	96.9000	0.6116	1583.68	818.43	1882.82	613.39	3588.68	598.68	8633.33	971.75
11/30/94	1.3006	1.3752	5.3785	1.5685	7.7344	98.9100	0.6382	1474.73	788.45	1941.77	608.9	3174.05	575.03	8636.58	938.45
12/30/94	1.2898	1.4030	5.3445	1.5495	7.7375	99.6000	0.6384	1505.85	816.01	1872.34	623.14	3062.9	590.19	8599.66	953.04
01/31/95	1.3201	1.4092	5.2850	1.5232	7.7355	99.4300	0.6323	1455.36	785.79	1801.26	599.99	2730.95	549.48	8375.34	980.01
02/28/95	1.3550	1.3937	5.1295	1.4567	7.7316	96.6000	0.6313	1544.85	809.6	1801.72	624.2	3110.03	507.25	8410.73	1019.27
03/31/95	1.3652	1.3993	4.8100	1.3785	7.7321	86.8500	0.6177	1539.75	850.57	1881.6	578.47	3207.29	496.49	8799.07	1047.99
04/28/95	1.3751	1.3597	4.9160	1.3856	7.7410	84.0400	0.6215	1655.71	843.37	1942.92	606.12	3129.17	504.14	9036.2	1079.31
05/31/95	1.3908	1.3698	4.9570	1.4140	7.7358	84.6500	0.6303	1640.28	881.67	1989.98	624.49	3525.3	476.07	9390.99	1119.75
06/30/95	1.4069	1.3738	4.8525	1.3835	7.7380	84.7000	0.6287	1647	900.14	1911.59	631.24	3464.11	458.11	9390.91	1150.99

(*Continued*)

EXCHANGE RATES AND STOCK MARKET INDEX VALUES FROM 1981 TO 2003

| | Exchange Rate (Foreign per USD) | | | | | | | Index Values | | | | | | | |
	Australia	Canada	France[a]	Germany[a]	Hong Kong	Japan	U.K.	Australia	Canada	France	Germany	Hong Kong	Japan	U.K.	U.S.
07/31/95	1.3537	1.3695	4.7840	1.3852	7.7382	88.1800	0.6258	1726.84	920.26	1977.76	666.55	3579.22	510.14	9880.91	1193.44
08/31/95	1.3303	1.3432	5.0450	1.4679	7.7414	98.9500	0.6445	1748.37	904.89	1963.61	666.53	3474.1	547.41	9956.58	1200.18
09/29/95	1.3236	1.3445	4.9250	1.4295	7.7320	99.7300	0.6331	1750.68	908.56	1897.89	655.38	3651.31	554.45	10061.79	1253.11
10/31/95	1.3132	1.3401	4.8860	1.4074	7.7319	101.6500	0.6326	1706.56	901.2	1909.77	646.88	3699.88	545.12	10055.92	1251.42
11/30/95	1.3470	1.3587	4.9930	1.4468	7.7350	101.4600	0.6535	1787.35	949.63	1919.66	661.47	3718.07	569.68	10424.28	1304.22
12/29/95	1.3455	1.3655	4.8975	1.4345	7.7323	102.8700	0.6437	1833.61	964.41	1961.23	670.84	3817.6	604.39	10563.79	1324.8
01/31/96	1.3435	1.3743	5.1090	1.4895	7.7325	107.2900	0.6624	1902.45	1014.3	2144.7	720.64	4338.39	616.59	10832.16	1367.59
02/29/96	1.3084	1.3728	5.0425	1.4703	7.7315	105.1200	0.6527	1908.89	1011.98	2165.85	720.11	4293.88	598.44	10841.23	1386.98
03/29/96	1.2796	1.3635	5.0365	1.4766	7.7348	107.0000	0.6552	1861.95	1021.54	2240	722.12	4253.97	626.68	10890.58	1400.27
04/30/96	1.2732	1.3615	5.1665	1.5302	7.7360	104.6300	0.6645	1945.58	1065.03	2353.54	719.98	4254.74	654.53	11345.36	1426.42
05/31/96	1.2531	1.3704	5.1670	1.5265	7.7370	107.9900	0.6454	1912.15	1092.5	2343.4	730.24	4369.49	642.76	11220.76	1464.63
06/28/96	1.2729	1.3657	5.1440	1.5210	7.7410	109.4800	0.6440	1903.88	1061.86	2357.63	748.91	4308.66	656.73	11113.78	1467.69
07/31/96	1.2928	1.3747	4.9970	1.4725	7.7340	106.7700	0.6428	1858.28	1039.25	2226.27	722.42	4189.22	611.13	11074.52	1401.23
08/30/96	1.2642	1.3685	5.0645	1.4801	7.7330	108.7000	0.6405	1941.69	1088.25	2218.76	742.39	4388.73	596.26	11612.28	1437.81
09/30/96	1.2639	1.3620	5.1670	1.5270	7.7332	111.6500	0.6389	1970.74	1126.07	2368.79	768.46	4666.04	628.75	11841.52	1523.45
10/31/96	1.2610	1.3409	5.1110	1.5141	7.7323	113.7900	0.6143	2027.67	1203.18	2404.19	767.7	4895.79	599.85	11964.33	1554.67
11/29/96	1.2290	1.3489	5.2235	1.5377	7.7325	113.8800	0.5945	2073.49	1301.23	2583.28	804.65	5331.98	606.67	12221.8	1667.25
12/31/96	1.2588	1.3697	5.1928	1.5387	7.7347	115.7700	0.5840	2113.82	1288.14	2608.45	815.58	5413.55	576.69	12436.5	1640.81
01/31/97	1.3115	1.3474	5.5235	1.6362	7.7490	121.2500	0.6245	2119.11	1335.76	2830.18	853.22	5385.26	541.28	12980.43	1739.75
02/28/97	1.2878	1.3670	5.6930	1.6872	7.7437	120.8300	0.6140	2150.67	1345.96	2942.71	913.14	5461.99	549.2	13148.96	1747.59
03/31/97	1.2755	1.3835	5.6165	1.6678	7.7485	123.7200	0.6080	2134.67	1295.7	2995.43	960.81	5142.59	544.2	13140.03	1674.62
04/30/97	1.2829	1.3971	5.8375	1.7330	7.7467	127.0300	0.6173	2211.55	1339.14	2985.35	968.05	5316.21	573.36	13440.71	1770.74
05/30/97	1.3106	1.3798	5.7720	1.7090	7.7490	116.4000	0.6112	2330.87	1436.53	2920.07	996.38	6022.79	594.82	13956.63	1886.63
06/30/97	1.3245	1.3810	5.8752	1.7438	7.7475	114.6100	0.6006	2457.47	1467.61	3199.49	1057.53	6299.66	621.83	13902.03	1968.91
07/31/97	1.3421	1.3820	6.1960	1.8379	7.7430	118.3700	0.6102	2481.23	1576.87	3440.09	1200.62	6697.1	622.81	14726.81	2130.34

(Continued)

APPENDIX A (Continued)

EXCHANGE RATES AND STOCK MARKET INDEX VALUES FROM 1981 TO 2003

| | Exchange Rate (Foreign per USD) | | | | | | | Index Values | | | | | | | |
	Australia	Canada	France[a]	Germany[a]	Hong Kong	Japan	U.K.	Australia	Canada	France	Germany	Hong Kong	Japan	U.K.	U.S.
08/29/97	1.3615	1.3890	6.0750	1.8050	7.7500	120.6500	0.6172	2352.01	1513.68	3158.21	1072.22	6019.62	576.43	14601.21	2026.82
09/30/97	1.3793	1.3824	5.9335	1.7671	7.7385	120.7100	0.6205	2529.14	1620.45	3368.48	1124.8	6197.8	564.59	15824.71	2140.79
10/31/97	1.4225	1.4099	5.7670	1.7220	7.7320	120.3900	0.5957	2265.55	1583.87	3112.4	1033.06	4389.33	519.52	14827.68	2074.64
11/28/97	1.4652	1.4245	5.9020	1.7650	7.7304	127.7400	0.5922	2285.61	1535.68	3244.08	1079.77	4276.59	513.41	14841.92	2167.65
12/31/97	1.5349	1.4288	6.0190	1.7991	7.7495	130.4500	0.6088	2439.75	1589.92	3409.27	1140.8	4377.04	487.63	15732.57	2212.92
01/30/98	1.4594	1.4562	6.1370	1.8315	7.7375	127.1000	0.6126	2480.37	1597.5	3613.61	1191.39	3620.51	522.2	16638.26	2238.96
02/27/98	1.4738	1.4236	6.0835	1.8141	7.7430	126.1200	0.6078	2518.81	1692.93	3907.14	1268.94	4582	522.8	17675.42	2402.16
03/31/98	1.5122	1.4180	6.1950	1.8500	7.7495	133.2900	0.5965	2585.75	1809.58	4391.82	1367.05	4573.39	515.57	18336.23	2528.6
04/30/98	1.5337	1.4302	6.0170	1.7944	7.7465	132.3700	0.5978	2612.87	1834.8	4430.95	1379.5	4134.4	507.21	18418.96	2557.15
05/29/98	1.5974	1.4571	5.9830	1.7840	7.7495	138.5000	0.6132	2578.4	1843.01	4657.45	1467.53	3566.57	507.06	18543.95	2496.87
06/30/98	1.6108	1.4717	6.0470	1.8033	7.7483	138.2900	0.5990	2521.5	1796.35	4805.8	1529.17	3346.08	511.1	118264.25	2607.8
07/31/98	1.6474	1.5112	5.9670	1.7790	7.7490	144.6500	0.6117	2562.71	1717.88	4763.36	1532.77	3095.68	527.11	18293.38	2570.08
08/31/98	1.7483	1.5745	5.9140	1.7584	7.7497	140.9000	0.5967	2380.06	1392.03	4199.1	1285.65	2796.68	463.2	16364.55	2190.76
09/30/98	1.6863	1.5262	5.5990	1.6702	7.7492	136.5900	0.5884	2485.89	1405.15	3716.16	1216.21	3123.54	438.33	15777.42	2341.08
10/30/98	1.6000	1.5432	5.5570	1.6565	7.7455	116.4500	0.5976	2649.84	1555.6	4069.01	1254.86	4016.44	433.58	16932.01	2531.76
11/30/98	1.5924	1.5235	5.6890	1.6966	7.7430	123.2100	0.6066	2812.71	1598.26	4398.67	1344.54	4142.05	478.02	17812.43	2694.61
12/31/98	1.6332	1.5375	5.5870	1.6670	7.7476	113.0800	0.6014	2890.03	1644.9	4505.36	1355.77	4010.92	456.86	18198.57	2876.82
01/29/99	1.5881	1.5095	5.7687	1.7200	7.7485	116.0000	0.6076	3027.28	1735.84	4821.52	1425.75	3746.69	474.76	18391.75	2997.14
02/26/99	1.6116	1.5090	5.9660	1.7788	7.7480	118.7000	0.6239	3004.44	1640.75	4672.14	1381.07	3842.17	475.69	19301.05	2899.72
03/31/99	1.5773	1.5092	6.0692	1.8096	7.7500	118.4300	0.6196	3105.09	1719.99	4822.18	1359.13	4259.16	540.69	19835	3021.04
04/30/99	1.5106	1.4578	6.2094	1.8514	7.7508	119.4300	0.6217	3227.08	1824.75	5077.41	1464.65	5200.98	572.65	20789.41	3153.01
05/31/99	1.5319	1.4725	6.2940	1.8766	7.7575	120.8800	0.6242	3023.7	1795.69	5070.82	1398.23	4800.01	554.81	19866.17	3075.91
06/30/99	1.5126	1.4735	6.3623	1.8970	7.7586	120.9400	0.6343	3145.41	1853.56	5295.07	1479.02	5407.59	613.51	20289.81	3232.3
07/30/99	1.5333	1.5070	6.1339	1.8289	7.7619	114.7000	0.6170	3188.42	1872.13	5161.76	1426.85	5300.09	642.5	20176.69	3128.1
08/31/99	1.5674	1.4965	6.1994	1.8484	7.7660	109.3000	0.6217	3118.31	1840.14	5420.98	1473.99	5401.14	634.78	20286.2	3103.66
09/30/99	1.5319	1.4695	6.1633	1.8377	7.7679	106.8200	0.6076	3055.93	1839.77	5448.27	1423.64	5119.71	660.41	19542.5	3020.64

(Continued)

EXCHANGE RATES AND STOCK MARKET INDEX VALUES FROM 1981 TO 2003

	Exchange Rate (Foreign per USD)							Index Values							
	Australia	Canada	France[a]	Germany[a]	Hong Kong	Japan	U.K.	Australia	Canada	France	Germany	Hong Kong	Japan	U.K.	U.S.
10/29/99	1.5684	1.4720	6.2365	1.8595	7.7690	104.2900	0.6088	3066.89	1930.2	5732.99	1515.59	5318.1	691.27	20151.13	3215.58
11/30/99	1.5696	1.4720	6.5094	1.9409	7.7665	101.8000	0.6275	3286.99	2009.95	6228.04	1605.99	6170.53	733.87	21459.85	3303.65
12/31/99	1.5244	1.4440	6.5140	1.9422	7.7740	102.1600	0.6192	3385.46	2241.05	6990.95	1837.49	6765.39	771.44	22576.97	3527.26
01/31/00	1.5669	1.4517	6.7229	2.0045	7.7810	107.3300	0.6180	3336.25	2235.91	6712.28	1811.24	6273.16	766.24	20695.34	3368.91
02/29/00	1.6483	1.4505	6.8024	2.0282	7.7833	109.8800	0.6337	3330.88	2389.73	7341.36	2035	6880.02	779.07	20763.48	3353.2
03/31/00	1.6466	1.4538	6.8372	2.0386	7.7867	102.7300	0.6281	3371.41	2504.7	7476.52	2035.26	7034.57	770.11	21778.08	3663.55
04/28/00	1.7241	1.4818	7.2218	2.1533	7.7890	107.9800	0.6427	3352.72	2468.47	7574.32	1993.16	6243.12	741.48	21007.62	3475.1
05/31/00	1.7479	1.4977	7.0321	2.0967	7.7927	107.7400	0.6681	3304.76	2460.14	7587.97	1916.66	5920.8	679.36	21153.05	3344.21
06/30/00	1.6678	1.4820	6.8723	2.0491	7.7960	106.1400	0.6609	3530.6	2677.15	7621.73	1860.06	6475.08	710.34	21238.05	3492.05
07/31/00	1.7227	1.4880	7.0792	2.1108	7.7988	109.6800	0.6674	3494.04	2737.48	7760.28	1913.08	6778.16	645.9	21472.21	3418.39
08/31/00	1.7346	1.4720	7.3886	2.2030	7.7992	106.6600	0.6889	3517.02	2940.23	7930.5	1912.63	6900.9	674.06	22566.47	3671.09
09/29/00	1.8349	1.5070	7.4228	2.2132	7.7971	107.9000	0.6763	3511.11	2745.52	7466.33	1800.49	6327.74	652.4	21432.95	3486.99
10/31/00	1.9131	1.5273	7.7299	2.3048	7.7995	109.1500	0.6894	3482.23	2591.64	7596.07	1851.36	5997.7	611.25	21855	3422.78
11/30/00	1.8615	1.5355	7.5449	2.2496	7.8000	110.9300	0.7037	3505.28	2409.79	7082.57	1675.05	5580.95	601.59	20987.23	3083.04
12/29/00	1.7986	1.4995	6.9872	2.0833	7.7999	114.3500	0.6687	3450.07	2437.59	7104.98	1672.38	6010.14	566.34	21316.96	3117.4
01/31/01	1.8051	1.4995	7.0472	2.1012	7.7995	116.3900	0.6843	3625.46	2524.96	7212.32	1742.33	6413.08	575.49	21681.1	3233.85
02/28/01	1.9004	1.5320	7.1207	2.1231	7.8000	117.2800	0.6929	3598.65	2261.59	6539.06	1624.57	5969.98	548.86	20561.55	2914.45
03/30/01	2.0713	1.5784	7.4591	2.2241	7.8003	125.5400	0.7047	3433.22	2149.05	6354.13	1534.43	5147.28	563.9	19506.55	2708.56
04/30/01	1.9316	1.5360	7.3919	2.2040	7.7990	123.5700	0.6990	3626.89	2240.6	6922.18	1626.02	5469.95	600.83	20693.76	2938.72
05/31/01	1.9670	1.5461	7.7582	2.3132	7.7998	118.8800	0.7055	3679.76	2285.66	6743.63	1590.15	5472.52	577.06	20313.33	2957.3
06/29/01	1.9585	1.5175	7.7408	2.3080	7.8000	124.7300	0.7104	3766.35	2187.97	6442.56	1567.29	5417.36	570.77	19760.89	2895.27
07/31/01	1.9354	1.5310	7.4949	2.2347	7.7997	125.0000	0.7017	3605.58	2176.14	6283.39	1517.77	5139.17	522.85	19357.59	2854.25
08/31/01	1.8950	1.5478	7.2162	2.1516	7.7998	118.7500	0.6892	3552.55	2114.28	5848.61	1373.37	4651.84	483.83	18867.79	2675.99
09/28/01	2.0313	1.5797	7.2091	2.1495	7.7996	119.2300	0.6807	3330.98	1962.8	5060.55	1153.63	4175.9	450.04	17075.45	2449.41
10/31/01	1.9662	1.5905	7.2941	2.1748	7.8002	122.0700	0.6880	3545.11	1967.02	5422.43	1226.28	4283.21	465.7	17708.73	2505.94
11/30/01	1.9294	1.5717	7.3226	2.1833	7.7988	123.8200	0.7015	3667.94	2109.08	5664.7	1344.16	4762.21	463.19	18497.36	2696.95

(Continued)

APPENDIX A   (Continued)

EXCHANGE RATES AND STOCK MARKET INDEX VALUES FROM 1981 TO 2003

	Exchange Rate (Foreign per USD)							Index Values							
	Australia	Canada	France[a]	Germany[a]	Hong Kong	Japan	U.K.	Australia	Canada	France	Germany	Hong Kong	Japan	U.K.	U.S.
12/31/01	1.9543	1.5925	7.3695	2.1973	7.7980	131.3000	0.6876	3762.78	2187.62	5850.26	1381.98	4834.96	455.2	18606.04	2732.31
01/31/02	1.9685	1.5915	7.6327	2.2758	7.7995	132.8400	0.7082	3812.68	2165.44	5680.01	1385.2	4606.52	428.87	18430.8	2687.57
02/28/02	1.9316	1.6049	7.5763	2.2590	7.7995	134.6300	0.7078	3762.18	2173.4	5663.69	1371.12	4538.48	446.71	18266.69	2631.73
03/29/02	1.8702	1.5958	7.5250	2.2437	7.8000	132.6100	0.7018	3781.75	2247.08	5997.37	1448.88	4782.91	468.82	18990.82	2738.53
04/30/02	1.8563	1.5681	7.2868	2.1727	7.7992	128.1300	0.6866	3712.24	2205.04	5748.74	1372.74	5003	478.36	18696.55	2586.09
05/31/02	1.7501	1.5275	7.0238	2.0943	7.8000	123.0800	0.6838	3740.62	2212.44	5537.61	1329.78	4956.72	495.83	18482.57	2562.58
06/28/02	1.7809	1.5190	6.6554	1.9844	7.8000	119.3800	0.6560	3578.53	2086.27	5048.55	1213	4672.74	454.18	16911.01	2372.78
07/31/02	1.8563	1.5845	6.6962	1.9966	7.8000	119.9000	0.6400	3443.25	1934.46	4514.39	1069.37	4508.75	427.87	15381.21	2198.91
08/30/02	1.8198	1.5585	6.6893	1.9945	7.8000	118.3400	0.6462	3490.83	1938.47	4480.19	1060.99	4405.77	417.73	15400.04	2214.68
09/30/02	1.8443	1.5863	6.6399	1.9798	7.7998	122.8600	0.6369	3335.01	1828.92	3748.98	835.4	4006.01	407.79	13613.38	1986.43
10/31/02	1.7873	1.5610	6.6386	1.9794	7.7995	122.9100	0.6398	3426.4	1842.9	4229.93	933.36	4160.54	383.22	14701.45	2147.29
11/29/02	1.7886	1.5658	6.6045	1.9692	7.7988	122.7200	0.6430	3471.75	1923.89	4513.96	969.17	4438.59	396.94	15230.08	2270.16
12/31/02	1.7778	1.5800	6.2561	1.8654	7.7988	118.7500	0.6213	3416.16	1936.23	4164.74	872.61	4158.93	375.72	14452.81	2142.78
01/31/03	1.7065	1.5235	6.1082	1.8212	7.8001	119.9600	0.6080	3384.62	1930.27	4029.82	840.33	4177.39	365.78	13185.19	2086.74
02/28/03	1.6461	1.4939	6.0855	1.8145	7.7991	118.2200	0.6354	3202.97	1928.8	3806.6	793.11	4131.99	364.42	13511.21	2053.18
03/31/03	1.6543	1.4673	6.0180	1.7943	7.7995	118.0700	0.6333	3297.72	1877.1	3660.12	768.31	3935.08	350.67	13378.81	2076.18
04/30/03	1.5969	1.4504	5.8672	1.7494	7.7991	119.0700	0.6250	3448	1950.39	4113.49	896.45	3973.52	355.2	14617.14	2243.73
05/30/03	1.5354	1.3867	5.5750	1.6623	7.7987	119.5000	0.6100	3473.52	2031.04	4220.63	914.02	4358.21	372.94	15271.98	2370.55
06/30/03	1.4896	1.3542	5.7030	1.7004	7.7984	119.8700	0.6050	3497.3	2072.99	4326.02	970.23	4436.54	402.38	15337.74	2403.07
07/31/03	1.5446	1.3857	5.8406	1.7415	7.7990	120.4200	0.6215	3623.85	2150.1	4528.19	1036.74	4714.92	419.81	15974.86	2453.92
08/29/03	1.5408	1.4022	5.9708	1.7803	7.7995	116.7100	0.6340	3742.15	2220.83	4687.5	1052.56	5116.37	447.73	16170.69	2506.57
09/30/03	1.4712	1.3547	5.6305	1.6788	7.7445	111.4300	0.6017	3704.34	2206.33	4519.93	1001.24	5305.25	458.25	15931.29	2479.5
10/31/03	1.4130	1.3098	5.6504	1.6848	7.7684	110.1000	0.5898	3836.52	2312.49	4864.13	1103.9	5766.92	472.21	16763.07	2622.79
11/28/03	1.3820	1.3045	5.4686	1.6305	7.7660	109.5300	0.5808	3754.35	2343.48	4954.76	1121.38	5827.04	452.86	16975.77	2655.43
12/31/03	1.3298	1.3103	5.2072	1.5526	7.7640	107.1300	0.5605	3883.44	2470.73	5108.24	1168.62	5993.55	472.21	17507.68	2776.34

[a]Exchange rates for France and Germany from 1999 are derived from the fixed exchange rates of the franc and deutschmark with the euro.

Source: Federal Reserve Statistical Release, Foreign Exchange Rates, Historical Data at ⟨http://www.federalreserve.gov/releases/h10/About.HTM⟩; Thomson Financial Datastream.

APPENDIX B

ANNUAL RETURNS OF EAFE AND S&P 500 FROM 1981 TO 2003

	EAFE	EAFE $	S&P 500
1981	12.2%	−1.03%	−4.9%
1982	10.1%	−0.86%	21.5%
1983	32.6%	24.61%	22.6%
1984	21.6%	7.86%	6.3%
1985	28.4%	56.72%	31.7%
1986	42.9%	69.94%	18.7%
1987	−2.0%	24.93%	5.3%
1988	34.0%	28.59%	16.6%
1989	21.7%	10.80%	31.7%
1990	−29.6%	−23.20%	−3.1%
1991	9.1%	12.50%	30.5%
1992	−5.8%	−11.85%	7.6%
1993	29.6%	32.94%	10.1%
1994	−1.8%	8.06%	1.3%
1995	9.8%	11.55%	37.6%
1996	11.6%	6.36%	23.0%
1997	13.8%	2.06%	33.4%
1998	12.6%	20.33%	28.6%
1999	33.8%	27.30%	21.0%
2000	−7.1%	−13.96%	−9.1%
2001	−16.0%	−21.21%	−11.9%
2002	−25.8%	−15.66%	−22.1%
2003	20.8%	39.17%	28.7%

Source: Thomson Financial Datastream.

INDEX VALUES OF S&P 500 AND EAFE FROM 1981 TO 2003

	S&P 500 Composite	EAFE	EAFE $
12/31/1980	99.7795	226.5120	325.3890
1/30/1981	95.6047	229.3330	320.9480
2/27/1981	97.2653	232.9080	316.7010
3/31/1981	101.1549	240.7800	328.1470
4/30/1981	99.1994	255.8420	337.0580
5/29/1981	99.4532	253.8560	322.8720
6/30/1981	98.8306	261.3220	325.1750
7/31/1981	99.0340	262.0790	312.0350
8/31/1981	93.3151	263.7310	319.4190
9/30/1981	88.7175	237.4400	287.6930
10/30/1981	93.5055	238.8340	292.4770
11/30/1981	97.3642	250.6270	325.0290
12/31/1981	94.8671	254.1480	322.0300
1/29/1982	93.6289	259.6880	319.9150
2/26/1982	88.3954	251.4310	299.5700
3/31/1982	87.9342	246.7030	285.0410
4/30/1982	91.9083	254.3540	303.5780
5/28/1982	88.7749	255.8580	299.6430
6/30/1982	87.4415	246.6030	277.2650
7/30/1982	85.8858	245.0880	274.0650
8/31/1982	96.3118	249.1810	274.2420
9/30/1982	97.5125	253.0020	272.5120
10/29/1982	108.7359	260.6160	273.6760
11/30/1982	113.1278	270.6160	295.6590
12/31/1982	115.3078	279.8430	319.2650
1/31/1983	119.5957	284.9260	316.5750
2/28/1983	122.3367	292.5150	325.3980
3/31/1983	126.8567	308.2740	338.1030
4/29/1983	136.8506	322.7420	357.4710
5/31/1983	135.6596	322.2640	355.7880
6/30/1983	140.9395	333.8790	363.9720
7/29/1983	136.7816	339.8690	364.8840
8/31/1983	138.8345	341.7110	359.1330
9/30/1983	140.7515	345.7270	373.1620
10/31/1983	139.1236	344.1350	372.9310
11/30/1983	142.0585	354.1510	381.8760
12/30/1983	141.3155	371.0370	397.8390
1/31/1984	140.5275	395.2350	415.7050
2/29/1984	135.5826	386.2070	419.5780
3/30/1984	137.9306	416.7720	459.0910
4/30/1984	139.2395	419.6850	451.5930

(Continued)

INDEX VALUES OF S&P 500 AND EAFE FROM 1981 TO 2003

	S&P 500 Composite	EAFE	EAFE $
5/31/1984	131.5316	382.5000	405.8690
6/29/1984	134.3886	390.2540	405.5050
7/31/1984	132.7216	377.7990	379.6420
8/31/1984	147.3805	407.2850	411.9460
9/28/1984	147.4155	416.1830	408.4490
10/31/1984	147.9835	427.9990	418.8040
11/30/1984	146.3265	433.7360	420.5280
12/31/1984	150.1814	451.3000	429.1260
1/31/1985	161.8823	468.8600	438.9080
2/28/1985	163.8653	482.2950	436.4470
3/29/1985	163.9733	491.8110	470.4440
4/30/1985	163.8193	491.2170	468.9790
5/31/1985	173.2842	509.5710	489.0520
6/28/1985	175.9992	513.9980	501.7670
7/31/1985	175.7422	507.4670	527.8440
8/30/1985	174.2422	527.4070	544.9600
9/30/1985	168.7923	528.1790	577.0230
10/31/1985	176.5882	551.2620	616.4590
11/29/1985	188.7010	554.4310	641.9500
12/31/1985	197.8289	579.5970	672.5430
1/31/1986	198.9339	580.3930	689.5990
2/28/1986	213.8038	607.1770	766.2000
3/31/1986	225.7327	698.4270	874.1570
4/30/1986	223.1907	702.8710	931.6320
5/30/1986	235.0645	704.4060	890.4220
6/30/1986	239.0365	714.6110	951.3620
7/31/1986	225.6667	729.6990	1010.2540
8/29/1986	242.4015	797.9440	1110.0800
9/30/1986	222.3627	791.9330	1098.9440
10/31/1986	235.1855	770.5740	1025.7790
11/28/1986	240.9015	798.0090	1085.1350
12/31/1986	234.7546	828.1400	1142.9150
1/30/1987	266.3652	883.8000	1264.5560
2/27/1987	276.8911	902.8460	1302.7240
3/31/1987	284.8800	941.8350	1409.7930
4/30/1987	282.3501	1012.1130	1559.2100
5/29/1987	284.7990	1032.1690	1559.4900
6/30/1987	299.1809	1013.0470	1510.0910
7/31/1987	314.3367	1029.7000	1507.7180
8/31/1987	326.0656	1063.4900	1621.0810
9/30/1987	318.9167	1069.4150	1595.8570

(Continued)

INDEX VALUES OF S&P 500 AND EAFE FROM 1981 TO 2003

	S&P 500 Composite	EAFE	EAFE $
10/30/1987	250.2344	872.8230	1372.5440
11/30/1987	229.6126	839.7500	1386.3740
12/31/1987	247.0800	811.2490	1427.8820
1/29/1988	257.4730	868.8570	1453.7000
2/29/1988	269.4750	930.5030	1550.9730
3/31/1988	261.1500	955.6410	1646.6300
4/29/1988	264.0380	974.9520	1670.8630
5/31/1988	266.3220	951.0360	1617.6750
6/30/1988	278.4950	985.7370	1575.3680
7/29/1988	277.4320	1016.3190	1625.1180
8/31/1988	267.9860	972.7690	1519.7730
9/30/1988	279.3840	1006.2650	1586.4820
10/31/1988	287.2700	1024.1790	1722.5980
11/30/1988	283.1760	1056.7450	1825.5690
12/30/1988	288.1160	1087.0850	1836.0720
1/31/1989	309.1760	1146.7310	1868.7540
2/28/1989	301.5090	1133.1510	1878.7210
3/31/1989	308.5040	1156.1880	1842.2090
4/28/1989	324.5620	1169.6890	1859.6590
5/31/1989	337.6930	1183.8100	1758.8040
6/30/1989	335.7780	1162.1670	1729.5880
7/31/1989	366.0950	1246.4410	1947.1430
8/31/1989	373.2520	1251.5090	1859.9350
9/29/1989	371.7380	1265.4140	1945.0000
10/31/1989	363.1060	1230.8580	1867.2340
11/30/1989	370.5110	1288.4540	1961.4820
12/29/1989	379.4090	1323.4200	2034.3270
1/31/1990	353.9370	1267.9890	1959.0450
2/28/1990	358.5360	1200.9960	1822.7290
3/30/1990	367.9950	1115.3030	1633.2180
4/30/1990	358.8150	1105.7740	1620.6910
5/31/1990	393.7950	1201.5090	1806.1090
6/29/1990	391.1390	1174.8610	1790.6340
7/31/1990	389.8900	1144.5500	1816.3190
8/31/1990	354.6480	1016.8090	1640.4310
9/28/1990	337.3880	858.4730	1412.2910
10/31/1990	335.9520	950.4650	1632.8060
11/30/1990	357.6680	905.9290	1536.9550
12/31/1990	367.6360	931.6640	1562.4520
1/31/1991	383.6420	940.8790	1613.4280
2/28/1991	411.0780	1056.2250	1786.8600

(Continued)

INDEX VALUES OF S&P 500 AND EAFE FROM 1981 TO 2003

	S&P 500 Composite	**EAFE**	**EAFE $**
3/29/1991	421.0320	1069.4740	1680.0220
4/30/1991	422.0290	1074.3390	1697.0080
5/31/1991	440.2350	1091.7870	1715.2160
6/28/1991	420.0670	1033.1140	1589.6290
7/31/1991	439.6460	1066.6410	1668.1620
8/30/1991	450.0520	1042.0800	1634.6930
9/30/1991	442.5300	1063.3980	1727.3130
10/31/1991	448.4800	1077.1670	1752.2320
11/29/1991	430.4090	1012.7160	1670.8950
12/31/1991	479.6330	1016.0700	1757.7090
1/31/1992	470.6950	1019.9880	1720.6800
2/28/1992	476.7910	1006.0420	1659.5650
3/31/1992	467.5180	955.8810	1550.4670
4/30/1992	481.2410	959.5830	1558.2300
5/29/1992	483.6000	989.4140	1663.0100
6/30/1992	476.4090	915.3800	1584.6820
7/31/1992	495.8720	884.4820	1544.6320
8/31/1992	485.7230	909.1430	1642.0390
9/30/1992	491.4310	904.4420	1610.1350
10/30/1992	493.1290	914.4070	1526.1650
11/30/1992	509.9200	947.6440	1540.9950
12/31/1992	516.1780	956.8650	1549.4320
1/29/1993	520.4940	959.9100	1549.7050
2/26/1993	527.5870	982.6400	1596.9750
3/31/1993	538.7190	1038.8820	1736.6420
4/30/1993	525.6980	1101.7270	1901.9310
5/31/1993	539.7610	1110.0420	1942.5640
6/30/1993	541.3410	1108.4980	1912.7040
7/30/1993	539.1640	1157.5480	1980.0980
8/31/1993	559.6210	1210.2110	2087.4390
9/30/1993	555.3300	1180.0600	2040.9100
10/29/1993	566.8170	1239.9550	2104.2540
11/30/1993	561.4140	1141.3060	1920.7620
12/31/1993	568.2020	1239.6970	2059.8910
1/31/1994	587.5190	1325.1580	2234.4890
2/28/1994	571.5730	1290.6820	2228.7590
3/31/1994	546.6540	1220.5990	2133.2380
4/29/1994	553.6640	1257.7940	2224.2240
5/31/1994	562.7500	1265.1130	2211.9290
6/30/1994	548.9560	1233.9750	2243.6830
7/29/1994	566.9820	1255.0910	2265.7550

(Continued)

INDEX VALUES OF S&P 500 AND EAFE FROM 1981 TO 2003

	S&P 500 Composite	EAFE	EAFE $
8/31/1994	590.2280	1281.9550	2319.8960
9/30/1994	575.7950	1222.6350	2247.3380
10/31/1994	588.7310	1235.6220	2322.6990
11/30/1994	567.2860	1209.3910	2211.5800
12/30/1994	575.7050	1217.6520	2225.9460
1/31/1995	590.6350	1158.9300	2140.9640
2/28/1995	613.6530	1137.7820	2135.3680
3/31/1995	631.7600	1123.5900	2269.1520
4/28/1995	650.3630	1157.0120	2355.0970
5/31/1995	676.3570	1154.9210	2327.6300
6/30/1995	692.0670	1129.8130	2287.4290
7/31/1995	715.0180	1212.1850	2430.4580
8/31/1995	716.8150	1246.8160	2338.3350
9/29/1995	747.0660	1257.1670	2384.6110
10/31/1995	744.3960	1237.8510	2321.1240
11/30/1995	777.0740	1284.8710	2386.3130
12/29/1995	792.0420	1337.3540	2483.0680
1/31/1996	819.0000	1386.9050	2493.8520
2/29/1996	826.5930	1372.4670	2502.9050
3/29/1996	834.5500	1410.2600	2556.6910
4/30/1996	846.8540	1458.9980	2631.6520
5/31/1996	868.6940	1441.9310	2583.8530
6/28/1996	872.0080	1456.3060	2599.0280
7/31/1996	833.4820	1385.2830	2523.7150
8/30/1996	851.0640	1397.1240	2529.8960
9/30/1996	898.9660	1462.0670	2597.7440
10/31/1996	923.7600	1444.7250	2571.8060
11/29/1996	993.5840	1502.8890	2674.7760
12/31/1996	973.8970	1492.9440	2641.0110
1/31/1997	1034.7410	1514.9210	2549.1930
2/28/1997	1042.8510	1551.6110	2591.5030
3/31/1997	1000.0020	1559.0670	2601.5260
4/30/1997	1059.7010	1605.6470	2615.9590
5/30/1997	1124.2190	1652.8020	2786.8380
6/30/1997	1174.5861	1742.3600	2941.1590
7/31/1997	1268.0450	1832.9050	2989.3450
8/29/1997	1197.0070	1699.4480	2766.7020
9/30/1997	1262.5630	1786.5500	2922.3140
10/31/1997	1220.3970	1618.2970	2698.3310
11/28/1997	1276.8920	1646.7630	2671.4460
12/31/1997	1298.8210	1699.2810	2695.3620

(Continued)

INDEX VALUES OF S&P 500 AND EAFE FROM 1981 TO 2003

	S&P 500 Composite	EAFE	EAFE $
1/30/1998	1313.1870	1780.2590	2819.2570
2/27/1998	1407.9010	1881.7760	3000.8120
3/31/1998	1479.9969	1978.1090	3093.8900
4/30/1998	1494.8870	1964.4300	3119.0830
5/29/1998	1469.1930	1982.9060	3104.6520
6/30/1998	1528.8700	2005.4530	3128.8460
7/31/1998	1512.5900	2037.1810	3161.2620
8/31/1998	1293.9041	1762.6060	2770.3130
9/30/1998	1376.7920	1646.3560	2686.1040
10/30/1998	1488.7830	1750.8620	2966.8610
11/30/1998	1579.0150	1889.7480	3119.5930
12/31/1998	1670.0060	1913.3990	3243.4150
1/29/1999	1739.8390	1954.5840	3234.5710
2/26/1999	1685.7670	1961.0850	3158.2310
3/31/1999	1753.2120	2053.9610	3290.8270
4/30/1999	1821.1060	2161.1640	3424.9240
5/31/1999	1778.1030	2076.9020	3249.2950
6/30/1999	1876.7830	2173.2710	3376.7250
7/30/1999	1818.1810	2158.6710	3477.8700
8/31/1999	1809.1860	2160.1680	3491.3480
9/30/1999	1759.5890	2144.1420	3527.2690
10/29/1999	1870.9370	2227.7520	3660.1570
11/30/1999	1908.9700	2350.2770	3788.0820
12/31/1999	2021.4010	2560.4310	4128.8090
1/31/2000	1919.8409	2457.8710	3867.1910
2/29/2000	1883.4990	2575.6580	3972.0260
3/31/2000	2067.7590	2626.8410	4126.7620
4/28/2000	2005.5490	2593.2700	3910.3440
5/31/2000	1964.4010	2534.2150	3815.6070
6/30/2000	2012.8300	2569.6270	3965.7210
7/31/2000	1981.3610	2533.8430	3800.2340
8/31/2000	2104.4319	2603.6570	3833.9980
9/29/2000	1993.3320	2490.5490	3648.0730
10/31/2000	1984.9050	2496.7420	3562.6400
11/30/2000	1828.4160	2393.4240	3429.8020
12/29/2000	1837.3650	2378.4010	3552.5110
1/31/2001	1902.5530	2411.3290	3550.8360
2/28/2001	1729.0699	2259.7820	3284.8960
3/30/2001	1619.5370	2195.0430	3067.4010
4/30/2001	1745.3920	2333.3030	3282.5390
5/31/2001	1757.0830	2282.0350	3169.2910

(Continued)

INDEX VALUES OF S&P 500 AND EAFE FROM 1981 TO 2003

	S&P 500 Composite	EAFE	EAFE $
6/29/2001	1714.3199	2222.2910	3040.8630
7/31/2001	1697.4449	2141.6720	2985.7770
8/31/2001	1591.1820	2018.0650	2910.7610
9/28/2001	1462.6899	1808.0670	2616.5960
10/31/2001	1490.5820	1879.1860	2683.5040
11/30/2001	1604.9189	1963.9840	2782.5990
12/31/2001	1618.9790	1996.9050	2799.1870
1/31/2002	1595.3530	1943.3680	2650.6660
2/28/2002	1564.5861	1950.1990	2669.3870
3/29/2002	1623.4590	2037.4870	2815.1200
4/30/2002	1525.0040	1995.1180	2835.5070
5/31/2002	1513.7690	1967.0440	2873.9730
6/28/2002	1405.9290	1810.7940	2760.6410
7/31/2002	1296.3440	1628.1870	2488.3210
8/30/2002	1304.8550	1625.5570	2483.2620
9/30/2002	1163.0439	1448.7260	2217.1920
10/31/2002	1265.4100	1528.4280	2336.5280
11/29/2002	1339.8920	1597.1010	2442.8710
12/31/2002	1261.1760	1481.3480	2360.9130
1/31/2003	1228.1379	1400.1840	2262.5300
2/28/2003	1209.7100	1374.3550	2210.8100
3/31/2003	1221.4561	1342.8600	2169.0290
4/30/2003	1322.0680	1458.2220	2384.1050
5/30/2003	1391.7240	1500.0980	2530.7760
6/30/2003	1409.4780	1552.3490	2593.4120
7/31/2003	1434.3290	1618.8440	2656.5780
8/29/2003	1462.3020	1671.0980	2721.1940
9/30/2003	1446.7700	1636.8210	2805.6200
10/31/2003	1528.6200	1721.8600	2980.6700
11/28/2003	1542.0699	1726.3540	3047.3630
12/31/2003	1622.9399	1789.1840	3285.5750

Source: Global Financial Data; Thomson Financial Datastream.

1.2

EXCHANGE RATES AND FIRMS

As a company's customers, suppliers, employees, and shareholders become more international, managers are forced to understand the implications of operating in a multicurrency environment. In particular, the identification and management of the risks that arise from international operations are a primary task for the CEOs, CFOs, and treasurers of major multinational firms. The three cases in this module examine how firms identify, measure, and manage currency exposures.

Movements in the currency market affect both large and small companies directly and indirectly. The impact of foreign exchange movements may be obvious, as in the case of building a factory abroad or entering into a long-term supply contract denominated in a foreign currency. Consider the decision by an American multinational to invest in a factory in Mexico. Construction of the factory requires an upfront payment of 100 million pesos and another payment of 100 million pesos upon completion, scheduled 14 months from now. If the current exchange rate is 10 pesos to the dollar, the American company is spending $10 million today, but it does not know what it will be spending *in dollars* in 14 months. If the peso weakens (depreciates) against the dollar—that is, if $1 buys more pesos in the future—the factory will ultimately cost less than $20 million, even though the company will still spend 200 million pesos. That, of course, is the rosy scenario. If the peso instead appreciates against the dollar, then the factory will cost more than $20 million.

Currency fluctuations affect all companies that do business across borders. The first case in this module, Hedging Currency Risks at AIFS, is an introduction to how firms manage their foreign exchange exposures. In this case, the company's revenues are in U.S. dollars, but most of its costs are in euros. The case illustrates how currency exposure is measured, and it explores available hedging techniques—particularly when volumes are uncertain.

Measuring, reporting, and managing currency risks are complex tasks for firms that have global operations. Managers have to make a multitude of decisions. Over what time horizon should exposures be measured? Should a multinational firm determine its net currency exposures, or should each subsidiary identify and manage its own currency exposures separately? What should a parent company do when two different subsidiaries have offsetting exposures—should it instruct each subsidiary not to hedge to avoid the costs of doing so? The issues become more complicated quickly. Reporting currency exposures raises further issues as the accounting rules are complex. Some foreign exchange losses flow through the income statement, creating a loss that reduces reported net income. Other foreign exchange losses flow straight to shareholders' equity as an adjustment on the balance sheet but never reduce reported net income. The second case in this module, Foreign Exchange Hedging Strategies at General Motors: Transactional and Translational Exposures, provides insights into the complexities faced by a huge multinational organization with subsidiaries around the world and with exposures to all the major currencies. It also addresses the accounting and financial reporting complications that arise when a public company issues financial statements based on consolidated operations of entities that may use different currencies as their primary medium of exchange.

The impact of currency fluctuations, however, may be subtle and more difficult to identify and measure. For example, the devaluation of a currency in a country where a significant competitor has much of its supply chain may lower a competitor's costs and give that competitor an edge. The third case, Foreign Exchange Hedging Strategies at General Motors: Competitive Exposures, investigates how currency movements may affect competitors' abilities to gain market share and how a firm can measure and respond to such currency risks.

Managing the risks of currency exposures is challenging. The market offers a number of alternatives to hedge foreign exchange risk, and managers must tailor the remedy to the risk. Currency options may be appropriate for some exposures, and currency futures for others. In today's sophisticated markets, a planner may find it useful to protect a transaction with a variety of derivative transactions. Real hedges, where firms adjust operations, may also be an important tool. Understanding how to use different financial instruments and devices is now a crucial part of the financial executive's toolbox, and these choices are detailed in these cases.

OVERVIEW OF THE CASES

Hedging Currency Risks at AIFS

AIFS organizes academic and cultural exchanges for students, sending over 50,000 American students abroad each year for study programs and tours. Most of the firm's revenues are in U.S. dollars, but its costs are in other currencies. AIFS sets prices for the programs months in advance and guarantees its prices once they are published in its catalog. Every year, Controller Christopher Archer-Lock and Chief Financial Officer Becky Tabaczynski must decide whether to hedge a euro-dollar exposure before they know the magnitude of the exposure. They have to make hedging decisions well before the company knows how many students will sign up for its programs. International crises can have a severe impact on sales volume, and on several occasions in recent years the company did not quite achieve its forecast sales. Archer-Lock and Tabaczynski must quantify exposures under different scenarios and also want to explore the implications of using various mixes of forwards and options in their hedging strategy.

In reading this case, one should pay particular attention to the problems driving AIFS to hedge. Currency risks arise naturally from the AIFS business model, but its core business is about providing a particular service abroad. The case examines the origins of foreign exchange exposures and the decisions a company must make on when to hedge, how much to hedge, and what instruments to use to hedge its exposure. Particular questions to consider are:

- What gives rise to the currency exposure at AIFS?

- What could happen if Archer-Lock and Tabaczynski did not hedge at all?

- What could happen with a 100% hedge with forwards and a 100% hedge with options? Use the forecast final sales volume of 25,000, and analyze the possible outcomes relative to the "zero impact" scenario described in the case.
- What happens when you consider alternate final sales volumes? 10,000? 30,000?
- What hedging decision would you advocate?

Foreign Exchange Hedging Strategies at General Motors: Transactional and Translational Exposures

The treasury team at General Motors (GM), headed by Eric Feldstein, is responsible for managing the corporation's monetary transactions and the risks associated with those transactions. With operations and subsidiaries all over the world, GM has exposure to numerous currencies. The company has formulated a hedging policy that covers the majority of its foreign exchange exposures, and Feldstein is responsible for approving exceptions to the policy. The GM treasury team is reviewing two proposals to deviate from the company's hedging policy, involving the Canadian dollar and the Argentinean peso. Feldstein and his team have to evaluate GM's exposure to each currency, determine the risks, consider other approaches to managing these currency risks, and decide if GM should depart from its formal hedging policy. If Feldstein does approve exceptional hedges for one or both of these currencies, he must also consider what instruments to use to implement the hedges.

In working through this case, it is valuable to think about both the policy and the necessity of having a procedure for making exceptions to the policy. The two currencies pose different problems for General Motors. The firm has a large transactional exposure to the Canadian dollar and also a very considerable translational exposure. Feldstein must determine how fluctuations in the U.S. dollar/Canadian dollar exchange rate would impact GM's income statement, and also consider the longer term implications of the firm's exposure to the Canadian dollar. In the case of the Argentinean peso, Feldstein has to decide how GM should deal with the widely anticipated devaluation of the peso. Would it be cost-effective for GM to hedge more of its exposure, or are there other actions that GM might take to mitigate the effects of a devaluation? Specific questions to consider in reading the case are:

- Should multinational firms hedge foreign exchange rate risk? If not, what are the consequences? If so, how should they decide which exposures to hedge?
- What do you think of GM's foreign exchange hedging policies? How would you advise them about possible changes to their policies?
- Should GM deviate and change its hedging decision on the Canadian dollar? Is such a deviation consistent with policy?
- If it does, what instruments should it use to accomplish that hedging?
- What would happen to GM's income statement if the Canadian dollar moved strongly, in either direction?
- Should GM increase its hedge with respect to the Argentinean peso? How costly would it be, and would it be worth it?

Foreign Exchange Hedging Strategies at General Motors: Competitive Exposures

Feldstein and the GM treasury team contemplate a third exception to GM's standard hedging policy in this case. They have to consider if GM should also manage its competitive exposures—the risk that currency movements may give its competitors a cost advantage. GM's major rivals—Toyota, Honda, and Nissan—are tied very closely to the Japanese yen, and movements in the U.S. dollar/yen exchange rate will affect their businesses. Feldstein faces the problem of predicting, first, how competitors would be affected by currency movements and, second, how competitors would react to foreign exchange market movements. Feldstein has to quantify GM's competitive exposure to the yen before he can recommend how to manage this exposure. In working through the case, consider:

- Why is GM worried about the yen? How important is the competitive exposure?
- What would happen if the exchange rate moved as hypothesized in the case? Trace the effects of that move all the way to GM's market value.
- What are the costs and benefits of hedging competitive exposures?
- Does it make sense to hedge against such exposures?

The jump from theory to practice—from what was introduced in Module 1.1 to what is explored in the cases in Module 1.2—is challenging. It is worthwhile to work through these chapters slowly and thoroughly.

ADDITIONAL READING

ADLER, MICHAEL, and BERNARD DUMAS. 1984. "Exposure to Currency Risk: Definition and Measurement." *Financial Management*, 13(2): 41–51.

FROOT, KENNETH A., DAVID S. SCHARFSTEIN, and JEREMY C. STEIN, 1993. "Risk Management: Coordinating Corporate Investment and Financing Policies." *Journal of Finance*, 48(5): 1629–1659.

4

Hedging Currency Risks at AIFS

Christopher Archer-Lock, London-based controller for student exchange organization American Institute for Foreign Study (AIFS) talked almost daily with his Boston-based counterpart, Becky Tabaczynski, CFO for the group's high school travel division ACIS. On this day in early July, 2004, their daily phone call had been especially invigorating.

As often before, they had discussed foreign exchange hedging, an area of key importance for the company. AIFS received most of its revenues in American dollars (USD), but incurred its costs in other currencies, primarily euros (EUR) and British pounds (GBP). The currency mismatch was natural given AIFS's business: it organized educational and cultural exchange programs throughout the world. Two of AIFS's major divisions served American students traveling abroad. The Study Abroad College Division, where Archer-Lock was controller and treasurer, sent college-age students to universities worldwide for semester-long programs, and the High School Travel Division, whose finances Tabaczynski managed, organized trips of one to four weeks for high school students and their teachers.

Currency hedging helped AIFS protect its bottom line from damaging exchange rate changes. Using currency forward contracts and currency options (Appendix 1 summarizes currency instruments), AIFS hedged its future cost commitments up to two years in advance. The problem was that the hedge had to be put in place before AIFS had completed its sales cycle, and before it knew exactly how much foreign currency it needed. The dilemma meant that Archer-Lock and Tabaczynski frequently discussed two points. First, what percentage of the expected costs should they cover? Currently, AIFS covered 100%. Second, in what proportions should AIFS use forward contracts and options? Today, Tabaczynski had promised Archer-Lock to put together scenarios for how changes in sales and exchange rates could affect the company. He was eager to see the results.

Professor Mihir A. Desai, Executive Director of the HBS Europe Research Center Vincent Dessain, and Research Associate Anders Sjöman prepared this case. Some names and data have been disguised for confidentiality. HBS cases are developed solely as the basis for class discussion. Cases are not intended to serve as endorsements, sources of primary data, or illustrations of effective or ineffective management.

AIFS ACTIVITIES AND BUSINESS MODEL

Through its family of companies, AIFS sent more than 50,000 students each year on academic and cultural exchange programs worldwide. Founded in the U.S. in 1964 by Sir Cyril Taylor (HBS MBA 1961) the group had annual revenues close to $200 million. Two of the group's main divisions focused on Americans traveling abroad:

- The College division organized study abroad programs for more than 5,000 American university-aged students during the academic year (Academic Year and Semester, AYS) or the summer (College Summer School, CSS). All courses were for academic credit, with most participants traveling to Europe, and a significant portion to the United Kingdom. Countries with study programs included Australia, Austria, the Czech Republic, France, Italy, Russia, South Africa and Spain.

- The Boston-based High School Travel Division had been founded in 1978 as the American Council for International Studies (ACIS) and organized chaperoned educational travel for about 20,000 high school students and teachers annually. The groups traveled on 1- to 4-week educational trips to Europe, China, Mexico, Africa, Australia and the Americas. For most participants, these trips were their first exposure to foreign countries, and so AIFS organized the whole trip: airfare, transportation, hotels, tour manager, guides, etc.

Overall, the College division had higher margins than the "low margin/high volume" operations of the ACIS division. ACIS was also more exposed to world events than the College division. High school travelers reacted immediately to news of war, terrorism or political uncertainty. Sales could drop up to 60% on such news. In the last 25 years, four events had led to such drops in ACIS sales: the 1986 terrorism acts, the 1991 Gulf War, the 2001 September 11 attacks and the Iraq war.

AIFS also ran several other programs, such as an Au Pair division which annually placed 4,000 young people in American homes to assist with child care, and the Camp America division, which placed 10,000 young people as camp leaders in U.S. summer camps. AIFS also arranged Academic Year in America (AYA) for students wanting to study in the U.S.

Catalogs, Guarantees, and Pricing

By and large, AIFS's business was "catalog-based." The College division distributed two main catalogs per year (one Summer and one Fall/Spring) and the High School division had one main Fall catalog, with several smaller catalogs distributed throughout the year. A key feature was that AIFS guaranteed that its prices would not change before the next catalog, even if world events altered AIFS's cost base. Although the idea often came up for discussion among AIFS management, it was always agreed that it would be hard to abandon the notion of guaranteed prices. The primary customer base (which was *not* the students, who changed from year to year, but their teachers and academic advisors) based their loyalty to AIFS on the fact that there would be no "price surprises."

When pricing the programs, both divisions took into account their cost base, competitive pricing and also the hedging activities. Their pricing schedules were, however, different.

College Pricing

The College worked on an academic planning year, from July 1 to June 30. Prices for any given year had to be set by June 30 the previous year. This meant that now in early

July 2004, Archer-Lock had just finalized the prices for the College division's "Summer 2005" and "Fall 2005/Spring 2006" catalogs. During the year, Archer-Lock met regularly with marketing and operations managers, to discuss sales forecasts and events that might affect sales. In addition, these managers put out weekly sales forecasts, on which Archer-Lock could base his hedging activities.

High School Travel Pricing

Combining tours, seasons and departure gateways, the ACIS catalog contained about 35,000 prices. Tabaczynski set these on a calendar year basis, January to December. One of her main goals was to see that ACIS followed a strategy of slow, but steady price increases year by year. She explained,

> We found that if we increased our own prices $200 from one year to another, the market reacted. So to avoid sudden price hikes, we instead raise prices in much smaller amounts, a little each year. Interestingly, if we become $200 more expensive than the competition, our customers don't seem to care. We have a very loyal customer base: over 70% of our teachers are returning customers.

HEDGING AT AIFS

At AIFS, Tabaczynski and Archer-Lock used currency hedging to help them manage three types of risk. First was the bottom-line risk, or the risk that an adverse change in exchange rates could increase the cost base. Explained Tabaczynski, "Say you have costs of EUR 20 million and that we set our catalog prices at parity with the dollar. Then the dollar goes to 1.30! We're now talking 30% of EUR 20 million. . . . It's a move that could take you out of business." Second was the volume risk, since foreign currency was bought based on projected sales volumes, which would differ from final sales volumes. Third was the competitive pricing risk, since no matter how currencies fluctuated, the AIFS price guarantee meant it could not transfer rate changes into price increases. Naturally, the competitive risk was closely linked to the other risks, especially the bottom line risk.

Hedging activities normally started about six months prior to a main pricing date. For the College division, this meant that hedging normally began in earnest in January. Figure 1 shows a sample timeline for pricing as well as hedging for the College division.

For the High School Travel division, hedging took place throughout the year, matched with various sales deals, but company policy was to hedge at least 25% by December, 40% by the end of March and a full 100% by the pricing date in June.

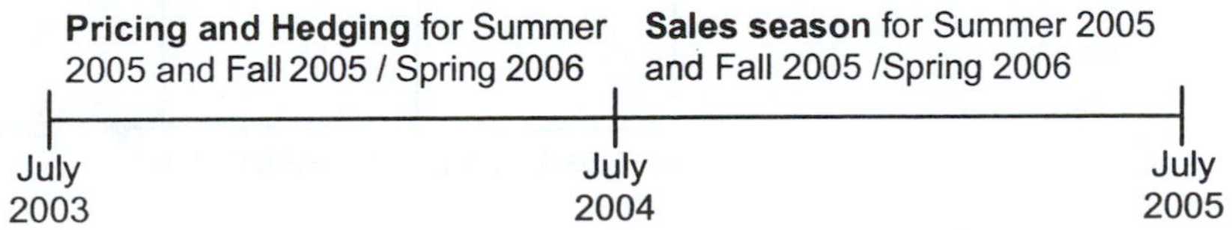

Pricing and Hedging for Summer 2005 and Fall 2005 / Spring 2006   **Sales season** for Summer 2005 and Fall 2005 /Spring 2006

July 2003   July 2004   July 2005

Figure 1   College Pricing and Hedging Timeline

Source: AIFS.

To track current hedges, Archer-Lock produced a daily report of currency rates and currency purchasing. (See Exhibit 1 for a sample daily report.) Archer-Lock explained the report,

> The report is circulated to a broad group of management, since currency rates and our hedging activity affect many aspects of our business and the issues are widely discussed. The report provides a snapshot of key market rates, both short and long term, alongside progress in our hedging activity. The top part of the report shows exchange rates for currencies, looking up to two years forward to match our catalog planning time scales, plus other data such as interest rates and currency policy guidelines. The lower part of the report shows forecast currency buying needs for the different sectors of the business, plus the percentage of hedging undertaken to date in contracts and options, and the rates achieved. These parameters are monitored in the light of sales and enrollment projections, market rates, currency policy and timing within the business cycle.

Archer-Lock also distributed a monthly report that reviewed currency purchasing and made recommendations for future hedging. (See Exhibit 2 for a sample monthly report.) When purchasing currency, AIFS worked with six different banks, with which it had long-standing relationships. The banks had all granted AIFS lines of credit, based on their own analyses of the business. Without the credit lines, AIFS would have had to deposit funds at each bank to cover its hedging activities. Currently, credit lines came close to $100 million. A similar level of deposits would have taxed AIFS considerably, compared to the company's annual turnover of $200 million.

The ultimate success of the group's hedging activities depended on the final sales volume and the ultimate market value of USD. Archer-Lock summarized the relationship between these two variables with a two-by-two matrix that he called the "AIFS shifting box." (See Figure 2.)

Archer-Lock explained,

> Square 1 means that we bought the currency but we don't need it, because our sales came in below our projections. It is a bad place, especially if we are locked into surplus forward contracts on which we would lose money. It's this box that makes us use options, and not just forward contracts. In square 2, the exchange gain hopefully compensates for the lower sales volume. The gain is larger with forward contracts than with options, since options cost roughly 5% of the nominal USD strike price. In square 3, volume came in higher than

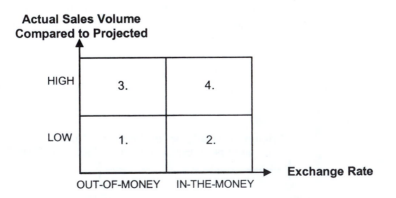

Figure 2 AIFS Shifting Box

Source: AIFS.

expected and so we are short foreign currency. The exchange rate moved out-of-money[1] though so we can just buy the extra volume we need, favorably, at spot rate.

Finally, we have the tricky square 4, which combines both good news and bad news. Our sales came in higher than expected, which is good, but it means that we need more currency. Unfortunately, the currency rate moved in-the-money, so we have to buy at a higher rate than the rate we used when we priced the catalog. This downside should be offset though by the sales increase—we just have to monitor where the breakeven is between these two.

To help inform its hedging decisions, AIFS had put in place a currency hedging policy (see Exhibit 3). In essence, the policy addressed two key questions. First, what percentage of the expected requirements should AIFS cover? Commented Tabaczynski,

> The bottom-line risk drives this. There was a time when we only covered 80% which is quite a reasonable cover. Then came that one bad year in 1995 where we got burned. Volume came in higher than expected, we were only covered 80%, and I think we lost $700,000 against the rate we used when we priced the catalog. So now we cover 100% of our needs.

Second, within the cover, what should be the proportion of contracts versus options? Currently, the policy let the College division use up to 30% in options, and ACIS up to 50%. Said Tabaczynski,

> In general, I believe that in the long run, no matter how you hedge, half the time you win, half the time you lose. You still need to hedge for the short run, though. With options, you can stabilize your earnings, your price increase. Assume we only bought contracts, at say 1.30. The dollar continues to be weak—but then just before we price the catalog, it goes to parity. Competitors who aren't hedging can buy at spot rate—but I have to price at 1.30. Now, with options I have the choice to step away—so options lead to a more stable company, with more stable infrastructure. I really like options.

In general, Archer-Lock believed the hedging policy had struck a happy balance between structure and adaptability, as well as between risk and cost. He commented,

> Although one could envisage a more prescriptive or mechanistic approach, we have generally been happy with the hedging process. The policy provides a framework, which is filled out by management discussion and some discretion. The key elements of the framework are that we cover 100% of the forecast and so do not speculate by leaving needs open at the pricing date, and that we match the options percentage to the perceived volume risk. This seems logical when you think of the risk in terms of the shifting box matrix, but there is always a critical debate to be had here, which events and markets keep very much alive.

Tabaczynski added,

> I believe another reason we do a good job of hedging is because we have a good working relationship across the board. In some companies, hedging is considered a financial decision, independent of the business needs. Here, we're trying to match the business needs.

---

[1] A call option is "out-of-the-money" if the spot exchange rate is less than the option's strike price of the option (and vice versa for a put option). An "out-of-the-money" option will have no value at expiry, and the option holder normally just lets it expire. By contrast, an "in-the-money" option has an intrinsic value, since there is money to be made from exercising the option. A call option is in-the-money if its strike price is below the spot exchange rate.

EXHIBIT 1

AIFS DAILY FOREIGN CURRENCY STATUS REPORT

CURRENT EXCHANGE RATES[1]

	Spot	Six Months	One Year	Two Years	Discount/(Premium) 1 Yr %
EUR	1.2273	1.2245	1.2258	1.2344	0.12
GBP	1.8458	1.8169	1.7930	1.7637	2.86
CHF	1.2434	1.2309	1.2258	1.2023	−1.42
AUD	0.7055	0.6919	0.6829		3.20
ZAR	6.3987	6.6057	6.7962		6.21
JPY	110.59	109.67	108.24		−2.13
CAD	1.3641	1.3681	1.3693		0.38

OTHER INFORMATION

	US	UK	EUR
Interest rate	1.00%	4.25%	2.00%
Last change	25 Jun 03	6 May 04	5 Jun 03

0.5 % rise in EUR spot this month
0.7 % rise in GBP spot this month

AIFS option purchasing guidelines—
ACIS: up to 50% of requirement in Options
College: up to 30% of requirement in Options

DEALING SUMMARY (EUR & GBP)

		ACIS 2003	ACIS 2004	ACIS 2005	College Sum/Fall 03	College Spring 04	College Sum/Fall 04	College Spring 05	College Sum/Fall 05	College Spring 2006
Date of pricing		June 2002	June 2003	June 2004	June 2002	June 2002	June 2003	June 2003	July 2004	July 2004
Enrolment		18,000	22,000	25,000	2,990	2,015	3,480	2,250	3,500	2,300
EUR										
Required	'000	16,000	20,100	23,500	4,500	3,300	5,400	3,800	5,600	4,000
Cover in place	contracts %	50.9%	51.3%	51.1%	70.0%	71.2%	70.4%	71.1%	71.4%	62.5%
	options %	49.1%	48.7%	48.9%	30.0%	28.8%	29.6%	28.9%	28.6%	29.4%
	Total %	100.0%	100.0%	100.0%	100.0%	100.0%	100.0%	100.0%	100.0%	91.9%
Rate (including option costs)		0.9633	1.0774	1.2155	0.9590	0.9832	1.0503	1.0921	1.2012	1.2215
Current year contracts matured %			59.7%			100.0%	9.3%			
GBP										
Required	'000	3,000	3,800	4,400	2,150	1,950	2,600	2,200	2,700	2,300
Cover in place	contracts %	51.7%	50.0%	51.1%	69.8%	71.8%	70.2%	70.5%	70.4%	54.3%
	options %	48.3%	50.0%	48.9%	30.2%	28.2%	29.8%	29.5%	29.6%	29.5%
	Total %	100.0%	100.0%	100.0%	100.0%	100.0%	100.0%	100.0%	100.0%	83.8%
Rate (including option costs)		1.4715	1.5820	1.7070	1.4610	1.4791	1.5908	1.6050	1.7273	1.7442
Current year contracts matured %			63.2%			100.0%	15.4%			

[1]Exchange rate conventions vary; here, the euro exchange rate is in the form of USD/EUR while the Japanese yen rate is cited as JPY/USD.

Source: AIFS. Numbers and levels have been disguised for confidentiality.

EXHIBIT 2

AIFS MONTHLY CURRENCY STATUS REPORT (ABRIDGED SAMPLE FROM 6 JULY 2004)

The following currency purchasing was arranged in June:

Division	Period	Instrument	Currency amount	Rate
ACIS	2005	Contract	EUR 750,000	1.2318
ACIS	2005	Contract	EUR 250,000	1.2335
ACIS	2005	Option	EUR 500,000	1.2320
ACIS	2005	Contract	GBP 100,000	1.7825
College	Sum/Fall 2005	Contract	EUR 350,000	1.2311
College	Spring 2006	Contract	EUR 600,000	1.2272

The dollar has continued to show a somewhat weaker tone in the past month, without breaking decisively out of previous ranges. Some of the main themes have been the record US current account deficit ($144.88bn for Qtr 1, vs. $127bn for Qtr 4 2003), weaker than expected US payrolls data, and in spite of the first US interest rate rise for a year, more caution about the pace of further rises. More positive factors have been seen improving US consumer confidence data, and speculation about the possible effect, if passed, of the US Homeland Investment bill, which may allow US companies to repatriate profits at a rate of 5.25% instead of 35% for a limited period. The purchases made in the month were mainly to complete buying for the June catalog deadlines.

ACIS

Cover for 2005 was completed based on projections of 25,000 participants. The Euro rate is 1.2155 (including option costs) and the sterling rate is 1.7070. Current market rates are worse than the 2005 hedged rates (especially since there is now a forward premium for Euros 2 years ahead), but consideration is being given to some early 2006 hedging (c. 10% of needs, as a contribution to protecting the sneak deal[1]), although the policy deadline is to cover 25% by the end of December. Recent range trading has been contained below 1.24 EUR and 1.85 GBP, so a move through these levels may signify further upward momentum and justify defensive option purchasing. As target spot levels, 1.21 and 1.1950 EUR and 1.79 GPB were set recently for buying opportunities at this stage.

College

Following additional purchases to top up catalogue needs, average rates for 2005/06 are at 1.2097 for the Euro and 1.7351 for sterling (including option costs.) Catalogue pricing has been agreed following a separate memo, and is also set out in the July meeting book notes. Cover for Spring 2006 is 92% of projected Euro needs and 84% of projected sterling. The remainder is the uncovered balance of Partnership needs at this stage, the decision having been taken to leave this to a later point in the year when Spring 2006 Partnerships pricing is being formulated.

In spite of concerns about the dollar, it seems early to be moving into 2006/07 AYS/CSS purchasing at this stage, a year ahead of catalogue pricing. It would be consistent with policy to make a small early move if the dollar strengthened within current technical channels to give some advantage over current pricing, e.g. to 1.19 vs. EUR.

Chris Archer-Lock, 6 July 2004.

---

[1]The "sneak deal" was a sales offer to ACIS customers. Those customers who signed up by March 31 would receive a significant discount to the price printed in the sales catalog.

Source: Adapted by casewriters from AIFS. Numbers have been disguised for confidentiality.

EXHIBIT 3

AIFS CURRENCY HEDGING POLICY
(ABRIDGED FROM JULY 2003 REVISION)

General Principles

1. *Cash flow hedging.* Currency hedging will take place in the context of a phased currency cash flow forecast (aggregating cash flows from all sources including foreign currency earnings).

2. *Hedge accounting.* As far as possible, currency deals will be designated against the forecast, to enable cash flow hedge accounting to be used. This is usually consistent with the economic purpose of the currency transactions. However in some circumstances, e.g. adjustments to forecast volume, economic hedging decisions may override hedge accounting requirements, resulting in hedging purchases having to be "marked to market".

3. *Proportions.* Generally 100% of forecast foreign currency exposure will be hedged by the time prices are set with a combination of options and contracts. When currency is purchased, the proportion of options will not exceed 20% of forecast requirement for Overhead, 30% for College programs, and 50% for ACIS.

4. *Instruments.* The portion hedged through "options" will be hedged by buying vanilla options, priced at the money forward or out of the money, for which AIFS will pay an option premium. In a situation where volume is at risk of declining, "put" options (options to sell currency) may be used to manage this form of volume risk. The portion of needs which is hedged through "contracts" will be hedged either (i) by outright forward contracts, or (ii) through structured instruments for which no initial premium is paid, but for which a worst case exchange rate is clearly identified, together with conditions upon which a more favorable exchange rate may apply on maturity (e.g. cylinders, forward plus contracts, bonus forwards, participating forwards). The majority of contract cover should be through outright forward contracts.

5. *Pricing date.* In general, this is the date by which prices have to be set for catalogue publication. Flexibility may be retained if the catalogue states that prices may change, or if another mechanism is used for communicating prices to the customer. A reasonable balance should be struck between obtaining protection in advance, and addressing the actual timing, competitive position, and certainty of commitments in these areas.

6. *Timing of purchase.* All things being equal, purchasing should begin more than six months prior to a main pricing date, and should build up to that date, but be phased so that rates combine being reasonably up to date at deadlines (and thus responsive to evolving circumstances, changing volumes, etc.) with the advantages of averaging. When current exchange rates permit the formulation of good business plans, e.g. a good net margin with minimal price increases, some currency purchases should be made early in the buying cycle. Where rates are adverse, or the external environment makes business volume uncertain, purchases may be later in the cycle in order to assess requirements and competitive position. Generally, purchasing should progress so that no more than 25% should be left to be covered in the month prior to pricing. Purchasing should make use of stop loss and target buying levels where circumstances permit.

7. *Reports.* Chris Archer-Lock will produce a daily status of currency rates and purchasing in place by division. A periodic report will be prepared by Chris Archer-Lock reviewing foreign currency purchasing and making recommendations for forthcoming hedging.

8. *Dealing controls.* Deals will be arranged with banks by telephone. Hardcopy confirmations from the banks will be signed off by an authorized individual separate from the dealer. Periodic checks of banks' outstanding deal listings will also be carried out by an independent individual.

9. *Bookkeeping.* A central company-wide bookkeeping rate will be set, which averages all forward contracts and takes account of period end cash balances. Book adjustments will provide businesses with appropriate individual exchange rates. The impact of spot deals and rolling

---

(Continued)

EXHIBIT 3   *(Continued)*

**AIFS CURRENCY HEDGING POLICY
(ABRIDGED FROM JULY 2003 REVISION)**

---

contracts will be charged to divisions. Option costs will be charged to and budgeted by divisions. FAS 133 valuations and accounting entries will be carried out quarterly.

The above principles apply generally. Additional guidance for specific divisions is set out below.

ACIS Division

1. *Instruments.* In order to allow for volume fluctuations, needs for a particular year will usually be covered by a combination of up to 50% of forecast needs in options and the remainder in forward contracts (or structured products with a set worst case rate and no initial option premium). An option premium budget will be set for each financial year.

2. *Timing.* Estimated currency needs for the next year will be covered by the time of pricing, typically the previous June. The timing of the marketing program requires the following stage deadlines:

	Amount	**Cumulative**	**Timing**
At least	25%	25%	By the end of December
At least	15%	40%	By the end of March
At least	60%	100%	By the pricing date in June

College Division

1. *College Division (AYS and CSS).* Estimated needs should generally be hedged 100% through options and forward contracts (or zero premium instruments) against the cash flow forecast by the time pricing decisions are taken in June. This applies to the extent that fees are fixed in June.

2. *Proportion.* Needs for an academic year will be covered by up to 30% of forecast needs in options and the remainder in contracts (or structured products with a set worst case rate and no initial option premium).

3. *Phasing.* Cover will be designated to mature in the spring, summer or fall of the relevant year, in order to provide an effective cash flow hedge.

Source: Adapted by casewriters from AIFS. Numbers have been disguised for confidentiality.

TABACZYNSKI'S SPREADSHEET

Although the company's hedging policy gave guidelines on how much to cover, and how to split the cover between contracts and options, the exact parameters could always be discussed. In the end, it was the two unknowns—final sales volume and final dollar exchange rate—that determined what economic impact the hedging activities had on the company. For the currency component, Archer-Lock followed rate movements for the key currencies. Specifically, he tracked the long term dollar movement against the euro (see Exhibit 4) and the British pound (see Exhibit 5), as well as the short and medium term movements of the euro and the GBP against the dollar (see Exhibit 6 for short term currency movements and Exhibit 7 for medium term currency movements). This involved technical analysis of the charts, where trends and key market levels were identified, as well as fundamental economic analysis. For the economic analysis, Archer-Lock followed in particular the development of the U.S. trade deficit against U.S. Gross Domestic Product (see Exhibit 8). At the moment, developments had experts arguing that a sharp USD movement might be imminent.

EXHIBIT 4

MONTHLY AVERAGE EXCHANGE RATES, USD/GBP (1971–2004, Q2)

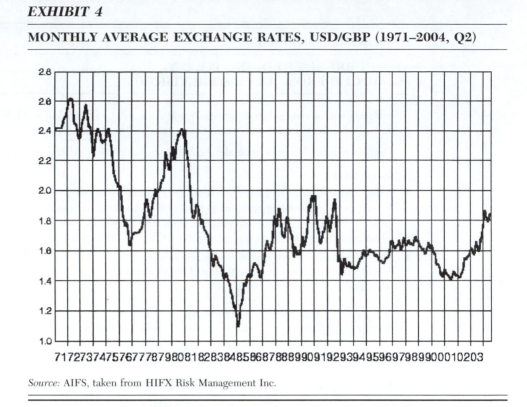

Source: AIFS, taken from HIFX Risk Management Inc.

EXHIBIT 5

MONTHLY AVERAGE EXCHANGE RATES, USD/EUR (1993–2004, Q2)

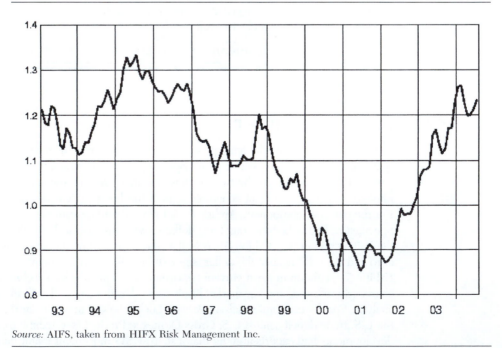

Source: AIFS, taken from HIFX Risk Management Inc.

EXHIBIT 6

CURRENCY DEVELOPMENTS, SHORT-TERM (MAY–JULY 2004)

a. EUR/USD

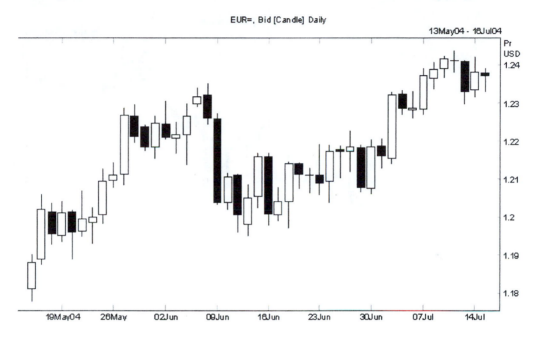

b. GBP/USD

Source: AIFS, taken from HIFX Risk Management Inc.

EXHIBIT 7

CURRENCY DEVELOPMENTS, MEDIUM TERM (APRIL 2002–JULY 2004)

a. EUR/USD

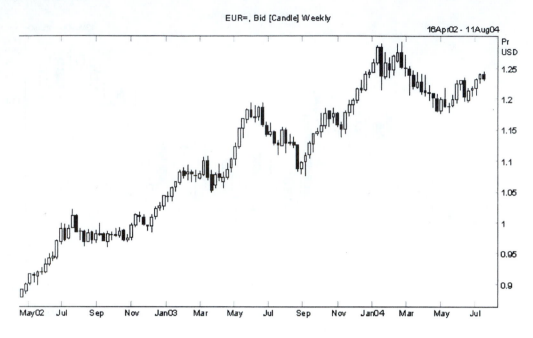

b. GBP/USD

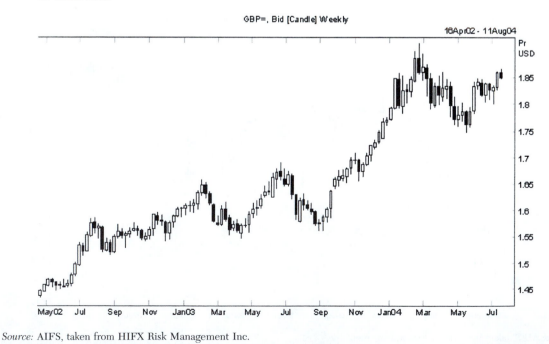

Source: AIFS, taken from HIFX Risk Management Inc.

EXHIBIT 8

US TRADE DEFICIT AS PERCENTAGE OF US GROSS DOMESTIC PRODUCT, 1970–2003

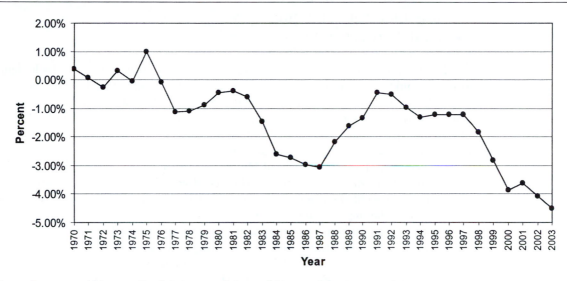

Source: International Monetary Fund, International Financial Statistics CD-ROM, June 2004.

Archer-Lock and Tabaczynski had often discussed how to best prepare for these volatilities. Taking the high school division as an example, Archer-Lock told Tabaczynski in their phone call, "It looks like ACIS will get around 25,000 participants this year. The dollar is hovering around 1.22 EUR. But that can all change. How should we prepare? This seems a critical year given the weaker dollar. We should plan carefully so we know for which levels we are ready to commit." Tabaczynski picked up on the challenge,

> OK, how about I put together a spreadsheet that models this? It'll look at the contract and option balance, and the overall level of our coverage. It'll take into account how much we achieve of our projected sales volume. In the end, it will show the additional benefit or loss we get, given coverage, USD exchange rate levels and sales volume results.

Tabaczynski recognized that a comprehensive model that covered different scenarios could be very useful in identifying the consequences of different hedging strategies. Such a model, though, would also generate a wide range of outcomes that could prove overwhelming. She therefore decided to focus first on the expected final sales volume of 25,000 and to analyze three simple hedging strategies. Mindful of AIFS's 100% hedging policy and the ongoing debate on the use of forwards versus options, Tabaczynski defined three alternative strategies:

- Do nothing (no hedge)
- 100% hedge with forwards
- 100% hedge with options

Next, in consultation with Archer-Locke, Tabaczynski defined the range of exchange rates that would be included in the model. The two agreed that the model should include three exchange rate levels for the dollar to the euro:

- stable dollar (1.22 USD/EUR)
- strong dollar (1.01 USD/EUR)
- weak dollar (1.48 USD/EUR)

Tabaczynski also had to decide how to measure the impact of each of the hedging strategies under different exchange rate scenarios. She decided that it would be most straightforward to quantify the impact on dollar costs. AIFS calculated that its average cost per participant was €1000. At the current exchange rate of 1.22 USD/EUR, dollar costs per participant would be $1220, or a total of $30.5 million for the projected sales volume of 25,000. Tabaczynski defined this level of dollar costs as the "zero impact" scenario; in other words, costs of $1220 per participant would have "zero impact", because they were the same as projected costs. If actual dollar costs were above this level, then there would be a negative impact. Similarly, if actual dollar costs were lower than expected, the impact would be positive.

Finally, Tabaczynski had to incorporate the price of each hedging strategy into her model. The Do Nothing strategy or a hedge using forwards incurred no additional expense. For the option strategy, AIFS would have to pay an option premium of 5% of the USD notional value. For example, if AIFS decided to use options to hedge projected costs of one million euros at the current exchange rate of $1.22/euro, it would pay an option premium of $61,000. Tabaczynski's analysis had to include the option premium since she wanted to measure the impact of different hedging strategies under different exchange rate scenarios on AIFS's costs.

Using the projected sales volume of 25,000 participants, Tabaczynski worked out a quick template to show the output of the model, as shown in Exhibit 9. First, she planned to analyze the three basic hedging policies she had defined. Then, she would complete the spreadsheet, analyzing different mixes of forwards and options, and then different levels of coverage.

Archer-Lock was eager to see the finished spreadsheet and to continue the discussion with Tabaczynski. He expected the model to be useful in defining alternative strategies for the expected final sales volume of 25,000. He also wanted to use the model to evaluate hedging strategies for a high final sales volume of 30,000 and a worst case scenario of a 10,000 final sales volume. Given AIFS's experiences in the aftermath of 9/11, such alternative volume outcomes were critical to consider when implementing hedging strategies.

Tabaczynski and Archer-Locke anticipated that the exercise would give them a comprehensive view of different hedging strategies under different assumptions. It might even give them arguments to assess AIFS's policy of 100% coverage, as well as the often debated questions of the options percentage. An exercise that had begun as a simple spreadsheet had morphed into something that enabled them to reevaluate the critical uncertainties AIFS faced and the goals of their hedging program.

EXHIBIT 9

TEMPLATE FOR ANALYZING HEDGING OPTIONS

The three simple hedging policies (no hedging, 100% hedging with forward contracts, and 100% hedging with options) are shown in the boxes. The empty cells should show the positive or negative impact of different hedging strategies at various USD exchange rate levels, measured relative to the scenario with "zero impact." One cell has been completed in the table below, for the "no hedge" scenario. The zero indicates that if there were no hedge and the exchange rate remained stable at $1.22/euro, there would be no impact on AIFS's costs.

Final volume: 25,000

			USD Exchange Rate (USD/EUR)		
% Cover	Contracts	Options	1.01	1.22	1.48
100%	0%	100%			
100%	25%	75%			
100%	50%	50%			
100%	75%	25%			
100%	100%	0%			
75%	0%	100%			
75%	25%	75%			
75%	50%	50%			
75%	75%	25%			
75%	100%	0%			
50%	0%	100%			
50%	25%	75%			
50%	50%	50%			
50%	75%	25%			
50%	100%	0%			
25%	0%	100%			
25%	25%	75%			
25%	50%	50%			
25%	75%	25%			
25%	100%	0%			
0%	—	—		0	

Source: Adapted by casewriters from AIFS. Numbers and levels have been disguised for confidentiality.

APPENDIX 1

BASIC HEDGING TECHNIQUES FOR MANAGING FOREIGN EXCHANGE RISK

All companies active on the international market have to consider the effect of movements in foreign exchange rates on their activities. For companies that work with more than one currency, several hedging techniques are available to guard against foreign exchange fluctuations.

- **Currency Accounts and Currency Loans**

  As a simple hedging tool, currency accounts (bank accounts set up in a foreign currency) work well for companies with a regular flow of both money out (payments) and money in (receipts) in a particular foreign currency. The matched in- and out-flows help the company avoid having to buy or sell currency for each transaction. Currency loans (borrowing money in a foreign currency) work similarly, in that the company can use future income streams in that currency to pay off the loan.

- **Spot Trading**

  Trading on the spot market is the most common foreign exchange transaction. The company simply converts foreign currency at today's market foreign exchange rate. Spot transactions are most commonly used for immediate payments in a foreign currency.

- **Forward Contracts**

  Forward contracts are the purchase (or sale) of a foreign currency at a specific date (the settlement date) in the future. Forward contracts allow companies to fix the exchange rate today for future payments or receipts of foreign currency. It gives the company the certainty of how much operating currency it would need to pay (or would receive).

- **Currency Options**

  The fixed rate in the forward contract protects the company from any unfavorable move in exchange rates. It, however, also stops the company from taking advantage of any *favorable* move. Currency options balance this situation. With currency options, the company has the right, but *not* the obligation, to purchase (a call option) or sell (a put option) a currency at an agreed exchange rate (the strike price). For this right without obligation, the buyer of the option pays a premium, making currency options a more expensive alternative to forward contracts. If there was an adverse movement in the exchange rate compared to the strike price, the holder of the option would allow the option to lapse. The holder could then instead buy or sell directly from the spot market.

Source: Casewriters.

Foreign Exchange Hedging Strategies at General Motors: Transactional and Translational Exposures

In September of 2001, Eric Feldstein, Treasurer and Vice President, Finance for General Motors Corp., paid little attention to his unobstructed view of Central Park from his office far above the Manhattan traffic. He was preoccupied with particular foreign currency exposures that required significant risk management decisions. An immediate priority was a decision on what to do about GM's billion dollar exposure to the Canadian dollar. Another pressing issue was GM's exposure to the Argentinean peso, in light of the expected devaluation in the months ahead.[1]

Feldstein and his treasury team were responsible for all of GM's monetary transactions and for managing the myriad risks associated with the timing of those transactions. They handled everything from investing excess cash from vehicle sales receipts to hedging currency risks when a foreign subsidiary like Opel Austria announced it would remit a dividend to the worldwide parent company. The GM Treasury program invested heavily in its people, rotating them through functional positions and offices around the world, developing their skills and experience. The unit continued to produce individuals who went on to senior finance positions with GM subsidiaries or elsewhere within the GM organization or left for senior roles at other major U.S. companies.

Professor Mihir A. Desai and Research Associate Mark F. Veblen prepared the original version of this case, "Foreign Exchange Hedging Strategies at General Motors," HBS Case No. 204-024. This version was prepared by Professor Mihir A. Desai and Research Associate Mark F. Veblen. HBS cases are developed solely as the basis for class discussion. Certain figures and details have been disguised and do not reflect the actual operations of General Motors Corp. Cases are not intended to serve as endorsements, sources of primary data, or illustrations of effective or ineffective management.

[1]The economic consequences of movements in the Japanese yen were also of significant concern and are the subject of Chapter 6.

As GM expanded around the world, the magnitude of its exposures to foreign currencies grew. Because exchange rate swings created gains and losses that flowed through GM's reported income statement, it was essential from a planning and management perspective to understand GM's foreign exchange flows and to manage the earnings and cash flow volatility they imposed on GM. Feldstein constantly followed news on volatile political situations around the world and kept abreast of macroeconomic trends that might affect GM's finances.

GM senior executives had implemented a number of formal policies with respect to foreign exchange risk management and hedging procedures. These policies guided the vast majority of treasury operations, but on occasion situations arose that required special attention and possibly a deviation from the stated policy. Feldstein, who had the authority to sign off on policy deviations, was currently reviewing such proposals for the Canadian dollar (CAD) and Argentinean peso (ARS). In his analysis, Feldstein paid particular attention to the transactional and translational consequences of these exposures, and pondered how these consequences should dictate his response.

OVERVIEW OF GENERAL MOTORS AND ITS TREASURY OPERATIONS

General Motors[2]

General Motors was the world's largest automaker, with unit sales of 8.5 million vehicles in 2001—15.1% worldwide market share—and had been the world's sales leader since 1931. Founded in 1908, GM had manufacturing operations in more than 30 countries, and its vehicles were sold in approximately 200 countries. In 2000, it generated earnings of $4.4 billion on sales of $184.6 billion (see Exhibit 1 for GM's consolidated income statement). The labor costs for its 365,000 employees in that year amounted to $19.8 billion, only $8.5 billion of which was for U.S.-based personnel. In addition to

---

EXHIBIT 1

GM CONSOLIDATED INCOME STATEMENT

December 31, ($ millions)	2000	1999	1998
Total net sales and revenues	184,632	176,558	155,445
Cost of sales and other expenses	145,664	140,708	127,957
Selling, general, and administrative	22,252	19,053	15,915
Interest expense	9,552	7,750	6,629
Earnings before taxes and minority interests	**7,164**	**9,047**	**4,944**
Income tax expense	2,393	3,118	1,636
Equity income (loss) and minority interests	(319)	(353)	(259)
Income from discontinued operations	—	426	(93)
Net income	**4,452**	**6,002**	**2,956**
Dividends on preference stocks	(110)	(80)	(63)
Earnings attributable to common stocks	**4,342**	**5,922**	**2,893**

Source: General Motors, December 31, 2000 10-K (Detroit: General Motors, 2001).

---

[2]Statistics drawn from General Motors, 2001 Annual Report (Detroit: General Motors, 2002) and General Motors, December 31, 2001 10-K (Detroit: General Motors, 2002).

EXHIBIT 2

GM SEGMENT BREAKDOWN OF SALES TO END CUSTOMERS, 2000

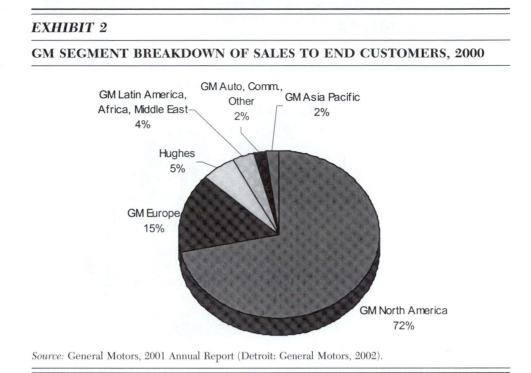

Source: General Motors, 2001 Annual Report (Detroit: General Motors, 2002).

vehicles, other major product lines included (i) financial services for automotive, mortgage, and business financing, and insurance services through General Motors Acceptance Corporation (GMAC), (ii) satellite television and commercial satellite services through Hughes Electronics, and (iii) locomotives and heavy duty transmissions through GM Locomotive Group and Allison Transmission Division. GM traded on the New York Stock Exchange and was a component of the Dow Jones Industrial Average.

While North America still represented the majority of sales to end customers and the largest concentration of net property, plant, and equipment (see Exhibit 2 and Exhibit 3), the importance of GM's international operations was growing as a percent of the overall business. With globalized production, these figures understated the degree to which intermediate goods in GM's supply chain moved around the world. Its market share in Latin America was 20% and in Europe had reached 10% (20% if Fiat's figures were included).[3] Increasing market share in Asia, which stood at 4%, was a major strategic objective for GM.

General Motors Treasurer's Office

GM's Treasurer's Office performed a full range of corporate treasury functions from its head office in New York and through additional locations in Brussels, Singapore and Detroit. The organizational structure shown in Exhibit 4 demonstrates the nature and extent of those activities.

One of the key functions of the Treasurer's Office was financial risk management. This included management of not only market risk (foreign exchange, interest rate and

---

[3]General Motors owned 20% of Fiat, and Fiat held an option to put the remaining 80% to GM.

EXHIBIT 3

GM GEOGRAPHIC BREAKDOWN OF NET PROPERTY, 2000

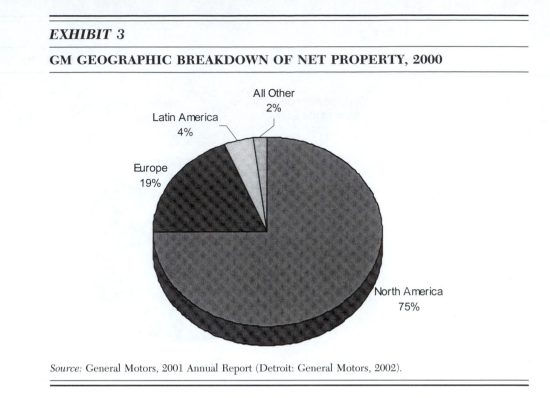

Source: General Motors, 2001 Annual Report (Detroit: General Motors, 2002).

---

commodities exposures) but also counterparty, corporate and operational risk. Exhibit 5 outlines the components of this function and demonstrates the high degree of centralization in approach.

All of GM's financial risk management activities were subject to oversight by the Risk Management Committee, which was composed of six of GM's most senior executives including Feldstein.[4] The committee met quarterly to review the performance of GM's financial risk management strategies and to set treasury policy for GM and its subsidiaries. Treasury policy included evaluating the parameters and benchmarks for managing market risks, determining criteria for assessing counterparty credit risk, determining thresholds for property and liability insurance coverage, as well as reviewing internal control aspects of operating policies and procedures. GM's formal, company-wide policies contained not only broad principles, but also detailed execution procedures such as, in the case of foreign exchange risk management, the types of instruments to be used and the appropriate time horizons.[5] At its meetings the committee also discussed any special topics that needed to be addressed. Such special topics often included precisely the deviations from usual policy Feldstein was currently considering.

Various groups within the Treasurer's Office were involved in the implementation of financial risk management policy. For foreign exchange, all of GM's hedging activities were concentrated in two centers:

---

[4]Other members of the Risk Management Committee were the Chief Financial Officer, the General Auditor, the Chief Accounting Officer, the Chief Economist, and a senior executive from General Motors Acceptance Corporation (GMAC), GM's financial services subsidiary.

[5]GM policy specified, for example, which risks were to be hedged using forward contracts rather than options contracts.

EXHIBIT 4

GM TREASURY GROUP—ORGANIZATIONAL STRUCTURE

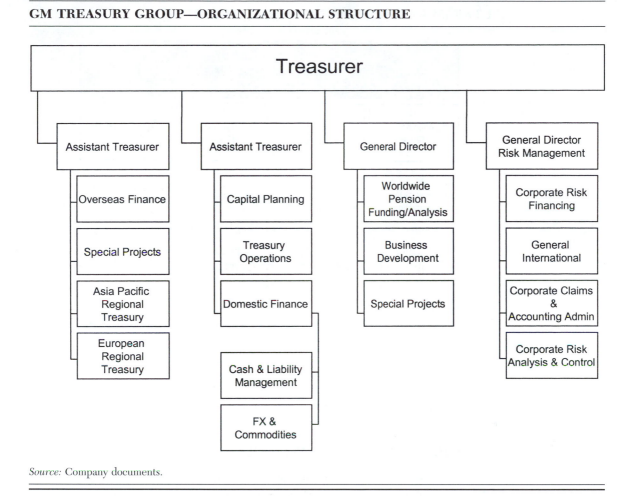

Source: Company documents.

- The Domestic Finance group in New York handled FX hedging for GM entities located in North America, Latin America, Africa and the Middle East
- The European Regional Treasury Center (ERTC) was GM's largest foreign exchange operation, covering European and Asia Pacific FX exposures

FX hedging activities were segregated in this way on the principle that there should be some geographic correspondence between where a business unit was actually managed and where treasury for that business was controlled. At the same time, though, it was considered desirable to reap the benefits of pooling exposures across groups. In a sense, the goal was to match treasury management to the footprint of the business. Having local market knowledge and a trading center in both the European and U.S. time zones was also very helpful, because GM was active in each of the major foreign exchange markets.

In managing the FX exposures, both the Domestic Finance group and the ERTC worked closely with other groups within Treasury that had the primary responsibility

EXHIBIT 5

GM TREASURY GROUP—FUNCTIONAL STRUCTURE

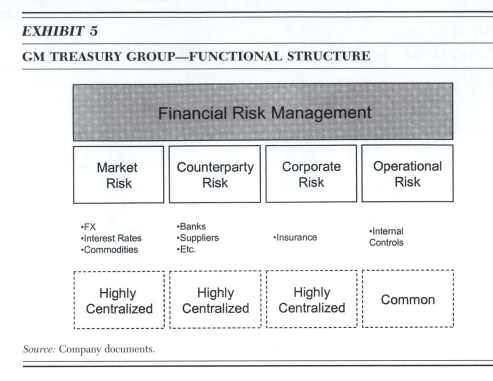

Source: Company documents.

of providing strategic support to GM entities within that region. These groups were also the global coordinators for intercompany loans, moved cash around the world to finance overseas mergers and acquisitions activities, and managed dividend repatriations.

REVIEW OF CORPORATE HEDGING POLICY

General Motors' overall foreign exchange risk management policy was established to meet three primary objectives: (1) reduce cash flow and earnings volatility, (2) minimize the management time and costs dedicated to global FX management, and (3) align FX management in a manner consistent with how GM operates its automotive business. The first constituted a conscious decision to hedge cash flows (transaction exposures[6]) only and ignore balance sheet exposures (translation exposures[7]). The second objective was a consequence of an internal study that determined that investment of resources in active FX management had not resulted in significant outperformance of passive benchmarks. As a result, policy was changed and a passive approach replaced

---

[6]Transaction exposures are the gains and losses that arise when transactions are settled in some currency other than a company's reporting currency. These exposures stem from buying and selling activities as well as financing decisions such as borrowing. For further detail see W. Carl Kester and Richard P. Melnick, "Note on Transaction and Translation Exposure," HBS Case No. 288-017 (Boston: Harvard Business School Publishing, 1987, rev. 1992).

[7]Translation exposures are the gains and losses that arise when the assets and liabilities of a multinational's foreign subsidiary are translated back into the multinational's reporting currency for the purposes of preparing consolidated financial statements. For further detail see W. Carl Kester and Richard P. Melnick, "Note on Transaction and Translation Exposure".

the active one. The third reflected a belief that financial management should somehow map to the geographic operational footprint of the underlying business.

Passive Policy: Hedge 50% of Commercial (Operating) Exposures

The policy adopted was generally to hedge 50% of all significant foreign exchange commercial (operating) exposures on a regional level.[8] GM policy differentiated between "commercial" exposures—cash flows associated with the ongoing business such as receivables and payables—and "financial" exposures such as debt repayments and dividends. GM policy also outlined what sorts of derivative instruments were to be used for hedging.

Commercial (Operating) Exposures

With operations, sales units, and investments spanning the globe, GM had direct or indirect commercial exposures to virtually every meaningful currency. Each regional center collected monthly forecasts of accounts receivable and accounts payable, usually for the twelve coming months, from all of the GM entities within its region and totaled the net exposures (receivables minus payables) by currency pair.[9] This information was compiled into a matrix presenting the exposure totals by currency pair for each regional unit (General Motors North America, General Motors Europe, General Motors Asian Pacific, and General Motors Latin America, Africa, Middle East) and then aggregating them up to a corporate grand total for General Motors as a whole. (See Exhibit 6 for the summary of exposures by currency pair.) In practical use, this provided GM executives with granular information about the currency exposures created by ongoing business operations.

A determination of *"riskiness"* was then made on a regional basis, deciding which FX exposures were significant enough to warrant hedging. This determination was governed by the following formula:

Implied risk = Regional notional exposure × Annual volatility of relevant currency pair

For example, if GM-North America's (GMNA) forecasted 12-month euro exposure was a $400 million net payable at December 31, 2000, this difference of euro receivables less euro payables would represent the notional euro exposure for GM's North America region. Given the euro's annual volatility versus the U.S. dollar of 12%, this suggested an implied risk of $48 million. For all implied risks of $10 million or greater, the regional exposure was required to be hedged. In the case of particularly volatile currencies, exposures were only hedged for the coming six months rather than twelve, and the implied risk threshold was lowered to $5 million. In practice, GM's overseas operations were large enough that all major currencies exceeded this threshold in one or more regions.

[8]The fact that exposures were managed regionally meant that although there might be offsetting exposures in different regions, each region's exposure would still be separately hedged. For example, if with respect to the British pound GM-Europe had a net receivables position $1 million and GM-Asia Pacific had a net payables position of $1 million, each region's GBP exposure would be hedged even though GM as a consolidated entity had no net exposure before or after this hedging activity took place.

[9]The business units were permitted some flexibility in netting across months so long as they established a currency hedge through their treasury center. For example, if $20 million net receivables exposure in one month was likely to be offset by a $15 million payables exposure in the next month in the ordinary course of business, the net exposure of $5 million could be hedged with a forward contract and a currency swap used to hedge the risk involved in the timing difference.

EXHIBIT 6

GM'S LARGEST CURRENCY EXPOSURES
(FORECASTED RECEIVABLES LESS PAYABLES)

As of 12/31/00 ($ millions)	USD	EUR	JPY	GBP	SEK	AUD	CAD	CHF	PLN	MXP	OTHER
GMNA	800	(400)	—	—	(200)	—	(1,400)	—	—	1,200	—
GME	400	(2,400)	(200)	1,400	(800)	400	(200)	400	200	—	800
GMAP	200	(200)	(200)	200	—	200	—	—	—	—	200
GMLAAM	600	(400)	(500)	—	—	—	—	—	—	—	—
GM Total	2,000	(3,400)	(900)	1,600	(1,000)	600	(1,600)	400	200	1,200	1,000

Figures have been disguised and do not reflect the actual operations of General Motors Corp.

NOTES:
    GMNA: General Motors North America
    GME: General Motors Europe
    GMAP: General Motors Asian Pacific
    GMLAAM: General Motors Latin America, Africa, Middle East

Source: General Motors.

Net exposures within a region were then hedged to a *benchmark hedge ratio* of 50%. For example, half, or $200 million, of GMNA's notional euro exposure of $400 million would be hedged.

Having calculated the forecasted net exposure to a particular currency for each of the coming twelve months, the regional treasury center was then bound to use *particular derivative instruments* over *specified time horizons*: forward contracts to hedge 50% of the exposures for months one through six and options to hedge 50% of the exposures for months seven through twelve. Assuming that GMNA's $400 million euro exposure was distributed evenly over the twelve months of 2001, the $200 million exposure for months one through six would be hedged through forward contracts on $100 million, and the $200 million exposure for months seven through twelve would be hedged through options on $100 million. In general, at least 25% of the combined hedge on a particular currency was to be held in options in order to assure flexibility.

The evolution of the rolling forward twelve months naturally became more complicated when the exposures were not evenly spread across time (see Exhibit 7). First, as months rolled closer (cash flow G from month seven to six in Exhibit 7), the Treasury group replaced or supplemented options-based hedge positions with forward contracts, sometimes selling options previously purchased. This meant that the balance of forwards and options used to hedge the year ahead was constantly changing—and according to policy, options had to make up 25% of hedge positions. Second, the forecasts that the Treasury group received from managers in the operating subsidiaries frequently changed from month to month. This created situations where hedging actions from the previous month left the Treasury group either over- or under-hedged due to changing expectations.

Treasury centers were also expected to monitor the economic performance of their hedges and to readjust cover to levels which matched the levels achieved by a simulated benchmark hedge portfolio. This was done on a *delta basis*. The delta provided a

EXHIBIT 7

EVOLUTION OF NET RECEIVABLES/PAYABLES EXPOSURE, ROLLING FORWARD TWELVE MONTHS

Month	1	2	3	4	5	6		7	8	9	10	11	12
			FORWARDS							OPTIONS			
t=0 CFs	A	B	C	D	E	F		G	H	I	J	K	L
t=1 CFs	B*	C*	D*	E*	F*	G*		H*	I*	J*	K*	L*	M

(°) Forecasts received from operations managers for future months may change from month to month.

Source: Casewriter analysis

measure of how effectively a particular instrument covered a risk, taking into account the probability that the instrument would be exercised. Forward contracts therefore had a delta of 100%. In purchasing currency options, GM sought to buy at-the-money-forward options that had an expected delta of 50% upon execution. Given the required mix of forwards and options in hedging an exposure, the hedge ratio of 50% initially corresponded, on a delta basis, to a hedge ratio of 37.5%. Taking again GMNA's euro exposure as an example, the first six months were hedged on a delta basis at the notional hedge ratio (50%) times the forward contract delta (100%) or a delta hedge ratio of 50%. Similarly the last six months were hedged notionally at 50% and using options with a 50% delta, which combined to a 25% delta hedge ratio. The average delta hedge ratio over the entire hedging horizon was therefore 37.5% at the outset.

Over time, the delta hedge ratios of both the actual and the benchmark hedge portfolios could be expected to depart from the initial 37.5%, primarily due to sensitivity of the value of options to movements in spot rates. Experience suggested that the delta hedge ratio of the benchmark portfolio would fluctuate somewhere between 30% and 45%. In addition, the delta hedge ratio of the actual portfolio would often vary from that of the benchmark portfolio because of the practical difficulties in executing exactly in line with the benchmark. A tolerance of +/− 5% was therefore allowed in matching the delta cover of the actual portfolio to the cover of the benchmark portfolio. It was also possible, on an exception basis, to deviate from a passive hedging strategy and take a view on the future direction of a particular FX rate. Regional approvals were required in any such case. Even then, delta and notional cover levels had to be kept within certain prescribed ranges.

Commercial Exposures (Capital Expenditures)

Because capital expenditures did not exhibit the same month-to-month volatility or changing forecasts, GM adopted a different approach to hedging them. Unlike uncertain cash flows, planned investments (purchases of fixed assets or equipment) that met either of the following two tests were hedged with forward contracts using a 100% hedge ratio to the anticipated payment date: (i) an amount in excess of $1 million, or (ii) an implied risk equivalent to at least 10% of the unit's net worth. Such exposures were generally treated separately from ordinary commercial exposures.

Financial Exposures

Other known cash flows, including loan repayment schedules and equity injections into affiliates were hedged on a case-by-case basis. Generally they were structured so as to create as little FX risk as possible, and as a rule of thumb they were also 100% hedged using forward contracts. Dividend payments, on the other hand, were only deemed hedgeable once declared, and even then were hedged in the same manner as ordinary commercial exposures, i.e., a 50% hedge ratio.

Translation (Balance Sheet) Exposures

Translation exposures were not included under GM's corporate hedging policy. Nonetheless, they could on occasion become large enough to warrant the attention of senior finance executives, and Feldstein therefore kept abreast of all such situations. Such exposures were closely related to management's determination of a subsidiary's functional currency, a topic discussed in Appendix B.

Accounting Treatment

One of the goals of GM's hedging policy was to reduce earnings volatility. This goal was challenging given that, under the prevailing accounting standards (FAS 133), the forwards and options GM would use generally had to be marked-to-market and the gains and losses flowed through the income statement. At the same time, the underlying exposure being hedged was, in the case of commercial exposures (forecasts of receivables and payables up to 12 months in advance), often not on the books at all, and therefore changes in its market value did not hit the income statement. This mismatch was a potential source of earnings volatility.

FAS 133, however, provided the possibility of hedge accounting treatment for an exposure and associated hedge position. If the requirements for hedge accounting treatment were met, the above described earnings volatility was neutralized by taking gains and losses on the hedges to a shareholder's equity account in the balance sheet pending the realization of gains and losses on the underlying hedged exposures. Ultimately, gains and losses on the hedges would be released through the income statement contemporaneously with the recognition in the income statement of the gains and losses on the underlying exposures. Unfortunately, due to the complexity of compliance with hedge accounting regulations only a few of GM's more significant currency pairs were initially targeted for compliance.[10]

Reporting

Hedging activities were closely tracked and regularly reviewed within the Treasury Group. The information was made available to senior management and to the Risk Management Committee to assist in policy review and creation. It was this internal moni-

---

[10]Compliance was at the discretion of the company: by providing extensive proof that derivative transactions were entered into for the purpose of hedging and by establishing the effectiveness of the hedge, companies could obtain hedge accounting treatment for the combined position and avoid asymmetric mark-to-market treatment of the underlying exposure and hedge position.

toring that had led, just a few years earlier, to the decision to shift away from active FX risk management to passive management.

MONTHLY REVIEW—THE CANADIAN DOLLAR

GM-Canada was an integral part of GM's worldwide production process. In addition to serving the Canadian domestic market, it served as a core supplier to other GM operations in North America, especially those in the United States, and it also relied on many U.S. based suppliers. At GM-Canada the U.S. dollar-denominated flows were so large that the U.S. dollar was effectively the primary operating currency of the company. As a result, accounting standards required that the U.S. dollar be selected as the functional currency despite GM-Canada's very large Canadian dollar assets and liabilities. The rules on determining the choice of a subsidiary's functional currency are explained in Appendix B, and Exhibit 8 provides an illustration of the impact of a change in exchange rates using different functional currencies.

Since GM-Canada's functional currency was the U.S. dollar, its exposure to the Canadian dollar was recognized as a foreign currency exposure. The income statement impact arose from gains and losses on both the CAD-denominated cash flows (see Exhibit 9) and on the balance sheet CAD net monetary liability position (see Exhibit 10). Both exposures were equivalent to short positions in the Canadian dollar. The net payable cash flow exposure resulted largely from payments due to Canadian suppliers, and the size of the net monetary liability stemmed mainly from future pension and postretirement benefit obligations to employees in Canada.

GM's passive hedging policy called only for hedging 50% of the CAD 1.7 billion cash flow exposure projected over the subsequent twelve months. Nonetheless, Feldstein acknowledged that GM's policy of not hedging the translation exposure stemming from the CAD 2.1 billion net monetary liability left a large CAD exposure that could impact GM's year-end financial results significantly.

Feldstein therefore met with his FX and Commodities Manager, Doug Ostermann, who was proposing to increase the hedge ratio for the CAD to the maximum allowed under GM policy—75%. The internal memorandum requesting permission to deviate so far from the standard 50% policy read as follows:

> Historically, GMNA has a short CAD commercial exposure of approximately CAD 1.6–1.8 billion, primarily due to CAD denominated supplier payments being larger than CAD denominated sales. . . . In order to reduce global earnings volatility at year-end, we recommend to hedge up to 75% of GMNA's commercial exposure (approximately 30% hedging ratio for the balance sheet exposure). According to the FX policy, any deviation from the passive hedging strategy (50% notional hedging ratio), requires the approval . . .

Feldstein felt he needed a comparison of the income statement impact of a 75% versus a 50% hedge ratio. The proposal suggested that the expected volatility of the CAD/USD exchange rate was plus-or-minus 3.1% around the 1.5780 exchange rate on the date of the memo. Using this volatility, Ostermann could do a sensitivity calculation with a favorable scenario (gain due to FX movements) and an unfavorable scenario (loss due to FX movements) based on the after-tax gain/loss impact from the projected CAD cash flow as well as from the CAD net monetary liability. By dividing this amount by the 550 million shares GM had outstanding, Ostermann could determine how much the proposed deviation would reduce EPS volatility. To simplify the calculation, Ostermann ignored the costs of hedging (such as option premiums). Additionally,

EXHIBIT 8

ILLUSTRATIVE EXAMPLE OF THE EFFECT OF A EUR DEPRECIATION/ USD APPRECIATION DEPENDING ON THE CHOICE OF FUNCTIONAL CURRENCY

	Exchange Rate (EUR / USD)		Impact on **GMWorldwide's** Financial Statements
	1.0	0.9	

USD Functional

GMS Net Assets

In functional currency	USD	100.0	100.0	
In foreign currency	EUR	50.0	50.0	
GMS - Reported	USD	150.0	145.0	

A

Income Statement:	USD	-5.0
Translation Adjustment:	USD	0.0
Shareholders' Equity:	USD	-5.0

EUR Functional

GMS Net Assets

In functional currency	EUR	50.0	50.0	
In foreign currency	USD	100.0	100.0	
GMS - Reported	EUR	150.0	161.1	

B

Income Statement:	USD	10.0
Translation Adjustment:	USD	-5.0
Shareholders' Equity:	USD	5.0

A A depreciation of the EUR against the USD causes a decline in the dollar value of GMS's foreign currency (EUR) net asset, generating a loss for GM Worldwide's income statement.

B The increase in the euro value of GMS's foreign currency net asset generates a gain for GM Worldwide's income statement. Given that the GMS functional currency is not GM's reporting currency, there is a translation adjustment of -$5.0.porting currency, there is a translation adjustment

Source: Casewriter analysis.

EXHIBIT 9

GM CANADA—PROJECTED CASH FLOW EXPOSURE

Cash Flows	Amount as of September 30, 2001
INFLOWS	
Canadian sales	10,564
Tax refunds (GST)	1,049
OUTFLOWS	
Material purchases	(10,180)
Capital expenditures	(113)
Other structural costs	(1,737)
Tax expenditures	(1,258)
Other expenditures	(6)
12 month C$ cash flow forecast	**(1,682)**

Figures have been disguised and do not reflect the actual operations of General Motors Corp.

Source: Company documents.

EXHIBIT 10

GM CANADA—NET MONETARY ASSET/LIABILITY EXPOSURE

Balance Sheet Account	Amount as of September 30, 2001
ASSETS	
Cash & cash equivalents	683
Accounts & notes receivable	271
Deferred income taxes	118
Pension asset	1,525
LIABILITIES	
Outside—all other	(93)
Other postretirement benefits	(1,949)
Warranty	(132)
Accounts payable and other	(2,565)
C$ Monetary asset / (liability) position	**(2,143)**

Figures have been disguised and do not reflect the actual operations of General Motors Corp.

Source: Company documents.

Osterman wanted his analysis to reflect the "excess cash" of CAD 660 million held by GM Canada.[11]

As Feldstein prepared to make a decision about the CAD deviation, he had to keep in mind both what economic risks he wanted to hedge and what was called for under GM's corporate hedging policy.

Implementing a Foreign Exchange Hedge

If Feldstein signed off on this deviation, Mercedes Michel and the team in Domestic Finance would oversee implementing the hedge. Michel was in regular communication with several of the largest currency-dealing banks and maintained up-to-date price quotations. On any day when GM was active in the market adjusting its hedge positions, she was on the phone with the banks virtually all day getting quotations and executing trades. On an ordinary day, she could get most of the information she needed from electronic data sources. When a hedge position was being created or modified, she handled transactions in both forward and options contracts.

Suppose on September 15, 2001 Michel needed to hedge a CAD 10 million cash outflow three months in the future (in other words, 50% of a CAD 20 million notional exposure). First, she checks the market price levels using a Bloomberg terminal. The spot price on the CAD/USD exchange rate is bid-ask of 1.5621–1.5624. (Spreads were very small when transacting in significant amounts in the currency markets; players typically only referred to the last two digits of the spread because it was assumed that buyers and sellers knew the levels to the 1/100th of a point.) With that information she dials one of her regular bankers:

Michel: Can you give me a two-way price on 10 Canada?

Trader: CAD spot is 21 to 24.

Michel: I'll do it at 21.

Trader: So, you are buying 10 million Canadian dollars against U.S. dollars at 1.5621.

Michel: Actually, I want to roll it 3 months out. Can you tell me the forward points?

Trader: That's 45 points.

Michel: Can you improve it a pip?

Trader: Humm . . . OK . . . You get it at 46.

Michel: Done. Thanks.

Trader: Good. Then GM buys 10 million Canadian dollars at 1.5667 and sells USD 6,382,842.92 with value December 17, 2001.

Michel: Agreed. Bye.

Now assume that instead of hedging the exposure with a forward contract, Michel needed to use a currency option to hedge the CAD 10 million exposure. Michel will buy a CAD call / USD put with a notional amount of CAD 10 million. Assume the spot price is 1.5621. Again, before calling the trader, Michel checks Bloomberg to find the forward rate—1.5667 in this example. Michel will use this as the strike price for a 3-month at-the-money-forward (ATMF[12]) CAD call / USD put.

---

[11]Total cash or cash equivalents held by GM Canada was CAD 683; Ostermann estimated CAD 660 of this amount was "excess cash."

[12]Rather than being at-the-money with respect to the spot price, such an option is at-the-money with respect to the forward price.

Michel: Can you give me a price for a CAD call / USD put with delta exchange?[13]

Trader: Sure. Give me the details.

Michel: I need a 10 Canada call, maturing on December 17th, with a strike price of 1.5667 and delta exchange at 1.5621. Can you give me the premium price as a percentage of USD?

Trader: Yes. Hold on a moment . . . So, the strike is at 50% delta[14] . . . the premium price is 1.45% of USD offered.

Michel: Let's see. The U.S. dollar put amount is 10 million divided by 1.5667, that's USD 6,382,842.92; that times 1.45% makes the premium amount 92,551.22 U.S. dollars. Let's do it.

Trader: Done. GM buys a 10 million Canadian dollar call / U.S. dollar put with maturity on December 17, value December 18, at a strike of 1.5667. On the delta exchange GM sells CAD 5 at 1.5621.

Michel: Agreed. Bye.[15]

Comparing Forward Contracts with Options

Because GM's hedging operations constituted a substantial volume of currency trading, GM was concerned with executing its hedging policies in a cost efficient manner. Forward contracts and options, however, were not easily comparable on straight cost basis. A forward contract was always a zero cost contract on the trade date, whereas buying an option involved paying a premium. Thus, the treasury group needed a way of analyzing the two strategies with respect to one another. The framework devised by the Treasury group involved comparing how one strategy or the other would have fared at the different possible exchange rates that might prevail at the future date (the date of the exposure to hedge).

Specifically, it compared: (1) the combination of the outright exposure plus a 50% hedge using forward contracts, with (2) the combination of the outright exposure plus a 50% hedge using options. On a graph of future spot prices (*x*-axis) against cash flow payoff (*y*-axis), these two produced lines that intersected. That point of intersection represented a sort of break-even point—if GM Treasury's expected future spot exchange rate was different from that point, GM could choose the strategy that was more profitable.

Forward Contracts

Continuing the example from Michel's conversations with traders above, Michel constructed a spreadsheet that considered a range of future spot rates of 1.4000 to 1.8000 CAD per USD. The outright exposure measured the foreign exchange gain or loss GM would recognize on the CAD 20 million position. At a 50% hedge, Michel knew she

---

[13]The delta exchange effectively allowed the bank to offer a price quotation based on a fixed spot rate (of 1.5621 in this case). As a result, GM was able to contact multiple banks and obtain competitive price quotations and select the best one for executing the options trade. Appendix A discusses the mechanics of a delta exchange in detail.

[14]An at-the-money-forward option was characterized by a delta (sensitivity to changes in the underlying exchange rate) of 50%.

[15]Michel might have asked the trader to hold the price quotation while she contacted other banks in search of a better price. The fact that she immediately executed the trade with this trader suggests that she had already called two other banks and that their price quotations were not as competitive.

had to layer on a CAD 10 million hedge at a forward price of 1.5667. This would produce a partially offsetting cash flow in the future. The sum of the outright gain/loss and the cash settlement of the forward contract amounted to the net consequence of a forwards strategy.

Options Contracts

Instead, Michel could layer on top of the outright exposure just calculated an option contract purchase. The sum of the outright exposure and the option payoff amounted to the net consequence of an options strategy. The option characteristics were as described above: a strike price equal to the forward price of 1.5667 and a premium cost of 1.45% of the notional hedge amount. When the option was in the money, the contract returned a profit (less the premium), whereas when it expired out of the money, the gain (loss) on the outright exposure was reduced (increased) by the premium amount.

SPECIAL SITUATIONS—THE ARGENTINEAN PESO

Argentina presented GM Treasury with a real headache for GM's extensive operations there. In order to cure rampant inflation, the government exercised control over foreign currency exchange and maintained a peg to the U.S. dollar at USD 1 : ARS 1. With a debt-to-GDP ratio of 45% and $16.5 billion coming due in 2002, the "zero-deficit" law passed by the Argentine Senate in 2001 put Argentina at serious risk of defaulting on its debt. Credit analysts at Standard & Poor's and Moody's had downgraded Argentina to six and seven grades below investment grade, respectively. GM Treasury's Latin America experts believed the short-term probability of default had reached 40%. In the medium term, the probability rose to 50% because Argentina had not addressed key issues such as trade liberalization, state reform, and pension and healthcare reform. A default would undoubtedly be accompanied by a massive devaluation.

The Argentina situation appeared grim. Feldstein reviewed the figures before him. The treasury analysts had provided the ARS and USD denominated components of the balance sheet (see Exhibit 11)—and described a potential devaluation of the peso against the dollar from 1:1 to 2:1. Feldstein saw two immediate impacts. First, local currency equivalent of USD borrowings by GM Argentina (a local currency functional subsidiary) would grow, putting financial pressure on the subsidiary. In fact, the $300 million USD net liability position would double in peso terms to an ARS 600 million liability. There would be a consequent ARS 300 million adverse income statement impact for the subsidiary. Second, there would be a substantial translation loss on GM Argentina's ARS denominated net assets when these net assets were consolidated in USD with all other assets of GM Worldwide. This loss would negatively impact consolidated shareholders' equity. With a few calculations, Feldstein figured the value at risk to GM—an amount that included the maximum EPS hit GM might be forced to take into net income in 2002 together with the shareholders' equity impact.[16]

---

[16]In fact, the accounting consequences were more complex. As a local currency functional entity, GM Argentina would first convert all non-ARS denominated asset and liabilities to ARS. The gain or loss would be reflected in GM Argentina's income statement and ultimately impact the consolidated net income of GM Worldwide. On consolidation, the entire GM Argentina balance sheet, now denominated exclusively in ARS, would be translated into USD, and any gain or loss would be reflected as an accumulated translation adjustment (ATA) flowing directly to shareholders' equity.

EXHIBIT 11

GM ARGENTINA BALANCE SHEET, MONETARY ASSETS AND LIABILITIES BY CURRENCY, AS OF SEPTEMBER 30, 2001

ARS Monetary Assets		ARS Monetary Liabilities	
Scrap incentive owed by govt.	45.8	Payables to local suppliers	24.1
Interest subsidy owed by govt.	3.2	Provisions to local suppliers	11.3
VAT credit and other tax owed by govt.	130.6	ARS loan (VAT financing)	13.7
Receivable (tax credit reimbursement)	2.7	Other provisions	9.8
Other	7.8	Tax payable	2.0
Total	**190.0**	**Total**	**60.9**
USD Monetary Assets		**USD Monetary Liabilities**	
Cash	2.5	Accounts payable	224.5
Receivables	20.5	Loans	101.3
Total	**23.0**	**Total**	**325.7**

Figures have been disguised and do not reflect the actual operations of General Motors Corp.

Source: Company documents.

Hedging the Peso Exposure

This time, Michel had sent some materials along with the policy deviation proposal. She reviewed the market for forwards and options on the ARS and suggested a method for thinking about how costly it would be to hedge the ARS exposure in the financial markets. Michel had compiled historical prices on one-, six-, and twelve-month forward rates of the peso vs. the dollar (see Exhibit 12). Feldstein's first observation was the rapid rise in forward rates over the recent months. With the peso pegged at 1:1 to the dollar, the forward premium, approximately 4.56% on a one-month contract, would be lost if the peso peg was maintained (since pesos could instead still have been purchased at 1:1). Michel extrapolated from the historical prices the costs of hedging a $300 million exposure based on rolling over shorter term contracts or purchasing year-long contracts (see Exhibit 13).

These figures led Feldstein to consider what alternative hedging opportunities might be available to mitigate the impact of a likely devaluation. He hoped to find some natural business hedges or creative ways to reduce peso-denominated assets and substitute peso-denominated liabilities for hard currency-denominated ones. Similarly, creating exports—even if to other GM affiliates—from Argentina could bring in revenues in more stable foreign currencies. GM Argentina had already eliminated peso cash balances and transferred them in USD to the European Regional Treasury Center. It was also considering the purchase of some materials locally in ARS for export to other entities in the region that would pay for them in hard currency. GM-Argentina's USD borrowings would certainly have to be addressed. The Argentina situation was more complex than most currency deviation requests—although Feldstein had to consider all of the same issues as with the CAD deviation, it was less clear how to accomplish an ARS deviation effectively.

Feldstein and Ostermann needed to decide how to proceed: was it worth the costs to increase the size of GM's hedge position beyond what was required by usual policy?

EXHIBIT 12

**ARGENTINEAN PESO/U.S. DOLLAR FORWARD RATES
BY CONTRACT MATURITY**

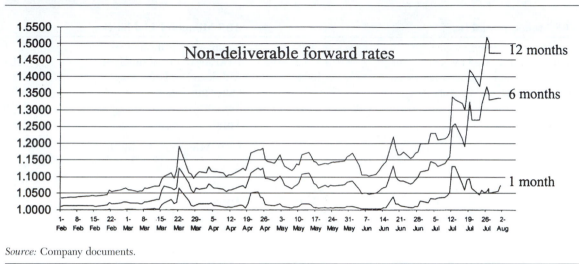

Source: Company documents.

CONCLUSION

Feldstein had a great deal of thinking to do. The two cases under consideration—the CAD deviation and the ARS deviation—were not simple ones. He had to balance the dictates of GM's hedging policy with concerns about how markets would respond to changes in the exchange rates and the potential consequences of GM's significant exposures to each of these currencies. It was important for him to understand not just what the policy permitted, but what the economics of each exposure were, and what was best for GM as a consolidated global entity in each case.

EXHIBIT 13

COST OF HEDGING THE ARS EXPOSURE IN ARGENTINA

Time Horizon / Hedging Period	Cost ($ millions)
One-month Forward	$6.4
Three-month Forward	18.2
Six-month Forward	28.7
Twelve-month Forward	40.3

Source: Company documents.

APPENDIX A

MECHANICS OF A CURRENCY OPTION PURCHASE WITH A DELTA EXCHANGE

Key Variables for a Currency Option

(1) Spot exchange rate, 1.5621; (2) forward rate (sometimes stated in forward points or forward premium), 1.5667; (3) strike price (an exchange rate), 1.5667; (4) risk free interest rate in both currencies, available instantly from Bloomberg; (5) time to expiration, three months; and (6) volatility of the currency pair, the price quoted by the bank.

What Happens When GM Buys an Option from a Bank?

After Michel and the trader agree on a price and the bank has written an option, the bank has taken on a naked option position. However, the bank usually does not take currency positions for the purpose of gain, but instead acts as an intermediary and earns a commission on each trade. As a result, it wishes to eliminate the exposure created by having written the option to GM. Typically the bank does so by immediately creating an offsetting position. It might be that the bank has another client who wants to take the exact opposite side of the option GM bought. This is rare, however, and the bank normally resorts to "delta hedging." At any given point in time, an option has some price sensitivity to the underlying asset price. For example, if an exchange rate appreciates one percent, this would increase the value of a call on that currency. The amount by which the call value increases is called the delta. If a bank is short an option on CAD 10 million but has bought CAD 5 million and the option has a delta of 50%, then the bank is perfectly hedged: if the CAD exchange rate appreciates one percent, the short option will lose one percent on CAD 10 million times 50%, but the long currency position will gain one percent on CAD 5 million times 100% in value. (The delta of a long position in the underlying asset is necessarily one.) As the spot rate changes, the bank will have to increase and decrease the size of its delta hedge position so that changes in the exchange rate will always create offset gains and losses on the option and delta hedge positions.

What if GM Wants to Get Competitive Price Quotations?

In order to get multiple price quotations, it is necessary to call several banks. This requires that the first bank called agrees to leave its quoted price open for some time while GM accumulates other price quotations. Spot rates, however, change constantly, so no bank will leave a price quotation open for long. GM must, therefore, find a device that protects the bank against changes in the spot rate between getting the price quotation and calling back to execute the trade. In effect, GM must promise to help the bank retroactively create the delta hedge that the bank would have created on its own, had the order been placed during the same phone call that the price quotations was given.

What is a "Delta Exchange"

Mechanically, by agreeing to the delta exchange, GM is agreeing to act as the counterparty for the bank's delta hedging transaction at the spot rate prevailing when the option price quotation was given. This protects the bank's ability to hedge the option exposure. It also requires that GM purchase CAD 5 million on the spot market before placing the option trade so that when it purchases the option from the bank it has CAD 5 million on hand to sell to the bank when it is called upon to complete the delta exchange.

UNDERSTANDING THE CHOICE OF A SUBSIDIARY'S FUNCTIONAL CURRENCY

When U.S. multinationals established new overseas subsidiaries, management was required to determine whether the functional currency for each overseas subsidiary would be the local currency or the U.S. dollar. Under FASB #52, the functional currency had to be the primary operating currency of that subsidiary. (There was one exception: parent companies were required to use their own reporting currency in highly inflationary economies.) A self-contained unit with substantial local currency receipts and expenses had to select the local currency as its functional currency. However, a subsidiary that purchased much of its raw inputs from a U.S. parent or sold a substantial part of its production to its U.S. parent each year—in short, operations that were essentially an extension of the parent company's business—had to select the U.S. dollar as its functional currency. The choice of functional currency did not impact the consolidated entity's reporting currency, which was always the U.S. dollar in the case of U.S. multinationals.

While the choice of functional currency did not change the economic realities of the business and its operations, it did change how a company reported the changes in value resulting from fluctuating exchange rates. The following example illustrates the consequences of the choice of functional currencies (see Exhibit 8 for an illustration of these issues).

Imagine that GM-Strasbourg (GMS) has nothing but cash held in a U.S. dollar-denominated checking account and a euro-denominated checking account. The respective balances are $100 and €50. The subsidiary is financed entirely with equity. Furthermore, assume for simplicity that the U.S. dollar and the euro are trading at parity. Suppose GMS has a choice whether to use the U.S. dollar or the euro as its functional currency.[17] The difference between these alternatives is examined by tracing the consequences of a 10% devaluation of the euro against the U.S. dollar.

When GMS's functional currency is the same as GM's reporting currency (U.S. dollars), GM's consolidated income statement will include a gain or loss on the changes in value, as measured in U.S. dollars, of GMS's foreign currency denominated monetary asset/liability.[18] (GMS's income statement will show the same.) When GMS instead uses its local currency (euros) as its functional currency,

1. GM's consolidated income statement will include a gain or loss on the changes in value, as measured in GMS's local currency of GMS's non-local currency denominated asset/liability (GMS's income statement will show the same)

2. GM's balance sheet will show an adjustment to shareholders' equity for the translation to U.S. dollars of GMS's assets/liabilities.

The critical insight is that, while the overall impact of the devaluation of the euro will be the same regardless of the functional currency chosen, there is a difference in what impact is recognized in the income statement and what impact is recognized directly in the shareholders' equity of GM.

---

[17]As described above, the functional currency was determined by objective standards rather than a choice. This example assumes a choice of functional currencies for illustrative purposes.

[18]For completeness, it should be noted that there would be an income statement impact resulting from any GMS foreign currency denominated non-monetary assets such as inventory and fixed assets if the historical exchange rate at which these assets were carried on the books needed to be adjusted retrospectively.

(Continued)

UNDERSTANDING THE CHOICE OF A SUBSIDIARY'S FUNCTIONAL CURRENCY

In the case where the dollar is chosen as the functional currency, the euro exposure is considered the foreign currency. The illustrative 10% depreciation of the euro against the U.S. dollar reduces the value of GMS's euro holdings: the €50 that used to be worth $50 are now only worth $45. This $5 loss is the economic impact on GM Worldwide (see Panel A in Exhibit 8 for an illustration). At the subsidiary level, that $5 loss is similarly recorded as a decrease in value of the €50 that are held in the euro-denominated account. Both the subsidiary and GM as a consolidated entity report on their income statements a foreign exchange loss of $5. This reduction in net income flows through to the balance sheet reducing equity (retained earnings) by $5.

In the next case, where the euro is the functional currency, GMS reports a $100 foreign exchange exposure. When the euro depreciates, the value of GMS's foreign exchange exposure ($100) changes. GMS's foreign currency-denominated asset (the $100 checking account balance) must be remeasured into the functional currency and the gain of €11.1 (or $10.0) is credited to the income statement. Upon consolidation, GMS's entire assets and liabilities of €161.1, including the $100 checking account after remeasurement into euros, are translated into U.S. dollars. (See Panel B in Exhibit 8 for an illustration.)

6

Foreign Exchange Hedging Strategies at General Motors: Competitive Exposures

In September of 2001, Eric Feldstein, Treasurer and Vice President, Finance for General Motors, Corp. turned his attention to a long-standing strategic concern: the economic consequences of fluctuations in the Japanese yen. The yen figured heavily in the cost structures of some of GM's competitors, and Feldstein had to anticipate how exchange rate movements might impact those competitors and GM itself.

Feldstein and his treasury team were responsible for managing the risks associated with foreign currency transactions and movements.[1] For the most part, currency risks arising from GM's worldwide operations were managed in accordance with the company's formal hedging policy. While GM's substantial exposure to the yen did not arise from specific foreign exchange transactions, it nonetheless presented real risks to the company. Feldstein had to understand the magnitude of the risks arising from GM's yen exposure, and determine how best to manage those risks.

Professor Mihir A. Desai and Research Associate Mark F. Veblen prepared the original version of this case, "Foreign Exchange Hedging Strategies at General Motors," HBS Case No. 204-024. This version was prepared by Professor Mihir A. Desai and Research Associate Mark F. Veblen. HBS cases are developed solely as the basis for class discussion. Certain figures and details have been disguised and do not reflect the actual operations of General Motors Corp. Cases are not intended to serve as endorsements, sources of primary data, or illustrations of effective or ineffective management.

[1]GM's Treasury operations and its management of currency risks arising from its global operations are described in detail in Chapter 5.

EXHIBIT 1

GM CONSOLIDATED INCOME STATEMENT

December 31, ($ millions)	2000	1999	1998
Total net sales and revenues	184,632	176,558	155,445
Cost of sales and other expenses	145,664	140,708	127,957
Selling, general, and administrative	22,252	19,053	15,915
Interest expense	9,552	7,750	6,629
Earnings before taxes and minority interests	**7,164**	**9,047**	**4,944**
Income tax expense	2,393	3,118	1,636
Equity income (loss) and minority interests	(319)	(353)	(259)
Income from discontinued operations	—	426	(93)
Net income	**4,452**	**6,002**	**2,956**
Dividends on preference stocks	(110)	(80)	(63)
Earnings attributable to common stocks	**4,342**	**5,922**	**2,893**

Source: General Motors, December 31, 2000 10-K (Detroit: General Motors, 2001).

OVERVIEW OF GENERAL MOTORS AND ITS CORPORATE HEDGING POLICY

General Motors[2]

General Motors was the world's largest automaker and, since 1931, the world's sales leader. In 2001, GM had unit sales of 8.5 million vehicles and a 15.1% worldwide market share. Founded in 1908, GM had manufacturing operations in more than 30 countries, and its vehicles were sold in approximately 200 countries. In 2000, it generated earnings of $4.4 billion on sales of $184.6 billion (see Exhibit 1 for GM's consolidated income statement). North America still represented the majority of sales to end customers and the largest concentration of net property, plant, and equipment (see Exhibit 2 and Exhibit 3), but the importance of GM's international operations was growing as a percent of the overall business.

GM's Corporate Hedging Policy

GM's global operations gave rise to significant currency risks, and the Treasurer's Office managed those risks. The key objectives of GM's foreign exchange risk management policy were to reduce cash flow and earnings volatility; minimize the management time and costs dedicated to FX management; and align FX management in a manner consistent with how GM operated its automotive business. These objectives were supported by the company's formal hedging policy. General Motors hedged cash flows (transaction exposures) only and ignored balance sheet exposures (translation exposures). The company followed a passive hedging strategy that limited management time spent on FX management, a consequence of an internal study that determined that investment of resources in active FX management had not resulted in significant outperformance of passive benchmarks.

[2]Statistics drawn from General Motors, 2001 Annual Report (Detroit: General Motors, 2002) and General Motors, December 31, 2001 10-K (Detroit: General Motors, 2002).

EXHIBIT 2

GM SEGMENT BREAKDOWN OF SALES TO END CUSTOMERS, 2000

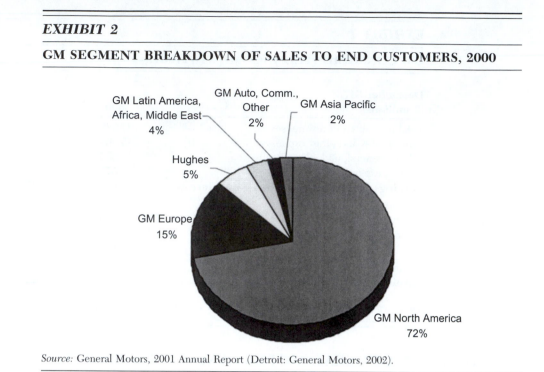

Source: General Motors, 2001 Annual Report (Detroit: General Motors, 2002).

EXHIBIT 3

GM GEOGRAPHIC BREAKDOWN OF NET PROPERTY, 2000

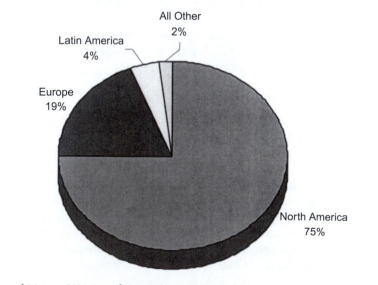

Source: General Motors, 2001 Annual Report (Detroit: General Motors, 2002).

The corporate hedging policy also required foreign exchange exposures to be managed on a regional (rather than world-wide) basis, so that financial management was consistent with the operational footprint of the underlying business.[3]

The passive hedging policy adopted by GM was generally to hedge 50% of all significant foreign exchange exposures arising from the cash flows associated with ongoing business, such as receivables and payables. Such commercial exposures were forecast on a regional basis, and a formula was used to determine the riskiness of the exposure and the amount to hedge on a rolling twelve-month basis. The corporate hedging policy also defined the instruments used for hedging activities. Forward contracts were used to hedge exposure arising within six months, and options used to hedge exposures arising within seven to twelve months. All deviations from these guidelines had to be approved by senior executives, and Feldstein scrutinized such requests closely.

Feldstein and his team also monitored foreign exchange exposures that were not covered by the company's hedging policy but could nonetheless have a direct or indirect impact on GM's business. Recently, Feldstein had paid increasing attention to the strength of the dollar against the Japanese yen and the question of how to manage GM's very substantial yen exposure. Typically, such "competitive" exposures were discussed heuristically but the absence of analytical approaches to quantify these exposures limited the ability to implement specific hedges.

UNDERSTANDING COMPETITIVE EXPOSURES

Source of Competitive Exposure

GM's exposure to the Japanese yen was not created by GM's inflows or outflows or how it chose to run its business. Rather, it was a result of competing against companies with different home currencies. The major Japanese automakers had large portions of their cost structure denominated in yen. As a result, any depreciation in the yen lowered their relative cost structure as compared to the U.S. and European auto manufacturers. If some of GM's competitors achieved significantly reduced costs through currency depreciations, this meant that the performance of GM's business faced currency risk: lower costs for Japanese firms would lead to lower required prices to achieve the normal profitability levels, thus eroding GM's market share—and market value.

The dollar/yen exchange rate had fluctuated widely over the past two decades and now the yen was depreciating (see Exhibit 4). Japanese automakers derived 56% and 43% of their revenues from the U.S. market in 1999 and 2000, respectively. In the most recent year, they sold 4.1 million units in the United States. Equity analysts had estimated that the yen appreciation from 117 to 107 during the first half of 2000 had reduced Japanese automakers' combined global operating profits by $4 billion. Feldstein reversed that statistic in his mind: for every 1 yen depreciation against the dollar, Japanese competitors' collective operating profit grew by more than $400 million. Rough estimates from

---

[3]Transaction exposures are the gains and losses that arise when transactions are settled in some currency other than a company's reporting currency. These exposures stem from buying and selling activities as well as financing decisions such as borrowing. Translation exposures are the gains and losses that arise when the assets and liabilities of a multinational's foreign subsidiary are translated back into the multinational's reporting currency for the purposes of preparing consolidated financial statements. For further information on GM's hedging policies see Chapter 5.

EXHIBIT 4

HISTORICAL JAPANESE YEN/U.S. DOLLAR EXCHANGE RATE (YEN PER DOLLAR)

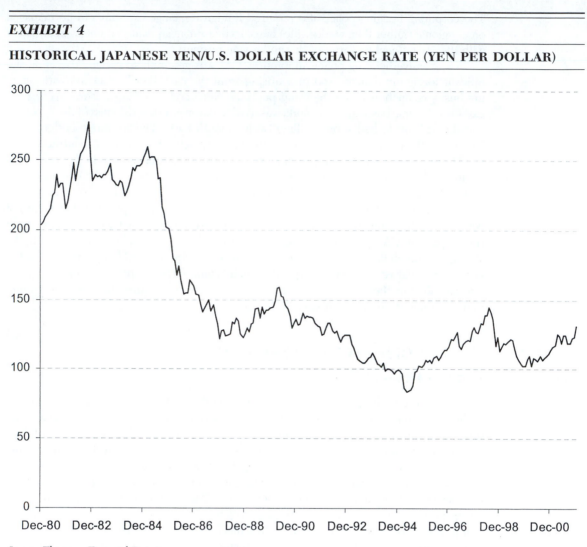

Source: Thomson Financial Datastream.

research reports suggested that the Japanese firms were unprofitable when the yen was stronger than 110 to the dollar and profitable at 120 or more yen to the dollar.

Measuring Competitive Exposures

Feldstein thought of this exposure as a competitive one rather than a financial one. There was no projected receivable or payable and no capital investment or loan to be repaid, yet there was still a bottom-line impact that stemmed from fluctuations in exchange rates. Because of the lack of an explicit transaction, Feldstein realized he was outside the usual territory of GM's hedging policy. Any action with respect to the yen based on this perceived competitive exposure would be setting a new precedent—something Feldstein felt he had to consider very carefully. At the very least, he needed an airtight story justifying the magnitude of the exposure and how it could be effectively hedged.

Feldstein felt that a compelling case could be made for the following chain of events. (1) A depreciation in the yen led to (2) additional gross margin for Japanese automakers, who (3) passed along some of this benefit to consumers in the form of lower prices, and (4) as a result of lower prices the Japanese automakers gained market share in the U.S., which (5) ate into unit sales at GM, which (6) lowered GM's profits, which (7) reduced GM's market value. The key was numerically estimating these variables and effects.

Of course, he would also need to place his estimated competitive exposure in the context of GM's overall yen exposure. This included a commercial exposure based on forecasted receivables and payables of $900 million; an investment exposure resulting from equity stakes in several Japanese companies (see Exhibit 5); and a financing exposure through a yen-denominated loan. GM had recently completed a yen bond issue, one of the objectives of which had been to partially offset the yen competitive exposure. Approximately $500 million worth of bonds were outstanding.

Feldstein realized that estimating the magnitude of the competitive exposure depended on a number of assumptions and involved a fair amount of guesswork. In any event, he could calculate sensitivities for each input variable later. After consultations with the business development team, he figured that the average Japanese car had between 20% and 40% Japanese content. This included parts sourced from suppliers in Japan as well as labor and plant expense incurred in Japan. A yen depreciation, therefore, had the potential to reduce cost of goods sold substantially. Hoping for insights into what portion of cost savings might ultimately be passed on to end buyers, Feldstein conferred with colleagues of his in GM's sales and marketing organizations. The feedback he received suggested that a reasonable estimate of what the Japanese automakers might give away in terms of added incentives or lower sticker prices would be between 15% and 45% of the cost savings. In 2000, Japanese automakers had given away relatively little in incentives in comparison to the rest of the industry (see Exhibit 6). GM, on the other hand, had given away more than the industry average—and almost one third of per vehicle profits.

The two most difficult factors to estimate were the consumer sales elasticity and the cross elasticity to GM sales. Feldstein consulted with one of the sales managers for dealer networks and was told that a 5% price increase could be expected to lower unit sales by around 10%. In an effort to isolate the impact on GM, Feldstein assumed that any market share losses to Japanese automakers would be shared equally among and entirely by the Big Three in Detroit.

EXHIBIT 5

GENERAL MOTORS INVESTMENTS IN JAPANESE AUTOMAKERS

Affiliate	Affiliate Exposure Long/(Short) ($ billions)	GM Ownership Stake
Fuji	(1.50)	20%
Isuzu	(1.02)	49%
Suzuki	(0.09)	20%

Figures have been disguised and do not reflect the actual operations of General Motors Corp.

Note: Exposures are net yen exposures (measured in dollars) and are presented for each affiliate entity. For example, Fuji's yen-denominated liabilities exceed its yen-denominated assets by $1.5 billion. GM's exposure is limited by the relevant ownership share in the affiliate.

Source: General Motors

EXHIBIT 6

2000 AVERAGE INCENTIVE PER UNIT IN THE UNITED STATES

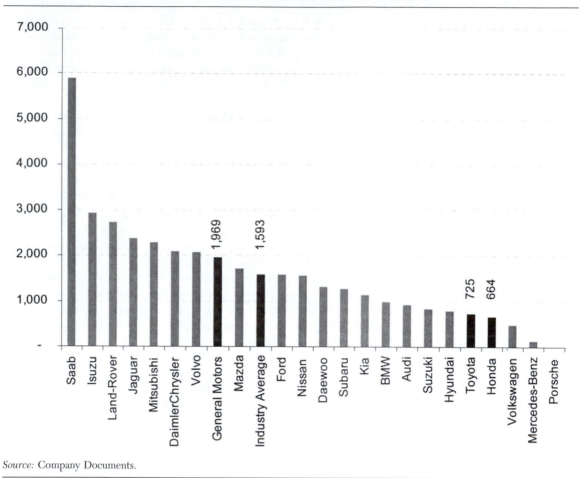

Source: Company Documents.

Feldstein figured that a rough calculation around a 20% yen devaluation would capture an upper bound of the likely exposure. The consequent annual impact on GM's income statement could then be valued as a perpetuity at a 20% discount rate—clearly a simplification, but if he needed more detailed figures he could ask his team to delve deeper into the numbers.

CONCLUSION

Feldstein had a great deal of thinking to do. While many auto executives complained about the value of the yen, Feldstein wanted to move past the standard rhetoric on exchange rates and quantify GM's yen exposure. Such an analysis, he concluded, had to underpin any recommendations or decisions on managing GM's risk, especially since the corporate hedging policy included no guidelines on managing such competitive exposures.

PART 2

MULTINATIONAL FINANCE

Levels of foreign direct investment (FDI) have mushroomed over the last decade. These trends reflect a true integration of operations across borders. FDI is no longer simply foreign sales offices or outsourced production facilities. Instead, tightly integrated production processes have made the distinction between home-country and foreign operations obsolete. These changes in the organization of multinational firms raise new issues for financial managers.

Specifically, managers must consider the most effective way to allocate capital across subsidiaries when capital controls, legal rules, and tax regimes influence those decisions. These financial factors must be balanced against the managerial perspective where such decisions can change managerial incentives. For example, whereas dividend repatriation policies and capital structure decisions can be tailored to minimize taxes, managers who run subsidiary operations may reject those decisions as distorting their financial performance. In addition, some countries restrict the ability to make payments in foreign currency, limiting a parent company's ability to extract either dividends from equity investments or interest payments on capital invested through intercompany borrowing. Such complexities also change the manner in which investment project evaluation takes place. The cases in Multinational Finance help managers appreciate the kinds of financing and investment decisions that have to be made once a firm operates beyond its borders.

FINANCING DECISIONS WITHIN THE FIRM

Managers have to make fundamental financial decisions before moving into a foreign market. Will the foreign operations be a branch office, a wholly owned subsidiary, or a joint venture with a local partner? Will the foreign operations be financed entirely with equity or with a mix of debt and equity? If debt is involved, will the debt be provided by the parent company or will the foreign operation be required to borrow on its own? If the foreign operation does its own borrowing, will the parent provide its credit rating through a guarantee of the debt? Going forward, will the capitalization structure change over time? For example, will the foreign operation be provided with some initial debt that will be paid down as the operation develops the capacity to support its own debt? This is only the first layer of questions. More nuanced analyses may also have to consider whether local markets permit financing secured by particular assets or whether local laws impose thin-capitalization rules that require a certain predetermined level of equity capital. In addition to these issues, managers also have to consider local business custom. In some countries, custom may effectively require a local partner and therefore raise the issues inherent in joint venture structures, complicated by the cross-border context.

The first case in Module 2.1 addresses many of these issues. The Refinancing of Shanghai General Motors case considers how a maturing subsidiary should refinance itself with particular attention to the currency characteristics of its debt, the switch from project finance to multinational finance, the conflicts between parent and subsidiary concerns, and the role of legal rules in constraining financial choices.

International tax rules are particularly vexing to managers operating in a cross-border setting. Although many firms capitalize aggressively on differences in tax rules, other firms find themselves disadvantaged by home-country tax rules. With increasingly integrated markets, tax differences—and the reactions of managers to them—can have a large impact on the competitive positioning of firms. The second case in Module 2.1, Corporate Inversions: Stanley Works and the Lure of Tax Havens, explores one response to the U.S. tax regime—expatriation—as a way of exploring how firms are impacted by tax rules. The case examines the costs and benefits of a strategic reincorporation to avoid the U.S. worldwide income tax system. It not only offers a primer on the incentives and complications of international taxation, but it also emphasizes the potential changes in shareholder value resulting from corporate expatriation.

The last case, The Continuing Transformation of Asahi Glass: Implementing EVA, addresses performance measurement and budgeting challenges in the context of managing a web of foreign operations. Analytically, it explores in depth the implementation of an economic value added model in an international setting. In the process, it sheds light on the differences in corporate governance practices across borders and how these affect managers of multinational concerns. It grapples with a tough issue: how can senior management successfully get subsidiaries across the globe to adopt a unified decision-making methodology?

OVERVIEW OF THE CASES

The Refinancing of Shanghai General Motors

Shanghai General Motors (SGM) was founded in 1997 as a 50/50 joint venture between General Motors and Shanghai Automotive Industry Corporation (SAIC), a local firm owned by the Shanghai Municipal Government. The partners contributed equal amounts of equity, and a consortium of banks provided debt financing for the new enterprise. SGM built a profitable automotive plant in 1999 that allowed SGM to capture a 5% share of the Chinese market in less than two years. SGM planned to add a smaller, more affordable family car in 2001 to its initial luxury sedan and minivan models.

SGM's original capitalization occurred in the aftermath of the Asian financial crisis when it had been challenging to convince banks to invest in a new Chinese enterprise. By late 2000, however, SGM had a track record of profitable operations, and SGM faced new strategic issues with China's forthcoming entry into the WTO. The CFO of SGM, Mark Newman, determined that it might be an opportune time to refinance SGM's long-term debt and its revolving credit facility. In particular, Newman wanted to increase the proportion of Chinese renminbi-denominated debt and to secure more favorable terms from SGM's lenders. In developing a proposal for refinancing SGM, Newman had to consider several issues: how China's entry into the WTO in 2001 would affect SGM's operations and profitability; how to construct a new financial strategy that would be acceptable to the host government and beneficial to SGM; and whether the proposed refinancing would be equally attractive to SGM's American and Chinese parent companies.

In reflecting on General Motors' choice about the initial capitalization of SGM, readers should consider how multinational firms should think about financial policy for their subsidiaries. More specifically, readers can consider:

- Why might GM have chosen to enter China through a joint venture? What conflicts might arise with the JV partner, and were sufficient actions taken to mitigate these conflicts?
- Why would GM want its Shanghai subsidiary to borrow funds directly when GM might be able to get more attractive terms?
- As Newman, how would you prioritize your goals in changing the financing?
- Why did the banks demand proportional borrowing and repayment? How did this make subsequent changes to the debt structure more difficult?
- If you were designing GM's worldwide policy on financing subsidiaries, what goals would you prioritize? What objections from country managers might you anticipate?

Corporate Inversions: Stanley Works and the Lure of Tax Havens

In February 2002, Stanley Works, the leading U.S. toolmaker, announced that it was moving its legal domicile to Bermuda. The company cited its increasingly global business and its need to remain competitive as reasons for the move. In particular, Stanley claimed that its effective worldwide tax rate would drop as much as 9% if it relocated to Bermuda. The stock market reacted favorably to Stanley's announcement, and its stock price rose significantly. A few months later, when Stanley apparently backed down from its plan, its stock price plunged. One of Stanley's U.S. competitors, American Handyworks, Inc., attempts to understand how the proposed change in Stanley's legal domicile could have such an impact on its market capitalization. An American Handyworks tax planner has to quantify the gains Stanley would realize if it relocated overseas, and determine if his own firm should pursue such a strategy.

This case provides an introduction to the labyrinthine rules of how the United States taxes multinational firms and describes the incentives this tax regime creates. These ideas are presented in the context of ferreting out what tax management strategies are worth to a company—measured by its stock price. While reading through the case, consider:

- What principles underlie the international tax regime employed by the United States? What is the difference between taxing one's citizens and one's residents? What are the consequences of this decision? In particular, how does this decision affect behavior?

- Stanley Works experienced extreme fluctuations in its market value when it made announcements related to its move to Bermuda. What were the sources of this change in market value? Please detail alternative sources of the value that might be reflected in the stock price change.

- What are the costs of an inversion transaction? Who pays them? Who makes the decision? Does this matter?

- Why is Stanley Works moving to Bermuda? Is this what it said when it announced the deal?

- Is what Stanley is doing problematic? Morally? Economically? If so, how do you solve the problem?

The Continuing Transformation of Asahi Glass: Implementing EVA

The final case in Module 2.1 explores the use of an EVA (economic value added) methodology at Asahi Glass. EVA is among the changes initiated by the CEO, Shinya Ishizur, aimed at transforming Asahi Glass from a traditional Japanese company to a global firm. Other changes included a corporate reorganization into worldwide business groups, the appointment of non-Japanese managers to key positions, and corporate governance reforms. The EVA methodology was introduced to improve resource allocation across Asahi's numerous businesses around the world and to evaluate the managerial performance of top executives. The case examines how the company implemented EVA and in particular how it calculated the weighted average cost of capital (WACC) for its different businesses in different countries. Is Asahi Glass gaining benefits from the EVA methodology, and does it contribute to the transformation of Asahi Glass into a truly international firm? Particular questions worth thinking about in analyzing the case include:

- How did main-bank relationships impact Japanese corporate governance?

- What do you view as the primary obstacles facing Ishizu as he continues to try to transform Asahi Glass?

- What is the premise of EVA systems? How do they relate to traditional discounted cash flow notions of net present value? Do EVA systems provide the right incentives?

- How would you evaluate the EVA system implemented by Asahi? Would you recommend any changes?

- Would you buy stock in Asahi?

ADDITIONAL READING

DESAI, MIHIR A. 2003. "The Divergence Between Book and Tax Income." *Tax Policy and the Economy*, 17: 169–206.

DESAI, MIHIR A., ALEXANDER DYCK, and LUIGI ZINGALES. 2004. "Theft and Taxes." NBER Working Paper no. 10124.

DESAI, MIHIR A., and JAMES R. HINES, JR. 2002, September. "Expectations and Expatriations: Tracing the Causes and Consequences of Corporate Inversions." *National Tax Journal,* 55(3): 409–440.

DESAI, MIHIR A., C. FRITZ FOLEY, and JAMES R. HINES, JR. 2004, August. "The Costs of Shared Ownership: Evidence from International Joint Ventures." *Journal of Financial Economics*, 73(2): 323–374.

DESAI, MIHIR A., C. FRITZ FOLEY, and JAMES R. HINES, JR. 2004. Dividend Policy Inside the Multinational Firm. Harvard University Working Paper.

DESAI, MIHIR A., C. FRITZ FOLEY, and JAMES R. HINES, JR. 2004, December. "A Multinational Perspective on Capital Structure Choice and Internal Capital Markets." *Journal of Finance,* 59(6): 2451–2458.

DESAI, MIHIR A., C. FRITZ FOLEY, and JAMES R. HINES, JR. 2001. Repatriation Taxes and Dividend Distortions. *National Tax Journal,* 54: 829–851.

ZIMMERMAN, JERROLD. 1997. "EVA and Divisional Performance Measurement." *Journal of Applied Corporate Finance*, 98–109.

The Refinancing of Shanghai General Motors

In late 2000, Mark Newman, Chief Financial Officer of Shanghai General Motors, glanced out his window as unpainted car bodies shuttled continuously through the glass skybridge between factory buildings. Obtaining initial funding for the operations in Shanghai several years earlier had been a protracted process requiring efforts by a number of key individuals at General Motors and its partner Shanghai Automotive Industry Corporation (SAIC) to get the deal done. While the efforts paid off, the resulting funding terms had proven to be restrictive and were priced above what Newman believed could now be obtained in the Chinese market. Newman wanted his finance team to help him prepare a request to the board of directors to refinance the entire borrowing facility. As he thought about the presentation to his board, Newman remembered some of the lessons from his days running investor relations for General Motors in New York. He wanted to weave a story to justify refinancing the old loan facility as well as present compelling figures to make his case.

Newman had arrived at Shanghai General Motors in November 1999, just six months after the start of operations and about two years after construction of the facility—with an approved capital outlay of $1.52 billion—had begun. Sales in 1999 had been brisk but growth in sales of the "upper medium" sedan and wagon models were well behind 2000 budget levels, resulting in a buildup in the company's inventories. Fortunately, pricing in the marketplace had been stronger than predicted and the Chinese renminbi (RMB) exchange rate had held stable at 8.2 RMB per dollar.[1] The net result was better than anticipated profits—in fact, operations had always been profitable. Additionally, funding requirements had been lower than anticipated, leaving a large portion of the current credit facility undrawn. This performance, however,

---

Professor Mihir A. Desai and Research Associate Mark F. Veblen prepared this case. HBS cases are developed solely as the basis for class discussion. Cases are not intended to serve as endorsements, sources of primary data, or illustrations of effective or ineffective management.

[1]The Chinese government maintained a policy of holding the RMB's value at approximately 8.2 per dollar. The currency was, however, not formally pegged to the dollar, and therefore stability of its exchange rate was not assured. Nor was the RMB a freely convertible currency; the Chinese government controlled all exchange transactions of RMB against foreign currencies.

concealed the strict terms and relatively high financing costs to which Shanghai General Motors had agreed when it first raised debt just after the Asian financial crisis. Armed with a board approval granted in early 2000 to explore funding options, Newman now needed to pitch the board on a $700 million refinancing transaction that would significantly change SGM's credit facilities. He needed to frame his presentation in such a way so as to gain the consent of both joint venture partners—General Motors, the architect of the original financing, and Shanghai Automotive Industry Corporation, which had strong relationships with several state-owned banks in China.

OVERVIEW OF THE JOINT VENTURE PARTNERS

General Motors[2]

General Motors was the world's largest automaker, selling 8.6 million vehicles in 2000—15% worldwide market share—and had been the world's sales leader since 1931. Founded in 1908, GM had manufacturing operations in more than 30 countries, and its vehicles were sold in approximately 200 countries. In 2000, it generated earnings of $4.3 billion on sales of $184.6 billion. The labor costs for its 389,000 employees in that year amounted to $20.9 billion, only $9.4 billion of which was for U.S.-based personnel. In addition to vehicles, other major product lines included (i) financial services for automotive, mortgage, and business financing, and insurance services through General Motors Acceptance Corporation (GMAC), (ii) satellite television and commercial satellite services through Hughes Electronics, and (iii) locomotives and heavy-duty transmissions through GM Locomotive Group and Allison Transmission Division. GM traded on the New York Stock Exchange and was a component of the Dow Jones Industrial Average.

Since the early 1990s GM had pursued growth in Asia as one of its key corporate objectives. Accordingly, it viewed China as a vital market through which GM could maintain its global leadership position by gaining market share in Asia. The plan to form the Shanghai GM partnership had originally been conceived in 1994, and the GM board later approved it as a major strategic initiative even though it was viewed as potentially risky. GM's project coincided with the desire of the Chinese government to bring in a U.S. automaker that would import new product and process technologies. Specifically, GM was awarded a permit in 1997 to bring a medium luxury car to market in cooperation with a joint venture partner, Shanghai Automotive Industry Corporation. The SGM project represented a major step toward growing GM's Asian presence and a strengthening of its relationship with China—one that dated back to 1922. By 2000, GM operated four joint ventures and two wholly owned subsidiaries in China and had participated in more than $2 billion of investment projects that employed some 3,500 workers throughout the country.

GM's market share in Asia, however, was relatively modest compared to its shares in other regions. By 2000, General Motors commanded the #1 spot in North and South America with approximate market shares of 28% and 16%, respectively. In Western Europe, GM's Opel Mark held nearly 10% of the market, and Fiat, in which GM had recently acquired a 20% stake, held approximately 10%, for a combined Western Europe market share of about 20%.[3] In Asia, however, GM had only about a 4% share through a fragmented network of holdings that included Holden in Australia, a 49% stake in Isuzu, and a 20% ownership in both Suzuki and Fuji Heavy Industries (Subaru) in Japan.

[2]Statistics drawn from GM annual report and SEC Form 10-K.

[3]General Motors owned 20% of Fiat, and Fiat held an option to put the remaining 80% to GM.

GM had also entered into discussions regarding the acquisition of the automotive assets of Daewoo Motor Corporation in South Korea. China was a relatively bright spot, where its operations had achieved 5% market share in a rapidly growing market (see Exhibit 1).

GM Internal Policy for Funding Subsidiaries

Since its forays into emerging markets (such as Brazil) in the 1920s, GM had developed a wealth of experience in funding overseas subsidiaries and more recently in financing joint venture companies. While GM evaluated funding approaches for these ventures on a case-by-case basis, it was fairly consistent in applying certain key principles in each situation.

Once an overseas investment (e.g., the initial investment in SGM) had received the appropriate corporate approvals, the GM Treasurer's Office was primarily responsible for determining the appropriate capital structure for the entity in which the investment was being made. GM endeavored to limit its equity investment in new entities so as to contain its incremental financial exposure. At the same time, this goal had to be balanced against the increased financial risk to the funded entity, resulting in a recommended capital structure that considered its downside funding requirements. Borrowing levels were

---

EXHIBIT 1

CHINESE CAR MARKET SHARE, 2000

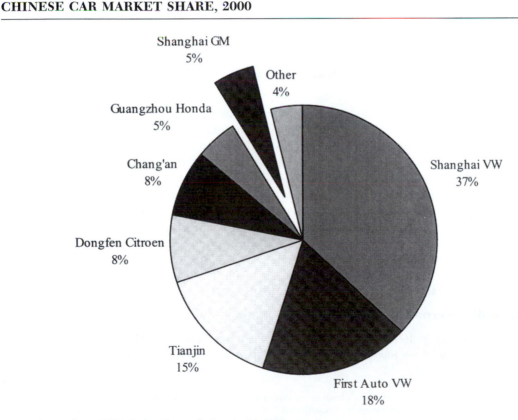

Source: Drawn from: CSFB Equity Research, January 14, 2002.

also reviewed against the local tax capacity of the invested entity in order to provide the most tax-efficient capital structure. Furthermore, new entities were encouraged to borrow debt in local currency as, more often than not, foreign entities were net importers of components, technology and engineering services and were already "short" on foreign currency exposure. In cases where overseas entities were GM-controlled, GM often used inter-company loans as temporary debt for foreign ventures but preferred to have entities obtain bank funding as part of their permanent capital structure where local funding sources were available. When debt was issued locally, GM relationship banks often took a leadership role in arranging credit facilities but GM welcomed the participation of "non-relationship" banks so as to keep credit capacity available with relationship banks for other global initiatives. Debt borrowed locally was issued on the basis of the local venture's credit profile with no parental guarantees. Once a venture was up and running, GM left sufficient cash in the entity to fund ongoing business requirements but endeavored to repatriate all excess cash to the parent where possible. In a joint venture investment, GM upheld these basic principles but had to reach agreement with the respective joint venture partner regarding key capital structure issues.

In the context of Newman's proposal to pursue a refinancing, he understood that GM and SAIC would not be providers of new capital. Given SGM's solid start-up performance, both shareholders believed that any additional funding could be obtained through debt and that even with significant future expansion, debt levels were unlikely to hit the peak levels forecasted when the SGM project was first approved. While neither shareholder would entertain further funding to SGM, Newman knew that GM would use its relationships with key overseas banks and SAIC would leverage its connections with key local banks to support SGM's efforts if the refinancing proposal was approved.

Shanghai Automotive Industry Corporation (SAIC)

SAIC was 100% owned by the Shanghai Municipal Government. In the 1950s it manufactured cars, motorcycles, and heavy trucks and tractors for final sale to customers, but in the 1980s it transitioned from this final manufacturing role to a component supplier and joint venture partner role. In 1984 SAIC joined forces with Volkswagen by taking a 25% stake in Shanghai VW, a brand that dominated the Chinese auto market for the next 15 years with its "Santana" model. (The Santana and Passat made throughout China still commanded a 55% market share.) Later SAIC also began forming joint ventures with other component suppliers such as Bosch, Delphi, Visteon, and others. SAIC was China's leading auto producer, while VW was China's leading brand.[4] On a consolidated basis in 2000, SAIC returned RMB 6 billion in profits on RMB 88 billion in sales.

OVERVIEW OF SHANGHAI GENERAL MOTORS

Formation and Governance

Founded in 1997, SGM was a 50/50 joint venture between GM and SAIC. Governance of the joint venture was split evenly between the parents. GM and SAIC each received

---

[4]SAIC was considered China's leading automaker if one calculated market shares based on output by ventures in which it was a partner (JVs with GM and VW). VW was China's leading brand similarly calculated: the combined output of VW's ventures (VW maintained joint ventures in China with both SAIC and FAW, an entity similar to SAIC) accounted for more cars than any other brand's network of ventures.

five board seats on the ten-member board and each appointed two executives on the four-person executive committee. The board met twice a year, and the executive committee met formally every week. Furthermore, each parent agreed to key terms in a joint venture agreement (summary in Exhibit 2) and also to provide certain "expertise assistance" (outlined in Exhibit 3). The joint venture's initial capitalization consisted of $700 million of equity injected by the owners and $821 million of debt through a syndicated loan facility (see Exhibit 4 and Exhibit 5 for capital structure and ownership details).

Products

SGM began operations in 1999 selling a medium luxury sedan based on the U.S.-based Buick Regal, but marketed under the SGM brand and Buick model name (see Exhibit 6 for an overview of models competing with the Buick sedan). In 2000, it added a mini-van model, the Buick GL8, based on the U.S.-based Pontiac Transport that shared a common powertrain with the Buick sedan. In 2001, SGM planned to introduce the Sail (based on an Opel Corsa design modified by GM Brazil), a small car designed to be an affordable family vehicle. The Buick sedan, priced at RMB 250,000–370,000, became the mainstay of the government limousine fleet and a prestigious car for well-to-do individuals. The Buick GL8, similarly priced at RMB 300,000–380,000, was initially designed as a functional premium car/van for families, but proved to be more successful among business buyers. At only one-third the cost (RMB 100,000), the Sail offered a strong value proposition. SGM had packed cutting-edge technology into a small car in a market dominated by the VW Santana, a model that had not changed significantly since its introduction in the mid-1980s.

Customs Duties and China's Entry into the World Trade Organization

Historically, the Chinese government had protected local markets and companies through high import duties. It also actively encouraged companies (especially foreign companies) to localize production of intermediate goods. In the case of automakers, manufacturers were required to attain local content of at least 40% and were rewarded for increasing localization ratios through preferential treatment with respect to duty rates, which could fall from 45% to as low as 25%–30% through achieving higher localization targets. SGM initially imported 60% of the components for its Buick model, but as that ratio fell to 40%, SGM was rewarded with lower duty rates on its imported components purchases. In comparison, Shanghai VW had achieved over 80% localization for the Santana model, and therefore enjoyed the most preferential treatment for customs duties. Import tariffs had created an opportunity for local suppliers (many whom were at least partially owned by SAIC) to demand pricing in excess of worldwide benchmarks. With WTO on the horizon, it was understood that pricing on both local and imported (provided primarily by GM) components would need to be reduced to meet the realities of a more open automotive market.

SGM's leadership viewed China's entry into the WTO, scheduled for late 2001 as a long-term positive for SGM, even though in the short term it could increase SGM's import costs due to loss of preferential duty rates. Opening trade and eliminating many of the frictions imposed by the Chinese government would clear the way for SGM and General Motors to optimize manufacturing and component sourcing on a global basis, without the redundant capital investment in China now needed to satisfy local regulations. For a capital-intensive industry like auto manufacturing, significant cost savings could be realized from local mass production of high-volume units and importing niche

EXHIBIT 2

JOINT VENTURE AGREEMENT SUMMARY TERM SHEET

Under the Joint Venture Agreement, SAIC and SAJSC are obligated to:

- Contribute US$350 million in equity;
- Assist SGM in the submission and application of all necessary approvals, permits, certificates and licenses required for manufacture, distribution and sale of the products;
- Assist with import and export licenses;
- Arrange for the transfer to SGM of the land use rights of the manufacturing facility;
- Assist SGM in contracting for or obtaining electricity;
- Assist the directors and foreign personnel of GMCI in obtaining all necessary visas, travel documents and work permits;
- Assist the smooth transfer of any employees from SAIC to SGM, and with the recruitment of any other Chinese personnel and management;
- Assist the SGM and GMCI in obtaining tax and custom reductions and/or exemptions;
- Generally assist the SGM in its relations with local government authorities and PRC companies;
- Assist SGM in obtaining adequate raw materials, local equipment, transport, and communication facilities;
- Assist SGM in obtaining RMB and foreign exchange loans from financial institutions in China.

GM and GMCI are obligated to:

- Contribute US$350 million in equity;
- Assist in the procurement of equipment and supplies from overseas;
- Assist SGM to recruit appropriate management and senior technical support;
- Enter into (1) a trademark and trade name license; (2) an import supply contract with SGM; (3) a services and secondment contract with SGM; and (4) a technology license contract with SGM.

SGM can be dissolved under the following events:

- SGM sustains significant losses for five (5) consecutive years after start of normal production and the parties are unable to agree on a method to improve the financial condition of the SGM;
- SGM is unable to continue operations for six months due to a force majeure event;
- Any of the "Additional Contracts" (e.g., implementation support, import supply, labor, land use, secondment, or trademark and trade name license) are not entered into within 3 months;
- The failure of any party or SGM to perform its obligations under the Joint Venture Agreement, the Articles of Association, or any of the Additional Contracts;
- Failure of any party to make a contribution to the registered capital of SGM in accordance with the articles of the Joint Venture Agreement which remains unresolved for more than three months;
- Expropriation or requisition of any material portion of the assets, property, or employees of SGM;
- Mutual agreement by the sponsors.

Source: Shanghai GM.

EXHIBIT 3

SGM PARTNER EXPERTISE ASSISTANCE (DISTRIBUTION/SALES)

Distribution Activities	Explanation	SAIC	GM
Direct Sales—Retail	Retail sales partners (possibly sales points)	X	X
Warranty Service	Aftersales network and technical expertise		X
Technical/Maintenance Service	Aftersales network and technical expertise		X
Technical Support	GM China Technical Assistance Center		X
Wholesale/Retail Systems	Software systems	X	X
Management Training	Facilities, expertise	X	X
Sales Training	Facilities, expertise		X
Technical Training	Facilities, expertise, GM China Tech. Service		X
Parts Warehousing	Land, facilities, organization	X	X
Part Sales—SGM Product	Network, expertise	X	X
Exports	Expertise, local networks	X	X
Warranty Administration	Systems, expertise	X	X

Source: Shanghai GM.

EXHIBIT 4

SGM CAPITAL STRUCTURE

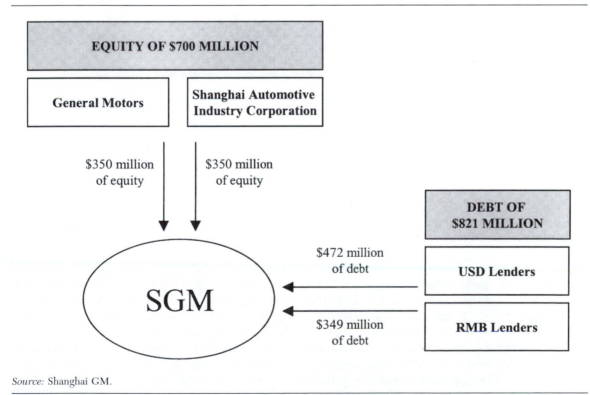

Source: Shanghai GM.

EXHIBIT 5

SGM SHAREHOLDING STRUCTURE

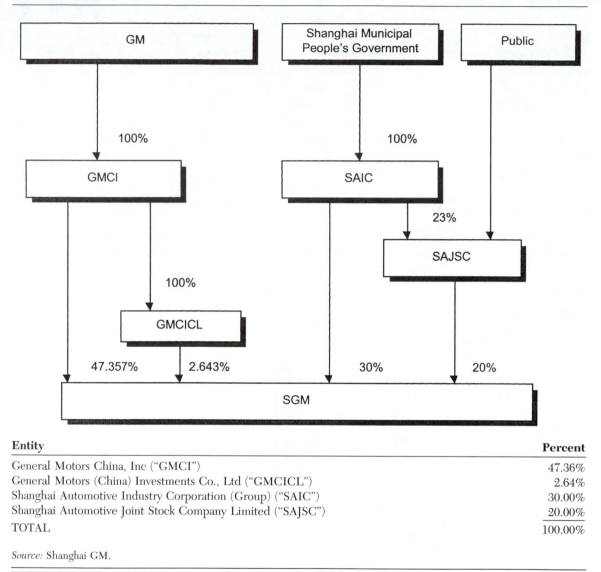

Entity	Percent
General Motors China, Inc ("GMCI")	47.36%
General Motors (China) Investments Co., Ltd ("GMCICL")	2.64%
Shanghai Automotive Industry Corporation (Group) ("SAIC")	30.00%
Shanghai Automotive Joint Stock Company Limited ("SAJSC")	20.00%
TOTAL	100.00%

Source: Shanghai GM.

(e.g., luxury sedans and SUVs) items from centralized facilities that could supply many markets. In the long run, WTO entry would enable SGM to fill out its product portfolio in China without building plants for every model it wanted to sell in that market.

In the short run, however, China's WTO entry meant that duty rates on components would fall from pre-WTO levels to world standard levels over a phase-in period. The preferential treatment that had been awarded to local automakers based on their localization ratios, however, would be eliminated immediately. The combination of these two effects resulted in a period of time when imposed duty rates would actually be higher than those realized by SGM before WTO. Rough internal estimates suggested that duty costs could rise by 5%.

EXHIBIT 6

POSITIONING OF MODELS VS. THE COMPETITION

Brand	Buick	Honda	Audi	Passat
Key Models and Their Date of Introduction	Jun 99—GL/GLX May/Jun 00—GS Aug 00—G	1H 99—Accord	Jan 00—A6	Mar 00—Passat
Positioning	Best-in-class value Business car	World class quality and service Practical car	Passion and Vision Government car	Business car or high class car
Perceived Strengths	Prestige presentable American heritage (safety, comfort)	Quality fit and finish Ease of maneuverability Fuel economy	Power symbol (official car) German technology Luxury	Modern looking Aftersales service network
Perceived Weakness	Fuel economy (however, the most fuel efficient V6 offered in PRC)	Advertising and communication Noisy	Entrenched official/ government image High price	Taxi cabs Mainstream brand but not premium
Price Range (RMB '000)	288–375	260–298	328–512	245–289
Unit Sales in 2000	30,542	32,233	15,888	26,152
Market Share in Sales[a]	4.8%	4.7%	2.8%	not available
2001 Target (unit sales)	68,000[b]	50,000	28,000	60,000

[a]Based on January–August 2000 data. Source: China National Automotive Industry Consulting & Development Co.
[b]Including family car.

Source: Shanghai GM.

Another more immediate effect was the forecasted increased competition from vehicle imports, particularly in the upper medium segment in which the Buick sedan belonged. Whereas the tariff imposed on imported vehicles had been 70% prior to WTO, that figure was forecast to be cut to just over 40% with WTO accession and drop to 25% by 2006. Slower sales in 2000 had been attributed to customers deferring automobile purchases in anticipation of significantly lower vehicle costs after WTO entry. To some degree, this effect might be mitigated by the quota system imposed on foreign car import permits, as buyers might worry that a shortage of imported cars just after China's WTO entry would prevent them from obtaining cars at all. In its forecasting, SGM was anticipating lowering its prices 5%–7% against the influx of competing models. On top of lower volume growth and price pressure, it was also assumed that the WTO could cause deterioration in SGM's sales mix toward lower-priced cars that faced less import competition.

Operating Performance

SGM was profitable in each year since inception. (See Exhibit 7 for summary financial results, both historical and projected; see Exhibit 8 for projected income statement; see Exhibit 9 for cash flow statement; and see Exhibit 10 for balance sheet.) Jennifer Li, a Manager in the Asia Pacific Regional Treasury Center working with Newman in evaluating the

EXHIBIT 7

SHANGHAI GENERAL MOTORS—ACTUAL AND PROJECTED FINANCIAL HIGHLIGHTS

RMB millions;

Years ending December 31,	1998A	1999A	2000A	2001	2002	2003	2004	2005	2006
INCOME STATEMENT									
Sales	33	5,966	8,847	12,426	17,911	20,565	24,593	26,984	27,278
Sales Growth	NA	NM	48.3%	40.5%	44.1%	14.8%	19.6%	9.7%	1.1%
EBITDA	NA	1,249	1,653	1,916	2,433	2,752	3,054	3,124	3,246
EBIT	NA	679	803	1,121	1,588	1,846	2,274	2,277	2,376
Net Interest Expense	NA	74	165	172	217	251	256	222	174
Depreciation and Amortization	NA	570	850	795	845	906	780	847	870
Net Income/(Loss)	(3)	605	638	753	819	1,318	1,674	1,782	1,939
Dividend	—	—	—	275	299	481	611	650	707
Dividend as % of Net Income	—	—	—	37%	36%	36%	37%	36%	37%
BALANCE SHEET									
Short-Term Debt	—	—	232	1,852	3,313	4,255	4,228	3,569	2,916
Long-Term Debt—US$ Facility	NA	NA	NA	1,152	747	446	275	93	—
Long-Term Debt—RMB Facilities	NA	NA	NA	554	343	198	119	40	—
Total Short-Term and Long-Term Debt	1,021	2,007	3,115	3,558	4,403	4,899	4,622	3,702	2,916
Total Liabilities	2,780	4,730	5,522	4,730	6,104	6,847	6,975	6,295	5,530
Shareholders' Equity	5,795	6,400	6,984	7,481	7,965	8,743	9,731	10,782	11,926
Tangible Net Worth (TNW)	5,577	6,159	6,754	7,026	7,510	8,288	9,276	10,327	11,471
Intangible Assets	218	241	230	455	455	455	455	455	455
CASH FLOW STATEMENT									
Cash Balance	1,893	1,607	858	429	449	465	478	485	490
Capital Expenditures	3,947	2,729	713	1,858	1,405	1,831	882	446	979
SELECTED FINANCIAL RATIOS									
Total Debt/Total Equity	18%	31%	45%	48%	55%	56%	47%	34%	24%
Total Debt/Tangible Net Worth	18%	33%	46%	51%	59%	59%	50%	36%	25%
EBIT/Net Interest Expense	NA	9.2x	4.9x	6.5x	7.3x	7.4x	8.9x	10.3x	13.6x
ASSUMPTIONS									
RMB/US$ (period end rate)	8.20	8.20	8.20	8.57	8.98	9.29	9.56	9.69	9.79
Interest % on RMB Facilities				5.27%	5.27%	5.27%	5.27%	5.27%	5.27%
Interest % on USD Facility				6.10%	6.10%	6.10%	6.10%	6.10%	6.10%

Source: Shanghai GM.

EXHIBIT 8

SHANGHAI GENERAL MOTORS—PROJECTED INCOME STATEMENT

Calendar Year (RMB millions)	2001	2002	2003	2004	2005	2006
Vehicle Sales	12,421	17,905	20,539	24,502	26,889	27,182
Net Component Sales	5	6	26	91	95	96
Total Revenue	**12,426**	**17,911**	**20,565**	**24,593**	**26,984**	**27,278**
Cost of Goods Sold	(9,080)	(13,402)	(15,531)	(18,820)	(21,053)	(21,045)
Gross Profit	**3,346**	**4,509**	**5,034**	**5,773**	**5,931**	**6,233**
Research and Development	(72)	(80)	(87)	(96)	(105)	(91)
Product Engineering	(348)	(469)	(570)	(881)	(937)	(1,100)
Royalties	(93)	(121)	(102)	(53)	—	—
Advertising/Commercial	(109)	(158)	(181)	(216)	(237)	(240)
Other Selling, General, and Administrative	(808)	(1,248)	(1,342)	(1,473)	(1,528)	(1,556)
EBITDA	**1,916**	**2,433**	**2,752**	**3,054**	**3,124**	**3,246**
Depreciation and Amortization	(795)	(845)	(906)	(780)	(847)	(870)
EBIT	**1,121**	**1,588**	**1,846**	**2,274**	**2,277**	**2,376**
Net Other Non-Operating Income/(Expense)	(48)	(11)	(9)	(7)	(7)	(7)
Interest Income/(Expense)	(172)	(217)	(251)	(256)	(222)	(174)
Exchange Gain/(Loss)	(87)	(475)	(161)	(119)	(35)	(4)
Pre-Tax Income	**814**	**885**	**1,425**	**1,892**	**2,013**	**2,191**
Enterprise Taxes	(61)	(66)	(107)	(218)	(231)	(252)
Net Income	**753**	**819**	**1,318**	**1,674**	**1,782**	**1,939**

Source: Shanghai GM.

EXHIBIT 9

SHANGHAI GENERAL MOTORS—PROJECTED STATEMENT OF CASH FLOWS

Calendar Year (RMB millions)	2001	2002	2003	2004	2005	2006
Net Income After Tax	753	819	1,318	1,674	1,782	1,939
Net Interest Expense	172	217	251	256	222	174
Foreign Exchange Gain/(Loss)	87	475	161	119	354	
Depreciation and Amortization	795	845	906	780	847	870
Capital Expenditures	(1,858)	(1,405)	(1,831)	(882)	(446)	(973)
Increase/(Decrease) in Managed WC	(251)	(747)	(333)	(596)	(526)	(250)
Cash Flow Before Financing	**(302)**	**204**	**472**	**1,351**	**1,914**	**1,764**
Net Interest Expense	(172)	(217)	(251)	(256)	(222)	(174)
Foreign Exchange Gain/(Loss)	(87)	(475)	(161)	(119)	(35)	(4)
Short-Term Debt Borrowing/(Retirement)	1,619	1,461	942	(27)	(658)	(653)
Long-Term Debt Borrowing/(Retirement)	(1,178)	(616)	(446)	(250)	(261)	(133)
Dividend Payment	(275)	(299)	(481)	(611)	(650)	(707)
Transfers to the Bonus and Welfare Fund	(34)	(37)	(59)	(75)	(80)	(87)
Increase/(Decrease) in Excess Cash	429	(21)	(16)	(13)	(8)	(6)
Total Financial Flow	**302**	**(204)**	**(472)**	**(1,351)**	**(1,914)**	**(1,764)**

Source: Shanghai GM.

EXHIBIT 10

SHANGHAI GENERAL MOTORS—PROJECTED BALANCE SHEET

Calendar Year (RMB millions)	2001	2002	2003	2004	2005	2006
Operating Cash	429	449	465	478	485	490
Accounts Receivable	511	736	844	1,007	1,105	1,117
Inventory	2,065	2,952	3,346	4,064	4,661	4,910
Other Current Assets	373	537	616	735	807	816
Total Current Assets	3,377	4,674	5,270	6,284	7,057	7,332
Net Fixed Assets	7,150	7,951	9,117	9,279	8,878	8,981
Net Capitalized Start-up Expenses	542	301	60	—	—	—
Deferred Assets	1,143	1,143	1,143	1,143	1,143	1,143
Total Assets	**12,211**	**14,069**	**15,590**	**16,706**	**17,078**	**17,456**
Accounts Payable	1,008	1,484	1,708	2,065	2,288	2,305
Short-Term Debt	1,852	3,313	4,255	4,228	3,569	2,916
Other Current Liabilities	159	214	240	288	305	310
Total Current Liabilities	3,019	5,011	6,203	6,581	6,163	5,530
RMB Term Debt	554	343	198	119	40	—
USD Term Debt (in RMB millions)	1,152	747	446	275	93	—
Other Liabilities	5	3	1	—	—	—
Total Liabilities	**4,730**	**6,104**	**6,847**	**6,975**	**6,295**	**5,530**
Paid in Capital	5,798	5,798	5,798	5,798	5,798	5,798
Reserve Fund	122	196	314	465	625	800
Joint Venture Expansion Fund	128	202	320	471	632	806
Bonus and Welfare Fund	88	125	184	260	340	427
Retained Earnings	1,346	1,645	2,126	2,738	3,388	4,095
Total Shareholders' Equity	**7,481**	**7,965**	**8,743**	**9,731**	**10,782**	**11,926**
Total Liabilities and Equity	**12,211**	**14,069**	**15,590**	**16,706**	**17,078**	**17,456**

Source: Shanghai GM.

refinancing transaction, shared the enthusiasm over SGM's first year. She commented, "1999 was a hot year: Shanghai GM cars were rumored to be selling on the black market for a $20,000 premium to retail prices and the company was in good operating condition." SGM sold 20,000 units between May and December 1999. With the GL8 minivan launched in the spring/summer of 2000, management budgeted 50,000 units for the year and saw significant upside potential to realize higher volumes. These estimates proved to be overly optimistic, and 2000 returned net income growth over 1999 but negative operating cash flow due to over-ordering of components in anticipation of higher unit sales. (See Exhibit 11 and Exhibit 12 for unit production figures, and see Exhibit 13 for market size estimates.)

Initially, SGM was able to sell cars to customers through its 80 retailers immediately for cash and therefore did not carry significant receivables. As the market became more competitive, however, retailers were no longer able to complete their sales to customers exclusively in cash. SGM accepted three- to six-month bank drafts from retailers and therefore saw a marked increase in notes receivable. In order to boost cash flow and to avoid bearing the costs of financing dealers' receivables, SGM devised a plan to

EXHIBIT 11

SHANGHAI GENERAL MOTORS—ACTUAL UNIT SALES BY MODEL

	Unit Sales June–December 1999	Unit Sales 2000
Buick Sedans	19,790	23,487
Buick GL-8 wagon	NA	7,055
Total	19,790	30,542

Source: Shanghai GM.

discount these notes receivable to banks. Retailers were allowed to pass notes receivable on to SGM and, if they exchanged the notes for cash within a short period of time, SGM would not assess any financing costs. However, if the retailers requested SGM to hold the notes for a longer period, SGM discounted the notes to banks and passed along the borrowing costs to the retailers. Allowing SGM to handle the receivables discounting was advantageous to retailers, who on their own could not have achieved as favorable rates. General Motors' finance arm, General Motors Acceptance Corporation (GMAC), was contemplating a joint venture with SAIC Finance Company (SAICFC). The finance company joint venture would ultimately assist retailers with wholesale financing and consumers with financing for their car purchases.

Assumptions and Near-term Forecasts

The projections presented in Exhibit 7 through Exhibit 10 reflected both China's entry into the World Trade Organization—resulting in more competition and thus lower

EXHIBIT 12

SHANGHAI GENERAL MOTORS—PROJECTED UNIT SALES BY MODEL AND COMPANY GROWTH

Ended December 31	2001	2002	2003	2004	2005	2006
Buick Sedans	25,500	34,500	40,000	56,000	66,000	68,075
Buick Wagons	12,500	15,000	14,500	14,200	14,200	14,836
Buick Sail	30,000	65000	87,500	100,000	100,000	102,089
Total Unit Sales	68,000	114,500	142,000	170,200	180,200	185,000
Total Unit Growth	123%	68%	24%	20%	6%	3%
Production Capacity	150,000	150,000	190,000	190,000	190,000	190,000
Manufacturing Headcount	2,335	3,127	3,260	4,015	4,171	4,169
Commercial Headcount	516	814	824	832	827	825
Total Headcount	2,891	3,941	4,084	4,847	4,998	4,994

Source: Shanghai GM.

EXHIBIT 13

PRC MOTOR VEHICLE OWNERSHIP 1990–1999

Year	Private	YoY Change	Commercial	YoY Change	Total	YoY Change
1990	816	11.6%	4,967	13.4%	5,784	7.8%
1991	960	17.7	5,101	2.7	6,601	4.8
1992	1,182	23.1	5,735	12.4	6,917	14.1
1993	1,558	31.8	6,618	15.4	8,176	18.2
1994	2,054	31.9	7,365	11.3	9,420	15.2
1995	2,500	21.7	7,900	7.3	10,400	10.4
1996	2,897	15.9	8,104	2.6	11,001	5.8
1997	3,584	23.7	8,607	6.2	12,191	10.8
1998	4,237	18.2	8,957	4.1	13,193	8.2
1999	5,041	19.0	9,811	9.5	14,852	12.6
1990–99 CAGR (%)		22.4		7.9		11.0

Source: China Statistical Yearbook 1999, and Shanghai GM.

volume growth—and SGM management's goal of introducing a new model every year, requiring significant capital expenditures. The projections did not, however, reflect the upside from the powertrain market. SGM saw significant export potential for manufactured engines both to other GM companies elsewhere in the world and to local plants that only assembled vehicles. Many GM affiliates had in the past imported engines from Japan, but SGM was quickly becoming recognized as a lower cost producer. The car market in India would probably follow a similar path as the Chinese market had in terms of consumer preferences for smaller vehicles with superior fuel economy, so India provided a likely outlet for SGM-made components and technology.

The pro forma operating figures constructed by Newman's team would assist in determining the business's capital needs. The new model introductions (SGM would soon need an intermediate car offering) and investments in refreshing the Buick, GL8, and Sail were projected to exhaust current manufacturing capacity in 2003/2004. Much of 2003 capex would go toward a $300 million investment to bring on an additional 150,000 or more units of assembly capacity (supplementing the 175,000 peak unit capacity[5] at the existing factory). The model also included substantial dividend payouts—up to nearly 40% of net income—to the joint venture parents.

SGM FINANCE DEPARTMENT

The SGM Finance Department had been established in a similar manner to the organizational structure of GM's Finance Staff. Reporting to the CFO were the four departmental heads of Treasury, Accounting, Comptrolling and Internal Controls. The

---

[5]Initially the factory was estimated to have a capacity of 100,000 based on two shifts, but because of productivity increases as the labor force became more skilled, the peak (three shift) capacity was expected to rise from 150,000 to 190,000 units over several years.

Accounting group handled accounts payable, accounts receivable, and general ledger. The Comptrolling group managed costing, operations analysis and pricing. The Internal Controls group oversaw the implementation and maintenance of appropriate control processes throughout the company and facilitated functional audits by both shareholders from time to time. Finally, the Treasury group was responsible for banking (essentially cash, debt, and foreign exchange management), tax planning and compliance, and insurance. Within the Treasury group there was also a small Business Development team that evaluated new investments and was now almost fully engaged with the GM Asia Pacific Regional Treasury Center in assessing the refinancing of SGM.

The Banking Team

Financing

The day-to-day money operations consisted mainly of cash management and integrating data with SGM's internal information systems. Cash management—managing collections and payments, and investing excess cash—was implemented through relationships with commercial banks that provided such services to large corporate clients. SGM was a cash-rich entity, but lived in a highly regulated financial environment with few short-term investment options. Returns on excess cash were as low as 0.72% at a time when SGM typically carried between RMB 300 million and RMB 900 million in cash balances. The banking team was devoting a great deal of time to working with banks on raising the return on excess cash. Other priorities included integrating electronic links to banks with SGM's SAP enterprise resource planning software and completing a SpeedCollect system that would eliminate the float in funds-transfer transactions with customers and suppliers.

Risk Management

As a result of its floating rate U.S. dollar-denominated borrowings, SGM faced both foreign-exchange exposures and interest-rate exposures. A second source of exchange-rate exposure came from the core operations of the business: 40% of the components used in SGM automobiles were sourced abroad and as a result had to be purchased in foreign currencies. The individuals tracking SGM's exposures paid particular attention to movements in U.S. interest rates, seeking to identify opportunities to lock in low fixed rates through swaps.

Hedging

Financial regulations in China regarding derivatives trading were very strict. The only allowed financial instruments for hedging currency risk were three- and six-month forward contracts on the RMB, and they could only be purchased through the Bank of China. Purchasing such contracts, however, was typically prohibitively expensive: forward rates were quite high despite the Chinese government's informal peg to the U.S. dollar.[6]

The Tax and Insurance Team

SGM's tax planning strategies hinged on optimizing its operations given the incentives created by local tax laws and duty levels. This included not only regulatory compliance,

---

[6]Hedging a future RMB 820 million cash inflow to dollars might only yield $90 million (a forward exchange rate of RMB 9 per dollar, or an 11% premium to the spot rate of 8.2), instead of the $100 million it would return if the informal peg were maintained. In the absence of price competition for selling such contracts, forward rates remained high.

but also seeking opportunities to structure operations in a tax-efficient manner and, where appropriate, disseminating knowledge within SGM so that line managers also acted in such a manner to achieve favorable tax treatment. A second priority was to look overseas and elsewhere within GM to ferret out tax strategies that might be applicable in the Chinese setting.

On the insurance side, SGM owned substantial fixed assets and land-use rights that needed to be insured. Second, as an automaker, it was subject to significant product liability for the automobiles that it sold. On both of these fronts, the treasury group interfaced with local and foreign insurers and negotiated for the lowest premiums and best coverage. Again, dissemination of knowledge within SGM was a crucial responsibility and generally took the form of providing training to line managers on risk management and general safety procedures.

THE INITIAL FINANCING

The first debt financing was raised in 1998. At the time, the credit markets were still in turmoil following the Asian financial crisis. Many foreign banks had pulled out of the region entirely, and very few were seeking to increase their credit exposure in China. Both foreign and local banks had significantly tightened their lending standards. General Motors' expansive worldwide operations necessitated deep relationships with a number of banks around the world. GM's willingness to leverage these relationships, combined with significant upfront bank fees, allowed the joint venture to amass the necessary funding.

The initial loan was closed on project finance terms with no guarantees from the joint venture's owners, with onerous restrictions and with pricing reflective of the difficult credit environment in Asia. A panel of 39 foreign and local banks provided the syndicated loan. The facility amount was $821 million USD equivalent: $472 million of long-term U.S. dollar-denominated debt provided by foreign and local banks, $267 million USD equivalent long-term RMB-denominated debt, and a $82 million USD equivalent local currency revolving working capital facility provided by local banks.[7] The dollar-denominated debt was priced at a floating rate of six-month Libor plus 105 basis points and the RMB piece carried a floating rate equal to the People's Bank of China (PBOC) rate (see Exhibit 14).[8] SAIC Finance Company also provided a backstop facility in local currency through a bilateral agreement with SGM to lend an additional RMB 1,490 million if necessary. Loan terms included:

- **Amount** The initial funding amount was based on a plan to introduce a sedan (the Buick) and a minivan (the GL8 minivan) built on a single platform. The required investment was projected to be $1.5 billion, of which $700 million came as equity from the joint venture's owners. The planned Jin Qiao factory in Shanghai was to be equipped with an engine and powertrain plant as well as an assembly plant that employed flexible manufacturing processes so that it could be expanded at a later date to produce other models as well. Because much of the initial expenditure would be made in USD, the Chinese government required that the initial financing contain a meaningful portion of dollar-denominated debt.

[7]The local currency facilities ($349 million USD equivalent) were available in RMB based on the prevailing USD exchange at the time of issuance. Thus, if the RMB depreciated, the nominal amount of available RMB from the local currency facility would increase. The RMB component was initially composed of RMB 2,216 million of long-term debt and RMB 680 million of revolving working capital.

[8]The PBOC rate was the primary corporate lending benchmark in China, analogous to the prime rate in the United States.

EXHIBIT 14

INTEREST RATES

Rate	As of December 31, 2000
People's Bank of China (PBOC)	5.85%
U.S. Dollar Libor	6.2%

Source: Thomson Financial Datastream and IMF, *International Financial Statistics.*

- **Amendments** The financing terms very specifically defined the project and approved particular capital expenditures. Any changes—such as new capital expenditures, new product launches, asset acquisitions or disposals—required supermajority approval of a bank committee on which all of the banks were represented.

- **Collateral** The facility was secured against SGM's physical assets, effectively pledging all existing and future assets of SGM as collateral.

- **Financial restrictions** Extensive covenants outlined various financial metrics that had to be maintained and also imposed a restriction on additional borrowing, limiting SGM to no more than $60 million of incremental, subordinated debt.

- **Reserve fund** During the repayment period, SGM was required to maintain a reserve fund where it deposited cash in anticipation of future payments, thus assuring the banks of SGM's ability to make the payments on the specified dates.

- **Equal use of USD and RMB** The loan agreement also stipulated that long-term borrowings would be made as evenly as practicable, drawing down equal amounts in USD and in RMB. Similarly, repayments of long-term debt would be made pro rata, with debt denominated in each currency being paid down at the same rate.[9]

Negotiating with the Bank Committee to Approve the Introduction of the Sail

During 1999, Newman's predecessor realized that SGM had secured more funding than was necessary to launch the two models identified in the scope of the original financing. Along with the rest of the management team, the CFO was anxious to make the necessary preparations for launching a third product—the Sail, a small car modeled after the Opel Corsa sold in Europe. It targeted the affordable family car segment, a level down from the premium Buick and GL8 minivan models. Newman's predecessor, with support from SAIC and GM, spent much of the first half of 1999 negotiating with the committee of lending banks to secure the necessary approvals to expand the scope of its initial project to include the Sail program. In the process, several of the banks responded to SGM's waiver request by seeking one-on-one informational briefings and making demands for additional fees.

[9]The USD and RMB credit facilities were provided by two different bank groups. SGM was a desirable credit for both groups of banks, and each group wanted to be assured that in providing the facility—which consumed a significant amount of the banks' internal credit exposure ceilings—all banks would be sure to benefit from the relationship with SGM. Similarly, if SGM's financial condition deteriorated materially, all of the banks wanted assurance that this risk would be spread across the combined bank group rather than concentrated on either the RMB or USD lenders.

The banks' formal waiver to include the Buick Sail investment in the original financing was received in July 1999 and provided availability for draws on the $821 million facility through September 2000[10] (the contemplated completion date for the Buick GL8 minivan investment). With the Sail launch planned for Q2 2001, the September 2000 date presented yet another challenge in funding this project. Without an extension of the availability date beyond September 2000, only the $82 million revolving facility would remain available out of the $821 million facility. Without approval to refinance the existing facility, Newman wanted to keep as much of the existing facility available for new draws while investments in the Sail program were still being funded. Armed with the knowledge that Chinese banks were flush with liquidity and anxious to increase exposure to good quality credits like SGM, Newman prevailed on the Chinese banks to extend availability through June 30, 2001 while capping the USD debt to foreign lenders at $160 million on the September 2000 date. Beyond the June 2001 date, Newman had two primary options for financing SGM: (1) draw down all remaining term loan availability on the RMB-denominated facility prior to June 2001 which could be further supplemented by accessing the $82 million RMB-denominated revolving facility and $60 million in subordinated debt; or (2) refinance the existing credit facility prior to June 30, 2001.

Impact of Capital Controls

The State Administration of Foreign Exchange (SAFE) tightly controlled the supply of all foreign currency in China. For trade purposes—and with an approved invoice—companies were able to purchase foreign currency from SAFE in order to import intermediate goods. This allowed SGM to source components from abroad with little administrative hassle. Capital controls, however, severely restricted companies' ability to execute financial transactions (particularly borrowing) in currencies other than the RMB. SGM had had to win SAFE approval for the dollar tranche of its initial financing. SAFE approved the exact amount as well as specific dates and amounts for the principal and interest payments over the subsequent five years. Any changes to this schedule would have to be approved by SAFE, and there were no assurances that approval would be granted. In effect, SAFE could prevent SGM from repaying the dollar portion of its outstanding debt by refusing to supply SGM with the dollars necessary to repay the loan. In SGM's case, because the loan agreement called for a proportional borrowing and repayment of long-term USD and RMB debt, SAFE could prevent SGM from making any net prepayment on its long-term USD debt.

Banks' Willingness to Lend

One of the primary concerns of credit officers in charge of commercial lending was finding clients who expected to draw down much of their facility. Typically, a lending operation was given a certain ceiling of funding commitments it could make. If it made commitments to customers far in excess of what those customers actually needed to borrow, then the lender effectively tied up part of his commitment quota even though those funds were not lent out earning interest.[11] From a bank's point of view, the ideal

[10]The September date applied to the US$472 million term loan and US$267 million RMB-denominated term loan. The US$82 million RMB-denominated revolving facility was available through 2006.

[11]This was commonly referred to as a bank tying up its balance sheet. For companies, this normally meant limiting their ability to borrow, but for banks it referred to limiting their ability to lend (and thus generate interest revenue).

customer was one that immediately wanted to draw down the full amount of the facility—this client was likely to be a much more profitable one. Of its initial credit facility, SGM had only drawn down approximately $400 million of the $821 million by the end of 2000, and of that amount $160 million was drawn down in U.S. dollars.

PRESENTING TO THE SGM BOARD

While many of Newman's presentations to the board had reported progress on increasing financial returns through improving volume utilization of a fixed asset base (reducing fixed cost-per-unit) or through lowering material costs through mandated cost reductions by suppliers (reducing variable unit costs), this presentation would be a pitch for the largest transaction since the formation of the joint venture. While Newman had previously reviewed the pros and cons of refinancing with the GM Regional Treasurer's Office in Singapore, he now needed a concise summary of why a refinancing would be strategically and financially advantageous and what terms would be critical to push for. Newman knew he would have to convince the very people who had pressured banks to help SGM with the original financing just three years ago into scrapping that arrangement. With the changing competitive situation—the impending entry into the WTO—Newman also realized that he had to bring the U.S. executives up to speed on local developments and convince the SAIC executives that the transaction was in the best interests of both parent companies.

Corporate Inversions: Stanley Works and the Lure of Tax Havens

Just after being promoted to head of tax planning at American HandyWorks, Inc., Roger Meyerson found himself buried in research on the practice of moving companies to tax havens. His company's largest competitor, Stanley Works, had announced on February 8, 2002, that it was moving the legal domicile of the company to Bermuda for strategic and tax reasons. HandyWork's Chief Financial Officer Jonathan Stern wanted Meyerson to stay on top of the issue and provide a detailed report on how Stanley planned to lower its effective tax rate by seven to nine percentage points as it had claimed it could in a press release. Stanley's market value had jumped $200 million dollars—a gain of over 5%—the day after they announced the deal; Stern wanted to know where these gains were coming from and whether HandyWorks could capitalize on the structure as well. As it had turned out, Stanley's announcement marked the beginning of a prolonged appreciation in Stanley's stock price that was also driven by several key alliances and positive results (see Exhibit 1 for stock price history and recent events). Three months later, on May 10, Stanley's shareholders had very narrowly approved the inversion transaction, but Stanley announced that it would need to hold a second vote because the first had shown "irregularities." Stanley lost $250 million of market value on May 10.

Meyerson reviewed these figures. First he wanted to understand what was driving Stanley to do this. Then he wanted to gauge the market's reaction to determine what opportunities this mechanism might offer HandyWorks—in particular, did HandyWorks have to follow suit in order to stay competitive? In order to do this, Meyerson knew that he had to understand the link between Stanley's motivations and the large swings in market value that the move to Bermuda had prompted.

Professor Mihir A. Desai of the Harvard Business School and Professor James R. Hines Jr. of the University of Michigan prepared this case with Research Associate Mark F. Veblen. American Handyworks and its executives are fictional. The material regarding Stanley Works has been drawn from published sources. HBS cases are developed solely as the basis for class discussion. Cases are not intended to serve as endorsements, sources of primary data, or illustrations of effective or ineffective management.

EXHIBIT 1

STANLEY WORKS ONE-YEAR ANNOTATED PRICE HISTORY

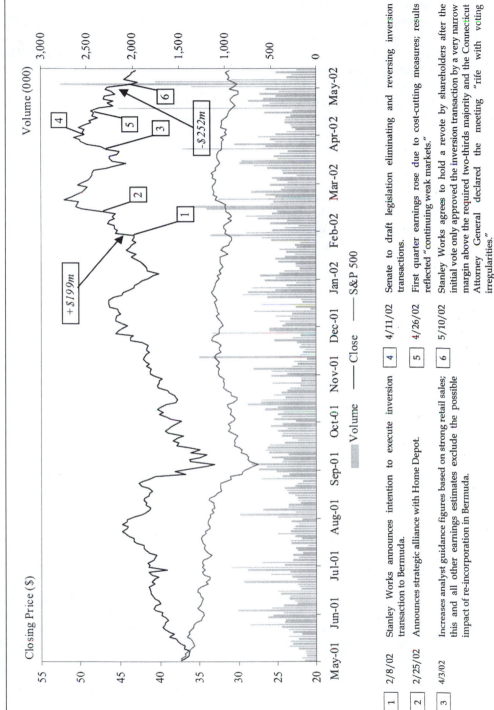

1	2/8/02	Stanley Works announces intention to execute inversion transaction to Bermuda.	4	4/11/02	Senate to draft legislation eliminating and reversing inversion transactions.
2	2/25/02	Announces strategic alliance with Home Depot.	5	4/26/02	First quarter earnings rose due to cost-cutting measures; results reflected "continuing weak markets."
3	4/3/02	Increases analyst guidance figures based on strong retail sales; this and all other earnings estimates exclude the possible impact of re-incorporation in Bermuda.	6	5/10/02	Stanley Works agrees to hold a revote by shareholders after the initial vote only approved the inversion transaction by a very narrow margin above the required two-thirds majority and the Connecticut Attorney General declared the meeting "rife with voting irregularities."

Source: Casewriter.

155

STANLEY WORKS

Founded in 1843 by Frederick T. Stanley, The Stanley Works had grown to nearly 15,000 employees, was a member of the Standard & Poor's (S&P) 500 Index, and was the leading toolmaker in the United States with sales of $2.6 billion. It divided its operations into two groups, Tools (77% of sales) and Doors (23% of sales). The Tools division manufactured hand tools for consumer and professional use, and mechanics' tools as well as pneumatic and hydraulic tools for industrial uses. The hand tools were distributed directly to retailers such as home centers and indirectly to end users through third-party distributors. Ultimately the products were used for everything from simple around-the-home fix-it jobs to major construction projects ranging from buildings to utilities to railroads. The more sophisticated products found their way onto assembly line equipment at major vehicle makers. The Doors division manufactured a full range of door systems, from ordinary doors for use in residential homes to reinforced commercial systems such as automatic and revolving doors. Door products were sold under a variety of brand names through both direct and indirect sales channels. Much of Stanley's sales were concentrated in a few mass market home centers—Home Depot, Sears, and Wal-Mart, for example—with Home Depot accounting for approximately 18% of 2001 revenues. Nonetheless, Stanley operated in over thirty countries, with foreign operations accounting for 30% of total sales. Meyerson glanced over the consolidated financial statement data he had retrieved from Stanley's most recent annual report to the Securities and Exchange Commission (see Exhibit 2). He also noted Stanley's equity beta of 0.89 and the 30-year Treasury Bond yield of 3.41%, as reported by Bloomberg.

Planned Reincorporation in Bermuda

A February 8th press release provided a general outline of Stanley's intentions—to "modify [its] corporate structure so that the company's place of incorporation will be changed from Connecticut to Bermuda." Chairman and Chief Executive John Trani cited increased operational flexibility, better access to international capital markets, and improved tax efficiency as strategic motivations for implementing the restructuring.

> This strategic initiative will strengthen our company over the long-term. An important portion of our revenues and earnings are derived from outside the United States, where nearly 50% of our people reside. Moreover, an increasing proportion of our materials are being purchased from global sources. This change will create greater operational flexibility, better position us to manage international cash flows and help us to deal with our complex international tax structure. . . . In addition to operational flexibility, improved worldwide cash management and competitive advantages, the new corporate structure will enhance our ability to access international capital markets, which is favorable for organic growth, future strategic alliances and acquisitions. Finally, enhanced flexibility to manage worldwide tax liabilities should reduce our global effective tax rate from its current 32% to within the range of 23%–25%.

At the same time, Trani assured investors (a) that the transaction would "be seamless and transparent for all stakeholders—employees, customers and vendors—around the world" and (b) that "corporate operations [would] continue to be managed from our current headquarters in New Britain, Connecticut, and these changes will not affect day-to-day operations."

EXHIBIT 2

FINANCIAL HIGHLIGHTS, THE STANLEY WORKS

(Millions of dollars, except per share data)	2001	2000	1999
INCOME STATEMENT			
Net sales	**2,624.4**	**2,748.9**	**2,751.8**
Cost of sales	1,701.3	1,751.5	1,813.9
Selling, general and administrative	593.7	656.6	703.0
Interest-net	25.6	27.1	27.9
Other-net	(5.3)	20.0	(2.5)
Restructuring charges and asset	72.4	—	(21.3)
Total Costs & Expenses	2,387.7	2,455.2	2,521.0
Earnings before income taxes	**236.7**	**293.7**	**230.8**
Income taxes	78.4	99.3	80.8
Net earnings	**158.3**	**194.4**	**150.0**
Net earnings per share of common	1.85	2.22	1.67
SUMMARY STATEMENT OF CASH FLOW			
Depreciation and amortization	82.9	83.3	85.6
Changes in operating assets and liabilities	(109.3)	(83.7)	(49.7)
Capital expenditures	(73.1)	(64.4)	(102.9)
Asset sales and business acquisitions	(69.5)	14.1	35.1
Proceeds from (payments on) total debt	43.3	27.0	(96.5)
Equity issuance (repurchase)	14.4	(99.7)	(11.4)
Cash dividends on common stock	(80.5)	(78.3)	(77.5)
Effect of exchange rate changes on cash	(7.4)	(9.6)	(5.0)
Increase (decrease) in cash and equivalents	21.6	5.6	(22.1)
BALANCE SHEET			
Cash and cash equivalents	115.2	93.6	
Accounts and notes receivable	551.3	531.9	
Inventories	410.1	398.1	
Property, plant and equipment	494.3	503.7	
Goodwill and other intangibles	236.1	175.9	
Other assets	248.7	181.6	
Total assets	**2,055.7**	**1,884.8**	
Short-term borrowings	177.3	207.6	
Accrued expenses	528.1	493.6	
Long-term debt	316.9	254.8	
Other liabilities	201.1	192.3	
Shareowners' equity	832.3	736.5	
Total liabilities and shareowners' equity	**2,055.7**	**1,884.8**	

Source: Stanley Works Form 10-K.

The journalistic and editorial ranks of the business press, however, were decidedly less enthusiastic about the transaction—as were politicians in Washington. Already several teams of Congressmen and Senators were making plans to introduce legislation banning such transactions.[1] A *New York Times* editorial quipped in a piece entitled "The Bermuda Tax Triangle":

> Stanley Works ought to change its name to Stanley Flees. The maker of distinctive black-and-yellow tools that for 159 years has made its home in New Britain, Conn., is planning to reincorporate in Bermuda in order to stiff Uncle Sam. Stanley is only the latest in an alarming exodus of greedy companies, but the prospect of the venerable firm taking off for a tax haven caused one local congressman to note that Benedict Arnold, too, left Connecticut and sailed off to Bermuda.[2]

The reaction to Stanley's decision, and Stanley's willingness to withstand it, only sharpened Meyerson's interest in understanding what made Stanley anxious to expatriate.

PRIMER ON INTERNATIONAL TAXATION

In order to figure out Stanley's motivation, Meyerson realized that he needed to revisit some of the foundations of how tax rules affect U.S. multinational firms. In particular, he wanted to understand how the income from foreign operations is taxed and what effects foreign operations have on a firm's overall tax position.

Concept of Residence of Domicile

The U.S. government taxes all companies that do business in the United States on their U.S. income. In addition, it taxes American firms on their foreign income. Accordingly, the United States is said to use a **worldwide income tax system**. This, naturally, makes the definition of what constitutes a domestic company crucially important. From a legal perspective, an American firm is any firm incorporated in the United States. A firm is free to choose its jurisdiction of incorporation, and (under U.S. law) is not required to produce or sell anything in the country that serves as its tax home. Many other countries, including Germany, the Netherlands, Canada, and France—not to mention tax havens—tax only income generated inside their borders. Because they tax their residents (regardless of "citizenship") only on domestic income, such countries are said to use a **territorial income tax system**.

Foreign Tax Credits

While the United States taxes the worldwide incomes of its corporations on top of taxes they pay to foreign governments, American firms are permitted to claim tax credits for foreign taxes paid (to avoid "double taxation"—levels of taxation that could erode the

---

[1]The Reversing the Expatriation of Profits Offshore Act (the REPO Bill), proposed in the Senate, would have required that an inverting company continue to be taxed as a domestic corporation if (1) the foreign entity held substantially all of the assets of the inverting domestic company, and (2) former shareholders of the domestic corporation owned at least 80% of the foreign company's stock. It also provided that if U.S. shareholders owned more than 50% but less than 80% of the foreign company, the IRS would scrutinize the transaction and the company's financials for the subsequent 10 years and would disallow various deductions. Several other proposals with similar features were also submitted in Congress.

[2]"The Bermuda Tax Triangle," *The New York Times*, May 13, 2002.

economic viability of business). Here, Meyerson struggled to get his hands around a complex set of rules and regulations. Since the foreign tax credit is intended to alleviate international double taxation, and not to reduce U.S. tax liabilities on profits earned *within* the United States, the foreign tax credit is limited to U.S. tax liability on foreign-source income. For example, an American firm with $200 of foreign income that faces a U.S. tax rate of 35% has a foreign tax credit limit of $70 (35% of $200). If the firm pays foreign income taxes of less than $70, then the firm would be entitled to claim foreign tax credits for all of its foreign taxes paid. If, however, the firm pays $90 of foreign taxes, then it would be permitted to claim no more than $70 of foreign tax credits.

Deferral of Taxes Due on Foreign Earnings

Meyerson also knew that American companies were permitted to defer any U.S. tax liabilities on certain unrepatriated foreign profits until they actually receive such profits in the form of dividends.[3] To illustrate deferral, Meyerson considered the case of a subsidiary of an American company that earned $500 in a foreign country with a 20% tax rate. This subsidiary paid taxes of $100 to the foreign country (20% of $500), and might have remitted $100 in dividends to its parent U.S. company, using the remaining $300 ($500 minus $100 of taxes minus $100 of dividends) to reinvest in its own (foreign) operations. The American parent firm then had to pay U.S. taxes on the $100 of dividends it received (and was eligible to claim a foreign tax credit of $20 for the foreign income taxes its subsidiary paid on the $100). But the American firm was not required to pay U.S. taxes on any part of the $300 that the subsidiary earned abroad and did not remit to its parent company. If, however, the subsidiary were to pay a dividend of $300 the following year, the firm would then be required to pay U.S. tax (after proper allowance for foreign tax credits) on that amount.

Limitations on Deferral and Anti-abuse Rules

While Meyerson saw a great opportunity in deferral, he quickly discovered the Controlled Foreign Corporations (CFC) rules and so-called Subpart F income classification. U.S. tax law contains these provisions to prevent American firms from delaying the repatriation of lightly taxed foreign earnings. These tax provisions apply to all CFCs, which are foreign corporations owned at least 50% by American individuals or corporations who hold stakes of at least 10% each. Under the Subpart F provisions of U.S. law, some foreign income of controlled foreign corporations is "deemed distributed" whether or not remittance actually (or ever) occurs, and therefore is immediately taxable by the United States.[4] Subpart F income includes passive income derived either through (a) insuring risks outside the CFC's home country or (b) so-called "foreign base company income." This latter category includes holding company income such as

---

[3]This deferral is available only on the active business profits of American-owned foreign affiliates that are separately incorporated as subsidiaries in foreign countries.

[4]Subpart F income consists of income from passive investments (such as interest and dividends received from investments in securities), foreign base company income (that arises from using a foreign affiliate as a conduit for certain types of international transactions), income that is invested in United States property, money used offshore to insure risks in the United States, and money used to pay bribes to foreign government officials. American firms with foreign subsidiaries that earn profits through most types of active business operations, and that subsequently reinvest those profits in active lines of business, are not subject to the Subpart F rules, and are therefore able to defer U.S. tax liability on their foreign profits until they choose to remit dividends at a later date.

dividends, interest, and royalties as well as sales, service, shipping, and oil and gas related income. In general, these rules prevent U.S. corporations from setting up affiliates in tax havens to hold investments (and therefore earn either deferred or tax-free returns on the investments).

Excess Credit or Deficit Credit Positions

Taxpayers whose foreign tax payments are larger (smaller) than the foreign tax credit limit are said to have "excess (deficit) foreign tax credits." American law permits taxpayers to use excess foreign tax credits in one year to reduce their U.S. tax obligations on foreign source income in either of the two previous years (carry-backs) or in any of the following five years (carry-forwards).[5] In practice, the calculation of the foreign tax credit limit relies on "worldwide averaging"—that is, all repatriated earnings, and their associated foreign tax credits, would be considered jointly.

Expense Allocations Under the FTC System

In addition to the rules governing the taxation of repatriated earnings, Meyerson knew that multinational firms such as Stanley also faced expense allocation rules. Firms with certain types of tax-deductible expenses, particularly interest charges, expenditures on research and development, and some general administrative and overhead expenses, are required to allocate fractions of these expenses between domestic and foreign source—even if the expenses were incurred entirely in the United States. The logic behind these rules appeared to be that raising investment capital, producing innovations, and managing firm operations all contribute to the worldwide income of the firm. The intention of the U.S. allocation rules is to retain the tax benefits of the deductibility of such expenses against domestic income only for the portion of expenses that contribute to producing domestic income.

U.S. tax rules implement this principle by allocating a certain portion (usually foreign assets as a pecent of total assets[6]) of particular expense items against foreign source income. These expenses reduce the amount of foreign income for the purpose of calculating the foreign tax credit limit, which is costly for firms with excess foreign tax credits (but not costly for firms with deficit foreign tax credits). Because interest expense is typically a firm's largest allocable expense, in practice firms with lightly-taxed foreign income and considerable U.S. interest expenses are likely to incur significant costs associated with the inability to receive the full benefits of interest expense deductions.

INVERSION TRANSACTIONS

Mechanics of Inversions

Meyerson consulted with Alison Lee, HandyWork's Vice President and General Counsel in order to understand the mechanics of inversions. After carefully defining an in-

---

[5]Foreign tax credits are not adjusted for inflation. Barring unusual circumstances, firms generally apply their foreign tax credits against future years only when unable to apply them against either of the previous two years. The most common reason why firms do not apply excess foreign tax credits against either of the previous two years is that they already have excess foreign tax credits in those years.

[6]While there is a long history of shifting definitions for these ratios, interest expenses were usually allocated between domestic and foreign source based on the fraction of assets located inside and outside the United States.

version transaction as a restructuring by a company of its corporate form such that it became a foreign company (with the same dispersed U.S. shareholders), she talked Meyerson through two slides she had prepared.

Lee proposed that the tax purpose of an expatriation was to avoid U.S. tax liabilities associated with foreign income (see Exhibit 3). The way this was accomplished was by removing foreign assets and foreign business activity from ownership by an

---

EXHIBIT 3

TRANSACTION SCHEMATICS—ENTITIES IN AFFILIATED GROUP SUBJECT TO U.S. TAXATION

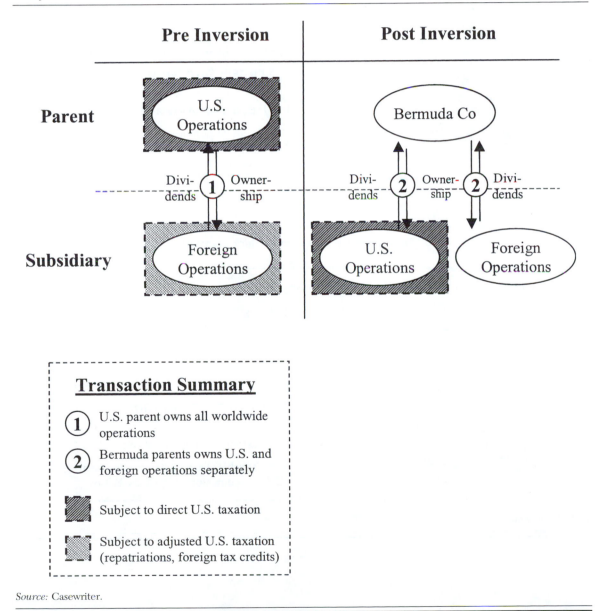

Source: Casewriter.

EXHIBIT 4

TRANSACTION SCHEMATICS—ASSET INVERSIONS AND STOCK INVERSIONS

Asset Inversion

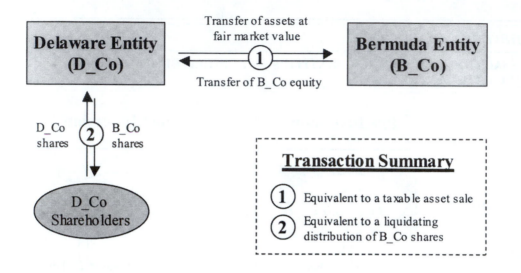

Stock Inversion (aka Taxable Stock Transfer)

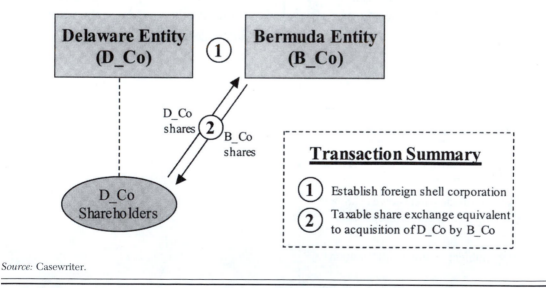

Source: Casewriter.

American corporation, thereby effectively eliminating U.S. taxes on any income it generated from these foreign operations. Prior to inverting, dividends from foreign operations were received by the American parent company, while subsequent to the inversion, dividends from foreign operations (as well as those from American operations) were received by the Bermuda (in this example) parent company.

Lee's second slide reflected the general requirement under U.S. law that foreign inversions be "recognition events" for capital gains tax purposes, meaning that taxpayers would incur capital gains tax liabilities for any previously unrecognized gains.[7] The nature of the capital gains taxes triggered by inversions depended on the way in which the inversion was structured; there were several possibilities, falling into two general categories (see Exhibit 4). In a taxable stock transfer, the new foreign parent company effectively exchanged its own shares for shares of the American company, a transaction that required individual and other shareholders to recognize capital gains equal to the difference between fair market values of the shares and tax basis. At the conclusion of such a transfer, shareholders owned shares in the new foreign parent company, and the American operations were typically organized as a subsidiary of the new foreign parent. In an asset transaction, the new foreign parent company acquired an American firm's assets, thereby triggering taxes on capital gains at the corporate level equal to the difference between fair market value and basis.[8]

Lee also pointed out a peculiarity of such transactions. In the Stanley case, as in several others, the inversion to Bermuda (i.e., reincorporation in Bermuda) was accompanied by structuring the deal so the new parent company would also be registered as an external company in Barbados. This permitted Stanley to take advantage of favorable withholding tax treatment of dividends and interest remitted from the United States to the foreign parent company.[9] Stanley and other companies are subject to rules requiring that tax-deductible interest payments from an American subsidiary to its foreign parent company not exceed interest payments that unrelated parties would require for the same loans. Furthermore, Stanley—or any other foreign-owned American subsidiary with a debt/equity ratio that exceeds 1.5—would not be permitted to deduct interest payments to a foreign parent in excess of 50% of the subsidiary's adjusted gross income. Lee also mentioned in passing that the deals also presented an interesting twist with respect to the incentive to engage in tax planning overseas—companies reducing their foreign taxes would no longer face higher U.S. taxes as a consequence.

The History of Inversions

Lee also provided details on selected corporate expatriations over the last 20 years (see Exhibit 5). Meyerson noticed that expatriating companies were historically dominated by the oil and gas and reinsurance businesses, but recent expatriates appeared to be drawn from a more broader range of American industrial companies. Indeed, seven of the firms

[7]This applied to gains only. Losses were not realized, but instead shareholders received carryover basis in the newly issued stock.

[8]There were variants, including drop-down transactions, that entailed a combination of these two transactions, and associated capital gains tax liabilities at both the individual shareholder and U.S. corporate level. Other structures allowed U.S. shareholders to elect to be treated differently from non-U.S. shareholders.

[9]The United States imposes withholding taxes of 30% on cross-border dividend and interest payments from foreign-owned American subsidiaries to their parent companies unless local tax rates are sufficiently high or a bilateral tax treaty specifies otherwise. Barbados and the United States have a tax treaty that eliminates the U.S. withholding tax on interest paid by an American subsidiary to its Barbados parent company, and reduces the corresponding withholding tax rate on dividend payments to 5%.

EXHIBIT 5

SELECTED HISTORICAL INVERSION TRANSACTIONS

Company (Ticker)	Announced	Destination	Transaction Detail	Market Value ($ millions)	Company Description
Mcdermott (MDR)	2/10/1983	Panama	Taxable Stock Transfer	727	Deepwater and subsea oil and gas production facilities
Helen Of Troy (HELE)	12/30/1993	Bermuda	Taxable Stock Transfer	104	Personal care products and accessories
Triton Energy (OILₗ)	2/8/1996	Cayman	Taxable Stock Transfer	1,945	International oil and gas exploration and production
Chicago Bridge & Iron (CBI)	12/18/1996	Netherlands	Subsidiary IPO	na	Storage tanks, natural gas processing plants
Tyco (TYC)	3/17/1997	Bermuda	Taxable Stock Transfer (M&A related)	9,713	Diversified manufacturer
Santa Fe International (GSF)	6/1/1997	Cayman		na	Offshore drilling
Fruit Of The Loom (FTL)	2/11/1998	Cayman	Taxable Stock Transfer	1,823	Basic and casual apparel
Playstar	5/5/1998	Antigua	F-Reorg.	na	Internet gaming and gambling
Gold Reserve (GLDR)	11/24/1998	Canada	Taxable Stock Transfer	27	Gold mining
Xoma (XOMA)	11/24/1998	Bermuda	Asset	160	Drug developer
Transocean (RIG)	3/15/1999	Cayman	Taxable Stock Transfer[a]	2,539	Offshore drilling
PXRE (PXT)	7/7/1999	Bermuda	Taxable Stock Trnasfer	223	Re/insurance
Everest Reinsurance (RE)	9/17/1999	Bermuda	Taxable Stock Transfer	1,311	Re/insurance
White Mountain Insurance (WTM)	9/23/1999	Bermuda	Asset	675	Re/insurance
Trenwick (TWK)	12/19/1999	Bermuda	Asset (M&A related)	279	Re/insurance
Applied Power	3/10/2000	Bermuda	Subsidiary Spin-off	na	Enclosures for electronic systems
R&B Falcon (FLC)	8/21/2000	Cayman	Acquired by Foreign Entity	4,906	Offshore drilling
Foster Wheeler (FWC)	11/29/2000	Bermuda	Taxable Stock Transfer[a]	183	Engineering & energy equipment
Cooper Industries (CBE)	6/11/2001	Bermuda	Taxable Stock Transfer	3,551	Electrical products
Global Marine (GLM)	9/4/2001	Cayman	Taxable Stock Transfer (M&A related)	2,667	Offshore drilling
Ingersoll Rand (IR)	10/16/2001	Bermuda	Taxable Stock Transfer	6,719	Tools & machinery
Nabors Industries (NBR)	1/2/2002	Bermuda	Taxable Stock Transfer	4,657	Offshore drilling
Noble Drilling (NE)	1/31/2002	Cayman	Taxable Stock Transfer	4,223	Offshore drilling
Stanley Tools (SWK)	2/8/2002	Bermuda	Taxable Stock Transfer	3,688	Hand- and industrial tools
NON-INVERSION EXPATRIATIONS					
Seagate Techology	4/20/2001	Cayman	"Ab Initio"	na	Hard disk drives
Accenture	7/19/2001	Bermuda	"Ab Initio"	na	Consulting

[a]F- or C-Reorganization with drop down.

Source: Compiled by casewriter from Compustat, CRSP, Hoovers, New York State Bar Association, and SEC Documents.

were members of the S&P 500.[10] Since the middle of 2001, firms with an aggregate market capitalization of over $25 billion had announced inversions. Meyerson also noticed the variety of transaction structures that were used to accomplish inversions and noted that a number were the consequence of normal M&A (merger and acquisition) activity.[11]

Meyerson pressed Lee for a bit of color on the stories behind the past inversions. She explained that there had been a trickle of such transactions in the 1980s and 1990s. The first occurred in 1983, when McDermott, a U.S. corporation, set up a Panamanian subsidiary, McDermott International, to acquire the American entity. Though the IRS challenged the transaction, McDermott's tax-favored treatment prevailed, and Congress subsequently adopted a rule making such transactions taxable to U.S. shareholders. In 1994, Helen of Troy announced an inversion designed to qualify as a tax-free share exchange to its shareholders, despite the new rules. In order to prevent this sort of transaction from becoming commonplace among American companies, new rules were again issued. The new rules made acquisitions of U.S. companies taxable to U.S. shareholders if the acquiring (foreign) company was not larger than the U.S. entity. Holding companies created to acquire U.S. operations (as in Helen of Troy) would therefore trigger taxes to U.S. shareholders. With such broad scope, these rules had the potential to complicate legitimate cross-border merger and acquisition transactions.[12]

FERRETING OUT THE MARKET'S ASSESSMENT

Meyerson puzzled over Stanley's recent stock price history—in particular, he stared at the $200 million jump in market value the day after the inversion was announced and the slightly larger drop in value the day the revote was announced. He realized that he was going to need much more detail on Stanley's international operations and capital structure, which he found in the footnotes to consolidated financial statements in Stanley's Form 10-K. First, Meyerson wanted a sense of the base in interest expense Stanley was using for its expense allocation calculations (see Note H in Exhibit 6). Then, he wanted to understand just how integral a part of Stanley's overall operations foreign divisions were (see Note O in Exhibit 7). Meyerson harbored the hope, however, that he could find extensive information on Stanley's tax situation in its income tax disclosure (see Note P in Exhibit 8). Estimating the average tax rate Stanley faced in foreign countries would allow him to make a more accurate determination of how large the repatriation tax savings might be.

Seeing how much shareholder value was at stake, Meyerson wanted to isolate how an inversion could generate such large market value swings. Looking over the numbers, Meyerson's biggest concern was that he might not be able to account for all of the market value change Stanley had experienced after announcing its inversion. Meyerson considered the possibility that these market value gains could represent tax savings or other economic consequences not proposed by Lee. Finally, Meyerson considered the tax consequences to Stanley shareholders and wondered if these consequences should figure into his calculations. With this understanding, Meyerson, Stern, and Lee could then decide if an inversion would be the right thing for American HandyWorks to undertake as well.

[10]These S&P 500 firms are Cooper, Ingersoll Rand, Nabors, Noble, Stanley, Transocean, and Tyco.

[11]Accenture and Seagate represented the initial capitalization of companies abroad and, as such, constitute non-inversion expatriations.

[12]In the case of large-scale transactions such as the formation of DaimlerChrysler, the merging parties requested private-letter rulings from the IRS prior to executing the merger stating that the transaction would not face scrutiny under these rules.

EXHIBIT 6

THE STANLEY WORKS NOTES TO CONSOLIDATED FINANCIAL STATEMENTS

Note H: Long-Term Debt and Financing Arrangements

(Millions of dollars)	Interest Rate	2001	2000
Notes payable in 2002	7.40%	100.0	100.0
Notes payable in 2004	5.80%	120.0	120.0
Notes payable in 2007	4.50%	75.0	—
Industrial revenue bonds due in varying amounts to 2010	5.8–6.8%	19.6	19.6
ESOP loan guarantees, payable in varying monthly installments through 2009	6.10%	22.5	27.9
Other, including net swap receivables		(20.2)	(12.7)
Total long-term debt		**316.9**	**254.8**
Less: current maturities		120.1	6.1
Long-term debt		**196.8**	**248.7**

Aggregate annual maturities of long-term debt for the years 2003 to 2006 are $7.1 million, $101.0 million, $2.8 million, and $0.6 million, respectively, and $85.3 million thereafter. Interest paid during 2001, 2000, and 1999 amounted to $33.4 million, $36.1 million, and $30.8 million, respectively.

Source: Stanley Works Form 10-K.

EXHIBIT 7

THE STANLEY WORKS NOTES TO CONSOLIDATED FINANCIAL STATEMENTS

Note O: Geographic Area

(Millions of dollars)	2001	2000	1999
Net sales			
United States	1,885.2	1,984.0	1,962.5
Other Americas	185.4	203.3	199.0
Europe	456.7	459.3	493.2
Asia	97.1	102.3	97.1
Consolidated	**2,624.4**	**2,748.9**	**2,751.8**
Long-lived assets			
United States	593.5	458.3	442.1
Other Americas	28.5	31.3	28.1
Europe	254.1	266.7	286.3
Asia	38.2	34.2	36.7
Other	—	—	6.4
Consolidated	**914.3**	**790.5**	**799.6**

Source: Stanley Works Form 10-K.

EXHIBIT 8

THE STANLEY WORKS NOTES TO CONSOLIDATED FINANCIAL STATEMENTS

Note P: Income Taxes

Significant components of the company's deferred tax liabilities and assets as of the end of each fiscal year were as follows:

(Millions of dollars)	2001	2000
Deferred tax liabilities:		
Depreciation	78.0	82.4
Other	5.8	16.4
Total deferred tax liabilities	**83.8**	**98.8**
Deferred tax assets:		
Employee benefit plans	16.5	26.4
Doubtful accounts	10.8	16.1
Inventories	7.7	13.8
Amortization of intangibles	14.7	16.4
Accruals	12.8	13.9
Restructuring charges	14.9	20.7
Foreign and state operating loss carryforwards	21.0	16.1
Valuation allowance	(21.0)	(16.1)
Other	0.8	6.9
Total deferred tax assets	**78.2**	**114.2**
Net deferred tax (liabilities) assets	**(5.6)**	**15.4**

Valuation allowances reduced the deferred tax asset attributable to foreign and state loss carryforwards to the amount that, based upon all available evidence, is more likely than not to be realized. Reversal of the valuation allowance is contingent upon the recognition of future taxable income and capital gains in specific foreign countries and specific states, or changes in circumstances which cause the recognition of the benefits to become more likely than not.

Income tax expense consisted of the following:

(Millions of dollars)	2001	2000	1999
Current:			
Federal	24.1	40.1	25.3
Foreign	19.6	16.7	13.7
State	5.9	7.0	5.6
Total current	**49.6**	**63.8**	**44.6**
Deferred (benefit):			
Federal	33.4	34.7	32.1
Foreign	(7.0)	(2.9)	0.8
State	2.4	3.7	3.3
Total deferred (benefit)	**28.8**	**35.5**	**36.2**
Total	**78.4**	**99.3**	**80.8**

Income taxes paid during 2001, 2000, and 1999, were $41.4 million, $59.7 million, and $22.4 million, respectively.

EXHIBIT 8 (Continued)

THE STANLEY WORKS NOTES TO CONSOLIDATED FINANCIAL STATEMENTS

Note P: Income Taxes (continued)

The reconciliation of federal income tax at the statutory federal rate to income tax at the effective rate was as follows:

(Millions of dollars)	2001	2000	1999
Tax at statutory rate	82.8	102.8	80.8
State income taxes, net of federal benefits	5.4	6.7	5.8
Difference between foreign and federal income tax	(15.9)	(7.0)	(4.5)
Other-net	6.1	(3.2)	(1.3)
Income taxes	**78.4**	**99.3**	**80.8**

The components earnings before income taxes consisted of the following:

(Millions of dollars)	2001	2000	1999
United States	212.9	267.5	201.0
Foreign	23.8	26.2	29.8
Total pretax earnings	**236.7**	**293.7**	**230.8**

Undistributed foreign earnings of $62.2 million at December 29, 2001 are considered to be invested indefinitely or will be remitted substantially free of additional tax. Accordingly, no provision has been made for taxes that might be payable upon remittance of such earnings, nor is it practicable to determine the amount of this liability.

Source: Stanley Works Form 10-K.

The Continuing Transformation of Asahi Glass: Implementing EVA

> Toshiya Iwasaki, who founded our company in 1907, succeeded in Japan's first commercial manufacturing of flat glass after numerous failures. He used to say, "Never take the easy way out, but confront difficulties." He built the corporate culture to challenge the most difficult problems.
>
> —Shinya Ishizu, President and CEO

Shinya Ishizu was in a difficult situation of his own devising. As president and CEO of Asahi Glass Company (AGC), he presided over a Japan-based multinational manufacturer of flat glass, chemicals, and electronics and displays, with annual sales of ¥1.3 trillion and the largest global market share in most of its product categories. Worldwide, AGC controlled a network of over 200 subsidiaries and affiliates in 25 countries, generating ¥52.4 billion in overseas operating profits in FY2003—sixth largest among all Japanese companies.[1] (See Exhibit 1 for financial information and Exhibit 2 for AGC's global presence.)

After he was appointed president and CEO in 1998, Ishizu began implementing a number of drastic changes to the company's structure and corporate culture in order to create a truly international enterprise. In 2002, he split AGC into four business units on a global basis which were dubbed "in-house companies" and appointed two non-Japanese executives to manage the glass business, which, at 53% of total sales and 56% of operating profits, was the core of the company. Many Japanese employees working for the company in Japan were placed under non-Japanese bosses for the first time, and many had to learn English.

Professor Mihir A. Desai and Masako Egawa, Executive Director, Japan Research Office, and Research Associate Yanjun Wang prepared this case. HBS cases are developed solely as the basis for class discussion. Cases are not intended to serve as endorsements, sources of primary data, or illustrations of effective or ineffective management.

[1]"Overseas Profits of Japanese Companies Rose 46%," *Nikkei Economic Journal*, June 19, 2003.

EXHIBIT 1

FINANCIAL INFORMATION

Consolidated Statements of Income (in ¥ millions)

	For the Year Ended:		
	3/31/01	3/31/02	3/31/03
Net Sales	**1,312,829**	**1,263,196**	**1,295,011**
Cost of Sales	**971,893**	**975,488**	**1,000,501**
Selling, General & Administrative Expenses	**229,283**	**228,720**	**227,034**
Operating Profit	**111,652**	**58,988**	**67,475**
Nonoperating Income			
Interest and dividend income	5,374	4,107	4,675
Gain on sales of marketable securities	—	—	—
Equity in earnings of nonconsolidated subsidiaries and affiliates	4,855	3,428	4,234
Other nonoperating income	4,677	7,909	5,900
Total Nonoperating Income	**14,908**	**15,445**	**14,811**
Nonoperating Expenses			
Interest expenses	24,268	22,252	16,634
Other nonoperating expenses	4,265	7,710	8,889
Total Nonoperating Expenses	**28,534**	**29,963**	**25,524**
Recurring Profit	**98,026**	**44,470**	**56,761**
Extraordinary Profit			
Gain on sale of fixed assets	6,425	5,884	15,332
Gain on sale of investments in securities	10,411	4,132	6,823
Gain on sale of investments in subsidiaries and affiliates	1,762	—	—
Gain on establishment of trust for retirement benefits	75,506	—	—
Others	6,933	3,735	6,782
Total Extraordinary Profit	**101,039**	**13,751**	**28,937**
Extraordinary Losses			
Loss on disposal of fixed assets	9,706	11,470	12,403
Exchange loss	6,524	—	—
Loss on sale of investments in subsidiaries	—	4,191	63
Loss on valuation of investments in securities	3,125	2,004	44,220
Loss on restructuring programs	13,917	42,294	18,720
Charge for full amount of transitional obligations for retirement benefits	84,256	—	—
Others	21,102	5,913	4,556
Total Extraordinary Losses	**138,632**	**65,874**	**79,964**
Net Income (Loss) Before Taxes	**60,433**	**(7,652)**	**5,734**
Taxes	**20,761**	**13,613**	**13,259**
Deferred Income Taxes	**744**	**(19,496)**	**(9,107)**
Minority Interests in Earnings of Consolidated Subsidiaries	**14,203**	**10,836**	**5,499**
Net Income (Loss)	**24,724**	**(12,605)**	**(3,918)**

(Continued)

EXHIBIT 1   (Continued)

FINANCIAL INFORMATION

Consolidated Balance Sheets (in ¥ millions)

	For the Year Ended:		
	3/31/01	**3/31/02**	**3/31/03**
ASSETS			
Current Assets:			
Cash on hand and in banks	47,143	50,195	56,880
Trade notes and accounts receivable	26,721	241,803	241,232
Inventories	204,169	203,607	187,324
Other current assets	67,424	60,284	63,817
Total Current Assets	582,458	555,890	549,255
Fixed Assets:			
Tangible fixed assets:			
Building and structures	202,244	215,198	217,202
Machinery, equipment, tools and fixtures	423,554	447,059	432,879
Land	99,813	108,044	109,462
Construction in progress	37,171	47,695	39,322
Total tangible fixed assets	762,784	817,998	798,867
Intangible fixed assets	107,956	104,506	111,758
Investments, etc.:			
Investments in marketable securities	382,024	343,876	241,002
Other investments	50,900	66,500	85,101
Total investments, etc.	432,926	410,378	326,104
Total Fixed Assets	1,303,667	1,332,883	1,236,730
Deferred Assets	689	610	527
TOTAL ASSETS	**1,886,815**	**1,889,384**	**1,786,513**
Current Liabilities			
Trade notes and accounts payable	190,068	155,247	161,495
Short-term bank loans	148,006	159,254	109,087
Commercial paper	80,563	95,638	58,845
Current maturities of bonds	43,178	22,103	77,266
Nontrade payables	64,705	60,715	60,058
Other current liabilities	107,104	95,708	103,119
Total Current Liabilities	633,629	588,670	569,874
Long-term Liabilities			
Bonds issued	282,999	320,331	295,496
Long-term bank loans	130,101	137,987	144,987
Long-term deferred tax liabilities	60,991	43,692	33,989
Accrued retirement benefits	42,877	46,236	57,025
Other long-term liabilities	37,267	72,648	59,303
Total Long-term Liabilities	554,237	620,895	590,803
Minority Interest	91,948	93,842	71,999

(Continued)

EXHIBIT 1   (Continued)

FINANCIAL INFORMATION

Consolidated Balance Sheets (in ¥ millions)

	For the Year Ended:		
	3/31/01	**3/31/02**	**3/31/03**
Shareholders' Equity			
Common shares	90,472	90,472	90,472
Additional paid-in capital	84,388	84,395	84,395
Retained earnings	441,906	419,644	404,817
Assets revaluation reserve	119	117	117
Revaluation of investment in securities	50,969	20,090	8,912
Adjustments on foreign currency translation	(60,851)	(28,438)	(33,752)
Treasury shares	(3)	(306)	(1,127)
Total Shareholders' Equity	607,000	585,975	553,835
TOTAL LIABILITIES, MINORITY INTEREST & SHAREHOLDERS' EQUITY	**1,886,815**	**1,889,384**	**1,786,513**

Source: Company documents.

This reorganization was accompanied by equally drastic reforms in corporate governance and the introduction of new management system for resource allocation and performance measurement based on economic value added (EVA). EVA had been introduced at AGC's Japanese operations in 1999 aiming at maximization of shareholders' value. However, Ishizu believed that drastic reforms had not been embraced widely. While younger and overseas staff accepted the changes, there was strong resistance from senior executives, who took comfort in AGC's traditionally strong position in the marketplace and who did not see the need to tamper with the present winning formula. Ishizu realized that the corporate culture of AGC, which had been 100 years in the making, would be difficult to change, and worried that a reaction by the old guard would jeopardize both his reforms and the future growth of the company. In November 2003, as he thought about his successor, he believed it was critical that he should ensure that AGC's reforms and its transition to a truly international enterprise should be embraced by all the executives and employees. He wondered how he could change the mindset of executives and employees and reform the management system to fit with AGC's operations, which were extremely diverse in terms of products as well as geography.

OVERVIEW OF ASAHI GLASS COMPANY

Around the turn of the 20th century, Toshiya Iwasaki (a nephew of the founder of Mitsubishi Group) chose to ignore the advice of his family and began experimenting with the industrial production of flat glass. At the time, nobody in Japan—including the

EXHIBIT 2

GLOBAL PRESENCE

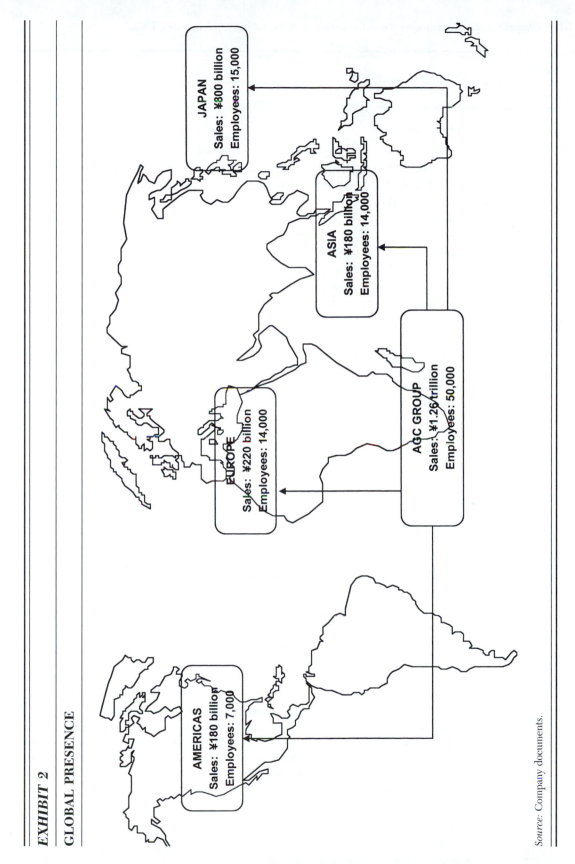

AMERICAS
Sales: ¥180 billion
Employees: 7,000

EUROPE
Sales: ¥220 billion
Employees: 14,000

ASIA
Sales: ¥180 billion
Employees: 14,000

JAPAN
Sales: ¥800 billion
Employees: 15,000

AGC GROUP
Sales: ¥1.26/trillion
Employees: 50,000

Source: Company documents.

EXHIBIT 3

HISTORY

Year	Progress and Development
1907	Asahi Glass Company established in Amagasaki, Hyogo Prefecture.
1909	Belgian-type hand-blown sheet glass manufacture begins (the first such production in Japan).
1914	The first shipment of sheet glass exported to England.
1917	Headquarters moved to Tokyo.
1956	The Indo-Asahi Glass Co., Ltd. established. Production of glass bulbs for TV picture tubes begins.
1963	Thai-Asahi Glass Public Co., Ltd. established.
1966	Asahi Glass and the U.S. firm PPG set up Asahi Penn Chemical Co., Ltd.
1972	P.T. Asahimas Flat Glass Co., Ltd. set up in Indonesia.
1979	Asahi Glass invests in MCIS Safety Glass Sdn. Bhd. In Malaysia.
1981	Asahi Glass acquired Glaverbel S.A. and MaasGlas B.V., glass companies in Belgium and the Netherlands.
1985	AP Technoglass Co. established in the U.S.A. Asahi TechnoVision Pte. Ltd. established in Singapore.
1989	Siam Asahi Technoglass Co., Ltd. established in Thailand.
1992	Dalian Float Glass Co., Ltd. established in China. Acquired AFG Industries, Inc. of the U.S.A.
1996	P.T. Video Display Glass Indonesia established.
1999	Acquired PTFE business in U.S. and U.K. of ICI. Acquired the majority interest of Hankuk Electric Glass, Co., Ltd. of Korea
2000	Asahi Glass Fine Techno Taiwan Co., Ltd. was established.
2001	Announced a public tender offer for shares in Glaverbel S.A.
2002	Creation of AGC Group Vision, "Look Beyond." Introduced an in-house company system.

Source: Company documents.

government—had succeeded in producing flat glass.[2] In 1907, Iwasaki founded AGC and two years later, after nearly ten years of trials, began the production of flat glass. (See Exhibit 3 for AGC's history.)

As the Japanese economy boomed in the aftermath of World War II, the demand for glass skyrocketed, especially in the construction, television-manufacturing, and automobile industries. By the early 1950s, AGC was producing automotive glass[3] and CRT (cathode ray tubes) glass bulbs for televisions. In 1956, the company established its first overseas company in India, manufacturing flat glass, and during the 1960s and 1970s expanded international operations by building manufacturing plants in Thailand, Indonesia, Singapore, and other Southeast Asian countries.

[2]Flat glass is primarily used for construction and automotive glass materials and includes flat glass, sheet glass or plate glass.

[3]Automotive glass is manufactured by tempering or laminating flat glass.

During the 1980s and 1990s, AGC expanded its reach by making inroads into the European and U.S. markets. In 1981, AGC purchased two companies from French conglomerate BSN (which was exiting the glass business); Glaverbel, a Belgian company; and MaasGlas, a Dutch company. In 1992, the acquisition of U.S.-based AFG Industries finally gave AGC a presence in all the major world markets.

In 2003, AGC's sales consisted of glass products (54% of sales), electronics and displays (24%), chemicals (19%), and other products (3%). In most product categories, AGC was either the market leader or second largest among global competitors. AGC accounted for 21% of the flat glass market and 30% of the automotive glass market. While display and electronics products accounted for 24% of sales, this segment accounted for 41% of operating profits, and it continued to grow rapidly. AGC was the world leader in CRT glass bulbs, with a 32% market share, and had a commanding 90% share of the PDP (plasma display panel) glass substrates market. Manufacture of chemicals such as fluorinated resins, soda ash, caustic soda, propylene oxide, and sodium bicarbonate accounted for 19% of total company sales, but incurred operating losses in 2002. The remainder of AGC's sales came primarily from ceramics. (See Exhibit 4 for the segment information and Exhibit 5 for market shares of glass products.)

AGC's global competitors in the glass trade included Saint-Gobain in France, Pilkington in the U.K., and Guardian in the U.S. Its domestic competitors, such as Nippon Sheet Glass and Central Glass, were substantially smaller.

FINANCE FUNCTION

Relationship with Banks

During the 1960s and 1970s, banks acted as the major providers of debt capital to AGC (as well as to many other Japanese companies) since the domestic capital market was not well developed. In Japan, the bank having the strongest relationship with the borrower was called the "main bank" and kept the largest amount of loans outstanding to, and equity interest in, the borrower. The main bank sometimes assumed the responsibility of monitoring the performance of the borrower on behalf of all the lenders, selectively intervening if the company's performance deteriorated.

The banks and corporations typically had cross-shareholding arrangements, owning small minority interests in each other. The implicit agreement was that each party would vote for the management at general shareholders' meetings and would not sell its shares without obtaining agreement from the other party (issuer). Some corporations invited senior bank managers as executive or non-executive board members. Being a member of Mitsubishi Group, AGC's main bank was Bank of Tokyo-Mitsubishi (BOTM). Historically, the bank was the seventh-largest shareholder of AGC with 3.8% interest. AGC simultaneously owned 0.9% of Mitsubishi Tokyo Financial Group, BOTM's holding company. At the peak of cross-ownership in early 1990s, Mitsubishi Bank (predecessor of Bank of Tokyo-Mitsubishi) owned 4.9% of AGC and AGC owned 1.5% of the bank. According to Takashi Matsuzawa, CFO and director, "the main bank used to act as the *'stable shareholder*,' which understood AGC's business and supported our management."

The troubles that plagued the Japanese economy in the 1990s—particularly the bad debt problems and the banking crisis—had a significant impact on the main bank system. Banks began to sell their stock portfolios to compensate for losses from bad debts (by realizing latent gains) and to reduce the volatility of earnings and capital.[4] Sales of

[4]Japanese banks were allowed by the Bank for International Settlements to include 45% of latent gains from equity holdings when calculating bank capital.

EXHIBIT 4

SEGMENT INFORMATION

Business Segment Information

	For the Year Ended:		
	3/31/01	**3/31/02**	**3/31/03**
(in ¥ millions)			
Glass			
Sales	625,240	666,470	708,439
Operating profit	35,852	40,267	37,776
Assets	845,007	845,704	835,397
Depreciation	47,755	56,977	53,462
Capital expenditures	40,391	58,282	53,261
Electronics and Displays			
Sales	386,174	314,947	309,884
Operating profit	65,587	23,838	27,559
Assets	344,401	369,458	405,997
Depreciation	28,959	30,545	32,761
Capital expenditures	34,828	45,719	26,665
Chemicals			
Sales	274,965	258,676	261,330
Operating profit	9,011	(5,390)	1,389
Assets	302,838	315,983	292,901
Depreciation	18,789	20,726	21,471
Capital expenditures	15,569	23,342	17,647
Other			
Sales	93,805	88,224	69,487
Operating profit	1,124	391	766
Assets	250,254	240,796	255,605
Depreciation	2,091	1,765	1,356
Capital expenditures	2,533	3,703	709
(in ¥ millions)			
Total Sales	**1,380,186**	**1,328,318**	**1,349,142**
Corporate or eliminations	(67,357)	(65,122)	(54,131)
Consolidated sales	1,312,829	1,263,196	1,295,011
Total Operating Profit	**111,575**	**59,107**	**67,492**
Corporate or eliminations	76	(119)	(17)
Consolidated operating profit	111,652	58,988	67,475
(in ¥ billions)			
Glass			
Flat glass		382	426
Automotive glass		219	242
Other		91	83
Eliminations		(26)	(42)
Total		666	708
Electronics and Display			
Display	242	196	200
Electronic materials	148	123	116
Eliminations	(4)	(4)	(5)
	386	315	310

(Continued)

EXHIBIT 4   (Continued)

REGIONAL SEGMENT INFORMATION (IN YEN MILLIONS)

	For the Year Ended:		
	3/31/01	**3/31/02**	**3/31/03**
Japan			
Sales	841,008	765,710	775,841
Operating profit	39,389	7,118	15,182
Assets	950,994	909,322	800,254
Asia			
Sales	214,493	190,746	217,124
Operating profit	46,627	24,728	26,637
Assets	191,066	207,789	277,194
The Americas			
Sales	171,359	180,306	183,337
Operating profit	7,781	3,226	6,280
Assets	254,543	245,824	213,998
Europe			
Sales	190,365	224,201	258,491
Operating profit	18,115	24,030	19,439
Assets	190,382	232,451	317,290
Overseas Sales			
Sales	576,217	595,253	658,952
Operating profit	72,523	51,983	52,356
Assets	635,991	686,064	808,482
Total Sales	**1,417,227**	**1,360,965**	**1,434,795**
Corporate or eliminations	(104,398)	(97,768)	(139,783)
Consolidated sales	1,312,829	1,263,196	1,295,011
Operating Profit	**111,914**	**59,103**	**67,540**
Corporate or eliminations	(261)	(115)	(64)
Consolidated operating profit	111,652	58,988	67,475
Exchange Rates (¥/Foreign Currency)			
U.S. dollar:			
At year-end	114.75	131.95	119.90
Average	108.42	122.21	124.83
Euro:			
At year-end	106.55	116.51	125.08
Average	99.60	109.04	118.29

Source: Company documents.

EXHIBIT 5

GLOBAL MARKET SHARES

Market Share of Glass Products

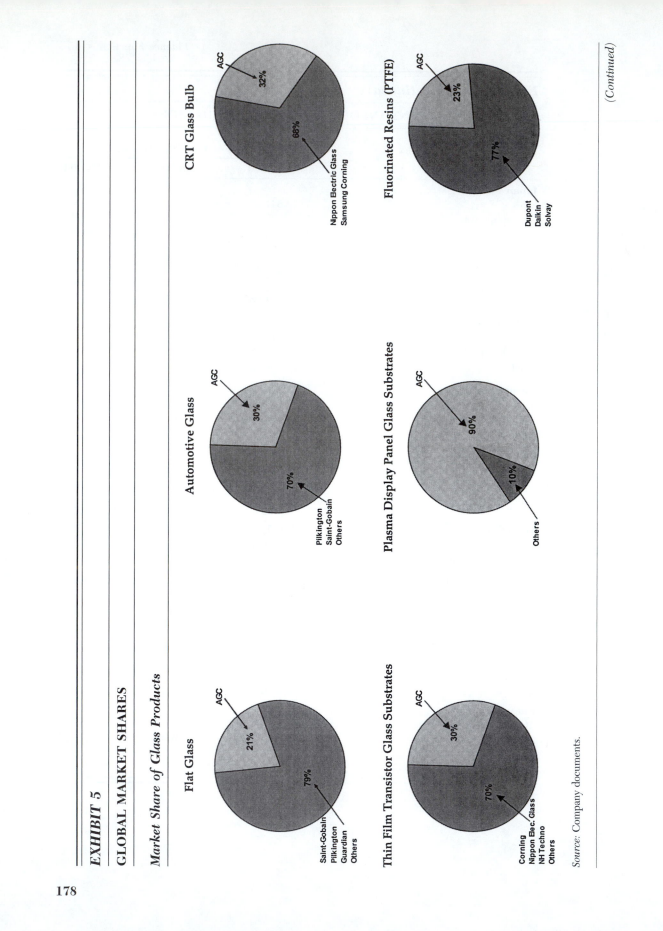

Flat Glass

Automotive Glass

CRT Glass Bulb

Thin Film Transistor Glass Substrates

Plasma Display Panel Glass Substrates

Fluorinated Resins (PTFE)

Source: Company documents.

(Continued)

EXHIBIT 5 *(Continued)*

GLOBAL MARKET SHARES

Global Market Share of Flat Glass (2001)

	Europe	North America	South America	Japan	Asia	TOTAL
Asahi Glass	**25**	**19**	**0**	**40**	**18**	**21**
Saint-Gobain	27	2	36	0	13	16
Pilkington	22	14	36	0	4	15
Guardian	11	18	28	0	13	14
PPG	0	23	0	0	0	6
Nippon Sheet Glass	0	0	0	33	8	4
Central Glass	0	0	0	27	0	1
Others	15	24	0	0	44	23
Total	100	100	100	100	100	100

Source: UBS Warburg: Asahi Glass (March 19, 2003).

equity holdings by both banks and corporations greatly reduced cross-shareholding; from 1991 to 2001, the percentage of cross-shareholding against the total market value of listed companies in Japan fell from 17.8% to 8.9%.

As Japanese capital markets became increasingly deregulated in the 1980s, Japanese companies including AGC began to use capital markets more actively. Takashi Matsuzawa commented on the change in the relationship with its main bank: "the main bank relationship meant a lot in the old days. But today the meaning of cross-shareholding has changed completely. I would like to divest those cross-shareholding shares and shrink our balance sheet." As the yield of cross-shareholding shares were around or less than 1%, investors did not want to see too much of the company's resources tied up with such low-yielding assets.

As of March 31, 2003, AGC held ¥137.5 billion in corporate stock, down from ¥224.5 billion the year before. During the year ending March 31, 2003, the company incurred ¥44.2 billion in losses on the write-down of investments in securities, most of which were bank shares. (See Exhibit 6 for the stock price performance of AGC and banks.)

In November 2003, AGC announced that its shares held by banks, which accounted for 6.1% of AGC's outstanding stock, would be sold in the public market. In return, AGC planned to sell its holdings of bank shares, including those of BOTM, thereby reducing its cross-shareholding.

Raising Funds Through Capital Markets

When AGC began investing in Southeast Asia in the 1960s, it relied upon loans from Japanese banks to fund the overseas operations. During the 1970s AGC began to raise funds in overseas markets such as Switzerland and Germany to fund its international operations. As the company expanded internationally, it realized the importance of capital markets and in 1983 obtained S&P ratings. Makoto Seki, director, finance division, explained how operations in each region were financed in 2003:

> In the U.S., operations are primarily funded by commercial paper (CP) and medium-term notes (MTNs) issued by a finance company. In Europe, 95% of funding is handled by a finance company, but through bank loans. In Japan the parent company issues CP and gives the proceeds to a finance company, which in turn on-lends to subsidiaries. In Asia outside Japan, we established a finance company in Singapore which is still small. Most of our Asian subsidiaries are borrowing from banks. Some of them are borrowing from Japanese banks, which are willing to treat them as AGC parent credit. So the main bank relationship is still very important for us.

Decentralized Funding Decisions

When AGC acquired Glaverbel in 1981, the company felt Glaverbel's operations were too large relative to AGC as a whole. AGC management hoped to take Glaverbel public after its turnaround to minimize the financial risk. Therefore, when Glaverbel management proposed an IPO in 1987, AGC management supported it even though the attendant dilution of earnings was not welcome from the parent company's viewpoint. The acquisition of AFG Industries in 1992 presented even bigger risks for AGC. AGC encouraged all of its major subsidiaries to manage their companies without relying on the parent company's credit.

Concerns about financial risk led senior management to decide to make each regional operation autonomous within the tri-polar organization of Japan/Asia, Europe and U.S. In addition, Japanese accounting rules which focused on the parent company

EXHIBIT 6

STOCK PRICE PERFORMANCE OF AGC AND BANKS

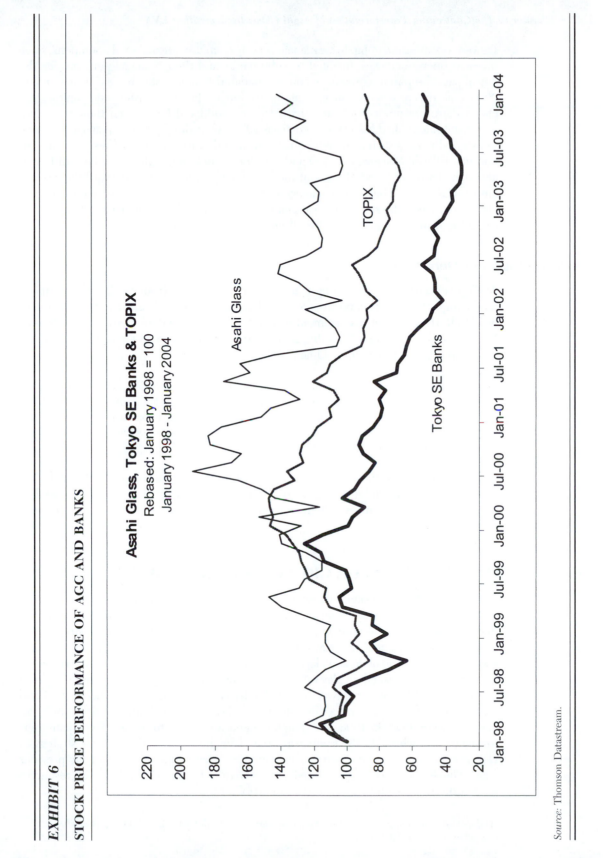

Asahi Glass, Tokyo SE Banks & TOPIX
Rebased: January 1998 = 100
January 1998 - January 2004

Source: Thomson Datastream.

skewed the attention of Japanese managers away from the international operations, since overseas operations were handled by subsidiaries and their financial performance did not impact the parent company's non-consolidated financial statements. It was only in 2000 that the primary financial statements for all Japanese listed companies were changed from a non-consolidated basis to a consolidated basis, even though consolidated statements had been required since 1978. Accordingly, senior managers as well as external parties such as investors had considered non-consolidated results more important. Takashi Matsuzawa, CFO and director, commented, "the financial staff like us always had a pretty good idea about the cash flow position and creditworthiness of the entire AGC group, but senior management focused on the parent company until the late 1990s, when the regulation was changed and consolidated financial statements became the primary requirement for all Japanese companies."

Credit Ratings and Debt Position

AGC was accorded an A2 rating from Moody's and an A- from S&P. The amount of total company debt declined from ¥735 billion as of March 31, 2002 to ¥686 billion as of March 31, 2003, but management planned to reduce the debt further (an additional ¥150 billion) to maintain favorable ratings. According to Hideki Goto, vice president, investment grade research, Goldman Sachs (Japan) Ltd.:

> AGC's credit is a combination of conservative business risk and better-than-average financial risk. AGC controls 41% of the domestic sheet glass market and is part of an oligopoly which has lasted for the past few decades. The company is also No. 1 globally. But it is shifting its business portfolio towards higher risk/higher growth potential as it allocates more resources to electronics and display products.[5]

It was unclear if those credit analysts welcomed AGC's focus on display and electronics business which led to higher risk. They believed that higher business risk had to be offset by more conservative financial profile in order for AGC to maintain its overall credit quality.

REORGANIZATION AND VALUE CREATION MANAGEMENT

Prior to the 1990s, management assessed the performance of each AGC subsidiary separately. However, it had become increasingly clear that coordination across national borders and product lines—assessing the performance of each company *as a part of AGC group*—was an essential step toward efficiently managing and optimizing the value for each business. Automobile and electronics companies, which were important customers for automotive glass and display business, respectively, had become increasingly global and demanded consistent service on a global basis. Global auto giants such as GM and Toyota asked for a single price for automotive glass, be it in Kentucky, Spain or Thailand. Consequently, in 1998 AGC implemented a strategy to focus on company performance as a whole. In the same year, AGC launched a "Shrink to Grow" strategy in response to weak domestic performance and the Asian economic crisis of the previous year. These paired strategies aimed at *selective* and *focused* allocation of resources among the various businesses in AGC's portfolio.

---

[5]Hideki Goto, vice president, investment grade research, Goldman Sachs (Japan) Ltd, interview by casewriter on July 3, 2003, Tokyo.

In 1999, AGC introduced in Japan a measurement system similar to economic value added (EVA) aimed at assessing the performance of each business unit, and linked the bonuses of managers and executives to these measures to provide proper incentives.

As a further change, AGC's resource allocation process was made a regular part of the company's three-year mid-term planning cycle. As each SBU prepared its mid-term plan, including investment and free cash flow projections, AGC ranked each business based on its fit with overall corporate strategy and its contribution to the value of the firm. The company aimed to fashion a "value portfolio" by selectively committing resources based on these rankings. According to Takashi Terashima, executive officer, general manager and corporate controller, "Flat panel display is ranked as *core*, electronics as *hope*, flat and automotive glass as *opportunistic*."

In April 2002, AGC announced a new group vision named "Look Beyond," an initiative aimed at clarifying shared values (innovation and operational excellence, integrity, diversity and environment) and providing long-term direction beyond the usual three-year planning cycles, and proposed further reorganizations to implement the change. Ishizu assembled a project team to draft the new group vision, handpicking 13 middle managers in their late 30s and early 40s. The reorganization encompassed three distinct changes: (1) the creation of in-house companies on a global basis; (2) corporate governance reform; and (3) the definition of group corporate and business operating functions.

Creation of In-House Companies

AGC had traditionally been organized and operated according to geographical regions, and management in Tokyo had respected the autonomy of U.S. and European operations. In 2002, the company established four "in-house companies," organized along product lines to foster international coordination. The reason for this change was to allow AGC to more effectively cater to major customers, including global players in the automobile and electronics industries. Two non-Japanese executives were appointed as heads of in-house companies: Luc Willame, CEO of Belgian-based Glaverbel S.A., became president of Flat Glass Company; and Jay Strong, an American who headed AP Technoglass (a subsidiary of AFG Industries, Inc. in the U.S.), became president of Automotive Glass Company. As previously mentioned, these companies together accounted for 55% of sales and 56% of AGC's operating profits. (See Exhibit 7a for the global management structure for the glass business and Exhibit 7b for the structure of the four in-house companies.)

Commenting on the reason for the changes, Ishizu remarked, "the market and customers for most of our products are global. So we have to coordinate ourselves globally and face our customers with 'one voice.' We now have to form a scrum among 50,000 employees globally; we are now together." Ishizu often used the word "cross-fertilization" to encourage employees from different countries to communicate closely and learn from each other. Masayuki Kamiya, director, corporate planning, explained, "the objectives of the global organization were delegation of authority, and quick decision and implementation of strategies." Ishizu, pleased with the outcome of the global reorganization, commented: "both [Luc and Jay] make quick decisions, expediting the decision making for our company. They demand clear accountability from their subordinates. Their appointment shook up the Japanese managers who were taking it easy, which was exactly what I intended."[6]

[6]"Industrial Power: Milestone for Revival and My Opinion (Interview with Shinya Ishizu, President and CEO, Asahi Glass), *Japan Economic Journal*, December 17, 2002, p. 17.

EXHIBIT 7A

GLOBAL MANAGEMENT STRUCTURE FOR GLASS BUSINESS

OPERATIONS FOCUSED ON THREE REGIONAL BASES

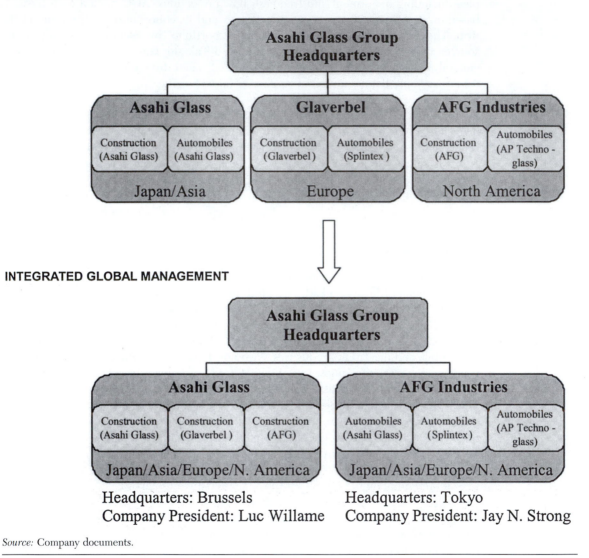

Source: Company documents.

Jay Strong, senior executive officer and president of Automotive Glass Company, shared his experience: "AGC used to be a federation of regional operations. Now it is a global, integrated organization. Since reorganization, we have not experienced any *inter-regional* conflicts, although there are many *intra-regional* ones, such as how to coordinate strategy and marketing." Some analysts considered that it might take time for AGC to fully implement the strategy and reap the benefits of the reorganization. Yusuke Ando, senior analyst at the Daiwa Institute of Research, sounded a cautionary note from

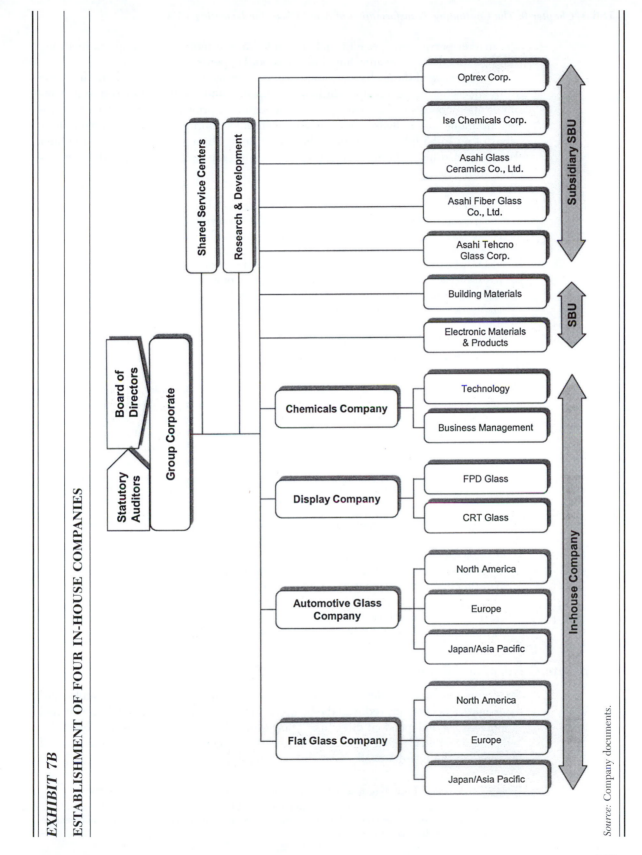

Source: Company documents.

185

the market perspective: "equity analysts wanted to see more stepped-up restructuring through the global reorganization, but it has not happened."[7]

In the wake of these changes, some managers began to feel uneasy about the scope of the decisions being left up to in-house companies and felt that inter-company communication about such decisions was not enough of a priority. For instance, upon reorganization, each in-house company was given the authority to make investment decisions of up to ¥5 billion, five times the earlier limit. Strong found the ¥5 billion limit had expanded his authority "staggeringly." Takashi Matsuzawa, CFO and director, expressed his views:

> We aim to treat each in-house company as independent. Delegation of authority to in-house company forces its president to become responsible for the division's capital structure and credit risk in the same way as AGC group CEO is responsible for those issues to the external market. This system will bring up excellent managers. But there is a risk that some presidents, who may not fully understand AGC's financial position, could make a decision which has significant impacts on the overall creditworthiness of the company. Group corporate is expected to act as a judge or an internal investor; sometimes in-house companies' decisions are restricted through the AGC group medium-term planning conference.

Takashi Wada, senior executive officer and general manager, corporate planning, described two major difficulties AGC faced:

> First, conflicts with minority shareholders. AGC had established a lot of joint ventures when we went into new overseas markets. As we began to manage business regionally and globally, however, we faced increasing conflicts of interests with local partners. For instance, it was not always easy for AGC to optimize manufacturing operations in Asia because local partners tended to pursue profits for each local company. To resolve such conflicts, we bought out the interests held by our partners. Second, communication. To facilitate communication globally, we need to rely on more in-depth, frequent communication and relocation of people across regions.

Shukichi Umemoto, director, tax and accounting division, pointed out another problem:

> The accounting system within AGC has not been standardized yet; Japanese operations are accounted for based on Japanese GAAP, U.S. operations on U.S. GAAP, and European operations on Belgian GAAP. The treatment of certain items differs significantly among three principles, creating inconsistency in decision making and performance evaluation across regions. These three GAAPs are headed in the direction of convergence. AGC should harmonize those three GAAPs until convergence is achieved.

Corporate Governance Reform

AGC implemented a series of reforms to separate management execution and board oversight. The company reduced the board of directors from 20 members to seven, and appointed two independent directors.[8] Many former board members became executive officers. Additionally, four of AGC's 22 executive officers, including Ishizu, continued to serve on the board as well.

---

[7]Yusuke Ando, Daiwa Institute of Research senior analyst, interview by casewriter on July 3, 2003.

[8]Haruo Shimada (professor at Keio University) and Kakutaro Kitashiro (then president of IBM Japan) were appointed as external directors. Hiromichi Seya, former president of AGC, who was not an executive director, served as chairman of the board.

AGC was at the forefront of the corporate governance reform among Japanese companies. Traditionally the boards of Japanese companies including AGC had been dominated by insiders. At the end of 2002, less than one third of listed companies appointed external directors, but about half of those companies had only one such director,[9] whereas AGC had two out of seven.

Delegation of authority to in-house company presidents allowed the board to narrow its focus to a few strategic issues. According to Takashi Wada, senior executive officer and general manager, corporate planning, "the number of agenda items declined from more than 10 to several key items. It allows us to have more in-depth discussions on each topic. Now our board meetings start at 9:30 but sometimes run through lunchtime."[10] The board meetings were held at least once a month.

In June 2003, AGC established a four-person nominating committee to oversee the executive succession process. The committee was structured so as to always include the two independent directors. This was again a departure from standard Japanese business practice: the majority of Japanese companies did not have nominating committees, and presidents picked their own successors.

Defining Group Corporate and Business Operating Functions

AGC carefully delineated *group corporate* functions and *business operating* functions. Group corporate was charged with oversight of each *business operating* organization, allocation of management resources, providing a common management platform, and developing new businesses — essentially acting as the framework within which in-house companies and SBUs functioned. Within this framework, in-house companies and SBUs assumed *business operating* functions and were given greater autonomy than they had previously enjoyed, with the expectation that this freedom would allow the unit to maximize the value of its constituent businesses. Group corporate would act as an "investor" within the company, diverting resources strategically as a given unit demonstrated its potential to create value. The resource allocation decision was extremely important as AGC operated a diversified portfolio of businesses.

Masayuki Kamiya, director, corporate planning, explained:

> The functions of group corporate consist of global corporate service and regional shared service. The former includes such functions as strategic planning, financial control, finance, investor relations, communication, group human resources management, and new business development. The latter is an integral part of operating divisions and includes such functions as purchasing, accounting and human resources management. The expenses of global corporate service are not charged to each business unit while the expenses of regional shared service are charged to operations.

Takashi Terashima, executive officer, general manager, corporate controller, mentioned that there is a possibility that *group corporate* "will ultimately become a holding company. If AGC forms a holding company, the advantage is to be able to implement a different compensation system for each company by tying the bonuses to individual performance. But the shareholders ultimately decide our organizational structure."

[9]The survey conducted by the Tokyo Stock Exchange (65% of 2,103 companies responded) indicated 29% of the respondents appointed external directors. Of those companies which had external directors, 52% had one and 25% had two external directors. (Source: Tokyo Stock Exchange, "The Results of the Survey on Corporate Governance," January 27, 2003.)

[10]"A Managerial Analysis: Asahi Glass," *Diamond Weekly*, April 12, 2003, p. 57.

As finance was centralized under the new structure, corporate management saw an opportunity to consolidate and streamline tasks such as financing, tax management and insurance. These matters had previously been arranged within each region, an approach that naturally did not minimize costs to the company as a whole.

Of these, tax management seemed the most promising area to generate savings. AGC appointed the European tax manager based in Belgium to the role of global tax coordinator, as he already had extensive experience managing pan-European tax issues for Glaverbel. He, along with each regional tax manager and Matsuzawa's staff in Tokyo, set out to optimize the company's worldwide tax.

Under the new organization, each in-house company became responsible for its own EBIT and operating assets, and EVA, and incentives of senior managers were tied to these performance measures. The bonuses for in-house company presidents were determined based on one-year operating profits, but investors scrutinized top management for both short-term and long-term financial performance. Some executives worried about possible inconsistencies between Ishizu's stated objectives and those of in-house company presidents. There were heated discussions within AGC whether each BU should be responsible for EBIT and operating assets as well as capital structure decisions. Some were concerned that BU managers, who might not be familiar with AGC's credit standing, could make significant investment decisions which might negatively affect the company's overall capital structure and credit ratings and argued that asset allocation and capital structure decisions should be left with group corporate.

AGC began to globalize human resources management as well, selecting about 100 senior managers and 200 "high potential" middle managers to train as candidates for future leadership. About 30% of these candidates were non-Japanese. This was consistent with the management's expectation that the percentage of Japanese employees at AGC, currently about 30% of total, would in 10 years decline to about 6%. Such a plan was revolutionary within Japanese business culture, which had long placed a high premium on retaining as many Japanese employees as possible, and fostering career-spanning relationships with them. Consequently, this strategy dismayed Japanese managers, who felt that AGC was choking off their future with the company.

USING EVA AT ASAHI GLASS

In 1999, AGC implemented EVA as a tool for resource allocation as well as for performance evaluation for managers and above. It was calculated using the formula:

$$EVA = NOPAT - CE \times WACC$$

NOPAT: Net Operating Profit After Tax
CE: Capital Employed
WACC: Weighted Average Cost of Capital

The 22 executive officers were evaluated based on improvement in EVA calculated using a WACC of 8%, which was the weighted average of country WACCs.

In practice, EVA rate instead of EVA was mapped to manager bonuses using a seven-grade rating system.

$$EVA\ Rate = NOPAT / (CE \times WACC)$$

Hence, an EVA rate of 1 is equivalent to an EVA of 0. About 1,400 lower level managers in Japan were evaluated based on the absolute EVA calculated using a WACC of 5%, which was based on the cost of capital in Japan in 1999. They planned to use 8% for the lower level managers as well starting 2004.

Calculating WACC for Each Country

WACC Formula

$$WACC = (1 - t)R_d \frac{D}{D + E} + R_e \frac{E}{D + E}$$

t: Tax rate

R_d: Cost of debt

R_e: Cost of equity

D: Amount of debt

E: Amount of equity

WACC measured the cost of capital using the weighted-average cost of debt and equity. Since interest payments were tax deductible, the cost of debt was reduced by the corporate tax rate.

Debt-to-Equity Ratio

A target debt-to-equity ratio of 0.7 was applied across the board for book-value basis as well as market-value basis as the assumption for the capital structure in order to reflect the company's medium-term plan. Since D/E was 0.7, one could calculate D/ (D + E) and E/ (D + E) by assigning E a value of 1 and D a value of 0.7. Therefore, for all countries:

D/(D + E) = 0.7/(0.7 + 1) = 0.41

E/(D + E) = 1/(0.7 + 1) = 0.59

Deriving Cost of Debt and Cost of Equity

Industrialized Countries In industrialized countries, the local currency was used for the calculations. The cost of debt was calculated by adding the risk-free rate in each country based on the information provided by the *Financial Times* to a credit spread of 100 basis points (a ballpark figure). Therefore, $R_d = R_{\text{risk-free}}$ + Credit Spread, where credit spread is 100 basis points.

The cost of equity was calculated using the CAPM model: adding the risk-free rate to the product of a beta[11] and the market premium based on the information provided by Ibbotson. Therefore, $R_e = R_{\text{risk-free}}$ + Beta × Market Premium.

Emerging Markets In emerging markets, the U.S. dollar was used for the calculations.

The cost of debt was calculated by adding the U.S. 10-year Treasury Bond yield, a credit spread of 100 basis points (again, a ballpark figure), and the country risk premium. Therefore, R_d = U.S. 10-year TB yield + Credit Spread + Country Risk Premium, where credit spread is 100 basis points.

---

[11]Beta is a measure of volatility of a stock relative to the overall market.

The cost of equity was estimated based on the information provided by Ibbotson and JP Morgan. CAPM was not very useful here due to the lack of historical information on the stocks.

Exhibit 8 illustrates the WACC calculation for each country.

Country Examples

Two examples of the calculations of the country WACCs performed by Michitoshi Yamada, manager at corporate controller, are as follows:

1. Industrialized Countries—Japan

$R_d = R_{risk-free} + $ Credit Spread $ = 0.84\%^{12} + 1.00\% = 1.84\%$

$R_e = R_{risk-free} + $ Beta $\times$ Market Premium $= 0.84\%^{13} + 1 \times 5.4\%^{14} = 6.24\%$

Tax rate in Japan = 42.05%

$\Rightarrow WACC_{Japan} = (1 - 42.05\%) \times 1.84\% \times 0.41 + 6.24\% \times 0.59 = 4.1\%^{15}$

2. Emerging Markets − Indonesia

$R_d = $ U.S. 10-year TB yield + Credit Spread + Country Risk Premium
$= 4.2\% + 1.00\% + 6.0\%^{16} = 11.2\%$

$R_e = (28.9\% + 15.9\%) / 2 = 22.39\%^{17}$

Tax rate in Indonesia = 30%

$\Rightarrow WACC_{Indonesia} = (1 - 30\%) \times 11.2\% \times 0.41 + 22.39\% \times 0.59 = 16.4\%^{18}$

Calculating WACC for Each Business Unit

Glass Business

AGC calculated the WACC for each BU of their glass businesses based on the weighted average of the WACC of each country in which a given business unit operated. For instance, the WACC of the flat glass business in Asia was 10.0%, which was a weighted average of the WACCs of Japan, China, Indonesia, Philippines, and Thailand. (See Exhibit 9a for WACC calculations for Asian flat glass business.)

In this calculation the cost of capital for each country was derived by modifying the cost of capital shown in Exhibit 8. The corporate controller took the average of the costs of capital of countries from Exhibit 8 for countries in each country risk categories developed by Rating and Investment Information, Inc. (R&I), a Japanese rating agency. For instance, countries such as Indonesia and Vietnam belonged to category D, and the average cost of capital of category D countries was approximately 15%. Therefore, 15% was used for all countries which belonged to category D. Similarly, 13% was used for category C countries such as China and Mexico, and 10% for category B countries such as Korea and Taiwan. For most industrialized countries or category A countries, the

---

[12]The company used the number provided by the *Financial Times*. See Exhibit 8, under Japan for Risk-Free Rate (long-term).

[13]The same as 12 above.

[14]The company used the number provided by Ibbotson. See Exhibit 8, under Japan for Market Risk Premium.

[15]Rounded to 4%.

[16]The company calculated the country risk premium based on JP Morgan Discount Rates.

[17]The company used an average of the estimates provided by JP Morgan and Ibbotson in this calculation. See Exhibit 8, under Indonesia for Equity Cost, Ibbotson, JP Morgan and Average.

[18]Rounded to 16%.

EXHIBIT 8

WACC CALCULATION FOR EACH COUNTRY

Local Currency	Risk-Free Rate (long-term)	Risk-Free Rate (short-term)	Spread (bps)	Debt Cost Before Tax	Tax Rate	Debt Cost After Tax	Market Risk Premium[a]	Cost of Equity	D/E Ratio	Debt Portion	Equity Portion	WACC	Rounded
Australia	5.46%	—	100	6.46%	30.00%	4.52%	3.50%	8.96%	0.70	1.86%	5.27%	7.13%	7%
Austria	4.35%	—	100	5.35%	34.00%	3.53%	2.50%	6.85%	0.70	1.45%	4.03%	5.48%	6%
Belgium	4.38%	—	100	5.38%	40.17%	3.22%	7.10%	11.48%	0.70	1.33%	6.75%	8.08%	8%
Canada	5.13%	—	100	6.13%	38.62%	3.76%	3.20%	8.33%	0.70	1.55%	4.90%	6.45%	6%
Denmark	4.40%	—	100	5.40%	30.00%	3.78%	9.80%	14.20%	0.70	1.56%	8.35%	9.91%	10%
France	4.31%	—	100	5.31%	34.33%	3.49%	6.90%	11.21%	0.70	1.44%	6.59%	8.03%	8%
Germany	4.29%	—	100	5.29%	38.90%	3.23%	4.70%	8.99%	0.70	1.33%	5.29%	6.62%	7%
Ireland	4.32%	—	100	5.32%	16.00%	4.47%	8.40%	12.72%	0.70	1.84%	7.48%	9.32%	9%
Italy	4.45%	—	100	5.45%	36.00%	3.49%	3.90%	8.35%	0.70	1.44%	4.91%	6.35%	6%
Japan	0.84%	—	100	1.84%	42.05%	1.07%	5.40%	6.24%	0.70	0.44%	3.67%	4.11%	4%
Netherlands	4.31%	—	100	5.31%	34.50%	3.48%	7.70%	12.01%	0.70	1.43%	7.06%	8.50%	8%
Singapore	2.60%	0.7%	100	3.60%	22.00%	2.81%	5.40%	6.10%	0.70	1.16%	3.59%	4.74%	5%
Spain	4.37%	2.6%	100	5.37%	35.26%	3.48%	5.40%	7.96%	0.70	1.43%	4.68%	6.11%	6%
Sweden	4.80%	3.6%	100	5.80%	28.00%	4.18%	12.20%	15.84%	0.70	1.72%	9.32%	11.04%	11%
United Kingdom	4.54%	—	100	5.54%	30.00%	3.88%	7.10%	11.64%	0.70	1.60%	6.85%	8.44%	8%
United States	4.18%	—	100	5.18%	39.50%	3.13%	5.30%	9.48%	0.70	1.29%	5.58%	6.87%	7%

[a]Based on short-term, risk-free rate if available.

(Continued)

EXHIBIT 8 (Continued)

WACC CALCULATION FOR EACH COUNTRY

US$	10 Year T Bond	Risk Premium	Spread	Debt Cost Before Tax	Tax Rate	Debt Cost After Tax	Equity Cost			D/E Ratio	Debt Portion	Equity Portion	WACC	Rounded
							Ibbotson	JP Morgan	Average					
China	4.18%	74	100	5.92%	33.0%	3.97%	17.4%	12.0%	14.69%	0.70	1.63%	8.64%	10.27%	10%
India	4.18%	280	100	7.98%	36.8%	5.05%	19.9%	12.6%	16.24%	0.70	2.08%	9.55%	11.63%	12%
Indonesia	4.18%	600	100	11.18%	30.0%	7.83%	28.9%	15.9%	22.39%	0.70	3.22%	13.17%	16.39%	16%
Korea	4.18%	140	100	6.58%	29.7%	4.63%	16.2%	14.7%	15.43%	0.70	1.90%	9.07%	10.98%	11%
Malaysia	4.18%	182	100	7.00%	28.0%	5.04%	18.0%	11.6%	14.79%	0.70	2.08%	8.70%	10.78%	11%
Pakistan	4.18%	850	100	13.68%	33.0%	9.17%	30.5%	20.7%	25.59%	0.70	3.77%	15.05%	18.83%	19%
Philippines	4.18%	541	100	10.59%	32.0%	7.20%	21.5%	15.2%	18.34%	0.70	2.97%	10.79%	13.75%	14%
Taiwan	4.18%	115	100	6.33%	25.0%	4.75%	13.8%	14.9%	14.37%	0.70	1.95%	8.45%	10.40%	10%
Thailand	4.18%	158	100	6.76%	30.0%	4.73%	19.8%	14.1%	16.94%	0.70	1.95%	9.97%	11.91%	12%
Vietnam	4.18%	650	100	11.68%	32.0%	7.94%	25.7%	18.7%	22.20%	0.70	3.27%	13.06%	16.33%	16%
Brazil	4.18%	1,356	100	18.74%	34.0%	12.37%	22.1%	23.4%	22.74%	0.70	5.09%	13.38%	18.47%	18%
Mexico	4.18%	305	100	8.23%	35.0%	5.35%	17.5%	12.9%	15.17%	0.70	2.20%	8.92%	11.13%	11%
Czech	4.18%	67	100	5.85%	31.0%	4.04%	16.5%	10.7%	13.58%	0.70	1.66%	7.99%	9.65%	10%
Russia	4.18%	350	100	8.68%	24.0%	6.60%	24.7%	13.7%	19.19%	0.70	2.72%	11.29%	14.00%	14%

Source: Company documents.

EXHIBIT 9A

WACC CALCULATION FOR A BUSINESS UNIT—
ASIAN FLAT GLASS BUSINESS

Country	Cost of Capital	Capital Employed	CE × CoC	WACC Contribution
Japan	7.0%	626.2	43.8	3.8%
United States	7.0%	—	—	—
United Kingdom	7.0%	—	—	—
Euro	7.0%	—	—	—
Australia	7.0%	—	—	—
Singapore	7.0%	—	—	—
China	13.0%	59.9	7.8	0.7%
India	13.0%	—	—	—
Indonesia	15.0%	120.2	18.0	1.5%
Korea	10.0%	—	—	—
Malaysia	13.0%	—	—	—
Pakistan	21.0%	—	—	—
Philippines	13.0%	101.7	13.2	1.1%
Taiwan	10.0%	—	—	—
Thailand	13.0%	258.2	33.6	2.9%
Vietnam	15.0%	—	—	—
Total		**1,166.2**	**116.4**	**10.0%**

Source: Company documents.

EXHIBIT 9B

WACC CALCULATION FOR A BUSINESS UNIT—
FLAT PANEL DISPLAY BUSINESS

Country	Cost of Capital	Capital Employed	CE × CoC	WACC Contribution
Japan	7.0%	776.0	54.3	6.2%
United States	7.0%	—	—	—
United Kingdom	7.0%	—	—	—
Euro	7.0%	—	—	—
Australia	7.0%	—	—	—
Singapore	7.0%	—	—	—
China	13.0%	—	—	—
India	13.0%	—	—	-
Indonesia	15.0%	—	—	—
Korea	10.0%	—	—	—
Malaysia	13.0%	—	—	—
Pakistan	21.0%	—	—	—
Philippines	13.0%	—	—	—
Taiwan	10.0%	105.7	10.6	1.2%
Thailand	13.0%	—	—	—
Vietnam	15.0%	—	—	—
Total		**881.7**	**64.9**	**7.2%**

Source: Company documents.

cost of capital was around 7%. Accordingly, 7% was used as the cost of capital for Japan, instead of 4% (the number shown in Exhibit 8). This was consistent with the general view that the current risk free rate of 0.8% was unusually low and that the historical risk free rate was around 4%.

In contrast, the WACC of AGC's flat panel display business was 7.4%. (See Exhibit 9b for WACC calculations for flat panel display business.) The difference was due to the fact that 46% of the capital employed in Asia by the flat glass business was in emerging markets with high WACCs, such as Thailand, Indonesia and Philippines, whereas 88% of the capital employed by the flat panel display business was in Japan with a relatively low country WACC of 7%.

Non-glass Businesses

For other (non-glass) businesses whose operations were primarily based in Japan, the WACC for Japan was used when calculating EVA. For instance, electronics and building materials were both assigned Japan's WACC of 7%. Initially, AGC calculated the cost of capital using the beta reflecting the risk of each business, but did not find meaningful difference across diverse business lines and resorted to the current method.

In the 18 major countries where AGC had substantial operations, WACC ranged between 7% and 15%, and tax rates ranged between 22% and 42%. At the in-house company/SBU level, WACC ranged between 7% and 10%, and tax rates between 35% and 42%. (Exhibits 10a and 10b tabulate the WACCs and tax rates of major countries and divisions, respectively).

Beta

In calculating beta for the company as a whole, AGC used the average beta of foreign glass companies such as San-Gobain, Pilkington and PPG, and also gave attention to global materials companies such as Bridgestone, Shin-Etsu Chemical and DuPont. AGC believed that the betas of domestic glass companies such as Nippon Sheet Glass and Central Glass (which held 33% and 27% of the Japanese flat glass market, respectively) were irrelevant as these companies were less global and less diversified than AGC. (Exhibit 11 shows an analysis of the competitors.) Deriving an unlevered beta of 0.7 from the average of six global materials companies and levering it by debt-to-equity ratio of 0.7, AGC used a beta of 1.0 throughout its WACC calculations.

Advantages and Shortcomings of EVA

The introduction of EVA immediately provided AGC with several advantages. For instance, all managers were more aware of the efficiency of capital and hence more sophisticated in resource allocation. EVA also made it easier to compare investment results from various countries. In the past, AGC had tended to over-invest in emerging market countries, since investment projects had been evaluated based on the deceptively low hurdle rate.

However, EVA was not a silver bullet. Many managers remained unpersuaded as to its worth, and therefore did not refer to it when making decisions. This was true at all levels; even senior management, which had made the decision to introduce EVA, still relied on operating profits to evaluate the performance of in-house companies and for developing medium-term plans. Moreover, use of EVA as a performance-evaluation measure was limited to executive officers and employees of the parent company, approximately 2.5% of the total work force. Even in these cases, EVA ended up competing

EXHIBIT 10A

WACC AND TAX RATE BY COUNTRY (FOR VALUATION)

Country	WACC	Tax Rate
Japan	7.0%	42.0%
United States	7.0%	40.0%
United Kingdom	7.0%	30.0%
Euro	7.0%	35.0%
Australia	7.0%	30.0%
Singapore	7.0%	22.0%
China	13.0%	33.0%
India	13.0%	36.8%
Indonesia	15.0%	30.0%
Korea	10.0%	29.7%
Malaysia	13.0%	28.0%
Philippines	13.0%	32.0%
Taiwan	10.0%	25.0%
Thailand	13.0%	30.0%
Brazil	13.0%	34.0%
Mexico	13.0%	35.0%
Czech	10.0%	31.0%
Russia	15.0%	24.0%

Source: Company documents.

EXHIBIT 10B

WACC AND TAX RATE BY DIVISION (FOR PERFORMANCE EVALUATION)

Division	WACC	Tax Rate
AGC Group	8.0%	38.0%
Flat Glass Co.	8.0%	37.0%
Flat Glass, Asia	10.0%	37.0%
Flat Glass, America	7.0%	40.0%
Flat Glass, Europe	7.0%	35.0%
Automotive Co.	8.0%	39.0%
Automotive, Asia	8.0%	40.0%
Automotive, America	7.0%	40.0%
Automotive, Europe	7.0%	35.0%
Display Co	8.0%	36.0%
Display, CRT	9.0%	34.0%
Display, FPD	7.0%	40.0%
Chemical	9.0%	39.0%
Electronic	7.0%	41.0%
Building Material	7.0%	42.0%
Ceramics	8.0%	40.0%
Asahi Fiber	7.0%	42.0%
ATG	7.0%	42.0%
Ise Chemical	7.0%	42.0%

Source: Company documents.

with other, older measures, such as cash flow, rather than being the sole evaluator of performance.

Some managers continued to hold fast to the belief that cash flow was a more appropriate tool for resource allocation and performance evaluation. The company was keen to improve its debt-to-equity ratio and ratings, and some felt management should focus on cash flow in the short run. Compared to conventional measures such as cash flow or ROE, EVA did not provide suitable performance targets which could be used for communication with investors.

CONCLUSION

Speaking on the challenges he faced in implementing the reform and transformation of AGC group, Ishizu commented:

> Our corporate creed says, "Never take the easy way out, but confront difficulties." But we have lost the challenging spirit. Now our culture is, "Never take the difficult way out." This is the revenge of our past success.[19]

[19]"Interview by Editor-In-Chief: Shinya Ishizu, President and CEO, Asahi Glass," *Diamond Weekly*, October 25, 2003, p. 128.

EXHIBIT 11

ANALYSIS OF COMPETITORS (IN ¥ BILLIONS)

	Shin-etsu (A)	Bridgestone (B)	Pilkington (C)	Saint-Gobain (D)	DuPont (E)	PPG (F)	Avg. (A-F)	Avg. (C,D,F)
Interest-bearing debt	178	766	242	1,093	894	314		
Short-term	114	331	123	483	192	91		
Long-term	64	435	119	610	702	223		
Shareholders' equity	812	835	134	1,385	1,895	404		
Market value	2,284	1,195	255	1,655	6,071	1,179		
Interest expense	6	27	12	70	77	22		
Interest rate before tax	3.4%	3.5%	5.0%	6.4%	8.6%	7.0%		
Tax rate	42%	42%	30%	36%	41%	41%	39%	36%
Interest rate after tax	2.0%	2.0%	3.5%	4.1%	5.1%	4.1%		
Risk-free rate	1.4%	1.4%	4.9%	5.0%	5.0%	5.0%		
Beta	1.07	0.91	0.83	0.84	0.86	0.83		
Market risk premium	6.2%	6.2%	7.9%	7.8%	6.0%	6.0%		
Required return on equity	8.0%	7.0%	11.5%	11.6%	10.2%	10.0%		
Beta, Unlevered	1.02	0.66	0.50	0.59	0.79	0.72	0.71	0.60
Beta, Levered w/ D/E 0.7	1.44	0.93	0.74	0.85	1.12	1.01	1.02	0.87
D/E, book value basis	0.22	0.92	1.81	0.79	0.47	0.78	0.83	1.12
D/E, market value basis	0.08	0.64	0.95	0.66	0.15	0.27	0.46	0.62
WACC, book value basis	6.9%	4.7%	6.3%	8.3%	8.5%	7.4%		
WACC, market value basis	7.6%	5.1%	7.6%	8.6%	9.5%	8.8%		
Total assets	1,289	2,444	535	3,734	5,287	1,108		
Enterprise value	2,462	1,961	497	2,748	6,965	1,493		

Source: Company documents.

Through the mid-1980s, AGC had experienced decades of rapid growth, enjoying the benefits of oligopoly in both the domestic and international markets. Looking back on his efforts, Ishizu admitted that he had underestimated how difficult it would be to transform the culture of a large, successful company with a century-long history. Now five years into a six-year expected term (at AGC, presidents traditionally retired after six years), he commented on his situation:

> My biggest concern is how to make all employees embrace the change. We have already crossed the Rubicon and there is no going back. So we must develop a culture to ensure transformation.

Ishizu's main objective was to implement a mechanism that would allow AGC to continually adapt itself to an ever-changing global business environment. He was asking himself how such a mechanism might be implemented.

VALUING CROSS-BORDER INVESTMENTS

Cross-border mergers and acquisitions activity accounts for approximately one-third of all global mergers and acquisitions activity. These transactions run the gamut from strategic acquisitions to leveraged buyouts in foreign markets. The deals also play out in both directions—not only are U.S. companies looking abroad for acquisition targets but foreign companies are increasingly adding U.S. companies to their portfolios. DaimlerBenz's acquisition of Chrysler in 1998 and IBM's sale of its personal computing division to Lenovo are only the most recognizable of many such transactions. The growth of this market, where corporate divisions and entire companies alike trade hands across borders, opens up new issues for the financial manager in a multinational company. Managers have to understand how to value such deals in order to navigate these broader markets.

The complications managers face start at the very foundation of financial analysis: how to discount expected cash flows. This is the focus of the first case in this module. Valuing a Cross-Border LBO: Bidding on the Yell Group sets the foundation by addressing how a bidder should value a firm with operations in two countries—the United States and the United Kingdom. The central questions are: how do managers value cash flows that are in multiple currencies? Should exchange rate effects be incorporated in discount rates or expected cash flows? The relative stability of the currencies involved allows the case to focus on the basics of cross-border valuation. In addition to the valuation issues, methods of financing—particularly for a leveraged buyout (LBO) setting—are also discussed and incorporated into the valuation.

Asking "what is the right discount rate?" in the emerging market setting is even more complex as country risk becomes a significant factor. Managers have to understand the assumptions underpinning country risk adjustments and the implications of such adjustments. This is especially true for managers responsible for a portfolio of international investments across countries. These issues are explored in Globalizing the Cost of Capital and Capital Budgeting at AES. With the market downturn in 2000, AES was forced to reevaluate its static capital budgeting procedures for its global network of operations, especially in developing countries. This case looks at the method for globalizing the cost of capital and the appropriateness of AES's model. Is there an emerging market discount rate? Does each emerging market have its own discount rate? How does a multinational financial manager balance the complexity costs of calculating different rates for each decision with the need to make decisions quickly? This case provides a rich setting for thinking about cross-border valuation when country-risk is involved.

The final case, Dow Chemical's Bid for the Privatization of PBB in Argentina, examines a strategic acquisition in a special international setting: a government-run privatization transaction. Argentina's decision to privatize a major petrochemical producer (PBB) opened the window for Dow Chemical to become the largest plastics producer in Latin America. In this case, readers imagine themselves in Dow's shoes and must grapple with a full valuation in an emerging market setting. Although the AES case emphasizes discount rates, the Dow case emphasizes adjustments to cash flows to reflect the idiosyncrasies of operating in an emerging market.

OVERVIEW OF THE CASES

Valuing a Cross-Border LBO: Bidding on the Yell Group

In this case, two of the largest firms in global private equity, Apax Partners and Hicks, Muse, Tate & Furst, join forces to bid for Yell, a division of British Telecom (BT). Yell publishes business directories in two countries: BT Yellow Pages in the United Kingdom and Yellow Book USA in the United States. BT anticipates raising as much as £2 billion from the sale of the Yell assets; this large transaction would be a significant event in the still-developing European private equity market. The private equity consortium must value Yell and decide how much to bid for the business.

The key issue in the case is how to value an enterprise with businesses in different countries and cash flows in different currencies. The proposed leveraged buy-out (LBO) of Yell also raises the question of the appropriate discounted cash flow method to use for a business that will assume a lot of debt, and poses the problem of how to build financial models for two very different businesses. These business differences—both in terms of strategic characteristics and growth rates—also complicate the valuation. Questions one should be able to answer include:

- Is Yell a good buyout candidate?
- How would you approach Yell's valuation? In particular, how will your valuation incorporate the fact that cash flows are in sterling and dollars?
- Do the management projections in Exhibits 6 and 7 make sense to you? In other words, if you were part of the Apax/Hicks Muse team, would you trust them?
- What is the effect of high leverage on those projections?
- Please consider the Capital Cash Flows (CCF) method in building your analytical model. How much is Yell worth? How much would you bid?
- How does your answer to the previous question change if you value the business with the adjusted present value (APV) method instead of the CCF method?
- If you were Apax/Hicks Muse would you do the deal? How much is this deal worth to the private equity investors?

Globalizing the Cost of Capital and Capital Budgeting at AES

AES is a global electricity firm with operations in 30 countries and on five continents. The company operates in four business segments: utilities, contract generation, competitive supply, and growth distribution. AES grew rapidly after it went public in 1991, and much of its growth came from its international expansion. The global economic downturn that began in late 2000, however, saw AES's market capitalization decline dramatically. The company was hit by currency devaluations in South America, lower energy prices, and changes in the regulatory regimes for energy in some countries.

The financial crisis led AES to create a new planning group, charged with revaluing the company's assets and developing a methodology for calculating the cost of capital for AES's diverse businesses around the world. In the past, AES used a 12% cost of capital to evaluate all projects. Rob Venerus, the director of the new planning group, aims to improve on this across-the-board approach. He is considering a methodology that incorporates both country and other risks specific to a project into the cost of capital for each project. The purpose of the new methodology is to provide a more accurate financial assessment of the company's diverse international businesses and projects, and Venerus has to decide if this approach would improve AES's financial decision making. The case builds an understanding of the finance theory and economic justification for applying discount rates that reflect country-specific risks. The following questions should help in working through the case:

- How would you evaluate the capital budgeting method used historically by AES? What is good and bad about it?

- If you implemented the methodology suggested by Venerus, what would be the range of discount rates one would use around the world?

- Does this make sense as a way to do capital budgeting?

- How big a value difference does this new approach make to the Pakistan project?

- How do these cost of capital modifications translate into changed probabilities in terms of real events?

Dow Chemical's Bid for the Privatization of PBB in Argentina

In 1995, the Argentine government announced plans to privatize 51% of PBB, a company that produced ethylene and polyethylene. The acquisition of PBB would make Dow Chemical Company the leading polyethylene producer in Latin America. Dow's regional executives have to assess the risks of the acquisition as well as its long-term potential. PBB is an attractive investment to Dow for several reasons. Polyethylene is used mainly in packaging, and the Latin American market for the product is projected to grow substantially as standards of living improve and consumers demand higher-quality packaging. Argentina appears to have achieved some economic stability in recent years, with the peso pegged to the U.S. dollar and the government committed to a program of economic reforms. The PBB production facilities, however, need to be upgraded to world standards, and Dow anticipates that additional investments in capacity will be required to consolidate its market position in polyethylene. The overall project, therefore, includes investments in addition to PBB, and this makes the valuation more complex. Given Argentina's long history of economic turmoil, Dow's executives have to consider how risks such as currency crises will affect the project. The Dow executives need to identify the project's key risks, decide how to incorporate these risks into the valuation, and determine what to bid for PBB.

This case explores the risks and opportunities for multinationals in emerging markets and how to incorporate them into valuation. It emphasizes understanding how helpful scenario analysis can be. Think about the following questions while evaluating Dow's situation:

- What risks *specifically* is Dow exposed to in Argentina?
- How should those risks be incorporated into a valuation of the privatization possibility?
- What would happen to these assets in the worst case?
- How does the fact that the state is the seller change your bidding strategy?
- What would you bid for these assets?

Each of these cases requires readers to use and to question familiar valuation approaches, and to explore how valuation is different in an international context.

ADDITIONAL READING

DESAI, MIHIR A., C. FRITZ FOLEY, and KRISTIN FORBES. 2004. "Financial Constraints and Growth: Multinational and Local Firm Responses to Currency Crises." NBER Working Paper No. 10545.

DIMSON, ELROY, PAUL MARSH, and MIKE STAUNTON. 2002, September. "Global Evidence on the Equity Risk Premium." *Journal of Applied Corporate Finance* (15:4): 27–38.

O'BRIEN, THOMAS. 2004. "Foreign Exchange and Cross-Border Valuation." *Journal of Applied Corporate Finance* (16): 147–154.

SABAL, JAIME. 2004. "The Discount Rate in Emerging Markets: A Guide." *Journal of Applied Corporate Finance* (16): 155–166.

10

Valuing a Cross-Border LBO: Bidding on the Yell Group

By Friday April 13, 2001, the team from Apax Partners and Hicks, Muse, Tate & Furst had been working around the clock all week. They were preparing their investment proposal for the largest European leveraged buyout transaction ever executed by a financial buyer: the acquisition of Yell Holdings from British Telecom (BT). Hicks Muse and Apax, two of the biggest names in the global private equity industry, had joined forces to acquire the directories business of BT, a business that owned and operated assets in both the United Kingdom and the United States. The team was under pressure to reach a final consensus on the valuation of Yell and how much to bid for it. The deal was crucially important to both Apax and Hicks Muse because of its high visibility—simply by virtue of its size and complexity, it would leave its mark on the reputations of both private equity firms.

The valuation of Yell was complicated by the cross-border nature of the deal. Yell consisted of two main assets: BT Yellow Pages, the market-leading classified directory business in the United Kingdom; and Yellow Book USA, the market-leading independent publisher of business directories in the United States. Not only were those businesses located in different markets, but they also were had by different growth rates and cash flow characteristics. Further complicating matters, each business unit faced an immediate uncertainty. The U.K.'s Office of Fair Trading (OFT) was reviewing BT Yellow Pages's leading position in the classified directories advertising services market. The OFT was expected to recommend the imposition of a limit on the annual increase in rates for advertising, thereby affecting BT Yellow Pages' valuation. It was critical to understand how much value was dependent on such regulatory imposition. At the same time, Yellow Book USA's management was projecting continued rapid expansion into new markets. Their financial forecasts were based on sustained future growth and high EBITDA margins from the business. The Apax and Hicks Muse professionals noticed

Professor Mihir A. Desai, Paolo Notarnicola (MBA '02), and Research Associate Mark F. Veblen prepared this case. Certain details have been disguised. HBS cases are developed solely as the basis for class discussion. Cases are not intended to serve as endorsements, sources of primary data, or illustrations of effective or ineffective management.

the assumption of significant investment to expand the business, and they wondered how sensitive the value of the combined entity was to these assumptions.

Two investment banks, Merrill Lynch and CIBC World Markets, had been chosen as partners for the deal. Provisionally, they would lead a syndicate contributing £1.45 billion of total debt to finance the acquisition. This borrowing would take the form of £950 million in senior debt and £500 million in bridge loans to be repaid with the proceeds of a future high-yield offering. BT would also contribute £100 million in the form of vendor loan notes. With the banks' documentation and all business projections in front of them, the two private equity groups had to decide whether to proceed further with the deal and, if so, how to arrive at an appropriate bid. The clock was ticking, and the Apax/Hicks Muse team needed concrete answers. How much was Yell worth? How much to bid? And, most importantly, was the Yell buyout a good deal for Apax Partners and Hicks Muse?

THE SPONSORS

Apax Partners and Hicks, Muse, Tate, & Furst were among the leading private equity groups in the world.[1]

Apax Partners was formed in 1977 when MMG (founded in 1972) joined forces with U.S.-based Alan Patricof Associates (founded in 1969). By 2001 Apax managed almost $12 billion on behalf of leading institutional investors around the world. The firm had 150 investment professionals operating in 10 countries across Europe, Israel, Japan, and the United States (through Patricof & Co. Ventures). Apax had a strong track record in the telecoms and media sector, with investments including Jazztel, The Stationery Office, Future Publishing, and Ginger Media Group. In 1999, Apax Funds acquired TDL Infomedia, Yell's main competitor in the United Kingdom, which it subsequently sold to SEAT Pagine Gialle in 2000 for a transaction value of 745 million euros.

The Dallas-based Hicks, Muse, Tate & Furst raised its initial fund in 1989. Since its inception, Hicks Muse had invested approximately $10 billion of equity capital in over 65 platform portfolio investments and over 300 add-on acquisitions with combined transaction values exceeding $50 billion. After opening its European office in London in 1998, the firm was looking to expand its presence on the continent. At that time, Hicks Muse was the largest private equity media owner in the world, with more than $4 billion invested in media sector transactions. Among Hicks Muse's key media investments were Clear Channel Communications, LIN Television, Davivo International, Mandeville Cable, International Outdoor Advertising, Marcus Cable, and Claxson Interactive Group. Hicks Muse had made a number of acquisitions in Europe including Media Capital, a Portuguese company with activities in television, radio, newspapers, and magazines. The firm had recently declared its return to a "back-to-basics" strategy, which meant investing in media, branded consumer goods, and manufacturing industries.

Apax managed one of the largest European private equity funds, worth €4.4 billion, while Hicks Muse would use its $1.5 billion dedicated European fund to help pay for the purchase, should the deal be closed.

---

[1]This section is based on the Offering Memorandum for the high-yield offering, "Yell Finance B.V.," August 6, 2001, Merrill Lynch International (Sole Book-Running Manager) and CIBC World Markets (Joint Lead Manager), p. 3; and the following press clippings: "Two buyout firms will acquire Yell of Britain," *The New York Times*, May 28, 2001, and "Hicks, Apax Take Yell from BT," *Buyouts*, June 4, 2001.

THE EUROPEAN PRIVATE EQUITY MARKET

Compared to the United States, the private equity market for large transactions in Europe was still at an early stage (see Exhibit 1 for a recent history of European LBOs). Nevertheless, increased attention from major players was bringing more competition into the market. Successful European funds (e.g., BC Partners, CVC Capital, Schroder Ventures) were aggressively targeting growth and restructuring opportunities mainly in the United Kingdom, France, and Germany. At the same time, some of the most prominent U.S. private equity funds were also moving into Europe. In particular, U.S. banks and private equity investors were shifting portfolios toward Europe because of a belief that Europe would in time mirror the size and depth of the U.S. buyout market.

Critical to the development of the European buyout market was the growth of the European high-yield debt market—the preferred instrument for financing these large leveraged acquisitions. Even though issuance was expected to increase significantly in the next two years, the European high-yield market was still developing as an asset class (see Exhibit 2). European high-yield markets did not offer either the diversification (bonds from telecoms, media, and cable companies made up almost 70% of the market value in 2000) or the depth (there was little liquidity in the European secondary market) of the U.S. markets. This exposed investors to greater risk (and therefore generally lowered pricing levels), because small amounts of selling pressure could lead to plummeting bond prices.[2]

By the middle of 2001, the high-yield funds began to experience net inflows, and fresh capital was being placed into new issues. Goldman Sachs's high-yield indices showed that spreads on high-yield debt had begun to reverse their steady increase since February (see Exhibit 3). In particular, spreads on CCC-rated paper were declining sharply. Some analysts interpreted such data as evidence of increasing investor risk appetite in the market.[3] Indeed, a record issue of almost $500 million was planned in May for Messer Griesheim, the industrial gases company in which Allianz Capital Partners and Goldman Sachs had bought a two-thirds share at the beginning of 2001. A £220 million issue that year to finance the buyout of United Biscuits by Cinven, PAI Management, and DB Capital had also been very successful.

YELL GROUP LIMITED

Yell Group Ltd. was the company to be created to act as a holding company for the Yellow Pages business in the United Kingdom and the Yellow Book business in the United States. British Telecom, under pressure to reduce its heavy debt load, had been wavering for months about the future of its two Yellow Pages divisions.[4] Investors in BT, one of the giants in the European telecommunication industry, were concerned about BT's high leverage and the generally adverse conditions BT was facing in the telecom market. Year-to-date its stock price had declined 15% compared with a 5% drop in the FTSE 100 stock index. (See Exhibits 4 and 5 for a history of financial results and stock price performance for BT.)

Shortly before Apax and Hicks Muse had initiated talks with BT executives about the future of Yell, the telecom giant had announced plans to raise £11 billion by selling

---

[2]See "Brightness fading fast," *The Financial Times*, November 1, 2000 available on line at http://specials.ft.com/.

[3]Dresdner Kleinwort Wasserstein Research report, "Credit Check," May 24, 2001, Dresdner Kleinwort Wasserstein, pp. 6–7.

[4]Anjana Menon and Tom Bawden, "Hicks Muse, Apax cut offer for BT Yellow Pages: Yell unit forced to lower ad rates," *National Post*, May 25, 2001; Charles Pretzik, "BT looks ready to sell Yell for GBP 2bn," *The Financial Times*, May 25, 2001.

EXHIBIT 1

EUROPEAN LEVERAGED BUYOUTS FOR A TRANSACTION VALUE OVER $1 BILLION, 1999–2001

Date	Target Name	Business Description	Acquirors	Value ($ millions)	Debt Providers
03/20/01	Fairbar	Pubs and bars	Morgan Grenfell Private Equity	2,328	Lehman
03/01/01	Messer Griesheim GmbH	Industrial gases	Allianz Capital, Goldman Sachs	2,467	N.A.
09/25/00	Laporte	Chemicals	Kohlberg Kravis Roberts & Company	1,182	Chase Manhattan, Merrill Lynch, Goldman Sachs
01/09/00	General Healthcare Group	Hospitals	BC Partners	1,860	Morgan Stanley
07/21/00	Tomkins PLC	Food manufacturing	Doughty Hanson & Company	1,700	JP Morgan
02/22/00	North Rhine Westphalia	Cable network	Callahan Associates International	2,785	Salomon Smith Barney
12/17/99	United Biscuits	Food manufacturing	PAI Management, Cinven, DB Capital	2,024	Deutsche Bank, DLJ European Private Equity
12/05/99	Zeneca Specialties	Chemicals	Cinven, Investcorp	2,100	Chase Manhattan, The Industrial Bank of Japan
02/22/99	William Hill	Betting shops	Cinven, CVC Capital Partners	1,337	The Industrial Bank of Japan

Source: Thomson Financial Securities Data.

EXHIBIT 2

EUROPEAN AND U.S. HIGH-YIELD BONDS ISSUANCE, TOP 10 UNDERWRITERS IN 2000

Managing Bank	Number of Issues	Total ($ millions)	Share (%)[a]
European Market			
Credit Suisse First Boston	7	3,115	34.3%
Merrill Lynch	6	1,147	12.6%
Citigroup/Salomon Smith Barney	4	907	10.0%
JP Morgan	5	854	9.4%
Goldman Sachs	4	744	8.2%
Lehman Brothers	2	269	3.0%
Dresdner Kleinwort Wasserstein	1	241	2.6%
ABN AMRO	1	198	2.2%
CIBC World Markets	1	193	2.1%
Morgan Stanley	1	144	1.6%
US Market			
Credit Suisse First Boston	26	6,913	20.3%
Goldman Sachs	12	4,586	13.4%
Morgan Stanley	15	4,492	13.2%
Citigroup/Salomon Smith Barney	16	4,366	12.8%
JP Morgan	15	2,750	8.1%
Deutsche Bank	13	2,484	7.3%
Banc of America Securities	11	2,177	6.4%
Merrill Lynch	9	1,769	5.2%
Lehman Brothers	6	1,686	4.9%
UBS Warburg	4	735	2.2%

[a]Based on share of total issuances in 2000 by all underwriters.

Source: Thomson Financial Securities Data.

---

assets and shares as it tried to pay down some of its £28 billion of debt.[5] In addition to an outright sale, BT had considered a demerger of the directories business or a partial stock market floatation. According to *The Financial Times*, the Apax/Hicks Muse consortium was just one of at least three groups understood to have approached BT about Yell. Another private equity consortium, including Kohlberg Kravis Roberts and Texas Pacific Group, was also interested, as was SEAT Pagine Gialle, the Italian Yellow Pages business.

The most serious competition for Apax/Hicks Muse and the other groups promoting a buyout came from the possibility of a demerger, which would result in a separation of the directories business (Yell) from BT followed by a distribution of 90% of the shares of the directories business to existing BT shareholders. In the demerger scenario, Yell would have carried up to £1 billion of BT debt onto its own balance sheet. A floatation of up to 20% of the directories business would have raised up to £1 billion, but was no longer under consideration because of the recent decline in stock prices. Investors, however, seemed to prefer an outright sale, welcoming the prospect of more than £2 billion of cash flowing into BT.[6]

[5]BT reported £12.1 billion of loans and other borrowings embedded in net current assets.

[6]"Apax and Hicks Muse head consortium to buy Yell," *PrivateEquityOnline.com*, April 5, 2001, ⟨http://www.privateequityonline.com/⟩; Clive Mathieson, "BT holds talks over Pounds 2.5bn trade sale of Yell," *The Times (London)*, April 6, 2001.

EXHIBIT 3

SPREADS ON THE GOLDMAN SACHS EUROPEAN HIGH-YIELD INDICES (BASIS POINTS)

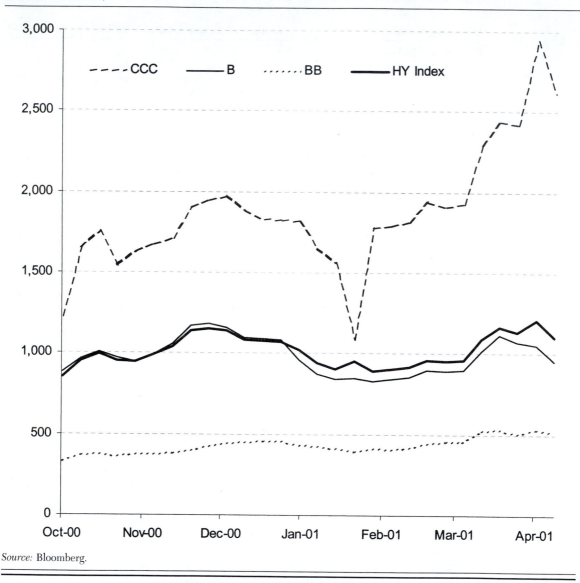

Source: Bloomberg.

BT Yellow Pages

BT Yellow Pages was a series of annual, regional, classified directories that listed the name, address, and telephone number of substantially all business telephone subscribers in the United Kingdom. The listings were organized into over 2,500 available classifications, with more than one classification potentially applicable to a business. In the 2000 fiscal year (ending on March 31), BT Yellow Pages directories contained 813,000 advertisements for approximately 390,000 advertisers. That represented nearly 85% of the U.K. classified directories advertising revenues.

EXHIBIT 4

BRITISH TELECOM-SELECTED HISTORICAL FINANCIAL INFORMATION, 1996–2000 (POUNDS IN MILLIONS, EXCEPT PER-SHARE DATA)

	Years Ended 31 March				
	1997	**1998**	**1999**	**2000**	**2001**
Income Statement					
Total turnover	17,379	17,411	18,223	21,903	29,666
Total operating profit (loss)	3,429	3,461	3,474	3,198	(336)
Profit on sale of fixed assets	8	63	1,107	126	619
Net interest payable	(174)	(310)	(286)	(382)	(1,314)
Profit (loss) before taxation	3,203	3,214	4,295	2,942	(1,031)
Profit (loss) after taxation	2,101	1,727	3,002	2,045	(1,683)
Minority interests	(24)	(25)	(19)	10	(127)
Profit (loss) for the financial year	2,077	1,702	2,983	2,055	(1,810)
Basic earnings (loss) per share	32.8p	26.6p	46.3p	31.7p	(27.7)p
Cash Flow Statement					
Cash flow from operating activities	6,185	6,071	6,035	5,849	5,887
Dividends from associates and JVs	7	5	2	5	10
Investment Return & Finance Servicing	(220)	(160)	(328)	(163)	(727)
Taxation paid	(1,045)	(1,886)	(630)	(1,311)	(669)
Capital expenditure and investment	(2,820)	(3,108)	1	(3,752)	(8,442)
Acquisitions and disposals	(252)	(1,501)	(1,967)	(6,405)	(13,754)
Equity dividends paid	(1,217)	(3,473)	(1,186)	(1,364)	(1,432)
Management of liquid resources	(504)	2,247	(2,447)	1,236	(480)
Financing	(224)	1,794	(458)	5,959	19,735
Incr. (decr.) in cash for the year	(90)	(11)	67	54	128
Decr. (incr.) in net debt for the year	849	(3,860)	3,146	(6,582)	(18,942)
Balance Sheet					
Intangible fixed assets	N/A	N/A	742	5,777	18,380
Tangible fixed assets	16,802	17,252	17,854	18,163	21,625
Fixed asset investments	1,273	1,708	1,832	5,878	5,204
Net current assets (liabilities)	(2,667)	(2,637)	(495)	(7,115)	(11,143)
LT loans and other borrowings	(2,693)	(3,889)	(3,386)	(5,354)	(18,775)
Provisions for liabilities & charges	(1,391)	(1,426)	(1,391)	(1,056)	(723)
Minority interests	(208)	(223)	(216)	(498)	(499)
Total equity shareholders' funds	11,116	10,785	14,940	15,795	14,069
Total assets	25,062	23,285	27,962	37,588	54,799

Source: British Telecom.

Yellow pages advertising expenditures tended to be more stable than other forms of media advertising and did not fluctuate widely with economic cycles. They were considered a "must buy" by many small and medium-sized businesses since the yellow pages were their principal means of reaching customers in the United Kingdom. The strength of the yellow pages as compared with other forms of advertising lay in its consumer reach, lasting presence, and cost-effectiveness. The following table illustrates the growth of the classified directories market in comparison to the overall advertising market in the United Kingdom.

TABLE A   Growth in the Advertising Market, 1985–1999

	Classified Directories Advertising Market			Total Advertising Market		
	1985–1999	1985–1995	1996–1999	1985–1999	1985–1995	1996–1999
Nominal	10.4%	12.0%	6.6%	7.9%	7.9%	8.0%
Real	6.1%	7.0%	3.8%	3.7%	3.1%	5.1%

Source: Apax Partners, adapted by casewriter.

The economics of the business were dependent on the number of advertisements sold in a given year and the advertisements' prices. Such prices varied according to different types and dimensions of advertisements. Premium options upgraded the appearance of advertisements by adding bold face or color type and graphics. For an additional charge, special placement in the directory—on the back cover, for instance—could be purchased. Management forecasted the business performance in terms of number of advertisements to be sold each year and average price per advertisement (see Exhibit 6). Management also provided estimates of costs for discounts and promotions, other direct costs, and overhead costs together with working capital and capital expenditures requirements for this business.

Regulation[7]

In 1995, the U.K. Office of Fair Trading, the government agency responsible for enforcing antitrust policy, undertook a review of the classified directories industry due to concerns regarding the market position of BT Yellow Pages. The Monopolies and Mergers Commission investigated the issue and concluded that BT Yellow Pages held a monopoly position in the classified directories advertising services market and that prices were "higher than would be the case if competition were effective."[8] The Commission recommended the imposition of a limit on the annual increase in rates for advertising in BT Yellow Pages. For a period of three years, BT Yellow Pages could increase the average price of its advertisements by the inflation rate (as indicated by the official U.K. Retail Price Index) minus 2%. This had happened each year for three years leading up to March 2001.

In April 2001, the Office of Fair Trading began investigating the issue again. Many sources indicated that the government agency would recommend a permitted rate of growth in prices of inflation less an even larger adjustment. Although Yell management was not as pessimistic, Apax/Hicks Muse speculated that the Office of Fair Trading would cap the advertising price growth rates at 6% below the inflation rate. In other words, starting from year 2002, the average advertisement price was expected to decline since projections for inflation were 2.4% in 2002, 2.3% in 2003, and 2.0% thereafter. As a result, the management's top-line revenue projections would have to be revised. The Office of Fair Trading was expected to announce its new recommendation for the following years soon, so it was crucially important for

[7]Offering Memorandum for the high-yield offering, "Yell Finance B.V.," August 6, 2001, Merrill Lynch International (Sole Book-Running Manager) and CIBC World Markets (Joint Lead Manager), p. 74.

[8]Monopoly and Mergers Commission report on classified advertising services, chapter 1, available at ⟨http://www.competition-commission.org.uk/rep_pub/reports/1996/383classified.htm⟩.

EXHIBIT 5

BRITISH TELECOM'S SHARE PRICE DATA (PENCE/SHARE)

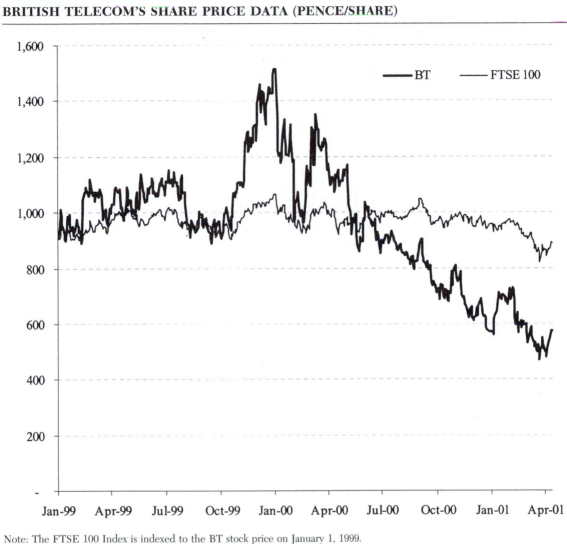

Note: The FTSE 100 Index is indexed to the BT stock price on January 1, 1999.

Source: British Telecom.

the sponsors to understand how sensitive the Yell valuation was to the price caps dictated by regulators.

Yellow Book USA

Yellow Book was the market-leading independent publisher of yellow pages directories in the United States. In 2001, Yellow Book published 270 directories with a combined circulation of over 26 million copies in 18 states east of the Mississippi River. It had approximately $330 million in revenues and $42 million in EBITDA. (See Exhibit 7 for

EXHIBIT 6

BT YELLOW PAGES—HISTORICAL FINANCIAL INFORMATION AND MANAGEMENT PROJECTIONS FOR THE BUSINESS, 1999–2005 (POUNDS IN THOUSANDS)

Year	Actual 31-Mar-00	Actual 31-Mar-01	Projected 31-Mar-02	Projected 31-Mar-03	Projected 31-Mar-04	Projected 31-Mar-05	Projected 31-Mar-06	Projected 31-Mar-07
Advertisement Volume (000s)	813	853	927	991	1,058	1,126	1,194	1,254
Weighted Average Advertisement Price (£)	641	645	644	648	649	649	649	649
Discounts and free ads (£000s)	42,402	47,276	78,180	86,585	84,324	86,615	85,366	86,049
Direct costs (£000s)	180,479	187,395	195,972	201,742	206,649	211,278	214,996	216,716
Overhead costs (£000s)[a]	102,530	88,870	74,930	77,137	79,013	80,783	82,204	82,862
Change in WC (£000s)	10,570	12,772	2,178	6,000	8,497	6,300	4,375	2,023
Capex (£000s)	7,380	9,760	10,220	9,730	9,230	8,380	8,000	8,000
Depreciation (£000s)	5,530	5,370	6,130	8,850	8,400	7,630	8,000	8,000
Other U.K. businesses:								
Capital cash flows after taxes (£000s)	(4,566)	(14,438)	(12,641)	(8,238)	1,362	1,956	10,000[b]	20,000[b]

[a]Does not include depreciation.

[b]Starting in 2006, cash flows from Other U.K. Businesses should grow dramatically into the tens of millions of pounds. Management, however, found it difficult to evaluate the cash stream post–2005 given the high uncertainty surrounding those future projections.

Source: Apax Partners; casewriter estimates; figures have been disguised.

EXHIBIT 7

YELLOW BOOK USA—HISTORICAL FINANCIAL INFORMATION AND MANAGEMENT PROJECTIONS FOR THE BUSINESS, 1999–2005 (DOLLAR FIGURES IN THOUSANDS)

Year	Actual 31-Mar-00	Actual 31-Mar-01	Projected 31-Mar-02	Projected 31-Mar-03	Projected 31-Mar-04	Projected 31-Mar-05	Projected 31-Mar-06	Projected 31-Mar-07
New launches (number)	n/a	n/a	7	8	7	8	0	0
Total Revenues ($000s)	217,500	330,000	421,600	483,200	544,050	598,600	688,390	757,229
Capex ($000s)	3,698	7,000	10,600	8,700	8,170	8,990	8,000	8,000
Depreciation	N/A	7,000	6,240	7,910	7,430	8,810	8,000	8,000

Source: Apax Partners; casewriter estimates; figures have been disguised.

213

historical financial information and management's projections for the business.) British Telecom had purchased Yellow Book USA in August 1999 for $665 million.

The U.S. yellow pages market was a $13 billion industry that had been growing at a steady 4%–5% per year. The yellow pages were an important source of new business for small to medium-sized enterprises (SMEs) throughout the country. It was estimated that 80% of consumer purchases in the United States were made within 20 miles from home. Recognizing this tendency, 75% of SMEs advertised in the yellow pages.

The industry had been historically dominated by the Regional Bell Operating Companies (RBOCs). RBOCs had continued to rely upon their well-established brands and had grown directory revenues primarily through rate increases. They had generally treated the directory business as a "cash cow" and had offered the directory as an added service rather than a main vehicle for growth. The industry dynamics had been slowly changing over the previous decade as independent directory providers had emerged. Independents experienced a growth rate of 19.8% in 2000 versus 4.3% for the RBOCs, and the independents were projected to increase their market share from 11% to 30% over the 2000–2005 period. For Yellow Book, this growth was to be fueled by expansion efforts such as launching new directories into contiguous markets and launching wide area books into cities without an independent presence.

New Market Launches

Hoping to capture much of the predicted market share gains, Yellow Book's growth plans were ambitious. Although the Apax/Hicks Muse team was confident that some organic growth could be achieved in the next few years, they thought that an aggressive strategy of new product launches would have to complement organic growth in order to achieve management projections on the revenue side. As a result, they built several new launches each year into their forecasts (see Exhibit 7).

Management expected EBITDA margins to increase as the portfolio matured. In their experience very low margins were achieved in the first year of operations for new launches. Margins could improve significantly and almost match margins on organic sales in the second year of operations. Accordingly, the sponsors thought it important to segregate organic revenues from new launch revenues and only apply an EBITDA margin to organic sales while separately adding in the impact of new launches in order to roll the two very different types of markets together. The sponsors believed that a 17% EBITDA margin on organic sales was a more realistic target for 2002, improving at a 2% increase per year as business went up until the 25% target rate was hit in 2005 and maintained thereafter.

Since the risk of a cold launch was perceived to be too high in a new market given a strong incumbent publisher or lack of Yellow Book brand awareness, management had opted in the past to give away advertising for one year for free. This approach involved identifying the advertisers in the incumbents' books and providing them with a similar advertisement at no cost in the first year. This required an investment in direct sales costs (first-year discounts, free copies, promotions, and costs of prototyping) of around $4 million in the first year of each launch. This initial-year investment was particularly significant when compared with first-year average revenues of $8.1 million for each launch. Moreover, there was significant uncertainty around these revenues figures (the sponsors believed they could range between $5 million and $11 million), so Apax/Hicks Muse felt it necessary to segregate out the organic revenues from the revenues associated with new launches, all of which management had rolled up into a single top-line forecast. This approach also afforded an opportunity to give a more so-phisticated treatment to operating income from new launches, which could not be derived as reliably from applying EBITDA margins to new launch revenues as could EBITDA from organic revenues.

Working Capital

It was the norm in the U.S. and the U.K. to take a very small up-front deposit and to bill the customer monthly over the 12 months post publication. As a rule of thumb it would take 180 days (on average) to receive payment from customers. (A $34 million increase in working capital in 2001 had been unusually low in management's view—an anomaly stemming from the early stage of the business.) On the contrary, payables turned over in approximately one month.

Other U.K. Businesses

In addition to its core directory business, BT Yellow Pages owned and operated four relatively small divisions in which the company had invested £14 million in 2001. These divisions were:

- Business Pages: six directory editions aimed at the business-to-business market.
- Talking Pages: a 24-hour, telephone-based, operator-assisted directory service.
- Business Database: direct marketing and database development services to businesses in the United Kingdom.
- Yell.com: an interactive, consumer-facing edition of Yellow Pages' U.K. listing data, searchable by business type, company name, and postcode.

While the sponsors recognized that such businesses could represent some potential good opportunities in the future, projections over the five-year time horizon of the prospective investment indicated that those businesses were still in their early stages. (Exhibit 6 details the expected cash flow after taxes from other U.K. businesses.)

DEAL STRUCTURE AND FINANCING

Merrill Lynch and CIBC World Markets had agreed to raise £1.45 billion of debt through £950 million of syndicated senior term loans and £500 million through a bridge loan to be refinanced via a high-yield offering on the U.K. and U.S. markets. The senior term loans and bridge loan would be drawn down in full at closing to fund the acquisition. Apax/Hicks Muse believed that the subsequent high-yield bond issuance to pay off the bridge loan would require a yield of between 10% and 11.5%. Moreover Apax/Hicks Muse had arranged for an additional vendor loan from British Telecom for £100 million (see Exhibit 8 for a summary of debt terms and conditions) and a £100 million revolving credit facility to provide a cushion for working capital swings.

Exhibit 9 illustrates the planned corporate structure (devised by accountants PwC and lawyers Weil, Gotshal & Manges) and the company's ownership following the buyout. The new parent company, Yell Group Limited, would establish a wholly owned subsidiary, Yell Finance B.V., to act as the issuer of the high-yield offering, and this

EXHIBIT 8

DEBT PACKAGE OFFERED BY MERRILL LYNCH—CBIC WORLD MARKETS (POUNDS IN MILLIONS)

Debt	Amount	Interest	Type
Senior Term Loan A	£600	Libor[a] + 2.5%	7-year amortizing[b]
Senior Term Loan B	£175	Libor + 2.75%	8-year bullet
Senior Term Loan C	£175	Libor + 3.0%	9-year bullet
High Yield bond	£500	10.75% expected	10-year instrument
Vendor Loan	£100	Libor (rolled)[c]	12-year bullet
Revolving Credit Facility	£100	Libor + 2.5%	undrawn at closing

[a]10-year LIBOR was 5.4% at the time.

[b]£50 million due in the second year, £75 million in the third year, £100 million in the fourth year, and equivalent amounts until maturity.

[c]Interest was tax deductible and accrued at a floating rate of six-month sterling LIBOR. Interest accrued and "rolled over," however, it was not payable until redemption. In that sense, it resembled a pay-in-kind (PIK) security.

Source: Adapted from Offering Memorandum, "Yell Finance B.V.," August 6, 2001; casewriter estimates.

EXHIBIT 9

CORPORATE STRUCTURE AND OWNERSHIP

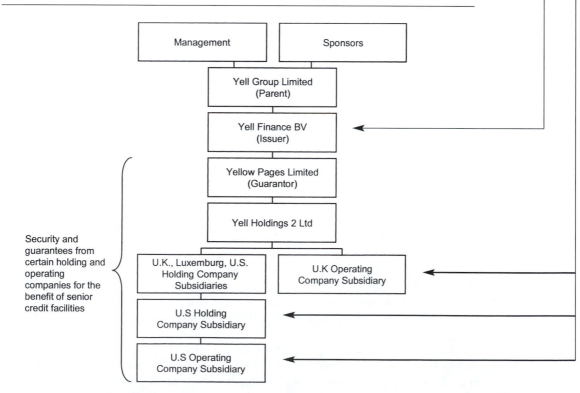

Source: Adapted from Offering Memorandum "Yell Finance B.V.," August 6, 2001, p. 22.

subsidiary would in turn own all of Yellow Pages Limited, the holding company that would guarantee all of the senior notes. Through various other subsidiaries, Yellow Pages Limited would own all of the operations of the former BT Yellow Pages and of Yellow Book USA. Yellow Pages Ltd.'s guarantees of the high-yield offering would be subordinated to its guarantee of the senior credit facilities.

Apax and Hicks Muse funds (the sponsor funds) would contribute 46.3% of the equity each, while 7.3% of equity was reserved for management participating in the buyout. BT's vendor loan would provide £100 million in additional capital. Funding provided by the sponsors and BT would flow first into Yell Group Limited, the parent company, and then from Yell Group Limited down to the U.K. and U.S. operating companies. Fees payable to bankers, accountants, lawyers, and equity providers were expected to account for no more than 5% of the transaction value.

BIDDING FOR YELL

The Apax/Hicks Muse team had the weekend to prepare an appropriate valuation for Yell. First they had to build their own projections for the U.K. and U.S. businesses, and they had to figure out which assumptions were critical and how changes in those assumptions could affect their valuation results. Second, they had to decide which method to choose for valuing the two businesses. In the context of high leverage and a changing capital structure over the investment period, one of the partners had suggested that the capital cash flow method might be preferred to the WACC or APV techniques. Third, they had to consider that the U.S. and U.K. businesses operated using different currencies. (Exhibit 10 provides further information on the betas and capital structures of comparable companies. Exhibit 11 shows data on U.S. and U.K. interest, exchange, and tax rates.) Finally, after valuing Yell, they had to recommend to their internal investment committees an exact bid value that would result in an attractive risk/reward proposition for doing the deal. After all, a significant portion of the compensation Apax and Hicks Muse received from their respective limited partners came in the form of a 20% carried interest in portfolio investments.

EXHIBIT 10

DATA FOR COMPARABLE LISTED COMPANIES (FIVE-YEAR AVERAGE UNLESS OTHERWISE INDICATED)

Company	Main Business Activities	Local Index	Beta vs. Local Index	Beta vs. S&P 500 Index	Beta vs. MSCI World Index	Debt/EV
SBC Communications	Long distance service, local service, wireless, and directory publishing	S&P 500	0.54	0.54	0.63	15.4%
Verizon	Long distance service, local service, wireless, and directory publishing	S&P 500	0.53	0.53	0.61	22.6%
BellSouth	Long distance service, local service, wireless, and directory publishing	S&P 500	0.41	0.41	0.42	17.5%
Qwest	DSL services, broadband and wireless communications, directory publishing	S&P 500	1.23	1.23	1.39	25.0%
Sprint	Long distance service, local service, product distribution, and directory publishing	S&P 500	0.66	0.66	0.68	16.4%
McLeodUSA	Internet access, system integration services, and yellow pages publishing	S&P 500	1.75	1.75	N/A	20.7%
WorldPages[a]	Independent directory publisher recently diversifying in Internet portal services	S&P 500	0.89	0.89	1.08	24.4%
SEAT Pagine Gialle	White and yellow pages telephone directories. More recently Internet access services	MIB 30 (Italy)	0.97	0.56	0.87	2.8%
Wanadoo[b]	Internet Service Provider. Also offers client portals, e-merchant services, and directories	CAC 40 (France)	1.46	1.19	1.47	1.1%
Telefonica Publicidad Informacion[c]	Directory publishing	IBEX 35 (Spain)	2.33	1.13	1.90	1.9%
Eniro[b]	Catalog and telephone directory publishing	OMX (Sweden)	0.43	0.67	0.79	8.2%

[a]Three-year data available.
[b]One-year data available.
[c]Two-year data available.

Source: Bloomberg International.

EXHIBIT 11

COUNTRY-SPECIFIC INFORMATION ABOUT INTEREST RATES, CURRENCY, AND TAXES

On April 12, 2001	United States	United Kingdom
Yield on 5-year T-bill	4.77%	5.06%
Yield on 10-year T-bill	5.17%	4.94%
Yield on 30-year T-bill	5.61%	4.52%
$/£ spot rate	1.439 bid—1.44 ask	
$/£ 1-year forward mid rate	1.4315	
$/£ 2-year forward mid rate	1.4290	
$/£ 3-year forward mid rate	1.4270	
$/£ 4-year forward mid rate	1.4245	
$/£ 5-year forward mid rate	1.4570	
Tax rate	35%	30%

Source: Adapted from Bloomberg International; Offering Memorandum, "Yell Finance B.V.," August 6, 2001.

11

Globalizing the Cost of Capital and Capital Budgeting at AES

In June 2003, Rob Venerus, director of the newly created Corporate Analysis & Planning group at AES Corporation, thumbed through the five-inch stack of financial results from subsidiaries and considered the breadth and scale of AES. In the 12 years since it had gone public, AES had become a leading independent supplier of electricity in the world with more than $33 billion in assets stretched across 30 countries and 5 continents. Venerus now faced the daunting task of creating a methodology for calculating costs of capital for valuation and capital budgeting at AES businesses in diverse locations around the world. He would need more than his considerable daily dose of caffeine to point himself in the right direction.

Much of AES's expansion had taken place in developing markets where the unmet demand for energy far exceeded that of more developed countries. By 2000, the majority of AES revenues came from overseas operations; approximately one-third came from South America alone. Once a critical element in its recipe for success, the company's international exposure hurt AES during the global economic downturn that began in late 2000. A confluence of factors including the devaluation of key South American currencies, adverse changes in energy regulatory environments, and declines in energy commodity prices conspired to weaken cash flow at AES subsidiaries and hinder the company's ability to service subsidiary and parent-level debt. As earnings and cash distributions to the parent started to deteriorate, AES stock collapsed and its market capitalization fell nearly 95% from $28 billion in December 2000 to $1.6 billion just two years later.

As one part of its response to the financial crisis, AES leadership created the Corporate Analysis & Planning group in order to address current and future strategic and financial challenges. To begin, the CEO and Board of Directors asked Venerus, as director of the new group, to revalue the company's existing assets, which required

Professor Mihir Desai and Research Associate Doug Schillinger prepared this case. HBS cases are developed solely as the basis for class discussion. Cases are not intended to serve as endorsements, sources of primary data, or illustrations of effective or ineffective management.

creating a new method of calculating the cost of capital for AES businesses. Central to the questions facing Venerus was the international scope of AES, as he explained:

> As a global company with operations in countries that are hugely different from the U.S., we need a more sophisticated way to think about risk and our cost of capital around the world. And, frankly, the finance textbooks aren't that helpful on this subject.

The mandate from the board of AES to create a new methodology presented an interesting but overwhelming challenge. As he prepared his materials for the board, Venerus wondered if his new approach would balance the complexities of the unique business situations around the world with the need for a simple, straightforward process that could be implemented accurately and consistently throughout the organization.

AES CORPORATION[1]

Roger Sant (HBS 1960) and Dennis Bakke (HBS 1970) founded AES Corporation (originally Applied Energy Services) in 1981 shortly after the adoption of federal legislation that became known as the Public Utility Regulatory Policy Act (PURPA). The legislation was part of the United States government's reaction to growing concern over American dependence on foreign oil. The act sought to diminish this dependence by requiring that electric utilities source some of their new power needs through qualified co-generators and small independent power producers, provided that the power generated by independents cost less than if the utility were to produce the power itself. Sant and Bakke recognized that in shielding small independent power producers from costly state and federal regulation, PURPA actually created a market for a new private sector power market. In practice, the act almost ensured that independent power producers could undercut a utility's cost of production.

The company initially struggled to raise financing but experienced rapid growth after the construction of its first cogeneration facility in Houston, Texas in 1983 and the subsequent development of a profitable cogeneration facility in Pittsburgh, Pennsylvania in 1985. By the time the company went public in 1991, revenues had grown to $330 million and net income had soared to $42.6 million from $1.6 million just three years earlier.

In the early 1990's, AES began to shift its focus overseas where there were more abundant opportunities for the company to apply its non-recourse, project finance model to the development of contracted generating facilities. In addition, foreign governments often provided incentives to attract foreign direct investment in infrastructure projects like power plants. The willingness of international development banks to invest alongside AES in volatile parts of the world helped mitigate the risk of expropriation and the increased breadth of the global financial markets provided greater access to capital.

AES initiated its international expansion in 1991–92 with the purchase of two plants in Northern Ireland. The following year, AES began what would become a massive expansion into Latin America with the acquisition of the San Nicolas generation facility in Buenos Aires, Argentina. A year later, AES created a separately listed subsidiary, AES China Generating Co., to advance Chinese development projects. As the pace of deregulation quickened around the world, AES was presented with an abundant supply of capital and a wealth of opportunities for investments in energy-related businesses,

---

[1]Much of this overview comes from Paula Kepos, ed., *International Directories of Company Histories*, Volume 10. (Detroit: St. James Press, 1995), pp. 25–27.

some of which were more complex than AES's portfolio of contract generation projects. In addition to expanding its line of business profile, it continued its geographic expansion and between 1996 and 1998 the company acquired several large utility companies in Brazil, El Salvador and Argentina. By this time the company was spending an estimated 80–85% of its capital investment overseas in places as diverse as Australia, Bangladesh, Canada, Cameroon, the Dominican Republic, Georgia, Hungary, India, Kazakhstan, the Netherlands, Mexico, Pakistan, Panama, Puerto Rico, Ukraine, The United Kingdom, and Venezuela.[2]

AES in 2002

By 2002, AES was one of the largest independent power producers in the world. (See Exhibits 1, 2, and 3 for AES consolidated financial statements.) The company was organized around four separate lines of business: Contract Generation, Competitive Supply, Large Utilities, and Growth Distribution.[3]

Contract Generation

In 2002, AES's Contract Generation business accounted for approximately 29% of AES revenue and consisted of generation facilities which sold electricity under long-term (five years or longer) contracts. The term of the contracts allowed AES to limit its exposure to volatility in electricity prices. The resulting stable production requirements enabled AES to accurately predict supply needs and enter into similarly long-term agreements for coal, natural gas, and fuel oil thereby limiting its exposure to fuel price volatility. Facilities varied considerably in size with plants as small as the 26 MW Xiangci-Cili hydro plant in China to the enormous ten-plant 2,650 MW Tiete hydro complex in Brazil.

Competitive Supply

Accounting for 21% of AES revenues, the Competitive Supply line of business sold electricity directly to wholesale and retail customers in competitive markets using shorter-term contracts or daily spot prices. Competitive Supply businesses, sometimes called "merchant plants," were highly susceptible to changes in the price of electricity, natural gas, coal, oil and other raw materials. AES's margin in U.S. dollars was influenced by a host of factors including weather conditions, competition, changes in market regulation, interest rate and foreign exchange fluctuations, and availability and price of emissions credits. Such price volatility had recently damaged several Competitive Supply businesses including the Drax plant in the United Kingdom, the largest plant in AES's Competitive Supply fleet.[4]

Large Utilities

By the end of 2002, the Large Utility business included only three major utilities, each in a different country: Indiana Power and Light Company in the U.S. (IPALCO),

---

[2]Paula Kepos, ed., *International Directories of Company Histories*, Volume 53. (Detroit: St. James Press, 1995), p. 17.

[3]The description for these lines of businesses comes largely from AES's annual reports; see AES Corporation, 2001 Annual Report (Arlington: AES Corporation, 2002) and AES Corporation, 2002 Annual Report (Arlington: AES Corporation, 2003).

[4]Energy companies typically refer to generation companies not as members of a "portfolio" but members of a "fleet."

EXHIBIT 1

AES CONSOLIDATED INCOME STATEMENT

Amounts in millions except per share figures	2002	2001	2000
Revenues			
Regulated	$4,317	$3,255	$2,661
Non-regulated	4,315	4,390	3,545
Total revenues	8,632	7,645	6,206
Cost of sales			
Regulated	(3,627)	(2,416)	(2,093)
Non-regulated	(3,086)	(3,052)	(2,210)
Total cost of sales	(6,713)	(5,468)	(4,303)
SG&A expenses	(112)	(120)	(82)
Severance and transaction costs	—	(131)	(79)
Interest expense	(2,031)	(1,575)	(1,262)
Interest income	312	189	201
Other income	219	116	51
Other expense	(87)	(65)	(52)
(Loss) gain on sale of investments and asset impairment expense	(1,600)	18	143
Goodwill impairment expense	(612)	—	—
Foreign currency transaction loss	(456)	(30)	(4)
Equity in pre-tax (loss) earnings of affiliates	(203)	176	475
(Loss) income before income taxes and minority interest	(2,651)	755	1,294
Income tax (benefit) expense	(27)	206	368
Minority interest (income expense)	(34)	103	120
(Loss) income from continuing operations	(2,590)	446	806
Loss from operations of dicontinued businesses (net of income tax benefit of $90, $10 and $5, respectively)	(573)	(173)	(11)
(Loss) income before cumulative effect of accounting change	(3,163)	273	795
Cumulative effect of change in accounting principle (net of income tax benefit of $72)	(346)	—	—
Net (loss) income	$(3,509)	$273	$795
BASIC (LOSS) EARNINGS PER SHARE:			
(Loss) income from continuing operations	$(4.81)	$0.84	$1.67
Discontinued operations	$(1.05)	$(0.32)	$(0.01)
Cumulative effect of accounting change	$(0.65)	$—	$—
Basic (loss) earnings per share	$(6.51)	$0.52	$1.66

Source: AES Corporation, 2002 Annual Report (Arlington: AES Corporation, 2003).

Eletropaulo Metropolitana Electricidade de Sao Paulo S.A. in Brazil (Eletropaulo), and C.A. La Electricidad de Caracas in Venezuela (EDC). These utilities combined generation, transmission and distribution capabilities and were subject to local government regulation and price setting. All three enjoyed regional monopolies and in total accounted for 36% of AES revenues. U.S. energy regulations had required AES to sell a fourth such company, Central Indiana Light and Power (CILCORP) when AES purchased IPALCO, a sale that was completed near the end of 2002.

EXHIBIT 2

AES CONSOLIDATED BALANCE SHEET

Amounts in millions; as of December 31,	2002	2001	2000	1999	1998
ASSETS					
Cash & Equivalents	$780	$802	$950	$669	$491
Other Short-Term Investments	211	215	1,297	164	35
Accounts Receivable	1,264	1,137	1,566	936	383
Inventory	384	468	569	307	119
Prepayments & Advances	218	215	1,193	327	155
Other Current Assets	1,492	1,855	209	184	71
Total Current Assets	4,349	4,692	5,784	2,587	1,254
Long-Term Investments	194	3,031	3,122	1,575	1,933
Property Plant & Equipment	23,050	21,127	21,874	14,210	6,029
Accum Depr. & Amort.	(4,204)	(3,015)	(2,632)	(763)	(525)
Property Plant & Equipment, Net	18,846	18,112	19,242	13,447	5,504
Goodwill/Intangibles	1,403	2,433	2,248	1,904	1,490
Other Long-Term Assets	8,984	8,544	2,642	1,367	600
Total Assets	33,776	36,812	33,038	20,880	10,781
LIABILITIES & SHAREHOLDERS' EQUITY					
Accounts Payable	1,139	727	743	381	215
Short-Term Debt	—	—	—	—	—
Curr. LT Debt and CLOs	3,341	2,449	2,462	1,216	1,413
Other Current Liabilities	2,031	1,752	1,834	973	348
Total Current Liabilities	6,511	4,928	5,039	2,570	1,976
Long-Term Debt	17,684	17,406	17,382	12,136	5,791
Total Long-Term Debt	17,684	17,406	17,382	12,136	5,791
Deferred Taxes	981	627	1,863	1,787	268
Other Long-Term Liabilities	8,941	8,312	3,212	1,750	952
Total Liabilities	34,117	31,273	27,496	18,243	8,987
Stockholder's Equity					
Common Stock	6	5	5	4	2
Additional Paid in Capital	5,312	5,225	5,172	2,615	1,243
Retained Earnings	(700)	2,809	2,551	1,120	892
Treasury Stock	—	—	(507)	—	—
Other Equity	(4,959)	(2,500)	(1,679)	(1,102)	(343)
Total Shareholders' Equity	(341)	5,539	5,542	2,637	1,794
Total Liabilities + Shareholders' Equity	33,776	36,812	33,038	20,880	10,781
Shares Outstanding	558	533	509	414	361

Source: "AES Annual Balance Sheet", December 2003, available from OneSource Information Services, ⟨http://www.onesource.com⟩

EXHIBIT 3

AES 2002 REVENUES BY LINE OF BUSINESS AND GEOGRAPHIC REGION

Line of Business

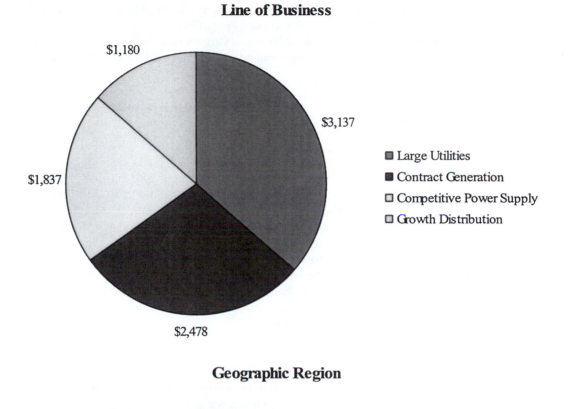

$1,180

$3,137

$1,837

$2,478

- ■ Large Utilities
- ■ Contract Generation
- □ Competitive Power Supply
- □ Growth Distribution

Geographic Region

$1,568

$2,783

$1,739

$2,091

- ■ South America
- ■ North America
- □ Europe/Africa
- □ Caribbean

Source: AES Corporation, 2002 Annual Report (Arlington: AES Corporation, 2003).

Growth Distribution

Growth Distribution businesses offered AES significant potential growth due to their location in developing markets where the demand for electricity was expected to grow at considerably faster rates than in developed countries. However, these businesses also faced notable risks relating to operating difficulties, less stable governments and regulatory regimes, and differing cultural norms regarding basic principles such as payment conventions and safety regulations. Two new Growth Distribution businesses in Ukraine (Kievoblenergo and Rivoblenergo) and one in Cameroon (SONEL) were acquired as recently as 2001.

RECENT DIFFICULTIES

AES's placement in foreign markets as well as poor performance at several new U.S. businesses nearly crippled the company during the global economic slowdown that began in 2001. AES's market value started to fall slowly in 2001 but fell precipitously in 2002. Having traded for more than $70 per share in October 2000, AES stock hovered around $1 per share in the same month of 2002 (see Exhibit 4). Wall Street began to question the company's ability to weather the storm, and one analyst wrote, "It is clear that AES's current stock price is reflecting the scenario that the company will not survive."[5] The collapse of the stock price and the subsequent $3.5 billion loss that included a substantial write-off in 2002 were brought on by several factors, the effect of which was amplified by AES's capital structure. Among these factors were adverse shifts in foreign exchange markets, regulatory policies and commodity prices, against many of which AES could not fully protect itself.

Currency Devaluations

During 2001, a political and economic crisis in Argentina brought about a significant devaluation of most South American currencies against the U.S. dollar. In December, the newly elected government abandoned the country's fixed dollar to Argentine peso exchange rate (1:1) and converted U.S. dollar denominated loans into pesos. On its first day of trading as a floating currency, the peso lost 40% of its value against the U.S. dollar.[6] By the end of the year, the peso was trading at a rate of 3.32 pesos to the US dollar and had been as high as 3.9 pesos.[7] The currencies in Brazil and Venezuela—equally important markets for AES—followed suit, with the Brazilian real and the Venezuelan bolivar each depreciating approximately 50% against the U.S. dollar during the same period (see Exhibit 5). As a result, AES recorded foreign currency transaction losses of $456 million in 2002.

Several of AES's subsidiaries in South America defaulted on their debt and were forced to restructure. The debt was non-recourse to the parent, AES Corporation, so AES was not obligated to service the subsidiary debt. However, the parent company did suffer from cash flow shortfalls as a result of lower than expected dividends from the subsidiaries. The impact of devaluation was increased when foreign businesses were paid in local currency but had obligations to repay debt denominated in U.S. dollars.

---

[5]Ali Agha and Ed Yuen, Banc of America Securities, "AES Corporation, Analysis of Sales and Earnings," October 25, 2002, available from The Investext Group, ⟨http://www.investext.com⟩, accessed July 15, 2003.

[6]"Argentina's Peso is Expected to Face Pressure This Week," *The Wall Street Journal*, January 14, 2002, available from Factiva, ⟨http://www.factiva.com⟩, accessed July 7, 2003.

[7]AES Corporation, 2002 Annual Report (Arlington: AES Corporation, 2003), p. 38.

EXHIBIT 4

AES STOCK PRICE HISTORY, MARCH 1996 THROUGH DECEMBER 2002

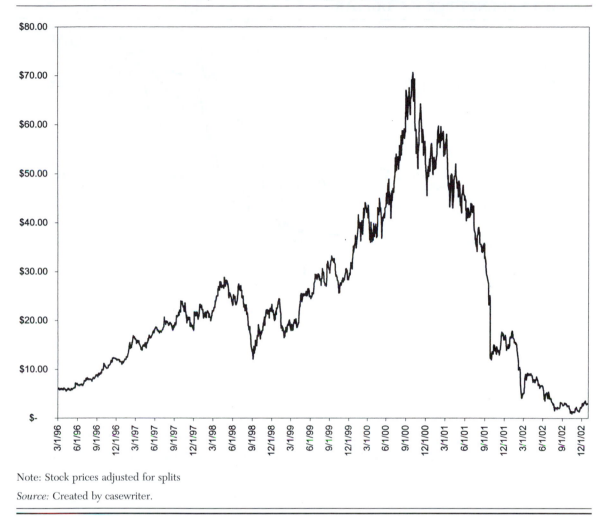

Note: Stock prices adjusted for splits

Source: Created by casewriter.

Adverse Regulatory Changes

During the late 1990s, the regulatory agencies in Brazil had failed to produce a market structure sufficiently attractive to encourage domestic construction of new generation assets. Demand exceeded supply, causing shortages. The majority of Brazil's generation capacity was hydroelectric, and energy deficiencies were exacerbated in 2001 and 2002 by below-average rainfall. In response, the Brazilian regulatory authorities began rationing energy consumption in June of 2001.[8] In addition to the loss of sales volume, the decline of the Brazilian real against the dollar triggered a regulatory conflict concerning the applicable exchange rate for the real to dollar energy-cost pass through provisions in AES's contract. In effect, the government of Brazil required AES to purchase energy in dollars while reimbursing the costs using an earlier period exchange rate, which lagged the deflation. In the fourth quarter of 2002, AES took a pre-tax

[8]Ibid., p. 20.

EXHIBIT 5

SELECTED SOUTH AMERICAN EXCHANGE RATES (2001–2002)
(LOCAL CURRENCY PER U.S. DOLLAR)

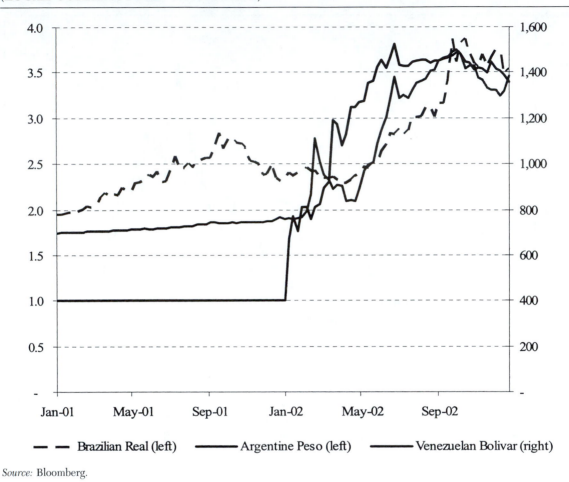

Source: Bloomberg.

impairment charge of approximately $756 million on Eletropaulo, one of its major Brazilian businesses.

Commodity Prices Decline

A 2001 change in the regulatory regime in the United Kingdom also adversely impacted AES by increasing competition and reducing prices in its generation markets. That, along with an unusually warm winter in the U.K., brought wholesale electricity prices down approximately 30%.[9] These pressures caused several counterparties to default on their long-term purchase agreements. This counterparty risk, coupled with changes in the commodity markets, enhanced the financial pressure on AES facilities and those that could not sell electricity above their marginal costs were taken off line or shut down.

[9]AES Corporation, 2002 Annual Report (Arlington: AES Corporation, 2003), p. 21.

Above and beyond the currency and regulatory difficulties at AES, the company was forced to take significant impairment charges on unprofitable or discontinued businesses. In 2002, the company took after-tax charges of $465 million on development and construction projects, $301 million on discontinued operations, and a massive $2.3 billion in asset impairments associated with several large utility and generation businesses.[10]

AES Reaction

In response to the financial crisis, AES successfully refinanced $2.1 billion of bank loans and debt securities. The refinancing arrangement came through the day before AES was to pay down $380 million of its outstanding debt. A group of 63 banks and investment funds agreed to provide $1.6 billion in new loans, and AES secured a two-year extension on another $500 million in notes due in 2002.[11]

AES also secured agreements to sell a number of its assets. Total proceeds from the sales were expected to be approximately $819 million. Proceeds from sales in 2003 were expected to be approximately $310 million.[12]

CAPITAL BUDGETING AT AES

Historically, capital budgeting at AES was fairly straightforward. When AES undertook primarily domestic contract generation projects where the risk of changes to input and output prices was minimal, a project finance framework was employed. Venerus explained that this framework consisted of a fairly simple set of rules—all non-recourse debt was deemed good, the economics of a given project were evaluated at an equity discount rate for the dividends from the project, all dividend flows were considered equally risky, and a 12% discount rate was used for all projects. In a world of domestic contract-generation projects where most risks could be hedged and businesses had similar capital structures, Venerus felt that this model worked fairly well.

Beginning in the early 1990s, with its international expansions, this model of capital budgeting was exported to projects overseas. Early on, the model worked well—such as with the initial expansion in Northern Ireland, as this project had many of the characteristics of domestic opportunities. Venerus explained that the model became increasingly strained with the expansions in Brazil and Argentina because hedging key exposures such as regulatory or currency risk was not feasible. In addition, the financial structure of a going-concern business like a utility is notably different than those of a limited-lifespan asset like a generating facility. Nonetheless, in the absence of an academic or other alternative, the basic methodology remained intact.

Another factor that created fundamental difficulties for transporting this model to overseas settings was the ever-increasing complexity in the financing of international operations.

As one example of this, Venerus described how international operations would be evaluated and financed. Exhibit 6 illustrates the typical structure: subsidiaries A and B were financed with debt that was non-recourse to the parent. The subsidiaries' creditors had claims on the hard assets at the power plants but not on any other AES

[10]Ibid., p. 37. The $2.3 billion in asset impairment charges included the $706 million after tax impairment charge at Eletropaulo.

[11]"AES Stock Shoots Up as Refinancing Keeps Bankruptcy at Bay," *The Washington Post*, December 17, 2002, available from Factiva, ⟨http://www.factiva.com⟩ accessed July 17, 2003.

[12]AES Corporation, 2002 Annual Report (Arlington: AES Corporation, 2003), p. 36.

EXHIBIT 6

TYPICAL STRUCTURE OF AN AES INVESTMENT

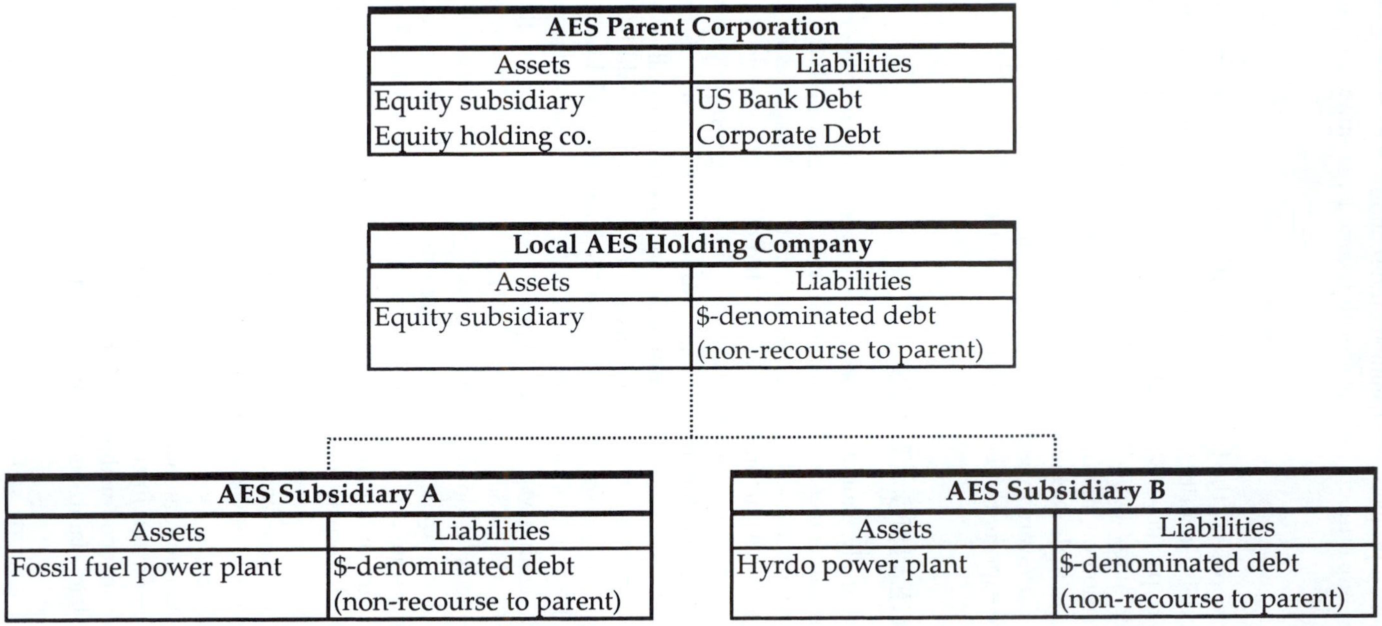

AES Parent Corporation

Assets	Liabilities
Equity subsidiary	US Bank Debt
Equity holding co.	Corporate Debt

Local AES Holding Company

Assets	Liabilities
Equity subsidiary	$-denominated debt (non-recourse to parent)

AES Subsidiary A

Assets	Liabilities
Fossil fuel power plant	$-denominated debt (non-recourse to parent)

AES Subsidiary B

Assets	Liabilities
Hyrdo power plant	$-denominated debt (non-recourse to parent)

Source: Company documents and casewriter analysis.

affiliate or subsidiary. The local holding company, which often represented multiple subsidiaries, also borrowed to finance construction or acquisitions and received equity in the various subsidiaries it held. In addition, the holding company had debt that was non-recourse to the parent, secured by dividends from the operating company. Finally, AES borrowed once again at the parent level in order to contribute equity dollars into holding companies and subsidiary projects. At the end of 2002, AES had $5.8 billion in parent company (recourse) debt and $14.2 billion in non-recourse debt.

Using this subsidiary structure, the parent company received cash flows in the form of dividends from each subsidiary (some of which were holding companies) and, because the structure of every investment opportunity was essentially the same, all dividend flows were evaluated at the same 12% discount rate. This had the benefit of making similar projects seemingly comparable. However, when subsidiaries' local currency real exchange rates depreciated, leverage at the subsidiary and holding company level effectively increased, and the subsidiaries struggled to service their foreign currency debt. Venerus recalled how the model started to crumble in early international investments:

> Imagine a real devaluation of 50%. That cuts EBITDA in dollar terms by 50% and coverage ratios deteriorate by more than 50%. The local holding company can not service its borrowing and dividends to the parent are slashed. Ultimately the consolidated leverage was well over 80% without any hedging of foreign exchange for any meaningful duration—this is where the model broke down.

Venerus's solution to the problem had to be consistent, transparent and accessible. He knew his solution would have to account for changes in required returns due to leverage, incorporate some understanding of a project's risk profile, potentially include country risks and still provide values that were consistent with market behavior, including trading multiples.

GLOBALIZING THE COST OF CAPITAL

To overhaul the capital budgeting process and evaluate each investment as a distinct opportunity with unique risks, Venerus knew he would have to calculate a cost of capital for each of the many diverse AES businesses. As a starting point, he considered the 15 representative projects shown in Exhibit 7a and, using the financial data in Exhibit 7b, he endeavored to derive a weighted average cost of capital (WACC) for each project using a standard methodology:

$$WACC = \frac{E}{V} r_e + \frac{D}{V} r_d(1 - \tau)$$

In order to calculate each WACC, Venerus knew he would have to measure all of the constituent parts for the 15 projects: the cost of debt, the target capital structure, the local country tax rates and an appropriate cost of equity. In order to find the cost of equity, he would first have to estimate a reasonable equity beta.

Venerus questioned whether the traditional CAPM model could help him calculate all of the necessary ingredients for AES businesses in emerging markets. He did not advocate the use of a "World CAPM" where beta measured the covariance of a project's return to the world market portfolio of equities. AES owned businesses in poorly integrated capital markets, so he feared the use of a World CAPM might yield artificially low costs of capital due to the low (or in some cases negative) correlation of

EXHIBIT 7A

AES PROJECT DATA

Business/ Project	Country	Line of Business	Project Description	Tax Rate	Debt to Cap.	EBIT Coverage	Default Spread	Sovereign Spread	Risk Scores						
									Construction	Operation/Technical	Regulatory	Currency	Counterparty	Contract enf./Legal	Commodity
Andres	Dominican Republic	CG	300 MW gas fired combined cycle plant currently under construction 30 km east of Santo Domingo	25.0%	35.1%	3.0x	3.57%	8.93%	3	3	3	3	3	3	3
Caracoles	Argentina	CS	123 MW hydroelectric power plant located on the San Juan river in western Argentina	35.0%	40.8%	3.0x	3.57%	16.25%	3	2	2	2	—	2	1
Drax	United Kingdom	CS	Largest coal-fired power station in western Europe. It can produce enough electricity—about 4000 MW—to meet the needs of approximately four million people	0.0%	29.5%	3.0x	3.57%	0.00%	—	2	2	—	2	2	3
Eletropaulo	Brazil	LU	Distribution company that serves a population of 14 million in São Paulo	34.0%	30.0%	3.5x	2.89%	8.93%	—	1	3	3	1	3	2
Gener	Chile	CG	277 MW fossil fuel plant located in Tocopilla, 1500 km north of Santiago	17.0%	35.2%	2.5x	4.34%	1.73%	—	—	1	1	1	—	2

(Continued)

EXHIBIT 7A (*Continued*)

AES PROJECT DATA

Business/ Project	Country	Line of Business	Project Description	Tax Rate	Debt to Cap.	EBIT Coverage	Default Spread	Sovereign Spread	Risk Scores						
									Construction	Operation/Technical	Regulatory	Currency	Counterparty	Contract enf./Legal	Commodity
Haripur	Bangladesh	CG	360 MW gas turbine facility located 25 kilometers southeast of Dhaka, capital of Bangladesh	0.0%	33.3%	2.5x	4.34%	5.23%	2	—	—	—	1	1	1
Kelvin	South Africa	CG	600 MW coal fired power plant	25%	32.9%	2.5x	4.34%	3.14%	1	—	1	2	2	1	—
Lal Pir	Pakistan	CG	337 MW coal fired power plant	23%	35.1%	3.0x	3.57%	9.90%	—	1	2	2	1	2	1
Los Mina	Dominican Republic	CG	210 MW Oil-fired facility supplying the capital city of Santo Domingo	25.0%	28.7%	4.0x	1.85%	8.93%	—	3	3	3	3	3	3
OPGC	India	CG	Joint Venture with the Government of Orissa. Two 210 MW P.C. coal-fired units	7.9%	30.4%	3.0x	3.57%	3.60%	—	1	3	2	3	2	—

(*Continued*)

EXHIBIT 7A (Continued)

AES PROJECT DATA

Business/ Project	Country	Line of Business	Project Description	Tax Rate	Debt to Cap.	EBIT Coverage	Default Spread	Sovereign Spread	Risk Scores							
									Construction	Operation/Technical	Regulatory	Currency	Counterparty	Contract enf./Legal	Commodity
Ottana	Italy	CS	Oil fired 140 MW cogeneration facility—under contracts of up to 10 years, electricity, steam, compressed air, dematerialized water and nitrogen to three chemical facilities adjacent to the plant	35.0%	42.5%	2.5x	4.34%	0.14%	—	—	—	1	3	—	—
Red Oak	USA	CG	832 MW natural gas-fired plant	37.5%	39.5%	3.0x	3.57%	0.00%	—	2	—	—	3	—	2
Rivnoblenergo	Ukraine	GD	Distribution Company serving 380,000 customers	30.0%	36.5%	2.5x	3.57%	9.98%	—	—	1	2	1—	—	
Telasi	Georgia	GD	Distribution Company serving Tbilisi, the capital of Georgia.	20.0%	26.1%	4.0x	1.85%	9.98%	—	2	3	3	3	3	3
Uruguaiana	Brazil	CG	600 MW gas-fired combined cycle power plant	34.0%	32.2%	4.0x	1.85%	8.93%	—	—	3	3	2	3	2

Source: Company document. Project descriptions taken from http://www.aes.com/businesses/default.asp.

EXHIBIT 7B

SELECTED AES FINANCIAL DATA

Select Financial Information

10 Year US Treasury Bond	4.5%
US Risk Premium	7.00%
Un-levered Equity Betas by Line of Business	
Contract Generation	0.25
Large Utility	0.25
Growth Distribution	0.25
Competitive Supply	0.50

Source: Company document.

---

developing economies with the world market. For example, a World CAPM might generate the unreasonable result of a WACC lower than the U.S. risk free rate due to its negative correlation with the world market portfolio.

Similarly, Venerus did not advocate the use of a "Local CAPM" where beta measured the covariance of a project's returns with a portfolio of local equities. Countries such as Tanzania or Georgia, where AES had projects, did not have any meaningful equity markets or local benchmarks.

Still, he knew he had to find a way to capture the country-specific risks in foreign markets. At a high level, Venerus developed an approach with two parts. First, he calculated a cost of debt and cost of equity for each of the 15 projects using U.S. market data. Second, he added the difference between the yield on local government bonds and the yield on corresponding U.S. Treasury bonds to both the cost of debt and the cost of equity. Venerus believed that this difference or "sovereign spread" approximated the incremental borrowing costs (and market risk) in the local country. Exhibit 8 summarizes Venerus's approach.

Calculating the Cost of Equity and the Cost of Debt

To estimate an equity beta for each project, Venerus first had the Corporate Analysis & Planning group take un-levered equity betas from comparable U.S. companies. They averaged the betas to yield one un-levered beta for each of the four lines of business. Since the equity betas reflected not only the market risk associated with each company, but also the differential effects of leverage, the group re-levered the equity betas at indicative capital structures for each of the 15 projects using the following equation:

$$\beta_{levered} = \frac{\beta_{unlevered}}{\dfrac{E}{V}}$$

Using the re-levered equity betas, Venerus had the group calculate the cost of equity for each project using the traditional CAPM equation:

$$\text{Cost of Equity} = r_f + \beta(r_m - r_f)$$

EXHIBIT 8

SUMMARY OF WACC CALCULATIONS FOR AES

Step	Required Information	Approach
1. Calculate un-levered equity beta	• Betas at comparable US companies	Un-lever and average equity betas for comparables in each AES line of business
2. Re-lever equity betas at target capital structure	• Target capitalization ratios	Estimated by project using cash flows to calculate desired EBIT coverage
3. Calculate cost of equity for each AES business	• Risk Free Rate • Equity Risk Premium • Re-levered equity beta	10-Year US Treasury Note Long-term avg. difference between S&P 500 and US treasuries
4. Calculate the cost of debt	• Risk Free Rate • Default Spread	10-Year US Treasury Note Observed relationship between EBIT coverage ratios for comparable companies and their costs of debt
5. Add country specific risk to the cost of debt and cost of equity.	• Local sovereign spread	The difference between local government dollar-denominated bond yields and the corresponding US treasury note

Source: Company document and casewriter analysis.

Finally, an appropriate cost of debt needed to be calculated. Given the significant regulatory and market changes impacting AES over the previous two years, Venerus decided not to use the historical cost of debt which might reflect market conditions that no longer existed. Instead, he attempted to estimate the return on debt demanded by investors given the cash flow risks of a given project. To do so, he applied the following equation:

$$\text{Cost of Debt} = r_f + \text{Default Spread}$$

The estimation of "default spread" was based upon the observed relationship between EBIT coverage ratios for comparable energy companies and their cost of debt (shown in Exhibits 9a and 9b). The group estimated the appropriate EBIT coverage ratio for each project given its volatility of cash flows and leverage. Then, using the observed relationship, they assigned the commensurate cost of debt. For example, a project with a target EBIT coverage ratio of 3.0x was assigned a default spread of approximately 300 bp.

Adding the Sovereign Spread[13]

Before plugging the cost of equity and cost of debt into the WACC equation, Venerus wanted to account for country specific market risk. He believed that risk could be cap-

---

[13]Also referred to as the "country spread model" or the "Goldman Model." See Jorge O. Mariscal and Rafaelina M. Lee, Goldman Sachs, "The Valuation of Mexican Stocks: An Extension of the Capital Asset Pricing Model", 1993.

EXHIBIT 9A

EBIT COVERAGE RATIOS AND DEFAULT SPREADS

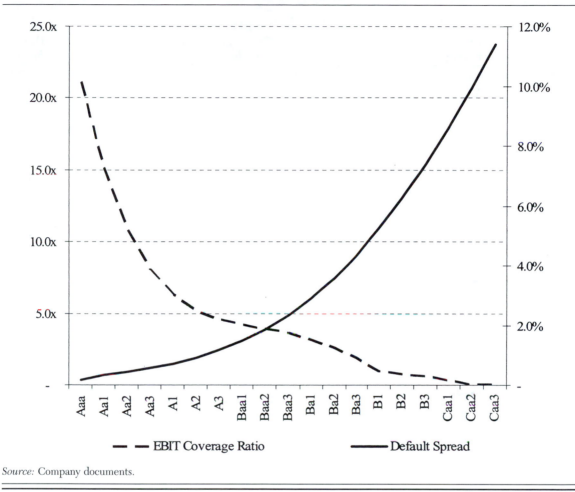

Source: Company documents.

---

tured in the difference between local government bond yields and the corresponding U.S. Treasury yields, or the "sovereign spread. " Thus, he added the spreads found in Exhibit 10 to both the cost of equity and cost of debt and used those values to generate a WACC for each project.

WACC ADJUSTMENTS FOR UNSYSTEMATIC RISK

Venerus felt that the above CAPM-based sovereign spread approach could provide AES with a useful WACC that reflected the systematic risk associated with each project according to its local market. However, was the approach reasonable in developing markets where access to capital was limited and information was less than perfect? Venerus believed that company-specific risk could not be easily diversified away in such markets. Moreover, AES—as an "investor" looking for potential projects—could

EXHIBIT 9B

EBIT COVERAGE RATIOS AND DEFAULT SPREADS

Credit Rating	EBIT Coverage Ratio	Default Spread
Aaa	21.1x	0.2%
Aa1	15.1x	0.3%
Aa2	10.9x	0.4%
Aa3	8.1x	0.6%
A1	6.3x	0.7%
A2	5.2x	0.9%
A3	4.6x	1.2%
Baa1	4.2x	1.5%
Baa2	3.9x	1.9%
Baa3	3.6x	2.3%
Ba1	3.2x	2.9%
Ba2	2.6x	3.6%
Ba3	1.9x	4.3%
B1	1.0x	5.2%
B2	0.8x	6.2%
B3	0.6x	7.4%
Caa1	0.4x	8.6%
Caa2	0.1x	10.0%
Caa3	0.1x	11.4%

Source: Company documents.

not diversify in the same way a portfolio manager might diversify. Perhaps most importantly, Venerus was concerned that calculating expected cash flows by a probability weighted average of various outcomes would be extremely difficult, if not impossible, to do accurately or consistently across the entire AES portfolio, even without the urgency of his present task. He felt budgeted cash flows would be more readily available. Thus, he believed the appropriate discount rate for AES businesses should account for some level of project specific risk. Even if expected cash flows were available, Venerus felt some degree of project-specific risk deserved consideration. Venerus illustrated his point with an example:

> Consider two hydro plants in Brazil that are identical in every respect except the hydrological risk of the rivers that feed them. Both plants have the same probability-weighted expected value cash flows. The hydrology of plant #1 produces cash flows that can vary by plus or minus 50% in a given year. The hydrology of plant #2 produces cash flows that can vary by plus or minus 10% in a given year. If both these plants are financed with 100% equity and pay no taxes, CAPM tells us that these plants are worth the same amount. That, to me, is unconvincing.

EXHIBIT 10

CREDIT RATINGS AND SOVEREIGN SPREADS USED BY AES

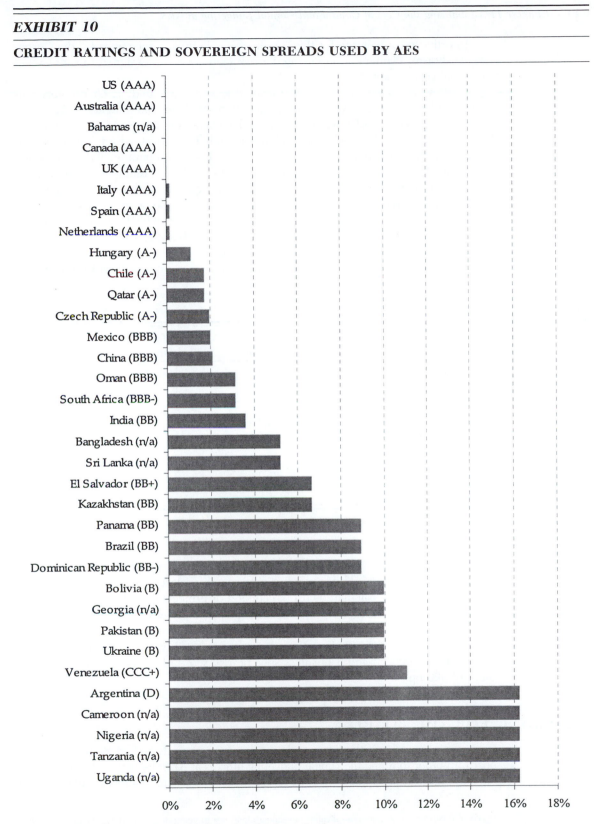

Source: Company document; Standard and Poor's and Lehman Brothers.

In order to compensate for this "un-diversifiable project specific risk," the Corporate Analysis & Planning group created a risk scoring system designed to supplement the initial cost of capital.

First, seven categories of project-level risk were identified. Each category was ranked and weighted according to AES's ability to anticipate and mitigate certain risks. For example, because AES was unable to hedge changes in currencies in certain markets, "currency risk" received a high weight and rank. In contrast, AES felt it could control for most technical or plant-related problems and as such "operational risks" received a relatively low weight. See Exhibit 11 for the seven risks and examples for each.

Second, projects were graded on their level of exposure to the seven categories of project risk. For each category, a project was assigned a grade between 0 (lowest exposure) and 3 (highest exposure). Next, the grades were multiplied by the respective weights and the seven categories added together to yield a single business-specific risk score. For example, Table A shows how the Lal Pir project, a contract generation business in Pakistan might be assigned grades that translated into a business specific risk score of 1.41:

TABLE A   Risk Score Calculation for Lal Pir Project

Categories of Risk	Weight	Grade for Lal Pir	Risk Scores (grade × weight)
Operational / Technical	3.5%	1	0.02
Counterparty Credit / Performance	7.0%	1	0.07
Regulatory	10.5%	2	0.21
Construction	14.5%	0	0.00
Commodity	18.0%	1	0.18
Currency	21.5%	2	0.43
Contractual Enforcement / Legal	25.0%	2	0.50
Sum of individual scores = business specific risk score			1.41

Source: Company document (actual assessments disguised).

Finally, the business-specific risk scores were used to calculate an adjustment to the initial cost of capital. The lowest business-specific risk scores (score = 0) received no adjustment to the calculated cost of capital. For projects with the highest business specific risk scores (score = 3), the cost of capital was increased by 1500 bp. The relationships between business-specific risk scores and adjustments to the cost of capital were linear. Thus, a business specific risk score of 2 would yield an adjustment to WACC of 1000 bp and a business specific risk score of 1 would yield an adjustment of 500 bp.[14]

PREPARING FOR THE BOARD

Venerus reviewed his methodology and considered the mandate he had received from the board. In order to refine the capital budgeting process at AES, he had to devise a coherent and practical way to define cost of capital in all of AES's international markets. In his

---

[14]AES also considered a more complicated non-linear algorithm to generate the WACC adjustment from the business-specific risk score.

EXHIBIT 11

PROJECT-SPECIFIC RISK CATEGORIES AND WEIGHTINGS

Risk Category	Example	Rank	Weight
Operational	An AES plant may fail to operate at capacity or fail to produce sufficient electricity to meet contractual obligations.	1	3.5%
Counterparty Credit / Performance	AES has offtake agreements that—like futures and other derivative instruments—require credit; the counterparty may either fail to post additional collateral as required or fail to pay.	2	7.0%
Regulatory	Contract settlement processes in a foreign country may change after AES has made investments in a generation facility. Regulatory agencies may choose not to adjust rates for a utility after inflation goes up or other market dynamics change.	3	10.5%
Construction	Construction of a specific plant is complete but the plant may not perform the way it is supposed to (the heat rate is too high, the output too low, the availability too low, etc.).	4	14.5%
Commodity	Prices of coal, oil, or other fuels may spike.	5	18.0%
Currency	AES may be unable to hedge the devaluation of foreign currencies like the Argentine peso.	6	21.5%
Contract Enforcement/ Legal	A local AES partner is in breach of contract and local government authorities may fail to enforce it. Alternatively, a foreign government may decide to nationalize assets.	7	25.0%

Source: Company document.

own mind, he went over the steps in his process: calculate the cost of equity and the cost of debt using U.S. market data, add the sovereign spread to each, calculate WACC using a target capital structure and finally, add a business specific risk adjustment to WACC.

Still, questions lingered in his mind. He reviewed the project cash flows for the AES Lal Pir contract generation plant in Pakistan presented in Exhibit 12 as a way of gauging the effect of his new methodology. In doing so, he considered the differences in value created by each of the adjustments to the discount rate. Was his discount rate an actual representation of the risk associated with the project? Did it yield the correct value? More generally, did the sovereign spreads accurately capture the market risk specific to a given country? Had he used the appropriate risk categories and suitable weights to reflect AES's appetite for risk?

It was time for him to decide. Should he move forward with the addition of the business-specific risk score or should he simply use the traditional sovereign spread model? The board's reaction was impossible to predict. What if the results were inconsistent with observable trading multiples? Would they accuse him of creating an over-complicated method or would they applaud the new technique as a pragmatic way to calculate the cost of capital in an international context?

EXHIBIT 12

PROJECT CASH FLOWS

Lal Plr (Pakistan) Contract Generation

Income	2004	2005	2006	2007	2008	2009	2010	2011	2012	2013	2014	2015	2016	2017	2018	2019	2020	2021	2022	2023
Revenue	312.5	313.6	314.7	315.8	316.9	318.0	319.1	320.2	321.4	322.5	323.6	324.7	325.9	327.0	328.2	329.3	330.5	331.6	332.8	333.9
EBITDA	100.0	100.4	100.7	101.1	101.4	101.8	102.1	102.5	102.8	103.2	103.6	103.9	104.3	104.6	105.0	105.4	105.7	106.1	106.5	106.9
Depreciation	(30.6)	(31.3)	(31.9)	(32.5)	(33.1)	(33.8)	(34.4)	(35.1)	(35.7)	(36.3)	(37.0)	(37.6)	(38.3)	(39.0)	(39.6)	(40.3)	(40.9)	(41.6)	(42.3)	(42.9)
Operating Profit	69.4	69.1	68.8	68.5	68.3	68.0	67.7	67.4	67.1	66.8	66.6	66.3	66.0	65.7	65.4	65.1	64.8	64.5	64.2	63.9
Interest	(44.1)	(42.7)	(41.1)	(39.4)	(37.5)	(35.4)	(33.2)	(30.7)	(28.0)	(25.0)	(21.8)	(18.2)	(14.3)	(9.9)	(5.2)	0.0	0.0	0.0	0.0	0.0
Taxes	(8.8)	(9.2)	(9.7)	(10.2)	(10.8)	(11.4)	(12.1)	(12.9)	(13.7)	(14.6)	(15.7)	(16.8)	(18.1)	(19.5)	(21.1)	(22.8)	(22.7)	(22.6)	(22.5)	(22.4)
Net Profit	16.4	17.2	18.0	19.0	20.0	21.2	22.4	23.9	25.4	27.2	29.1	31.3	33.6	36.2	39.1	42.3	42.1	41.9	41.8	41.6
Cash Flow																				
Operating Profit	69.4	69.1	68.8	68.5	68.3	68.0	67.7	67.4	67.1	66.8	66.6	66.3	66.0	65.7	65.4	65.1	64.8	64.5	64.2	63.9
Addback Depreciation	30.6	31.3	31.9	32.5	33.1	33.8	34.4	35.1	35.7	36.3	37.0	37.6	38.3	39.0	39.6	40.3	40.9	41.6	42.3	42.9
Maintenance CapEx	(12.5)	(12.5)	(12.6)	(12.6)	(12.7)	(12.7)	(12.8)	(12.8)	(12.9)	(12.9)	(12.9)	(13.0)	(13.0)	(13.1)	(13.1)	(13.2)	(13.2)	(13.3)	(13.3)	(13.4)
Pre-Tax, Pre-Finance Cash Flow	87.5	87.8	88.1	88.4	88.7	89.0	89.4	89.7	90.0	90.3	90.6	90.9	91.2	91.6	91.9	92.2	92.5	92.9	93.2	93.5
Interest	(44.1)	(42.7)	(41.1)	(39.4)	(37.5)	(35.4)	(33.2)	(30.7)	(28.0)	(25.0)	(21.8)	(18.2)	(14.3)	(9.9)	(5.2)	0.0	0.0	0.0	0.0	0.0
Principal	(14.2)	(15.5)	(16.9)	(18.4)	(20.1)	(22.0)	(24.1)	(26.4)	(29.0)	(31.8)	(34.9)	(38.3)	(42.1)	(46.2)	(50.8)	(0.0)	(0.0)	(0.0)	(0.0)	(0.0)
New Debt	0.0	0.0	0.0	0.0	0.0	0.0	0.0	0.0	0.0	0.0	0.0	0.0	0.0	0.0	0.0	0.0	0.0	0.0	0.0	0.0
Taxes	(8.8)	(9.2)	(9.7)	(10.2)	(10.8)	(11.4)	(12.1)	(12.9)	(13.7)	(14.6)	(15.7)	(16.8)	(18.1)	(19.5)	(21.1)	(22.8)	(22.7)	(22.6)	(22.5)	(22.4)
Levered Equity Cash Flow	20.3	20.4	20.4	20.4	20.3	20.2	20.0	19.7	19.3	18.9	18.3	17.6	16.8	15.9	14.8	69.4	69.8	70.3	70.7	71.1
Lev Equity Cash Flow with TV	20.3	20.4	20.4	20.4	20.3	20.2	20.0	19.7	19.3	18.9	18.3	17.6	16.8	15.9	14.8	69.4	69.8	70.3	70.7	71.1
Unlevered Cash Flow	63.2	63.6	64.0	64.4	64.8	65.2	65.7	66.1	66.5	66.9	67.3	67.7	68.2	68.6	69.0	69.4	69.8	70.3	70.7	71.1
Unlevered Cash Flow with TV	63.2	63.6	64.0	64.4	64.8	65.2	65.7	66.1	66.5	66.9	67.3	67.7	68.2	68.6	69.0	69.4	69.8	70.3	70.7	71.1
Capitalization																				
Initial PP&E	612.5	625.0	637.6	650.3	662.9	675.7	688.4	701.2	714.1	727.0	739.9	752.9	766.0	779.0	792.2	805.3	818.6	831.8	845.1	858.5
Goodwill	22.4	22.4	22.4	22.4	22.4	22.4	22.4	22.4	22.4	22.4	22.4	22.4	22.4	22.4	22.4	22.4	22.4	22.4	22.4	22.4
Accum Depreciation	(30.6)	(61.9)	(93.8)	(126.3)	(159.4)	(193.2)	(227.6)	(262.7)	(298.4)	(334.7)	(371.7)	(409.4)	(447.7)	(486.6)	(526.2)	(566.5)	(607.4)	(649.0)	(691.3)	(734.2)
Total Assets	604.3	585.6	566.3	546.4	525.9	504.9	483.2	461.0	438.1	414.7	390.6	365.9	340.7	314.8	288.3	261.2	233.5	205.2	176.3	146.7
Debt	416.5	401.0	384.1	365.7	345.6	323.6	299.4	273.0	244.1	212.3	177.4	139.1	97.0	50.8	(0.0)	(0.0)	(0.0)	(0.0)	(0.0)	(0.0)
Equity	187.8	184.6	182.1	180.7	180.3	181.3	183.8	187.9	194.1	202.4	213.2	226.8	243.6	264.0	288.3	261.2	233.5	205.2	176.3	146.7
Total Capital	604.3	585.6	566.3	546.4	525.9	504.9	483.2	461.0	438.1	414.7	390.6	365.9	340.7	314.8	288.3	261.2	233.5	205.2	176.3	146.7

note: values disguised

Source: Company document.

Dow Chemical's Bid for the Privatization of PBB in Argentina

On November 10, 1995, Oscar Vignart, vice president of business development for Latin America for Dow Chemical Company (Dow), and Luis Marcer, CFO of Dow Quimica Argentina, considered the bidding price on Petroquímica Bahia Blanca S.A. (PBB), which was being privatized by the Argentine government. PBB produced both ethylene and polyethylene. It was part of a petrochemical complex located in Bahia Blanca, 700 km south of the Argentine capital, Buenos Aires.[1] Vignart believed that the acquisition of PBB offered Dow a once in a lifetime opportunity to become the leading polyethylene player in Latin America.

Vignart and Marcer had reviewed Dow headquarters' projection of polyethylene consumption in Latin America and built cash flow projections for the project. They now had to incorporate Argentina's country risk into their model. While Vignart thought that Argentina's current political and economic conditions favored the investment, he also recognized that there were many uncertainties about the project which he had to address to justify the investment to the parent company. With the offer price for the privatization due in ten days, there was little time left to finalize the valuation and make a decision on the project.

Professor Mihir A. Desai and Alexandra de Royere, Senior Researcher at the HBS Latin America Research Center in Buenos Aires, prepared this case with the cooperation of Gustavo Herrero, Executive Director of the LARC, and Mark Veblen and Kathleen Luchs, Research Associates. HBS cases are developed solely as the basis for class discussion. Cases are not intended to serve as endorsements, sources of primary data, or illustrations of effective or ineffective management. Selected data have been disguised to protect confidentiality.

[1]In the case, PBB refers to a set of assets that included PPB's stake in Indupa, S.A.

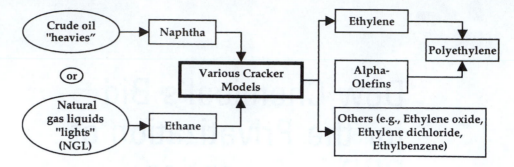

Figure A   Production of Ethylene and Polyethylene

Source: Prepared by casewriter.

OVERVIEW OF THE ETHYLENE AND POLYETHYLENE INDUSTRIES IN 1995

Ethylene, produced from oil or natural gas, was used to produce polyethylene, the world's most widely used plastic. Polyethylene accounted for approximately three-quarters of ethylene demand. Polyethylene plastic's principal application was in packaging, from trash bags to milk jugs.

Ethylene

Ethylene plants, known as hydrocarbon "crackers," separated either naphtha molecules (derived from crude oil) or ethane molecules (derived from natural gas).[2] The ethylene derived from this process was used to produce polyethylene (See Figure A).

Cracking naphta (the raw material derived from crude oil) required much more energy, manufacturing intensity, and equipment than cracking ethane (derived from natural gas). A plant for cracking ethane was estimated to cost $400–$500 million, a plant for cracking naphtha cost about $1 billion.[3] Roughly half of the world's ethylene plants, particularly those in gas-poor regions such as Japan and Western Europe, utilized naphtha. Plants in gas-rich regions such as North America and the Middle East more frequently employed ethane from natural gas streams.[4]

Large plant sizes and the need for economies of scale rendered the ethylene industry highly capital intensive. Consequently, capacity additions or reductions could significantly affect balance of supply and demand, influencing capacity utilization rates, prices, and profit margins. Ethylene profitability was tightly linked to its global operating rate. Among the investors in the ethylene business were oil companies, governments, pure chemical companies, conglomerates, private investors, and joint ventures. According to UBS Warburg plc, financial return objectives ranged from loss leader to zero return to beating the cost of capital. The loss leader or zero-return player was often a government operator that was, directly or indirectly, financing capital-intensive ethylene

---

[2]Cracking described a refining process whereby large, complex molecules were broken down into smaller molecules with a lower boiling point and then formed into new, lighter, higher-value compounds.

[3]Andrew Cash, Lara Palevitza, Gregg Goodnight, "Dow Chemical Report," UBS Warburg, January 31, 2001, pp. 23 and 24.

[4]*Ibid.*, p. 23.

plants in order to stimulate downstream business. This was the case in Brazil, where the government sponsored a "tri-partite" model, in which private Brazilian capital, multinationals holding the technology, and the government would each contribute one third of the investment. Because producers of ethylene and first order derivatives (mostly plastics) were highly integrated, margins for both products were highly correlated.

Polyethylene Plastic

Polyethylene plastic, produced from ethylene, was widely used in the manufacture of everything from trash bags, picnic cutlery and garbage pails to plastic toys. Polyethylene also replaced glass, wood, and metal in certain applications. There were three types of polyethylene, each with distinctive physical properties and commercial applications (see Table A).

TABLE A   Types of Polyethylene and Main Applications

Type of Polyethylene	Physical Properties	Examples of Commercial Applications
LDPE Low-density polyethylene	optical clarity, soft feel, printability	supermarket-related film and sheet applications such as bread bags
HDPE High-density polyethylene	tough, opaque, rigid	milk jugs (nearly half of this plastic's blow-molded volume)
LLDPE Low linear density polyethylene	strength, optical clarity, soft feel, printability	garbage bags

Source: Glenn W. Mierendorf, Dow Chemical Company Report, Prudential Securities, September 10, 1996, p. 7.

LDPE was first commercialized in the late 1930s, and HDPE was introduced in the mid-1950s. The fastest growing polyethylene, LLDPE, introduced in the 1970s, enjoyed a cost advantage over LDPE. However, it fell short of replacing LDPE totally because customers were required to upgrade their equipment to process the newer product.

Polyethylene was a global commodity product and pricing worldwide typically fell into a narrow band, inside which variations reflected different transportation costs. Polyethylene customers were typically small and medium-sized plastic processing companies.

Dow's Ethylene and Polyethylene Interests

In 1995, Dow generated annual revenues of $20.2 billion from its three major businesses: chemicals, plastics, and agricultural products. The Chemicals & Metals Division (that included ethylene) accounted for $3.3 billion and the Plastics Division (that included polyethylene) accounted for $3.9 billion. Dow held the leading market position worldwide in numerous chemical product lines, including ethylene and polyethylene. In a historically fragmented industry, Dow accounted for 7% of global capacity.[5]

[5]Glenn W. Mierendorf, Dow Chemical Company Report, Prudential Securities, September 10, 1996, p. 7.

TABLE B   Major Polyethylene Producers

Company	Polyethylene Capacity (in billions of pounds as of year-end 1995)	Share of Global Capacity
Dow Chemical	6.3	7%
Union Carbide	6.1	6%
Exxon	5.4	5%
Quantum	4.6	5%
Borealis	3.2	3%

Source: Glenn W. Mierendorf, Dow Chemical Company Report, Prudential Securities, September 10, 1996, p. 7.

Besides being a low cost producer, Dow embraced a strategy of horizontal and vertical integration, technological leadership, and international presence. Dow's capacity for ethylene, its largest volume chemical, was 11.3 billion pounds.[6] Nearly half of its internal ethylene consumption was accounted for by seven sites that manufactured 6.3 billion pounds of polyethylene annually. The remainder of internal consumption was used in the production of other products.[7] Polyethylene represented approximately 15% of Dow's total sales and 35% of its operating profits (Exhibit 1A shows sales by industry segment; Exhibit 1B shows sales by geographic region).

Dow had actively expanded globally by locating world scale petrochemical complexes in emerging economies. In 1995, it counted 94 plants in more than 30 countries. In Latin America Dow was present in Colombia, Chile, Brazil, and Argentina, with most of its investments concentrated in Brazil where Dow had built a petrochemical complex that manufactured products other than ethylene and polyethylene. Dow entered Argentina in 1957, and in the 1960s Dow Quimica S.A. invested in a facility that produced petrochemicals, herbicide, insecticides, and fungicides. Dow invested approximately US$100 million in this business over four decades.

DEVELOPMENT OF THE BAHIA BLANCA PETROCHEMICAL COMPLEX

Dow had long been interested in expanding its interests in Argentina and, 20 years earlier, the company had urged the Argentine government to develop a petrochemical complex in Bahia Blanca. It cited the natural competitive attributes of the region: availability and proximity of the two largest Argentine gas basins; easy access to maritime, rail, and road transport; proximity to the city of Buenos Aires (which represented nearly 50% of the domestic market); adequate service infrastructure; and the requisite human resources owing to the existence of institutions of higher learning in Bahia Blanca. At that time, it was critical to involve the government since the state owned the power, gas and oil supplies. (See Exhibit 2 for maps of the petrochemical sites in Brazil and Argentina.)

Ethylene and Polyethylene Industries in Argentina

The Argentine government did decide to develop a petrochemical complex in Bahia Blanca, but Dow did not participate. Instead, in September 1977, the government

[6]*Ibid.*, p. 4.
[7]*Ibid.*, p. 6

THE DOW CHEMICAL COMPANY—HISTORIC PERFORMANCE BY INDUSTRY SEGMENT (IN MILLIONS, EXCEPT FOR SHARE AMOUNTS)

	Chemicals & Metals[a]	Performance Chemicals	Plastics[b]	Performance Plastics	Hydrocarbons Energy	Diversified Bus. and Unallocated	Corporate Elim. & Disc. Oper.	Consolidated
1995								
Sales to unaffiliated customers	$3,322	$4,240	$3,932	$5,369	$2,371	$966	—	$20,200
Intersegment transfers	710	26	106	19	2,247	—	($3,108)	—
Operating income (loss)	1,136	670	1,475	1,056	(83)	(363)	—	3,891
Identifiable assets	2,660	4,066	3,422	3,962	2,743	717	6,012	23,582
Depreciation	280	320	327	294	104	44	—	1,369
Capital expenditures	516	274	81	175	342	29	—	1,417
1994								
Sales to unaffiliated customers	$2,471	$3,672	$3,064	$4,538	$2,044	$953	—	$16,742
Intersegment transfers	680	28	104	18	2,365	—	($3,195)	—
Operating income (loss)	337	514	531	611	74	(247)	—	1,820
Identifiable assets	2,705	3,842	3,785	3,834	2,108	699	9,572	26,545
Depreciation	241	273	311	263	92	44	—	1,224
Capital expenditures	152	253	83	134	388	64	109	1,183
1993								
Sales to unaffiliated customers	$2,301	$3,390	$2,510	$4,116	$1,808	$927	—	$15,052
Intersegment transfers	683	42	85	17	2,338	—	($3,165)	—
Operating income	154	403	89	304	46	78	—	1,074
Identifiable assets	2,519	3,631	3,525	3,570	1,933	692	9,635	25,505
Depreciation	246	279	318	269	94	46	—	1,252
Capital expenditures	215	204	126	173	426	60	193	1,397

(a) The ethylene business is included within this division.

(b) The polyethylene business is included within this division.

Source: The Dow Chemical Company, December 31, 1995 10-K (Midland, Michigan: Dow Chemical Co, 1995), available from Thomson Research, ⟨http://research.thomsonib.com⟩.

EXHIBIT 1B

THE DOW CHEMICAL COMPANY—HISTORIC PERFORMANCE BY GEOGRAPHIC AREA (IN MILLIONS, EXCEPT FOR SHARE AMOUNTS)

	United States	Europe	Rest of the World	Discontinued Operations & Eliminations	Consolidated
1995					
Sales to unaffiliated customers	$ 9,035	$6,411	$4,754	—	$20,200
Intersegment transfers	1,728	515	454	($2,697)	—
Operating income[a]	1,603	1,112	1,176	—	3,891
Identifiable assets	10,127	6,914	6,541	—	23,582
Gross plant properties	12,416	7,466	3,336	—	23,218
Capital expenditures	1,008	295	114	—	1,417
1994					
Sales to unaffiliated customers	$ 8,093	$4,809	$3,840	—	$16,742
Intersegment transfers	1,424	447	341	($2,212)	—
Operating income[a]	1,024	237	559	—	1,820
Identifiable assets	9,399	5,516	4,867	6,763	26,545
Gross plant properties	11,729	6,725	3,337	1,419	23,210
Capital expenditures	692	234	148	109	1,183
1993					
Sales to unaffiliated customers	$ 7,486	$4,299	$3,267	—	$15,052
Intersegment transfers	1,042	325	304	($1,671)	—
Operating income[a]	795	23	302	—	1,074
Identifiable assets	9,475	5,010	4,034	6,986	25,505
Gross plant properties	11,326	5,901	3,165	1,216	21,608
Capital expenditures	762	266	176	193	1,397

(a) Latin American operations represented approximately 10% of Dow Chemical Company's total sales in 1995.

Source: The Dow Chemical Company, December 31, 1995 10-K (Midland, Michigan: Dow Chemical Co, 1995), available from Thomson Research, ⟨http://research.thomsonib.com⟩.

began development of the complex in association with the local petrochemical private sector through mixed companies (owned partly by the state, partly by private companies), including the creation of PBB. The PBB assets consisted of a cracker and one polyethylene plant. Although ready in 1977, the cracker remained idle awaiting completion of the polyethylene facilities. Ethylene from PBB and polyethylene from Polisur finally started to be produced in 1982. In 1987, PBB began to operate an HDPE plant based on technology from the German company Hoechst AG.

In addition to PBB, the Bahia Blanca development included another mixed company set up to invest in ethylene, Polisur. In 1985, Polisur brought its first LDPE plant on line and in 1987 Polisur purchased from Union Carbide a "swing plant" capable of producing both LDPE and HDPE.

EXHIBIT 2

MAPS OF THE PETROCHEMICAL SITES IN ARGENTINA AND BRAZIL

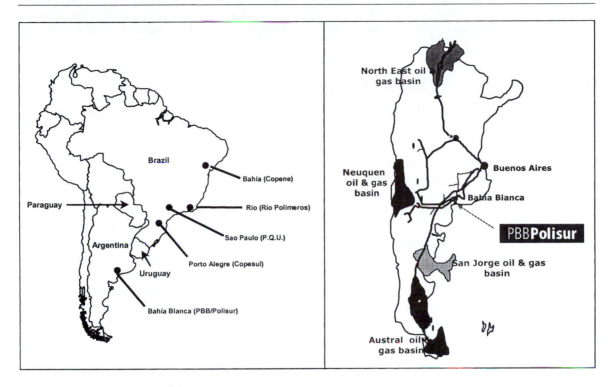

Source: Dow Quimíca Argentina S.A.

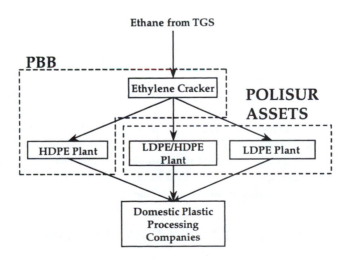

Figure B PBB and Polisur Assets

Source: Prepared by casewriter.

In 1994 PBB and Polisur, the only local players, controlled a 70% share of the Argentine polyethylene market. PBB's and Polisur's customers included more than 100 local small and medium-sized plastic-processing firms. Brazilian competitors supplied the rest of the Argentine market. (See Exhibit 3 for Latin American ethylene and polyethylene capacity.)

PRIVATIZATION IN ARGENTINA

Throughout the 1980s, Argentina experienced periods of hyperinflation, stagflation, and huge fiscal deficits. When Carlos Menem was elected President in 1989, the nation was gripped by hyperinflation with rates approaching 5000% per annum. Menem's policies achieved a quick, decisive success in March 1991 with the Convertibility Plan. This was the brainchild of his newly appointed economics minister, Harvard-trained economist Domingo Felipe Cavallo. The Convertibility Law ensured that the money supply was fully backed with external reserves and fixed the Argentine peso at exactly one U.S. dollar. Almost immediately, inflation converged to international levels. Convertibility also seemed to tame inflation without incurring a significant economic slowdown.

Concurrently, Menem and Cavallo implemented policies, sanctioned by the International Monetary Fund, aimed at reducing trade barriers, deregulating industries and capital markets, and privatizing businesses. The State Reform Law declared 32 state-owned enterprises eligible for privatization. Included were oil, natural gas, electricity, telecommunication, steel, transportation, and petrochemicals. Privatizations included the Ministry of Defense's sale of its minority stake in Polisur to its existing majority shareholder, Ipako, a local company. Approximately 90% of state-owned companies were privatized between 1991 and 1994, with proceeds exceeding $19 billion used largely to refinance and reduce public debt (see Exhibit 4A for sale proceeds for selected privatizations and Exhibit 4B for privatization cash proceeds).

The Decision to Privatize PBB

The Argentine economy became even more open in 1995 with the elimination of all duties, charges and other restrictions in the reciprocal trade among the members of Mercosur, a trading bloc created in 1991 that included Argentina, Brazil, Paraguay and Uruguay. (See Exhibit 5 for macroeconomic data on the Mercosur participants.) Argentine petrochemical producers would now compete directly with their Brazilian competitors and would likely lose market share to them because the technology and scale of the Bahia Blanca complex was no longer in line with international standards. Consequently, the government decided to privatize PBB. On October 2, 1995 the Argentine government announced a public bidding to execute the sale of 51% of PBB.

Given PBB's relative importance to the Argentine economy, Cavallo transferred the supervision of its privatization from the Ministry of Defense to the Ministry of Economy. The government retained Credit Suisse First Boston and a local investment bank as advisors, and a respected local law firm to organize the privatization. (See Exhibit 6 for the principal provisions of the tender.)

DOW'S INTEREST IN THE PBB PRIVATIZATION

As Dow's vice president for business development in Latin America, Oscar Vignart had watched the rapid transformation occurring in Argentina. He anticipated continued improvement in standards of living, leading to increased demand for polyethylene in

EXHIBIT 3

PROJECTION OF ARGENTINE AND BRAZILIAN POLYETHYLENE DEMAND AND PRODUCTION

Total Polyethylene (MM lb)	1990	1991	1992	1993	1994	1995	1996	1997	1998	1999	2000	2001	2002	2003	2004	2005
ARGENTINA																
Population	33.0	33.5	33.8	34.1	34.6	35.1	35.5	35.9	36.4	36.8	37.3	37.7	38.2	38.6	39.1	39.5
Capacity	666	666	666	666	666	666	666	666	666	666	783	1,603	1,603	1,603	1,603	1,603
Demand	359	487	580	697	787	755	847	944	1,035	1,139	1,256	1,371	1,499	1,643	1,804	1,984
Production	500	503	542	531	569	531	595	594	665	665	666	782	1,602	1,602	1,602	1,602
Operating Capacity	79%	80%	86%	84%	90%	80%	89%	89%	100%	100%	100%	100%	100%	100%	100%	100%
Consumption per Capita	11	15	17	20	23	22	24	26	28	31	34	36	39	43	46	50
BRAZIL																
Population	145.0	147.0	150.0	152.6	155.2	157.8	160.2	162.6	165.0	167.5	170.0	172.5	175.1	177.8	180.4	183.1
Capacity	2,313	2,313	2,313	2,886	2,908	3,073	3,157	3,510	3,675	4,105	4,546	4,546	5,648	5,648	5,648	5,648
Demand	1,629	1,592	1,570	1,828	2,088	2,414	2,577	2,740	2,937	3,155	3,396	3,621	3,869	4,140	4,438	4,765
Production	2,112	1,971	2,026	2,525	2,719	2,680	2,784	3,104	2,976	3,379	3,783	3,795	4,798	4,810	4,822	4,834
Operating Capacity	91%	85%	88%	87%	94%	87%	88%	88%	81%	82%	83%	83%	85%	85%	85%	86%
Consumption per Capita	11	11	10	12	13	15	16	17	18	19	20	21	22	23	25	26
MERCOSUR																
Population	185	188	191	194	198	201	204	207	210	213	216	219	222	225	229	232
Capacity	2,979	2,979	2,979	3,552	3,574	3,740	3,823	4,176	4,341	4,771	5,329	6,149	7,251	7,251	7,251	7,251
Demand	2,019	2,115	2,191	2,573	2,927	3,221	3,479	3,743	4,035	4,361	4,724	5,068	5,449	5,869	6,334	6,848
Production	2,612	2,474	2,568	3,056	3,288	3,211	3,379	3,699	3,641	4,045	4,449	4,577	6,401	6,412	6,424	6,436
Operating Capacity	88%	83%	86%	86%	92%	86%	88%	89%	84%	85%	83%	74%	88%	88%	89%	89%
Consumption per Capita	11	11	11	13	15	16	17	18	19	20	22	23	25	26	28	30
TOTAL LATIN AMERICA[a]																
Population	423	432	441	449	457	464	472	479	485	492	500	507	515	523	531	539
Capacity	4,616	4,661	4,661	5,234	5,366	5,756	5,840	6,215	6,437	6,951	7,590	9,056	11,358	11,878	11,878	11,878
Demand	4,537	4,836	5,187	5,749	6,537	6,579	7,314	7,913	8,470	9,084	9,762	10,417	11,135	11,922	12,785	13,735
Production	4,178	4,112	4,286	4,662	4,990	4,972	5,251	5,796	6,516	6,931	7,721	8,262	9,832	10,867	11,515	12,233
Operating Capacity	90%	88%	92%	89%	93%	86%	90%	93%	101%	100%	102%	91%	87%	91%	97%	103%
Consumption per Capita	11	11	12	13	14	14	15	17	17	18	20	21	22	23	24	25

(a) Mercosur + Chile + Andean pact + Caribbean & Central America + Mexico.

Source: Dow Química Argentina S.A.

EXHIBIT 4A

SALE PROCEEDS FOR SELECTED PRIVATIZATIONS (IN MILLIONS OF US DOLLARS)

Enterprise	Cash	Debt[a]
YPF	3,040	855
Telephone	2,271[b]	5,000
Aerolíneas Argentinas	260	1,610
Petrochemicals	53	0
Oil fields	1,560	0
Power (SEGBA, AYE)	308	955
Real estate	107	0
Steel companies	143	40
Natural gas	300	2,651
Ports	14	0
TOTAL	**8,056**	**11,111**

(a) Face value.

(b) Plus $380 million in promissory notes.

Source: Adapted from Argentina's Privatization Program: World Bank Publication, 1993. This exhibit was taken from HBS case No. 9-702-002, "Argentina's Convertibility Plan," by Rafael di Tella and Huw Pill, p. 14.

EXHIBIT 4B

FOREIGN DIRECT INVESTMENT AND PRIVATIZATIONS, 1990–1995

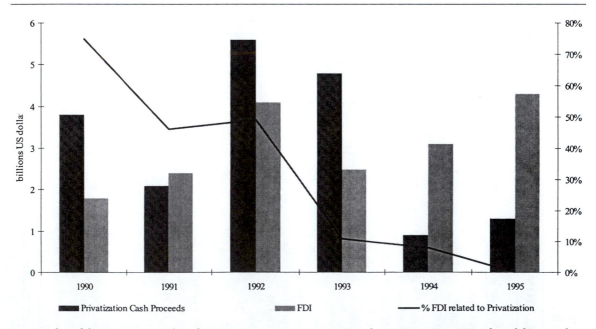

Source: Adapted from Japan External Trade Organization, "Privatization in Developing Countries," 1998. This exhibit was taken from HBS case No. 9-702-002, "Argentina's Convertibility Plan," by Rafael di Tella and Huw Pill, p. 14.

EXHIBIT 5

MACROECONOMIC DATA ON MERCOSUR COUNTRIES

Data series	Unit	1995			
		Argentina	Brazil	Uruguay	Paraguay
Real GDP (PPP US$ at 1996 prices)	mil USD	322,139	1,088,000	23,786	17,222
GDP per capita	USD	7,421	4,321	7,325	3,498
International reserves/total debt	%	16.2	32.0	31.5	43.2
Exchange rate LCU:US$ (av)	LC/USD	1.0000	0.9177	0.1575	0.00059
Private consumption (real change p.a.)	%	−4.4	16.4	−3.7	2.6
Consumer Prices (end-period change p.a.)	%	1.6	22.4	35.2	10.5
Recorded unemployment	%	15.4	4.6	10.3	8.1
Population	(million)	35	163	3	5

Source: EIU Country Data database at http://80-countrydata.bvdep.com.ezp2.harvard.edu/cgi/template.dll?product=101&user=ipaddress. Accessed 08/27/2003.

Argentina. The food and packaging industries and the supermarket/hypermarket sector (including multinationals such as Carrefour and Wal-Mart) had experienced dramatic growth since 1991. Competition from imported products in modern attractive packaging was forcing local manufacturers to upgrade their presentations. The Brazilian plastics market, three times the size of Argentina's, had also experienced significant growth during this period.

The expected growth in polyethylene demand made PBB a potentially attractive acquisition (see Exhibit 3 for Latin American ethylene and polyethylene capacity). As Vignart observed:

> The Bahia Blanca petrochemical pole has structural disadvantages, but there is an abundant supply of primary materials (petroleum and gas) and energy is competitively priced. If we were to get into the privatization, the project would require the modernization of existing facilities and a considerable increase in production capacity through the expansion of existing plants and the construction of new plants, in order to become internationally competitive. By planning to produce not just for the domestic market, but also for all of Mercosur, and especially Brazil, the Bahia Blanca complex would be able to justify its new scale.

PBB's Growth Potential

The acquisition of PBB would be the first step towards consolidating all of Bahia Blanca's polyethylene activity under Dow's control, a plan Vignart believed was consistent with Dow's business model. To achieve this goal, Dow would also have to acquire Polisur's two polyethylene plants and expand existing capacity. According to Dow engineers, the expansion of its polyethylene capacity in Bahia Blanca would require the company to build a world-class competitive cracker. Doing so would nearly triple PBB's ethylene capacity.

Marcer and Vignart therefore, had to consider not just what to bid for PBB in the privatization, but also develop an overall plan for the development of Dow's polyethyl-

EXHIBIT 6

PBB PRIVATIZATION TERMS

The Argentine government offered for sale shares representing 51% of the total capital stock of Petroquímica Bahia Blanca S.A. (PBB).

The tender was designed as follows:

(a) Bidders were invited to participate in a 45-day "due diligence" process. For that purpose, every bidder had access on assigned days to PBB's "data rooms" and could ask for additional information about the companies. Information provided to any bidder was made available to the other participants.

(b) Following the due diligence process the bidders were required to present their offers in two envelopes.

(c) Bidders were to submit in envelope number 1 the fulfillment of legal and accounting requirements:
   a. by-laws and most recent balance sheets;
   b. a board resolution accepting the terms and conditions of the bid;
   c. a statement of net worth of at least US$5 billion;
   d. an offer guaranty (deposit of money or letter of credit issued by a first class bank) in favor of the government for an amount of US$15 million.

(d) Offers submitted in envelope number 2 were to be:
   a. unconditionally subject to the terms of the bid;
   b. inclusive of all the offered shares of PBB;
   c. expressed in U.S. dollars without any reserve.

(e) Once the government determined that a bidder had satisfactorily complied with the requirements set forth for the contents of envelope 1, envelope 2 was to be opened. The only consideration open to the seller in assigning the shares was price, the minimum accepted price being US$150 million.

(f) The price was inclusive of all offered shares. The seller made no other representation than that the shares were validly issued and free of any encumbrances and that their owners would be accorded the right of vote and dividends as set forth in the by-laws and other corporate documents. The seller's sole liability was for any contingency unknown at, and that arose after, the date of transfer; any contingency discovered within two years of the transfer date would be compensated up to the amount of US$8 million.

(g) The price had to be paid in cash within three days of the seller officially accepting the offer.

Source: Dow Quimica Argentina S.A.

ene business in Argentina. Gaining control of PBB would be the first step in a project, which they defined in three stages:

- *Stage 1* involved taking control of PBB, which comprised the ethylene cracker and a polyethylene plant and then upgrading the facilities in order to make them internationally competitive
- *Stage 2* involved acquiring Polisur's two polyethylene plants
- *Stage 3* involved building a new ethylene cracker and a polyethylene plant

The production capacity and investment required for each stage of the project are described in Exhibit 7. Vignart and Marcer also sought to identify the main issues for each stage of the project.

EXHIBIT 7

DESCRIPTION OF THE DIFFERENT STAGES OF THE PROJECT

	Production Capacity MM lb. as of 1995	Increased Capacity MM lb.	Total Investments MM $ between 1996 and 2000
Stage 1			
PBB Ethylene Cracker	540	66	128.9
PBB Polyethylene Plant	203	—	28.0
Stage 2			
Polisur—2 Polyethylene Plants	463	—	45.8
Stage 3			
New Ethylene Cracker	—	937	376.3
New Polyethylene Plant	—	595	160

Source: Dow Quimica Argentina S.A.

In Stage 1, Vignart and Marcer had to consider Dow's competitors in the bidding for PBB. Two major regional players—the Brazilian privately owned petrochemical company Copesul and the family-owned Argentine firm Perez Companc—had teamed up for the purpose of taking over PBB.[8] Typically in its acquisitions, Perez Companc had sought foreign partners with the capacity to issue debt in the international financial markets in order to bid jointly. Copesul, which had been privatized in 1992, produced petrochemicals including ethylene in Brazil and was interested in expanding internationally into petrochemicals (see Exhibit 8A for Perez Companc financial data and Exhibit 8B for Copesul financial data).

In Stage 2, Dow would have to negotiate with Ipako, a private company owned by local businessmen that owned 100% of Polisur.

For Stage 3 to be successful, the supply of ethane would have to be secured, and a key issue for Vignart was how to secure additional ethane for a new cracker. The current supplier was TGS, but Vignart believed that the magnitude of the project required an alliance with a larger player. He knew that YPF, which produced approximately 50% of the natural gas in Argentina, was looking for alliances downstream. YPF was Argentina's largest enterprise and the eleventh-largest oil and gas company in the world. Vignart had been impressed by YPF's restructuring which led to its successful privatization,[9] and he considered it a potentially credible partner. Vignart wondered whether building a strategic alliance that went beyond a long-term ethane contract might enhance the project's probability of success.

VALUATION

Marcer and Vignart worked on the valuation in collaboration with the corporate M&A department. The valuation team included two economic valuators, one based in Buenos

---

[8]In the recent Argentine privatizations, Perez Companc had already made several acquisitions in the telecommunication and energy sectors. It was granted major gas and oil concessions, part of the San Lorenzo refinery and TGS that provided ethane to PBB.

[9]YPF was privatized in June 1993 in an international public offering which yielded $3.04 billion.

EXHIBIT 8A

MAIN FINANCIAL DATA ON PEREZ COMPANC S.A. (IN MILLIONS OF U.S. DOLLARS)

Perez Companc Sales (MM US$)	1993	1994	1995
Oil and Gas Production and Services	560	594	672
Petrochemicals and Refineries	38	212	482
Telecommunications	148	158	138
Construction	165	139	144
Farming, Forestry and Agro Industrial	37	40	42
Other Investments	100	119	115
Sub-total	1,048	1,262	1,593
Eliminations	53	111	126
Total sales	995	1,151	1,467

Perez Companc Other Key Financial Data (MM US$)	1993	1994	1995
Operating Income	129	154	186
Net Financial Expense	(23)	(42)	(26)
Total Assets	2,496	2,567	2,830
Current Liabilities	514	467	501
Non Current Liabilities	720	691	748
Sub-total	1,234	1,158	1,249
Minority Interest	113	122	120
Shareholders' Equity	1,149	1,288	1,461
Total Liabilities and Shareholders' Equity	2,496	2,568	2,830

Source: Perez Companc S.A., 1995 Annual Report (Argentina: Perez Companc, 1995), pp. 29 and 35.

EXHIBIT 8B

MAIN FINANCIAL DATA ON COPESUL

Copesul Shareholders	1995
Odebrecht Group (Brazilian company)	29%
Ipiranga Group (Brazilian company)	29%
Petroquisa (subsidiary of Petrobras, the state-owned oil company)	15%
Others (banks, pension funds, and others)	27%

Copesul Key Financial Data (thousand U.S.$)	1993	1994	1995
Total Net Sales	637,959	662,759	677,780
Operating Income	(21,566)	12,918	96,755
Net Financial Income (Expense)	17,663	21,518	58,288
Net Income	(476)	21,121	65,950
Total Assets	1,250,191	1,166,993	1,221,815
Current Liabilities	105,189	99,877	160,834
Non Current Liabilities	41,130	80,540	131,443
Sub-total	146,319	180,417	292,277
Shareholder's Equity	1,103,872	986,576	929,538
Total Liabilities and Shareholders' Equity	1,250,191	1,166,993	1,221,815

Source: Company Reports and Economatica.

Aires, the other at headquarters. The board of directors had retained Chase Manhattan Bank to provide an independent assessment of the value of PBB. Marcer and the economic valuator used standard Dow procedures based on net present value to evaluate the different stages of the project. The Dow methodology emphasized building a cash flow model and then running sensitivity analyses.

Stage 1 Cash Flows

For Stage 1, the Dow team developed two cash flows, one for the PBB ethylene cracker and one for the PBB polyethylene plant.

The cash flow for the PBB ethylene cracker is given in Exhibit 9A. Cash flow items for the PBB cracker included:

- *Revenues*   Approximately 95% of cracker revenues derived from the sale of ethylene, the remainder from by-product credits. All the ethylene produced would be sold internally at the Bahia Blanca complex at the international ethylene market price in U.S. dollars.

- *Variable costs*   Ethane represented 85% of the cracker's variable costs. A cracker's competitiveness depended in part on its "ethane ratio" (the volume of ethane consumed per pound of ethylene produced). The existing PBB cracker had a higher ethane ratio than new crackers; that is, it consumed more ethane to produce the same amount of ethylene. The price of ethane from the local supplier was based on the international market price of ethane in U.S. dollars. Utilities (fuel, gas, energy, chemicals) accounted for the balance of the variable costs.

- *Fixed costs*   Overhead (mainly labor) and maintenance were for the most part a local currency cost. At PBB, fixed costs would gradually be reduced to approximately 15% of the total costs of the plant producing at a 100% operating rate.

The cash flow for the PBB polyethylene plant is given in Exhibit 9B. Cash flow items for the PBB polyethylene plant included:

- *Revenues*   Polyethylene was sold at the international market price in U.S. dollars.
- *Freight and duty*   The incidence of transport and duties in the net sales price (net sales price = gross sales prices − freight and duties) made the business mix by geographic area a key factor for profitability. Transport cost represented around 3% of the net sales price in the case of selling locally, 10% in the case of selling to the Mercosur, and 17% in the case of selling to the rest of Latin America. When selling to the Extra Zone (the United States, Europe, or Asia), transport cost represented around 24% of the net sales price.

  For the PBB plant, it was anticipated that all production would be sold in the local market.

- *Variable costs*   Ethylene consumption represented approximately 85% of total variable costs denominated in U.S. dollars. A plant's competitiveness depended in part on its "ethylene ratio" (the volume of ethylene consumed per pound of polyethylene produced).

- *Fixed costs*   Overhead (mainly labor) and maintenance were largely local currency costs. At PBB, fixed costs represented 15% of the total costs of a plant producing at a 100% operating rate.

EXHIBIT 9A

STAGE 1—PBB BASE CASE CASH FLOW—ETHYLENE CRACKER

STAGE 1-PBB

Ethylene Cracker	1995	1996	1997	1998	1999	2000	2001	2002	2003	2004	2005	2006	2007	2008	2009	2010
REVENUE																
Ethylene Production Capacity (MM lb)	540.1	540.1	540.1	540.1	606.0	606.0	606.0	606.0	606.0	606.0	606.0	606.0	606.0	606.0	606.0	606.0
Operating rate	90.2%	90.0%	100.0%	100.0%	100.0%	100.0%	100.0%	100.0%	100.0%	100.0%	100.0%	100.0%	100.0%	100.0%	100.0%	100.0%
Ethylene Volume Production (MM lbs)	**487.0**	**486.1**	**540.1**	**540.1**	**606.0**	**606.0**	**606.0**	**606.0**	**606.0**	**606.0**	**606.0**	**606.0**	**606.0**	**606.0**	**606.0**	**606.0**
Ethylene International Net Sales Price (US$/lb)	0.273	0.219	0.250	0.220	0.190	0.222	0.285	0.358	0.297	0.247	0.218	0.229	0.261	0.304	0.346	0.306
Ethylene revenue	**132.9**	**106.4**	**135.2**	**119.0**	**115.4**	**134.7**	**172.6**	**216.9**	**180.2**	**149.9**	**132.0**	**138.9**	**158.3**	**184.0**	**209.7**	**185.5**
By product credit sales	**5.0**	**5.4**	**5.7**	**6.1**	**9.2**	**8.4**	**8.4**	**8.3**	**8.5**	**8.9**	**9.0**	**9.6**	**9.9**	**10.2**	**10.4**	**10.7**
TOTAL REVENUES	**137.9**	**111.8**	**140.9**	**125.1**	**124.6**	**143.1**	**181.0**	**225.2**	**188.7**	**158.8**	**141.0**	**148.5**	**168.2**	**194.2**	**220.1**	**196.2**
COSTS																
Ethane international price (US$/lb)	0.0625	0.0638	0.0625	0.0617	0.0625	0.0743	0.0776	0.0810	0.0844	0.0878	0.0911	0.0945	0.0979	0.0979	0.0979	0.0979
Ethane ratio (volume of ethane consumed per lb. of ethylene)	1.2670	1.2670	1.2670	1.2670	1.2670	1.2670	1.2670	1.2670	1.2670	1.2670	1.2670	1.2670	1.2670	1.2670	1.2670	1.2670
Ethylene Volume Production (MM lbs)	487.0	486.1	540.1	540.1	606.0	606.0	606.0	606.0	606.0	606.0	606.0	606.0	606.0	606.0	606.0	606.0
Ethane cost	**38.6**	**39.3**	**42.8**	**42.2**	**48.0**	**57.0**	**59.6**	**62.2**	**64.8**	**67.4**	**69.9**	**72.6**	**75.2**	**75.2**	**75.2**	**75.2**
Other variable costs (5% of sales)	**6.9**	**5.6**	**7.0**	**6.3**	**6.2**	**7.2**	**9.1**	**11.3**	**9.4**	**7.9**	**7.0**	**7.4**	**8.4**	**9.7**	**11.0**	**9.8**
Total variable costs	**45.5**	**44.9**	**49.8**	**48.5**	**54.2**	**64.2**	**68.6**	**73.5**	**74.2**	**75.4**	**77.0**	**80.0**	**83.6**	**84.9**	**86.2**	**85.0**

(Continued)

EXHIBIT 9A *(Continued)*

STAGE 1—PBB BASE CASE CASH FLOW—ETHYLENE CRACKER

STAGE 1-PBB Ethylene Cracker	1995	1996	1997	1998	1999	2000	2001	2002	2003	2004	2005	2006	2007	2008	2009	2010
Total fixed costs	**25.2**	**26.1**	**18.3**	**14.5**	**14.8**	**15.3**	**14.5**	**15.0**	**15.4**	**15.9**	**16.3**	**16.9**	**17.4**	**18.0**	**18.5**	**19.1**
Depreciation	**4.2**	**4.9**	**12.2**	**14.1**	**15.3**	**16.3**	**17.0**	**17.8**	**18.6**	**19.5**	**16.1**	**16.3**	**9.9**	**9.0**	**8.8**	**8.9**
PROFIT BEFORE TAX	**63.1**	**35.9**	**60.6**	**48.0**	**40.3**	**47.4**	**80.9**	**118.9**	**80.5**	**48.1**	**31.5**	**35.3**	**57.3**	**82.3**	**106.6**	**83.3**
Tax (31% until 1999 then 36%)	19.6	11.1	18.8	14.9	12.5	17.1	29.1	42.8	29.0	17.3	11.4	12.7	20.6	29.6	38.4	30.0
PROFIT AFTER TAX	**43.5**	**24.8**	**41.8**	**33.1**	**27.8**	**30.3**	**51.8**	**76.1**	**51.5**	**30.8**	**20.2**	**22.6**	**36.7**	**52.7**	**68.2**	**53.3**
Plus: Depreciation	4.2	4.9	12.2	14.1	15.3	16.3	17.0	17.8	18.6	19.5	16.1	16.3	9.9	9.0	8.8	8.9
Less: Change in working capital (6% of sales)	8.3	(1.6)	1.7	(1.0)	(0.0)	1.1	2.3	2.6	(2.2)	(1.8)	(1.1)	0.5	1.2	1.6	1.6	(1.4)
Less: Investments	—	7.5	72.9	18.5	12.0	9.9	7.6	7.9	8.1	8.4	8.7	9.0	9.2	9.5	9.8	10.2
Plus: PBB Positive Cash Treasury Position U.S.$	74.0	—	—	—	—	—	—	—	—	—	—	—	—	—	—	—
CASH FLOW ETHYLENE - Stage 1	**113.4**	**23.8**	**(20.6)**	**29.7**	**31.1**	**35.6**	**58.9**	**83.4**	**64.2**	**43.6**	**28.7**	**29.4**	**36.2**	**50.6**	**65.7**	**53.4**

Source: Dow Química Argentina S.A.

EXHIBIT 9B

STAGE 1—BASE CASH FLOW—PBB POLYETHYLENE PLANT (IN MILLIONS OF US DOLLARS)

STAGE 1-PBB POLYETHYLENE PLANT

	1995	1996	1997	1998	1999	2000	2001	2002	2003	2004	2005	2006	2007	2008	2009	2010
VOLUME																
Polyethylene Production Capacity (MM lbs)	202.8	202.8	202.8	202.8	202.8	202.8	202.8	202.8	202.8	202.8	202.8	202.8	202.8	202.8	202.8	202.8
Operating rate	65.0%	65.0%	65.0%	100.0%	100.0%	100.0%	100.0%	100.0%	100.0%	100.0%	100.0%	100.0%	100.0%	100.0%	100.0%	100.0%
Polyethylene Total Volume Production (MM lbs)	131.8	131.8	131.8	202.8	202.8	202.8	202.8	202.8	202.8	202.8	202.8	202.8	202.8	202.8	202.8	202.8
Polyethylene Sales Breakdown																
Sold locally	100.0%	100.0%	100.0%	100.0%	100.0%	100.0%	100.0%	100.0%	100.0%	100.0%	100.0%	100.0%	100.0%	100.0%	100.0%	100.0%
Exports Mercosur	—	—	—	—	—	—	—	—	—	—	—	—	—	—	—	—
Export Latin America	—	—	—	—	—	—	—	—	—	—	—	—	—	—	—	—
Export Extra Zone	—	—	—	—	—	—	—	—	—	—	—	—	—	—	—	—
Polyethylene Total Volume Production (MM lbs)																
Sold locally	131.8	131.8	131.8	202.8	202.8	202.8	202.8	202.8	202.8	202.8	202.8	202.8	202.8	202.8	202.8	202.8
Exports Mercosur	—	—	—	—	—	—	—	—	—	—	—	—	—	—	—	—
Export Latin America	—	—	—	—	—	—	—	—	—	—	—	—	—	—	—	—
Export Extra Zone Total	131.8	131.8	131.8	202.8	202.8	202.8	202.8	202.8	202.8	202.8	202.8	202.8	202.8	202.8	202.8	202.8

(*Continued*)

EXHIBIT 9B (Continued)

STAGE 1—BASE CASH FLOW—PBB POLYETHYLENE PLANT (IN MILLIONS OF US DOLLARS)

STAGE 1-PBB

POLYETHYLENE PLANT	1995	1996	1997	1998	1999	2000	2001	2002	2003	2004	2005	2006	2007	2008	2009	2010
PRICE																
Polyethylene International Gross Sales																
Price (US$/lb)	0.581	0.483	0.522	0.486	0.450	0.491	0.561	0.641	0.560	0.494	0.461	0.475	0.514	0.565	0.616	0.571
Polyethylene Freight & Duties cost:																
Sold locally	0.017	0.017	0.017	0.017	0.017	0.017	0.017	0.017	0.017	0.017	0.017	0.017	0.017	0.017	0.017	0.017
Exports Mercosur	0.054	0.054	0.054	0.054	0.054	0.054	0.054	0.054	0.054	0.054	0.054	0.054	0.054	0.054	0.054	0.054
Export Latin America	0.077	0.077	0.077	0.077	0.077	0.077	0.077	0.077	0.077	0.077	0.077	0.077	0.077	0.077	0.077	0.077
Export Extra Zone	0.100	0.100	0.100	0.100	0.100	0.100	0.100	0.100	0.100	0.100	0.100	0.100	0.100	0.100	0.100	0.100
Polyethylene International Net Sales Price (US$/lb)																
Sold locally	0.565	0.466	0.506	0.469	0.434	0.475	0.544	0.625	0.543	0.477	0.444	0.459	0.497	0.548	0.599	0.554
Exports Mercosur	0.527	0.428	0.468	0.432	0.396	0.437	0.506	0.587	0.506	0.439	0.406	0.421	0.460	0.510	0.561	0.516
Export Latin America	0.504	0.406	0.445	0.409	0.373	0.414	0.484	0.564	0.483	0.417	0.384	0.398	0.437	0.488	0.538	0.493
Export Extra Zone	0.482	0.383	0.423	0.386	0.350	0.391	0.461	0.541	0.460	0.394	0.361	0.376	0.414	0.465	0.516	0.471
TOTAL REVENUE	**74.5**	**61.5**	**66.7**	**95.2**	**87.9**	**96.3**	**110.4**	**126.7**	**110.2**	**96.8**	**90.1**	**93.1**	**100.9**	**111.2**	**121.5**	**112.4**

(Continued)

EXHIBIT 9B (Continued)

STAGE 1—BASE CASH FLOW—PBB POLYETHYLENE PLANT (IN MILLIONS OF US DOLLARS)

STAGE 1-PBB POLYETHYLENE PLANT	1995	1996	1997	1998	1999	2000	2001	2002	2003	2004	2005	2006	2007	2008	2009	2010
TOTAL REVENUE	**74.5**	**61.5**	**66.7**	**95.2**	**87.9**	**96.3**	**110.4**	**126.7**	**110.2**	**96.8**	**90.1**	**93.1**	**100.9**	**111.2**	**121.5**	**112.4**
COSTS																
Ethylene international net price US$/lb	0.273	0.219	0.250	0.220	0.190	0.222	0.285	0.358	0.297	0.247	0.218	0.229	0.261	0.304	0.346	0.306
Ethylene ratio (volume of ethylene consumed per lb. of polyethylene)	1.007	1.007	1.007	1.007	1.007	1.007	1.007	1.007	1.007	1.007	1.007	1.007	1.007	1.007	1.007	1.007
Polyethylene Total Volume Production (MM lbs)	131.8	131.8	131.8	202.8	202.8	202.8	202.8	202.8	202.8	202.8	202.8	202.8	202.8	202.8	202.8	202.8
Ethylene cost	**36.2**	**29.1**	**33.2**	**45.0**	**38.9**	**45.4**	**58.2**	**73.1**	**60.7**	**50.5**	**44.5**	**46.8**	**53.4**	**62.0**	**70.7**	**62.5**
Other variable costs (10% of sales)	**7.4**	**6.1**	**6.7**	**9.5**	**8.8**	**9.6**	**11.0**	**12.7**	**11.0**	**9.7**	**9.0**	**9.3**	**10.1**	**11.1**	**12.1**	**11.2**
Total variable costs	**43.7**	**35.2**	**39.9**	**54.5**	**47.7**	**55.0**	**69.2**	**85.8**	**71.8**	**60.2**	**53.5**	**56.1**	**63.4**	**73.1**	**82.8**	**73.7**
Total fixed costs	**10.6**	**13.6**	**9.0**	**6.8**	**6.9**	**6.4**	**5.9**	**6.1**	**6.3**	**6.5**	**6.7**	**6.9**	**7.1**	**7.3**	**7.6**	**7.8**
Depreciation	**8.8**	**9.1**	**9.9**	**10.6**	**10.9**	**11.2**	**11.5**	**11.6**	**11.7**	**11.9**	**3.2**	**3.1**	**2.5**	**1.9**	**1.7**	**1.6**
PROFIT BEFORE TAX	**11.4**	**3.6**	**8.0**	**23.3**	**22.4**	**23.6**	**23.8**	**23.2**	**20.5**	**18.2**	**26.7**	**27.0**	**27.9**	**28.8**	**29.3**	**29.2**
Tax (31% until 1999 then 36%)	3.5	1.1	2.5	7.2	6.9	8.5	8.6	8.4	7.4	6.6	9.6	9.7	10.0	10.4	10.6	10.5

(Continued)

EXHIBIT 9B   (Continued)

STAGE 1—BASE CASH FLOW—PBB POLYETHYLENE PLANT (IN MILLIONS OF US DOLLARS)

STAGE 1-PBB

POLYETHYLENE PLANT	1995	1996	1997	1998	1999	2000	2001	2002	2003	2004	2005	2006	2007	2008	2009	2010
PROFIT AFTER TAX	**7.8**	**2.5**	**5.5**	**16.1**	**15.5**	**15.1**	**15.2**	**14.9**	**13.1**	**11.7**	**17.1**	**17.2**	**17.9**	**18.5**	**18.8**	**18.7**
Plus: Depreciation	8.8	9.1	9.9	10.6	10.9	11.2	11.5	11.6	11.7	11.9	3.2	3.1	2.5	1.9	1.7	1.6
Less: Change in working capital (20% of sales)	14.9	2.6	(1.0)	(5.7)	1.5	(1.7)	(2.8)	(3.3)	3.3	2.7	1.3	(0.6)	(1.6)	(2.1)	(2.1)	1.8
Less: Investments	—	2.6	8.2	7.3	3.1	6.8	7.5	1.3	1.4	1.4	1.5	1.5	1.6	1.6	1.7	1.7
CASH FLOW																
POLYETHYLENE - Stage 1	**1.7**	**6.4**	**8.2**	**25.1**	**21.8**	**21.2**	**22.0**	**28.4**	**20.1**	**19.4**	**17.5**	**19.4**	**20.3**	**20.8**	**20.9**	**16.7**

CONSOLIDATED PBB

CASH FLOWS - STAGE 1	1995	1996	1997	1998	1999	2000	2001	2002	2003	2004	2005	2006	2007	2008	2009	2010
Cash flow ethylene	113.4	23.8	(20.6)	29.7	31.1	35.6	58.9	83.4	64.2	43.6	28.7	29.4	36.2	50.6	65.7	53.4
Cash flow polyethylene	1.7	6.4	8.2	25.1	21.8	21.2	22.0	28.4	20.1	19.4	17.5	19.4	20.3	20.8	20.9	16.7
TOTAL CASH FLOW - STAGE 1	**115.2**	**30.1**	**(12.4)**	**54.7**	**52.9**	**56.7**	**80.9**	**111.8**	**84.3**	**63.1**	**46.2**	**48.9**	**56.5**	**71.4**	**86.6**	**70.1**

Source: Dow Química Argentina S.A.

Stage 2 Cash Flows

In Stage 2, Dow would acquire control of Polisur, the only other polyethylene firm in Argentina. Exhibit 10 provides the cash flows for the Polisur polyethylene plants. The cash flows for Stage 2 of the project were projected using the same model as for the PBB polyethylene plant in Stage 1, taking into account the greater efficiency of the Polisur plants in terms of their variable and fixed costs. Also, while the existing Polisur production was sold within Argentina and Mercosur, it was anticipated that eventually all of the production would be sold in the local market.

Stage 3 Cash Flows

Stage 3 of the project involved building a new ethylene cracker and a new polyethylene plant.

Exhibit 11A provides the cash flow projections for the new ethylene cracker, using the same model as for the PBB cracker in Stage 1. The new cracker would be more efficient than the PBB cracker, with an improved ethane ratio, and fixed costs for the new cracker would account for only 6% of total costs.

Exhibit 11B provides the cash flows for the new polyethylene plant, using the same model as for the PBB plant in Stage 1. The new plant, however, would be more efficient and fixed costs would be reduced to 10% of total costs.

The new polyethylene plant would start to operate in 2001, exporting 70% of its production. Demand in the Mercosur trade bloc was projected to escalate at a rate such that in 2010 all of the new plants' sales would be concentrated in Argentina (43% of the volume) and Mercosur (57%). For projections of polyethylene demand, Vignart explained, industry planners used a multiple of GDP growth (1.5 to 2 times). If demand in Argentina and the rest of Mercosur fell short of expectations, exports to other regions could always be increased, albeit at the expense of profitability.

Terminal Values

In their financial analysis, Vignart and Marcer also had to incorporate the terminal value of each stage of the project. Since demand and prices were subject to cyclical changes, they decided that the future cash flows for each stage of the project could best be estimated by using the average of the last five years of cash flows. They used 3.3% as the terminal growth rate for the project.

Risk Measurement

To assess whether the project would earn an acceptable return on the investment, Vignart and Marcer had to consider Dow's weighted average cost of capital and determine a risk premium for doing the project in Argentina. The risks of political instability or expropriation appeared small since Argentina had had a stable democratic government for the past twelve years and there had been no case of expropriation in the previous 50 years.

Currency risk and the possible impact of government policies on the project were more difficult to evaluate. Argentina had experienced no less than eight major currency crises between the early 1970s and 1991, and in 1995 the banking and credit crisis—known as the Tequila crisis—affected Argentina.[10] The Convertibility Law, which tied

---

[10]The Tequila crisis was attributed to the loss of confidence following the Mexican peso devaluation in December 1994, and uncertainty regarding the Argentine presidential elections in May 1995, in which President Menem was ultimately re-elected.

EXHIBIT 10

STAGE 2—POLISUR BASE CASE CASH FLOW (IN MILLIONS OF US DOLLARS)

STAGE 2- POLISUR POLYETHYLENE PLANTS	1995	1996	1997	1998	1999	2000	2001	2002	2003	2004	2005	2006	2007	2008	2009	2010
VOLUME																
Polyethylene Production Capacity (MM lb)	462.6	463.0	463.0	463.0	463.0	463.0	463.0	463.0	463.0	463.0	463.0	463.0	463.0	463.0	463.0	463.0
Operating rate	86.0%	100.0%	100.0%	100.0%	100.0%	100.0%	100.0%	100.0%	100.0%	100.0%	100.0%	100.0%	100.0%	100.0%	100.0%	100.0%
Polyethylene Total Volume Production (MM lbs)	**397.8**	**463.0**	**463.0**	**463.0**	**463.0**	**463.0**	**463.0**	**463.0**	**463.0**	**463.0**	**463.0**	**463.0**	**463.0**	**463.0**	**463.0**	**463.0**
Polyethylene Sales Breakdown																
Sold locally	84.0%	85.0%	89.0%	91.0%	95.0%	98.0%	100.0%	100.0%	100.0%	100.0%	100.0%	100.0%	100.0%	100.0%	100.0%	100.0%
Exports Mercosur	16.0%	15.0%	11.0%	9.0%	5.0%	2.0%	—	—	—	—	—	—	—	—	—	—
Export Latin America	—	—	—	—	—	—	—	—	—	—	—	—	—	—	—	—
Export Extra Zone	—	—	—	—	—	—	—	—	—	—	—	—	—	—	—	—
Polyethylene Total Volume Production (MM lbs)																
Sold locally	334.1	393.5	412.0	421.3	439.8	453.7	463.0	463.0	463.0	463.0	463.0	463.0	463.0	463.0	463.0	463.0
Exports Mercosur	63.6	69.4	50.9	41.7	23.1	9.3	—	—	—	—	—	—	—	—	—	—
Export Latin America	—	—	—	—	—	—	—	—	—	—	—	—	—	—	—	—
Export Extra Zone	—	—	—	—	—	—	—	—	—	—	—	—	—	—	—	—
Total	397.8	463.0	463.0	463.0	463.0	463.0	463.0	463.0	463.0	463.0	463.0	463.0	463.0	463.0	463.0	463.0

(Continued)

EXHIBIT 10 (*Continued*)

STAGE 2—POLISUR BASE CASE CASH FLOW (IN MILLIONS OF US DOLLARS)

STAGE 2-POLISUR POLYETHYLENE PLANTS

	1995	1996	1997	1998	1999	2000	2001	2002	2003	2004	2005	2006	2007	2008	2009	2010
PRICE																
Polyethylene International Gross Sales Price (US$/lb)	0.581	0.483	0.522	0.486	0.450	0.491	0.561	0.641	0.560	0.494	0.461	0.475	0.514	0.565	0.616	0.571
Polyethylene Freight & Duties cost:																
Sold locally	0.017	0.017	0.017	0.017	0.017	0.017	0.017	0.017	0.017	0.017	0.017	0.017	0.017	0.017	0.017	0.017
Exports Mercosur	0.054	0.054	0.054	0.054	0.054	0.054	0.054	0.054	0.054	0.054	0.054	0.054	0.054	0.054	0.054	0.054
Export Latin America	0.077	0.077	0.077	0.077	0.077	0.077	0.077	0.077	0.077	0.077	0.077	0.077	0.077	0.077	0.077	0.077
Export Extra Zone	0.100	0.100	0.100	0.100	0.100	0.100	0.100	0.100	0.100	0.100	0.100	0.100	0.100	0.100	0.100	0.100
Polyethylene International Net Sales Price (US$/lb)																
Sold locally	0.565	0.466	0.506	0.469	0.434	0.475	0.544	0.625	0.543	0.477	0.444	0.459	0.497	0.548	0.599	0.554
Exports Mercosur	0.527	0.428	0.468	0.432	0.396	0.437	0.506	0.587	0.506	0.439	0.406	0.421	0.460	0.510	0.561	0.516
Export Latin America	0.504	0.406	0.445	0.409	0.373	0.414	0.484	0.564	0.483	0.417	0.384	0.398	0.437	0.488	0.538	0.493
Export Extra Zone	0.482	0.383	0.423	0.386	0.350	0.391	0.461	0.541	0.460	0.394	0.361	0.376	0.414	0.465	0.516	0.471
TOTAL REVENUE	222.3	213.3	232.3	215.8	199.8	219.4	251.9	289.1	251.6	220.9	205.7	212.4	230.3	253.8	277.3	256.5

EXHIBIT 10 (*Continued*)

STAGE 2-POLISUR BASE CASE CASH FLOW (IN MILLIONS OF US DOLLARS)

STAGE 2-POLISUR POLYETHYLENE PLANTS	1995	1996	1997	1998	1999	2000	2001	2002	2003	2004	2005	2006	2007	2008	2009	2010
TOTAL REVENUE	222.3	213.3	232.3	215.8	199.8	219.4	251.9	289.1	251.6	220.9	205.7	212.4	230.3	253.8	277.3	256.5
COSTS																
Ethylene international price (US$/Lb)	0.273	0.219	0.250	0.220	0.190	0.222	0.285	0.358	0.297	0.247	0.218	0.229	0.261	0.304	0.346	0.306
Ethylene ratio (volume of ethylene consumed per lb. of polyethylene)	0.979	0.979	0.979	0.979	0.979	0.979	0.979	0.979	0.979	0.979	0.979	0.979	0.979	0.979	0.979	0.979
Polyethylene Total Volume Production (MM lbs)	397.8	463.0	463.0	463.0	463.0	463.0	463.0	463.0	463.0	463.0	463.0	463.0	463.0	463.0	463.0	463.0
Ethylene cost	106.3	99.2	113.5	99.8	86.3	100.8	129.1	162.2	134.8	112.1	98.7	103.9	118.4	137.6	156.8	138.7
Other variable costs	25.6	31.1	32.9	31.1	32.1	33.1	33.9	34.7	36.1	37.7	39.1	40.3	41.5	42.7	43.9	45.4
Total variable costs	131.9	130.3	146.4	130.9	118.4	133.9	163.0	196.9	170.9	149.8	137.8	144.2	159.9	180.3	200.7	184.1
Total fixed costs	15.1	15.1	15.5	15.9	16.3	16.6	17.0	17.4	17.9	18.3	18.7	19.2	19.6	20.1	20.6	21.1
Depreciation	2.1	4.3	4.9	5.6	6.4	7.1	4.4	5.9	6.5	7.1	7.7	8.3	9.0	6.8	6.9	7.0
PROFIT BEFORE TAX	73.1	63.5	65.4	63.3	58.8	61.7	67.5	68.8	56.3	45.7	41.5	40.7	41.8	46.6	49.1	44.2
Tax (31% until 1999 then 36%)	22.7	19.7	20.3	19.6	18.2	22.2	24.3	24.8	20.3	16.5	14.9	14.7	15.0	16.8	17.7	15.9

(*Continued*)

EXHIBIT 10 *(Continued)*

STAGE 2-POLISUR BASE CASE CASH FLOW (IN MILLIONS OF US DOLLARS)

STAGE 2-POLISUR POLYETHYLENE PLANTS	1995	1996	1997	1998	1999	2000	2001	2002	2003	2004	2005	2006	2007	2008	2009	2010
PROFIT AFTER TAX	50.5	43.8	45.2	43.7	40.6	39.5	43.2	44.1	36.1	29.3	26.5	26.1	26.8	29.8	31.4	28.3
Plus: Depreciation	2.1	4.3	4.9	5.6	6.4	7.1	4.4	5.9	6.5	7.1	7.7	8.3	9.0	6.8	6.9	7.0
Less: Change in working capital (20% of sales)	44.5	(1.8)	3.8	(3.3)	(3.2)	3.9	6.5	7.4	(7.5)	(6.1)	(3.0)	1.3	3.6	4.7	4.7	(4.2)
Less: Investments	—	10.1	6.8	7.0	7.3	14.6	15.4	5.5	5.7	5.9	6.1	6.3	6.4	6.6	6.7	6.9
CASH FLOW POLYETHYLENE - Stage 2	8.1	39.8	39.5	45.6	42.8	28.2	25.7	37.0	44.3	36.6	31.2	26.8	25.7	25.3	26.9	32.6

Source: Dow Quimíca Argentina S.A.

STAGE 3—BASE CASE CASH FLOW—ETHYLENE CRACKER (IN MILLIONS OF US DOLLARS)

Stage 3-New Ethylene Cracker	1997	1998	1999	2000	2001	2002	2003	2004	2005	2006	2007	2008	2009	2010
REVENUES														
Ethylene Production Capacity (MM lb)	—	—	—	116.8	937.0	937.0	937.0	937.0	937.0	937.0	937.0	937.0	937.0	937.0
Operating rate	—	—	—	100.0%	100.0%	100.0%	100.0%	100.0%	100.0%	100.0%	100.0%	100.0%	100.0%	100.0%
Ethylene Volume Production (MM lbs)	—	—	—	**116.8**	**937.0**	**937.0**	**937.0**	**937.0**	**937.0**	**937.0**	**937.0**	**937.0**	**937.0**	**937.0**
Ethylene International Net Sales Price (US$/lb)	—	—	—	0.2223	0.2849	0.3579	0.2974	0.2473	0.2178	0.2292	0.2612	0.3036	0.3460	0.3061
Ethylene revenues	—	—	—	**26.0**	**266.9**	**335.4**	**278.7**	**231.8**	**204.1**	**214.7**	**244.8**	**284.5**	**324.2**	**286.8**
By product credit sales	—	—	—	**0.5**	**3.8**	**3.8**	**3.8**	**3.8**	**3.8**	**3.8**	**3.8**	**3.8**	**3.8**	**3.8**
TOTAL REVENUES	—	—	—	**26.5**	**270.8**	**339.2**	**282.5**	**235.6**	**207.9**	**218.6**	**248.6**	**288.3**	**328.0**	**290.6**
COSTS														
Ethane ratio (volume of ethane consumed per lb. of ethylene)				1.2300	1.2300	1.2300	1.2300	1.2300	1.2300	1.2300	1.2300	1.2300	1.2300	1.2300
Ethylene Volume Production (MM lbs)	—	—	—	116.8	937.0	937.0	937.0	937.0	937.0	937.0	937.0	937.0	937.0	937.0
Ethane international price (US$/lb)	—	—	—	0.074	0.078	0.081	0.084	0.088	0.091	0.095	0.098	0.098	0.098	0.098
Ethane cost	—	—	—	**10.7**	**89.4**	**93.4**	**97.3**	**101.2**	**105.0**	**108.9**	**112.8**	**112.8**	**112.8**	**112.8**
Other variable costs (5% of sales)	—	—	—	1.3	13.5	17.0	14.1	11.8	10.4	10.9	12.4	14.4	16.4	14.5
Total variable costs	—	—	—	**12.0**	**103.0**	**110.3**	**111.4**	**113.0**	**115.4**	**119.8**	**125.3**	**127.2**	**129.2**	**127.4**
Total fixed costs	—	—	—	**7.0**	**7.0**	**7.2**	**7.4**	**7.5**	**7.7**	**7.9**	**8.1**	**8.1**	**8.2**	**8.4**
Depreciation	—	—	—	**37.6**	**37.6**	**37.6**	**37.6**	**37.6**	**37.6**	**37.6**	**37.6**	**37.6**	**37.6**	**37.6**
PROFIT BEFORE TAX	—	—	—	**(30.1)**	**123.2**	**184.1**	**126.1**	**77.5**	**47.2**	**53.2**	**77.6**	**115.4**	**153.0**	**154.9**
Tax (31% until 1999 then 36%)	—	—	—	—	44.4	66.3	45.4	27.9	17.0	19.2	27.9	41.5	55.1	55.7
PROFIT AFTER TAX	—	—	—	**(30.1)**	**78.8**	**117.8**	**80.7**	**49.6**	**30.2**	**34.1**	**49.7**	**73.8**	**97.9**	**99.1**
Plus: Depreciation	—	—	—	37.6	37.6	37.6	37.6	37.6	37.6	37.6	37.6	37.6	37.6	37.6
Less: Change in working capital (6% of sales)	—	—	—	1.6	14.7	4.1	(3.4)	(2.8)	(1.7)	0.6	1.8	2.4	2.4	(2.2)
Less: Investments	4.5	50.1	247.7	74.0	—	—	—	—	—	—	—	—	—	—
CASH FLOW ETHYLENE - Stage 3	**(4.5)**	**(50.1)**	**(247.7)**	**(68.1)**	**101.8**	**151.3**	**121.7**	**90.0**	**69.5**	**71.0**	**85.5**	**109.0**	**133.1**	**101.4**

Source: Dow Química Argentina S.A.

EXHIBIT 11B

STAGE 3—EXTENSION BASE CASE CASH FLOW—ONE POLYETHYLENE PLANT (IN MILLIONS OF US DOLLARS)

STAGE 3-NEW POLYETHYLENE PLANT	1997	1998	1999	2000	2001	2002	2003	2004	2005	2006	2007	2008	2009	2010
VOLUME														
Polyethylene Production Capacity in (MM lb)					595.2	595.2	595.2	595.2	595.2	595.2	595.2	595.2	595.2	595.2
Operating rate					88.9%	96.3%	100.0%	100.0%	100.0%	100.0%	100.0%	100.0%	100.0%	100.0%
Polyethylene Total Volume Production (MM lbs)					**529.1**	**573.2**	**595.2**	**595.2**	**595.2**	**595.2**	**595.2**	**595.2**	**595.2**	**595.2**
Polyethylene Sales Breakdown														
Sold locally					31.0%	31.0%	32.0%	34.0%	38.0%	42.0%	42.0%	43.0%	43.0%	43.0%
Exports Mercosur					44.0%	44.0%	47.0%	53.0%	58.0%	56.0%	56.0%	56.0%	56.0%	57.0%
Export Latin America					11.0%	11.0%	11.0%	12.0%	4.0%	2.0%	2.0%	1.0%	1.0%	—
Export Extra Zone					14.0%	14.0%	10.0%	1.0%	—	—	—	—	—	—
Polyethylene Total Volume Production MM lbs														
Sold locally					164.0	177.7	190.5	202.4	226.2	250.0	250.0	256.0	256.0	256.0
Exports Mercosur					232.8	252.2	279.8	315.5	345.2	333.3	333.3	333.3	333.3	339.3
Export Latin America					58.2	63.1	65.5	71.4	23.8	11.9	11.9	6.0	6.0	—
Export Extra Zone					74.1	80.2	59.5	6.0	—	—	—	—	—	—
Total					529.1	573.2	595.2	595.2	595.2	595.2	595.2	595.2	595.2	595.2
PRICE														
Polyethylene International Gross Sales Price (US$/lb)					0.561	0.641	0.560	0.494	0.461	0.475	0.514	0.565	0.616	0.571
Polyethylene Freight & Duties cost:														
Sold locally					0.017	0.017	0.017	0.017	0.017	0.017	0.017	0.017	0.017	0.017
Exports Mercosur					0.054	0.054	0.054	0.054	0.054	0.054	0.054	0.054	0.054	0.054
Export Latin America					0.077	0.077	0.077	0.077	0.077	0.077	0.077	0.077	0.077	0.077
Export Extra Zone					0.100	0.100	0.100	0.100	0.100	0.100	0.100	0.100	0.100	0.100
Polyethylene International Net Sales Price (US$/lb)														
Sold locally					0.544	0.625	0.543	0.477	0.444	0.459	0.497	0.548	0.599	0.554
Exports Mercosur					0.506	0.587	0.506	0.439	0.406	0.421	0.460	0.510	0.561	0.516
Export Latin America					0.484	0.564	0.483	0.417	0.384	0.398	0.437	0.488	0.538	0.493
Export Extra Zone					0.461	0.541	0.460	0.394	0.361	0.376	0.414	0.465	0.516	0.471
TOTAL REVENUE					**269.4**	**337.9**	**304.0**	**267.3**	**250.0**	**259.8**	**282.8**	**313.3**	**343.6**	**316.9**

STAGE 3—EXTENSION BASE CASE CASH FLOW—ONE POLYETHYLENE PLANT (IN MILLIONS OF US DOLLARS)

STAGE 3-NEW POLYETHYLENE PLANT

	1997	1998	1999	2000	2001	2002	2003	2004	2005	2006	2007	2008	2009	2010
TOTAL REVENUE					269.4	337.9	304.0	267.3	250.0	259.8	282.8	313.3	343.6	316.9
COSTS														
Ethylene international price (US$/lb)					0.285	0.358	0.297	0.247	0.218	0.229	0.261	0.304	0.346	0.306
Ethylene ratio (volume of ethylene consumed per lb.of polyethylene)					0.920	0.920	0.920	0.920	0.920	0.920	0.920	0.920	0.920	0.920
Polyethylene Total Volume Production MM lbs					529.1	573.2	595.2	595.2	595.2	595.2	595.2	595.2	595.2	595.2
Ethylene cost					138.7	188.7	162.9	135.5	119.3	125.5	143.1	166.3	189.5	167.6
Other variable costs (8% of sales)					21.6	27.0	24.3	21.4	20.0	20.8	22.6	25.1	27.5	25.4
Total variable costs					160.2	215.8	187.2	156.8	139.3	146.3	165.7	191.3	217.0	193.0
Total fixed costs					4.9	4.2	4.2	4.1	4.0	4.0	4.1	4.2	4.2	4.2
Depreciation					14.0	14.0	14.0	14.0	14.0	14.0	14.0	14.0	14.0	14.0
PROFIT BEFORE TAX					90.3	104.0	98.6	92.3	92.7	95.5	99.0	103.8	108.4	105.7
Tax at 36%					32.5	37.4	35.5	33.2	33.4	34.4	35.6	37.4	39.0	38.1
PROFIT AFTER TAX					57.8	66.5	63.1	59.1	59.3	61.1	63.4	66.4	69.4	67.7
Plus: Depreciation					14.0	14.0	14.0	14.0	14.0	14.0	14.0	14.0	14.0	14.0
Less: Change in working capital (20% of sales)					53.9	13.7	(6.8)	(7.3)	(3.5)	2.0	4.6	6.1	6.0	(5.3)
Less: Investments		30.0	70.0	60.0	—	—	—	—	—	—	—	—	—	—
CASH FLOW POLYETHYLENE - Stage 3		**(30.0)**	**(70.0)**	**(60.0)**	**17.9**	**66.8**	**83.9**	**80.4**	**76.8**	**73.2**	**72.8**	**74.3**	**77.3**	**87.0**
CASH FLOW ETHYLENE PLUS POLYETHYLENE - Stage 3														
Cash flow - ethylene - Stage 3	(4.5)	(50.1)	(247.7)	(68.1)	101.8	151.3	121.7	90.0	69.5	71.0	85.5	109.0	133.1	101.4
Cash flow - polyethylene - Stage 3		(30.0)	(70.0)	(60.0)	17.9	66.8	83.9	80.4	76.8	73.2	72.8	74.3	77.3	87.0
TOTAL CASH FLOW - Stage 3	**(4.5)**	**(80.1)**	**(317.7)**	**(128.1)**	**119.7**	**218.1**	**205.6**	**170.5**	**146.3**	**144.2**	**158.3**	**183.4**	**210.5**	**188.4**

Source: Dow Química Argentina S.A.

the peso to the U.S. dollar, had remained in force despite the Tequila crisis, and by November 1995, the availability and cost of funds in Argentina had significantly improved over January 1995, albeit not to the pre-Tequila level. Most of the business and financial communities, having witnessed the robustness of convertibility, were confident that it would last for several years. However, Vignart and Marcer had to consider the possibility of future crises and their likely impact on the project. They also examined government policies relevant to foreign investments. The Menem government had dismantled many of the laws and regulations on repatriation of capital. Capital repatriation in hard currency was now permitted through the free foreign exchange market without limits. No limits were imposed on payments of foreign loan principal and interest, and there were no restrictions on borrowing abroad by non-resident companies or private individuals. Vignart and Marcer debated whether to cover for exchange rate risk in the event that the Argentine convertibility law came to an end, and discussed how to assess the risk that the laws on capital repatriation might change.

Vignart and Marcer were aware that Dow had analyzed a similar project in the United States using discount rates in the range of 8 to 10% and they debated the country risk premium required for the Bahia Blanca project. As part of their analysis, they examined interest rates and yield spreads in the U.S. and Argentina over the last five years (see Exhibit 12) and reviewed the various currency, economic and political risks they had identified.

Financing Alternatives

Marcer, working with Dow's corporate M&A department, had to determine the best way to finance the acquisition of PBB as well as the subsequent stages of the project. To invest in the Bahia Blanca project, Dow would create a holding company, Dow Investment Argentina. The alternatives for the PBB bid were either to use general corporate funds or to raise debt. Marcer emphasized that the decision would be a function of the company's global financial position (see Exhibit 13 for Dow Chemical's balance sheet). In the case of raising debt, Dow would have to analyze the options of pledging the assets or giving a corporate guarantee. Because Dow had a cost advantage in raising corporate debt, it might prefer to use internal funds rather than secure project loans. Dow would be faced with the same options for Stage 2. In Stage 3, project finance aimed at funding the construction of new facilities would have to be considered as a third alternative.[11] The appetite for project finance in Argentina would depend on the country risk at the time.

PREPARING FOR THE BID

Vignart and Marcer reviewed the different scenarios they had built and the uncertainties they had identified for each stage of the project. In Stage 1, they had to decide if Copesul/Perez Companc were serious bidders and how Dow would finance the acquisition. In Stage 2, Dow would have to acquire Polisur, which would require successful negotiations with its owner. For Stage 3, Vignart believed that securing a partnership with YPF would significantly drive down the level of investment risk. Reaching a pricing agreement acceptable to both parties, however, would not be an easy task. In addition to these uncertainties, Vignart had to consider the political and economic factors that were relevant in determining the country risk for the project.

[11]Project finance was not available for funding improvements/capacity increases of existing facilities.

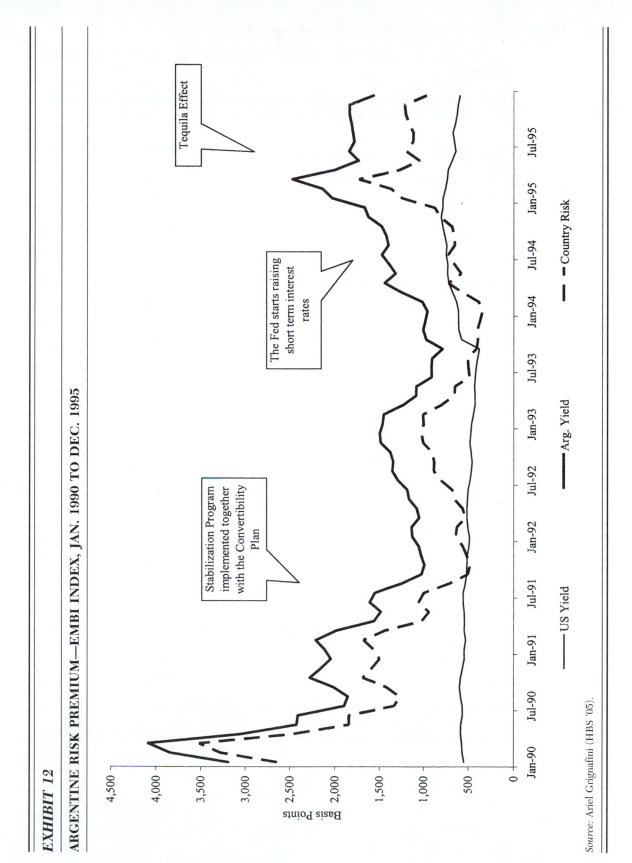

EXHIBIT 12

ARGENTINE RISK PREMIUM—EMBI INDEX, JAN. 1990 TO DEC. 1995

Tequila Effect

The Fed starts raising short term interest rates

Stabilization Program implemented together with the Convertibility Plan

Basis Points

4,500 · 4,000 · 3,500 · 3,000 · 2,500 · 2,000 · 1,500 · 1,000 · 500 · 0

Jan-90 · Jul-90 · Jan-91 · Jul-91 · Jan-92 · Jul-92 · Jan-93 · Jul-93 · Jan-94 · Jul-94 · Jan-95 · Jul-95

——— US Yield   ——— Arg. Yield   — — Country Risk

Source: Ariel Grignafini (HBS '05).

EXHIBIT 13

THE DOW CHEMICAL COMPANY CONSOLIDATED BALANCE SHEET (IN MILLIONS OF US DOLLARS, EXCEPT PER SHARE AMOUNTS)

December 31,	1995	1994
Assets		
Cash and cash equivalents	2,839	569
Other current assets	7,715	8,124
Total Investments	2,720	2,790
Net plant properties	8,113	8,726
Total Other Assets	2,195	6,336
Total Assets	**23,582**	**26,545**
Liabilities and Stockholders' Equity		
Notes payable	323	741
Long-term debt due within one year	375	534
Accounts payable	2,246	2,562
Other current liabilities	2,657	2,781
Total current liabilities	5,601	6,618
Long term debt	4,705	5,303
Total other non-current liabilities	3,799	3,884
Minority Interest in Subsidiary Companies	1,775	2,506
Temporary equity—other	313	—
Preferred stock (authorized 250,000,000 shares of $1.00 par value each; issued Series A- 1995: 1,521,175; 1994: 1,549,014) at redemption value	131	133
Guaranteed ESOP obligation	(103)	(111)
Total temporary equity	341	22
Common stock (authorized 500,000,000 shares of $2.50 par value each; issued 1995 and 1994: 327,125,854)	818	818
Additional paid-in capital	315	326
Retained earnings	10,159	8,857
Unrealized gains (losses) on investments	62	(21)
Cumulative translation adjustments	(349)	(330)
Treasury stock, at cost (shares 1995: 76,168,614; 1994: 50,002,967)	(3,644)	(1,438)
Net stockholders' equity	7,361	8,212
Total Liabilities and Stockholders' Equity	**23,582**	**26,545**

Source: The Dow Chemical Company, December 31, 1995 10-K (Midland, Michigan: Dow Chemical Co, 1995), available from Thomson Research, ⟨http://research.thomsonib.com⟩.

Vignart believed that Dow had the opportunity to become the number one player in the Latin American polyethylene industry. His immediate concern was to decide on the price to bid for PBB in the upcoming privatization. He also needed to complete the valuation of the entire project to justify the investment in Argentina to the parent company.

PART 3

CROSS-BORDER FINANCING

CROSS-BORDER FINANCIAL DECISIONS

Multinational firms often turn to foreign markets to raise capital rather than tapping domestic markets alone. This shift represents both an integration of markets across borders and a deepening of the available sources of financing for companies able to take advantage of global financing markets. Equity markets are also now international, and companies can choose what country to use for stock listing purposes. As a result, it is common for both debt and equity capital to be raised and/or listed outside an issuer's home country.

International differences in legal rules, capital market depth, and tax regimes create opportunities and difficulties. Every country regulates its own financial markets, and governance structures and reporting requirements differ around the world. As a consequence, a broad set of questions emerges: What are the benefits and costs of cross-listing? How can tax rate differences create arbitrage opportunities for issuers? What risks arise from the currency composition of debt? The cases in this section of the book consider these questions.

In each of the cases in this module, managers attempt to tailor financing solutions to the opportunities created by global capital markets. In Drilling South: Petrobras Evaluates Pecom, the Brazilian firm Petrobras considers the acquisition of a foreign firm. Pecom is an Argentine oil company severely affected by the national financial crisis in Argentina. Petrobras must consider the governance implications of a cross-border listing, the effects of currency crises on a company, and the uncertainties inherent in valuing a distressed foreign company. In the next case, Nestlé and Alcon—The Value of a Listing, executives at Nestlé, a Swiss company, consider the effect of taking their independently successful Texas-based eye-care subsidiary, Alcon, public. Managers have to decide on which stock exchange to list Alcon, and consider how the listing will affect the valuation of both Nestlé and Alcon. The first note in this module, Cross-Border Listings and Depositary Receipts, explains how companies list their shares on foreign stock exchanges, and looks at both the pros and cons of doing so. The note addresses some of the complexities of cross-border listings: How are ADRs structured? Who are the parties involved? Who handles converting dividends from one currency into another? It also considers some of the managerial incentives and economic consequences of cross-border listings.

Tax-Motivated Film Financing at Rexford Studios examines how different tax jurisdictions create opportunities for tax arbitrage. Rexford managers must consider how to value such an opportunity and identify just where the value comes from. The film industry has been something of a pioneer in exploiting cross-border financial opportunities. The second note in this module, The Strategy and Sources of Motion

Picture Finance, provides a detailed look at how tax incentives and policies, both domestic and foreign, have changed the financing patterns of a particular industry.

OVERVIEW OF THE CASES

Drilling South: Petrobras Evaluates Pecom

In July 2002 the Brazilian oil company, Petrobras, considered the acquisition of an Argentine oil company, Pecom. The proposed acquisition raises complex issues for both companies. The valuation of Pecom is not straightforward because of the economic turmoil in Argentina. Although Pecom has attractive assets, the financial crisis in Argentina and the devaluation of the Argentine peso brought the company to the brink of ruin because of its dollar-denominated debt. Country risk is a key issue in the acquisition, since the economic turmoil in Argentina has caused a huge rise in its country risk premium. João Nogueira Batista, Chief Financial Officer of Petrobras, and his team have to consider how to incorporate these factors in their valuation of Pecom.

The situation at home in Brazil raises other issues. Petrobras is majority owned by the Brazilian government. Although the state's control over Petrobras has relaxed in recent years, a different government could challenge the company's governance and strategy. One of the leading candidates in the upcoming general elections in Brazil, Luiz Inácio Lula da Silva of the Workers' Party, does not fully support Petrobras's increasing autonomy. Should Petrobras make a major acquisition when its own future is politically uncertain? Will Petrobras's acquisition of a large but distressed foreign company help it become more independent of the Brazilian government? Consider the following questions in trying to understand how multinationals in emerging markets woo global investors and pursue expansion opportunities:

- Would you invest in Petrobras stock? What would you be most worried about?
- Why did Petrobras cross-list? Why do firms cross-list? What are the consequences of cross-listing?
- How should Petrobras value Pecom? Why is Pecom for sale today?

Nestlé and Alcon—the Value of a Listing

Nestlé, the world's largest food company, counts among its corporate assets the world's leading opthalmology company, Alcon, as well as a significant stake in cosmetics giant L'Oréal. In response to a perceived undervaluation of the parent company by the capital markets, Nestlé is considering divesting a part of Alcon and must decide on a listing location and what form of security to issue. Executive Vice President Francisco Castañer and Chief Financial Officer Wolfgang Reichenberger consider the various legal and business issues involved and assess the proposals made by an investment banking house. In the process, the two executives wrestle with the tradeoffs involved in listing in the United States versus Europe, the appropriate valuation of the subsidiary and the consolidated company, and the incentives and tax consequences of a listing decision. The following questions accompany this case:

- Why specifically does Nestlé believe it is undervalued? How does that question relate to Nestlé's choice of how to list Alcon?
- Do you think this cross-listing will work in rectifying the valuation issue?
- The investment bank proposed a complicated hybrid structure—why? Does this seem necessary given Nestlé's objectives?

Cross-Border Listings and Depository Receipts

This note provides readers with information on the varied instruments that have evolved to facilitate investments in foreign corporations, with an emphasis on American Depositary Receipts (ADRs). The note describes the different types of ADRs and the regulatory requirements foreign corporations must meet to list their shares on U.S. stock exchanges. The evolution of cross-border listings is examined, as are recent developments such as Globally Registered Shares (GRSs). The note also reviews the academic research on the motivations for cross-border listings, and provides information on managerial views on the advantages and disadvantages of cross-border listings.

Tax-Motivated Film Financing at Rexford Studios

Rexford Studios is a midsized film studio with a track record of successful films. The company is ready to start its next film project and plans to produce as many as 15 films over the next three years. Responsibility for arranging financing for these films rests with Rexford's president, Charles O. Shaw. In the past, Rexford relied largely on bank financing, but Shaw is now considering a proposal from a group of German investors who want to participate in the financing of Rexford's next film. Shaw has to analyze the proposed deal, both to quantify the benefits to Rexford and to understand the incentives for the investors. Shaw also needs to assess the risks of the deal and decide if he can negotiate better terms for Rexford.

This case uncovers a cross-border investment opportunity based on tax arbitrage. Parsing the cash flows and attributing them to the various players in the sale-leaseback structure are essential to evaluating the offer. So, too, is choosing the appropriate discount rate based on the project risk. The following questions are helpful to consider while reading the case:

- Generally, what risks do film studios face in production and distribution of a film? Are the risks the same for all studios? Why or why not?
- How do studios use financing to manage their risk? When does financing externally make sense? Internally?
- What does the structure of the proposed deal from Film Fund International II look like? Who are the potential parties involved? What are their roles?
- If Shaw decides to fund *Bait and Wait* with the structure proposed, how much will he have to deposit into Neue Landesbank when the deal closes? In determining the amount of the deposit, what is the appropriate discount rate to be applied to the cash flows?
- Based on this deposit, does the deal provide any value to Rexford Studios? If so, how much? To which other parties is value allocated? How? Please quantify.
- Should Shaw pursue the proposed deal? Should he propose any changes? If so, what would make the deal better for Rexford?
- What risks does the deal pose for each party? How could these risks be effectively mitigated?

The Strategy and Sources of Motion Picture Finance

This note is a detailed examination of financial innovations in the U.S. film industry, with particular attention to how tax considerations have changed film financing in the United States and around the world. The note provides managers with insights into how countries use financial incentives to compete for film production and why countries provide such incentives.

ADDITIONAL READING

DOIDGE, C., R. STULZ and A. KAROLYI. 2004. "Why Are Foreign Firms Listed in the U.S. Worth More?" *Journal of Financial Economics*, 71(2): 205.

KAROLYI, G. ANDREW, 2004. "The Role of American Depositary Receipts in the Development of Emerging Equity Markets." *Review of Economics and Statistics,* 86(3): 670.

STIGLITZ, JOSEPH E. 1985. "The General Theory of Tax Avoidance." *National Tax Journal,* 38(3): 325–338.

AUGUSTE, SEBASTIAN, KATHRYN M. E. DOMINGUEZ, HERMAN KAMIL, and LINDA L. TESAR. 2002. "Cross-border Trading as a Mechanism for Capital Flight: ADRs and the Argentine Crisis." NBER Working Paper No. 9343.

13

Drilling South: Petrobras Evaluates Pecom

If you live in our neighborhood, you've got to look at Argentina. It's going through a major crisis today, but it is the second largest market in South America.[1]

— Francisco Gros, CEO, Petrobras

João Nogueira Batista, Chief Financial Officer of the Brazilian firm Petrobras, reflected on Gros's words as he prepared for a Board of Directors meeting in July 2002. The main item on the Board's agenda was the proposed acquisition of an Argentinean firm, the Perez Companc Group, or Pecom.[2] The acquisition would significantly increase Petrobras's oil and gas production and add to its oil reserves. It would also provide the mainly Brazilian-based Petrobras with considerable foreign interests. Petrobras would have access to Pecom's management team, which had worked in most of the major Latin American countries and under different operating environments, enhancing Petrobras's ability to manage an international portfolio.

Recent corporate governance changes meant that Petrobras now had more independence from the Brazilian government, and some managers were eager to explore new opportunities for the company, including the possible acquisition of Pecom. Others were more cautious. General elections would be held in a few months, and one of the leading candidates for president, Luiz Inácio Lula da Silva of the Workers' Party, did not fully support Petrobras's increasing autonomy. If Lula won the election,

---

Professor Mihir Desai and Ricardo Reisen de Pinho, Senior Researcher at the Harvard Business School Latin America Research Center, prepared this case with the collaboration of Gustavo Herrero, Executive Director fo the HBS LARC and the assistance of Research Associate Kathleen Luchs. This case was developed from published sources. HBS cases are developed solely as the basis for class discussion. Cases are not intended to serve as endorsements, sources of primary data, or illustrations of effective or ineffective management.

[1]Andrew Kelly, "New Petrobras chief focused on returns and ratings," *Reuters News*, March 26, 2002, available from Factiva, ⟨http://www.factiva.com⟩.

[2]The company was constituted as a holding company under the legal name of PC Holding S.A. Since its main asset was Pecom, an energy company, the name Pecom stands for Perez Companc, unless noted otherwise.

Petrobras's new structure and its strategy could be challenged. At the same time, the acquisition of Pecom would give Petrobras even more weight and could increase the company's already substantial contribution to the Brazilian economy.

Batista had spent the previous weeks debating the merits of the acquisition and how to value Pecom with his team. There had been numerous discussions on the cost of capital for the acquisition, and especially on how to incorporate country risk given the current economic upheaval in Argentina. Uncertainty over the appropriate discount rate to use in a cash flow model led some team members to advocate other approaches to the valuation, such as multiples. It was Batista's responsibility to present these different perspectives to the Board. The uncertainties inherent in valuing Pecom were bound to give rise to interesting discussions at the forthcoming Board meeting.

PETROBRAS

Petrobras was created as a symbol of Brazil's natural wealth under the slogan "the oil is ours," in 1953. It was incorporated as a mixed-capital company[3] with a government-granted monopoly for all crude oil and gas production, refining and distribution in Brazil. Petrobras's official monopoly ended in January 2002, when the Brazilian government deregulated domestic prices for crude oil and oil products.

Petrobras's first discoveries were made onshore in the Northeast of Brazil in the 1950s and 1960s. In the mid 1980s, when the giant deepwater pools in the Campos Basin were discovered and developed, the profile of the company started to shift upstream toward exploration, development, and production.

Upstream and Downstream Activities[4]

By 2001, almost 50 years after its inception, Petrobras had become a fully integrated oil and gas company. Petrobras was the seventh largest publicly traded oil and gas company in the world based upon proven reserves, the largest Brazilian corporation, the third largest Latin American corporation, and the 185th largest global company, by 2001 consolidated revenues.

In Brazil, Petrobras had a dominant position in both upstream and downstream activities. The company's combined oil and gas production was 1,621 tbpd and it had proven reserves estimated at around 9.3 billion boe.[5] (Exhibit 1 provides selected oil and gas data for Petrobras and other oil companies.) Most of the firm's proven reserves were located in very deep waters (more than 400 meters) and Petrobras was the world's pioneer in deep water oil exploration and production. Furthermore, with approximately

---

[3]According to Law 2004, a mixed-capital company was a Brazilian enterprise in which the majority of the voting capital was to be owned by the Brazilian federal government, a state or a municipality.

[4]The following section is based on Petróleo Brasileiro S.A.–Petrobras, December 31, 2001 20-F (Brazil: Petrobras, 2001), available from Thomson Research, ⟨http://research.thomsonib.com⟩; "Fortune Global 5 Hundred: The world's largest corporations," *Fortune*, July 22, 2002; Alexandra Strommer, "Muscle and Brains," J.P. Morgan Securities Inc., July 16, 2002; Geir Sagemo and Erik Mielke, "Riding out the Storm," Dresdner Kleinwort Wasserstein, August 1, 2001; and Emerson Leite and Gustavo Santos, "Notes from meeting with CEO Francisco Gros," Credit Suisse First Boston, February 18, 2002.

[5]tbpd signifies thousand barrels per day. boe stands for barrel of oil equivalent, a unit of measure to equate oil and natural gas volumes. Each barrel of oil equals 0.1589 cubic meters of natural gas. Petrobras's proven reserves were 7.7 billion barrels of oil and condensate and 255 million cubic meters of natural gas.

EXHIBIT 1

2001 SELECTED OIL AND GAS DATA

		Proven Oil and Gas Reserves			Combined Oil and Gas Production		
		Reserves (bboe) 2001	Life (years) 2001	CAGR (%) 1996–2001	Production (tbpd) 2001	CAGR (%) 1996–2001	CAGR (%) 2001–2005
Super Majors	Exxon Mobil	20.8	13.4	1%	4,256	0%	3%
	Royal Dutch/Shell	18.8	13.8	1%	3,722	0%	5%
	BP Amoco	16.3	13.3	14%	3,370	3%	6%
	Chevron Texaco	11,8	12.0	4%	2,695	0%	0%
	Total Fina Elf	11.0	13.7	10%	2,197	4%	6%
Majors	ENI	6.9	13.9	9%	1,369	7%	5%
	Repsol-YPF	5.6	NA	NA	370	15%	6%
	Ameralda Hess	1.1	6.7	4%	433	4%	5%
Emerging Oils	LUKOil	16.6	28.9	7%	1,573	5%	2%
	PetroChina	16.4	19.2	6%	2,349	1%	2%
	Yukos	13.3	31.3	6%	1,166	11%	9%
	Pemex[a]	53.0	33.4	(3)%	4,338	2%	NA
	PDVSA	103.0	71.3	1%	3,973	1%	NA
	Petrobras	9.3	15.6	3%	1,621	11%	10%
	CNOCC	1.8	18.9	5%	261	7%	20%
	Pecom	1.0	15.0	20%	184	10%	17%

[a]CAGR 1998–2001.

Source: Compiled and adapted by the casewriter from Frank J. McGann and Marcus Sequeira, "Petrobras—The music is still playing, but will somebody change the tune?" Merrill Lynch, September 24, 2002, Alexandra Strommer, "Muscle and Brains," J.P. Morgan Securities Inc., July 16, 2002, and companies reports.

60% of its reserves undeveloped, Petrobras had a large pool of assets to engender long-term production growth.

In downstream activities, Petrobras was the fifth-largest refiner in the world among traded companies, with a virtual monopoly in the Brazilian downstream business. It owned and operated 11 out of 13 refineries in Brazil, accounting for 98.6% of the Brazilian refining capacity. Petrobras also owned the largest oil distribution company in Brazil. Exhibits 2 and 3 show the organization of the firm's main activities within its corporate and management structures.

The Restructuring of Petrobras[6]

Until the late 1990s, the Brazilian government owned 84% of the voting shares of Petrobras and the Brazilian President appointed the company's board and its executive

[6]This section is adapted from Alexandra Strommer, "Muscle and Brains," J.P. Morgan Securities Inc., July 16, 2002; Brian Singer and Tatiana Andrade, "Petrobras S.A, (ADR) (PBR)," Goldman Sachs, March 7, 2002; and Petróleo Brasileiro S.A.–Petrobras, December 31, 2001 20-F (Brazil: Petrobras, 2001), available from Thomson Research, ⟨http://research.thomsonib.com⟩.

EXHIBIT 2

PETROBRAS CORPORATE STRUCTURE—TOTAL CAPITAL

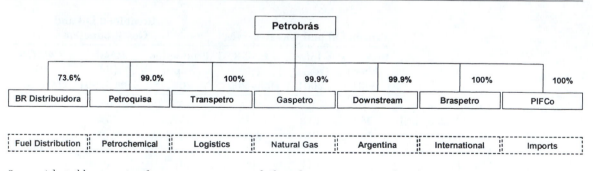

Source: Adapted by casewriter from company reports and Alexandra Strommer, "Muscle and Brains," J.P. Morgan Securities Inc., July 16, 2002.

directors. For many years, there was a market perception that several governments had used Petrobras as a tool to contain inflation[7] or to advance development policies for specific industrial groups. Beginning in 1997, Petrobras became more independent of the government. Responsibility for appointing the board shifted from the Brazilian president to Petrobras's shareholders, and the government was allowed to sell up to 34% of its voting shares in the capital markets. The government lifted restrictions on the ownership of shares by non-government entities and permitted foreign ownership of

EXHIBIT 3

PETROBRAS' MANAGEMENT STRUCTURE

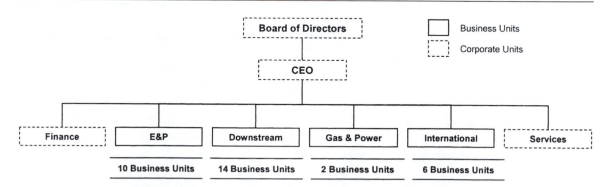

Source: Adapted by the casewriter from João N. Batista, "Abamec Nacional 2002," PowerPoint Presentation, May 27, 2002. Petrobras S.A, Investor Relations available from Petrobras Web site, http://www2.petrobras.com.br/ri/port/ApresentacoesEventos/ Apresentacoes/pdf/abamec_fin_270502.pdf.

[7]According to the Instituto Brasileiro de Geografia e Estatística (IBGE), gasoline itself accounted for approximately 4% of the official IPCA inflation index, and also served as a trigger for other important items, such as transportation, which accounted for 22% of the official index.

EXHIBIT 4

PETROBRAS'S GOVERNANCE: MAJOR CHANGES AND EVENTS

Before 1997	• The government had absolute power over Petrobras's businesses and interests • The government owned 84% of the voting shares, with the rest spread among Brazilian individuals and corporations subject to ownership caps • Petrobras's board members and executive directors were all the same, and appointed by the Brazilian President • Petrobras's CEO had veto power over any decision
From 1997 to 1999	• The board was appointed in shareholder meetings, and the executive directors by the board, necessarily with different members • Minority shareholders could appoint one board member • Any entity, individual or corporate, Brazilian or foreign, was allowed to buy shares without restrictions or limitation • Up to 34% of the voting shares that were owned by the government could be sold in the capital markets
From 1999 to 2001 The Reichstul Years	• Phillippe Reichstul CEO • Adoption of a new long-term strategic plan • Introduction of the concept of business groups and imposed performance targets • Simultaneously, Petrobras streamlined its management structure, and empowered management, strengthening its capacity, flexibility and ability to react to new situations • Integration of some of Petrobras's subsidiaries to become divisions of the controlling company, inducing synergies and avoiding functional overlaps • Petrobras was listed on the NYSE • Off-balance-sheet arrangements were recognized and restated in the balance sheet • Pension fund liabilities related to retired employees were redeemed through an exchange with non-tradable government securities • Petrobras increased its free-float through public offerings from the government and from federal agencies, such as Banco Nacional de Desenvolvimento (BNDES, the Development National Bank)
From 2001–Present The Gros Years	• Francisco Gros CEO • The role and responsibilities of the board and executive directors were defined • Committees were created to oversee and advise top management • Different communication channels with the market were put in place • Guidelines for corporate governance, best practices and ethical conduct were issued

Source: Adapted by casewriter from Alexandra Strommer, "Muscle and Brains," J.P. Morgan Securities Inc., July 16, 2002, p. 40, and Petróleo Brasileiro S.A.–Petrobras, December 31, 2001 20-F (Brazil: Petrobras, 2001), available from Thomson Research, http://research.thomsonib.com.

---

shares (see Exhibit 4 for major changes in the ownership and governance of Petrobras). In August 2000, Petrobras was listed on the NYSE through an ADR Level II program, and in July 2002 it was listed on Latibex, the euro market for Latin American equity shares.[8] The shareholder structure of Petrobras is shown in Exhibit 5.

[8]Petrobras's NYSE ticker was PBR. Under the ADR Level II program, Petrobras started reporting quarterly under U.S. Generally Accepted Accounting Principles (GAAP), following disclosure regulations issued by the Securities and Exchange Commission (SEC). Petrobras's Latibex listing meant that the stock was traded and settled like any other Spanish security. Latibex was created in conjunction with the Bolsa de Madrid in December 1999.

EXHIBIT 5

PETROBRAS SHAREHOLDER STRUCTURE

	Major Shareholders	Voting Shares	Preferred Shares	Total Shares
Directly or indirectly controlled by the Government	União Federal (Government)	55.7%	0.0%	32.5%
	BNDESPar[a]	2.0%	16.3%	7.9%
	Other Brazilian public entities	0.2%	0.1%	0.1%
Others	Bovespa[b]	4.6%	24.9%	13.1%
	Annex V[c]	3.4%	18.8%	9.8%
	ADR—Level I, II and III	22.7%	34.0%	27.4%
	FGTS—Fundo de Garantia do Tempo de Serviço[d]	7.4%	0.0%	4.3%
	Other	4.1%	5.9%	4.8%
Total		100.0%	100.0%	100.0%

[a]A subsidiary of the National Development Bank, Banco Nacional de Desenvolvimento Economico e Social (BNDES).

[b]Sao Paulo Stock Exchange.

[c]Shares bought by foreign investors in Brazil and exchanged for ADRs at a later date.

[d]Social Security Fund.

Source: Adapted by casewriter from Alexandra Strommer, "Muscle and Brains," J.P. Morgan Securities Inc., July 16, 2002, and Petróleo Brasileiro S.A.–Petrobras, December 31, 2001 20-F (Brazil: Petrobras, 2001), available from Thomson Research, ⟨http://research.thomsonib.com⟩.

In 2002 another significant change affected Petrobras's financing strategy. Petrobras had played a key role in the government's fiscal policy. It was the largest Brazilian taxpayer, as well as the largest distributor of dividends and royalties. Petrobras's net profit represented almost 25% of the overall primary surplus of the consolidated public sector, or roughly 1% of the Brazilian GDP. Petrobras's capital expenditures were included in the government's budget and the company's investments and indebtedness were therefore subject to restrictions tied to the country's fiscal policy. From July 2002 on, The International Monetary Fund (IMF) no longer considered Petrobras's investments part of the government's budget, thus removing any restrictions on its financing strategy.

Along with the changes in its ownership and control, Petrobras streamlined its management structure and implemented new management policies. The changes included the adoption of a new long-term strategic plan, the introduction of business units, the integration of some subsidiaries into the company as divisions to promote synergies and minimize functional overlaps, and the introduction of performance targets. Under the leadership of the current CEO, Francisco Gros, the company defined the role and responsibilities of the board and the executive directors, created committees to advise top management, and issued guidelines for corporate governance, best practices and ethical conduct.

The main objective of these changes was to transform Petrobras into a state-owned company able to compete with the same agility and freedom as a privately owned corporation. These changes appeared to be paying off. Statistical studies indicated that from 1999 to 2001, Petrobras migrated from a typical Brazil-risk stock, trading in close correlation with country risk, to something closer to a global oil company, reacting more to swings in crude oil prices. The market capitalization of Petrobras almost tripled during this period. Exhibit 6 provides data on the company's stock price history.

EXHIBIT 6

TIMELINE OF STOCK PRICE PERFORMANCE AND MAJOR EVENTS
(WEEKLY PETROBRAS PN AND PECOM ADR PRICES IN $—JANUARY 28, 2000 = 100)

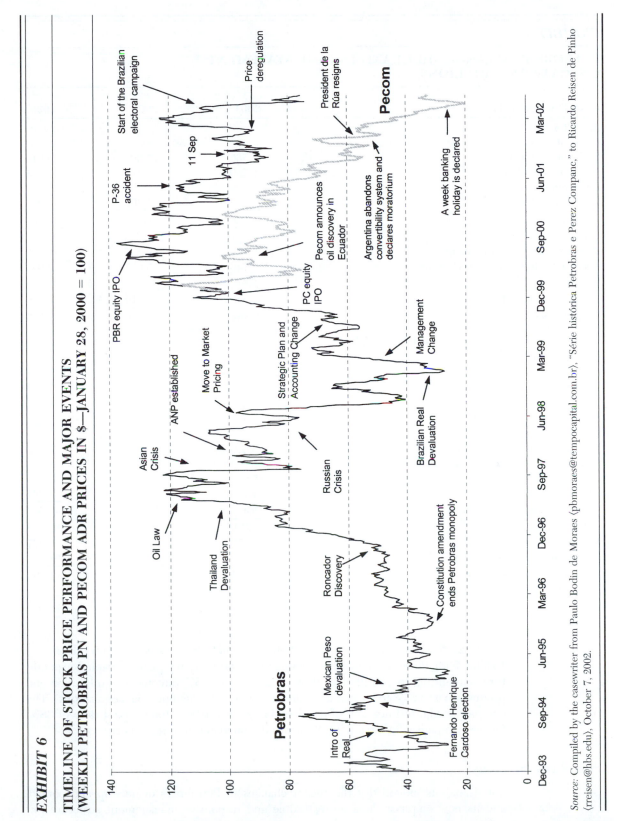

Source: Compiled by the casewriter from Paulo Bodin de Moraes ⟨pbmoraes@tempocapital.com.br⟩, "Série histórica Petrobras e Perez Companc," to Ricardo Reisen de Pinho ⟨rreisen@hbs.edu⟩, October 7, 2002.

EXHIBIT 7

PETROBRAS BALANCE SHEET AND INCOME STATEMENT
U.S. GAAP (IN $ MILLIONS)

As of December 31	2001	2000	1999
ASSETS			
Current Assets			
Cash and cash equivalent	7,360	5,826	3,015
Accounts receivable	2,759	2,211	1,575
Inventories	2,399	3,087	2,270
Other current assets	1,808	1,402	1,307
Total current assets	14,326	12,526	8,167
Permanent Assets			
Property, plant and equipment	19,179	19,237	18,426
Receivables from Brazilian Government	746	5,051	4,925
Others	2,613	2,322	2,215
Total non-current assets	22,538	26,610	25,566
Total Assets	**36,864**	**39,136**	**33,733**
LIABILITIES AND STOCKHOLDERS' EQUITY			
Current liabilities			
Trade accounts payable	1,783	2,011	1,314
Short-term debt	2,041	4,080	5,765
Other current liabilities	4,220	3,549	2,732
Total current liabilities	8,044	9,640	9,811
Non-current liabilities			
Employees post-retirement benefits	3,380	4,319	5,163
Project financings and capital lease obligations	5,083	3,426	1,781
Long-term debt	5,908	4,833	4,778
Other liabilities	1,123	2,060	1,241
Total non-current liabilities	15,494	14,638	12,963
Total Liabilities	**23,538**	**24,278**	**22,774**
Minority Interests	79	153	237
Total Stockholders' Equity	**13,247**	**14,705**	**10,722**
Total Liabilities + Equity	**36,864**	**39,163**	**33,733**

(Continued)

In 2001, on a consolidated basis, Petrobras's net revenues were $24.5 billion (see Exhibit 7 for Petrobras's financial statements). The company planned capital expenditures amounting to $28.2 billion through 2005, with 45% directed to exploration and production and 23% to international projects (not including potential acquisitions). The company's adjusted net debt of $11.1 billion gave a debt-to-total-capital ratio of 38%. Of the company's financial debt, 88% was denominated in foreign currency.

Petrobras' Strategy

Some analysts judged that the recent changes in Petrobras's ownership and control and its new emphasis on a more flexible and responsive management structure put

EXHIBIT 7   (Continued)

PETROBRAS BALANCE SHEET AND INCOME STATEMENT
U.S. GAAP (IN $ MILLIONS)

As of December 31	2001	2000	1999
Total Revenues	**34,145**	**35,496**	**23,467**
Value-added taxes, freight, and specific parcel price	(9,596)	(8,541)	(7,109)
Net Revenues	**24,549**	**26,955**	**16,358**
CoGS	(12,807)	(13,449)	(8,210)
Gross Profit	**11,742**	**13,506**	**8,148**
Total depreciation, depletion and amortization	(1,729)	(2,022)	(2,262)
Exploration	(549)	(477)	(295)
Selling, general, and administration expenses	(1,751)	(1,450)	(1,282)
Research and development expenses	(132)	(152)	(132)
Total Cost and Expenses	**(4,161)**	**(4,101)**	**(3,971)**
Operating Income	**7,581**	**9,405**	**4,177**
Non–operating Items	(1,361)	(1,126)	(723)
Income before Financial Items	6,220	8,279	3,454
EBITDA	**8,498**	**10,778**	**6,011**
Financial Income (Expenses)	567	204	213
Net Income before Extraordinary Items	4,749	5,821	2,487
Net Income (average tax rate of 35%)	**3,491**	**5,342**	**727**

Source: Adapted from F. J. McGann and M. Sequeira, "US GAAP results show no surprises," Merrill Lynch, July 1, 2002.

Petrobras in a different league from state-owned Latin American oil companies such as Pemex and PDVSA (see Exhibit 8 for key statistics on Petrobras and other Latin American oil companies). Alexandra Strommer, a J. P. Morgan senior analyst, explained:

> Petrobras had a very peculiar position within the oil industry. The company could not be considered a typical Latin American oil company like PDVSA or Pemex because it was already much more market-oriented and had more of a private-company mentality. Also, it was not a net exporter, focused on the external markets, but very much Brazil-centric. Additionally, despite its size, Petrobras did not seem to fit among the major oil companies, since it was not really global, even though it has a sizable integrated structure.[9]

While Petrobras was not yet a global oil company, it was committed to geographic diversification. Petrobras's stated objective was to build a portfolio of upstream assets in Latin America, the Gulf of Mexico, the Caribbean, and West Africa. The common theme behind that geographic focus was for Petrobras to leverage its deepwater expertise acquired in the Campos Basin. Moreover, since 95% of Petrobras's upstream reserves were exposed to the risks of a single country, Brazil, the company had a strong strategic rationale for enlarging its international activities. The acquisition of an Argentinean company was in line with Petrobras's strategy of expanding outside Brazil.

[9]Alexandra Strommer, "Muscle and Brains," J.P. Morgan Securities Inc., July 16, 2002, p. 22.

EXHIBIT 8

PETROBRAS, PEMEX, PDVSA, AND PECOM—KEY STATISTICS

	Petrobras[a]	Pemex[b]	PDVSA[c]	Pecom
Operating Figures—2001				
Combined reserves (billion boe)	9.3	53.0	103.4	1.1
Combined production	1,568	4,338	3,973	184
Lifting and production costs ($)	3.26	3.34	2.17	2.72
Production cost per barrel ($)	4.85	4.06	3.76	6.40
Financial Data (in $ million)—2001				
Total assets	32,390	60,913	57,542	6,194
Total debt	18,491	37,994	12,273	2,656
Shareholder's Equity (book value)	12,483	13,439	37,098	2,817
Net Debt	11,118	36,414	11,348	1,674
EBITDA	9,362	26,668	11,167	693
Net Income	4,194	(3,729)	3,993	102
Stock Returns				
(as of March 28, 2002)				
1 Year	15%			(43%)
3 Years	127%			(47%)
5 Years	44%			(67%)

[a]Brazilian GAAP.

[b]Petroleos Mexicanos, Mexican state-owned oil company.

[c]Petroleos de Venezuela, S.A., Venezuelan state-owned oil company.

Source: Compiled and adapted from Rodrigo Lopes ⟨rodrigo.lopes@chase.com⟩, "Dados—Relatorio Petrobras," to Ricardo Reisen de Pinho ⟨rreisen@hbs.edu⟩, March 7, 2003, and March 13, 2003, and companies reports.

PECOM

The origins of Pecom went back to 1946, when the Perez Companc family incorporated the firm as a shipping company. However, it was only in 1960 that the company got involved in the oil business. Gradually, Pecom developed an appetite and skills for the oil industry and, in 1990, the company gained its first major oil concession. In 1994, Pecom took another important step when it started operations in Venezuela and then expanded into Brazil, Bolivia, Ecuador and Peru. In 1998 Pecom was consolidated as a vertically integrated energy company. The firm listed its shares on the Buenos Aires Stock Exchange in January 2000 and launched an ADR program on the New York Stock Exchange. Pecom's corporate structure is shown in Exhibit 9.

Upstream and Downstream Activities[10]

Pecom's exploration and production activities were its main cash source, with drilling accounting for 69% of its adjusted EBITDA. Pecom's proven developed and undevel-

[10]The following section is based on Petróleo Brasileiro S.A.– Petrobras, December 31, 2001 20-F (Brazil: Petrobras, 2001), p. 20, available from Thomson Research, ⟨http://research.thomsonib.com⟩; Patricia Bueno-Kearns and Carla Arellano, "Oil Companies–Majors–Perez Companc," Salomon Smith Barney, June 15, 2001, p. 13.

EXHIBIT 9

PECOM CORPORATE STRUCTURE

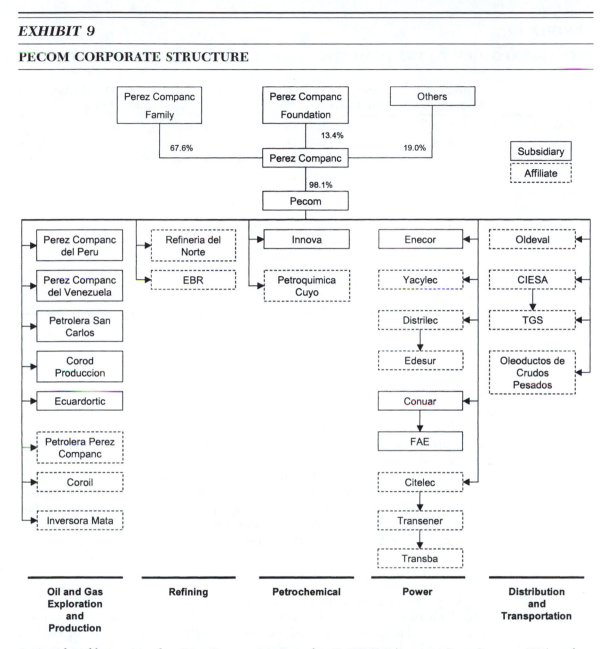

Source: Adapted by casewriter from Perez Companc S.A., December 31, 2001 20-F (Argentina: Perez Companc, 2001), available from Thomson Research, http://research.thomsonib.com.

oped reserves were estimated around one billion boe.[11] About 42% of Pecom's total reserves were in Argentina, and 58% were in operations in five other South American countries. Pecom forecast that its total production in 2005 would reach 400 tbpd, with most of this coming from outside Argentina.

[11]Composed of 739 million barrels of oil and condensate, and 43 million cubic meters of natural gas.

EXHIBIT 10

PECOM—EXPOSURE TO THE DOMESTIC MARKET AND EXPORT OPPORTUNITIES

Product	Revenues: Main Currency	Costs: Main Currency	Markets	Export Opportunity	Devaluation Impact
Oil & Gas	USD	AR$ and other	Domestic, Exports	Yes	Positive
Refining	AR$	USD	Domestic	Limited	Neutral to negative
Petrochemicals	AR$	USD	Domestic, Exports	Yes	Neutral to negative
Power Generation, Transmission, and Distribution	AR$	AR$	Domestic	No	Negative
Oil and Gas Transportation	AR$	AR$	Domestic	No	Negative

Source: Adapted by casewriter from Perez Companc S.A., December 31, 2001 20-F (Argentina: Perez Companc, 2001), available from Thomson Research, ⟨http://research.thomsonib.com⟩ and Edmo Chagas and Andrea Kannebley, "Oil Companies, Secondary—Perez Companc," UBS Warburg, August 28, 2001, p. 8.

Pecom's downstream activities included refining operations in Argentina and Bolivia. Although these interests represented just 7% of Pecom's adjusted EBITDA as of December 2001, refining was a key part of Pecom's long-term strategy, representing an important link in the business value chain. Petrochemicals represented 8% of Pecom's adjusted EBITDA in 2001. It had the region's largest capacity for styrene and polystyrene production, and was a leader in Argentina in these products. In addition, Pecom had over a one-third share of the fertilizer market in Argentina. Among Pecom's other activities were its investment in TGS, the largest transporter of natural gas in Argentina, and interests in the generation, transmission, and distribution of electricity in Argentina. Pecom operated 75% of the country's high-voltage power transmission system, and had an exclusive license to serve both the residential population and commercial firms in the central and southern Buenos Aires metropolitan area.

Pecom and the Financial Crisis in Argentina

Like many oil companies with hard, bankable assets, Pecom opted for relatively low-cost dollar borrowings in the 1990s, on the assumption that its primary products—crude, gas, and refined products—would remain priced in dollars (see Exhibit 10 for Pecom's exposure to the domestic market and export opportunities). In July 2001, for instance, Deutsche Bank, a commercial bank, led a syndicate of banks to underwrite a four-year, $220 million unsecured floating rate note with a 9.3% all-in cost, substantially below the 16% Argentine sovereign bonds for Pecom.[12]

In January 2002, however, the Argentine government abandoned its Convertibility Law, which fixed the Argentine peso at exactly one U.S. dollar and opted for a "pesification" of the economy. All U.S. dollar-denominated deposits in the financial system were converted at a rate of 1:1, while all U.S. dollar-denominated debts incurred in the Argentine financial system were converted at a rate of 1.40:1. The government decided to compensate financial institutions for the difference with a bond that had not yet been

[12]"Capitalizing on oil," *Latin Finance,* February 1, 2002, available from Factiva, ⟨http://www.factiva.com⟩.

EXHIBIT 11A

PECOM: SEVEN-YEAR DEBT REFINANCING SCHEDULE (ESTIMATES AS OF MARCH 31, 2002 IN $ MILLIONS)

	1 Year	2 Years	3 Years	4 Years	5 Years	6 Years	7 Years
Bank Loans	834	159	147	86	20	20	6
Bonds	93	285	0	0	189	378	0
Total	**927**	**444**	**147**	**86**	**209**	**398**	**6**

Source: Adapted by casewriter from Frank J. McGann and Marcus Sequeira, "Perez Companc—Can it weather the storm?" Merrill Lynch, June 3, 2002, p. 5.

issued in July 2002. Firms that had incurred debt in U.S. dollars abroad were forced to cancel them through the open exchange rate market. On July 15, 2002, the U.S. dollar was quoted at AR$3.58.

The financial crisis in Argentina had a severe impact on Pecom. Less than 10% of Pecom s loans, and none of its foreign bond debt, were covered by the pesification. Pecom still faced mostly dollar-based debts, but revenues from some of its commercial agreements denominated in dollars and adjusted per the U.S. producer price index were converted into pesos at a 1:1 rate, and indexation was eliminated. These peso revenues were far below world market prices since domestic prices did not rise at the same rate as the devaluation. Pecom also faced a pending export tax that could be levied on up to 40% of the company's Argentine oil export revenue. In March 2002, Pecom held $231 million in cash and short term investments and its debt and other financial obligations to the end of the year amounted to $840 million (see Exhibits 11a and 11b for Pecom's debt profile). Pecom's vice chairman, Oscar Vicente, painted a grim picture of Pecom's situation: "I have half or less of the pesos I need to buy the dollars I have to pay. A group like Perez Companc is not viable in this situation."[13]

[13]"Argentine Perez Companc seeks to renegotiate debt," *Reuters News*, March 14, 2002, available from Factiva, ⟨http://www.factiva.com⟩.

EXHIBIT 11B

PECOM: DEBT BREAKDOWN BY TYPE (ESTIMATES AS OF MARCH 31, 2002 IN $ MILLIONS)

	1 Year	Years 1–7 Total	Year 1 % of Total
Bonds	93	945	10%
Foreign Banks	435	802	54%
Trade Finance	292	364	80%
Local Banks	51	52	98%
Accrued Interest	56	56	100%
Total	**927**	**2,219**	**42%**

Source: Adapted by casewriter from Frank J. McGann and Marcus Sequeira, "Perez Companc—Can it weather the storm?" Merrill Lynch, June 3, 2002, p. 5.

EXHIBIT 12

PECOM CASH FLOW FORECAST (IN $ MILLIONS)

CASH FLOW	1999A	2000A	2001A	2002E	2003E	2004E	2005E	2006E	2007E
Net income from operations	175	235	151	32	79	125	192	290	347
Depreciation	196	220	305	265	267	284	317	317	317
Exploration expense	13	7	19	12	12	10	10	10	10
Gross Cash Flow—Perez Companc	**384**	**462**	**475**	**309**	**358**	**418**	**519**	**617**	**674**
Earnings—unconsolidated affiliates	(99)	(89)	(92)	(50)	(37)	(40)	(41)	(43)	(45)
Dividends—unconsolidated affiliates	67	84	64	0	0	0	0	0	0
Gross Cash Flow—adjusted for equity affiliates	**352**	**456**	**447**	**258**	**321**	**379**	**478**	**574**	**629**
Capital Expenditures	(496)	(576)	(794)	(98)	(196)	(295)	(491)	(491)	(491)
Dividends	(63)	(65)	(64)	0	(39)	(43)	(48)	(52)	(58)
Net Gross Cash Flow—Discretionary	**(175)**	**(178)**	**(382)**	**210**	**122**	**80**	**(19)**	**73**	**125**
Net Gross Cash Flow—Discretionary—adjusted for equity affiliates	**(207)**	**(184)**	**(411)**	**160**	**85**	**41**	**(61)**	**30**	**80**

Source: Adapted by casewriter from Frank J. McGann and Marcus Sequeira, "Perez Companc—Can it weather the storm?" Merrill Lynch, June 3, 2002, pg. 6.

Although the medium- and long-term business view was still promising, the short-term scenario had put the company at a crossroad. Pecom and its external advisors had been working on different alternatives since the end of 2001, without a clear or easy solution. The company owned sound assets, but it could not simply divest selected assets without jeopardizing its longer-term growth prospects (see Exhibit 12, 13, and 14 for Pecom's actual and estimated financial statements). Simultaneously, the local banking system was in crisis and international bankers were reluctant to increase their

EXHIBIT 13

PECOM PROJECTED BALANCE SHEET
(IN $ MILLIONS UNLESS OTHERWISE STATED)

As of December 31	1999A	2000A	2001A	2002E	2003E	2004E	2005E	2006E	2007E
ASSETS									
Current Assets									
Cash and cash equivalent	254	274	581	485	655	691	616	622	693
Accounts receivable	641	627	566	453	491	518	579	679	755
Inventories	147	170	156	113	123	130	145	170	189
Total current assets	1,042	1,071	1,303	1,051	1,269	1,339	1,340	1,471	1,637
Non-current Assets									
Accounts receivable	50	77	96	76	82	86	97	113	126
Inventories	77	93	97	63	68	72	80	95	105
Investments	1,194	1,251	1,126	357	395	435	477	521	567
Fixed assets	2,661	2,990	3,550	2,310	2,071	1,922	1,942	1,964	2,026
Others	9	5	8	8	8	9	9	9	9
Total non-current assets	3,991	4,416	4,877	2,814	2,624	2,524	2,605	2,702	2,833
Total Assets	**5,033**	**5,487**	**6,180**	**3,865**	**3,894**	**3,863**	**3,944**	**4,173**	**4,470**
LIABILITIES AND STOCKHOLDERS' EQUITY									
Current liabilities									
Accounts payable	180	249	318	239	260	274	306	359	399
Short-term debt	305	739	1,269	1,274	1,279	1,284	1,289	1,294	1,299
Other current liabilities	159	141	269	217	234	247	276	324	360
Total current liabilities	644	1,0129	1,856	1,730	1,773	1,805	1,871	1,977	2,058
Non-current liabilities									
Long-term debt	1,612	1,410	1,403	1,003	1,003	903	803	703	603
Other liabilities	204	172	114	77	83	88	98	115	128
Total non-current liabilities	1,816	1,582	1,517	1,080	1,086	991	901	818	731
Total Liabilities	**2,460**	**2,711**	**3,373**	**2,810**	**2,860**	**2,796**	**2,772**	**2,795**	**2,789**
Minority Interests	17	68	71	75	79	83	87	91	95
Total Stockholders' Equity	**2,556**	**2,708**	**2,736**	**980**	**955**	**984**	**1,085**	**1,287**	**1,586**
Total Liabilities & Equity	**5,033**	**5,487**	**6,180**	**3,865**	**3,894**	**3,863**	**3,944**	**4,173**	**4,470**

(Continued)

EXHIBIT 13 (Continued)

PECOM PROJECTED BALANCE SHEET
(IN $ MILLIONS UNLESS OTHERWISE STATED)

	1999A	2000A	2001A	2002E	2003E	2004E	2005E	2006E	2007E
Balance Sheet Ratios									
Total LT Debt/Capital	37%	33%	33%	49%	49%	46%	40%	33%	26%
Total LT Liabilities/ Capital	42%	37%	36%	52%	53%	50%	45%	39%	32%
Total LT Liabilities & ST Debt/Capital	45%	46%	50%	71%	71%	70%	67%	62%	56%
Total Debt/Capital	41%	42%	48%	67%	67%	65%	62%	57%	51%
Net Debt/Net Capital	38%	39%	42%	62%	59%	56%	54%	48%	40%
Book Value/Share (in $)	3.28	3.47	3.51	1.26	1.23	1.26	1.39	1.65	2.03
Return on average capital	7.2%	9.2%	5.8%	1.8%	8.4%	13.3%	1 9.2%	25.2%	24.9%
Total Debt	1,917	2,149	2,672	2,277	2,282	2,187	2,092	1,997	1,902
Debt less Cash	1,663	1,875	2,091	1,792	1,627	1,496	1,476	1,375	1,209

Source: Adapted by casewriter from Frank J. McGann and Marcus Sequeira, "Perez Companc—Can it weather the storm?" Merrill Lynch, June 3, 2002, p. 31.

exposure to an emerging market company. Pecom's management and shareholders had to come up with a solution before they were out of cash or credit. A senior analyst from Merrill Lynch explained:

> It is necessary to look at whether the company really does have the cash flow to continue to endure the crisis. Whatever the long-term cash-flow generation capability of the company, the ability to meet its debt maturities and interest payments is key to preserving equity value.[14]

PETROBRAS'S PROPOSED ACQUISITION OF PECOM

The acquisition of Pecom by Petrobras offered the Argentinean firm a solution to its current financial problems and it was in line with Petrobras's strategy of geographic diversification. It was not clear, however, if the acquisition would be feasible. The deal would require regulatory approval, Argentina was in the midst of a financial crisis, and Brazil faced economic challenges of its own. Many Brazilians feared that the crisis would spread to their country, and were concerned about the fiscal deficit and the continuing depreciation of the Brazilian real against the U.S dollar (see Exhibit 15 for average monthly exchange rates). There was also considerable political uncertainty in Brazil because of the upcoming general elections in October 2002. Some businesses feared that the leading candidate for president, Luiz Inácio Lula da Silva of the Workers' Party,

[14]Frank J. McGann and Marcus Sequeira, "Perez Companc—Can it weather the storm?" Merrill Lynch, June 3, 2002, p. 5.

EXHIBIT 14

PECOM CONSOLIDATED EARNINGS MODEL
(IN $ MILLIONS UNLESS OTHERWISE STATED)

	1999A	2000A	2001A	2002E	2003E	2004E	2005E	2006E	2007E
Sales									
Oil & Gas Production	589	719	891	674	784	829	927	1,115	1,284
Assumptions:									
Oil Sales (thousand of barrels per day)	96	100	125	120	119	125	134	158	176
Gas Sales (million of cubic meters per day)	6	6	10	9	9	9	10	11	11
WTI ($ per barrel)	19	30	26	22	25	23	24	24	25
Average oil sale price ($ per barrel)	15	17	16	14	16	16	17	17	18
Average gas sale price ($ per thousand cm)	40	45	42	20	24	27	29	30	32
Adjustments/Eliminations	(2)	(3)	(6)	(6)	(7)	(7)	(8)	(9)	(10)
Petrochemical & Refining	543	717	750	460	539	559	591	625	662
Electricity	140	158	164	70	96	110	155	217	229
Distribution & Transportation	8	35	38	19	21	23	25	28	31
Non-energy Sales	59	56	49	28	31	34	37	41	45
Eliminations	(99)	(139)	(238)	(95)	(105)	(115)	(127)	(139)	(153)
Total Consolidated Sales	**1,240**	**1,546**	**1,654**	**1,155**	**1,366**	**1,440**	**1,608**	**1,887**	**2,097**
Operational Income									
Oil & Gas Production	189	246	266	201	279	313	362	447	524
Petrochemical & Refining	21	65	35	11	24	42	47	49	52
Electricity	80	93	99	29	32	42	57	82	86
Distribution & Transportation	56	56	47	8	3	3	3	3	4
Non-energy Operational Income	10	4	9	35	25	26	28	29	31
Corporate & Eliminations	(44)	(62)	(70)	(25)	(27)	(29)	(31)	(3 3)	(35)
Total Operational Income	**312**	**402**	**386**	**259**	**335**	**397**	**466**	**578**	**662**
EBITDA	**521**	**633**	**716**	**541**	**619**	**696**	**799**	**912**	**995**
Net-Financial Expenses	(134)	(157)	(206)	(220)	(230)	(225)	(195)	(165)	(165)
Pre tax Income	**178**	**260**	**175**	**39**	**105**	**172**	**271**	**414**	**497**
Tax (average tax rate of 35%)	(8)	(15)	(14)	(10)	(19)	(40)	(69)	(111)	(135)
Minority Interest	5	(10)	(10)	(5)	(6)	(8)	(10)	(13)	(15)
Net Income before Extraordinary Items	**175**	**235**	**151**	**26**	**81**	**129**	**198**	**297**	**358**
Extraordinary Items	130	41	(55)	26	0	0	0	0	0
FX Gains (Losses)— Parent/Subsidiaries	0	0	0	(514)	(66)	(55)	(49)	(44)	0
Income on non-current investments—YPF	33	0	0	0	0	0	0	0	0
Net Income	**338**	**283**	**102**	**(463)**	**15**	**74**	**149**	**255**	**358**

Source: Adapted by casewriter from Frank J. McGann and Marcus Sequeira, "Perez Companc—Can it weather the storm?" Merrill Lynch, pp. 16, 17, and 29.

EXHIBIT 15

AVERAGE MONTHLY FOREIGN EXCHANGE RATE

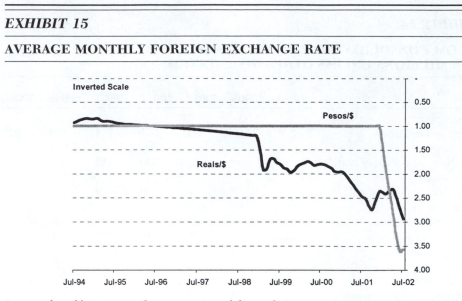

Source: Adapted by casewriter from Banco Central do Brasil, "Economia e Finanças—Séries Temporais—código 3698 e 3932," Banco Central do Brasil Web site, ⟨http://www.bcb.gov.br⟩.

would change Brazil's existing economic and legal framework if elected president. A roll back of privatization, or at least a freeze on it, was among the Workers' Party's proposals, and it was not clear what impact this might have on Petrobras.

Batista therefore faced a demanding task in evaluating the proposed acquisition of Pecom. The transaction initially envisioned by Petrobras's CEO Gros and Batista covered Petrobras's purchase of 58.6% of the total capital of Pecom from the Perez Companc family and the Perez Companc Foundation. In a separate transaction, Petrobras would also acquire 47.1% that the Perez Companc family held in Petrolera Perez Companc.[15] Batista and his team prepared pro forma consolidated figures to detail the increases in oil and gas reserves and refining capacity that would be gained, and to show how the acquisition would affect debt and income (see Exhibits 16a for Pro Forma Operating Figures and Exhibit 16b for Pro Forma Financial Data).

To assess whether the acquisition would add value to the shareholders through an acceptable return on investment, Petrobras had to estimate a weighted average cost of capital for the transaction. After having implemented a policy of stricter capital discipline, only projects with a return on invested capital above 14% were acceptable to Petrobras.[16]

Valuation Approaches

Batista had emphasized the need to build a cash flow model and run sensitivity analysis in the valuation of Pecom. The most complex issue confronting Batista was how to account for country risk in the cost of capital. Latin America's long tradition of economic and political instability exposed companies to a myriad of risk factors, including

[15]Perez Companc had a 19.2% stake in Petrolera Perez Companc.
[16]Alexandra Strommer, "Muscle and Brains," J.P. Morgan Securities Inc., July 16, 2002, p. 22.

EXHIBIT 16A

PRO FORMA OPERATING FIGURES (AS OF DECEMBER 2001)

	Petrobras	Pecom	Pro Forma
Proven Reserves			
Oil (million bbl)	7,749	739	8,488
Gas (billion cubic meters)	253	46	299
Combined (million boe)	9,257	1,010	10,267
Production			
Oil (thousand barrels per day)	1,379	125	1,504
Gas (million cubic meter per day)	36	10	46
Combined (thousand boe per day)	1,596	181	1,777
Downstream			
International Refining Capacity (thousand bpd)	91	124	155
Gas Stations in Argentina	707	128	835
Gas Transportation Lines (kilometers)	7,500	7,000	14,500

Source: Adapted by casewriter from "Perez Companc Acquisition Overview," PowerPoint Presentation, July 2002. Petrobras S.A, Investor Relations.

currency devaluation, repatriation, capital controls, and expropriation, but these risks changed over time and varied from country to country. Over the last decade, both Argentina and Brazil had embraced reforms backed by the International Monetary Fund (IMF) and the World Bank. Measures such as exchange rate stabilization, freer capital flow mechanisms, lower import tariffs to encourage trade, and privatization of state-owned companies were put into practice to pave the way toward integration with global

EXHIBIT 16B

PRO FORMA FINANCIAL DATA (AS OF MARCH 31, 2002)

	Petrobras	Pecom	Pro Forma
Balance Sheet and Market Data			
Total Assets	37,119	3,446	40,565
Total Debt	14,016	2,330	16,346
Shareholder's Equity (Book value)	12,656	700	13,066
Cash and cash equivalents	6,445	236	5,926
Net Debt	7,571	2,094	10,420
Income and Cash Flow Statement Data			
Sales	22,724	1,555	24,279
EBITDA	8,544	689	9,233
Net Income	2,883	(392)	2,653
Capital Expenditures (CAPEX)	4,629	747	5,376

Source: Adapted by the casewriter from "Perez Companc Acquisition Overview," PowerPoint Presentation, July 2002. Petrobras S.A, Investor Relations.

EXHIBIT 17

SOVEREIGN RISK (EMBI—STRIP SPREAD—BPS)

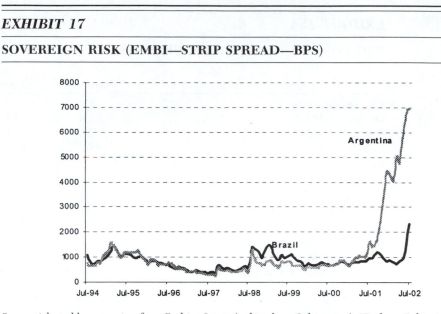

Source: Adapted by casewriter from Rodrigo Lopes ⟨rodrigo.lopes@chase.com⟩, "Dados – Relatorio Petrobras," to Ricardo Reisen de Pinho ⟨rreisen@hbs.edu⟩, March 7, 2003, and March 13, 2003.

economies.[17] Argentina, however, was again in financial crisis, and determining the appropriate country risk premium to use for the Pecom valuation proved challenging for Batista and his team.

Country risk premiums were most commonly derived from J. P. Morgan's Emerging Market Bond Index (EMBI), which measured the spread between external sovereign debt instruments of emerging markets with U.S. Treasury Bills of similar duration. As shown in Exhibit 17, Argentina and Brazil had similar country risk premiums up to mid-2001. By 2002, Argentina's country risk had increased so much that some team members argued that incorporating this risk premium into the discount rate for the Pecom valuation was problematic (see Exhibit 18 for sovereign risk premiums and market valuation indicators). They suggested that the cost of capital could instead be derived from current analyst estimates of the weighted average cost of capital for oil companies, including Petrobras and Pecom (see Exhibits 19a and 19b for cost of capital estimates), or from cost of equity estimates for different countries, including Brazil and Argentina (see Exhibit 20). Other team members, though, questioned how relevant such estimates were to the Pecom valuation.

The uncertainty about the country risk premium and the appropriate cost of capital to use in a cash flow model led Batista and his team to consider other valuation approaches in their analysis. They compared the valuations of selected companies, examining their multiples on a range of variables including reserves, EBITDA, cash flow and earnings (see Exhibit 21). BOE multiples were another common valuation measure used in the oil industry, and Exhibit 22 provides information on the BOE multiples for recent transactions. BOE multiples, however, did vary considerably across transactions, and also according to the location of reserves, as shown in Exhibit 23. In analyzing the

---

[17]"The slow road to reform," *The Economist*, November 30, 2000.

EXHIBIT 18

MARKET VALUATION INDICATORS
(AS OF MARCH 28, 2002, UNLESS NOTED OTHERWISE)

	Petrobras (PBR)	Pecom (PC)		Market Indicators
Beta 1 Year	0.69	0.77	Brazilian Sovereign Risk (bps)	718
Beta 3 Years	0.94	0.87	Argentine Sovereign Risk (bps)	5,013
Market price	$26.47	$8.12	Treasury 10 Years	5.400%
			Treasury 30 Years	5.799%

Source: Adapted by casewriter from Rodrigo Lopes ⟨rodrigo.lopes@chase.com⟩, "Dados—Relatorio Petrobras," to Ricardo Reisen de Pinho ⟨rreisen@hbs.edu⟩, March 7, 2003, and March 13, 2003.

different market-based valuations, team members debated which companies were most comparable to Pecom and which transactions could usefully be compared to the proposed acquisition.

Funding Strategy

Another point the board would raise was the question of Petrobras's financing strategy for the acquisition. Funding the acquisition with cash, securities, or a combination of both would be a sensitive matter. Petrobras was a well-recognized name, but market conditions were deteriorating by July 2002. Raising local funds meant paying high local interest rates with maturities shorter than 3 years. International markets were

EXHIBIT 19A

2002 ESTIMATES OF THE WEIGHTED AVERAGE COST OF CAPITAL (WAAC) FOR PETROBRAS AND GLOBAL OIL CORPORATIONS

Company	Estimated WAAC
Petrobras	15.0%
Ocean Energy	9.0%
KerrMcgee	9.0%
Exxon Mobil	8.9%
Shell	8.8%
Noble Affiliates	8.5%
Chevron Texaco	8.1%
BP	7.6%

Source: Adapted by casewriter from Christian Audi and Richard Wu, "Petrobras—Foreign expansion makes sense, at the right price," Morgan Stanley Dean Witter & Co, January 18, 2002, p. 5.

EXHIBIT 19B

ESTIMATES OF THE COST OF CAPITAL FOR PETROBRAS AND PECOM

Company	WACC Estimate	Date	Source	Details
Petrobras	13.20%	March 30, 2001	Dresdner Kleinwort Wasserstein[a]	n/a
Petrobras	16.40%	December 20, 2001	Goldman Sachs[b]	n/a
Petrobras	19.40%	July 16, 2002	J. P. Morgan[c]	Risk free rate: 5% Country risk premium: 12% Market risk premium: 7% Beta: 1.0 Debt-to-total-capital ratio: 38.5% Cost of debt: 12%
Pecom	12.60%	June 8, 2001	Santander Central Hispanico[d]	n/a
Pecom	13.25%	August 28, 2001	UBS[e]	Risk free rate: 3.75% Equity risk premium: 5.5% Pecom premium: 4%
Pecom	18.00%	December 20, 2001	Goldman Sachs[b]	n/a

[a]Geir Sagemo et al., "Energy Valuation in Emerging Markets," Dresdner Kleinwort Wasserstein, March 30, 2001, p. 19.

[b]Brian Singer, Tatiana Andrade, and Gordon Lee, "Perez Companc (ADR) (PC)/Transportadora de Gas del Sur (ADR) (TGS)—Energy: Oil and Gas," Goldman Sachs, December 20, 2001, p. 5.

[c]Alexandra Strommer, "Muscle and Brains," J.P. Morgan Securities Inc., July 16, 2002, p. 10.

[d]Fernando Pérès, "Perez Companc—Pumping up profits," Santander Central Hispanico, June 8, 2001, p. 7.

[e]Edmo Chagas and Andrea Kannebley, "Oil companies, secondary—Perez Companc," UBS, Equity Research, August 28, 2001, p. 11.

Source: Compiled by casewriter.

EXHIBIT 20

COST OF EQUITY COMPARISON (JULY 2001)

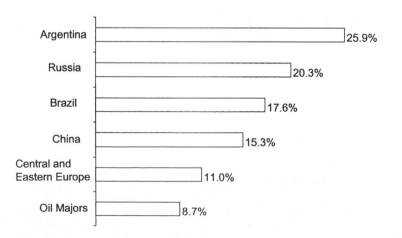

Source: Dresdner Kleinwort Wasserstein equity research estimates in Geir Sagemo and Erik Mielke, "Riding out the Storm," Dresdner Kleinwort Wasserstein, August 1, 2001, p. 13.

EXHIBIT 21

VALUATION TABLES FOR SELECTED COMPANIES (AS OF MARCH 28, 2002)

Company	Ticker	Price (US$)	Market Cap	EV Reserves 2002	EV EBITDA 2001A	EV EBITDA 2002E	EV EBITDA 2003E	EV Debt Adjusted Cash Flow 2001A	EV Debt Adjusted Cash Flow 2002E	EV Debt Adjusted Cash Flow 2003E	Price Cash Flow 2001A	Price Cash Flow 2002E	Price Cash Flow 2003E	Price Earnings 2001A	Price Earnings 2002E	Price Earnings 2003E
Supermajors																
BP	BP	53.1	198.0	10.4	6.9	8.1	6.2	9.0	8.3	7.1	10.2	7.3	7.3	13.0	15.7	10.9
Chevron Texaco[a]	CVX	90.3	98.8	7.0	5.1	5.9	5.0	7.0	7.3	6.3	6.3	6.3	5.5	10.0	13.0	10.3
Exxon Mobil	XOM	43.8	294.9	11.5	7.1	8.9	7.7	9.2	11.4	9.6	9.1	10.9	9.3	15.2	20.7	15.6
Royal Dutch	RD	54.3	113.1	4.8	4.9	5.4	4.7	6.7	7.8	6.8	6.8	7.6	6.4	12.0	13.7	10.6
Shell Transport	SC	44.3	71.3	3.3	4.9	5.5	4.8	6.9	7.9	6.9	6.9	7.7	6.5	12.2	14.1	10.8
Total Fina Elf	TOT	76.6	101.8	9.1	5.7	5.9	5.0	6.9	7.3	6.5	7.2	6.6	6.1	14.0	14.5	11.5
Weighted Average[b]				9.0	6.2	7.3	6.1	8.1	9.0	7.7	8.3	8.4	7.4	13.4	16.6	12.5
Majors																
Occidental	OXY	29.2	10.9	6.8	4.8	5.7	4.8	5.2	6.2	5.3	4.1	5.0	4.4	8.5	11.8	9.9
Murphy	MUR	48.8	2.2	6.9	3.6	6.3	3.9	3.7	5.0	3.7	2.8	3.4	2.4	7.7	21.2	6.7
BG	BRG	22.3	15.7	10.0	14.2	14.6	9.0	18.6	14.2	11.7	20.9	7.6	6.2	20.9	9.7	8.0
ENI	E	72.1	57.6	9.4	7.0	4.9	4.7	8.1	8.3	6.8	5.3	5.4	4.9	5.3	5.4	4.9
Norsk Hydro	NHY	47.9	12.3	6.9	4.3	3.0	3.3	17.7	16.9	14.7	3.9	3.7	2.7	3.9	3.7	2.7
Conoco Phillips	COP	62.8	42.6	16.6	8.6	10.4	5.0	16.3	19.8	10.9	4.0	6.9	5.1	8.8	14.5	10.2
Repsol YPF	REP	12.7	15.5	4.7	6.6	3.1	3.7	5.2	5.4	5.5	3.1	4.5	3.8	3.1	4.5	3.8
Statoil	STO	7.8	17.1	5.0	4.5	2.5	2.6	2.2	2.9	2.3	3.8	5.3	4.1	3.8	5.3	4.1
Weighted Average[b]				9.3	7.0	6.3	4.6	9.8	10.6	7.8	5.6	5.7	4.7	7.3	8.9	6.7

(Continued)

EXHIBIT 21 (Continued)

VALUATION TABLES FOR SELECTED COMPANIES (AS OF MARCH 28, 2002)

Company	Ticker	Price (US$)	Market Cap	EV Reserves 2002	EV EBITDA 2001A	EV EBITDA 2002E	EV EBITDA 2003E	EV Debt Adjusted Cash Flow 2001A	EV Debt Adjusted Cash Flow 2002E	EV Debt Adjusted Cash Flow 2003E	Price Cash Flow 2001A	Price Cash Flow 2002E	Price Cash Flow 2003E	Price Earnings 2001A	Price Earnings 2002E	Price Earnings 2003E
Emerging Oils																
Lukoil	LUKOY	59.0	11.1	1.1	3.8	4.5	3.0	4.6	5.4	3.6	3.8	4.5	3.0	5.0	6.1	3.5
MOL	MOLHB	4,950.0	1.7	NA	8.5	NA	NA	8.9	NA	NA	6.8	NA	NA	21.3	NA	NA
Sibneft	SBKYY	17.0	8.0	3.4	6.3	7.0	5.0	6.8	7.6	5.9	6.5	7.4	5.7	31.9	48.7	33.0
Yukos	YUKOY	124.0	18.4	2.2	5.2	5.2	3.8	6.2	6.8	5.0	6.6	7.0	5.2	14.7	17.5	13.5
Surgut	SNGSRU	11.4	13.0	1.2	2.9	2.6	2.4	NA	NA	NA	5.1	4.6	4.1	209.2	189.3	170.4
PetroChina	PTR	20.9	3.6	2.6	3.2	3.1	2.8	4.4	4.2	3.8	3.5	3.4	3.2	6.4	6.2	5.6
Sinopec	SNP	16.2	0.3	7.6	8.4	8.7	6.3	5.5	5.5	4.6	3.2	3.2	2.7	7.7	8.7	6.1
PKN	PKNPW	18.7	1.9	NA	5.6	5.8	4.1	6.0	6.3	4.6	4.7	4.9	3.5	25.3	18.5	7.6
Weighted Average[b]				**3.2**	**4.8**	**4.9**	**3.8**	**4.8**	**5.0**	**3.9**	**4.6**	**4.7**	**3.8**	**31.9**	**31.7**	**26.4**
Petrobras	PBR	26.5	28.7	2.9	2.8	3.1	2.8	3.7	3.6	4.3	2.5	2.2	2.6	3.6	4.3	3.8
Overall Weighted Average				6.1	5.2	5.4	4.3	6.6	7.1	5.9	5.3	5.3	4.6	14.0	15.4	12.3

[a]Proven reserves for Chevron Texaco is the sum of the individual proven reserves reported by both Chevron and Texaco.

[b]Weighted average by market capitalization.

Source: Compiled and adapted from Alexandra Strommer, "Muscle and Brains," J.P. Morgan Securities Inc., July 16, 2002, p. 14, and from Rodrigo Lopes (rodrigo.lopes@chase.com), "Dados—Relatorio Petrobras," to Ricardo Reisen de Pinho (rreisen@hbs.edu), March 7, 2003, and March 13, 2003.

EXHIBIT 22

SELECTED TRANSACTION COMPARABLES (IN $ PER BOE)

	Acquirer	Target (Oilfield Service controlled by)	Country	BOE Multiple
2000	Canadian Hunter	Sipetrol	Argentina	2.38
2000	Pecom	CGC	Argentina	3.69
2000	Pecom	Sudelektra	Argentina	4.05
2000	Repsol-YPF	Astra	Argentina	5.14
2000	Crestar Energy	CMS Energy	Ecuador	2.93
1999	Chevron	Petrolera San Jorge	Argentina	4.44
1999	Pioneer Natural	Pecom	Argentina	4.37
1999	Repsol	YPF (outstanding shares)	Argentina	3.83
1999	Repsol	YPF	Argentina	4.56
1999	Vintage Petroleum	Total / YPF	Argentina	2.09
1999	Alberta Energy	Pacalta Resources	Ecuador	4.59
1999	ENI SpA	Atlantic Richfield	Ecuador	2.49
1999	Vintage Petroleum	Petrobras	Ecuador	1.00

Source: Adapted by casewriter from Christian Audi and Richard Wu, "Perez Companc—A defensive play in case of a devaluation?" Morgan Stanley Dean Witter & Co, August 2, 2001, p. 11.

EXHIBIT 23

BOE MULTIPLES OF PROVEN RESERVES IN 2001 ($ PER BOE)

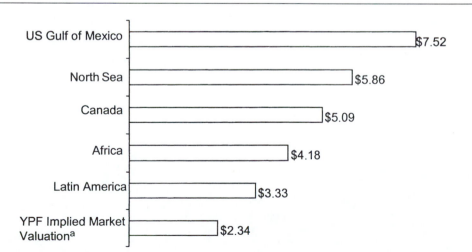

[a]Based on Repsol's purchase of the Argentine company Yacimientos Petroliferos Fiscales SA (YPF) in 1999.

Source: Adapted by casewriter from "Perez Companc Acquisition Overview," PowerPoint Presentation, July 2002. Petrobras Investor Relations, referencing Herold Transaction Review, 1996–2002 YTD, http://www.herold.com/research/disp_home.

virtually closed to corporate bonds coming from emerging markets.[18] Finally, floating equity at that point could send a troublesome signal regarding Petrobras's current price and the degree to which it truly reflected its inherent equity value, thus jeopardizing the market expectation that Petrobras could lower its cost of capital, and consequently boost future results and market performance.[19]

As Batista organized his notes for the board meeting, he reflected on the issues he and his team had discussed in the previous weeks. Was the Pecom acquisition a sound opportunity to increase Petrobras's diversification, or was it a risky venture during an unsettled time? The price offered for Pecom would at least in part determine the answer, and Batista wanted to be sure that his valuation of Pecom provided the board with the information it needed to make a decision.

[18]"Jittery Petrobras heads for own goal," *Upstream*, June 21, 2002, available from Factiva, ⟨http://www.factiva.com⟩.

[19]Alexandra Strommer, "Muscle and Brains," J.P. Morgan Securities Inc., July 16, 2002, p. 40.

14

Nestlé and Alcon—
The Value of a Listing

Wolfgang Reichenberger, Chief Financial Officer (CFO) at Swiss food giant Nestlé, and Francisco Castañer, Executive Vice President (EVP), stepped into the offices of Peter Brabeck-Letmathe, Chief Executive Officer (CEO). On this day in early September 2001, they had important business to discuss with the company's CEO.

As EVP, Castañer was responsible for the non-food business of the Nestlé Group worldwide. Although Nestlé was primarily known for its food brands—such as Nescafé, Perrier and Buitoni—the company had some select activities in other sectors. Its two largest non-food holdings were in fully-owned eye-care company Alcon, a producer of ophthalmic drugs, equipment for ocular surgery, and contact lens solutions, and a large stake in cosmetics giant L'Oréal.

For a while now, Nestlé had discussed carving out a part of Alcon for a public listing. The larger question then, that Reichenberger and Castañer wanted to discuss with Brabeck, was what effect a carve-out would have on Nestlé's overall valuation. Assuming further that they did list Alcon, two other questions followed suit. First, how should they arrive at an appropriate valuation of Alcon? Second, on what stock exchange should they list their Texas-based, but Switzerland-incorporated, subsidiary: in New York or Zürich?

NESTLÉ, THE WORLD'S LARGEST FOOD COMPANY

At the beginning of the new millennium, Nestlé was the world's number one food company.[1] It was the world leader in soluble coffee, mineral water, dairy, and infant

Professor Mihir A. Desai together with Executive Director Vincent Dessain, and Research Associate Anders Sjöman of the HBS Europe Research Center prepared this case. The authors gratefully acknowledge the help of Research Associates Mark F. Veblen and Anaïs Loizillon. Some names and data have been disguised for confidentiality. HBS cases are developed solely as the basis for class discussion. Cases are not intended to serve as endorsements, sources of primary data, or illustrations of effective or ineffective management.

[1]The information in this section is based in part on Ray Goldberg and Harold F. Hogan, "Nestlé S.A.", HBS Case No. 902-419 (Boston: Harvard Business School Publishing, 2002).

nutrition, and also very active in the ice cream, chocolate, and pet food segments. (See Exhibit 1 for brand examples.) In 2000, net profits for the group were Swiss Francs (CHF) 5.7 billion (about $3.4 billion USD) on annual sales of CHF 81.4 billion (about $48.2 billion). (See Exhibit 2 for Nestlé 2000 financials and Exhibit 3 for a 7-year overview.) Estimates of global market share gave 1.4% of the food and beverage industry and 2.6% of processed and branded products to Nestlé. The top six brands—Nestlé, Nescafé, Nestea, Maggi, Buitoni and Friskies—contributed approximately 70% of sales. The two leading business segments—"Beverages" and "Milk products, nutrition and ice cream"—represented almost 60% of sales, with the remainder covered by "Prepared dishes, cooking aids and pet care", "Chocolate, confectionary and biscuits" and "Pharmaceutical products."

Nestlé employed more than 250,000 people in 508 factories and offices in over 80 countries. Sales were geographically spread fairly evenly across Europe and the United States—about 30% each—and somewhat lower for Africa, Asia and Oceania

EXHIBIT 1

NESTLÉ BRAND PORTFOLIO

Segment	Brands
Soluble coffee	Nescafé, Taster's Choice, Ricoré, Ricoffy
Roast & ground coffee	Nespresso, Bonka, Zoégas, Loumidis
Water	Nestlé Pure Life, Nestlé Aquarel, Perrier, Vittel, Contrex, S. Pellegrino, Valvert, Panna, Levissima, Vera, Fürst Bismarck, Viladrau, Arrowhead, Poland Spring, Zephyrhills, Santa Maria, La Vie
Other beverages	Nestea, Nesquik, Nescau, Milo, Carnation, Libby's, Caro
Dairy products	Shelf stable: Nestlé, Nido, Nespray, Ninho, Carnation, Milkmaid, La Lechera, Moça, Klim, Gloria, Svelty, Molico, Nestlé Omega Plus, Bear Brand, Coffee-mate Chilled: Nestlé, LC1, Chamyto, La Laitiäre, Sveltesse, Yoco, Svelty, Molico
Breakfast cereals	Nestlé
Infant foods	Nestlé, Nan, Lactogen, Beba, Nestogen, Cérélac, Neslac, Nestum, Guigoz
Performance nutrition	PowerBar
Clinical nutrition	Nutren, Peptamen, Modulen, Build-up, Nesvita
Culinary products	(Soups, seasonings, prepared dishes, canned food, pasta, sauces :) Maggi, Buitoni, Crosse & Blackwell, Libby's, Thomy, Winiary
Frozen foods	Maggi, Buitoni, Stouffer's
Ice cream	Nestlé, Frisco, Motta, Camy, Savory, Peters
Refrigerated products	(Yogurts, desserts, pasta, sauces :) Nestlé, Buitoni, Herta
Chocolate and confectionery	Nestlé, Crunch, Cailler, Galak/Milkybar, KitKat, Quality Street, Smarties, Baci, After Eight, Baby Ruth, Butterfinger, Lion, Aero, Polo, Frutips, etc.
Food Services	Chef, Davigel, Minor's, Santa Rica
Petcare	Friskies, Fancy Feast, Alpo, Mighty Dog, Gourmet, Mon Petit, Felix
Flavors for the food industry	Food Ingredients Specialities (FIS)
Pharmaceutical products	Alcon, Galderma
Cosmetics	L'Oréal (significant interest)

Source: Nestlé web site, ⟨http://www.nestle.com/all_about/at_a_glance/aag-main_brands.html⟩, accessed 23 Aug 2002.

EXHIBIT 2

NESTLE FINANCIAL STATEMENTS 2001 (IN MILLIONS OF SWISS FRANCS, CHF)

CONSOLIDATED INCOME STATEMENT	2000	1999
Sales to customers	81,422	74,660
Cost of goods sold	−38,121	−35,912
Distribution expenses	−5,884	−5,268
Marketing and administration expenses	−26,467	−23,887
Research and development costs	−1,038	−893
Restructuring costs	−312	−402
Amortization of goodwill	−414	−384
Trading profit	**9,186**	**7,914**
Net financing cost	−746	−998
Net non–trading items	−99	−57
Profit before taxes	**8,341**	**6,859**
Taxes	−2,761	−2,314
Net profit of consolidated companies	**5,580**	**4,545**
Share of profit attributable to minority interests	−212	−160
Share of results of associated companies (°)	395	339
Net profit for the year	**5,763**	**4,724**

CONSOLIDATED BALANCE SHEET		
Liquid assets	10,131	6,670
Trade and other receivables	12,685	12,443
Inventories	7,168	7,383
Tangible fixed assets	18,625	19,218
Other assets (incl. Financial assets and goodwill)	16,915	13,225
Total Assets	**65,524**	**58,939**
Trade and other payables	10,001	9,635
Total debt	13,173	12,547
Other liabilities (incl. Employee benefits and tax liabilities)	11,837	11,679
Minority interests	609	625
Shareholders' equity	29,904	24,453
Total liabilities and equity	**65,524**	**58,939**

CONSOLIDATED CASH FLOW STATEMENT		
Cash flow from operating activities	**8,851**	**8,187**
Capital expenditures	−3,305	−2,806
Expenditure on intangible assets	−188	−139
Sale of tangible fixed assets	355	363
Acquisitions	−2,846	−440
Disposals	780	253
Other movements	146	10
Cash flow from investing activities	**−5,058**	**−2,759**
Dividend for the previous year	−1,657	−1,469
Bonds issued/(repaid)	−127	−72
Increase/(decrease) in other medium/long term debt	−155	500
Increase/(decrease) in short term debt	921	−3,488
Decrease/(increase) in short term investments	1,452	12
Other	−1,856	−2,856
Cash flow from financing activities	**−1,422**	**−7,373**

Note: (°) Includes Nestlé's 26% stake in L'Oréal.

Source: Nestlé S.A., 2000 Annual Report. Cham and Vevey, Switzerland, 2001.

EXHIBIT 3

NESTLE FINANCIAL INFORMATION (7 YEAR REVIEW)

In millions of CHF (except for per share data)	2000	1999	1998	1997	1996	1995	1994
Results							
Consolidated sales	81,422	74,660	71,747	69,998	60,490	56,484	56,894
Trading profit	9,186	7,914	7,081	7,057	6,053	5,658	5,628
as % of sales	11.30%	10.60%	9.90%	10.10%	10.00%	10.00%	9.90%
Taxes	2,761	2,314	2,000	1,842	1,552	1,561	1,647
Consolidated net profit	5,763	4,724	4,205	4,182	3,592	3,078	3,250
as % of sales	7.10%	6.30%	5.90%	6.00%	5.90%	5.40%	5.70%
as % of average equity	21.20%	20.00%	19.50%	21.90%	22.90%	23. 30%	19.90%
Total amount of dividend	2,127	1,657	1,469	1,376	1,180	1,043	1,040
Depreciation property, plant, equipment	2,737	2,597	2,609	2,677	2,305	2,103	2,321
as % of sales	3.40%	3.50%	3.60%	3.80%	3.80%	3.70%	4.10%
Amortization of goodwill	414	384	301	140	102	42	—
Balance sheet							
Current assets	30,747	27,169	26,467	25,671	23,070	20,927	21,420
of which liquid assets	10,131	6,670	7,963	8,102	5,860	5,124	5,132
Non-current assets	34,777	31,770	30,236	25,910	23,605	19,189	23,807
Total assets	65,524	58,939	56,703	51,581	46,675	40,116	45,227
Current liabilities	23,174	22,182	22,567	20,985	19,859	17,410	17,297
Non-current liabilities, minority interests	12,446	12,304	11,321	9,990	9,239	8,862	10,986
Equity	29,904	24,453	22,815	20,606	17,577	13,844	16,944
Capital expenditure	3,305	2,806	3,061	3,261	3,054	3,056	3,029
as % of sales	4.10%	3.80%	4.30%	4.70%	5.00%	5.40%	5.3 0%
Data per share							
Consolidated net profit	14.91	12.21	10.70	10.63	9.13	7.85	8.37
Equity	77.40	63.20	58.10	52.40	55.70	45.90	43.60
Dividend	5.50	4.30	3.80	3.50	3.00	2.65	2.65
Pay-out ratio	36.90%	35.20%	35.50%	32.90%	32.90%	33.80 %	31.70%
Stock exchange prices (high/low)	389.3/254.0	310.7/250.8	349.8/212.2	219.2/142.1	148.7/125.0	129.8/109.0	143.7/106.3
Yield	1.4/2.2	1.4/1.7	1.1/1.8	1.6/2.5	2.0/2.4	2.0/2.4	1.8/2.5
Number of personnel	224,541	230,929	231,881	225,808	221,144	220 ,172	212,687

Source: Nestlé S.A., 2000 Annual Report, Cham and Vevey, Switzerland, 2001.

combined at 19% (see Exhibit 4 for sales by segment and geography.) As a result of its international expansion, the Swiss company now had only just over 1% of its sales actually in Switzerland. Nestlé's international profile was also reflected in its executive board, where the ten-man board included eight different nationalities (see Exhibit 5).

Company History

The history of Nestlé began in 1866 in the city of Vevey, close to Lausanne, in Switzerland, when pharmacist Henri Nestlé introduced a wheat-based infant formula product for mothers unable to breast-feed. The formula met with huge success in curbing infant malnutrition and mortality rates. Incorporating the formula into a company, Nestlé began selling to other European countries. Growth increased when the Red Cross started to use the formula in developing countries. In 1905, Nestlé merged with its chief rival, Anglo-Swiss Condensed Milk Company, founded by two American brothers, Charles and George Page.

Adding more food activities, Nestlé grew throughout the century into Switzerland's largest industrial company. The growth built largely on a steady stream of acquisitions. For instance, in 1929, it bought Cailler, the first company to mass-produce chocolate bars. An investment in Brazil led to a request from Brazilian coffee growers to develop

---

EXHIBIT 4

NESTLE SALES BY BUSINESS SEGMENT AND BY GEOGRAPHIC REGION

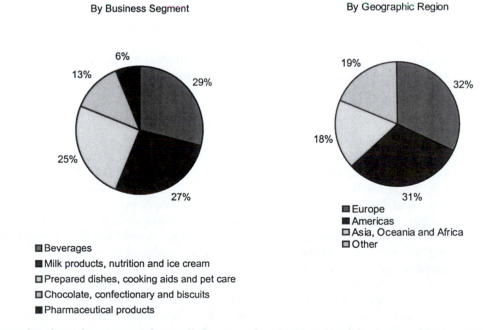

By Business Segment

29%
6%
13%
27%
25%

- ■ Beverages
- ■ Milk products, nutrition and ice cream
- □ Prepared dishes, cooking aids and pet care
- □ Chocolate, confectionary and biscuits
- ■ Pharmaceutical products

By Geographic Region

19%
32%
18%
31%

- ■ Europe
- ■ Americas
- □ Asia, Oceania and Africa
- □ Other

Source: Nestlé web site, http://www.nestle.com/all_about/at_a_glance/aag-main_brands.html, accessed 23 Aug 2002.

EXHIBIT 5

NESTLE EXECUTIVE BOARD, 2001

Name	Title	Nationality
Chief Executive Officer		
• Peter Brabeck-Letmathe	Direct responsibilities: Nutrition Strategic Business Division, Perrier Vittel Group	Austrian
Senior Vice Presidents		
• Francisco Castañer	Pharmaceutical and Cosmetic Products, Liaison with L'Oréal, Human Resources, Corporate Affairs	Spanish
• Frank Cella	Strategic Business Units, Marketing	American
• Michael W. O. Garrett	Asia, Oceania, Africa, Middle East	British/Australian
• Rupert Gasser	Technical, Production, Environment, R&D	Swiss/Austrian
• Lars Olofsson	Europe	Swedish
• Wolfgang H. Reichenberger	Finance, Control, Legal, Tax, Purchasing, Export	Swiss/Austrian
• Carlos Eduardo Represas	United States of America, Canada & Mexico	Mexican
• Chris Johnson	Deputy EVP, GLOBE Programme, Information Systems, Logistics, eNestlé	American

Source: Nestlé website, http://www.nestle.com/Data/MediaCenter/management.asp?menu=2, accessed 24 February 2004.

a water-soluble "coffee cube." The result, Nescafé, was launched in 1938. (For a more detailed list of acquisitions, see Exhibit 6.)

Nestlé also learned first-hand the challenge of operating internationally. In the early 1970s, for instance, non-governmental organizations accused Nestlé of unethical promotion of its infant formula in developing countries. They claimed Nestlé failed to warn of potential dangers from incorrect use on the product labels, and that Nestlé marketers were dressed as health care professionals. An international consumer boycott became a global media event. Helmut Maucher, who was named chairman and CEO in 1981, acknowledged the boycotters, met with them and other critics, and was instrumental in setting up a commission to police adherence to the World Health Organization's International Code of Marketing for Breast Milk Substitutes.

Maucher remained as CEO for 16 years, during which time Nestlé, among other things, expanded its food base into pet care. In 1997, Maucher was succeeded by Peter Brabeck-Letmathe. A native Austrian, and a company veteran with over 33 years of experience for Nestlé in South America and in Europe, Brabeck announced that revenue would from now on be derived two-thirds internally and one-third externally. The target rate for Real Internal Growth (growth excluding acquisitions and divestitures) was set at 4% annually. Brabeck also cut into the business, and disposed of under-performing units, such as the U.S. roast and ground coffee and Libby's canned meat products. He also closed some R&D plants, and merged several production facilities. During his first three years in office, Brabeck combined divestitures with selective acquisitions (see Exhibit 7). Analysts took this as a sign that Nestlé was seriously looking at its growth numbers and at divesting non-strategic activities.

Brabeck did stay true, though, to the Nestlé tradition of giving power to the various country heads. Central units, such as production, R&D and logistics, had no profit-and-loss responsibility of their own. Instead, local entities were run as autonomous fi-

EXHIBIT 6

NESTLE ACQUISITION HISTORY (SELECTED)

Year	Milestone
1866	Company's foundation
1905	Merger between Nestlé and Anglo-Swiss Condensed Milk Company
1929	Merger with Peter-Cailler-Chocolates Suisses S.A. Acquisition of Swiss General, inventor of milk chocolate
1947	Merger with Alimentana S.A. (Maggi)
1971	Merger with Ursina-Franck (Switzerland)
1985	Acquires Carnation (USA), acquires Carnation Friskies brand (UK)
1988	Acquires Buitoni-Perugina (Italy)
1988	Acquires Rowntree (GB)
1992	Acquires Perrier (France)
1997	Nestlé, through the Perrier Vittel Group, expands its mineral water activities with the outright acquisition of San Pellegrino
1998	Acquires Spillers Petfoods, UK, and strengthens position in the pet food business
1999	Divestiture of Findus brand (except in Switzerland and Italy) and parts of Nestlé's frozen food business in Europe. Divestiture of Hills Bros, MJB and Chase & Sanborn coffee brands (USA)
2000	Acquisition of PowerBar

Source: Nestlé web site, ⟨http://www.nestle.com/all_about/at_a_glance/aag-historical_dev.html⟩, accessed 23 Aug 2002.

nancial entities which should develop their own capital structures and be evaluated as independent entities. Dividend remittances to headquarters were made annually and were expected to be based on annual profits. In the group, debt was generally allocated among the subsidiaries, which were responsible for making their own, independent, borrowing decisions.

In January 2001, Nestlé announced its largest acquisition to date. It would buy pet food company Ralston-Purina, with brand names such as Dog Chow, Fit & Trim, Purina O.N.E. and Purina Veterinary Diets. Nestlé would pay $11 billion in cash for the St. Louis, Missouri-based company, in a deal that was expected to go through at the end of 2001. Merging it with Nestlé's existing pet food activities would create the world's largest pet food company, Nestlé Purina PetCare.

Non-Food Investments

Outside of the food sector, Nestlé had two significant investments. The company was a minority partner in Gesparal, the holding company for French cosmetics company L'Oréal. Gesparal was run by the family Bettencourt, the founders of L'Oréal. With its 49% stock in Gesparal, Nestlé held 26% of L'Oréal and had the first right of refusal of the Bettencourt family's shares. The 26% holding had in 2001 an EBITDA value of approximately CHF 0.5 billion. In 1989, Nestlé and L'Oréal had created a joint venture in dermatology, Galderma. Galderma sold products worldwide for skin ailments such

EXHIBIT 7

NESTLE MAIN ACQUISITIONS AND DIVESTITURES 1997–2001

Company	Business	Country	Deal	Stake (%)	Sales (CHFmn)
2001 (until Sep 2001)					
Ralston Purina[a]	Pet food	United States	Acquisition	100%	4,930
Schöller	Ice cream and frozen food	Germany	Acquisition	100%	N/A
Black Mountain	Mineral water	United States	Acquisition	100%	60
Dar Natury	Mineral water	Poland	Acquisition	50%	N/A
Dreyers	Ice cream	United States	Incr. in participation	from 21% to 24%	N/A
Fonterra	Dairy	Americas	Joint venture	N/A	N/A
Hoji Food	Bouillons	China	Acquisition	60%	N/A
Mineralbrunnen	Mineral water	Germany	Disposal	42%	N/A
2000					
Powerbar	Performance nutrition	Unites States	Acquisition	100%	220
UCC	Vending for beverages	Japan	Acquisition	100%	616
Cargill s.a.c.i	Pet food	Argentina	Acquisition	100%	72
Summit Autonomous	Eye care	United States	Acquisition	100%	150
Joe	Confectionary	Romania	Acquisition	100%	N/A
Nestlé Mackintosh	Confectionary	Japan	Incr. in participation	from 66% to 100%	200
Consomate/Rosa Blanca	Bouillons	Mexico	Acquisition	100%	N/A
Wyeth-Ayerst	Infant formula	Canada	Acquisition	100%	N/A
Kekkuti	Mineral water	Hungary	Acquisition	90%	N/A
Aberfoyle	Mineral water	Canada	Acquisition	100%	135
Valvita & Schoonspruit	Mineral water	South Africa	Acquisition	100%	N/A
Fresh Water	Mineral water	Argentina	Acquisition	100%	N/A
Findus brand and related assets	Frozen food	Europe	Disposal	N/A	900
Frozen potatoes business	Frozen potatoes	United States	Disposal	100%	N/A
Vismara	Processed meat	Italy	Disposal	100%	N/A
1999					
La Cocinera	Frozen food	Spain	Acquisition	100%	N/A
Svitoch	Confectionary	Ukraine	Acquisition	75%	N/A
Totole	Bouillons	China	Acquisition	80%	N/A
La Universal	Biscuit	Ecuador	Acquisition	100%	N/A
Haagen-Dazs	Ice cream	United States	Joint venture	50%	N/A
Quilmes	Mineral water	Argentina	Joint venture	N/A	N/A
Hills Bros, MJB, Chase & Sanborn	Roast and ground coffee	United States	Disposal	100%	N/A
Laura Secord	Chocolate retail	Canada	Disposal	100%	N/A
Cocoa processing	Cocoa processing plants	Malaysia & Italy	Disposal	100%	N/A
Alder/Bavaria	Cheese	Argentina	Disposal	100%	N/A

(*Continued*)

EXHIBIT 7 *(Continued)*

NESTLE MAIN ACQUISITIONS AND DIVESTITURES 1997–2001

Company	Business	Country	Deal	Stake (%)	Sales (CHFmn)
1998					
San Pellegrino	Mineral water	Italy	Incr. in participation	from 50% to 100%	N/A
Borden/Klim	Milk powder	Regional	Acquisition	100%	N/A
Spillers	Pet food	United Kingdom	Acquisition	100%	N/A
Nestlé Philippines	Nestlé products	Philippines	Incr. in participation	from 55% to 100%	N/A
Libby's	Canned meats	United States	Disposal	100%	N/A
1997					
Ault and Dairy World	Ice cream	Canada	Acquisition	100%	N/A
Shanghai Fuller	Ice cream, milk	China	Acquisition	100%	N/A
D'Onofrio	Ice cream, confectionary	Peru	Acquisition	81%	N/A
Basotherm	Eye care and dermatology	Germany	Acquisition	100%	N/A
Cremo	Ice cream and dairy	Venezuela	Acquisition	100%	N/A
Dairy Farm	Ice cream and dairy	China	Inc. in participation	from 51% to 100%	N/A
Contadina	Canned tomato	United States	Disposal	100%	N/A

Note: a. Closing subject to customary regulatory approval.

Source: Nestlé documents, as presented in Ray Goldberg and Harold F. Hogan, "Nestlé S.A.", HBS Case No. 902-419 (Boston: Harvard Business School Publishing, 2002).

as acne, psoriasis, rosacea and nail fungus. In 2000, Galderma reached sales of €525 million, growing 32.2% on the previous year. (Exhibit 8 shows L'Oréal's 2000 financials.)

Nestlé's second large non-food holding was the wholly-owned ophthalmology[2] company Alcon.

ALCON, THE EYE-CARE SUBSIDIARY

Alcon was founded in 1945 by two pharmacists, Robert Alexander and William Connor, in Fort Worth, Texas. The company specialized in ophthalmic products at a time when most eye care patients would ask their local pharmacy to make drugs to order. The results varied greatly from pharmacy to pharmacy—and contaminations from eye care solutions often led to eye infections, even blindness. As an early entrant into this corner of the market, Alcon experienced early success and continued growth; by 1970 sales reached $25 million, and the company was publicly listed in 1971.

Then, in 1977, Alcon was wholly acquired off the New York Stock Exchange by Nestlé. From then onwards, Alcon held most of its intellectual property rights with

[2]Ophthalmology is the branch of medical science concerned with the structure, functions, and diseases of the eye.

EXHIBIT 8

L'OREAL 2000 FINANCIALS, ALL NUMBERS IN MILLIONS OF EURO, €

Consolidated Balance Sheet	31.12.2000	31.12.1999
Assets (net values)		
Unissued share capital	0.10	0.10
Goodwill (note 1)	506.50	109.70
Intangible fixed assets	4,134.60	3,293.90
Tangible fixed assets	1,611.60	1,408.90
Financial assets	230.40	134.60
Investments in associated companies	1,121.90	970.70
Sum Fixed Assets	**7,605.10**	**5,917.90**
Current assets	6,013.40	4,944.10
Unrealized translation losses	16.00	16.50
TOTAL ASSETS	13,634.50	10,878.50
Liabilities		
Shareholders' equity (after minority interests)	6,590.40	5,797.60
Minority interests	9.90	10.40
Provisions for liabilities and charges	722.30	500.80
Loans and debts	3,423.60	1,913.90
Current liabilities	2,882.00	2,638.80
Unrealized translation gains	6.30	17.00
TOTAL LIABILITIES	13,634.50	10,878.50

Consolidated Profit and Loss Accounts	2000	1999
Net sales	12,671.20	10,750.70
Purchases and variation in stocks	−2,307.40	−2,038.90
Personnel costs	−2,217.80	−1,882.50
External charges	−5,988.80	−5,102.70
Taxes other than on income; depreciation; charges to provisions	−616.40	−460.70
Operating profit	1,540.80	1,265.90
Exchange gains and losses	−59.50	−36.00
Adjusted operating profit	1,481.30	1,229.90
Financial expense—net	−159.30	−104.60
Profit before taxation of fully consolidated companies	1,322.00	1,125.30
Income tax	−488.50	−428.70
Net profit before capital gains, losses, and minority interests of consolidated companies	833.50	696.60
Group's share of net profit before cap gains, losses, and min interests of equity affiliates	199.90	136.50
Net profit before capital gains and losses and minority interests	1,033.40	833.10
Capital gains/losses on disposals of fixed assets; restructuring costs, goodwill amortization	−58.60	−40.10
Net book profit before minority interests	974.80	793.00
Minority interests	−5.40	−5.80
Net book profit after minority interest	**969.40**	**787.20**
Net profit before capital gains and losses and after minority interests	**1,027.80**	**827.50**
Number of shares outstanding	676,062,160	676,062,160
Earnings per share in euros	1.52	1.22

Source: L'Oréal, 2000 Annual Report, Paris, 2001.

Nestlé in Switzerland, with patents licensed to the U.S. operations which returned royalty payments. Alcon legally became a Swiss-domiciled company in 1992, incorporated in Hünenberg, Switzerland. Top management and central R&D efforts all remained, though, in Fort Worth.

In 2000, Alcon was the world's leading ophthalmology company with net earnings of $331 million on sales of $2.5 billion. (See Exhibit 9 for financials.) The company developed, manufactured and marketed ophthalmic pharmaceuticals (such as glaucoma treatments, anti-infectives, and allergy relievers), ophthalmic surgical equipment (for cataract removal and laser vision correction), and contact lens care products and other consumer eye care products (such as contact lens solutions brand Opti-Free.) Alcon was not active in the glasses and contact lenses areas. Alcon operated directly in about 75 countries with almost 11,000 employees, and its products were present in over 180 countries. Of a sales staff of around 2,200, 1,500 focused on markets outside the U.S. However, more than half of company sales and earnings were generated in the U.S. (Exhibit 10 shows the company's geographic spread.)

Alcon was a leader in nearly every product category it entered. As a whole, Alcon was twice as large as its nearest competitor, and held about a quarter of the $11 billion dollar global market for ophthalmic products. Its global sales represented 19% of the ophthalmic pharmaceutical market, 45% of the ophthalmic surgical market and 19% of the ophthalmic consumer market. Top management argued that not only did this make Alcon the largest and most profitable, but also the purest ophthalmic company in the world. The business performance went hand-in-hand with a strong commitment to research and development: Alcon had invested approximately $1 billion in R&D over the last five years and had accumulated over 1,400 patents.

In addition to a strong focus on R&D, Alcon also prioritized managerial longevity and stability. For instance, almost everyone on the executive board had been with the company for over 20 years. (See Exhibit 11 for Alcon's 2001 executive board.) Top managers received two thirds of their compensation in stock options, valued according to a phantom stock program.[3]

In the industry, Allergan of Irvine, California, was considered Alcon's closest comparable competitor. Allergan shared Alcon's three business areas, and was also active in an area that the company called "Skin Care & Botox." However, Allergan had recently announced plans to spin off its ophthalmic surgical and consumer eye care businesses, to create a more pure pharmaceutical company, consisting of the ophthalmic pharmaceutical and "Skin Care & Botox" divisions.

In 2001, Alcon stood to benefit from several future growth trends. An aging population and rising incomes in emerging markets were expected to create both an increase in eye-related disorders and the number of customers who could afford eye care products. The ophthalmology market was also relatively insensitive to short-term economic cycles. Recently, Nestlé CEO Brabeck had asked the Alcon top management to prepare a 10-year growth plan. The plan had revealed a more than promising R&D pipeline. Combined with Allergan's announcement to divest its ophthalmic products, and fellow Swiss pharmaceutical Novartis's apparent intention to also move away from ophthalmology, Alcon could potentially become *the* one-stop-shop for ophthalmologists worldwide.

---

[3]Phantom stock plans are management tools. The plans mimic stock plans, by providing payments based on hypothetical holdings in company stock. These holdings are valued based on the assumed market value of one share of company stock.

EXHIBIT 9

ALCON FINANCIALS (ALL NUMBERS IN MILLIONS OF USD). REPORTING ESTABLISHED UNDER THE GAAP RULES.

Balance Sheet	Dec 31, 1999	Dec 31, 2000
Assets		
Current assets		2,044.8
Property, plant and equipment, net		613.4
Intangible assets, net		1,138.8
Long term deferred income tax assets, other assets		84.5
Total assets		**3,881.5**
Liabilities and Shareholders' Equity		
Current liabilities		1,794.5
Long term debt, net of current maturities		699.8
Long term deferred income tax liabilities		45.5
Other long term liabilities		240.3
Total shareholders' equity		1,101.4
Total liabilities and shareholders' equity		**3,881.5**

Income Statement	1999	2000
Sales	2,401.0	2,553.6
Cost of goods sold	719.1	749.7
Selling, general and administrative	805.2	855.8
Research and development	213.1	246.3
In process research and development	—	18.5
Amortization of intangibles	46.4	86.5
Operating income	**617.2**	**596.8**
Other income (expense):		
Gain (loss) from foreign currency, net	10.7	0.1
Interest income	13.7	44.1
Interest expense	−54.4	−86.3
Other	—	—
Earnings before income taxes	**587.2**	**554.7**
Income taxes	240.3	223.0
Net earnings	**346.9**	**331.7**

Cash Flow	1999	2000
Cash flow from operating activities	**451.8**	**392.8**
Proceeds from sale of assets	3.7	107.9
Purchases of property, plant and equipment	−99.4	−117.1
Purchase of intangible assets	−15.2	—
Acquisitions, net of cash acquired	—	−863.0
Net cash from investing activities	**−110.9**	**−872.2**
Proceeds from issuance of long term debt	1.3	612.8
Net proceeds (repayment) from short term debt	198.8	307.3
Dividends to shareholder	−112.6	−4.2
Repayment of long term debt	−66.1	−32.9
Other	—	—
Net cash from financing activities	**21.4**	**883.0**
Effect of exchange rates on cash and cash equivalents	−1.6	−2.1
Net increase in cash and cash equivalents	**360.7**	**401.5**
Cash and cash equivalents, beginning of year	149.8	510.5
Cash and cash equivalents, end of year	510.5	912.0

Source: Alcon, 2001 Annual and Corporate Report, Hünenberg, Switzerland, 2001.

EXHIBIT 10

ALCON GEOGRAPHIC SPREAD

Region	Corporate headquarters	US general office	Country main office	Manu-facturing	Other office branch	R&D
North America		1	4	6	3	3
Latin America			11	2	1	
Europe	1		20	6	11	2
Middle East & Africa			1		2	
Asia & Oceania			11	1	37	

Source: Adapted from Alcon, 2001 Annual and Corporate Report, Hünenberg, Switzerland, 2001.

EXHIBIT 11

ALCON EXECUTIVE MANAGEMENT, 2001

Name	Title	Nationality	With Alcon since	In current position since
Chief Executive Officer				
• Tim Sear	Chairman, President and CEO, Alcon Inc	British	1971	1997
Senior Vice Presidents				
• Andre Bens, Ph.D.	Global Manufacturing. Technical Support, Alcon Manufacturing, Ltd	Belgian	1982	2001
• Gerald Cagle, Ph.D.	Research & Development Alcon Research, Ltd	American	1976	1997
• Fred Pettinato	International Operations Alcon Laboratories, Inc	American	1989	2001
• Charles Miller	Finance and CFO Alcon Laboratories, Inc	American	1971	1997
• Cary Rayment	U.S. Operations Alcon Laboratories, Inc	American	1974	2001

Note: In the U.S., Alcon built on a diverse group of legal entities.

- **Alcon Manufacturing, Ltd.** was the U.S. manufacturing arm, with operations in Texas, California, Pennsylvania, and West Virginia.
- **Alcon Laboratories, Inc.** was the selling, marketing, and distribution arm with physical locations in Texas, California, Maryland, Hawaii, and Florida. Alcon Laboratories, Inc. also maintained sales and technical service staff in almost all 50 states and the District of Columbia.
- **Alcon Research, Ltd.** was the research arm with operations primarily in Texas, California, and Florida.
- **Falcon Pharmaceuticals, Ltd.** was the generic company brand with headquarters in Texas.
- **Alcon Pharmaceuticals, Inc.** was a distribution operation based in Nevada.

    Alcon's international companies were primarily selling, marketing, and distribution entities, but several of these companies also had manufacturing operations and a few had small research facilities.

Source: Alcon, 2001 Annual and Corporate Report, Hünenberg, Switzerland, 2001 (Note from Alcon 2003 Annual Report).

DISCUSSING ALCON'S IMPACT ON NESTLE'S FINANCING STRATEGY

Currently, Alcon was but a small part of the overall Nestlé group, representing 5% of sales and 12% of EBIT. However, despite its small relative size within Nestlé, Alcon was a large specialty pharma company in its own right. To CEO Brabeck, Alcon's value was completely buried in the food and beverages ocean that was Nestlé. He had recently told Castañer and Reichenberger,

> Alcon has had a great development as a division of Nestlé—which has not been recognized by the financial world. The best way to show the intrinsic value of this fantastic company might be to make it public, to let the market decide what the real value should be.

Castañer, a 56-year old Spaniard who had been with Nestlé since 1964, reasoned that,

> A food analyst on Wall Street does not understand ophthalmology. We report Alcon as part of Nestlé's consolidated operations—but Alcon has growth rates sometimes twice the Nestlé group growth rate. Alcon should also have higher valuation multiples than Nestlé's much larger food businesses. So analysts are not recognizing the true value of Alcon. Conversely, this also means that the Alcon business stops Nestlé from truly exposing its value.

Nestlé executives were aware that Nestlé's 12.7x EBITDA multiple appeared to be in line with its competitors. At the same time, they felt that the other businesses embedded in that multiple masked a food & beverage business that was trading at a discount to its peers. (Exhibit 12 compares Nestlé and its competitors.) Alcon was one part of the explanation; the 26% stake in L'Oréal— which was consolidated only at the level of net profit under "Share of results of associated companies"—was another. Theoretically, a good valuation would break down a company into its business types, and apply the proper multiple to each type. This would essentially build the value of Nestlé up as the sum of its component parts. However, Nestlé found that analysts grouped the businesses, applying blended multiples that did not reflect the underlying businesses. Ironically this meant that no one at Nestlé knew what multiple was being applied to *either* business, food & beverage or Alcon. By extracting the non-food subsidiaries and forcing analysts to decompose the various businesses, Nestlé management wondered what the valuation effect might be—for both Nestlé and Alcon.

Beyond valuation changes, examining the values of the component parts separately would produce numbers that might paint a more revealing picture of the company as a whole. The underlying theory of a multiples analysis was predicated on comparability. Intrinsic differences among companies might lead to multiple differentials. A company that had expanded higher up the value chain, capturing higher margin businesses, could generally be expected to trade at a higher EBITDA multiple than one that had not; a company with better growth potential or more product R&D under development might similarly trade at a higher multiple than its slower growth peers. In short, the multiples were valuable not only for the valuations they produced but also for the underlying stories they told. Reichenberger therefore wanted to know not only the valuations of Nestlé and Alcon at the proper multiples, but wanted to understand what accounted for the differences, if any, as compared to competitors.

In addition to the valuation discussion, Castañer saw another reason for an Alcon IPO (Initial Public Offering). He explained, "It would help us give the top executives of Alcon incentives through a real stock options program, instead of the phantom stock program we use now, which basically always trails the competition." Concerns for the

EXHIBIT 12

COMPANY COMPARISONS (AMOUNTS IN MILLION USD)

a. Food and Beverage (F&B) Industry

Company	% F&B industry	Market Cap.	Enterprise Value	EBITDA	ROE (est.) Ave 3-yr (1999–2001)	Revenues 1999	Revenues 2000	Revenues 2001E	EPS 1999	EPS 2000	EPS 2001E	EPS 5-yr Future Growth (est.)
Cadbury Schweppes	51%	13,138	15,518	1,511	22.1	6,946	6,842	8,026	2.02	1.47	1.56	12.0
Campbell	91%	12,237	16,254	1,475	188.8	6,424	6,267	6,664	1.63	1.65	1.55	n.a.
Damone	n.a.	17,203	21,854	2,136	n.a.	14,178	13,201	12,955	4.91	4.47	0.84	5.0
General Mills	100%	18,947	28,104	1,484	462.3	6,700	7,078	n.a.	2.00	2.28	n.a.	5.0
Heinz	100%	14,394	19,855	1,912	46.8	9,408	9,430	9,431	2.47	1.41	2.36	5.0
Kellogg	100%	12,235	18,262	1,640	54.1	6,984	6,955	8,853	0.83	1.45	1.18	10.0
Kraft	100%	18,887	33,082	6,608	11.8	26,797	26,532	33,875	1.20	1.38	1.17	31.0
Nestlé	94%	84,056	97,500	7,662	19.9	46,745	50,254	51,029	1.89	2.28	2.58	9.0
Unilever	n.a	32,929	50,038	n.a.	18.9	29,425	30,415	31,673	3.08	1.04	1.19	13.0

Source: Nestlé (EPS 5-yr growth from Nestlé, and originating with Morgan Stanley reports and Goldman Sachs presentation).

b. Pharma Industry

Company	% Pharma industry	Market Cap.	Enterprise Value	EBITDA	ROE (est.) Ave 3-yr (1999–2001)	Revenues 1999	Revenues 2000	Revenues 2001E	EPS 1999	EPS 2000	EPS 2001E	EPS 5-yr Future Growth (est.)
Allergan	63%	9,846	9,728	434	25.8	1,452	1,626	1,746	1.39	1.61	1.69	21.7
Bausch & Lomb	15%	2,019	2,150	222	6.8	1,756	1,772	1,712	1.75	1.49	0.78	10.1
King	86%	10,349	10,429	426	17.9	348	620	872	0.47	0.47	0.99	23.8
Teva	88%	7,682	8,345	448	16.3	1,282	1,750	2,077	0.94	1.14	2.04	25.0
Forest	100%	14,584	14,128	449	17.0	873	1,175	1,567	0.64	1.18	1.82	28.9

Source: Nestlé (based in part on in-house presentation by CSFB).

Alcon top executives would also justify why only a part, and not all, of Alcon would be listed. Explained Brabeck, "Alcon management delivers results so they need to be rewarded [through a stock option program]—but they also value keeping Nestlé as a main shareholder."

Nestlé itself needed to discuss how much effective control of Alcon it wanted to keep. An IPO might make Alcon lose its long-term perspective, as the company would have to meet the demands for quarterly results. Management also risked becoming too conservative, avoiding investment risks to preserve the stock price level. Nestlé would have to keep its eye on Alcon to make sure that the long term would not be forgotten. To Brabeck, it was never the pressure of analysts that made a board more responsible: "It is not because you have a teacher watching over your shoulder that you necessarily perform better."

Guarding the Credit Rating

Although not related to the Alcon discussion at first glance, Reichenberger also needed to discuss Nestlé's financial situation after the Ralston Purina acquisition. His main concern was how market analysts and rating agencies would view the deal, expected to go through in early 2002 when Nestlé would pay $10.3 billion in cash for the pet food company. Currently, Ralston Purina had a net income of $530 million on annual sales of $2.7 billion. By paying in cash rather than with stock, Nestlé had negotiated a smaller price premium.[4] To finance the cash acquisition, however, Nestlé had to borrow additional funds. The purchase would in fact be completely debt financed.

To soften concerns among analysts and rating agencies, Nestlé had publicly committed itself to undertake a debt reduction program after the acquisition. However, some analysts questioned Nestlé's current AAA credit rating. In fact, in the spring of 2001, S&P and Moody's analysts put the company on its watch list. To Nestlé management, this was big news, as Nestlé was one of relatively few companies (see Exhibit 13) that firmly kept the highest credit rating possible. Few companies in the world had achieved that status and even fewer non-American companies. Brabeck felt that the rating provided several concrete sources of value. He explained,

> [The rating] is an amazing weapon that allows for reduced financing costs. When Nestlé suddenly needs to borrow $10 billion for an acquisition this can be done in an afternoon. The rating is also a crystal clear indication of financial soundness and stability. Nestlé has a very wide investor base of more than 200,000 shareholders, so stability matters a lot. Very few companies in the world still have a triple-A credit rating—and none in the food sector.

However, the company always made sure the markets knew that for strategically important acquisitions, it would be willing to accept a rating downgrade.

CONSIDERING THE CARVE-OUT

Assuming that Nestlé did list Alcon, Castañer and Reichenberger asked themselves *where* Alcon should be listed. 48-year old Reichenberger, who had been with Nestlé since 1977, framed the issue, "What is the natural shareholder base for a Swiss-

---

[4]Shareholders of firms being acquired often preferred cash because its value was certain. Stock, in contrast, was riskier, but allowed them to maintain an interest in the business and defer capital gains taxes until they sold the shares.

EXHIBIT 13

STANDARD & POOR'S AAA RATED COMPANIES SEPTEMBER 2001

Company	Country	Industry
North America		
American International Group	U.S.	Insurance, Financial Services
Automatic Data Processing	U.S.	Business Services (Outsourcing)
Berkshire Hathaway	U.S.	Investment Firms
Bristol Myers Squibb	U.S.	Pharmaceuticals
Exxon Mobil Corp	U.S.	Energy & Utilities
General Electric Co	U.S.	Automotive, Transport, Aerospace & Defense
Johnson & Johnson	U.S.	Pharmaceuticals
Massachusetts Mutual Life	U.S.	Insurance, Financial Services
Merck & Co	U.S.	Pharmaceuticals
Northwestern Mutual Life Ins	U.S.	Insurance, Financial Services
Pfizer Inc	U.S.	Pharmaceuticals
Shell Oil Co	U.S.	Energy & Utilities
State Farm Insurance	U.S.	Insurance
Teachers Insurance and Annuity Association—College Retirement Equities Fund (TIAA-CREF)	U.S.	Financial services
United Parcel Service Inc	U.S.	Transportation Services
United Services Auto Assn	U.S.	Insurance
Wesco Financial Corp	U.S.	Financial services, investment firms
Imperial Oil Ltd	Canada	Energy & Utilities
Europe		
Nestlé SA	Switzerland	Food
Novartis AG	Switzerland	Pharmaceuticals
Swiss Reinsurance Co	Switzerland	Insurance, Financial Services
Royal Dutch/Shell Group Comb	The Netherlands	Energy & Utilities
Asia		
Toyota Motor Corp	Japan	Automotive & Transport, Manufacturing
Toyota Motor Credit Corp	Japan	Financial services

Source: Adapted by casewriter from Standard & Poor's Research Insight.

incorporated company that has more than half of its sales generated in the U.S., and its top management and research staff in Texas?"

In fact, Nestlé had already asked some investment bankers to consider the question. Credit Suisse First Boston (CSFB) had provided advice on how the choice of listing affected investor base. CSFB had given Nestlé four alternatives: a Swiss listing, a dual listing in Switzerland and the United States, a U.S. listing, or an American Depositary Receipt issue.

Swiss Listing

It would be simple to IPO Alcon in Zürich. As a Swiss subsidiary of another Swiss company, Alcon already operated under Swiss securities laws. A Swiss listing would simplify relations between Nestlé and Alcon, who would be on the same reporting schedules for financial statements and investor announcements. This would minimize future administrative costs of the outstanding common shares. Such an equity issue, however, would limit Nestlé and its underwriters to the pool of capital in Switzerland. While this was a sophisticated investor group, there were few large institutional investors with market expertise in Alcon's niche.

Dual Listing

The Swiss capital pool could however be supplemented by issuing Alcon shares (still structured as a Swiss company) in the U.S. This would help target specialty pharmaceutical investors. However, it was unclear if these investors were interested in foreign companies. Maybe the U.S. buyers in the end would just be the diversified international funds? Also, offering shares to a broader set of investors came with a cost. Alcon would be forced to abide by U.S. as well as Swiss securities laws, which were not always consistent with each other. For example, securities laws between the two countries differed in their requirements of how much notice investors must be given before annual meetings, in what form that notice should come, of how proxy voting was handled, and what disclosure duties Alcon had if it made an offer to acquire another public company. Finally, dual listings in general had a limited success rate. It seemed as if few companies had the size to support two liquid markets with their shares. Instead, trading normally seemed to center on one market, even if the shares were initially introduced in two places.

U.S. Listings

Nestlé could also choose to reincorporate Alcon as a U.S.-based subsidiary, and then offer shares in the United States. This should remove any reservations U.S. specialty pharmaceutical investors might have. The downside, however, was that the entity would be fully subject to U.S. corporate income tax, and therefore not able to claim deductions in the United States for royalty payments paid to the Swiss parent company.

However, Brabeck had already signaled that this was not an option. The benefits of moving Alcon to the U.S. did not outweigh the costs—Nestlé would not move Alcon out of Switzerland. Nestlé could nevertheless go to market with a Swiss company structure that looked in every respect possible like an American company. This would include steps in the following areas:

- Corporate governance:
  1. Rename the firm Alcon, Inc. rather than Alcon, AG.
  2. Amend the incorporation documentation to conform to U.S. standards wherever possible.
  3. Create a board of directors, with prominent independent U.S. business figures; structure the board to resemble other U.S. boards with characteristics such as staggered terms.

- Financial reporting:
  1. Institute regular quarterly reporting of earnings under US GAAP even though Nestlé followed a policy of half yearly reporting under international accounting standards.
  2. Make dividend payments in USD by establishing a hedging facility converting dividends declared in Swiss francs (required by Swiss law) into dollar-denominated payments.

- Exchange listing:
    1. Issue common shares on the NYSE rather than listing an American Depositary Receipt (ADR), because the ADR would have highlighted Alcon's foreign status.
    2. Engage major settlement and custodian banks to create a share registry system to make procedures for trading shares and voting rights more like those for other U.S. companies.
- Operations:
    1. Keep headquarters, top management, and R&D facilities in Texas.
    2. Highlight in corporate presentations the operating statistics of 53% of revenues and 58% of operating income generated in the United States.

American Depositary Receipt (ADR)

The fourth and final option was to create an ADR.[5] An ADR offered many of the benefits of a U.S. listing. It was a security that most U.S. institutional investors were familiar with, and would help target the U.S. specialty pharmaceutical funds as investors. However, ADRs were a device customarily used by foreign companies and therefore ran the risk of being placed in the investment universe for international diversified funds rather than those specializing in Alcon's market niche. Depositary banks were experienced in minimizing the cross-national differences in securities regulations and trading conventions—they handled all aspects from paying dividends in U.S. dollars and handling proxy voting procedures to making sure the trade was as transparent as buying an ordinary share of a typical U.S. company.

LISTING?—BUT AT WHAT PRICE?—AND WHERE?

As Brabeck, Reichenberger and Castañer sat down, they summarized the discussion at hand as: "Should we list, and at what price, and where?" The first question naturally influenced the others, and no clear-cut strategy had emerged in earlier discussions. As the question of where and how to list Alcon was secondary, they returned once more to the larger question: What effect would a public listing of Alcon really have on the valuation and financing of the two companies involved?

---

[5]ADRs represent shares in a foreign corporation, and trade in the U.S. just like regular stock. ADRs are issued by U.S. banks or brokerage firms that purchase a bulk of shares from the foreign company, bundle the shares into groups, and reissue them.

15

Cross-Border Listings and Depositary Receipts

In 1927, the same year that Charles Lindbergh completed the first trans-Atlantic flight, JP Morgan launched the first American Depositary Receipt (ADR) for Selfridges Provincial Stores, a British retail company. The facility provided American investors with the opportunity to participate in the ownership of a foreign corporation while sparing them the inconvenience of dividend conversion into dollars, illiquidity, and other costs involved in investing in foreign securities. Through a variety of financial instruments, the U.S. market has been connecting U.S. investors and foreign firms ever since that first ADR.

At the end of 2001, the total worldwide market capitalization of non-U.S. issuers (462 firms) listed on the New York Stock Exchange (NYSE) reached $4.9 trillion (or 30% of total NYSE global market capitalization). The securities these issuers listed on the NYSE had a market value of $500 billion, a collective trading volume of 29 billion shares, and a cumulative traded value of $788 billion dollars. Furthermore, total non-U.S. equity investment[1] consistently captured approximately 10% of total U.S. equity investment through the mid- and late 1990s.

This note describes the varied instruments that have evolved to facilitate cross-listings and explores some of the reasons investors and firms turn to overseas markets. Section 1 describes the different instruments available in the world capital markets for firms to list their shares abroad. Because most cross-listing in the U.S. takes place in the form of American Depositary Receipts, this instrument is described in greater detail. Section 2 examines the evolution of cross-border listings beginning in the late 1950s, and recent trends. Section 3 reviews academic research and practitioners' views on the motivations for cross-border listings. Finally, Section 4 examines some of the consequences of cross-border listings.

Professor Mihir Desai and Research Associates Maria Raga-Frances, Ami Dave, Mark Veblen and Kathleen Luchs prepared this note as the basis for class discussion.

[1]U.S equity investment includes non-U.S. equities listed on a U.S. exchange as well as securities listed on overseas exchanges.

EXHIBIT 1

VOLUME OF OUTSTANDING DEPOSITARY RECEIPTS AND NEW ISSUANCES, 1980–2001

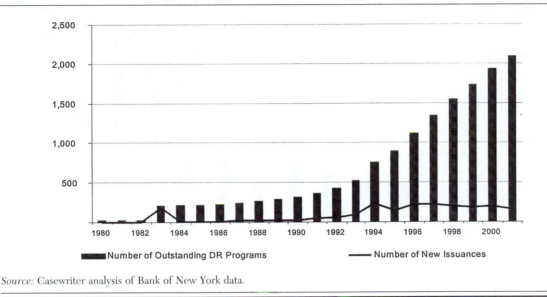

Source: Casewriter analysis of Bank of New York data.

CROSS-BORDER LISTING MECHANISMS

Cross-border listings come in two forms: (1) a company can engage a foreign depositary bank[2] to establish a depositary receipt program in the bank's home market, or (2) a company can list its shares directly on a foreign stock exchange upon fulfillment of the foreign regulatory and disclosure requirements. The majority of all non-U.S. companies that list their shares on U.S. exchanges do so through deposit agreements with U.S. banks. Over 70% of foreign companies listed on the NYSE in 2001 traded in the form of depositary receipts. Trading in these receipts accounted for 77% of total foreign stock trading volume.[3] Because these receipts are issued in the U.S., they are called American Depositary Receipts (ADRs). Exhibit 1 shows changes in the number of ADR programs since 1980 and reveals the gradual growth in the importance of ADRs. Exhibit 2 shows the total value of U.S. investment in non-U.S. entities and illustrates that, over the last decade, ADRs have accounted for a steadily increasing share of the investment in non-U.S. equity.

Depositary Receipt Features

ADRs facilitate low-cost investment in companies that trade on foreign stock exchanges without the inconvenience of accessing an overseas market directly. ADRs can be traded

---

[2]A depositary bank acts as the intermediary, owning common shares traded in the issuers' home market and issuing depositary receipts to investors in the cross-listing market.

[3]New York Stock Exchange, *Factbook*, 2001.

EXHIBIT 2

U.S. EQUITY INVESTMENT IN NON-U.S. EQUITIES, 1990–2001

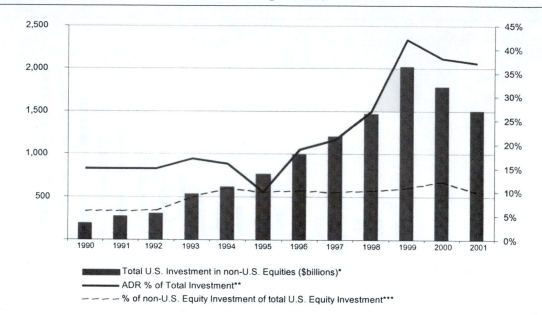

■ Total U.S. Investment in non-U.S. Equities ($billions)*

—— ADR % of Total Investment**

– – – – % of non-U.S. Equity Investment of total U.S. Equity Investment***

*"Total U.S. Investment in Non-U.S. Equities" is the stock of U.S Equity Investment in non-U.S. Equities in ordinary share and in depositary receipts form.

**"ADR % of Total Investment" is the percentage of U.S. Equity Investment in non-U.S. Equities that is held in the form of ADRs. Estimates from Citibank analysis based on 1993, 1997 and 2000 figures from the U.S. Treasury.

***"% non-U.S. Equity Investment of total U.S. Equity Investment" is the share of non-U.S. Equities in U.S. Equity Holdings.

Source: Compiled by casewriter from U.S. Treasury, "Flow of Funds of the United States, Flows and Outstanding, First Quarter of 2002"; U.S. Treasury, "Report on U.S. Holdings of Foreign Long-Term Securities as of December 31 of 1997" (April 2000); U.S. Treasury, "1994 Benchmark Survey of Ownership of Foreign Securities as of March 31, 1994" (July 1998); Thomson Financial and Citibank analyses.

and settled either on one of the U.S. exchanges (NYSE, NASDAQ, or AMEX) or in the over-the-counter (OTC) market. Receipt holders effectively possess the same ownership rights they would if they owned the underlying security outright, subject to any restrictions of the deposit agreement.

The structure of ADRs, common across various types, consists of a depositary bank that acquires ordinary shares of the non-U.S. company (either in the local stock market or directly from the company), deposits those shares in a custodian bank (usually an affiliate of the depositary), and then issues certificates for delivery to U.S. investors.[4] Subsequent ADR trading is tracked by the Depository Trust Company (DTC)—the clearing and settlement organization for securities traded in the U.S.[5]

[4]In practice, investors do not take physical delivery of the certificates. Instead these certificates are tracked in an electronic register.

[5]Depository Trust Company (DTC) is the national clearinghouse for the settlement of securities, and it performs asset services for its participating banks and brokerage houses. DTC's network links dealers, custodian banks, institutional investors and other agents.

Bundling and Share Ratios

To align the trading price of the receipt to customary price levels in its trading market, the structure of ADRs commonly includes a ratio, which corresponds to the number of underlying shares per ADR. This is often termed "bundling." In the example of a 1:10 ratio, one depositary receipt (also referred to as a certificate) evidences ownership of 10 American Depositary Shares (ADS), each of which represents ownership of one common or preferred share in the issuer's local market. While the terms ADR and ADS are frequently used interchangeably, the ADS is the actual share, and the ADR is the certificate.

Corporate Actions

In fulfilling its responsibilities as the facilitator of an ADR program, the depositary bank maintains a register of holders to reflect share transfers, distributes dividends to investors in U.S. dollars, and provides company information and other assistance to the ADR holders.

Issuances and Cancellations

As compensation for the abovementioned services, a depositary bank charges a fee (payable by the broker) when an ADR is either issued or cancelled. This fee depends on the price of the receipts, and it ranges from $0.01 (for receipts priced under $0.99) to $0.05 (for receipts priced above $10).[6] The depository bank does not charge traders or investors for ordinary domestic trading of certificates. Issuances and cancellations occur when, instead of finding a counterparty for an ADR trade in the U.S., the broker instead (in the case of a buy order) instructs the depositary bank to buy additional shares in the issuer's local market and issue new receipts on the newly acquired shares. Similarly, for a sell order, the broker would instruct the depositary bank to release locally held shares and cancel receipts, returning the cash from the local sale to the selling investor. The choice of whether to find a U.S. counterparty or to issue/cancel is entirely at the discretion of the broker and is transparent to the broker's client. Efforts at cross-market arbitrage can result in on-going issuances and cancellations. A massive cancellation of ADRs is called "flow back" because of the net selling by U.S. investors and the displacement of trading activity to the home country.

Types of Depositary Receipts

Exhibits 3a and 3b illustrate the different types of depositary receipts that can be issued in the U.S. markets. ADRs are termed "unsponsored" if the depositary bank issues them in response to investor demand or "sponsored" when an agreement between the foreign company and the depositary bank exists.

Unsponsored ADRs

As depicted in Exhibit 3a, the depositary acts as an intermediary, making foreign markets accessible to U.S. investors. Unsponsored ADRs can only trade in the OTC market. Brokers subscribe to the "pink sheet" for daily stock price information and for the list of market makers who trade each ADR. Unsponsored ADRs were more widely

---

[6]Depositary banks also historically charged issuers an upfront fee which has subsequently become minimal.

EXHIBIT 3A

MECHANICS OF AN UNSPONSORED ADR PROGRAM

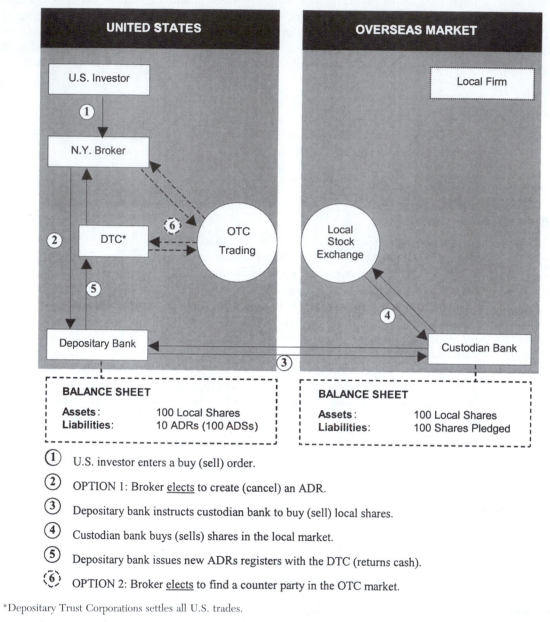

① U.S. investor enters a buy (sell) order.

② OPTION 1: Broker <u>elects</u> to create (cancel) an ADR.

③ Depositary bank instructs custodian bank to buy (sell) local shares.

④ Custodian bank buys (sells) shares in the local market.

⑤ Depositary bank issues new ADRs registers with the DTC (returns cash).

⑥ OPTION 2: Broker <u>elects</u> to find a counter party in the OTC market.

°Depositary Trust Corporations settles all U.S. trades.

Source: Casewriter analysis.

EXHIBIT 3B

VOLUME MECHANICS OF A SPONSORED ADR PROGRAM

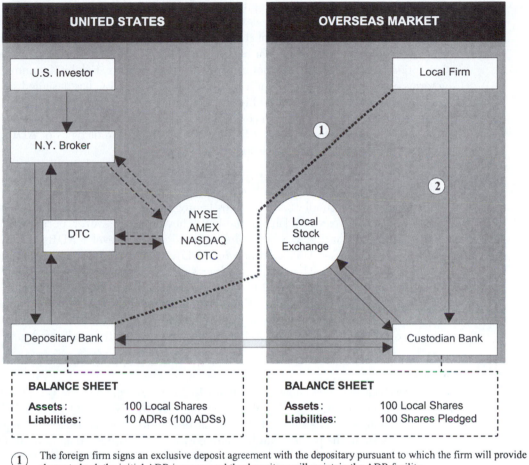

UNITED STATES

OVERSEAS MARKET

U.S. Investor

Local Firm

N.Y. Broker

NYSE
AMEX
NASDAQ
OTC

Local
Stock
Exchange

DTC

Depositary Bank

Custodian Bank

BALANCE SHEET

| Assets: | 100 Local Shares |
| Liabilities: | 10 ADRs (100 ADSs) |

BALANCE SHEET

| Assets: | 100 Local Shares |
| Liabilities: | 100 Shares Pledged |

(1) The foreign firm signs an exclusive deposit agreement with the depositary pursuant to which the firm will provide shares to back the initial ADR issuance and the depositary will maintain the ADR facility.

(2) While secondary trading occurs as in the prior exhibit, the local firm issues shares directly into the custodian as underlying securities for the ADRs.

Source: Casewriter analysis.

used than sponsored programs until 1982, when the SEC began requiring the depositary bank to register with the SEC by filing a Form-F6 for every ADR issue.[7] Although the form did not require any substantive disclosure, the foreign firm now had knowledge of the cross-border activity in its shares. Since the introduction of the Form F-6, unsponsored programs have become obsolete (only 2 of 161 new issues in 2001 were unsponsored).

[7]The Form F-6 is used to register ADRs as a U.S. security.

Sponsored ADRs

Sponsored ADRs have gradually supplanted unsponsored ADRs. Exhibit 3b depicts the mechanics of a sponsored ADR facility. The foreign firm signs an exclusive agreement making a single depositary the sole agent for its ADRs. This deposit agreement is a contract that details the legal relationship between the depositary bank, the custodian, and the issuing company. This agreement also details the services provided by the depositary to the ADR investor throughout the program. The deposit agreement might differ according to the laws of the foreign company's country of registration. For instance, subscription rights are frequently not available to ADR holders. Exhibit 4 summarizes key terms of a deposit agreement for a sponsored ADR. The SEC has designed several types of sponsored ADR programs—Level I, Level II, Level III and private placements through Rule 144a—which differ in cost, disclosure requirements and the type of market on which they can trade. Exhibit 5 characterizes the different types of ADR programs and highlights key characteristics of each type.

Level I ADR

Level I ADRs are the simplest and least costly program for a foreign firm to undertake in order to make its shares tradable in the U.S. They do not, however, permit the firm to raise new capital in the U.S. Like unsponsored ADRs, Level I ADRs trade only through the OTC market. Unlike unsponsored ADRs, however, the company is actively involved in the program. The company engages a U.S. depositary bank to implement the program and it files with the SEC those documents that it is required to file in its home country. In addition to filing a Form F-6 announcing the program, the company must also file for an exemption from SEC reporting Rule 12g3-2(b).[8] Generally this process requires eight weeks from an initial filing until an ADR actually trades.

Level II ADR

Level II ADRs also do not allow the company to raise new capital in the U.S., but they can be listed on a recognized U.S. stock exchange (NYSE, NASDAQ, or AMEX). Issuing an exchange-listed security, however, carries more onerous disclosure requirements and, as such, the process can be more costly for the issuer. In addition to filing a Form F-6, foreign issuers must, on an on-going basis, file comprehensive annual reports with the SEC (Form 20-F) within 180 days of their fiscal year end. The Form 20-F includes, though with less extensive detail, the key elements required of all issuers of public equity securities in the U.S. on the Form 10-K, including annual financial statements under its local accounting standards, management biographies, major shareholders, and related-party transactions. Perhaps most significantly, firms must partially reconcile their annual accounts to the U.S. Generally Accepted Accounting Principles (US GAAP). Like Level I ADRs, any interim financial statements released at home must also be filed in the U.S. U.S. exchanges also impose minimum conditions (e.g., annual turnover, firm market value, breadth of current shareholder base) before allowing a firm to list ADRs.[9]

---

[8]Companies that qualify under Rule 12g3-2(b) are exempt from periodic reporting requirements.

[9]James Shapiro of the NYSE estimates annual costs of preparing GAAP reports each year of $300,000–$500,000. In addition, the NYSE charges first year listing fees of $150,000 with an ongoing fee of $35,000. See "The Changing Landscape: Japanese ADRs," Roundtable discussion sponsored by *FinanceAsia* and Citibank, 2001 available at http://wwss.citissb.com/adr/www/adr_info/jar.pdf.

EXHIBIT 4

KEY TERMS OF A DEPOSIT AGREEMENT

Section	Content
ARTICLE 1. Definitions	Describes the terms used in the Agreement such American Depositary Shares, Beneficial Owner, Deposited Securities, Securities Act of 1933, etc.
ARTICLE 2. Form of the Shares, Deposit of the Shares, Execution and Delivery, Transfer and Surrender of Receipts	Details the mechanism involved in the trading of shares, such as execution and transfers.
ARTICLE 3. Certain Obligations of Owners and Beneficial Owners of the Receipts	Filing proofs, tax benefits and warrants on deposit of shares.
ARTICLE 4. The Deposited Securities	Outlines administrative procedures for distributing shares and exercising voting rights.
ARTICLE 5. The Depositary, the Custodian, and the Company	Specifies the duties of each party including exclusivity granted to the depositary bank in administering an ADR program for the company.
ARTICLE 6. Amendment and Termination	Explains the process for altering the terms of the ADR program or discontinuing it.
ARTICLE 7. Miscellaneous	Covers a number of legal topics frequently contained in securities agreements.

Sample of an ADR Certificate:

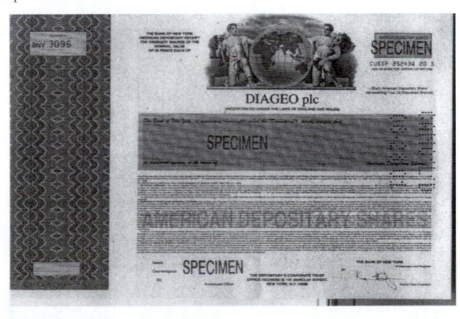

Source: Casewriter analysis of Bank of New York data.

EXHIBIT 5

ADR CHARACTERISTICS BY TYPE

	Listing Only				Source of Capital		
	Unsponsored	Level I	Level II	Level III	Rule 144a	Reg S (GDR)	Global Depositary Receipt (GDR)
Offering Type	Public	Public	Public	Public	Private	Private	Public/private
Description	Foreign firms trade in the U.S.; issuer not involved	Facility for foreign equities to be traded in the U.S.	Foreign equities can list on a recognized U.S. exchange	Foreign firms raise capital in U.S. public market	Foreign firms offer shares to QIB investors	DRs sold to non-U.S. investors	Offering in two or more foreign markets
Trading	OTC	OTC and "Pink Sheets"	NYSE, AMEX, NASDAQ	NYSE, AMEX, NASDAQ	PORTAL	Global offering	Varies
SEC Registration	Form F-6	Form F-6	Form F-6	Form F-1, Form F-6	None	After 40 days / Form F-6	Varies
U.S. Reporting Requirements	None	Exemption under Rule 12g-3-2(b)	Form F-20 filed annually and 6-K	Form F-20 and 6-K Form F-2	Exemption under Rule 12g-3-2(b) or agree to provide info on request	Home country	Varies
Accounting Methods	Home country	Reconciliation not required	Reconciled partially with US GAAP	Reconciled fully with US GAAP	Reconciliation not required	Reconciliation not required	Reconciliation not required
Advantages	Satisfies investor demand	Low disclosure/ cost	High visibility/ liquidity	Maximum liquidity and visibility	Fungibility, update into Level 1	Update into Level I after 40 days	Varies
Disadvantages	Lacks transparency: illiquidity	Limited liquidity: no listing or capital raising	Costly and full SEC disclosure	Costly and full SEC disclosure	Flow back	Flow back	Varies
Costs	No cost for issuer	$25,000 or less	$200,000– $700,000	$500,000– $2,000,000	$250,000– $500,000	$500,000– $2,000,000	Varies

Source: Casewriter analysis based on Karolyi, A., "Why Do Companies List Their Shares Abroad? (A Survey of the Evidence and its Managerial Implications)," Salomon Brothers Monograph Series, 7 (1998); data from Bank of New York, Citibank, JP Morgan.

Level III ADR

Level III ADRs allow foreign firms to raise new capital through a public offering on a recognized U.S. stock exchange. The foreign firm must prepare the financial statements reported on its Form 20-F and its interim statements in accordance with US GAAP and in compliance with all applicable SEC rules. Their legal obligations under securities laws are the same as for U.S. corporations. An additional registration document, Form F-1, is required at the time of issuance. It discloses the issuer's principal reasons for raising equity capital in the U.S., risk factors, and information regarding dilution of current shareholders' ownership interests.

Rule 144a ADR

Rule 144a permits foreign firms to raise capital from U.S. qualified institutional buyers (QIBs[10]) through ADRs without the heightened disclosure requirements of a Level III ADR. The capital is raised through a private placement sold to QIBs that are sufficiently sophisticated that the SEC imposes fewer reporting and registration requirements (no annual report on Form 20-F or US GAAP reconciliation). A Rule 144a ADR issue can therefore be a quicker and simpler way to access the U.S. market than a Level III ADR. To create liquidity, QIBs are permitted to buy and sell Rule 144a ADRs amongst themselves through PORTAL,[11] a marketplace organized by the NASDAQ. At the end of the three-year restricted period, a Rule 144a ADR issue can be converted into a Level I ADR without any further registration.

Reg S GDR

Companies may use depositary receipt programs to raise capital outside the U.S. as well. Global Depositary Receipts (GDRs) operate on the same principle as ADRs, but are issued, traded, and settled outside the U.S., usually in London or Luxembourg. Nonetheless, they are denominated in U.S. dollars. Most commonly, they are issued as the non-U.S. tranche of a Rule 144a offering but are exempted from SEC regulation by a special rule, Regulation S.[12] They are a vehicle for companies to tap an international investor base, selling Rule 144a ADRs to U.S. investors and Reg S GDRs abroad without the disclosure requirements of public U.S. offering. Reg S GDRs also offer the feature that, after 40 days, they may be converted into a Level I ADR, thus creating secondary market liquidity for the foreign buyers of a Reg S GDR issue.

Other Depositary Receipts

A European Depositary Receipt (EDR) generally is identical to a GDR in all respects except that it is denominated in euros rather than dollars. Like a GDR, it is frequently used in conjunction with a U.S. Rule 144a ADR issue. It gives non-Euro-zone corporations an opportunity to increase their investor base through a private placement to institutional investors in Europe. An International Depositary Receipt (IDR) is issued by a

---

[10]Qualified institutional buyers are institutions, which the government deems to be capable of assessing the risks of investment opportunities without the same protections the SEC provides to individual investors.

[11]PORTAL is an acronym for Private Offering, Resales and Trading through Automated Linkages. It was developed by the NASD (National Association of Security Dealers) to support the trading and facilitate liquidity of private placements.

[12]Regulation S deals with sales of securities outside the U.S. that are not subject to U.S. securities laws. Reg S securities must be either registered in the U.S. or granted an exemption from such registration before they can be resold in the U.S.

non-Euro-zone company in Brussels. These securities are similar to EDRs but disclosure standards depend on the issuer's home market. The shares are also held in bearer form, i.e. not registered on the books of the issuing corporation. This facility provides a listed, euro-denominated instrument that has historically been used primarily by Canadian and South African companies. If IDR holders want to sell their securities in the United States, procedures exist through which they may exchange their IDRs for ADRs.

Equity Listings

Ordinary Shares

"Direct" listing of an ordinary share refers to the issuance of a common share of the issuing corporation in a foreign market that will trade in all respects like an ordinary share of a domestic company in that market. Exhibit 6a illustrates the mechanics of this process. The issuing company must meet all of the regulatory requirements imposed

---

EXHIBIT 6A

MECHANICS OF A DIRECT LISTING OF AN ORDINARY COMMON SHARE

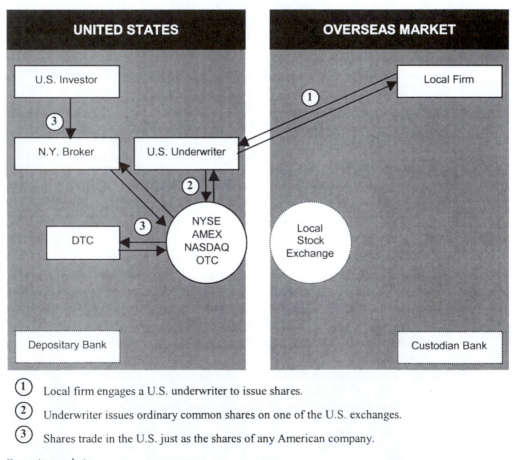

① Local firm engages a U.S. underwriter to issue shares.

② Underwriter issues ordinary common shares on one of the U.S. exchanges.

③ Shares trade in the U.S. just as the shares of any American company.

Source: Casewriter analysis.

EXHIBIT 6B

MECHANICS OF A GLOBAL REGISTERED SHARE

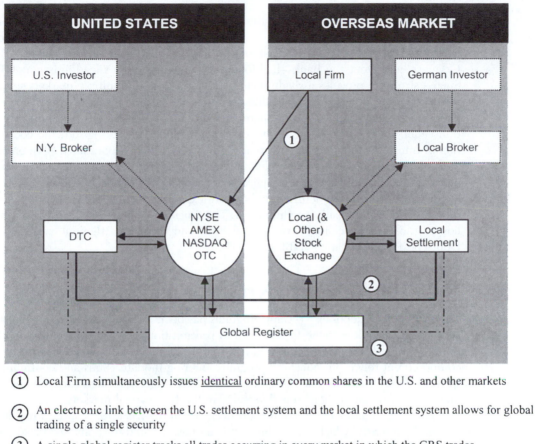

① Local Firm simultaneously issues <u>identical</u> ordinary common shares in the U.S. and other markets

② An electronic link between the U.S. settlement system and the local settlement system allows for global trading of a single security

③ A single global register tracks all trades occurring in every market in which the GRS trades

Source: Casewriter analysis.

by the securities laws of the country where it is listing ordinary shares. For example, when listing on American stock exchanges, the process requires extensive SEC registration materials and the same level of regular disclosure as domestic firms (quarterly and annual financial reports prepared in accordance with US GAAP). A company may choose to conduct its initial public offering in a foreign market, thereby issuing ordinary shares, or it may choose to list ordinary shares abroad in parallel with its already publicly traded shares at home. In this latter case, each ordinary share is subject to the securities laws of the country in which it trades. Accordingly, an issuer may have to meet several differing sets of rules.

Most of the ordinary share listings in the U.S. are from Canada, where the costs of a dual listing are significantly reduced by the fact that the Canadian accounting system is very similar to US GAAP. Similarly, direct "ordinary" listing is even more common among European countries because of similarities in stock exchange requirements and geographic proximity. The integration of capital markets of the European Union has brought about innovations such as "Euro-list," which permits investors in Frankfurt to buy London-listed shares directly through a broker in Frankfurt without dealing with conversion costs.

Global Registered Shares

In 1998, DaimlerChrysler AG took the cross-border listing concept one step further by issuing ordinary shares on 21 stock exchanges around the world in the form of a Global Registered Share (GRS)—the first of its kind. By 2001, three companies—UBS, Celanese, and Deutsche Bank—had followed DaimlerChrysler's lead in issuing GRSs. Such a structure provides a single security that can trade in multiple markets simultaneously, conforming to all applicable securities laws, and is supported by an infrastructure to handle cross-border share transactions. As illustrated in Exhibit 6b, the transaction required the establishment of a new "global" share register, the coordination of transfer agents and an electronic linking of clearing corporations, all in order to facilitate its trading, settlement and seamless, fungible transfer from one market to another. While the infrastructure requirements and need to abide by various securities laws suggest that this structure may be more expensive to maintain, the costs of employing a depositary bank are eliminated. The crucial innovation in the GRS structure lies in the electronic link between the local and foreign settlement systems (e.g. Deutsche Bourse Clearing (DBC) and DTC).

EVOLUTION OF CROSS-BORDER LISTINGS AND RECENT TRENDS

The evolution of depositary receipt programs has been markedly shaped by regulatory actions and macroeconomic factors such as privatizations. From its inception in 1927 until the mid 1950s (when sponsored ADRs were first allowed), the ADR market was composed entirely of unsponsored programs. During the late 1960s and continuing to the mid 1970s, the ADR market experienced its first surge, as foreign corporations grew interested in obtaining heightened visibility in the U.S. capital markets.

The second and larger growth spurt occurred in the early 1980s after a regulatory change by the SEC which shifted interest from unsponsored to sponsored programs.[13] As discussed previously, Exhibit 1 illustrates the consistent trend of new issuances of ADRs since 1980. Exhibit 2 illustrates the dramatic growth of ADR programs since 1990, as a share of U.S. investment in non-U.S. equities. In part, this growth stemmed from a wave of privatizations in Western Europe—initiated by Thatcher's administration in the U.K. in the late 80's—and by emerging markets following suit in the 1990s. Exhibit 7 illustrates that more than 60% of capital raised in 1990 through ADR programs came from European privatizations and that emerging markets have contributed gradually to the share of privatization ADRs deals. Since the mid 1990s, capital raised through privatization has decreased as a share of total capital raised.

A second wave of ADRs in the 1990s was stimulated by massive consolidations in the European Union, as large European corporations began actively acquiring U.S. firms. ADRs were a useful currency in executing stock swap transactions. Exhibit 8 shows that ADRs constituted the vast majority of consideration paid in many of the

---

[13]In creating the Form F-6 filing requirement, the SEC altered the competitive landscape for depositary banks. Whereas in the past they could create programs at will, now they were required to consult with the company first. That contact quickly became a forum where banks requested exclusivity in maintaining an ADR program for the company.

EXHIBIT 7

ADR PRIVATIZATION PROGRAMS BY REGION AND AS A % OF TOTAL CAPITAL RAISED THROUGH ADR PROGRAMS, 1984–2001

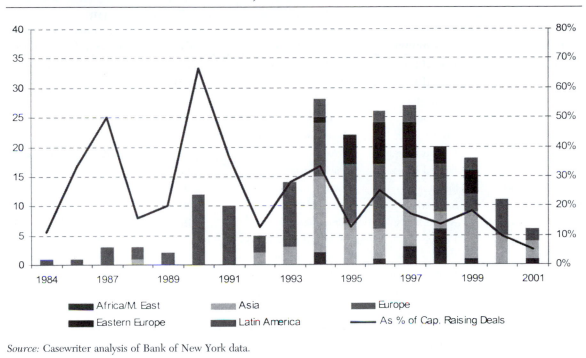

Source: Casewriter analysis of Bank of New York data.

largest acquisitions of U.S. companies by foreign buyers. By the late 1990s, annual issues by European companies reached triple-digit levels and Latin American companies had raised over $8 billion, cumulatively, through ADR programs. At the end of 2001, there were 2,100 active depositary programs around the world.

ADRs By Security Type

Exhibit 9 tracks the share of new issues by depositary receipt type since 1980. Of all outstanding programs at the end of 2001, 10% were unsponsored, 31% Level I, 13% Level II, 14% Level III, 18% Rule 144a, and 14% were GDRs sold to non-U.S. investors. In comparison to the cross section of ADRs two decades earlier, several trends emerge. First, with very few new unsponsored listings, that form of ADR is slowly shrinking as programs get cancelled (either through thin trading volume or as a result of the issuer being acquired). Second, the private market, which developed after the public market, has proven to be a large source of U.S. capital. Exhibit 10 illustrates that since the introduction of Rule 144a in 1990 private placements almost immediately accounted for 50% of all issues and three quarters of capital raised. Since then, it has slowly eroded to approximately one quarter of issues and capital raised. As depicted in Exhibit 11, since the early 1990s, the U.S. market has provided over $10 billion annually to foreign companies. Annual issuance in number and dollar terms has, however, fluctuated widely from year to year.

EXHIBIT 8

LARGEST M&A TRANSACTIONS WITH U.S. TARGETS EMPLOYING ADRS

Company	Country	U.S. Target	Date	ADR Share in Financing %	Value ($bn)
Vodafone Group	United Kingdom	AirTouch Comm	1999	91	60.3
BP	United Kingdom	Amoco	1998	100	54.3
Daimler Benz	Germany	Chrysler	1998	100	40.5
Deutsche Telecom	Germany	Voice Stream	2000	85	50.7
Vivendi	France	Seagram Co. (Canada)	2000	100	34.0
BP Amoco	United Kingdom	Arco	1999	100	26.8
Scottish Power	United Kingdom	Pacificorp	1998	100	12.6
Terra Networks	Spain	Lycos	2000	100	12.5
UBS	Switzerland	PaineWebber	2000	50	12.0
Aegon	Netherlands	Transamerica	1999	70	9.7
Alcatel	France	Newbridge Networks	2000	100	7.1
Alcatel	France	DSC Communications	1998	100	5.1
Serra Group	United Kingdom	LHS Group	2000	100	4.7
WPP Group	United Kingdom	Young & Rubicam	2000	100	4.7
Aegon	Netherlands	Providian	1996	75	3.5
Stora Enso	Finland	Consolidated Papers	2000	50	4.0
ING Group	Netherlands	Equitable of Iowa	1997	49	2.6
Fresenius	Germany	Fresenius USA	1996	100	2.2
New Corp.	Australia	Snyder Communications	1996	100	2.2
Havas Advertising	France	New World Comm.	2000	100	2.1
Lucas	United Kingdom	Varity Corp.	1996	100	2.0
Alcatel	France	Genesys Tele.	1999	100	1.5
Adecco	Switzerland	Olsten Corporation	1999	59	1.5

Source: JP Morgan, "ADRs as acquisition currency in cross-border M&A," August 2000, p. 3 available at ⟨http://www.adr.com/pdf/acquisition_currency.pdf⟩ © 2004 J.P. Morgan Chase & Co.

ADRs by Region of Origin & Industry

Companies from virtually every continent have utilized ADRs since 1985. Exhibit 12 illustrates that Western Europe accounts for the largest share, 42% of outstanding issues, with Asia comprising 37%. Latin American issuers account for 14%, and Africa and the Middle East constitute 5% and 2%, respectively, of the total ADR market.

In Western Europe, the bulk of issues are from the larger economies (especially the U.K.) where economic and corporate ties to companies in the U.S. are strongest. Exhibits 13a and Exhibit 13b emphasize the large proportion of total U.S. investment in foreign issuers that is associated with U.K companies (14% of total outstanding ADR programs and 13% of ADR trading volume). Exhibit 14 provides data on the top twenty ADR programs by trading volume in 2001. The exhibit also provides comparative trad-

EXHIBIT 9

DEPOSITARY RECEIPT ISSUANCES BY ADR TYPE, 1980–2001

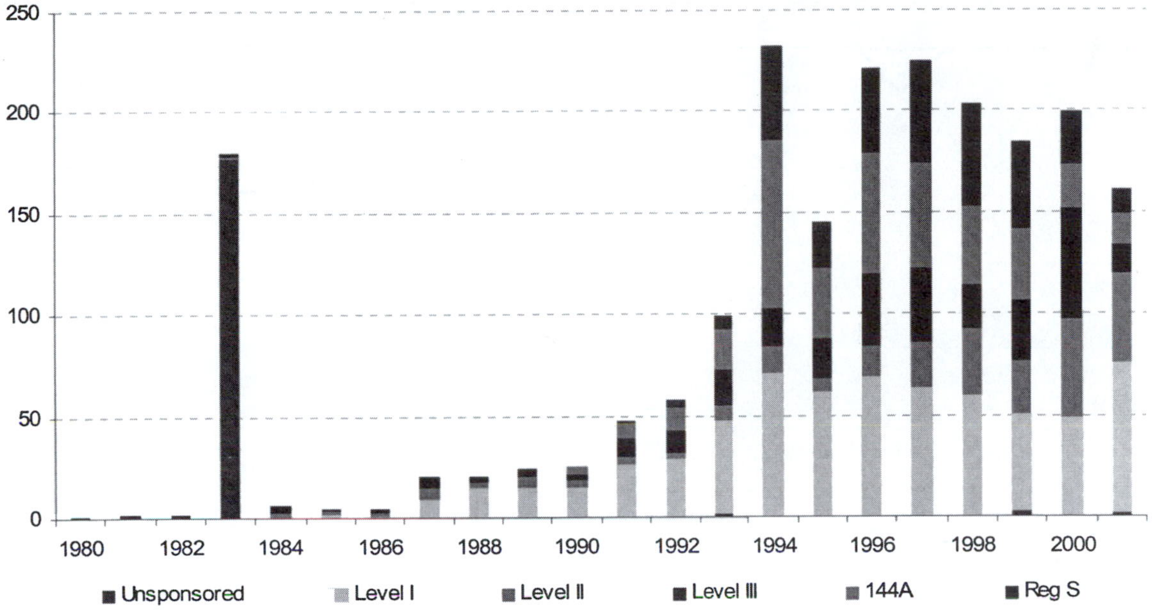
250
200
150
100
50
0
1980
1982
1984
1986
1988
1990
1992
1994
1996
1998
2000
Unsponsored
Level I
Level II
Level III
144A
Reg S

Source: Casewriter analysis of Bank of New York data.

ing volumes for local and ADR trading and demonstrates the significant role played by ADRs in the total trading activity of these firms. As evidenced in this exhibit, European programs tend to be the largest in terms of both dollar value and trading volume.

Industry Composition

ADR programs were initially concentrated in mineral and mining companies, diversified conglomerates, and financial services. In the early 1980s, chemicals firms and some construction companies joined the market. In the 1990s, pharmaceutical and food companies became a significant portion of the market. As the technology boom took off, however, technology companies from around the world turned to the U.S. capital markets and ADR issuances shifted toward this new industry segment. Exhibit 15 illustrates that by 2001 only two industries—technology and financial services—each accounted for over 10% of outstanding ADR programs and that the remaining activity is spread across industries.

Evolution of Direct Equity Listings

"Direct" listing on U.S. exchanges by non-U.S. firms has increased dramatically over the past two decades, from 62 outstanding issues during the early 1980s to more than 540 firms at the end of 2001. The geographic origin of firms listing directly has remained roughly constant since the 1980s. As shown in Exhibit 16, by the end of 2001, outstanding non-U.S. direct listings came predominantly from (i) Canadian firms,

EXHIBIT 10

PERCENT OF CAPITAL RAISED THROUGH LEVEL III PUBLIC OFFERINGS (VS. RULE 144A & REG S PRIVATE OFFERINGS), 1980–2001

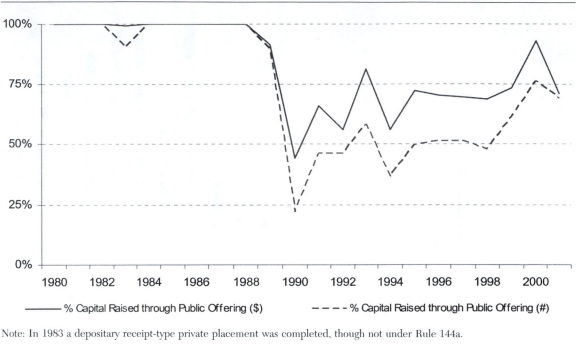

——— % Capital Raised through Public Offering ($)   − − − − % Capital Raised through Public Offering (#)

Note: In 1983 a depositary receipt-type private placement was completed, though not under Rule 144a.

Source: Casewriter analysis of Bank of New York data.

evidencing similarities in accounting standards and geographic proximity (54% of the total); and (ii) high-tech Israeli firms listing on the NASDAQ to benefit from higher valuations of technology firms in the U.S. (15% of the total). "Flag of convenience" firms account for 17% of non-U.S. firms with direct equity listings. These are firms such as Tyco International and Accenture that are registered in a different country from their country of operations.

Exhibit 17 lists the largest direct listed non-U.S. firms on American stock exchanges by market capitalization. The exhibit demonstrates that the NYSE is by far the most popular exchange (66% of listings). Three of the top four firms by market capitalization (UBS, Deutsche Bank, and DaimlerChrysler) trade in the form of Global Registered Shares.

MOTIVATIONS FOR CROSS-BORDER LISTING DECISIONS

There are a host of incentives for (i) foreign corporations to access capital markets abroad, and (ii) investors to pursue investment opportunities outside their home countries. Some of these incentives relate to specific characteristics of the local or foreign market (such as depth and cost of transacting), and others stem from subtler devices such as signaling methods to convey credibility to investors. This section reviews the academic and practitioner literature on cross-listed shares.

EXHIBIT 11

CAPITAL RAISED THROUGH DEPOSITARY RECEIPT PROGRAMS, 1980–2001

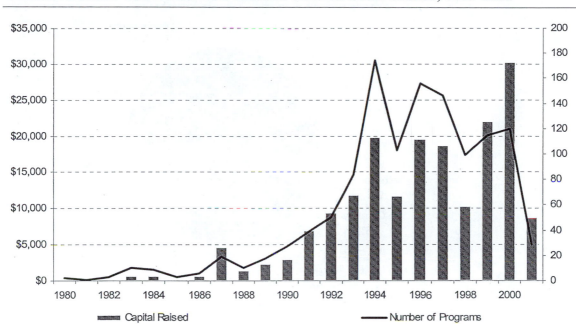

Source: Casewriter analysis of Bank of New York data.

EXHIBIT 12

DEPOSITARY RECEIPT ISSUANCES BY REGION, 1980–2001

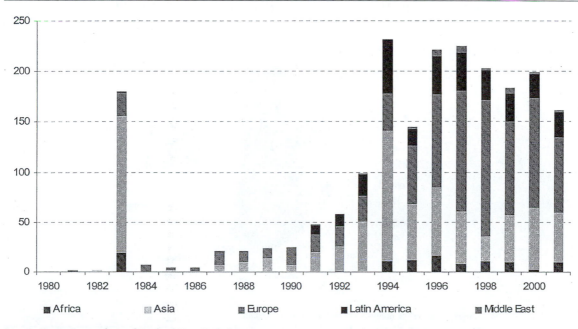

Source: Casewriter analysis of Bank of New York data.

OUTSTANDING ADR ISSUANCES BY COUNTRY, 2001

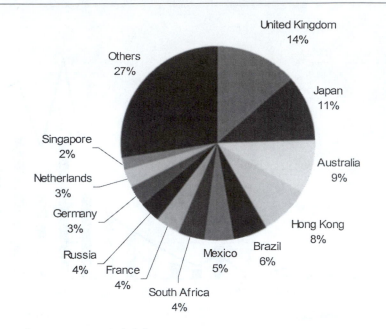

Note: Private placements are not included.

Source: Casewriter analysis of Bank of New York data.

EXHIBIT 13B

ADR SHARE OF TRADING VOLUME BY COUNTRY ($ VOLUME)

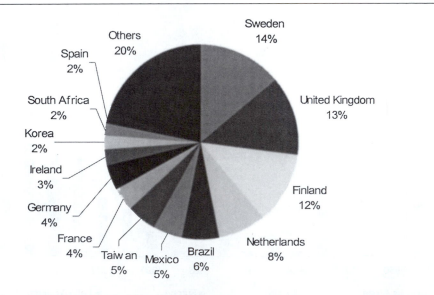

Source: Casewriter analysis of Bank of New York data.

EXHIBIT 14

TOP 20 LARGEST ADR PROGRAMS BY U.S. $ TRADED VOLUME AS OF DECEMBER 2001

Company	Country	Shares Outstanding (million shares)	ADRs Outstanding (million shares)	Bundling Ratio	% ADRs over Shares Outstanding (million shares)	ADR Trading Vol. (million shares)	U.S. Vol. ($millions)	ADR Turnover
Nokia Corporation	Finland	4,737.5	1,554	1:01	32.8%	3,565	88,381	229.3%
Vodafone Group	United Kingdom	65,012.5	799	1:10	12.3%	1,277	33,759	62. 6%
BP PLC	United Kingdom	22,432.1	6,937	1:06	30.9%	601	29,818	1,154.2%
Ericsson Tel 'B'	Sweden	8,065.5	1,083	1:01	13.4%	4,245	27,818	25.5%
Royal Dutch Petroleum	Netherlands	2,099.3	648	1:01	30.9%	417	24,412	155.2%
Elan Corporation	Ireland	350.4	315	1:01	89.9%	437	22,179	72.0%
Teva Pharma.	Israel	128.2	83	1:01	64.7%	347	19,857	23.9%
Telefonos de Mexico	Mexico	13,164.9	548	1:20	83.2%	445	16,010	123.0%
Deutsche Telecom	Germany	4,835.1	598	1:01	12.4%	598	17,503	100.0%
ASML Holding	Netherlands	467.0	127	1:01	27.3%	756	15,756	16.9%
Taiwan Semiconductor	Taiwan	18,622.9	351	1:05	9.4%	938	15,182	37.4%
STMicroelectronics	Netherlands	889.7	75	1:01	8.5%	363	13,886	20.7%
Alcatel	France	1,240.8	95	1:01	7.6%	398	13,463	23.8%
Shire Pharma.	United Kingdom	160.9	n.a.	1:03	n.a.	283	13,252	n.a.
Glaxo SmithKline	United Kingdom	6,173.0	293	1:02	9.5%	179	9,632	164.1%
Unilever	Netherlands	1,299.5	n.a.	1:04	n.a.	156	8,729	n.a.
Total Fina Elf.	France	705.9	35	2:01	5.0%	108	7,611	32.3%
Business Objects	France	61.9	19	1:01	30.5%	229	7,507	8.3%
Telebras	Brazil	334,398.0	n.a.	1:50	n.a.	153	7,391	n.a.
SAP	Germany	314.8	30	4:01	2.4%	222	7,366	13.5%
Smartforce	Ireland	56.9	57	1:01	100.0%	266	7,069	21.4%
Vivendi Universal	France	1,085.8	108	1:01	9.9%	113	6,929	1.6%
AstraZeneca	United Kingdom	1,766.5	88	1:01	5.0%	139	6,540	2.1%

Source: Compiled from company data and Bank of New York, "Depositary Receipts: 2001 Year-End Market Review," available at ⟨http://www.adrbny.com/files/MS1637.pdf.⟩

EXHIBIT 15

**COMPOSITION BY INDUSTRY FOR OUTSTANDING ADR
PROGRAMS, 2001**

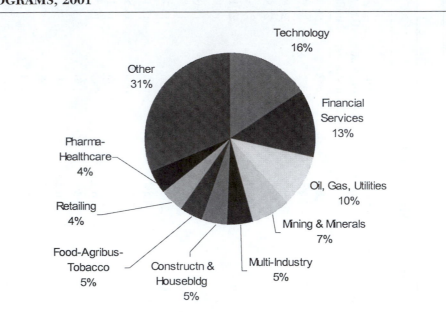

Source: Casewriter analysis of Bank of New York data.

EXHIBIT 16

ORDINARY SHARE LISTINGS BY COUNTRY, 2001

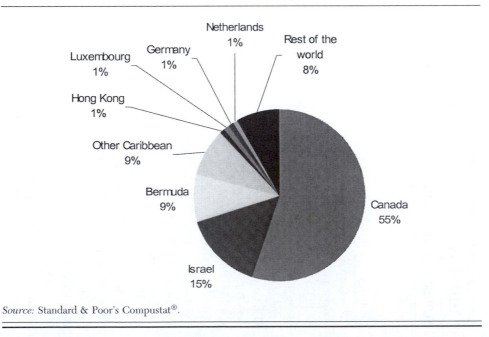

Source: Standard & Poor's Compustat®.

EXHIBIT 17

TOP ORDINARY SHARE LISTINGS BY MARKET CAPITALIZATION, DECEMBER 2001

Company Name	Country of Incorporation	U.S. Listing	Market Value	Trading Volume (Mil. Shares)
Tyco International	Bermuda	NYSE	88,064	2,464
UBS°	Switzerland	NYSE	62,023	55
Deutsche Bank°	Germany	NYSE	43,105	4
DaimlerChrysler°	Germany	NYSE	41,806	143
Schlumberger	Netherlands Antilles	NYSE	31,645	991
Nortel Networks	Canada	NYSE	23,975	4,342
BCE	Canada	NYSE	18,434	81
Carnival	Panama	NYSE	15,305	458
Accenture	Bermuda	NYSE	13,924	230
Manulife Fin.	Canada	NYSE	12,561	60
XL Capital	Cayman Islands	NYSE	12,309	262
Alcan	Canada	NYSE	11,530	320
Transocean	Cayman Islands	NYSE	10,782	909
Imperial Oil	Canada	AMEX	10,571	19
Ace Limited	Cayman Islands	NYSE	10,433	428
Check Point Software	Israel	NASDAQ	9,686	2,705
Flextronics Int'l	Singapore	NASDAQ	9,362	2,595
Sun Life Finl Svcs	Canada	NYSE	9,331	49
Canadian Nat. Rlwy	Canada	NYSE	9,304	88
Celestica	Canada	NYSE	9,278	675

Note: "Market value" refers to the total market capitalization from the firm's fiscal year end. "Trading volume" is the sum of the monthly number of shares for 12 months from the firm's fiscal year end.)

°Firms that trade in the form of Global Registered Shares.

Source: Standard & Poor's Compustat®.

Firm Value, Risk and Cost of Capital

When foreign firms list their shares abroad, the evidence indicates that the market value of the firm increases. Firms with cross-border listings are perceived as less risky and therefore the expected returns required by investors decrease, as does the cost of capital for the issuer. Theoretical and empirical studies have aimed to determine the factors that explain this phenomenon and academics have proposed several alternative hypotheses.

Market Segmentation Hypothesis

In this context, market segmentation refers to barriers that deter capital flows among countries. Examples of such barriers include transaction costs or foreign ownership restrictions. The segmentation hypothesis predicts that highly segmented markets should be characterized by an increased risk premium for local firms (Stulz, 1981).

When a foreign firm decides to raise capital by using a U.S. exchange, it is increasing the size of its investor pool. As such, equity ownership risk is spread across more individuals. This should result in lower risk and thus a lower expected return on equity and a lower cost of equity capital for the issuer. The degree to which this effect prevails should, according to the segmentation hypothesis, depend on the degree of segmentation in the local market of the foreign issuer.

The International Asset Pricing Model (IAPM) predicts that cross-listing acts to integrate capital markets and accomplish risk sharing in a manner that helps firms in segmented markets overcome some barriers to cross-border investment (Stapleton and Subrahmanyam, 1977). Errunza and Losq (1985) propose a theoretical model of asymmetric investment barriers to support this notion. They model a world with two sets of securities—one set free of restrictions and universally tradable and one set limited to trading in a single segmented market. They show that, because the latter is vulnerable to national market fluctuations and specific risks, its issuers face higher costs of capital than issuers of the unrestricted security. Perhaps the most important consequence of such theories is that cross-listing reduces a firm's cost of capital and therefore its internal hurdle rate, and should thus increase its equilibrium market value (Alexander et al. 1987).

Empirical work testing these hypotheses has focused on two methods. The first is observing stock price fluctuations around the period of the cross-listing. Alexander et al. (1988) produce results consistent with the segmentation hypothesis. They find that after completing cross-listings, firms exhibit lower expected returns, suggesting a lower cost of equity. The choice of timeframe for the study significantly affects the results. Miller (1999) shows positive abnormal returns around the announcement of an ADR program and insignificant abnormal returns in the post announcement period. The second method relies on estimating changes in the cost of capital for foreign firms after cross listing in the U.S. Errunza and Miller (2000) find that, after controlling for confounding effects, introducing an ADR program reduces the cost of capital in their sample of firms by 42.2%.

Liquidity Hypothesis

Empirical evidence suggests that cross-listing enhances the liquidity in a firm's traded equity shares. The increased liquidity is generally thought to result from (i) enlarging the shareholder base (more individual and institutional investors can access the shares) and (ii) decreasing information asymmetries resulting from heightened disclosure requirements. Theoretical models of multi-market trading posit that, when there is competition among capital markets for order flow, one market typically becomes dominant and, in turn, provides higher liquidity because of the concentration of information and liquidity in that market (Chrowdhry and Nanda 1991). Others suggest simply that the lengthening of trading hours inherently increases the trading volume of the shares (Karolyi 1998).

Empirical tests of these hypotheses utilize a number of distinct methods. Amihud and Mendelson (1986) find that cross-listed firms experienced an increase in trading volume and a decrease in bid-ask spread, and consequently a decrease in the cost of capital and an increase in stock price. Smith and Sofianos (1997) document systematic differences in the trading volume of NYSE-listed non-U.S. shares depending on the firms' nationality and other firm-specific factors. Foerster and Karolyi (2000) found that the returns of non-U.S. firms issuing equity on major U.S. exchanges were related to their trading volumes in the U.S. Examining trading volumes at the time of cross-listing, Bailey et al. (2002) find that a greater increase in trading volume is observed for firms from developed countries with relatively weak disclosure requirements. Madhavan (1995) suggests that when cross-listing firms are not required to disclose information on a regular basis, then fragmented markets problems are not solved and enhanced liquidity is not achieved.

Investor Recognition Hypothesis

A reduction in the cost of capital from cross-border listing is also associated with Merton's (1987) "investor recognition hypothesis." As a firm gains recognition, the size of the investor pool grows, decreasing expected returns for investors, in turn lowering the cost of equity and increasing market value. Miller (1999) found that foreign firms listing on major U.S. exchanges had larger abnormal returns than foreign firms traded in the OTC market, supporting the hypotheses that increased liquidity and greater investor recognition increase firm value. Other empirical tests of the investor recognition hypothesis have emphasized increased coverage by equity research analysts and increased media coverage after cross-listings (Baker et al., 2002).

Shareholder Protection Hypothesis

Markets vary in the kinds of legal protection available to minority shareholders. There is evidence that better shareholder protection leads to higher valuations of firms since investors are willing to pay more for shares when they have legal protection against expropriation (La Porta, 2002). Firms whose home markets provide weak protection for minority shareholders may, therefore, cross-list their shares in markets with stronger shareholder safeguards to demonstrate their commitment to shareholder rights and thereby increase the firm's share value. Stulz (1999) and Coffee (1999) argue that by binding themselves to extensive disclosure requirements in the cross-listing market, managers may decrease information asymmetry between themselves and investors, alleviating agency problems. Doidge et al. (2001) investigate this, finding that cross-listed firms tend to be those with low agency costs associated with controlling shareholders. Others have examined whether the structure of U.S. capital markets provides better protection for shareholders and translates into disincentives for managers to extract benefits from the firm. Conforming to SEC regulations may lower agency costs, thus increasing investor appetite for equity shares, lowering the firm's cost of capital, and increasing market value. Reese et al. (2002) demonstrate that greater commitment to maintaining shareholder rights (i) improves a firm's ability to raise capital and (ii) is associated with higher levels of equity issuance.

Corporate Visibility

Some practitioners believe that having a capital markets presence in an overseas market provides concrete business benefits. It may facilitate product market transactions by making customers more comfortable with the long term viability of the business. It may enhance a firm's strength in the labor market as compensation mechanisms such as stock options become available to the firm. Finally, it may improve its standing among institutional investors in the capital markets, insofar as it draws the attention of institutional investors specializing in the firm's industry rather than diversified international fund managers.

Product Market

Just as cross-listing enhances investor awareness of a firm, it may increase consumer knowledge about a firm and its products. Managers may have reason to believe that this will ultimately increase sales volume. A survey by Bancel and Mittoo (2001) reports that "16% of European cross-listed companies rate easier implementation of global marketing and production as a motive for cross-listing." They also claim that firms belonging to a given industry prefer to list on the same stock exchange.

Labor Markets

As stock option programs have become more prominent features of corporate compensation schemes in the U.S., those firms lacking a U.S. traded security (or the immediate prospect of issuing one in an IPO) are placed at a disadvantage relative to their competitors. They may find recruiting new employees and retaining talented employees more difficult as a consequence. Depositary receipt programs solve this problem by providing foreign firms with a U.S.-traded security desirable to employees that can serve as the underlying security for employee stock options. Several practitioners claim that cross-border listings are frequently motivated by the desire to create and proliferate employee option programs (Schneiber, 2001).

Capital Markets

One consequence of the highly developed fund management industry in the U.S. is that institutional investors generally purchase securities that meet a specific investment strategy (e.g. small-cap domestic equities or large-cap technology equities). Institutional investors may not be allowed to buy non-U.S. equities. Depositary receipt programs may circumvent a fund's formal restrictions by creating a domestically traded security.

Domestically traded securities may also facilitate mergers and acquisitions for foreign firms. A primary concern of acquirers in stock swap transactions is whether the target shareholders will choose to hold the shares they receive as consideration or immediately sell them. Foreign acquirers face this concern to a greater extent, because domestic investors may not find a share traded on a foreign exchange desirable. In this context, a foreign acquirer of a U.S. firm would prefer to exchange a U.S. traded security—an ADR, for example—for the target's outstanding shares. Because of the time lags involved in issuing a publicly traded ADR, foreign firms may initiate ADR programs to gain the option of executing a significant M&A transaction in the U.S.

CONSEQUENCES OF CROSS LISTINGS

The litany of benefits available to firms through cross listings must be weighed against the possibility of the market ultimately shunning the issuance. A primary concern is the phenomenon of "flow back"—when trading volume in the ADR, though initially well received, falters and trading migrates back to the home market. This effect negates the benefits of the ADR, as the home market once again becomes the most liquid market for trading. It is a concern of both foreign issuers and of market regulators.

Flow Back

Technically, flow back refers to the net flow of shares back to the local market after an overseas issuance. Flow back can be caused by both intrinsic characteristics of the issuer and external factors. A cost-effective ADR program requires a critical mass of trading volume in the ADR market. The costs of maintaining a program—management time, SEC disclosures, investor relations services, etc.—suggest that the firm must be of enough interest to foreign investors to build a foothold investor base. Virgin Atlantic, for example, delisted from the NASDAQ in July 2002 because it could not sustain the minimum trading volume requirements (2000 shares a day).

External factors that may produce flow back include index rebalancing and the desire of institutional investors to consolidate their holdings of a particular equity investment in its most liquid market. Institutional investors might sell or buy equity immediately upon notification of its "reweighting" or omission from indices. As illustrated in Exhibit 18, in October 1998, when the S&P 500 decided to drop Chrysler after its merger with Daimler Benz, a significant amount of Daimler trading flowed back to Frankfurt. Furthermore, after the merger in November 1998, DaimlerChrysler global

EXHIBIT 18

DAIMLERCHRYSLER TRADING ACTIVITY BEFORE AND AFTER THE MERGER

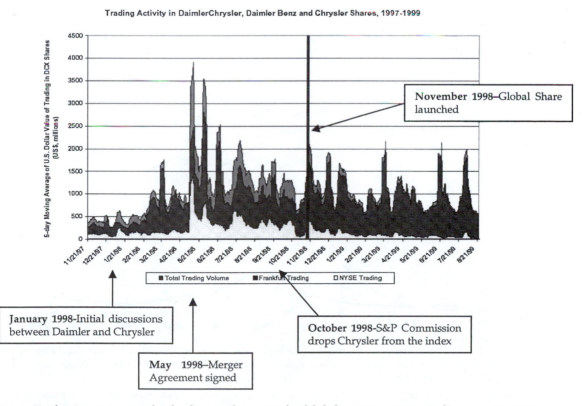

Trading Activity in DaimlerChrysler, Daimler Benz and Chrysler Shares, 1997-1999

Source: Karolyi, George A., "DaimlerChrysler AG, The First Truly Global Share," Dice Center Working Paper No. 99-13 (September 1999): 41; later published in *Journal of Corporate Finance*, vol. 9, 2003, pp. 409–430.

shares continued to experience flow back. The extended effect was spurred in part by institutional investors who previously had owned securities of both companies in both countries and upon the merger decided to sell the new global shares trading in the U.S.

Migration of Shares to International Exchanges

When large multinationals cross list abroad, a portion of trading activity emigrates to the international exchange. In the case of emerging markets, where there is limited local liquidity, cross listings of large companies may have a range of effects on the remaining local entities and for the local exchange. The issuance of ADRs in the U.S., by increasing the visibility and disclosure of a firm, may encourage institutional investors to buy ordinary shares directly in their local markets. Additionally, by issuing an ADR, foreign firms are signaling confidence in their growth strategies, which may translate into increases in local investors' confidence. At the same time, migration of stocks from exchanges in emerging economies to international centers make local exchanges less necessary, with little domestic activity to sustain the exchange (Claessens et al., 2002). One such example is the Bolsa de Mexico where 25% of the trading volume is in Telmex stock, which trades primarily abroad. Exhibit 19 illustrates that aggregated traded value of cross-listed firms for a sample of emerging markets is larger in those overseas exchanges where they are listed than in their local market.

EXHIBIT 19

VALUE TRADED OF CROSS-LISTED FIRMS IN INTERNATIONAL AND DOMESTIC MARKETS VS. LOCAL FIRMS

Note: "International firms in international market" refers to the traded volume of cross-listed firms in international exchange. "International firms in domestic market" refers to traded volume of those cross-listed firms in their local exchanges. "Domestic firms" refers to traded volume of public companies that do not trade abroad.

Source: Claessens, S., Klingebiel, D., and Schmukler, S., "Explaining the Migration of Stocks from Exchanges in Emerging Economies to International Centres, " CEPR Discussion Paper no. 3301 (London, Center for Economic Policy Research, 2002).

REFERENCES

ALEXANDER, G., EUN, C., JANAKIRAMANAN, S., 1987. "Asset Pricing and Dual Listing on Foreign Capital Markets: A note," *Journal of Finance* 42: 151–158.

ALEXANDER, G., EUN, C., JANAKIRAMANAN, S., 1988. "International Listings and Stock Returns: Some Empirical Evidence," *Journal of Financial and Quantitative Analysis* 23: 135–151.

AMIHUD, Y., MENDELSON, H., 1986. "Asset Pricing and the Bid-Ask Spread," *Journal of Financial Economics* 17: 223–249.

BAILEY, W., KAROLYI, A., SALVA, C., 2002. "The Economic Consequences of Increased Disclosure: Evidence from International Cross-Listings," Working Paper, Ohio State University.

BAKER, K., NOFSINGER, J., WEAVER, D., 2002. "International Cross-Listing and Visibility", *Journal of Financial and Quantitative Analysis* 37: 4950–5211.

BANCEL, F., MITTOO, U., 2001. "European Managerial Perceptions of the Net Benefits of Foreign Stock Listings," *European Financial Management* 7(2): 213–236.

CHROWDHRY, D., NANDA, V., 1991. "Multimarket Trading and Market Liquidity," *The Review of Financial Studies* 4: 483–511.

CLAESSENS, S., KLINGEBIEL, D., AND SCHMUKLER, S., 2002. "Explaining the Migration of Stocks from Exchanges in Emerging Economies to International Centres," CEPR Discussion Paper no. 3301. London, Centre for Economic Policy Research.

COFFEE, J., 1999. "The Future as History: The Prospects for Global Convergence in Corporate Governance and its Implications," *Northwestern University Law Review* 93: 641–707.

DOIDGE, C., STULZ, R., KAROLYI, A., 2001. "Why are Foreign Firms listed in the U.S. worth more?" Working Paper 8538, NBER [Forthcoming in *Journal of Financial Economics*].

ERRUNZA, V., LOSQ, E., 1985. "International Asset Pricing under Mild Segmentation: Theory and Test," *Journal of Finance* 40: 105–124.

ERRUNZA, V., MILLER, D., 2000. "Market Segmentation and Cost of Capital in International Equity Markets," *Journal of Finance and Quantitative Analysis* 35: 577–600.

FOERSTER, S., KAROLYI, A., 1999. "The Effects of Market Segmentation and Investor Recognition on Asset Prices: Evidence from the Foreign Stocks Listings in the United States," *Journal of Finance* 54: 981–1013.

FOERSTER, S., KAROLYI, A., 2000. "The Long-Run Performance of Global Equity Offerings," *Journal of Finance and Quantitative Analysis* 35, 4, 499–528.

KAROLYI, A., 1998. "Why Do Companies List Their Shares Abroad? (A Survey of the Evidence and its Managerial Implications)," Salomon Brothers Monograph Series, 7.

KAROLYI, A., 2003. "DaimlerChrysler AG, The First Truly Global Share," *Journal of Corporate Finance* 9: 409–430.

LA PORTA, R., LOPEZ-DE-SILANES, F., SHLEIFER, A., 1999. "Corporate Ownership around the World," *Journal of Finance* 54: 471–517.

LA PORTA, R., LOPEZ-DE-SILANES, F., SHLEIFER, A., VISHNY, R., 2002. "Investor Protection and Corporate Valuation," *Journal of Finance* 57: 1147–1170.

MADHAVAN, A., 1995. "Consolidation, Fragmentation, and the Disclosure of Trading Information," *Review of Financial Studies* 8(3): 579–603.

MERTON, R., 1987. "A Simple Model of Capital Market Equilibrium with Incomplete Information," *Journal of Finance* 42: 483–510.

MILLER, D., 1999. "The Market Reaction to International Cross-Listing: Evidence from Depositary Receipts," *Journal of Financial Economics* 51: 103–123.

PAGANO, M. AND P.VOLPIN, 2001. "The Political Economy of Corporate Governance," *Oxford Review of Economic Policy* 17: 502–519.

PAGANO, M., ROELL, A., ZECHNER, J., 2002. "The Geography of Equity Listing: Why do Companies List Abroad?" *Journal of Finance* 57: 2651–2694.

REESE, W., WEISBACH, M., 2002. "Protection of Minority Shareholder Interests, Cross-Listings in the United States and Subsequent Equity Offerings," *Journal of Financial Economics* 66: 65–104.

SCHNEIBER, KURT, cited in "The Changing Landscape: Japanese ADRs," Roundtable discussion sponsored by *FinanceAsia* and Citibank, 2001, available at ⟨http://wwss.citissb.com/adr/www/adr_info/jar.pdf⟩

SMITH, K., SOFIANOS, G., 1997. "The Impact of a NYSE Listing on the Global Trading of non-U.S. Stocks," Working paper 97-08, New York Stock Exchange.

STAPLETON, R., SUBRAHMANYAM, M., 1977. "Market Imperfections, Capital Market Equilibrium, and Corporate Finance," *Journal of Finance* 32: 307–319.

STULZ, R., 1981. "On the Effects of Barriers to International Investment," *Journal of Finance* 36: 923–934.

STULZ, R., 1999, "Globalization of Equity Markets and the Cost of Capital," Working Paper 7021, National Bureau of Economic Research.

16

Tax-Motivated Film Financing at Rexford Studios

Charles O. Shaw, president and head of production for Rexford Studios, Inc., stared through his windshield at the bumper-to-bumper traffic on Highway 101, just north of Melrose in Hollywood. Given Rexford's box office successes in 2000 and 2001, Shaw realized that the next few years would truly define the midsize studio's place in the competitive production industry. A new slate of 15 films was ready to be "green-lighted" for production over the next three years, but Shaw was under increasing pressure from the Rexford board of directors to reduce financing costs and mitigate the risks associated with film production.

On Shaw's mind on this hot afternoon in September 2002 was a film-funding proposal from Film Fund International II, GmbH (FFI) in Germany to fund a single film—the first on Rexford's new slate—scheduled to begin production in January of 2003. FFI was a relatively new financing source for funding U.S. films via film-specific investment vehicles. Shaw knew that the major studios had finance groups that sourced funds from around the world—possibly through similar structures—but without a finance group of his own to support him, Shaw had to quickly learn more about the mechanics and risks involved in the proposed deal.[1]

More specifically, Shaw knew that if the deal closed, he would have to immediately deposit a substantial amount of cash in a German bank. Part of his decision to go ahead with the deal, however, depended on how much he would have to deposit. Even if he decided to go ahead with this deal and deposit the money, he wondered how much it

Professor Mihir A. Desai, Gabriel J. Loeb (MBA '02), and Research Associate Mark F. Veblen prepared this case. HBS cases are developed solely as the basis for class discussion. The companies in this case are fictional. Cases are not intended to serve as endorsements, sources of primary data, or illustrations of effective or ineffective management.

[1]German film funds have been used widely throughout the U.S. film industry since the late 1990s. Merrill Lynch estimated that German funds cofinanced 15%–20% of all major Hollywood movies in 2001, listing 22 large film funds that closed or were in the process of closing in 2000 and 2001. These 22 funds raised over 2.8 billion euros (€) in capital, financing approximately 150 projects. Bernard Tubeileh and Stephan Seip, "German Film Funds: Competition or Co-Operation for Film Companies?" Merrill Lynch, October 4, 2001, p. 5.

would benefit Rexford and how much value each of the other parties involved was receiving. Was there room to negotiate with them for a better deal? He needed to come up with answers quickly so he could advise Rexford's board at its meeting next week.

VALUE CHAIN IN THE MOTION PICTURE INDUSTRY[2]

The year 2001 was a banner one for the movie industry: theaters grossed a record $8.14 billion, a 9% increase over 2000, and five films grossed over $200 million at the domestic box office.[3] While U.S. box office results were the most visible phase in the life cycle of a film, theatrical exhibition was only one part of an industry value chain spanning six broad functions that integrated many players of varied sizes and strategic scopes (see Exhibit 1 for a schematic outlining the industry's stages, activities, and players).

Talent

Actors and actresses, writers, directors, and even producers with the skill and reputation for creating successful film projects significantly influence filmmaking, through box office generating power, creative influences, and the ability to recruit other talent. Frequently, stars work through agencies and management companies such as Creative Artists Agency, the William Morris Agency, and Brillstein-Grey to be matched with production companies and studios[4] to back their work. In many instances, top talent commands a great deal of bargaining power in terms of extracting large percentages of gross revenue from studios as "success" fees for their performances.

Development

The first stage in the actual process of creating a film is development—discovering scripts, acquiring the rights, and modifying them into attractive packages for production. Generally, producers "pitch" a studio an idea, and upon selling this idea receive development funding to find a writer to generate a script. Scripts are also discovered by direct submissions from writers through their agents. Studios subsequently buy or option the rights to promising scripts and together with the producer prepare them to become a commercially viable screenplay. The studio and producer may make slight adjustments, attach talent or other creative elements, and then submit this package—along with a production budget—to studio executives to be green-lighted.

Financing

Once green-lighted, a film's financing is typically obtained from some combination of banks, individual investors, insurance companies, film funds, independent distributors, and major studios and media companies. Enough is raised to cover production and

---

[2]For further background and analysis on the motion picture industry, see Arturo Litwak, "Summit Entertainment," HBS Case No. 701-065 (Boston: Harvard Business School Publishing, 2001).

[3]Carl Diorio, "Record box office is qualified corker," *Daily Variety*, January 1, 2002.

[4]For purposes of this case, *studios* will be defined as entities that finance, own, and distribute films. These may be major studios such as Disney and Universal or independents such as Artisan and Intermedia. Moreover, *producers* or *production companies* will be defined as entities that may help arrange financing for films, hire personnel, manage the film production process, and receive a producer credit but are paid on a fee-for-service basis and do not generally own rights to a film property. In reality, the lines between these types of entities often blur.

EXHIBIT 1

FILM INDUSTRY VALUE CHAIN

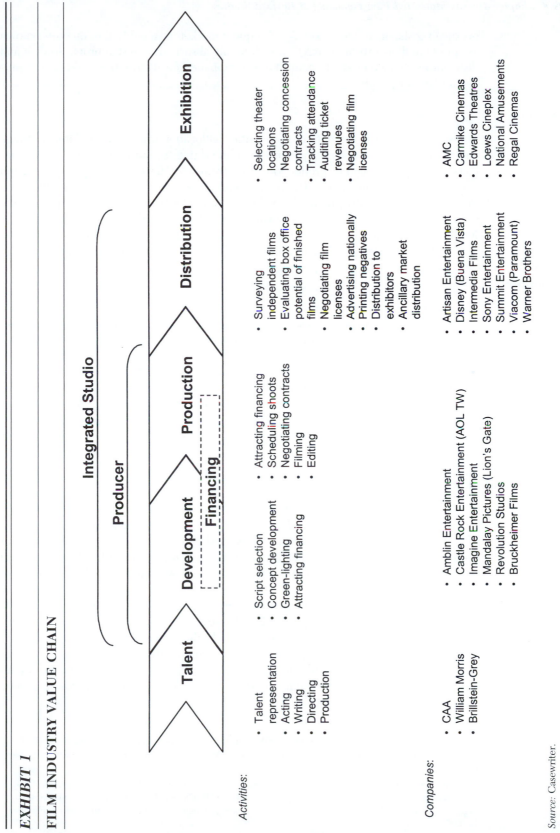

Integrated Studio

Producer

| Talent | Development | Production | Distribution | Exhibition |

Financing

Activities:

Talent
- Talent representation
- Acting
- Writing
- Directing
- Production

Development
- Script selection
- Concept development
- Green-lighting
- Attracting financing

Production
- Attracting financing
- Scheduling shoots
- Negotiating contracts
- Filming
- Editing

Distribution
- Surveying independent films
- Evaluating box office potential of finished films
- Negotiating film licenses
- Advertising nationally
- Printing negatives
- Distribution to exhibitors
- Ancillary market distribution

Exhibition
- Selecting theater locations
- Negotiating concession contracts
- Tracking attendance
- Auditing ticket revenues
- Negotiating film licenses

Companies:

- CAA
- William Morris
- Brillstein-Grey

- Amblin Entertainment
- Castle Rock Entertainment (AOL TW)
- Imagine Entertainment
- Mandalay Pictures (Lion's Gate)
- Revolution Studios
- Bruckheimer Films

- Artisan Entertainment
- Disney (Buena Vista)
- Intermedia Films
- Sony Entertainment
- Summit Entertainment
- Viacom (Paramount)
- Warner Brothers

- AMC
- Carmike Cinemas
- Edwards Theatres
- Loews Cineplex
- National Amusements
- Regal Cinemas

Source: Casewriter.

overhead costs, or "negative costs." Subsequent marketing and distribution costs, known as "prints and advertising (P&A)," are generally absorbed by distributors. Studios and distributors finance production and P&A in exchange for distribution rights and a percentage of net profits.[5]

Production

The screenplay has to be shot onto film either on location or on a studio lot soundstage and then passed through post-production film editing, sound editing, and special effects. The typical length of production varies from 3 to 12 weeks, and post-production may last up to several months. Upon completion, the master negative reel resides with the rights holder and is prepared for distribution. The highly fragmented production industry has seen nominal costs escalate substantially over the past two decades (see Exhibit 2). This increase in costs has increased the incentive for coproduction for studios seeking to spread the risk of a flop at the box office across several players.

Distribution

The distributor develops a marketing strategy, determines the number of screens on which the film should open, chooses an appropriate release window, and delivers trailers and the movie prints to various first-run exhibitors. In the process, the distributor negotiates the film rental contracts with exhibitors and collects and audits revenues received from the box office. Increased competition has forced P&A costs up over time (see Exhibit 2). Distributors face considerable performance risk for each film and therefore demand a fairly significant fee (see Exhibit 3) from producers. Distributors either purchase the film rights outright, in which case they need to recoup a fixed cost and then draw profits thereafter, or charge a fee as a percent of box office receipts for their services.

Exhibition and Ancillary Markets

While other sources of revenue streams, such as television and home video, have increased in importance, first-run U.S. theatrical exhibition remains the flagship distribution channel of any motion picture release and provides the most critical barometer for success in the ancillary markets. Exhibitors generally acquire films through direct negotiation with distributors and then sell tickets to moviegoers (as well as tracking attendance and handling local advertising of schedules and concession sales). Between 1990 and 2000, the number of movie screens exploded, growing by 13,000 to over 37,000 total screens. While this development affords moviegoers numerous options, the heavy debt loads incurred in the expansion have made the economics of exhibition less attractive and resulted in bankruptcy filings by several of the largest exhibitors.[6] Ancillary markets such as foreign exhibition, home video, cable television, and network television all provide additional revenue opportunities and are continuing to grow as a share

---

[5]See Chapter 17, "The Strategy and Sources of Motion Picture Finance," for a detailed overview of film-financing strategy, the various sources of funds, and a history of tax-motivated financial innovation in the industry.

[6]See Jill Goldsmith, "Edwards caught in exhib slide," *Daily Variety*, August 23, 2000; Carl Diorio, "Chapter 11 curtain to fall on GC," *Daily Variety*, October 11, 2000; Diorio, "Loews completes bankruptcy reorg.," *Daily Variety*, March 21, 2002; and Lindsay Chaney, "Mogul's new crown," *Daily Variety*, October 14, 2001.

EXHIBIT 2

FILM INDUSTRY COST TRENDS ($ MILLIONS)

Year	Average Negative Cost[a]	Average Prints & Advertising Cost	Average Total Cost	Growth	New Releases[b]	Growth
1980	9.4	4.3	13.7	na	134	na
1981	11.3	4.4	15.7	14.6%	145	8.2%
1982	11.8	4.9	16.7	6.4%	150	3.4%
1983	11.9	5.2	17.1	2.4%	166	10.7%
1984	14.4	6.7	21.1	23.4%	152	−8.4%
1985	16.8	6.5	23.3	10.4%	138	−9.2%
1986	17.5	6.7	24.2	3.9%	133	−3.6%
1987	20.1	8.0	28.1	16.1%	122	−8.3%
1988	18.1	8.4	26.5	−5.7%	153	25.4%
1989	23.5	9.2	32.7	23.4%	157	2.6%
1990	26.8	11.6	38.4	17.4%	158	0.6%
1991	26.1	12.1	38.2	−0.5%	150	−5.1%
1992	28.9	13.5	42.4	11.0%	141	−6.0%
1993	29.9	14.1	44.0	3.8%	156	10.6%
1994	34.3	16.1	50.4	14.5%	166	6.4%
1995	36.4	17.7	54.1	7.3%	212	27.7%
1996	39.8	19.8	59.6	10.2%	215	1.4%
1997	53.4	22.3	75.7	27.0%	219	1.9%
1998	52.7	25.3	78.0	3.0%	221	0.9%
1999	51.5	24.5	76.0	−2.6%	213	−3.6%
2000	54.8	27.3	82.1	8.0%	191	−10.3%
2001[c]	47.7	31.0	78.7	−4.1%	189	−1.0%

[a]Negative costs include production costs, studio overhead, and capitalized interest.

[b]MPAA releases only; other releases may come from independents or from abroad.

[c]Due to accounting changes, abandoned movie costs are no longer included in studio overhead and are therefore not part of negative costs.

Source: Adapted from "2001 U.S. Economic Review," Motion Picture Association of America, MPAA Worldwide Market Research.

of total film revenue. Major studios increasingly own key distribution rights for these ancillary products.

Exhibit 3 breaks down how the average box office dollar[7] is allocated across the value chain. "Gross rentals"—the amount of box office receipts that a distributor receives—equal roughly 50% of the box office dollar (with the other 50% equaling the exhibitor's net revenues). After taking a distribution fee of 30% ($0.50) on the rentals, and subtracting 25% in P&A costs from rentals, a film might only have $0.23 out of the

[7]"Box office" refers to the aggregate ticket sales by exhibitors before any distribution fees or other expenses are deducted.

EXHIBIT 3

SPLIT OF SAMPLE BOX OFFICE DOLLAR

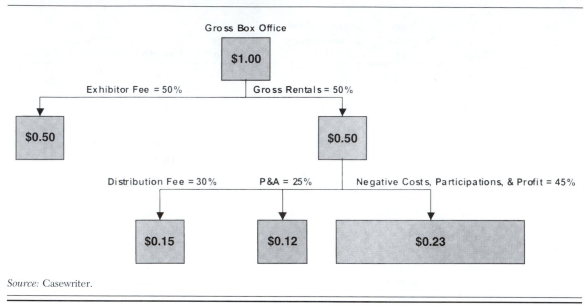

Source: Casewriter.

original box office dollar to pay for production and overhead, financing, and talent costs. Generally, this leaves the production company and any equity investors as the residual claimants on the remaining profit.

REXFORD STUDIOS AND ITS COMPETITION

Rexford started as an independent development and production company during the mid-1980s and had gone through several affiliations with the major studios for coproduction and distribution. In the mid-1990s, Rexford's founders (and Shaw's superiors) ended their studio contracts, acquired an independent distribution company, and decided to pursue their dream of running a full-fledged movie studio, financing and owning the films they produced.

Enjoying initial box office and critical successes with its earlier films, Rexford had enough cash in its coffers for development, some production, and distribution. In addition, Rexford had historically relied on strong relationships with film-focused bank lenders to help finance its production costs since becoming an independent. While the current slate of films appeared quite promising to Shaw and the studio chiefs, increased costs of production and marketing had begun to make financing more difficult. As the company wished to maintain some cash to provide for its future investment and growth, Shaw was given the task to find alternative—and less expensive—financing sources.

Although the company was privately held, the trade press often compared Rexford to upstart companies of the late 1990s such as Lion's Gate and Intermedia. Privately, however, Rexford wished to surpass these small studios and become a major player competing with the film studios of such companies as MGM, Disney, and Fox (see Exhibit 4 for company financial statements and Exhibit 5 for segment data). Shaw also urged his

EXHIBIT 4

COMPARABLE ENTERTAINMENT COMPANY CONSOLIDATED FINANCIALS ($ MILLIONS)

	Metro-Goldwyn-Mayer			The Walt Disney Company			Fox Entertainment			Lion's Gate Ent.		
	1999	2000	2001	1999	2000	2001	1999	2000	2001	1998	1999	2000
Total Sales	**1,142**	**1,237**	**1,388**	**23,455**	**25,418**	**25,269**	**8,057**	**8,589**	**8,504**	**118**	**271**	**282**
Cost of Goods Sold	958	772	766	20,030	21,660	21,670	6,220	6,482	6,274	93	223	156
SG&A Expense	291	340	585	—	—	—	806	1,011	1,101	24	31	38
Depreciation	25	29	33	456	1,233	767	315	440	477	5	7	10
Unusual Inc/Exp	301	(4)	—	172	92	1,454	—	—	—	1	3	53
Total Expenses	**1,575**	**1,136**	**1,385**	**20,658**	**22,985**	**23,891**	**7,341**	**7,933**	**7,852**	**123**	**264**	**257**
Interest Expense	(86)	(51)	(52)	612	497	417	(223)	(297)	(345)	4	4	10
Other—Net	(3)	15	7	218	697	322	(146)	(94)	84	6	87	—
Pre-Tax Income	**(521)**	**65**	**(41)**	**2,403**	**2,633**	**1,283**	**347**	**265**	**391**	**(14)**	**(5)**	**9**
Income Taxes	10	14	14	1,014	1,606	1,059	142	120	185	—	—	—
Net Income	(531)	51	(56)	1,389	1,027	224	205	145	206	(14)	(5)	9
Assets												
Current Assets	620	506	1,306	9,727	7,563	7,029	2,662	3,815	4,063	87	127	194
Long-Term Investments	—	—	—	2,434	2,270	2,061	—	—	—	162	192	306
PP&E, Net	48	47	39	11,346	12,310	12,907	1,321	1,478	1,454	41	45	44
Goodwill/Intangibles	2,711	2,954	2,552	18,657	21,456	19,775	8,439	11,274	11,350	32	29	35
Other Assets	45	41	27	1,515	1,428	1,927	741	1,363	989	6	9	15
Total Assets	**3,424**	**3,548**	**3,923**	**43,679**	**45,027**	**43,699**	**13,163**	**17,930**	**17,856**	**328**	**402**	**594**
Liabilities												
Current Liabilities	190	168	199	7,707	8,402	6,219	3,862	4,746	4,281	57	89	283
Long-Term Debt	719	710	836	9,278	6,959	8,940	53	974	1,032	90	41	66
Other Liabilities	398	360	399	5,719	5,566	5,868	2,580	3,964	4,575	14	24	24
Total Liabilities	**1,308**	**1,239**	**1,434**	**22,704**	**20,927**	**21,027**	**6,4 95**	**9,684**	**9,888**	**161**	**154**	**373**
Shareholders' Equity	2,117	2,310	2,490	20,975	24,100	22,672	6,668	8,246	7,968	167	206	197
Liabilities + Equity	**3,424**	**3,548**	**3,923**	**43,679**	**45,027**	**43,699**	**13,163**	**17,930**	**17,856**	**328**	**360**	**570**
Shares Outstanding	201	207	240	2,071	2,069	2,019	672	724	724	31	31	42
Other Financial Data												
Debt : Market Equity (%)	15.2%	21.0%	15.9%	21.7%	11.7%	26.1%	0.3%	4.4%	5.1%	59.2%	204.5%	218.2%
Return on Assets (%)	−15.5%	1.4%	−1.4%	3.2%	2.3%	0.5%	1.6%	0.8%	1.2%	−4.3%	−1.3%	1.5%
Recent Debt Rating			A-			A-			B			na
Recent Equity Beta			0.98			0.90			1.60			0.89

Source: Adapted from Compustat Research Insight, Company 10-Ks, Datastream International, Bloomberg, First Call.

EXHIBIT 5

COMPARABLE ENTERTAINMENT COMPANY FINANCIAL DATA BY SEGMENTS ($ MILLIONS)

	Total Revenue			Operating Profits			Assets			Capital Expenditures		
	1999	2000	2001	1999	2000	2001	1999	2000	2001	1999	2000	2001
Metro-Goldwyn-Mayer												
Feature Films	888	1,058	1,218	na	na	na	2,256	2,480	2,184	13	11	9
Television Programs	206	139	138	na	na	na	423	402	3.35	2	2	1
Cable Channels	15	33	78	na	na	na	9	12	845	na	na	na
Other	33	7	(46)	na	na	na	736	654	560	0	0	—
Consolidated Total	**1,142**	**1,237**	**1,388**	**na**	**na**	**na**	**3,424**	**3,548**	**3,923**	**15**	**12**	**10**
The Walt Disney Company												
Media Networks	8,012	9,836	9,569	1,512	1,985	1,758	na	21,932	20,357	168	249	207
Theme Parks and Resorts	6,141	6,809	7,004	1,494	1,615	1,586	na	10,884	11,369	1,699	1,524	1,278
Studio Entertainment	6,176	6,011	6,106	162	126	260	na	7,298	6,614	51	50	36
Consumer Products	3,126	2,762	2,590	592	386	401	na	1,173	1,041	114	73	70
Corporate/Other	—	—	—	(1,357)	(1,479)	(2,722)	na	3,740	4,318	102	117	204
Consolidated Total	**23,455**	**25,418**	**25,269**	**2,403**	**2,633**	**1,283**	**na**	**45,027**	**43,699**	**2,134**	**2,013**	**1,795**
Fox Entertainment Group												
Filmed Entertainment	4,416	3,856	3,585	355	128	286	3,355	4,620	4,382	116	72	58
Television Stations	1,469	1,635	1,550	557	585	499	6,659	6,213	6,106	133	85	22
Television Broadcast Network	1,743	1,751	1,823	(32)	29	(65)	1,576	1,382	1,534	49	12	11
Other Television Businesses	118	97	91	(7)	(11)	(9)	363	364	308	—	—	—
Cable Network Programming	311	1,250	1,455	(157)	(75)	(59)	424	3,841	4,033	9	78	54
Investments in Equity Affiliates	na	na	na	na	na	na	785	1,510	1,493	na	na	na
Segment Total	**8,057**	**8,589**	**8,504**	**716**	**656**	**652**	**13,163**	**17,930**	**17,856**	**307**	**247**	**145**
Lion's Gate Entertainment[a]												
Studio Facilities	6	7	6	4	5	3	na	na	na	na	na	na
Motion Pictures	78	147	174	13	27	100	na	na	na	na	na	na
Television	12	82	71	2	8	12	na	na	na	na	na	na
Animation	22	36	30	5	9	8	na	na	na	na	na	na
CineGate	—	—	2	—	—	2	na	na	na	na	na	na
Segment Total	**118**	**271**	**282**	**25**	**48**	**126**	**na**	**na**	**na**	**na**	**na**	**na**

[a]Lion's Gate data is as of March of the column year.

Source: OneSource Global Business Browser, SEC Documents (Lion's Gate Entertainment).

management team to benchmark performance goals and internal hurdle rates against estimates of the cost of capital for these larger, public companies (see Exhibit 4).

THE DEAL

On July 8, 2002, Shaw had approved a $50 million budget for the first film in Rexford's new slate, *Bait and Wait*—the true story of the Fargo State College ice fishing team. FFI was proposing a sale-and-leaseback transaction, scheduled to close on December 31, 2002, wherein it would buy the film, along with all of the associated rights, for $50 million. Rexford would then agree to lease back the film over a 20-year period, meaning that it would make yearly lease payments to FFI in exchange for all the copyrights and exploitation rights associated with the film over that period. Shaw noted that there were three key players in the deal as structured: Rexford Studios, Neue Landesbank AG, and FFI.

Rexford Studios

The proposal called for the production company to receive the purchase price in cash and subsequently be responsible for the lease payments. Rexford would immediately discharge this future lease obligation by transferring sufficient funds to a third-party bank that would then handle all of the future payments.

Purchase Price

FFI would purchase the rights to the completed master negative, including all copyrights, distribution rights, and so on, from Rexford for $50 million—a number that represented the expected book value of the film's production costs and overhead. Shaw noted that FFI specifically required that the film be purchased from Rexford prior to the start of production.

Leaseback

After the purchase, the deal stipulated that FFI would lease the master negative and all the rights back to Rexford in return for a stream of escalating (at a rate of 5% per annum) lease payments over a 20-year period, starting at the time of the film's release— one year from the date the deal would close (see Exhibit 6). Although Rexford would receive the $50 million upon the deal's December 31 closing, in order to meet the leasing obligation it would immediately have to deposit a significant amount at Neue Landesbank (which would subsequently make the lease payments out of this deposit). At the end of the lease term, all rights would revert back to Rexford.

Risk Allocations

An industry veteran, Shaw knew that until a film negative was complete, all kinds of risks remained that might prevent the film from being completed or might drive costs over budget. In addition to the risks of on-time completion and cost overruns on the production budget, Shaw wondered if Rexford would also be dealing with risks arising from an overseas investment denominated in euros, in an entirely different tax jurisdiction where tax rates or policies might change. Shaw wondered how and if FFI would absorb these risks or if he might be exposed to them.

EXHIBIT 6

**REXFORD STUDIO LEASE PAYMENT SCHEDULE
TO FILM FUND INTERNATIONAL II**

Date: December 31,	Payment: ($000)
2002	0
2003	2,485
2004	2,609
2005	2,740
2006	2,877
2007	3,021
2008	3,172
2009	3,330
2010	3,497
2011	3,672
2012	3,855
2013	4,048
2014	4,250
2015	4,463
2016	4,686
2017	4,920
2018	5,166
2019	5,425
2020	5,696
2021	5,981
2022	6,280

Source: Casewriter.

Other Considerations

Shaw noted that nothing in the prospectus called for Rexford to move production abroad. This was of particular concern to Shaw because he wanted to film the movie in its authentic North Dakota locale. Moreover, labor unions and other trade groups had been angered since the late 1990s, when film production was increasingly moved overseas to meet regulatory requirements to exploit the tax benefits offered in Australia, the United Kingdom, Canada, and many other countries. Regarding the deal's financial source, Shaw had seen anecdotal evidence that other studios, including New Line, Fox, and Paramount, had been increasingly using German investor funds to help finance their films since 2000, and he felt he would be irresponsible if he did not fully understand whether or not this deal offered Rexford any value.

Neue Landesbank

Neue Landesbank was referred to as the defeasance bank because its role in the transaction would be to discharge Rexford's lease obligation. Initially, the defeasance bank would issue a letter of credit on behalf of Rexford to guarantee the payments to FFI. On the closing date of the deal and upon receipt of the $50 million, Rexford would be required to immediately deposit the present value of the lease payments and fees into an account at this third-party bank. For a small fee, the bank would take the deposit principal in advance and then transfer the annual lease payments to FFI as they came due (every lease payment would occur at the end of the given year, starting December 31, 2003).

While the prospectus did not describe the amount of this initial deposit, it did provide several assumptions. First, the deposit balance would earn a fixed rate of interest of 6%. Second, as payment for its services, the defeasance bank was to receive a one-time fee at closing of 0.5% of the $50 million purchase price. Finally, each year the defeasance bank would also receive a fee of 0.2% of the deposit balance at the beginning of the year.

FFI

From the deal prospectus, Shaw noted that the fund would be structured as a limited partnership for a group of high-net-worth German investors specifically related to *Bait and Wait* and its $50 million budget—it was not seeking to fund a portfolio of films. In exchange for certain administrative fees, the fund arrangers would act on behalf of the investors to handle the sale and leaseback transaction and also regulatory requirements that had to be met during the production of the film.

According to the prospectus, FFI's individual investors had each agreed to contribute a minimum of €100,000, against which additional funds would be borrowed by FFI. Overall, the fund would raise a total of $51 million, $41 million of equity raised from investors and $10 million of debt maturing in 20 years.[8] The fund arrangers would immediately take a $1 million fee and use the rest in the film sale/leaseback. Shaw noticed a footnote that described some tax rules for Germans investing in films; it stipulated that because films were considered intangible assets in Germany, any investment in a film could not be capitalized and had to be expensed in the year incurred. The administrative fee was immediately deductible, and the interest expense was deductible over time. As Shaw continued to read, he saw that the prospectus emphasized the personal tax rates in Germany, forecasted to be 51.2% in 2002, dropping to 49.6% in 2004, 44.3% in 2006, and finally to 44.2% after 2012. Subject to some technical requirements, therefore, FFI's investors would receive a deduction of the full $50 million principal investment in *Bait and Wait* for the 2002 tax year. At the same time, investors would be taxed on the annual lease payments that Rexford would pay to FFI over the 20-year life of this deal.

EVALUATING THE PROPOSAL

Now back in his office sipping a nonfat mocha, Shaw struggled with his first impressions about the proposal. He knew that his studio chiefs and board of directors would be full of pointed questions about getting involved in such a complex structure. Shaw needed to understand exactly how the transaction worked and how much value it generated for Rexford and the other parties. How much would he have to deposit? He knew what the lease payments would be, but how would the interest rate data

[8]The third-party debt would carry an interest rate of 6% also and would be repaid through a bullet payment in 2020 at the end of the transaction.

EXHIBIT 7

U.S. GOVERNMENT AND CORPORATE BOND INTEREST RATES

Government or Int'l Debt	Yields	Corporate Bond Ratings (U.S. Industrials—10 Year)	Yields
U.S. Prime Rate	4.75%	AAA	6.00%
1-Month Treasury Rate	1.78	AA	6.20
1-Year Treasury Bond	2.75	A	6.43
10-Year Treasury Bond	5.41	BBB	6.88
20-Year Treasury Bond	6.03	BB	8.42
		B	9.41

Source: Bloomberg, Datastream International.

(see Exhibit 7) and betas for comparable companies he had put together help him find the appropriate discount rate? Or would using the return earned by the defeasance bank as a discount rate make more sense?

Shaw also wanted to understand the risks Rexford would face if he went through with the deal. Perhaps there was room for negotiating either less risk or greater economic gain. While he was confident about his slate of films, Shaw knew that as a mid-size studio in a risky business, Rexford would be challenged to keep its financing costs down. He needed to determine if this deal was the right way to face this challenge.

17

The Strategy and Sources of Motion Picture Finance

> There's no place for private investors in the film business. It's a business for studios, distributors and exhibitors, but not for private investors. They might as well throw their money down a rat hole.
>
> —Jake Eberts, CEO, Goldcrest Films

Along with technology, capital innovations have been among the most important forces shaping the motion picture industry throughout its history. The application and packaging of increasingly large amounts of capital for production have given rise to numerous financing innovations, which in turn have created a complex, often confusing capital structure for the industry. In the United States, the world's most prominent production market, these innovations have evolved both from within the industry as well as from external sources.

Many of the reasons for financial innovation in the motion picture industry have to do with the somewhat unusual economic structure of the industry itself. According to industry analyst Harold Vogel:

> Industries requiring sizable capital investments can normally be expected to evolve into purely oligopolistic forms: steel and automobile manufacturing are examples. But because movies—each uniquely designed and packaged—are not stamped out on cookie-cutter assembly lines, the economic structure is somewhat different. Here, instead, we find a combination of large oligopolistic production/distribution/financing organizations regularly interfacing with and being highly dependent on a fragmented assortment of small, specialized service and production firms.[1]

Professor Mihir A. Desai, Gabriel J. Loeb (MBA '02), and Research Associate Mark F. Veblen prepared this note as the basis for class discussion.

[1]Harold L. Vogel, *Entertainment Industry Economics: A Guide for Financial Analysis*, Fifth Edition (Cambridge, U.K.: Cambridge University Press, 2001), p. 41.

Even within this unusual industry structure, motion picture production has grown over the last 40 years, with over 480 total films released in the United States in 2001 compared with only 248 in 1960.[2]

This note serves as a primer on fundamental issues related to the financing of motion pictures in the United States. The first section explains the link between financing and production strategies for producers and studios and their approach to risk management. The second section describes internal and external sources studios draw upon to finance film production.[3] Each major source is evaluated based on whether it more closely resembles debt or equity financing. The last section describes how U.S. producers and studios have historically used tax-related incentives to help reduce the cost of producing films.

MOTION PICTURE FINANCING STRATEGY

One of the critical elements of film production involves the risk each film faces from inception to release. Broadly, there are three main risks films face—completion risk, performance risk, and financial risk. Like many large-scale investments, films often face completion risk due to the high level of required investment and the changing motivations and relationships between producers, talent, and financiers. Often, this means that millions of dollars are spent on a film that may not be completed or even fully produced.

Behind any completed film are investments for production, overhead, and marketing—all made prior to commercial release, a period of one to three years. Moreover, star power, critical reviews, the reaction of fickle audiences, and other factors all play a role in the box office success of a particular film. The resulting difficulty in accurately predicting revenues and profits creates a substantial amount of performance risk for a given film.

Since the 1980s, the competitive risks in the industry have become more pronounced. As production and marketing costs have increased, the level of risk for equity investors has increased as well—with higher dollar returns required in order to make investments in films positive net present value (NPV) for investors. High-net-worth individuals, once a standby source of funds through nonrecourse loans and limited partnerships, have abandoned such vehicles and can generally no longer afford to take on such high-risk investments. Other investors, such has insurance companies, have been disappointed by the unpredictable nature of film investments and have exited the market, further reducing the pool of interested investors. The "cash waterfall" in Exhibit 1 outlines the many parties (talent, distributors, creditors, etc.) that take a cut of revenues before the residual profits are distributed to a studio or an equity investor. Managing increased costs with fewer potential investors has created a serious funding problem for independent and major studios alike. In this "hit-or-miss" environment, financial payoffs have become more skewed, and studios have continuously attempted to mitigate and share their risks through various mechanisms.

---

[2]*2001 U.S. Economic Review*, Motion Picture Association of America (MPAA), Worldwide Market Research. Available at ⟨www.mpaa.org⟩.

[3]For purposes of this note, *studios* will be defined as entities that finance, own, and distribute films. These may be major studios such as Disney and Universal or independents such as Artisan and Intermedia. Moreover, *producers* or *production companies* will be defined as entities that may help arrange financing for films, hire personnel, manage the film production process, and receive a producer credit but are paid on a fee-for-service basis and do not generally own rights to a film property. In reality, the lines between these types of entities often blur.

EXHIBIT 1

WATERFALL OF CASH FLOW FOR A SAMPLE FILM AFTER EXHIBITOR SHARE

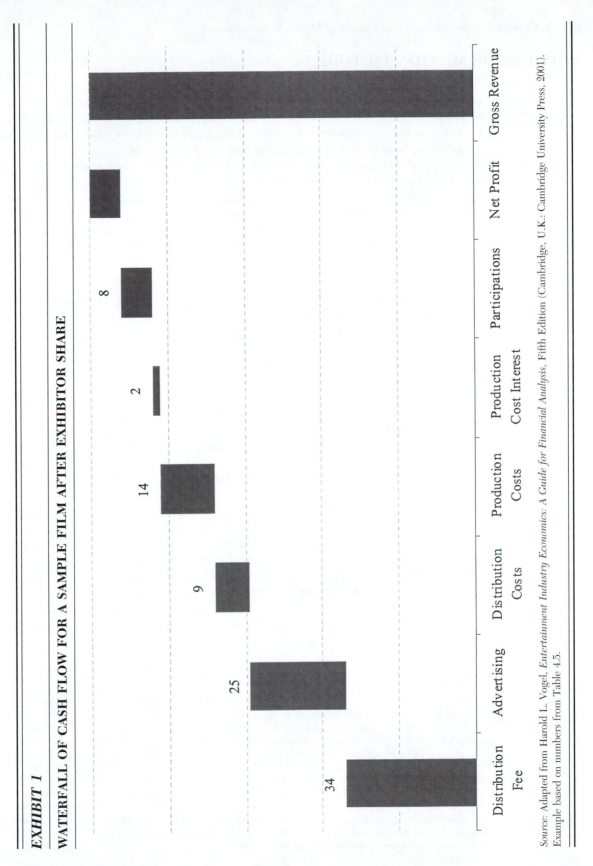

Source: Adapted from Harold L. Vogel, *Entertainment Industry Economics: A Guide for Financial Analysis,* Fifth Edition (Cambridge, U.K.: Cambridge University Press, 2001). Example based on numbers from Table 4.5.

SOURCES OF MOTION PICTURE FINANCE[4]

The most basic source of film finance for a studio is retained earnings from previously successful films. While this source is often used, large budgets and numerous productions have made it necessary for production companies to bring in additional capital. Exhibit 2 provides a classification of various financing methods by placing them along a continuum from pure debt financing to pure equity financing.

There are two main types of studios that seek financing—major studios (e.g., Disney, Universal, Warner Brothers) and independent, smaller studios (Artisan, Intermedia, Revolution Studios). Here, the size and scope of the company and of the film (or portfolio of films) produced affect the availability and choice of financing type. This section addresses which sources these two types of studios use most often and most successfully as well as how these sources address strategic issues of risk management.

Lenders

Lenders are generally industry-knowledgeable institutions that have specific groups focused on lending for film production. Examples include banks (Imperial Bank/Comerica, Societé Generale) and insurance companies (MetLife, Mariner, American International Group). Because many entities, such as insurance companies, have been disappointed by the returns from lending for film production, the bulk of lending for production since 2000 has come from banks.

The means by which a studio borrows funds often depends on its size and its ability to collateralize any bank loans. Established studios have historically been able to raise capital fairly easily through commercial bank loans for their production facilities. Because of these studios' large corporate structures, they are able to collateralize loans against numerous types of assets, providing them considerable flexibility in financing structures. More specifically, major studios often create a portfolio of films for production that helps diversify the risk of any one particular film.

From the perspective of a lender providing debt capital to a studio, there is a strong preference to lend against a portfolio of films for two main reasons. First, the portfolio provides for cross-collateralization, whereby the exposure to any single film is minimized.[5] Second, portfolio financing provides lenders a better mechanism to avoid adverse selection, known as "cherry picking," by studios that might otherwise ask for outside funding only for the least promising films and internally fund the most promising.

The use of film portfolios for financing is almost exclusively a major-studio phenomenon. Most small studios do not have the scale in resources or production capability to

---

[4]For a detailed overview of financial sources for film production described in this note, see Chapters 3 and 4 of Vogel's *Entertainment Industry Economics*.

[5]"Cross-collateralization" refers to an accounting practice in which major studios finance a portfolio of films together and use the most successful, profitable films to create a reserve fund, a cash trap that helps pay the debt used to produce the least successful films. The mechanics are such that the studio cannot draw profits from the portfolio of films until the reserve fund reaches a certain level (adequate to assure repayment of debt, for example). Instead of paying out on the winners and absorbing the losers, the studio smoothes its earnings across portfolios of films and is able to maintain stronger relationships with lenders. While portfolio financing has risk benefits—it limits the downside effects of any one movie—a studio using it often gives up some of the financial benefits of their highly successful internally financed films. One side effect of such vehicles is that it becomes very difficult to assess the profitability of an individual film. In the event that the studio has agreed to pay other parties based on the profitability of the film, those parties may not be able to collect the fair value based on the *individual* profitability of the film because its profits are first diverted to satisfy the reserve fund requirements.

EXHIBIT 2

SCHEMATIC OF DEBT EQUITY FINANCIAL SOURCES CONTINUUM

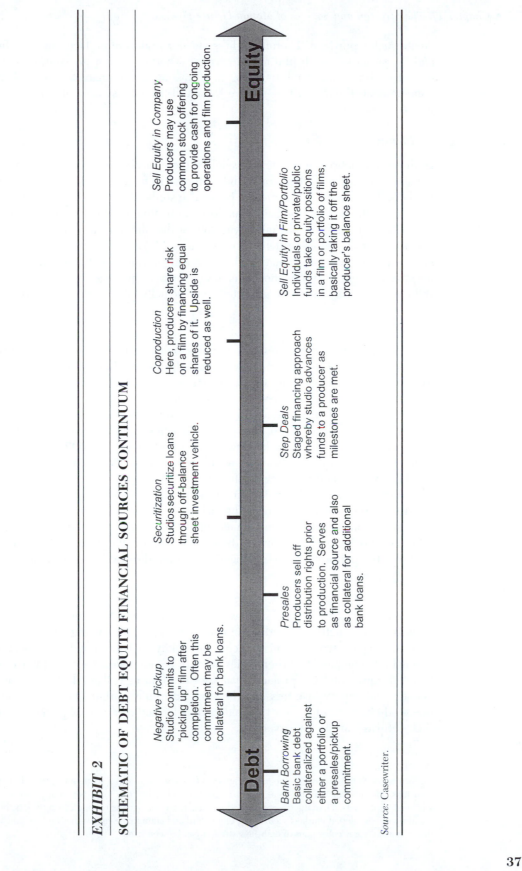

Debt

Bank Borrowing
Basic bank debt collateralized against either a portfolio or a presales/pickup commitment.

Negative Pickup
Studio commits to "picking up" film after completion. Often this commitment may be collateral for bank loans.

Presales
Producers sell off distribution rights prior to production. Serves as financial source and also as collateral for additional bank loans.

Securitization
Studios securitize loans through off-balance sheet investment vehicle.

Step Deals
Staged financing approach whereby studio advances funds to a producer as milestones are met.

Coproduction
Here, producers share risk on a film by financing equal shares of it. Upside is reduced as well.

Sell Equity in Film/Portfolio
Individuals or private/public funds take equity positions in a film or portfolio of films, basically taking it off the producer's balance sheet.

Sell Equity in Company
Producers may use common stock offering to provide cash for ongoing operations and film production.

Equity

Source: Casewriter.

create such a portfolio. Therefore, these smaller studios often face "one-off" financing, and the success of each film may determine whether a company continues as a going concern. Thus, while bank financing may have attractive characteristics relative to financing deals the studio may receive from a distributor, smaller players are less likely to access such sources.

Packages/Negative Pickups

In these transactions, a producer assembles the critical parts of a project and attempts to gain studio interest. Based on a studio promise to finance the film, a producer will often be able to secure a loan from a bank. The studio then "picks up" the film upon its completion, taking over the bank loan (by consolidating it into or financing it with a new loan). While the studio may take ownership of the film after its completion, the film is essentially produced using debt until that time. Major studios rarely need to use such structures due to the availability of debt financing through their parent organizations. In negative pickups, the production company generates a funding source for production but still holds the risk of the film until the studio actually takes out the bank loan.

Presales

Producers and studios often resort to presales to finance their movie without explicit major-studio backing. Here, the company will sell off various exhibition and distribution rights to the completed picture prior to its production. These may include rights to home video, foreign distribution, cable television, pay-per-view, network television, and so on over a specific period (e.g., 5 to 15 years) or up to a gross revenue cap. In addition to rights, presales often include some sort of equity or participation in the film for the distribution partner. As a rule of thumb, presales usually can provide only up to 60% of a film budget in cash;[6] however, they may also serve as collateral against additional bank loans necessary to fill the remaining funding gap. Although presale deals are more prevalent for small studios, they may be used by major studios for areas such as foreign distribution in which the studio prefers to not take on additional performance risk. Presales are based on risk-mitigation motivations. By giving up any upside associated with the distribution rights it sells, a studio "locks in" returns for these rights through the presales. However, the studio holds the performance risks remaining with the distribution rights it keeps.

Securitization

Since the late 1990s, studios such as Fox, Universal, and Dreamworks have used loan securitization structures.[7] Studio film slates serve as the underlying assets for such transactions. A typical structure might include an equity contribution by investors into a limited liability company that then issues notes or commercial paper and pledges the contributed equity and the projected value of the film as collateral. A rights agreement between the equity investors and the studio carefully outlines how the residual cash flows—those remaining after the holders of notes and commercial paper have received their returns—are to be carved up.

[6]Vogel, p. 114.

[7]Securitization is the process of pooling many assets (usually loans) into a single entity, which then issues securities. This is often referred to as asset-backed finance because the entity is issuing securities based on a collection of assets. The largest asset-backed markets use mortgages as the underlying assets, but there are also very developed markets securitizing credit card and automobile receivables and student loans. In theory, virtually any collections of cash flow streams can be securitized.

As a practical matter, major studios are more likely to benefit from these deals because they have both the critical mass of films in production and the ability to handle the financial complexities of the structures. Securitization effectively provides studios with another means of funding their production schedule and taking the costs off their balance sheets; however, while some of the risk may be shared with investors in this way, the underlying film assets still face performance risk for the studio.

Step Deals

This mechanism provides staged financing, in which a studio advances additional funds or may terminate involvement depending on whether or not various criteria (generally, production schedule and budget milestones) are met. Step deals may be done for any production company, studio related or independent. However, the step deal may be fairly risky for a producer, who by the very nature of this deal may be fired by a studio at any point during the development or production of the film. Step deals essentially mitigate the risks for a studio financing the production by providing it with several opportunities to exit its investment or to pursue it further.

Coproductions

Studios and other distributors often make coproduction deals with one another for one or more territories in order to share distribution risk. For example, a domestic and a foreign distributor may "split rights" by each contributing half of a picture's production cost and then being entitled to distribution fees and box office shares in their respective territories.[8] Both small and major studios have increasingly used coproduction since the 1990s as a risk management tool.

Selling Equity in a Film or a Portfolio of Films

A studio can sell partial or complete ownership interests in a film. There are two main types of buyers: individual investors and private/public funds.

Most individual investors associated with film finance help fund smaller, independent productions. However, some high-net-worth investors may provide significant sums of cash for larger-budget films. Although many of these individuals provide funds as an investment on which they expect substantial returns, the historical economics of film investments seldom justify returns as an adequate investment rationale. Additionally, due to the high costs of production, an individual investor is likely to buy significant equity in only one film at a time, rather than in a portfolio.

While private and public funds are also made up of individual investors, here the individuals combine their investments into a fund mandated for certain types of film investments. Most often, these funds take the form of limited partnerships—conduits that allow investors to enjoy income and potential tax benefits from the investments, while limiting their liability to the amount of their initial investment. Depending on the structure, funds may hold a perpetual equity ownership stake in a film or may own a film only as part of a sale-leaseback transaction. Funds have the capital to invest not only in individual films but also in large film portfolios (e.g., Disney's Silver Screen IV partnership

---

[8]Depending on the deal and the film's success, these deals may be profitable for all parties or only for some. Indeed, while studios may enter into coproduction deals to share downside risk, these may prove very costly in the event that a film is extremely successful. Disney faced this problem when *The Sixth Sense* brought in over $200 million at the domestic box office, but the studio had to share revenues above a certain threshold with Spyglass, which cofinanced the surprisingly successful film.

raised $400 million for 33 films in 1987).[9] While limited-partnership funds have faded in popularity in the United States, large numbers exist in countries such as the United Kingdom and Germany, where they provide significant tax benefits for individual investors.

Common Stock *Offerings*

Raising capital through common stock offerings has historically been a difficult task because of (1) the long time horizon for any significant return on investment, (2) the hit-or-miss nature of films as assets, and (3) the low value of the initial associated assets (the film itself is often the only tangible asset and may be several years in the making). However, in bullish markets, individual investors may be attracted to the excitement and risk of a small investment in a production. For example, Kings Road Entertainment successfully completed an IPO in 1985 for 1.5 million shares priced at $10 per share, with several films and some optioned screenplays as assets.[10] In 1986, DeLaurentiis Entertainment sold 1.85 million shares of common stock as well as $65 million in 12.5% subordinated debentures, listing as its primary asset a large previously acquired film library.[11]

Major studios have generally refrained from offering common stock, perhaps because their parent media groups were already publicly held. As such, it is independent studios that are most likely to take advantage of this source of financing. Recent examples of independents selling common stock include Internationalmedia AG on the German Neuer Market in May of 2000 and Pixar Animation Studios in the United States in November of 1995.

TAX-MOTIVATED INNOVATION IN U.S. MOTION PICTURE FINANCE

Historically, films in Hollywood were most commonly funded from internal cash flows or through bank loans. While this worked for many years when studios had control over exhibition and when films were relatively inexpensive to produce, once film costs and interest rates began rising, the studios began to struggle financially. When the government stepped in with tax-related legislation during the 1970s, alternative methods of financing became more popular (see Exhibit 3 for a timeline of the evolution of film-financing structures).

U.S. Tax Incentives

The use of tax incentives for films began in the United States during the early 1970s when the government provided specific incentives for small business through the tax code. While independent producers making low-budget films initially used these tax incentives, the major studios began to capitalize upon them in 1975, with Columbia Pictures and United Artists funding films such as *Taxi Driver*, *The Man Who Would be King*, and *Sinbad and the Eye of the Tiger*.[12] The government permitted "gearing," through which an investor could leverage his or her investment and gain a tax write-off in excess of the initial outlay. For example, for every dollar invested by an individual, $3 could be borrowed, and the investor was then able to write off the full $4.

For entities unable to access such loans, nonrecourse loans were used as a substitute for gearing. Nonrecourse loans were loans granted to the producers or studios based

[9]Silver Screen Partners IV 10-K, 1997.

[10]Vogel, p. 75.

[11]Vogel, p. 76.

[12]Martin Dale, *The Movie Game* (London, U.K.: Cassell, 1997), p. 295.

EXHIBIT 3

TIMELINE OF ALTERNATIVE U.S. FILM FINANCING

Historical Financing

Internally Generated Cash Flow and Bank Borrowing were the traditional sources of funding for most producers

Pre-1976

Tax Shelters and gearing allowed investors to write off even more than their invested capital. Using tax shelters made a return on this investment unnecessary and led to many abuses

1976

The U.S. government passed laws making it necessary to have money "at risk" in order to qualify for tax shelters. The investment tax credit and the Small Business Administration (SBA) allowed companies to gain not only write-offs but government loans and tax credits for investments that included films.

1977

Goldcrest Films and International Film Investors raised $10 million from investors and borrowed another $25 million from the SBA through a limited-partnership fund

1981–1987

During this period, approximately 19 limited partnerships were created by companies such as Delphi and Silver Screen Partners in order to take advantage of some tax benefits but also for potential returns on invested capital.

1986

Tax Reform Act of 1986 instituted the end of investment tax credits and passive loss rules, which prevented losses from passive investments from offsetting ordinary income. This made limited partnerships based on tax shelters obsolete

1987

Black Monday—October 19, 1987. The U.S. stock markets crashed, with the Dow Jones Industrial Average losing 23% of its value. After this, many individual investors became wary of film investments, especially with no significant tax benefits. No public limited partnerships created in U.S. after this time.

1990

Disney made a $600 million equity/debt offering to Touchwood—representing a group of Japanese investors seeking tax benefits.

Mid-1990s

Disney raised $400 in Eurobond offering with contingent interest. Fox used $960 New Millennium credit revolver for film working capital needs. Completion bonds used as guarantees to complete films within a certain budget.

1998-2001

Numerous countries, including the U.K., Ireland, the Netherlands, Australia, Canada, and Iceland, created incentives to produce movies in their respective countries. "Runaway production" in countries such as Canada became a common trend

Source: Casewriter.

on the success of the film itself, with no personal liability. Numerous investors used these nonrecourse loans to leverage their tax-offsetting losses without having to be responsible for the extra cash. With marginal tax rates approaching 70% at the time for individuals in the highest tax brackets, in addition to the ego satisfaction of investing in movies, there existed a powerful incentive for investment in tax-motivated film vehicles.

In 1976, however, after numerous abuses by individuals and organizations,[13] the government repealed its support of gearing and also created "at risk" rules, limiting direct write-offs to invested capital. However, the government did establish two other sources of financing that were used by the film industry—investment tax credits (ITCs) and the Small Business Administration (SBA). Disney won two key court cases in 1974 and 1976 that set the precedent for feature films to be accepted as capital assets for purposes of depreciation schedules and the ITC. Films were subsequently written off over a three-year useful life by investors. Additionally, the investors were able to write off an additional 6.67% credit against their investment, as long as 80% of the picture was produced in the United States.[14] Some producers managed to increase this credit to 10% in the mid-1980s. The ITC, therefore, served as a stimulus for independent U.S. production and curbed runaway production toward Canada and Europe.[15] Moreover, the ITC was most effective in combination with the SBA, which was designed to stimulate small business through government-subsidized loans. International Film Investors, set up in 1977 by Jake Eberts of Goldcrest Films and Josiah Childs, used the SBA to create a fund worth $35 million and used it to produce such films as *Gandhi* and *The Killing Fields*.[16]

The 1986 Tax Reform Act repealed the ITC and additionally instituted the "passive loss rules." These rules stated that passive losses (losses in which investors had no active role in managing the investment) could no longer be used to offset ordinary wage, salary, interest, or dividend income. Accordingly, tax-motivated transactions in film financing all but disappeared after 1986 in the United States. However, as described later in this note, the tax incentives adopted in many foreign countries in the 1990s imported these original U.S. structures and ultimately stimulated runaway production.

Limited Partnerships and Off-Balance Sheet Financing

Limited partnerships were the dominant structure used by investors to take advantage of tax incentives from the 1970s through the mid-1980s because they limited investors' liability to the amount invested. However, while tax incentives intended for small studios and producers were rolled back during the mid-1980s, profit-motivated rather than tax-motivated limited partnerships began to proliferate among the major studios. As film costs continued to increase rapidly during this period, limited partnerships played a substantial role in financing Hollywood studios.

During a short bubble from 1981 to 1986, 19 limited partnerships involving major studios were created. As Exhibit 4a and Exhibit 4b show, over $1.7 billion was raised

---

[13]For example, in *Burpee vs. Commissioner* the defendant, a chiropractor, invested approximately $100,000 in a movie entitled *The Adultress* and used a nonrecourse loan to shield over $700,000 of his income. The film never came close to paying back the nonrecourse loan, and Burpee was eventually forced to pay back taxes on the movie investment, which was deemed to have a value of only $25,000.

[14]Dale, p. 296.

[15]Runaway production is considered to be U.S. studio production that takes place in other countries in order to take advantage of investment, labor, and tax incentives.

[16]Jake Eberts and Terry Ilott, *My Indecision is Final: The Spectacular Rise and Fall of Goldcrest Films, the Independent Studio that Challenged Hollywood* (New York: The Atlantic Monthly Press, 1990), p. 40.

EXHIBIT 4A

NUMBER OF LIMITED-PARTNERSHIP FILMS CREATED IN THE UNITED STATES

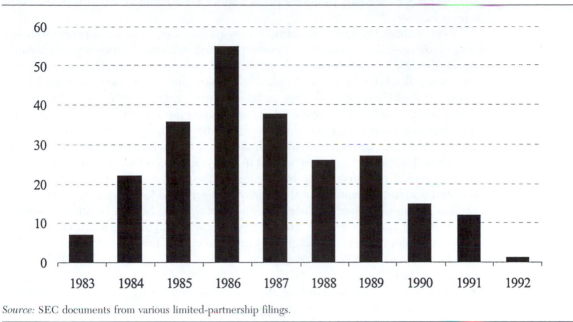

Source: SEC documents from various limited-partnership filings.

EXHIBIT 4B

DOLLAR AMOUNT OF FUNDS RAISED IN U.S. FILM-RELATED LIMITED PARTNERSHIPS ($ MILLIONS)

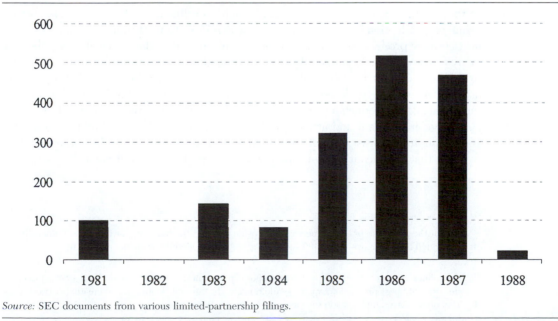

Source: SEC documents from various limited-partnership filings.

during this period, with funds investing in over 230 films, including *Poltergeist*, *The Karate Kid*, *Flashdance*, *Ghostbusters*, and *Crocodile Dundee*.[17] While numerous studios, including Columbia-TriStar and HBO, used these limited partnerships, Disney garnered the most funds from this period, with over $1 billion raised through Silver Screen Partners.[18]

Even without tax-related benefits, limited-partnership financing appealed to major studios for several reasons. First, limited-partnership financing was kept off balance sheets, thereby helping studios to keep their balance sheets clean while also allowing them some flexibility to borrow funds, if necessary, for nonpartnership-related films. Second, the additional capital from partnerships allowed for further diversification of production portfolios. With expanded cash resources, the studios were able to produce more films for their related distribution organizations. Finally, studios were often able to cover their fixed costs on films through distribution earn-outs and other mechanisms, even if the limited partners were unable to earn a return on their investments.

In a typical partnership, the invested capital would be allocated to specific films. The studio would guarantee that the principal be returned to investors in five years regardless of the films' performances (therefore precluding any tax benefit because no money was technically "at risk"). However, often the studio insisted on capping the upside that the limited partners might receive—the typical fund earned a relatively low cumulative return over its life (e.g., Silver Screen funds averaged a 13%–18% return over five years).[19]

After the stock market crash of 1987, investors were wary of investing in the hit-or-miss movie business and limited-partnership funds evaporated as a funding source for major studios. Subsequently, while a few studios managed to raise significant capital through methods such as common stock offerings (e.g., Pixar and Internationalmedia IPOs), most studios returned to the traditional means of financing, through internal cash flow and bank financing relationships.

Foreign Tax Incentives and Runaway Production

In the 1990s, U.S. studios began innovating and film financing started to move abroad. While co-production had always existed, in which U.S. studios produced abroad through host country production facilities, incentives introduced in the 1990s changed the way many films were made abroad. As of 2002, many foreign countries (see Exhibit 5), desiring the economic benefits that film production provides,[20] began marketing existing tax incentives (e.g., Goldcrest used tax-based sale-leasebacks in the United Kingdom to fund some of its productions in the late 1970s) as well as creating new ones that would encourage investment and attract production activity by U.S. studios. Disney's 1990 $600 million Touchwood equity and nonrecourse debt offering to Japanese investors signaled that significant foreign capital would be available to Hollywood.[21]

[17]Limited-partnership SEC filings.

[18]Note that the partnerships did not necessarily provide 100% of the financing for the films. Rather, they often provided a large share—up to 40%—while the studio provided the remainder of the funds.

[19]Dale, p. 297.

[20]Film productions involve capital investments, labor expenses in the country where filming takes place, and also pre- and post-production expenses. Additionally, the cultural significance of creating "British" or "Irish" content, for example, is also seen as important for national pride.

[21]Lisa Gubernick, "Mickey Mouse's sharp pencil," *Forbes*, January 7, 1991, p. 39.

EXHIBIT 5

EXAMPLES OF INTERNATIONAL FILM-BASED TAX INCENTIVES

Country	Benefit	Requirements	Regime Dates
U.K.	• 100% capital allowances		• 1979–1984
	• Business-expansion scheme—maximum write-off of £40,000 at tax rate up to 40%	• Only £750,000 could be raised this way • Shares had to be held for 5 years and could then be sold free of capital gains taxes	• 1984–1992
	• Section 42—Allows all investment in British movies to be written off over three years	• No minimum British cultural content • 70% of total production costs must be spent on activity carried out in the U.K. • At least 70% of total labor cost must be payable to citizens in the U.K., the EU, or a Commonwealth country	• 1992–Present
	• Section 48—Allows 100% of investment to be written off in first year, if qualifying British film and less than £15M	• Similar requirements as above • Often combined with sale-leasebacks and limited partnerships, which allow tax breaks at higher personal rates	• 1997–2005
Australia	• Division 10BA—Taxpayers resident in Australia are provided a deduction of 100% of an investment in the year of expenditure for qualifying Australian films	• Must be feature film for exhibition in cinemas or TV • Investment must not be made in obtaining an initial copyright interest • Made wholly or substantially in Australia, with significant Australian content, or by agreement between Australia and government of another country	• 1936–Present
	• Division 10B—For those ineligible for 10BA provides write-off of capital expenditure in acquiring rights over two years	• Similar to above requirements • Recently, usage of this provision through film special-purpose companies was prohibited due to tax avoidance	• 1936–Present
	• Canadian-style rebate fixed at 12.5% for qualifying expenditure on films	• Films $A15M–$A50M must spend 70% of budget in Australia • Cannot get both 10B and this rebate—one or the other	• 2001–Present
Ireland	• Section 481—Allows investors tax deduction for investment in qualifying films (80% against total profits in period in which investment is made) • Based on a sliding scale—only a certain percentage of budget is allowed to be raised this way	• Production company must be incorporated and be a tax resident in Ireland (and nowhere else) • Company must exist solely to produce films • Must be produced for exhibition through public • Films must be certified by Minister of Arts and Heritage • 75% of production work must take place in Ireland	• 1997–Present
	• 10% tax on profits—to companies involved in manufacturing, including film production	• Must be a production company that produces films for theatrical or television release • 75% of the production work must take place in Ireland	• Present–2010

(Continued)

379

EXHIBIT 5 (*Continued*)

EXAMPLES OF INTERNATIONAL FILM-BASED TAX INCENTIVES

Country	Benefit	Requirements	Regime Dates
Canada	• Federal Canadian Film Tax Credit—tax credits available for film productions that qualify as distinctly Canadian • Film tax credit is equal to 25% of qualified labor expenditures, with eligible labor expenditures limited to 48% of total budget (maximum 12% of total negative cost) • Noncertified tax credit—related to certified tax credit, but different restrictions • New legislation will likely wipe out loopholes in the law that allow for U.S. studios to shelter tax (2001) • Almost all provinces have their own incentives in addition to the federal laws	• Productions must qualify for "Canadian" status according to complex point system • Audio-Visual Certification Office must certify production • Productions must be completed within two years after the end of the tax year in which photography started • 75% of total remuneration must be paid to services provided by Canadians • Canadians must own 100% of copyrights • For noncertified tax credit, costs must exceed CN$1M, main activity of corporation must be film production, and a significant portion of Canadian labor must be hired. The only dollars that receive any benefit are based on the services rendered by Canadian citizens	• 1996–Present
Netherlands	• Contribution to any Dutch film production considered subordinated loan with full repayment obligation • Entrepreneurs entitled to accelerated depreciation on production costs • Film-related partnership liquidation proceeds may be realized partially tax free • Sale-leasebacks similar to U.K. schemes	• Only up to 50% of the budget may be funded through the tax incentive (70% prior to 1/1/2002) • As of 1/1/2002, 50% of budget must be spent in Holland • 50% of the funding must come from Dutch sources	• 1998–Present • 2001–Present

(*Continued*)

EXHIBIT 5 *(Continued)*

EXAMPLES OF INTERNATIONAL FILM-BASED TAX INCENTIVES

Country	Benefit	Requirements	Regime Dates
Germany	• Pre-1999—Up to 200% of actual losses could be allocated to specific investments • No general restrictions on loss compensation or deduction	• No specific German qualifications	• Pre-1999
	• Tax Amendment of 1999—Cut tax-saving opportunities with funds for ship, plane, and other financing, but left 100% deductibility for film investment • March 2001 Amendment—Added new criteria for film investment, while still allowing investors 100% deductibility if criteria met against income	• No German qualifications for content, production, or labor • Investment deductible for films because it is for intangible film rights assets • Funds must be set up as a limited partnership • Fund must be the actual producer of the movie—responsible for all business risks and decisions • Fund must be involved in film before production • Fund must retain rights to film property • Fund's main purpose must be to make a profit—otherwise, it is considered tax avoidance	• 1999–Present
Iceland	• 24% VAT tax refunded on production costs spent in Iceland • 12% rebate available on film production costs spent in Iceland	• Previously, 80% of production budget had to be spent in Iceland • After May 2001, any production costs are eligible for rebate	• 2001–Present
	• When 80% of total production costs are spent in Iceland, any money above that spent in the EU, Iceland, Norway, and Liechtenstein is also eligible for 12% rebate • 5% tax on income	• Companies must set up an international trading company for distribution	• Previously existing

Source: Adapted from *The Ernst & Young Guide to International Film Production*, Ernst & Young, 2001 edition.

As Exhibit 5 describes, the incentives for U.S. studios range from tax rebates to studios to accelerated depreciation for investors. Requirements for these benefits vary by country, with some countries—such as Germany—having no specific production requirements at all. Many movies have been produced using these incentives, including *Braveheart* (Ireland), *The Matrix* (Australia), and *Shallow Hal* (Germany), although the laws surrounding the benefits are constantly in a state of flux.[22]

The trend toward runaway production in the late 1990s created by these incentives has become a major concern for U.S. film-industry labor groups, who are adversely affected. These groups are lobbying Congress now to reinstate various federal incentives for U.S. production. However, at present, foreign incentives and the capital provided are powerful mechanisms that keep U.S. studios producing abroad. Two illustrative cases involving the use of foreign incentives for production are those of Canada and Germany, each of which uses tax incentives for different reasons and with different results.

Canada

Runaway production has been almost defined since the late 1990s by Canada, which offers not only broad tax incentives for U.S. production (see Exhibit 5) but also a more cost-effective means of production. Production in countries such as Australia and the United Kingdom is often based on films whose story lines fit with these locales; however, proximity, cheaper labor, an established infrastructure, and an English-speaking workforce make production in Canada an excellent substitute for production in the more expensive United States. Reflecting this trend, 37 feature films were made in Canada in 2000, up from 18 in 1999. At the same time, the number of movies made in the United States fell from 122 to 108. Moreover, American filmmakers accounted for about 85% of the $1.1 billion spent on foreign productions in Canada in the year ended March 2001. While U.S. studios have increasingly used Canadian production since the late 1990s, U.S. labor unions and other groups have been lobbying heavily for change, including tariffs on such production exportation.[23]

Germany

The market for film funds has exploded in Germany over the past two years. In 2000 and 2001 alone, at least 22 funds have closed, raising almost $2.5 billion. U.S. studios have been tapping into this pool, which provided funding for 15%–20% of all Hollywood-made movies in 2001.[24] Two tax amendments—one in 1999 and one in 2001—have allowed films to keep certain tax advantages whereby they are considered intangible assets. Investments in intangible assets are required to be expensed in the year incurred. As such, in limited-partnership film funds, 100% of investments must be deducted from

---

[22]Foreign-partnership financing creates the same adverse selection incentives that faced limited partnerships in the 1980s. For example, Disney refused to allow Silver Screen Partners to invest in its animated films, historically its largest and most predictable box office winners, but it did allow investments in such films as *Turner and Hooch* and *Ernest Goes to Camp*—both box office flops. As a consequence, studios are increasingly asked to share in the risk exposure of the films.

[23]Bernard Simon, "Using Tariffs to Discourage Movie Production Outside the U.S.," *The New York Times*, March 29, 2002.

[24]Bernard Tubeileh and Stephan Seip, "German Film Funds: Competition or Co-Operation for Film Companies?" Merrill Lynch & Co., October 4, 2001, p. 5.

taxes in the year the investment is made. Moreover, leverage may be used within the limited partnership to increase the tax deduction for each individual investor.[25]

While the benefits have remained in Germany since 1999, new requirements have made it more difficult for film funds and their limited partners to successfully qualify for tax incentives. Two major requirements are critical in order to qualify under the provision:

- *Producer attribution.* In order to qualify for any tax deductions, the fund itself must legally be the producer for the movie. That is, the fund must bear the financial risk of the film and must also make all the essential production decisions. In fact, the U.S. studio is usually "hired" to produce the film on behalf of the fund.

- *Profit intent.* The fund may not be advertised or intended to be a "tax-avoidance" scheme. Here, the burden of proof is on the fund itself. Detailed prospectuses, with calculated expected returns and minimum guaranteed revenues, must be provided to investors. Moreover, post-tax profits must not exceed twice the pretax profit in order to avoid being classified as a tax-avoidance device.

Funding models in Germany have moved from straight sale-leaseback mechanisms in 1999 to more equity-based approaches in 2001 and 2002.

---

[25]For German taxpayers, there are considerable cash flow consequences as well as tax savings from these transactions given the importance of advance payments made on estimated taxes. Interview with Michael Braun, president of Media Entertainment Funding GmbH, February 2002.

PART 4

INSTITUTIONS AND FINANCE

The interaction between institutions and finance is apparent in the cases throughout this book. The role of the Monetary Authority of Singapore in determining that country's exchange rate is one example of such an interaction. Other examples include the ways in which the financing of Shanghai General Motors was influenced by Chinese foreign exchange controls and business ownership restrictions, and how the tax policies of the German government created a financing opportunity for Rexford Studios.

In this section, the case studies look at institutions and their influence on finance more broadly. Specifically, a growing body of scholarship in finance and economics examines how the laws that govern investor protections and the contractual environment more generally impact the depth of capital markets, the size and growth trajectories of firms, and the growth rates of countries. This scholarship has emphasized large-sample studies, and this part of the book shows how many of these results are manifest in the experiences of firms in these uncertain institutional environments. In addition, multinational firms can avail themselves of several legal regimes; the cases in this chapter discuss how overlapping legal regimes can create opportunities and difficulties for multinational firms.

FINANCE IN WEAK INSTITUTIONAL ENVIRONMENTS

The institutional environment facing firms differs markedly around the world. Investor protections, regulatory obstacles, the ability to enforce contracts and protections from state expropriation all vary tremendously globally. This variation in contractual and property rights institutions must be addressed globally by firm strategies, their financing decisions, and by investors contemplating entering these markets. Firms unfamiliar with the prevailing 'rules of the game' are likely to suffer. But how should firms and investors respond? And what recourse do they have in a globalized world when they are expropriated?

The two cases in this module explore how firms respond to the institutional setting in which they operate and how firms are influenced by their institutional environment. The first case, Growing Up in China: The Financing of BabyCare Ltd., looks at a company that has developed a unique model to deal with the challenges of doing business in China but finds it challenging to raise third-round expansion capital. The case considers how this business model deals with the absence of safeguards common in better institutional environments and how the negotiations between entrepreneurs and venture capitalists reflect the institutional environment.

The following chapters, Czech Mate: CME and Vladimir Zelezny (A–E) explore investment in a newly privatized Czech television station. Although the TV station became enormously successful, the combination of a strong local partner and the Czech Republic's weak investor protections almost destroyed CME. In addition to depicting the mechanisms of an expropriation, these cases also afford a unique perspective on the tools available to international investors in recouping their investment. The cases in this section offer a glimpse at some of the issues confronting firms that operate in different institutional environments—one where the market for entrepreneurial finance is undeveloped, and the other in a legal regime that fails to protect basic property rights.

OVERVIEW OF THE CASES

Growing Up in China: The Financing of BabyCare Ltd.

This case explores the dynamics of venture capital and entrepreneurial finance in China and provides a rigorous valuation exercise. Christopher Mumford, the CFO of this infant nutritional products company, must choose among competing financing offers. The interplay of Chinese legal and customs restrictions and venture capitalists' bargaining techniques challenges the CFO to navigate a tricky negotiation and to devise a unique business model given these constraints. Underpinning the case is a valuation exercise involving a subscriber model of the business that tests core business assumptions and assesses the temporal distribution of funding needs and how milestones affect the choice of which term sheet to accept. The case also highlights some of the difficult questions a discerning venture capitalist might ask, requiring the CFO to justify his overall business model and working-capital needs. To help understand how venture capital and entrepreneurial finance differ in an emerging market setting, consider the following questions:

- What are the specific differences between venture capital transactions in developing markets relative to more advanced markets?
- How is (or isn't) BabyCare's business model tailored to the idiosyncrasies of an emerging market?
- How would you value BabyCare using a subscriber model? Is a subscriber model useful here or not?
- How would you evaluate funding opportunities as Mumford?

Czech Mate: CME and Vladimir Zelezny (A–E)

These cases examine how insiders can expropriate value from shareholders in emerging markets when property rights are ill defined. As such, they provide a platform for considering how institutions and legal rules impact financing patterns and economic outcomes. CME, controlled by the former U.S. ambassador to Austria, Ronald Lauder, and its Czech partners won the bidding for the first private broadcast frequency with national coverage in the Czech Republic in 1993. The Czech Media Council approved a split structure for the new station: the broadcast license was held by a Czech-owned company, and CME created a separate company to operate the station. The operating company had exclusive use of the broadcast license. The new station, called TV Nova, became wildly popular under the direction of Dr. Vladimir Zelezny. TV Nova gained a 70% audience share within a year of its launch and had strong advertising revenues. Several of CME's original local partners sold out to CME, and it accumulated over 93% ownership of TV Nova's operating company. Now, Zelezny also wants to sell his shares in TV Nova's operating company. He is willing to sell the shares to CME but claims there are other interested buyers. Zelezny is largely responsible for TV Nova's remarkable success, and CME does not want to jeopardize its relationship with him. However, CME is not eager to buy his shares. It already owns 93.2% of the station's operating company and does not want to provoke controversy over complete foreign ownership of the country's most popular television station. Also, since Zelezny controls the company that holds TV Nova's license, his ownership interest in the station's operating company helps ensure continued agreement between TV Nova's license holder and operating company. The CEO of CME must decide whether to purchase Zelezny's shares and, if so, what price to offer to Zelezny.

The B-series of cases deal with merger talks in which CME is engaged with SBS, a European broadcasting company. These cases present the issues surrounding the merger from the perspectives of CME, SBS, and Vladimir Zelezny. The C case explores the increasing tension between CME and its local partner, Zelezny, and the D and E cases provide the final chapter of the CME story. After CME fails to recover control of its investment in TV Nova through the Czech courts, it turns to international arbitration tribunals for redress. The company requests arbitration from the International Chamber of Commerce in its complaint against Zelezny. CME also requests arbitration according to the terms of investment treaties between the Czech Republic and the United States, and the Czech Republic and the Netherlands. It charges the Czech Republic with failing to protect its legal investment in TV Nova. The various tribunals issued different decisions in each case. "The Stockholm Tribunal" found in favor of CME and in May 2003 ruled that the company was entitled to compensation totaling $354.9 million from the Czech Republic.

This series of cases chronicles the difficulties that foreign investors can face entering unfamiliar turf. The following questions are useful in identifying some of the key issues in this series of cases:

- What value is Vladimir Zelezny providing to TV Nova?
- What value is CME providing to TV Nova?
- As CME, would you purchase the shares from Zelezny? If so, what would you worry about? If not, what would you worry about?

ADDITIONAL READING

DESAI, MIHIR A., AND ALBERTO MOEL. 2004. "Czech Mate: Expropriation and Investor Protection in a Converging World." ECGI Working Paper Series, No. 62/2004.

GLAESER, E., S. JOHNSON, AND A. SHLEIFER. 2001. "Coase vs. the Coasians." *Quarterly Journal of Economics,* 116: 853–899.

HANSMANN, H., AND R. KRAAKMAN. 2001. "The End of History for Corporate Law." *Georgetown Law Journal,* 89: 439–469.

KAPLAN, STEVEN N., AND PER STROMBERG. 2004. "Characteristics, Contracts, and Actions: Evidence from Venture Capitalist Analyses." *Journal of Finance,* 59(5): 2177–2210.

LAPORTA, RAFAEL, et al. 1997. "Legal Determinants of External Finance." *The Journal of Finance,* 52(3): 1131–1151.

LERNER, JOSH, AND ANTOINETTE SCHOAR. 2004. "The Illiquidity Puzzle: Theory and Evidence from Private Equity." *Journal of Financial Economics*, 72 (April): 3–40.

Growing Up in China: The Financing of BabyCare Ltd.

On June 26, 2002, Chris Mumford, Chief Financial Officer of BabyCare Ltd., returned to the office with Chief Executive Officer Matthew Estes after a long day of meetings with Franklin Templeton Investments, a potential third-round investor. The two executives were seeking $2–$3 million of expansion capital to fund the first major wave of new center openings in large cities throughout China. BabyCare had already received two term sheets from potential investors. Any offer would have to be approved by the board, which was ready to approve a small financing from current shareholders at a low valuation, thereby diluting management's stake significantly. Mumford and Estes were hoping that Templeton would come through with a better offer than those on the table.

The partner spearheading the Templeton team was Choong-Huei Seow. Seow wanted to focus on several key assumptions in the BabyCare valuation. Mumford and Estes had built their model based on top-line revenue estimates derived from average sales per salesperson and growth in salespeople rather than customer additions and purchase rates; Seow wanted to see a reconciliation of the two methods. This would give Seow an immediate sanity check on whether the revenue growth assumptions corresponded to realistic operating growth of the business. In large part, Seow's concern stemmed from the lack of comparable sales data to benchmark BabyCare against other companies. A second line of inquiry developed out of Mumford's presentation on the rapid cash cycle of the business and its zero-receivables model. Seow questioned why BabyCare had working capital funding requirements—after all, shouldn't a cash business be light on working capital?

Despite these two open questions, Estes and Mumford felt confident they had highlighted the big picture—why BabyCare's business model was so well adapted to the emerging markets environment and how it capitalized on obstacles unique to China. Estes touted BabyCare's promising future to establish itself as the premium brand of nutritional and vitamin supplements for the lucrative mother-and-child segment. BabyCare also provided training and health education to current and expecting parents. While this demographic group supported the business proposition, actually executing

Professor Mihir A. Desai and Research Associate Mark F. Veblen prepared this case. HBS cases are developed solely as the basis for class discussion. Cases are not intended to serve as endorsements, sources of primary data, or illustrations of effective or ineffective management.

in China proved to be a significant challenge. Venture stage financing was still uncommon in the Chinese business environment, and inefficient distribution channels and tight regulations complicated implementing the business plan.

ABOUT BABYCARE

Mumford and Estes originally met while studying Mandarin in Taiwan in 1991. Over the years they discussed a number of ways of working together, and in 1996, Estes approached Mumford with the BabyCare concept. The three founders who had originally developed the business idea were: (1) Estes, previously the head of hospital marketing and sales for SmithKline Beecham and then Managing Director of Wella Cosmetics–Greater China; (2) Michael McNabb, a Managing Director of Coopers & Lybrand Consulting; and (3) Vivek Kapur, one of the first foreign brand managers of Proctor & Gamble and subsequent Marketing Director of Heinz.[1]

The BabyCare concept was a novel business model that would directly address the real-world challenges to be overcome in achieving profitability in China, the world's largest baby care market. First, the concept relied upon a unique sales strategy of direct marketing. Second, the underlying economics were far more favorable than those of a normal consumer products company because BabyCare controlled distribution internally. Third, the plan sought to capitalize on a keen understanding of the dynamics of the Chinese consumer products market by focusing on the fundamental consumer need.

The BabyCare business grew to fill a market demand for information and products to help mothers, each of whom wanted to provide the very best care for her only child.[2] BabyCare delivered a product line of premium nutritional products via a well-trained direct sales force that was equipped to answer the consumer's need for information on pregnancy and child rearing. Training courses offered in BabyCare Centers by medical professionals on child nutrition, physical development, and other related topics supported branded product sales in four categories: (1) "Nutrimed" nutritional supplements, (2) "Naturesource" formula and protein drinks, (3) "DQ 168" educational toys, and (4) BabyCare breast-feeding accessories.[3]

In effect, BabyCare offered an "implicit promise that if a woman followed this program from her first trimester of pregnancy through the baby's early childhood, her child would have the best opportunity to develop to his or her fullest potential."[4] The dimensions of developmental potential included nutritional and physical fitness, intellectual capacity, and emotional intelligence.

---

[1]Wella was one of the world's leading cosmetics suppliers, focused on the hair and beauty products segment for both consumers and salon professionals. It employed 17,000 people in R&D, manufacturing, and distribution spread across 48 countries. Its products were ultimately distributed in over 150 countries.

[2]China was unique in that the government enforced a one-child policy to control population growth. This policy had long been highly controversial both inside and outside of China, because it raised a host of human rights concerns. (See ⟨http://axe.acadiau.ca/~043638z/one-child/links.html⟩ for references to perspectives from both the Chinese government and those opposing the policy.)

[3]The breast-feeding accessories product line was offered through an exclusive arrangement with the world's second largest player in the market for breast-feeding accessories. The relative health impact on a baby of consuming breast milk versus formula was also an internationally contentious issue, and the United Nations and World Health Organization had both taken stances opposing aggressive promotion of formula by multinationals. (See "Promoting proper feeding for infants and young children," March 13, 2002, available at ⟨http://www.who.int/⟩.) BabyCare's policy was to encourage breast feeding and to explicitly discuss in its training sessions and sales promotions scientific evidence supporting the claim that it was definitively better for babies than formula.

[4]Source: BabyCare information memorandum.

UNIQUE SALES STRATEGY

Unlike traditional consumer products companies in China that relied on distributors, wholesalers, and retailers, BabyCare took a direct approach to selling, handling every stage of the supply chain from packaging to the sale to end-customers. Customer representatives who were BabyCare employees formed the core of the sales and distribution mechanism. Customer representatives were responsible for attracting new customers, maintaining customer relationships, and recruiting and managing "downline" customer representatives.[5] Accordingly, their compensation reflected their performance in these three categories. Commissions were structured to reward customer recruitment, with customer representatives keeping 20% of sales to new customers, 10% of sales to repeat customers, and additional awards based on performance. Performance levels triggered automatic promotions, giving a customer representative a monthly base salary and the ability to recruit downlines whose performance could increase the rep's earnings.

The Chinese government was initially receptive to the direct selling model, one that had developed in the United States in the 1950s, because it relied on employing large numbers of people. Soon, however, the Chinese government reversed course for two reasons: (1) pyramid schemes appeared, and (2) it was difficult to enforce and collect the value-added tax applied to the final sale of goods. In 1998, regulations were passed that banned "multi-level marketing" (MLM) organizations.[6] Legitimate direct marketing businesses were allowed to open retail outlets and thereby operate essentially as hybrid retail-MLMs. BabyCare obtained a national license as a manufacturing entity that was allowed to open its own sales outlets, selling its own branded products.

BabyCare's direct-to-consumer model differed from typical MLMs in several key respects:

1. All BabyCare products were sold at standard retail prices at BabyCare centers. MLMs, on the other hand, marked up the price at each level (from manufacturer to sales rep and then again from sales rep to consumer). The government preferred standard retail prices because they facilitated collecting the appropriate sales tax.

2. BabyCare customer reps were bona fide employees who received a base salary and benefits. MLM companies instead used agent relationships with their sales force. The government strongly preferred the traditional employer-employee relationship rather than agent relationships.

The economics associated with the position, however, were trumped by the fact that most customer representatives were mothers themselves. They identified with their customers. They were enthusiastic about sharing advice and information. At the same time as they were providing meaningful income to their own families, they were also helping other mothers. Mumford attributed much of BabyCare's success to developing a model that recognized the emotional nature of this time in a woman's life and supported it by developing trusting relationships that provided honest and accurate health advice. As Mumford elaborated:

---

[5]As in many direct marketing organizations, customer representatives were compensated both on their own performance and on the performance of customer representatives they recruited. In this sense, every customer representative had a network of "downlines" whom they had recruited.

[6]Multi-level marketing referred to organizations in which one salesperson derived compensation both from his or her own selling activity and also from the selling activities of salespeople he or she was able to recruit and bring into the organization. MLM and direct marketing frequently overlapped.

It is universal. Mothers tend to spend time with other mothers. While the information sharing is important, the emotion sharing is a must. We have found that groups of mothers with same-age children create tight communities. The emotive bond tied in with capitalism makes a very convincing business model. What is more emotional than talking about your child?

Staff

The typical customer representative was female, age 25 to 40, with a secondary education, and ideally a mother. At a time when many traditional positions did not offer job security or benefits, BabyCare provided the rep with full benefits, continuous training and development, and an opportunity to earn significantly more than her peers. BabyCare regularly attracted top sales staff from organizations such as Amway, Mary Kay, and Avon (all of which operate profitable businesses in China), as well as pharmaceutical companies.

Retail Centers

While rewarding for the employee, the BabyCare model also benefited the business overall. BabyCare was able to move a high volume of sales through a relatively small retail space adjacent to the training facilities that drew mothers into the center. Typically, the customer reps made purchases on behalf of members using the members' cards—allowing BabyCare's member database to track each member's purchases—and then delivered the products personally. These visits to customers' homes and offices by customer reps provided BabyCare with a direct-to-consumer delivery system that was much less expensive than the distribution methods used by traditional consumer products companies and also strengthened the connection to members.

The prototype BabyCare center had a carefully planned design, providing for retail space where product samples were displayed, conference- and theater-style presentation rooms with audio-visual equipment to hold mother and child training sessions for large groups, and a series of small, private rooms where one-on-one counseling sessions were conducted or where a mother had the privacy to breastfeed her baby. Throughout the center, play areas for babies were strategically located so that a parent always had easy access to a bit of distraction for the baby to facilitate conversations with a fellow parent, customer representative, or counseling specialist. This model of a training/retail space was reinforced by personal relationships.

Technology

BabyCare invested in an Oracle enterprise resource planning (ERP) system that made tracking of daily sales and exact inventory counts possible. In the Chinese market, this technology investment provided a significant competitive advantage over companies such as Wyeth and Lederle because it allowed BabyCare full visibility throughout the inventory and sales cycle, while those companies that worked with local distributors received little information about true stock levels and real consumer offtake.

ECONOMICS OF THE BUSINESS

The large sales and marketing infrastructure BabyCare had developed required paying high commissions to the individual customer representatives. In order to offset this sales and marketing cost, products flowing through the channel needed to carry high gross margins. BabyCare was typically able to realize gross margins of 65% on food products and 70% to 80%-plus on nutrition products. These were sourced through a partner in the United States and packaged under the BabyCare brand. The commitment to high-quality ingredients helped BabyCare maintain premium pricing on the shelves. Instead of paying out nearly half of sales to distributors like other consumer products companies in China did, BabyCare controlled its own distribution channel through its sales force.

Information and Product Matrix

The company developed a proprietary "Mother & Child Physical & Mental Development Needs Matrix" that tracked mother, child, and father through nine[7] stages which included three trimesters of pregnancy, three stages of infancy, two stages of toddler years, and "pre-school" years from ages three to six. Furthermore, it mapped BabyCare products to cells in the matrix corresponding to the stages of development where those products were most appropriate (see Exhibit 1 for recommended unit consumption levels by year). This framework was the centerpiece of the training program, which was composed of a different curriculum for each stage of development. Mothers were provided with a color diagram, a single laminated page, that traced the trajectory for parents and child through the line of BabyCare products. Products could be purchased individually or where available as a bundle for each phase of development. Training sessions were complimentary for regular customers or could be purchased without a commitment to buy other BabyCare products. The products described in the lower panel of Exhibit 1 were the top sellers.

In addition to educating mothers about their evolving needs and product usage, the matrix provided a roadmap for the sales force in determining specific customers' needs. Customer representatives could be quickly trained to deliver a simple message to mothers seeking a structure for providing care to their new child. In essence, the matrix addressed a key challenge of direct-to-consumer marketing organizations—new product development and customer retention. Because the child's development path was known, the customer was always presented with the right product at the right time. There was no need to introduce new products in order to "get in front of the customer" as there was with traditional direct marketing organizations.

Cash Cycle

By design, the business could operate with minimal working capital requirements. Sales all occurred at BabyCare centers and were paid in cash. BabyCare had no credit sales and no receivables. Not having any receivables was a rarity for all businesses in China. The supply side of the equation, however, was substantially complicated by virtue of being located in China. While BabyCare's U.S. suppliers required payment at the time an order was placed, it took eight weeks before the goods were ready to be shipped and four more weeks for BabyCare to transport the product to China. Sometimes a shipment could clear customs immediately, and at other times it took up to three weeks. This created problems not only in tying up capital but also in terms of lost flexibility in the event of a stock-out. Once in China, the goods were packaged at a BabyCare facility in one week. With the delivery-to-home distribution model, BabyCare found it often held little more than two weeks of finished inventory in stock. As a result, the supply chain was around 15 weeks, creating the need to hold five months inventory in a high-growth environment.

---

[7]In fact, the financial model for the investor presentation was simplified: it combined phases early on and broke later phases into pieces in order to analyze periods of one year at a time.

EXHIBIT 1

ANNUAL UNIT CONSUMPTION OF PRODUCTS IN THE CHILD DEVELOPMENT MATRIX

Product	Yr 1	Yr 2	Yr 3	Yr 4	Yr 5	Yr 6	Yr 7
DHA	2	4	6	3	2	2	2
Ca+D	3	6	4	3	2	2	2
Infant Liquid	0	3	3	0	0	0	0
Children's Multi	0	0	0	4	4	4	4
Colostrum	2	3	2	2	1	2	3
Protein Drink	2	4	4	1	1	1	1
Follow on Formula	0	30	40	60	80	0	0

Product	Unit Price	Description
DHA	$14.00	Nutrimed™ Brain Support DHA (Docosahexaenoic Acid) was a substance required for normal brain development and was the primary structural fatty acid in the gray matter of the brain and retina of the eye, and was necessary for proper mental and visual functioning.
Ca+D	$16.00	Nutrimed™ Bone Enhancing Ca+D provided the calcium required for a child to achieve and maintain peak bone mass and helped counter the increased risk for developing osteoporosis faced by individuals who do not store sufficient amounts of calcium. Vitamin D assisted in the absorption of calcium.
Infant Liquid	$18.00	Nutrimed™ Infant Liquid was a precisely calibrated formulation of multiple vitamins for overall physical development of infants and children, generally a nutritional support for overall well-being.
Children's Multi	$13.00	Nutrimed™ Children's Tasty Vits supplied a precisely calibrated formulation of multi-vitamins and minerals for children's overall physical development.
Colostrum	$18.00	Nutrimed™ whole pure colostrum whey was derived from the first milking of drug-free cows. BabyCare's exclusive lyophilization process (freeze-dried vacuum process) guaranteed the protection of all nutrient and enzyme activity. Colostrum was super rich in natural immune system supporting agents, including the immunoglobulins IgG, IgA and IgM, nucleotides, gamma interferon, orotic acid and enzymes.
Protein Drink	$28.00	Naturesure™ Protein Drink Mix, with its unique amino acid profile derived from SUPRO® (the most advanced soy protein isolate available at the time) was most effectively used as a high protein supplement, but also inhibited fat absorption and accelerated fat metabolism, promoting lean body mass and reducing the risk of future heart disease.
Follow on Formula	$3.00	Nutrisource™ Follow on Milk Formula was a balanced nutrition formula designed to be as close as possible to breast milk. Follow-on formula was further fortified with calcium to fill the extra nutritional demand during the transition period to maintain a child's growth.

Note: While the model was constructed according to nine phases, the table above is based on annual periods.

Source: BabyCare; for illustrative purposes only.

The local packaging of many products and manufacturing of other products was in large part a response to laws that prohibited consumer products companies from importing finished goods for resale in China. Under the regulations, all companies had to manufacture their goods locally, but manufacturing was defined such that packaging was a part of the manufacturing process. As a result, BabyCare sourced intermediate goods (its food and nutrition products) in bulk from abroad and set up a packaging plant in China where the goods were put into their final retail packaging. This complied with local laws.

Market Growth and Expansion Opportunities

The PRC health supplement market doubled from $3 billion in 1998 to $6 billion in 2000 primarily via increased sales volumes, rather than margins, according to market research firm Pro Re Nata (PRN). This $6 billion market was BabyCare's addressable market. Of the 500 million urban residents in China, an estimated 350 million bought health supplements. PRN conservatively forecasted that the PRC market would represent 20%, or $10 billion, of worldwide sales of $51 billion by 2010. BabyCare expected this trend to continue in light of the current low base of personal income in China and consumptive patterns of its members. During the prior three years, a typical member purchased $250 of nutritional products over 13 months.

One fundamental factor driving the sales of nutritional supplements was a growing interest in self-medication, as busier lifestyles, coupled with rising levels of affluence, led more people to take a proactive stance regarding their general well-being. Governments in countries such as China and Japan supported this trend through campaigns encouraging consumers to self-medicate and thus reduce the increasing financial burden being placed by an aging population on medical systems.

The market was highly fragmented. Only 40% of producers had registered capital of more than $600,000 and the largest 50% of producers accounted for only one-third of all sales. By contrast, the top 20% of China's cosmetic companies commanded 80% of sales in that market. One reason for the persistent fragmentation was a lack of product differentiation and investment in marketing rather than product development.

Estes figured that near-term growth for BabyCare depended on a combination of within-city growth, geographic expansion within China, and increasing member lifecycle values. Expansion plans ultimately called for centers in up to 90 second-tier cities with populations of two million or more. Healthcare delivery systems in second-tier cities were ill-equipped to deliver prenatal and infant care education, leaving an acute, unsatisfied demand for information. Furthermore, the required investment to enter second-tier cities was substantially lower than in Beijing, Shanghai, and Guangzhou, and attracting employees would be easier because good job opportunities were more limited in second-tier cities. This concept was validated in the period from January 2001 to June 2002, when the company opened its first center outside Beijing in Dalian. The Dalian operation broke even in three months instead of seven and returned stronger-than-budgeted revenue growth.

DYNAMICS OF THE CONSUMER PRODUCTS MARKET IN CHINA

Mumford and Estes refined their pitch around a framework they called the "two Ds and four Hs." They believed it encapsulated the opportunities and challenges of the consumer products markets in China. The Ds illustrated the pressing market need for BabyCare's core product line and the Hs reviewed the impediments to profitability unique to the Chinese market.

D1. Demographics

China's long-standing one-child policy was designed to prevent uncontrolled population growth. With births hovering around 22 million per year in China, the population was expected to stabilize at approximately 1.6 billion. The combination of the political upheavals of the twentieth century together with an overburdened healthcare system had created a significant information gap with respect to childbirth. Young adults expecting children would naturally have turned to their parents for advice, but their parents suffered from a knowledge deficit due to the turmoil of the Cultural Revolution and its detrimental impact on formal health education. Information channels such as books and advertising media were helpful, but did not command the necessary levels of trust to truly drive spending patterns. Unlike in the United States, where medical spending on services far outpaced prescription expenditures, in China healthcare spending was 90% on prescriptions and only 10% on services (including education relating to childbirth). Mumford interpreted this statistic as showing that the Chinese healthcare system did provide basic medical care but did not have the resources to provide the auxiliary health services such as education that were essential to childrearing. In short, Estes focused on what he saw as a huge unfulfilled demand for information and advice.

D2. Disposable Income

On a macroeconomic level, China was expected to be one of the world's fastest growing markets, and this economic expansion would raise per capita income levels. Exhibit 2 highlights the relationship observed throughout the region between a country's gross domestic product and baby formula consumption. Mumford could extrapolate its impact on demand for BabyCare's products. The population growth was, moreover, distributed throughout China. In the context of funding a geographic expansion, Mumford's investor presentation included data on the robustness of spending out of disposable income allocated to child-related expenses. While the largest cities in China initially provided both the largest pools of targeted customers and the highest income levels, the drop in spending as one moved to second- and third-tier cities was much lower than the drop in disposable incomes (see Exhibit 3). Mumford attributed the resilience of spending on children to what he dubbed the "six pockets, one mouth" phenomenon: Chinese parents had long relied on their children for support in retirement, and the one-child policy resulted in every child having two parents and four grandparents, all dependent on this child's future success.[8]

Having set out the major demand drivers behind the BabyCare concept, Estes and Mumford then turned to the key challenges.

H1. High Media Cost Inflation

Advertising costs were growing consistently at double-digit rates annually in China. However, the typical investment of 70%–90% of companies' media budgets in television and newspaper advertising resulted in reaching general audiences rather than targeting families with the necessary disposable income to purchase premium baby nutri-

---

[8]Because China lacked a comprehensive and credible social security system, parents were especially concerned with the future success of their children. *The New York Times* reported that a book entitled *Harvard Girl* was the best-selling book in 2001 in China, where "proud parents . . . scientifically prepared their little darling, from age 0, to get into America's most prestigious university." Source: "A Chinese Dad in Defense of the Average Child," *The New York Times*, June 8, 2002.

EXHIBIT 2

FORMULA CONSUMPTION VS. GDP

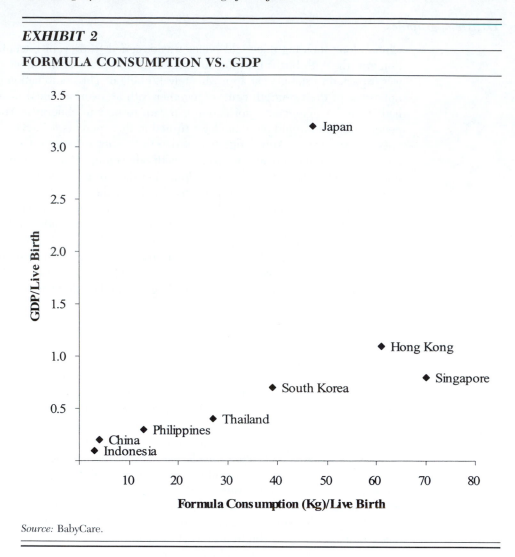

Source: BabyCare.

---

tion products. As a result, Mumford believed that media spending did not provide sufficient returns: "You lose one order of magnitude when using print or broadcast media. . . . Only one in ten viewers or listeners is likely to be a pregnant mother or mother with an infant or young child." Further, BabyCare faced the challenge that its information-led products required educating the consumer in a manner that could not effectively be communicated through a 30-second television spot or a newspaper ad.

H2. High Channel Costs

Consumer products companies found distribution to be one of the key challenges to operating in China. Using local distributors was a costly proposition—sometimes consuming 35–50 cents out of every revenue dollar—and offered poor service. Estes criticized distributors as "ineffective at providing real inventory counts, resulting in a lack of channel transparency and reliable data on end-customer sales."

EXHIBIT 3

RESILIENCE OF SPENDING ON A CHILD AS DISPOSABLE INCOME FALLS (IN RMB)

	Baby care related products from pregnancy to age 3	
	Large City	**2ⁿᵈ Tier City**
Average monthly spend:	743	540
Average monthly income:	2,400	1,600
Spend / total family income	23%–36%	34%–50%

Source: BabyCare.

H3. High Receivables

In addition to their high cost and poor service, distributors and retailers frequently forced manufacturers to extend generous trade terms. Often manufacturers found themselves with accounts receivable days of 120–190 days, because they had little bargaining power against the distributors, which were frequently state-owned entities. Sometimes the problems were even more severe, and bad debt expenses could become a significant cost with little remedy provided for manufacturers.

H4. Hard

Finally, the combination of high media costs, high channel costs, and high receivables made selling consumer products profitably in China just plain hard. The obstacles were not insurmountable, but they were substantial. To illustrate this point, Mumford used a slide that set side-by-side the cost structures of BabyCare and a typical consumer products company (see Exhibit 4).

FIRST ROUND OF FINANCING: STARTUP CAPITAL

Raising venture capital in China in the late 1990s was a challenge. Earlier in the decade many multinationals had entered China, and a number of venture capital firms had followed. In the mid-1990s many of these businesses found the realities of doing business in China far more challenging than expected. This left few sources of venture capital in China when Mumford and Estes needed to raise their first round of funding. Accordingly, they initially approached U.S. investors with the concept for BabyCare, but found little appetite for emerging markets and China exposure in venture portfolios in 1998. Discussions continued with the Hong Kong branches of private equity firms and venture capital firms. The venture funds and angel investors typically cut checks for up to $2 million for startup ventures and the private equity firms generally invested between $5 million and $20 million in more developed businesses. Raising the $9.8 million that BabyCare projected would be necessary was beyond the size of the venture players, but too early stage for the private equity firms. As an entrepreneur raising capital, Mumford believed that "from management's perspective two kinds of businesses

EXHIBIT 4

BABYCARE BUSINESS MODEL COMPARED TO A TYPICAL CONSUMER PRODUCTS COMPANY

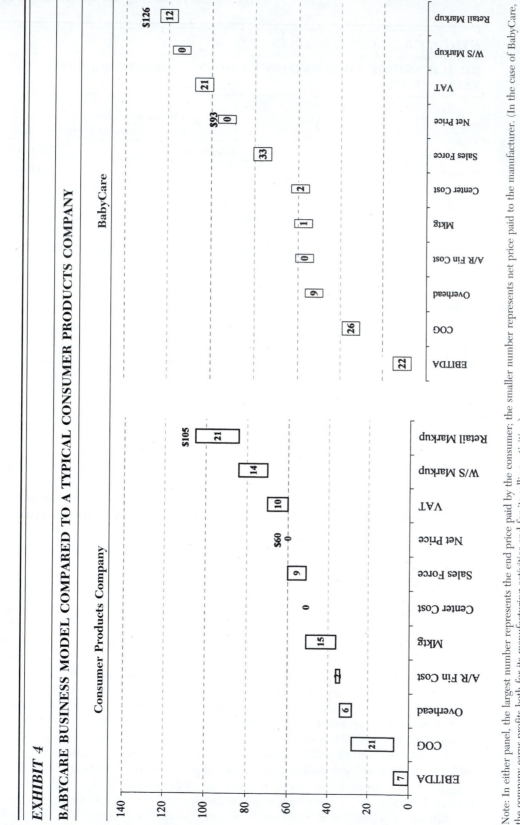

Note: In either panel, the largest number represents the end price paid by the consumer; the smaller number represents net price paid to the manufacturer. (In the case of BabyCare, the company earns profits both for its manufacturing activities and for its selling activities.)

Source: BabyCare.

make sense: (1) capital non-intensive business that you own 80% of, or (2) capital-intensive ones where you own very little but you take a carry and earn a percentage."

After a yearlong marketing process, BabyCare received two terms sheets, each offering a $10 million valuation for the enterprise. There were no good comparables at the time to justify the valuation. One of the term sheets came from the San Francisco-based venture firm Orchid Asia, and the other from the Hong Kong venture arm of a U.S. investment bank. The venture firm was financially motivated and was prepared to act quickly. The investment bank's venture arm had several years of experience in China and some operational expertise, which was advantageous, but would likely seek to become more involved in daily operations. Moreover, it asked for specific milestones not demanded by Orchid.

The negotiation of final terms with Orchid unexpectedly took eight months and ultimately included the milestones that BabyCare management had hoped to avoid. The funding was also cut back to $7.5 million, of which Orchid provided only $6.25 million and management provided the rest. Management later learned that some of the delay had been a result of Orchid's desire to place the investment in its second fund—a fund that was only being raised when discussions with BabyCare commenced.

During the first fund-raising effort, Estes had predicted that the likely exit strategy would be either a sale to a strategic buyer or an initial public offering in Hong Kong. The latter typically required two to three years of profitability and was normally done for the purpose of raising expansion capital. The Hong Kong market was sophisticated and able to provide appropriate valuations for companies in businesses ranging from cement to semiconductors.

SECOND ROUND OF FINANCING: A DOWN ROUND

By the end of 2000 the business concept—that 75%+ margins could be generated and consumers would follow through with the program—had been demonstrated, but the business was not scaling as quickly as expected. By slowing growth plans, management had stretched the initial funding, expected to last 14–18 months, to 30 months. In late 2000, the fund-raising environment was difficult, as the NASDAQ slide in the U.S. shut down the IPO market around the world and spooked private equity and venture investors. Orchid declined to provide follow-up financing. After canvassing the market, BabyCare successfully found a venture fund willing to both inject the needed capital and move quickly.

Pacific Group Ltd, a Hong Kong based investment firm founded by William Kaye, a former board member of Paine Webber, Inc. and head of that firm's risk arbitrage activities in 1980s and early 1990s, invested $3 million at a pre-money valuation of $2.6 million. Existing investors who were at that point unwilling or unable to provide more funds were severely diluted by Pacific Group's terms, but the shareholders voted in favor of the deal as it permitted operations to continue.

THIRD ROUND OF FINANCING: EXPANSION CAPITAL

Estes and Mumford felt that BabyCare was still too young to undertake a full-scale public offering. Six months away from breakeven and having demonstrated success in the Dalian market, BabyCare needed $2.5 million of financing to get to the point where expansion capital was self-generating from existing markets. Working capital requirements were also growing as a result of the long supply chain and growing demand. Estes and Mumford got approval from the BabyCare board to raise $2.5 million at a $20–$30 million valuation. Management had three options, and hoped that the Templeton team would provide a fourth:

1. **Small investment, low valuation**. Existing investors offered to provide $1 million in expansion capital at an $8 million valuation. The model would be further tested and expanded and additional capital could be raised once the market had another six months to recover.

2. **Large investment, higher valuation**. One of the leading private equity firms in healthcare offered to invest $6 million at a $26 million valuation. Based in the U.S., the firm prided itself on having impeccable connections with all the major healthcare companies, which could support BabyCare in product expansion.

3. **Desired investment, mid-range valuation**. A Hong Kong-based baby accessory company offered $2.5 million at a $19 million valuation. The company offered synergy opportunities in terms of product development, market expansion, and cost savings. Mumford worried that having a strategic investor might complicate a later sale of the company.

4. **Desired investment, innovative structure**. Franklin Templeton Investments was contemplating a convertible instrument that would provide $2.5 million in a four year 10% convertible note with a conversion at a $22 million valuation. Templeton further offered a 12% $1 million fixed-rate note to sweeten the deal and allowed them to put more funds to work in a transaction otherwise considered small for the firm's normal "sweet spot."

GETTING THE FRANKLIN TEMPLETON INVESTMENTS TERM SHEET

Mumford and Estes agreed that BabyCare should command a premium sales multiple because of its high net income margins, but before discussing valuation levels, they needed to convince Seow that their top-line revenue growth projections were realistic and that their working capital model was robust. Seow had, in effect, called them on their biggest assumptions and was demanding that they back them up.

Internal Financial Projections

Seow had reviewed BabyCare's financials (see income statement in Exhibit 5 and cash flow statement in Exhibit 6) and believed that Mumford and Estes had made estimates of how fast revenues would grow without providing a detailed build-up to support the top-line numbers. Along with his concern about backing into how quickly BabyCare would have to attract new members each year, Seow was also curious to see what percentage of the membership base and sales volume stemmed from new members. Seow realized, however, that he did not have enough information himself to answer these questions, and so he had asked Mumford to do the legwork.

Member Attrition and Growth

Before even they could answer the questions, Mumford and Estes had to hammer out some reasonable assumptions about the underlying business. In the fiscal year of operations ended June 30, 2001, BabyCare had signed on 10,000 members, 4,000 of whom had continued with the program. Looking at the more recent results from the second

EXHIBIT 5

BABYCARE PROJECTED INCOME STATEMENT

($000s)	2001	2002	2003	2004	2005	2006	2007
# Markets with Sales	2	6	13	24	36	48	60
# New Markets Invested	1	4	7	11	12	12	12
Gross Revenues	**2,142**	**5,718**	**13,572**	**33,787**	**59,311**	**82,501**	**107,912**
% Growth	n/a	166.9%	137.4%	148.9%	75.5%	39.1%	30.8%
VAT	242	567	1,530	5,744	10,083	14,025	18,345
Retail Offers	43	113	271	676	1,186	1,650	2,158
Net Revenues	**1,857**	**5,038**	**11,771**	**27,368**	**48,042**	**66,826**	**87,409**
Cost of Goods Sold	(522)	(1,390)	(2,825)	(6,568)	(11,050)	(15,370)	(20,104)
Gross Profit	**1,336**	**3,648**	**8,946**	**20,800**	**36,992**	**51,456**	**67,305**
Sales, General & Admin.	(1,292)	(2,819)	(6,003)	(13,234)	(24,496)	(32,882)	(42,830)
HR Expense	(1,161)	(1,248)	(1,530)	(2,574)	(3,347)	(3,848)	(4,233)
Operating Expenses	(502)	(369)	(520)	(729)	(947)	(1,089)	(1,898)
Product Development	(7)	(119)	(235)	(350)	(400)	(400)	(400)
Depreciation	(361)	(204)	(294)	(365)	(411)	(501)	(637)
Pretax Income	**(1,988)**	**(1,112)**	**362**	**3,548**	**7,390**	**12,735**	**17,305**
Income Tax	—	—	—	—	—	—	—
Net Income	**(1,988)**	**(1,112)**	**362**	**3,548**	**7,390**	**12,735**	**17,305**

Source: BabyCare.

EXHIBIT 6

BABYCARE PROJECTED CASH FLOW STATEMENT

($000s)	2001	2002	2003	2004	2005	2006	2007
Net Income	(1,988)	(1,112)	362	3,548	7,390	12,735	17,305
Capital Expenditure	(140)	(429)	(992)	(770)	(3,851)	(5,411)	(2,320)
Change in Working Capital	(134)	(1,021)	(240)	(1,642)	(1,120)	(2,722)	(2,304)
Deprecation	361	204	294	365	411	501	637
Change in Cash	(1,901)	(2,358)	(575)	1,501	2,830	5,102	13,319
Cash on Hand	n/a	1,099	(1,258)	(1,833)	(332)	2,498	7,600
Cash Investment	3,000	—	—	—	—	—	—
Cumulative Cash	1,099	(1,258)	(1,833)	(332)	2,498	7,600	20,919

Source: BabyCare.

year, it appeared that approximately 80% of the 1,000 members who had stayed on for a second year in 2001 would continue for a third. Mumford and Estes discussed what churn rates they should assume for later years. Both agreed that the first year was the telling year—if a mother kept up with the program after the birth of her baby, then she was likely to be committed to the program. They settled on a 10% attrition rate in the third through sixth years of the mother's involvement with BabyCare. After the seventh year, all remaining members would roll off the program because the child had outgrown the product offering. Having settled on those assumptions, Mumford had what he needed to answer Choong Huei's questions. Both he and Estes hoped that their top-line growth projections would return reasonable member growth statistics.

Working Capital

Estes asked Mumford to pull together an explanation of why BabyCare actually did need to fund working capital and how those funding needs would be reduced once they built local manufacturing facilities. Though not contained in any of the projections, Estes was already planning to build a local manufacturing plant at an estimated cost of $6 million in 2006. Although this would not change the cost of inputs, it would reduce manufacturing time to two weeks and entirely eliminate transportation and customs delays. In addition, Estes reckoned that as BabyCare became more established, it would no longer have to pay up-front for its input purchases, but would be able to obtain 60-day terms from suppliers. These changes, taken together, would dramatically alter BabyCare's working capital cycle.

Because the Chinese government had maintained the value of the RMB against the dollar at a steady 8.3 RMB per dollar, Mumford converted all of his projections into dollars and assumed that there would be no devaluation (or revaluation) of the local currency.

GETTING TO A DEAL

I have a love/hate relationship with fund-raising: on the one hand it is exciting to be on the road selling your wares, but at the 11th hour you always find yourself standing hat in hand at the service entrance of the Ritz Carlton.

—Chris Mumford

Mumford and Estes together realized that in gathering the information Seow wanted to see, they would create an informative benchmark for how their business was performing. Understanding how the cohort of BabyCare members would evolve over time and how their growth would translate into profitability would provide an operating gauge, while working through the working capital consequences of the changing supply chain would provide a financial efficiency gauge.

At the same time, they felt confident about their position—even in a difficult market, BabyCare had attracted financing alternatives. Estes and Mumford wanted to draw upon their experiences during the first two financing rounds to apply lessons learned there and generate a financing option that minimized dilution to current investors and management.

Czech Mate: CME and Vladimir Zelezny (A)

In the summer of 1997, Len Fertig, president and CEO of Central European Media Enterprises (CME), a holding company for television operations through Central and Eastern Europe, turned his attention to the negotiations between CME and Dr. Vladimir Zelezny. Zelezny was the managing director of CME's hugely successful Czech television station, TV Nova. A few months earlier, Zelezny had announced his desire to sell his holding in the station's operating company. While Zelezny was willing to sell his interest to CME, it was possible that he would seek another buyer if CME declined to purchase his shares.

Fertig recognized Zelezny's contribution to the television station's remarkable success and did not want to jeopardize the relationship between CME and Zelezny. The proposed deal, however, posed problems for CME. CME already owned 93.2% of TV Nova's operating company and did not seek complete ownership. As a foreign firm, CME was wary of provoking controversy about foreign ownership of the most popular Czech television channel and wanted to retain a local partner. Furthermore, Zelezny's holding in the station's operating company helped ensure that his interests were aligned with those of CME. If CME did consider buying Zelezny's shares, Fertig would have to decide on a price acceptable to both CME and to Zelezny. In deciding whether CME should buy Zelezny's shares, and if so at what price, Fertig had to find a way both to satisfy Zelezny and protect the interests of CME.

THE FOUNDERS OF CME AND CZECH PRIVATE TELEVISION

The Origins of CME[1]

CME originated in 1991 as a development corporation focused on opportunities in Eastern and Central Europe following the fall of communism in the region. Its founders

Professor Mihir A. Desai and Professor Alberto Moel of Hong Kong University of Science and Technology and Research Associate Kathleen Luchs prepared this case. This case was developed from published sources. HBS cases are developed solely as the basis for class discussion. Cases are not intended to serve as endorsements, sources of primary data, or illustrations of effective or ineffective management.

[1]This section is based on Central European Media Enterprises Ltd., Prospectus, October 13, 1994 (Bermuda: CME, 1994) available from Thomson Research, ⟨http://research.thomsonib.com⟩; Lisa Gubernick, "Chip off the Old Block," *Forbes*, February 24, 1997, pp. 103–4.

were Ronald Lauder, a former U.S. ambassador to Austria and one of the heirs of the Estée Lauder cosmetic fortune, and Mark Palmer, who had served as U.S. ambassador to Hungary. Palmer and Lauder recognized that anticipated economic growth in the former Soviet Bloc would increase demand for consumer goods. Advertising revenues would also grow, making media investments potentially attractive. Across the region, there were plans to privatize broadcast frequencies that had been state-controlled under the communist regimes. CME therefore focused on the nascent opportunities in commercial television. Lauder's and Palmer's experience in the region, their political connections, and their considerable financial resources put them in a strong position as investment partners in these new commercial television ventures.

Czech Private TV

In 1992, the Czech Republic announced it would privatize a broadcasting frequency with national coverage, the first former Soviet Bloc country to do so. A Media Council, whose members were elected by the Czech Parliament, would set programming standards and license conditions. It also had authority to issue broadcasting licenses. Among the interested bidders for the frequency was a group of five Czech professionals and intellectuals who were excited about the cultural and educational opportunities of private television. Vladimir Zelezny, a journalist, producer, and a former press official for the Czech government of Vaclav Havel, joined the original group and became its spokesman. The group named itself Central European Television for the 21st Century, or CET 21.

CET 21 needed financial backing to make its bid for the television license credible, and CME sought local partners to facilitate its bids for broadcasting licenses and also to ensure locally appropriate programming. The two groups worked together to submit a bid for the first Czech commercial TV station.

LICENSE NEGOTIATIONS[2]

During 1992, the Media Council reviewed proposals and held public hearings for the broadcasting license from more than twenty applicants, including a group with political ties to the ruling party in parliament and a group that included CNN.[3] The Media Council aimed to assess the suitability of each group's plan for the television station, and its viability. CET 21 and CME negotiated terms between themselves and consulted with the Media Council on their joint proposal. The new Czech media law did not forbid foreign ownership of television stations, and the Media Council accepted that foreign capital was required to launch a successful station. Nonetheless, the Media Council preferred a combination of domestic and foreign capital. The original plan was for CME to provide substantial capital for the new television station in return for 49% ownership of CET 21. After a number of hearings, the Media Council awarded the television license to CET 21 on January 30, 1993.

---

[2]This section is largely based on UNCITRAL Arbitration, Ronald S. Lauder vs The Czech Republic, Final Award, September 3, 2001 available at ⟨http://www.cetv-net.com/ne/articlefiles/439-lauder-cr_eng.pdf.⟩ (accessed July 21, 2003.)

[3]Burton Bollag, "Czechs Learning to Release Government's Control of TV," *The New York Times*, June 14, 1993, p. D6.

The decision provoked an outcry in the Czech Parliament from the ruling party. There were charges that the decision was too hasty, objections to the leftist political ties of CET 21's founders, and outrage over the extent of foreign investment in Czech television being allowed by the Media Council.

The Media Council responded to the uproar by asking CET 21 and CME to revise their plans for the television station before it actually issued the license. In particular, the Media Council declared it would not permit foreign ownership of the license. The founders of CET 21 and CME, in consultation with the Media Council, devised an alternative arrangement. CET 21 would be owned exclusively by its founders, including Zelezny, who were all Czech or Slovak nationals. The license would be granted to CET 21 and CET 21 would function solely as a license holder. A new company, to be established by CME and its local partners, would operate the television station. This new company would have exclusive use of the license held by CET 21 and assume all operating responsibility for the new station, including buying and producing programs and the sale of advertising. This arrangement left the license itself in Czech hands but allowed the participation of CME through the operating company.

The new operating company, CNTS, was owned by CME, CET 21, and the Czech Savings Bank (CSB). CME contributed 75% of CNTS's capital and received 66% ownership. The Czech Savings Bank contributed 25% of the capital and received 22% ownership. CET 21 contributed the use of its television license to CNTS and received 12% ownership. Exhibit 1 shows the ownership and structure of CNTS. These arrangements were finalized in a Memorandum of Agreement and approved by the Media Council in February 1993.[4] The public name of the new station operated by CNTS was TV Nova. Zelezny became director of TV Nova and began planning the station's launch.

TV NOVA

TV Nova enjoyed spectacular success under the direction of Zelezny. It first went on air in February 1994 and gained an astonishing 70% audience share within a year (see Exhibit 2 for the audience shares of Czech TV stations). Some analysts described TV Nova as the most successful launch ever of a new television station.

The station's programming was a mix of dubbed American shows and locally produced programs aimed at a mass-market audience. In contrast to the state-owned television stations, TV Nova followed the U.S. practice of scheduling regular time slots for its daily and weekly shows. The station purchased the rights to American series and films from major producers such as Walt Disney and Twentieth Century Fox and produced its own news, sports, variety, and game shows.[5]

TV Nova's news programs prominently featured gruesome car crashes and crime reports, and its news teams sought out stories of political chicanery. The station won such a huge market share, Zelezny explained, because "We never overestimate our viewer. We accept the fact that our viewer is a well-educated normal European, he's not over-educated with very sophisticated or unique cultural needs. Our programming

---

[4]UNCITRAL Arbitration, CME Czech Republic B.V. (The Netherlands) vs. The Czech Republic, Partial Award, September 13, 2001 available at ⟨http://www.cetv-net.com/ne/articlefiles/439-cme-cr_eng.pdf⟩ (accessed July 20, 2003).

[5]Central European Media Enterprises Ltd., Prospectus, October 13, 1994 (Bermuda: CME, 1994) available from Thomson Research, ⟨http://research.thomsonib.com⟩.

EXHIBIT 1

STRUCTURE OF TV NOVA

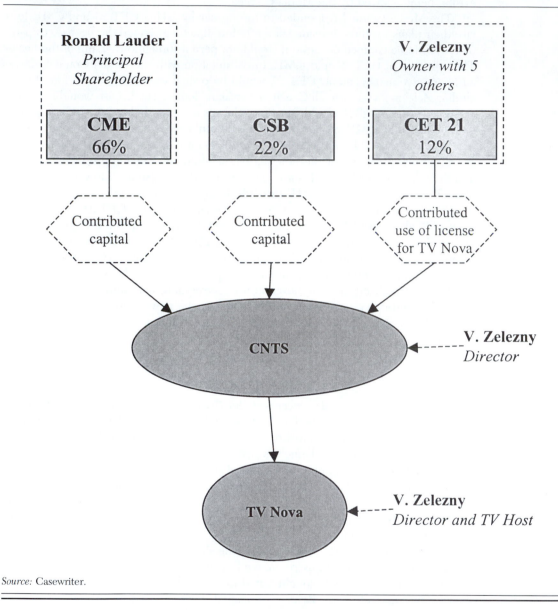

Source: Casewriter.

reflects this."[6] Zelezny himself presented a weekly program, "Call the Director" which aired on Saturdays at noon.

    Ronald Lauder reflected on the reasons for TV Nova's success: "There were several points. The most important was competition. When TV Nova started, there was no other commercial channel in the Czech Republic. And the state television at that time

[6]Normandy Madden, "Bridge Builder" [Interview with Vladimir Zelezny], *Television Business International*, September 1, 1996 available from Factiva, ⟨http://global.factiva.com⟩.

EXHIBIT 2

CZECH TV STATIONS, SHARE OF VIEWING, 1993–1996

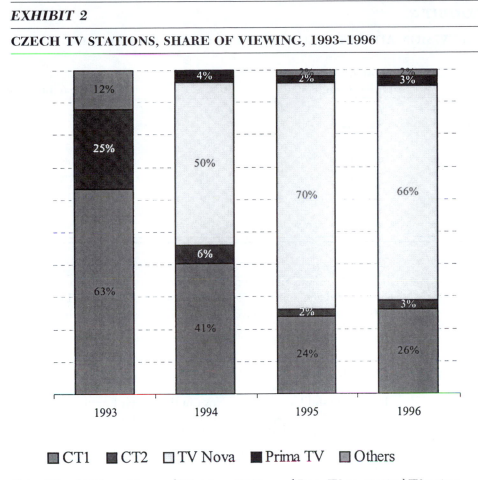

Note: CT1 and CT2 are state-owned TV stations. TV Nova and Prima TV are privatized TV stations.

Source: Created by casewriter based on data from Zenith Media, *Television in Europe to 2008*, August 1999, p. 23.

---

was not that good. The second was Vladimir Zelezny was brilliant about how he did it. The third was timing. The fourth was the fact that there are many American programs and the Czech people are very pro-American. They really loved to see that. So all the things together worked beautifully."[7]

The station's popularity with viewers was a strong draw for advertisers, especially large multi-nationals such as Procter & Gamble and Unilever who were eager to establish their brands in the new market economy of the Czech Republic. Spending on television advertising increased substantially in the Czech Republic in the mid-1990s, as shown in Exhibit 3. Advertisers favored TV Nova both because of its popularity and because of the availability of advertising time on the commercial station. The two Czech state-owned stations were limited to using 1% of their broadcasting time for advertising[8]

[7]Jana Ciglerova, "Interview with Ronald Lauder," *Lidovky Centrum,* August 12, 2002 at ⟨http://lidovky. centrum.cz/⟩ accessed August 13, 2002.

[8]The public television stations also received revenue from the television license fees levied on households.

EXHIBIT 3

TELEVISION ADVERTISING SPEND IN THE CZECH REPUBLIC

Year	Television % Share of All Advertising Spend	U.S. $M	Year-on-Year Increase
1991	—	—	
1992	—	—	
1993	43%	57	
1994	46%	109	90%
1995	47%	117	7%
1996	52%	167	43%

Source: Zenith Media, *Television in Europe to 2008*, August 1999, p. 24.

but TV Nova was permitted to broadcast advertising up to 20% in any one hour, with an overall daily limit of 10% of broadcast time.[9] By 1996, TV Nova had net revenues of $109 million. CNTS received all of TV Nova's revenues and paid CME a dividend of $8.4 million in 1996.

GROWTH OF CME

The successful launch of TV Nova in the Czech Republic spurred the overall growth of CME. The company incorporated in Bermuda and raised $68 million in its IPO in October 1994.[10] At that time, CME's ventures included TV Nova and two regional stations in Germany. Len Fertig explained CME's focus on Eastern and Central Europe:

> There's an opportunity there. The fall of the wall has opened up the economy . . . And why there, in particular? The founders of the company are familiar with the area. It's an opportunity for a new venture and startup that's not dominated by the multinational media players and we have a particular expertise in getting TV licenses and starting new operations. So it's just a great opportunity. There's a window now for a few years in which we can start new television stations.[11]

By 1996, the company owned television stations in Romania, Slovenia, the Ukraine, and the Slovak Republic. It had won a broadcasting license in Poland and was competing for a license in Hungary (see Exhibit 4 for CME's ventures). CME's television stations reached 93.9 million people (see Exhibit 5 for a breakdown of CME's broadcast reach.)

CME financed its ambitious growth strategy through two additional public offerings, in 1995 and 1996. Revenues grew to $136 million in 1996, but the company was

[9]Central European Media Enterprises Ltd., Prospectus, October 13, 1994 (Bermuda: CME, 1994) available from Thomson Research, http://research.thomsonib.com.

[10]CME traded on the NASDAQ under the trading symbol CETV.

[11]Jane Guva, "Interview with Leonard Fertig," *Dow Jones Investor Network*, Feb. 2, 1996 available from Factiva, http://global.factiva.com.

EXHIBIT 4

CME VENTURES

Entity	Ownership	Territory
TV Nova	93.2%	Czech Rep.
Holding Companies	100.0%	Germany
Videovox	97.0%	Hungary
Under development	95.0%	Hungary
Under development	33.0%	Poland
Media Pro Int'l	77.5%	Romania
MobilRom	9.5%	Romania
STS	80.0%	Slovak Rep.
Pro Plus	72.0%	Slovenia
Studio 1+1	50.0%	Ukraine

Source: Adapted from CME, Dec. 31, 1996 10-K (Bermuda: CME, 1996) available from Thomson Research, ⟨http://research.thomsonib.com⟩.

not yet profitable (see Exhibit 6 for CME's financial statements). The company's regional German stations, in Berlin and Brandenburg, suffered ongoing losses, and CME curtailed its investments in them. While the company's recently acquired television stations in Eastern Europe required substantial investments in programming and time to build their audiences, the outstanding success of TV Nova provided a model for these

EXHIBIT 5

CME BROADCAST REACH

Television Broadcast Operations	Territory	Broadcast Reach (millions of people)	CME Economic Interest
TV Nova	Czech Republic	10.2	93.2%
Markiza TV	Slovak Republic	4.3	80.0%
Pro TV	Romania	12.5	77.5%
Pop TV	Slovenia	1.6	72.0%
PULS	Berlin-Brandenburg	6.0	58.0%
Studio 1+1 Group	Ukraine	48.5	50.0%
Nuremberg Station	Nuremberg	1.2	37.4%
Leipzig Station	Saxony	0.7	16.7%
Dresden Station	Saxony	1.1	16.7%
TV Wisla	Poland	7.8	16.2%
Total		**93.9**	

Source: CME, Dec. 31, 1996 10-K (Bermuda: CME, 1996) available from Thomson Research, ⟨http://research.thomsonib.com⟩.

EXHIBIT 6

CME CONSOLIDATED STATEMENT OF OPERATIONS

(In thousands of U.S. dollars) For the years ended December 31,	1996	1995	1994
Gross revenues	170,114	121,113	64,389
Discounts and Agency Commissions	(34,129)	(22,194)	(10,823)
Net revenues	**135,985**	**98,919**	**53,566**
Station expenses:			
Other operating costs and expenses	50,188	28,972	21,907
Amortization of programming rights	21,599	16,319	10,403
Depreciation of station fixed assets and other intangibles	13,314	7,251	3,773
Total station operating costs and expenses	85,101	52,542	36,083
Selling, general and administrative expenses	21,357	7,725	6,009
Corporate expenses:			
Corporate operating costs and development expenses	15,782	10,669	3,699
Stock compensation charge		858	5,833
Amortization of goodwill and allowance for development costs	2,940	3,442	985
Capital registration tax	809	1,375	
Total corporate expenses	**19,531**	**16,344**	**10,517**
Operating Income	**9,996**	**22,308**	**957**
Equity in loss of unconsolidated affiliates	(17,867)	(14,816)	(13,677)
Interest and other income	2,876	1,238	179
Interest expense	(4,670)	(4,959)	(1,992)
Foreign currency exchange (loss)/gain	(2,861)	324	(245)
Net income (loss) before provision for income tax	**(12,526)**	**4,095**	**(14,778)**
Provision for income tax	(16,405)	(16,340)	(3,331)
Net loss before minority interest	**(28,931)**	**(12,245)**	**(18,109)**
Minority interest in loss of consolidated subsidiaries	(1,072)	(6,491)	(2,396)
Net loss	**(30,003)**	**(18,736)**	**(20,505)**

Source: CME, Dec. 31, 1996 10-K (Bermuda: CME, 1996) available from Thomson Research, ⟨http://research.thomsonib.com⟩.

newer stations. As Len Fertig explained, "We can duplicate Nova's financial success in Poland, Hungary, all of Eastern Europe."[12] TV Nova, however, was the only national station that had achieved profitability. Operating results for CME's largest TV stations are shown in Exhibit 7.

TV NOVA: CRITICS AND CHALLENGES

While TV Nova's success provided a model for CME's other broadcast ventures in Eastern Europe, the Czech television station had its share of critics. Some commentators

[12]Robert Frank, "Cultural Fare," *The Wall Street Journal*, April 30, 1997, p. A1.

EXHIBIT 7

OPERATING RESULTS FOR NATIONAL BROADCAST ENTITIES, YEAR ENDED DEC. 31, 1996

Consolidated Entities	Nova TV	Pro TV	Pop TV	Subtotal	Markiza TV	Total Adjusted
Territory	Czech Republic	Romania	Slovenia		Slovak Republic	
Net revenues	**109,242**	**15,803**	**9,080**	**134,125**	**7,462**	**141,587**
Station operating expense	(54,578)	(16,497)	(12,764)	(83,839)	(9,570)	(93,409)
Selling, general and administrative expense	(9,247)	(6,351)	(3,989)	(19,587)	(1,605)	(21,192)
Station operating income	**45,417**	**(7,045)**	**(7,673)**	**30,699**	**(3,713)**	**26,286**
Depreciation of assets	8,024	2,678	2,516	13,218	1,473	14,691
EBITDA	**53,441**	**(4,367)**	**(5,157)**	**43,917**	**(2,240)**	**41,677**
Amortization of programming rights	16,207	3,725	1,667	21,599	2,401	24,000
Cash program rights costs	(16,520)	(4,648)	(2,904)	(24,072)	(4,663)	(28,735)
Broadcast cash flow	**53,128**	**(5,290)**	**(6,394)**	**41,444**	**(4,502)**	**36,942**

Note: Broadcast cash flow is a broadcasting industry measure of performance and defined as net broadcast revenues, less broadcast operating expenses excluding depreciation and amortization, broadcast selling, general and administrative expenses, and cash program costs.

Source: CME, Dec. 31, 1996 10-K (Bermuda: CME, 1996) available from Thomson Research, ⟨http://research.thomsonib.com⟩.

disapproved of TV Nova's programming and influence, charging that the station was too sensational in its news coverage and too limited in its educational and cultural programming. In response, Fertig observed: "Sure, Nova news covers auto crashes as well as everything else. We are not the BBC. But people are interested in things that touch their lives, not meetings of ministers. Certain public TV journalists believe that TV should be centrally planned as opposed to viewer-responsive."[13]

Zelezny also vigorously defended TV Nova, sometimes using his own television show as a platform to answer those who criticized the station or its foreign ownership. He argued, "The intellectuals believed Czechs were special, more sophisticated. We proved they were wrong. We showed that Czechs are like all other Europeans, whose first interest is soccer, with erotica a close second. For that, we will never be forgiven."[14]

The Media Council Challenge

TV Nova confronted another challenge when the Media Council launched an investigation into its operations. The Czech Parliament had liberalized the media law at the start of 1996, and this change prompted the Media Council to re-examine the

[13]Janet Guyon, "CME Sticks with Fast-Growth Plan in Central Europe," *The Wall Street Journal Europe,* August 14, 1996, p. 4.

[14]Robert Frank, "Cultural Fare," *The Wall Street Journal,* April 30, 1997, p. A1.

arrangements between TV Nova's license holder (CET 21) and its operating company (CNTS), to ensure that the Council did not lose all authority over the country's most popular television station. The Council particularly wanted to affirm that CET 21, the license holder, had not, for all practical purposes, transferred its television license to CNTS.[15] As a member of the Media Council explained, "It's like transferring your driver's license . . . You can't just give it to someone else."[16]

Zelezny, the director of CNTS and by now a majority owner of CET 21, took a prominent part in the negotiations with the Media Council in the following months. He and Len Fertig protested that the Media Council had itself approved the structure of TV Nova, but they agreed to provide a draft contract that defined the services between CET 21 and CNTS and their legal relationship for discussion.[17] The Media Council continued to raise objections, however, and in July 1996 it commenced administrative proceedings against CNTS for broadcasting without a license. The police also launched a criminal investigation to determine if CNTS was broadcasting illegally.

While CNTS representatives continued to uphold the legitimacy of TV Nova's split structure, the company also sought to compromise with the Media Council to avoid possible sanctions against TV Nova. The Media Council had the authority to impose substantial financial penalties on CNTS if it was found in breach of the broadcasting law, and it also had the right to withdraw CET 21's broadcasting license. Zelezny considered the license to be seriously endangered and conveyed these fears to CME executives.[18] In May 1997, CNTS agreed to alter its agreement with CET 21, bowing to pressure from the Media Council. Instead of CET 21 granting CNTS exclusive "use of the license," the new agreement gave CNTS the right to use the "know-how concerning the license." CNTS also agreed to other requests made by the Media Council, including changing the description of its business in the company registry. While the Media Council expressed satisfaction with these concessions, it did not withdraw its administrative proceedings against CNTS at that time.

CNTS Ownership

The discussions with the Media Council on TV Nova occurred as CME acquired a larger ownership share in CNTS. Exhibit 8 shows how the ownership of CNTS changed between 1994 and 1997. As shown in the exhibit, CME's original stake in CNTS was 66%; the Czech Savings Bank (CSB) owned 22%, and CET 21 had a 12% stake. In 1996, CSB decided to sell its holding in CNTS as the Czech government began pressuring banks to sell their large equity holdings in Czech companies. CME agreed to purchase CSB's 22% share in CNTS for about $36 million, increasing CME's holding in CNTS to 88%. CSB lent CME funds for the purchase of its holding. Fertig described this as "the best deal of my life," explaining, "we increased our holding in our most valuable asset by one-third, buying an immense amount of future cash flow for very little of other

[15]UNCITRAL Arbitration, CME Czech Republic B.V. (The Netherlands) vs. The Czech Republic, Partial Award, September 13, 2001 available at ⟨http://www.cetv-net.com/ne/articlefiles/439-cme-cr_eng.pdf⟩ (accessed July 20, 2003).

[16]Robert Frank, "Cultural Fare," *The Wall Street Journal*, April 30, 1997, p. A1.

[17]UNCITRAL Arbitration, Ronald S. Lauder vs The Czech Republic, Final Award, September 3, 2001 available at ⟨http://www.cetv-net.com/ne/articlefiles/439-lauder-cr_eng.pdf.⟩ (accessed July 21, 2003).

[18]UNCITRAL Arbitration, CME Czech Republic B.V. (The Netherlands) vs. The Czech Republic, Partial Award, September 13, 2001 available at ⟨http://www.cetv-net.com/ne/articlefiles/439-cme-cr_eng.pdf⟩ (accessed July 20, 2003).

EXHIBIT 8

CNTS OWNERSHIP STRUCTURE, 1994–1997

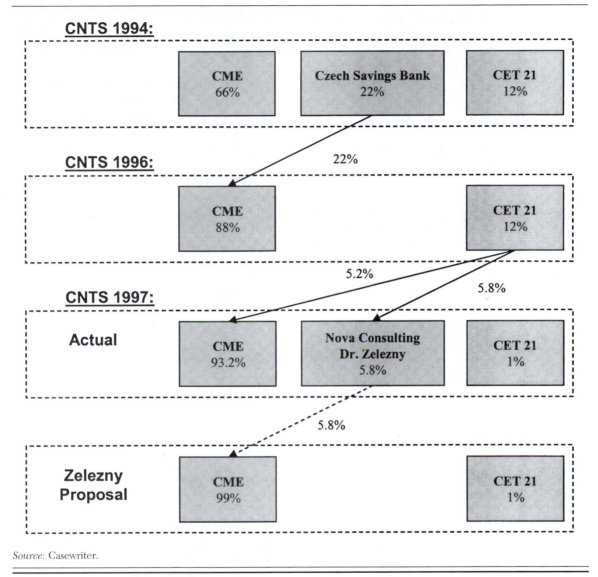

Source: Casewriter.

people's money."[19] Fertig also announced that CME intended to make a public offering of part of its holding in CNTS "to assure increased Czech participation in the future."[20]

A short time later, four of the original founders of CET 21 informed CME that they also wanted to cash out their investment. CET 21 held the broadcast license and

[19]Janet Guyon, "CME Sticks with Fast-Growth Plan in Central Europe," *The Wall Street Journal Europe*, August 14, 1996, p. 4.

[20]Kevin Done, "CME Buys Bank's Stake in Czech TV Group," *The Financial Times*, August 5, 1996, p. 17.

a 12% ownership stake in CNTS. CME considered that it was in the company's interest to ensure that ownership of the license company did not pass to possibly unfriendly outsiders.[21] CME therefore lent Zelezny a total of $5.2 million to buy out four of the original five founders of CET 21. At this time, CET 21's founders also transferred some of CET 21's original shares in CNTS to Nova Consulting, a company owned by Zelezny. This transaction gave Zelezny a 5.8% ownership stake in CNTS, through Nova Consulting. Zelezny also now had a controlling interest in CET 21, which itself held 6.2% of CNTS.

The terms of CME's loan to Zelezny required him to vote the acquired CET 21 shares as directed by CME until the loan was repaid.[22] The loan was forgiven the next year when Zelezny transferred 5.2% of CET 21's holding in CNTS to CME. As a consequence of this transfer, CME's ownership stake in CNTS rose to 93.2%. CET 21 retained 1% ownership in CNTS, and Zelezny owned 5.8% of CNTS through Nova Consulting.

Later that year, CME attracted unwelcome attention when journalists examining CME's filings with the SEC via the internet discovered details of the loan CME made to Zelezny to buy out the founders of CET 21. When these stories surfaced, critics charged that CME sought to control CET 21 through Zelezny and the controversy over foreign control of Czech television resurfaced. Len Fertig objected that the press coverage was unfair: "This has been twisted around in the Czech press about how CME is trying to take over the license company. We have no interest in the license company."[23] Zelezny also protested that he purchased the CET 21 shares "because I wanted to own a television station . . . not because the Americans wanted control. I'm Czech . . . I am not a puppet."[24] The controversy over the CME loan to Zelezny erupted just as CNTS was in discussions with the Media Council over the television license, raising suspicions about CME's motives. The Media Council demanded an explanation from Zelezny, who assured its members that the terms of the loan would not be fulfilled, meaning that he would not be required to vote his acquired CET 21 shares as directed by CME.[25]

ZELEZNY'S STAKE IN CNTS

Zelezny now wanted to sell the 5.8% stake in CNTS that he held through his company, Nova Consulting. He claimed that there were other interested buyers who would purchase his shares if CME did not do so.

Fertig had to consider several issues in deciding whether to purchase Zelezny's shares. If Zelezny sold his shares to another party, CME might be saddled with a troublesome minority shareholder. If CME bought the shares, other problems might arise. CME ownership of CNTS would increase to 99%, and Fertig knew from experience that this might provoke controversy over foreign ownership of Czech television. The Media Council posed another problem. While the Council had accepted the revised

[21]Normandy Madden, "'Iron Man' May Be Coming on Too Strong in Eastern Europe," *Advertising Age International*, May 15, 1997, p. I14.

[22]CME, September 30, 1996 10-Q (Bermuda: CME, 1996) available from Thomson Research, ⟨http://research.thomsonib.com⟩.

[23]"TV Nova Celebrates Third Birthday with High Profits and Controversy," *European Media Business & Finance*, February 10, 1997 available from Factiva, ⟨http://global.factiva.com⟩.

[24]Robert Frank, "Cultural Fare," *The Wall Street Journal*, April 30, 1997, p. A1.

[25]UNCITRAL Arbitration, CME Czech Republic B.V. (The Netherlands) vs. The Czech Republic, Partial Award, September 13, 2001 available at ⟨http://www.cetv-net.com/ne/articlefiles/439-cme-cr_eng.pdf⟩.

agreement between CNTS and CET 21, it had not yet formally rescinded administrative proceedings against CNTS. It was not known how the Media Council would react if CME bought Zelezny's shares in CNTS.

Fertig knew that several CME executives opposed buying Zelezny's shares. They argued that since Zelezny now controlled CET 21, it was important for him to retain an ownership interest in CNTS to ensure continued agreement between CET 21 and CNTS. Zelezny, however, was increasingly insistent on selling his CNTS shares, and he was pressing hard for a good price. It was up to Fertig to find a solution acceptable to both CME and Zelezny—and if that solution including purchasing the shares, Fertig also had to decide what price to offer Zelezny for those shares.

20

Czech Mate: CME and Vladimir Zelezny (B)— CME Negotiates

In January 1999, CME CEO Michel Delloye focused intently on the merger negotiations between his firm and SBS Broadcasting SA (SBS). As SBS completed its due diligence of CME, the relationship between CME, CNTS and Vladimir Zelezny came to preoccupy all merger participants. Delloye reviewed the agreements and arrangements between CME and Zelezny, Director of CME's most successful television station, TV Nova. While Zelezny himself had no ownership interest in CME or its Czech subsidiary, CNTS, his role as the head of TV Nova and the controlling shareholder of CET 21, the company holding TV Nova's broadcasting license, made him a significant player in these negotiations.

In August 1997, Zelezny had persuaded CME to purchase his 5.8% share of CNTS for $28.5 million, leaving Zelezny with no shares in CNTS. At that time, Zelezny had signed a share agreement with CME that included non-compete clauses preventing him from engaging in activities against the interests of CNTS. He continued to serve as General Director of CNTS as well as Director of TV Nova. Zelezny controlled CET 21, the company holding TV Nova's broadcasting license. (See Exhibit 1 for a diagram of the relationships among CME, CNTS and CET 21.) Over the past few months, Zelezny had repeatedly insisted that the agreement governing TV Nova's operation had to be restructured. Uncertainty over TV Nova's future could undermine the merger negotiations between CME and SBS, and Delloye needed to resolve the issues raised by Zelezny as soon as possible.

Professor Mihir A. Desai and Professor Alberto Moel of Hong Kong University of Science and Technology and Research Associate Kathleen Luchs prepared this case. This case was developed from published sources. HBS cases are developed solely as the basis for class discussion. Cases are not intended to serve as endorsements, sources of primary data, or illustrations of effective or ineffective management.

EXHIBIT 1

RELATIONSHIPS AMONG CME, CNTS, AND CET 21

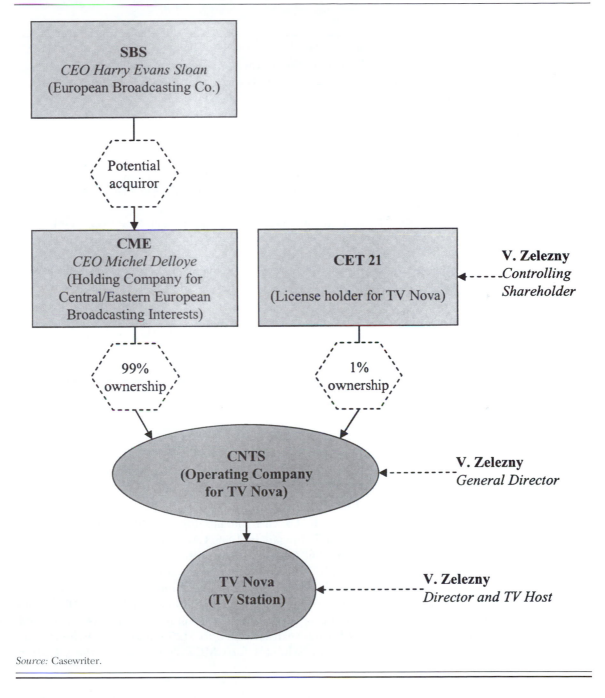

Source: Casewriter.

EXHIBIT 2

KEY DEVELOPMENTS AT CME

1997

June	CME fails in its bid for a national broadcasting license in Hungary
August	CME agrees to purchase Vladimir Zelezny's shares in CNTS for $28.5 million
September	Czech Media Council stops administrative proceedings against CNTS
September	CME acquires stake in TV 3, a small private Hungarian TV station
October	CME launches TVN in Poland
December	CME terminates its German operations

1998

March	Michel Delloye appointed CEO of CME, replacing Len Fertig. CME announces a change in its strategy from aggressive growth to a focus on improving the operating results of its existing assets
August	CME announces it will take a write-down on its Hungarian operations and freezes further investments in its Polish station pending a restructuring of its agreement with its local partner
August	S&P's Rating Service downgrades CME's corporate credit rating and changes its outlook for the company from positive to negative
November	CME receives an equity investment of $22.725 million from Ronald Lauder through RSL Capital LLC
December	CME sells its interest in its Polish station, TVN, and takes a write-down on its investment

Source: Casewriter.

DEVELOPMENTS AT CME[1]

A pioneer in commercial television ventures in Eastern and Central Europe, CME operated stations in Germany, the Czech Republic, Romania, Slovenia, the Ukraine, the Slovak Republic, Poland and Hungary by 1998. CME's flagship station, TV Nova, was profitable from the start, but CME ran into problems in some of the region's other larger markets (see Exhibit 2 for key developments at CME). In 1997, the company lost its bid for a national broadcasting license in Hungary and the next year it wrote down the value of its Hungarian programming library. In 1998 CME sold its interest in its Polish station, taking large write-downs on its investments. At the end of 1998, CME's net losses for the year amounted to $125 million (see Exhibit 3 for CME's financial statements and Exhibit 4 for CME's share price history). CME's

---

[1]The following section is largely based on the annual reports of CME 1996-1998: CME, Dec. 31, 1996-1998 10-K (Bermuda: CME, 1996, 1997, 1998) available from Thomson Research, ⟨http://research.thomsonib.com⟩.

EXHIBIT 3

CME CONSOLIDATED STATEMENT OF OPERATIONS

(In thousands of U.S. dollars) For the years ended December 31,	1998	1997	1996
Gross revenues	234,878	194,373	170,114
Discounts and Agency Commissions	(52,511)	(44,108)	(34,129)
Net revenues	**182,367**	**150,265**	**135,985**
Station expenses:			
Other operating costs and expenses	73,993	60,697	50,188
Amortization of programming rights	55,226	22,770	21,599
Depreciation of station fixed assets and other intangibles	17,056	15,184	13,314
Total station operating costs and expenses	146,275	98,651	85,101
Selling, general and administrative expenses	28,806	22,953	21,357
Corporate expenses:			
Corporate operating costs and development expenses	22,670	25,467	15,782
Amortization of goodwill and allowance for development costs	16,809	14,845	2,940
Capital registration tax			809
Restructuring charge	2,552	—	—
Total corporate expenses	**42,031**	**40,312**	**19,531**
Operating Income	**(34,745)**	**(11,651)**	**9,996**
Equity in loss of unconsolidated affiliates	(3,398)	(10,340)	(17,867)
Loss on impairment of investments in unconsolidated affiliates	—	(20,707)	—
Net interest and other income	(18,591)	(6,009)	(1,794)
Foreign currency exchange (loss)/gain	(8,412)	(5,857)	(2,861)
Net income (loss) before provision for income tax	**(65,146)**	**(54,564)**	**(12,526)**
Provision for income tax	(15,856)	(14,608)	(16,405)
Net loss before minority interest	**(81,002)**	**(69,172)**	**(28,931)**
Minority interest in loss of consolidated subsidiaries	(156)	1,066	(1,072)
Net loss from continuing operations	**(81,158)**	**(68,106)**	**(30,003)**
Discontinued operations:			
Operating loss of discontinued operations	(15,289)	(16,986)	—
Loss on disposal of discontinued operations	(28,805)	—	—
Net Loss	**(125,252)**	**(85,092)**	**(30,003)**

Source: CME, Dec. 31, 1998 10-K (Bermuda: CME, 1998) available from Thomson Research, http://research.thomsonib.com.

EXHIBIT 4

CME SHARE PRICE HISTORY

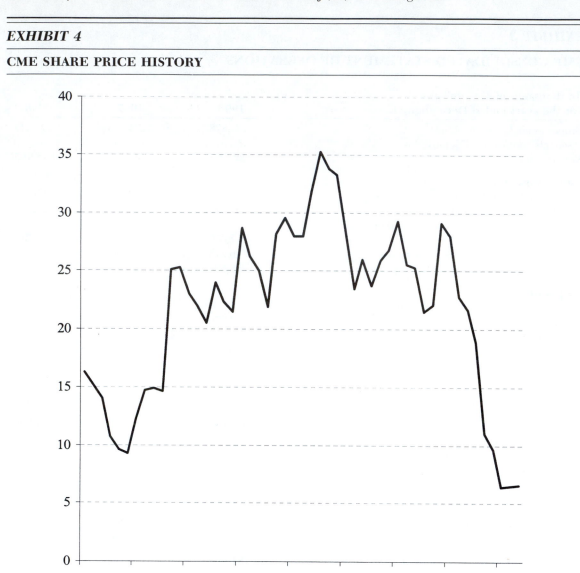

Source: Created by casewriter.

founder, Ronald Lauder, continued to support the company, providing $22.725 million in additional equity capital as CME searched for a possible merger partner. Due to the success of CNTS and TV Nova, CME still operated the most successful television station in central Europe and the possibility of SBS acquiring CME looked increasingly promising. SBS owned television stations in Scandinavia, Belgium, the Netherlands, and Hungary and wanted to expand its interests in Eastern and Central Europe.

DISCUSSIONS WITH DR. ZELEZNY[2]

Over the previous months, Zelezny had repeatedly demanded changes in the existing agreement between TV Nova's operating company, CNTS (99% owned by CME), and its license holder, CET 21. Since the founding of TV Nova, CNTS had held the exclusive right to operate the station and to its revenues, while CET 21 had contributed the use of its broadcasting license. In 1997, however, the Media Council had insisted that CNTS and CET 21 change the wording of their agreement. Instead of CNTS having "the exclusive use of the license" held by CET 21, the revised agreement stated that CNTS had exclusive "use of the know-how of the license." Now, Zelezny argued that CNTS could not continue as the exclusive operator of TV Nova because the Media Council opposed exclusive agreements between television license holders and operating companies. Zelezny proposed that CET 21 assume more responsibility for TV Nova's operations. Delloye knew that Zelezny had formed a program acquisition company named AQS. He had warned Zelezny not to acquire any programming for TV Nova from AQS since this function was the sole prerogative of CNTS. CME, as the parent of CNTS, would not surrender CNTS's exclusive right to operate TV Nova and receive all its revenues.

CME's Plan

Although Delloye was confident of CME's legal right to operate TV Nova through CNTS, Zelezny's disaffection could undermine the merger talks with SBS. CME therefore proposed a merger between CNTS and CET 21 so that there would no longer be two entities—one with the license and one as an operating company. Combining the two companies would simplify the structure of TV Nova and resolve the ongoing question of the respective rights of the operating company and license holder. As the majority shareholder of CET 21, Zelezny could anticipate receiving a considerable financial benefit from joining CET 21 with CNTS.

When Delloye had outlined this plan a few weeks earlier, Zelezny responded, "such a merger would not come easily and cheaply."[3] As Delloye prepared for the next round of talks, he considered the value to CME of combining CNTS and CET 21, and what it would cost to secure Zelezny's agreement. He knew he had to prepare an offer that would satisfy Zelezny and also reassure SBS that TV Nova had a secure future.

[2]This section is based on the UNCITRAL Arbitration, CME Czech Republic B.V. (Netherlands) vs The Czech Republic, Final Award, March 14, 2003, available at ⟨http://www.cetv-net.com/ne/articlefiles/ 439-Final_Award_Quantum.pdf⟩.

[3]Ibid., p. 67.

Czech Mate: CME and Vladimir Zelezny (C)— The Struggle for Control

As the merger negotiations between CME and SBS advanced in early 1999, Vladimir Zelezny's hold over TV Nova worried executives of both companies. SBS executives noted that, "the Feudal Lord may continue to resist operational control making it difficult to institute 'best practices.'"[1] CME tried to find a means of satisfying Zelezny without ceding its exclusive rights to operate TV Nova. CME and SBS offered various financial incentives to Zelezny aimed at securing his cooperation in order to advance the merger.

THE "PRICE OF PEACE" AND ZELEZNY'S ULTIMATUM

CME needed to assure SBS that it had secure control of TV Nova through its subsidiary, CNTS, and tried to get Zelezny's agreement on combining CNTS and CET 21. According to Zelezny, CME's founder, Ronald Lauder, "offered him $100 million to $140 million to buy CET 21 and lock up Nova's license."[2] SBS, in its own valuation of CME in February 1999, calculated that Zelezny should be offered 18% of TV Nova's new operating and license company worth $72 million, and a bonus worth $27 million

Professors Mihir A. Desai and Alberto Moel of Hong Kong University of Science and Technology and Research Associate Kathleen Luchs prepared this case. This case was developed from published sources. HBS cases are developed solely as the basis for class discussion. Cases are not intended to serve as endorsements, sources of primary data, or illustrations of effective or ineffective management.

[1]UNCITRAL Arbitration, CME Czech Republic B.V. (Netherlands) vs The Czech Republic, Final Award, March 14, 2003, p. 120, available at ⟨http://www.cetv-net.com⟩.

[2]Craig Mellow, "Ron Lauder's Disappearing TV Station," *Institutional Investor*, Jan. 1, 2000, p. 54.

upon renewal of the broadcast license. SBS executives characterized the $100 million offer to Zelezny as the "price of peace in the Czech Republic."[3]

Zelezny had not accepted any offer from CME when the CNTS Board met on February 24, 1999. Zelezny continued as General Director of CNTS, and at this meeting he put his position on record: CNTS could not continue as the exclusive operator of TV Nova and the existing contractual arrangements had to be changed. No compromise was possible, according to Zelezny, because the Media Council opposed exclusive agreements between operating companies and license holders. Zelezny declared that "his proposal was an ultimatum, which meant that CME could either accept or not."[4]

After this meeting, Zelezny directly solicited the support of the Media Council with a request that the Council clarify its position in writing. A few days later, the Council wrote a letter stating that exclusive agreements between operating companies and license holders were "incorrect," in the language of the Council. This letter dealt a serious blow to CME, since it challenged the company's right to control TV Nova. Nonetheless, CME continued to negotiate with Zelezny through its new CEO, Fred Klinkhammer, who replaced Delloye as CEO on March 23.

By the end of March 1999, CME and SBS had upwardly revised their estimates of the 'price of peace' with Zelezny; the cost rose to $125 million, and now included a fee payable to CET 21 of 4% of TV Nova's revenues. Although Zelezny had still not signed any agreement, SBS and CME publicly announced their merger on March 29. SBS offered $615 million in stock for CME. SBS included a release clause in the merger agreement, allowing it to withdraw on payment of a termination fee.

CME FIRES ZELEZNY

The impasse between CME and Zelezny continued up to the April meeting of the CNTS Board. At that meeting, Klinkhammer accused Zelezny of violating CNTS's exclusive right to acquire programming for TV Nova by authorizing AQS, a separate entity controlled by Zelezny, to buy programs for the station. Not convinced by Zelezny's denial, Klinkhammer fired him as General Director of CNTS. Klinkhammer deplored Zelezny's dealings with AQS, declaring, "such bad faith actions could hardly been expected, especially after CME purchased a 5.8% interest in CNTS from Dr. Zelezny for over $28 million less than two years ago and he agreed not to compete with CNTS as a condition of that purchase."[5] Zelezny claimed, "the law says TV Nova is CET 21" and reportedly claimed, "I am the executive of CET 21, owner of the name and Nova's licence. I am Nova."[6] Despite being dismissed as Director of CNTS, Zelezny continued as Director of TV Nova and still controlled CET 21.

Zelezny's sacking caused an uproar in the Czech Republic, with both sides in the dispute seeking media support. The Czech Media Council ordered the two parties to cease their public pronouncements but declined to intervene in the dispute.

---

[3]UNCITRAL Arbitration, CME Czech Republic B.V. (Netherlands) vs The Czech Republic, Final Award, March 14, 2003, p. 122, available at ⟨http://www.cetv-net.com⟩.

[4]UNCITRAL Arbitration, Ronald S. Lauder vs The Czech Republic, Final Award, September 3, 2001, p. 27 available at ⟨http://www.cetv-net.com/ne/articlefiles/439-lauder-cr_eng.pdf⟩ (accessed Oct. 21, 2003).

[5]"Zelezny Dismissed from CNTS," *PR Newswire*, April 19, 1999 available from Factiva at ⟨http://global.factiva.com⟩.

[6]"CME Company Wants to Prevent Zelezny from Heading Nova," *CTK Business News*, April 20, 1999 available from Factiva at ⟨http://global.factiva.com⟩.

ZELEZNY FIRES CNTS

Zelezny retaliated a few months after CME sacked him. On August 5, 1999, CET 21 terminated its service agreement with CNTS and withdrew the use of its license. CET 21 cited as grounds for its actions the failure of CNTS to deliver the daily log for TV Nova the previous day—a technical violation of the agreement between CNTS and CET 21. CME immediately sought a hearing from the Media Council and decried Zelezny's actions in the press. Klinkhammer declared, "Zelezny had less than $200 when he started with TV Nova. We have paid him more than $35 million in salary and other benefits. Now he is probably the first or second richest man in the country. We have created a monster."[7] Zelezny responded with a book entitled "We Shall Not Surrender This Television Station" and maintained, "CME is a flop . . . When it started it had a fantastic chance to win the television market in half of Europe, but it has been awfully managed and many decisions amounted to disasters."[8]

Lacking the use of a broadcast license, CNTS could not operate TV Nova. The Media Council refused to intervene in what it characterized as a commercial dispute, and the Czech courts offered no speedy remedy. CNTS was out of business.

TV Nova, however, continued to broadcast, with CET 21 securing the services of other companies to provide programming and sell advertising.

CME'S POSITION

With the loss of TV Nova, CME lost its major source of revenue and its share price plunged (see Exhibit 1 for CME's share price history). SBS reassessed its planned merger with CME and exercised its right to withdraw from the agreement in September.[9] Zelezny expressed some satisfaction with this outcome, explaining, "Lauder found he couldn't sell me or my generosity to SBS, and without me the SBS deal was off."[10]

CME, in serious financial straits after losing control of TV Nova, initiated various actions in the Czech courts to try and recover its control over TV Nova. Lauder used his considerable political influence to gather support for his cause in the United States. In November 1999, when the Czech Prime Minister visited Washington, D.C., Lauder paid for full page notices in *The New York Times* and *Washington Post* warning potential investors that the Czech Republic lacked safeguards for foreign investors (see Exhibit 2). Some observers judged that Lauder and CME would gain little satisfaction now that Zelezny controlled TV Nova, and the Director of the American Chamber of Commerce in Prague concluded, "No Czech politician who has any desire to continue being a politician is going to cross swords with Zelezny."[11]

[7]Kevin Done, "Czechs Watch CME TV battle," *Financial Times,* September 17, 1999, p. 30.

[8]*Ibid.*

[9]SBS paid CME a termination fee of $8.25 million. SBS did purchase selected assets from CME in separate transactions.

[10]Craig Mellow, "Ron Lauder's Disappearing TV Station," *Institutional Investor,* Jan. 1, 2000, p. 54.

[11]*Ibid.*

EXHIBIT 1

CME SHARE PRICE, 1999

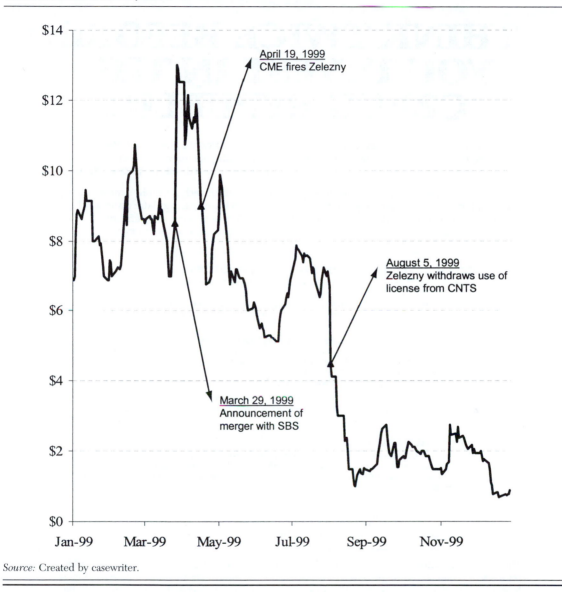

Source: Created by casewriter.

EXHIBIT 2

PAID ANNOUNCEMENT IN *THE NEW YORK TIMES*, NOVEMBER 8, 1999

THINK TWICE BEFORE YOU INVEST IN THE CZECH REPUBLIC

This may seem like a time of exciting opportunities for investment in the Czech Republic. For example, the Czech government is in the process of selling its interests in certain banks and, in the near future, in ands to privatize its interest in a national cellular phone company.

However, if our recent experience as principal investor in the Czech Republic's most successful broadcasting company is any indication, Czech business, regulatory and legal practices fall woefully short of international standards. Before making a significant investment in the Czech Republic, you may want to consider this cautionary tale:

CZECH GOVERNMENT WOOS FOREIGN INVESTORS...

When Central uropean Med (CME) wanted to establish a Western-style television station in the Czech Republic, the government welcomed CME's influx of capital and business expertise with open arms. Working with a local partner, CME developed TV Nova—which quickly emerged as the most opular private television station in Eastern Europe.

But then CME s local partner, Vladimir Zelezny, exploited his political influence and his network of contacts to undermine the partnership With the assistance of the government-controlled Czech Media Council, the regulatory body that grants television licenses and oversees broadcast operations, Zelezny cut out his foreign investors so that he could profit more fully from TV Nova's unparalleled success.

Under Zelezny's influence, the Czech Media Council has refused to protect CME's legal rights. According to a recent ed't rial in the European Wall Street Journal, the council "seems willing to let CME twist in the wind."

...BUT THEN ABUSES THEM

Under a 1991 U.S.-Czech treaty, the Czech government promised to protect U.S. investments from violations of the law. But it has been unwilling to handle this hot potato because—due to TV Nova's success—CME's local partner has acquired too much political clout.

Ronald S. Lauder, the controlling shareholder of CME and a U.S. citizen entitled to treaty protection, has instituted arbitration proceedings, through the UN Commission on International Trade Law, to ensure that the Czech government is held accountable for its discrimination against foreign investors and for failing to protect CME's rights.

The U.S. Ambassador to Prague has said that a just and speedy solution to this dispute would send a strong signal to foreign investors that the Czech Republic has an environment conducive to foreign investment. And leading U.S. Congressmen have rightly called for hearings into the Czech government's conduct. But, so far, *the Czech government has failed to act*.

Until this matter is resolved, we urge the international financial community to think twice before investing in the Czech Republic. Otherwise, you too could be left to "twist in the wind."

On behalf of its shareholders,

Central European Media Enterprises Ltd.
c/o RSL Investments Corporation, 767 Fifth Avenue, New York, NY 10153

Source: *New York Times*, Nov. 8, 1999, available from ProQuest Historical Newspapers at ⟨http://80-proquest.umi.com⟩.

Czech Mate: CME and Vladimir Zelezny (D)— Resolution

CME continued to try to regain control of TV Nova through appeals to the Media Council and the Czech courts, without success. CME and Ronald Lauder, as its principal shareholder, turned to international tribunals to hear their case. CME charged Zelezny with breaking the non-compete clauses in his agreement with the company and sought damages from him personally. In separate actions, CME and Lauder claimed that the Czech Republic and its regulatory commission, the Media Council, violated international treaties by failing to protect CME's legal investment in TV Nova. Separate tribunals held hearings in different cities, and the press dubbed the actions accordingly: "The Amsterdam Tribunal," "The London Tribunal," and "The Stockholm Tribunal."

TRIBUNAL DECISIONS

"The Amsterdam Tribunal"[1]

The International Court of Arbitration of the International Chamber of Commerce (ICC) heard CME's complaint against Zelezny, as provided for in the share agreement between CME and Zelezny. The two parties had signed the agreement in 1997 when CME purchased Zelezny's shares in CNTS. In February 2001, the Court found that Zelezny breached the terms of his non-compete agreement with CME by authorizing AQS to purchase programming for TV Nova. The Court nulled the original agreement

Professors Mihir A. Desai and Professor Alberto Moel of Hong Kong University of Science and Technology and Research Associate Kathleen Luchs prepared this case. This case was developed from published sources. HBS cases are developed solely as the basis for class discussion. Cases are not intended to serve as endorsements, sources of primary data, or illustrations of effective or ineffective management.

[1]This section is based on ICC International Court of Arbitration Case No. 10435/AER/ACS CME Media Enterprises B.V. (The Netherlands) vs Vladimir Zelezny (Czech Republic), Award Sentence, Feb. 9, 2001 available at http://www.cetv-net.com/iFiles/1439-CME_Zelezny_en.pdf.

between the parties, and ordered Zelezny to repay to CME the $23.35 million he had received to date for his CNTS shares.[2] CME was ordered to return to Zelezny the CNTS shares it had purchased from him, once it received repayment.

CME also claimed damages against Zelezny of $470 million for the destruction of CNTS. The Court found that CME had not proved this case and granted no damages to CME.

"The London Tribunal"[3]

Lauder, as the principal shareholder in CME, requested arbitration according to the terms of the treaty between the United States and the Czech Republic on the protection of investments. On behalf of CME shareholders, he claimed $500 million in damages from the Czech Republic for failing to protect his investment in TV Nova. This tribunal issued its decision on September 3, 2001. The tribunal found that the Czech Republic had arbitrarily discriminated against Lauder as a foreign investor at the time of the founding of TV Nova. At that time, the Media Council refused to allow CME's direct investment in TV Nova's license-holding company although such foreign investments were permitted under Czech law. The tribunal ruled, however, that Lauder failed to prove that CME's subsequent losses were caused by this discrimination and awarded no damages.

This was a clear victory for the Czech Republic and a spokesman for the government explained, "Mr. Lauder invested here; the investment was not really a success, and it has nothing to do with Czech laws."[4] Zelezny, still host of a show on TV Nova, declared, "Everything ended well. We've won and it is clear that only Ronald Lauder himself is to blame for his business failures."[5]

The Czech Republic enjoyed its victory only briefly. Ten days later, in a separate action, the arbitrators in "The Stockholm Tribunal" decided in favor of CME.

"The Stockholm Tribunal"[6]

CME, with a wholly-owned subsidiary registered in the Netherlands, pursued its own suit against the Czech Republic, accusing the Czech Republic of breaching its investment treaty with the Netherlands.[7] On September 13, 2001, this tribunal decided in favor of CME. The tribunal ruled that the Media Council's 1997 demand for changes in the agreement between CNTS's and CET 21 weakened CNTS's control over TV Nova and caused CME to be wrongly deprived of its investment in TV Nova two years later. The Tribunal's decision stated that CME's acceptance of the new agreement in 1997

[2]The original price of the shares was $28.5 million, but CME had stopped its installment payments to Zelezny for the shares when it fired him.

[3]This section is based on UNCITRAL Arbitration, Ronald S. Lauder vs The Czech Republic, Final Award, September 3, 2001 available at http://www.cetv-net.com/ne/articlefiles/439-lauder-cr_eng.pdf.

[4]Marius Dragomir, "TV Nova Courtroom Drama Set to Continue after London Episode," *Prague Business Journal*, September 10, 2001 available from Factiva at http://global.factiva.com.

[5]"Swedish Ruling Deals Blow to State as Zelezny's Accomplice," *CTK Daily News*, September 1, 2001 available from Factiva at http://global.factiva.com.

[6]This section is based on UNCITRAL Arbitration, CME Czech Republic B.V. (The Netherlands) vs. The Czech Republic, Partial Award, September 13, 2001, p. 139 available at http://www.cetv-net.com/ne/articlefiles/439-cme-cr_eng.pdf.

[7]The Czech government had refused to join this case to the Lauder action against the Czech Republic ("The London Tribunal"), and the two cases were decided by separate arbitration tribunals.

was irrelevant: "Such a decision for a compromise, however, does not make the Council's unlawful acts legal and cannot be deemed as a waiver of CME's rights under the Treaty."[8] The tribunal ruled that CME was entitled to compensation from the Czech Republic for the value of its investment, which would be determined separately.[9]

COMPENSATION CALCULATIONS[10]

To determine the compensation due to CME for the loss of its investment in TV Nova, the tribunal first established the fair market value of CNTS at the time it lost use of the license. The tribunal considered different valuation approaches presented by both parties, including discounted cash flow models, reports of stock market analysts, previous transactions in CNTS stock, and the merger offer by SBS. In March 2003, the tribunal ruled that the fair market value of CNTS in August 1999 was $400 million. Using this as a starting point, the tribunal determined the compensation due to CME from the Czech Republic as follows:

Market value of CNTS	$400.0 million
Less Residual value of CNTS[11]	38.5 million
Less "Zelezny Factor"	72.0 million
Adjusted value of CNTS	$289.5 million
CME compensation for 93.2% of CNTS[12]	$269.8 million plus 10% interest from February 2000 to date of payment

The tribunal reduced CME's compensation by the "Zelezny Factor"—or $72 million—on the basis that Zelezny's business and managerial skills accounted for $72 million of the value of CNTS. The tribunal ruled that the Czech Republic and its Media Council was not responsible for this part of CME's lost investment.

AFTERMATH

The Czech government tried to get Zelezny and TV Nova to accept some financial responsibility for the award. Zelezny, however, did not even mention the damages awarded to CME on his weekly TV show and a TV Nova spokesperson described the judgment as "a dispute between the Czech Republic and CME."[13] In May 2003 the Czech

---

[8]UNCITRAL Arbitration, CME Czech Republic B.V. (The Netherlands) vs. The Czech Republic, Partial Award, September 13, 2001, p. 139 available at ⟨http://www.cetv-net.com/ne/articlefiles/439-cme-cr_eng.pdf⟩ (accessed July 20, 2003).

[9]The decision of the tribunal was not unanimous. The arbitrator chosen by the Czech government refused to sign the decision and issued a separate opinion. His action had no legal force, and a new arbitrator was chosen for the next phase of the proceedings.

[10]This section is based on UNCITRAL Arbitration, CME Czech Republic B.V. (Netherlands) vs The Czech Republic, Final Award, March 14, 2003, available at ⟨http://www.cetv-net.com⟩.

[11]The residual value of CNTS included dividends paid to CME by CNTS after August 1999, the value of property and assets subsequently sold by CNTS, and the value of property and assets still held by CNTS.

[12]CME owned 93.2% of CNTS after the ICC Tribunal ("The Amsterdam Tribunal") ruled that Zelezny should repay CME for the CNTS shares it purchased from him and that CME should then return the CNTS shares to Zelezny.

[13]Marius Dragomir, "Pay TV," *Prague Business Journal*, March 24, 2003 available from Factiva at http://global.factiva.com.

government paid CME a total of $354.9 million, including the compensation for its lost investment, interest, and a share of legal costs. The Czech Premier pointed out that the sum "represented three times the annual budget of the Ministry of Environment, or the annual budget of the Ministry of Health."[14] One analyst estimated the cost of the award at about "$40 per person in a country where the average monthly wage is less than $600."[15] The government dismissed the Media Council and launched an inquiry into the affair.

CME collected the award from the Czech Republic but did not consider the matter closed. In August 2003 it filed another arbitration claim—in Vienna—against CET 21 for $275 million, seeking to recover the remainder of its investment losses. CME announced that, if it won, it would keep $72 million, the amount of its losses that the "Stockholm Tribunal" attributed directly to Zelezny and CET 21. CME would return $203 million of the potential award to the Czech Republic. CEO Fred Klinkhammer explained, "Czech citizens are entitled to a significant lowering of the burden brought upon them by the actions of the previous Media Council and CET 21."[16] CME stopped this action in October 2003 when PPF, one of the owners of CET 21, agreed to buy CNTS for $53.2 million. With the sale of CNTS, CME ended its legal actions concerning TV Nova in the Czech Republic.

Zelezny was elected to the Czech Senate in November 2002 but stripped of his parliamentary immunity in early 2003 to allow police to investigate fraud charges against him, some stemming from his failure to repay CME for the CNTS shares. His interest in CET 21 passed to a large Czech financial group (PPF) that paid the money he owed to CME. In May 2003, CET 21's new owners dismissed Zelezny as Director of TV Nova, hoping to distance the station from the lost arbitration.

In early 2004, Zelezny won a case in Prague city court in support of his claim that he owned 60% of CET 21. The court declared invalid all decisions and contracts made by CET 21 since May 2002; these decisions included Zelezny's dismissal as Director of TV Nova by PPF. Zelezny announced that he would negotiate with PPF over the ownership of CET 21 and declared, "I am not interested in upsetting the situation around TV Nova."[17]

[14]"Revenge of the Nerd, Part One," *Prague Business Journal*, May 19, 2003 available from Factiva at http://global.factiva.com.

[15]Richard Morgan, "Ron Lauder's Prague Spring," *Daily Deal*, May 26, 2003 available from Factiva at http://global.factiva.com.

[16]CME Press Release, August 6, 2003 available at ⟨http://www.cetv-net.com⟩.

[17]"Zelezny – I am Closer to a Stake in CET 21 Than is PPF," *CIA – Daily News*, Jan. 29, 2004 available from Factiva at http://global.factiva.com.

23

Czech Mate: CME and Vladimir Zelezny (E)— CME Returns

CME returned to the Czech Republic, once again as owners of TV Nova. On December 13, 2004, CME announced that it would acquire a controlling interest in TV Nova from the station's current owners, the Czech financial group PPF. TV Nova remained a highly successful television station, with a peak-time audience share of 44.6%, and CME would double its revenues with the acquisition.[1] The initial transaction was for 85% of PPF's interests in TV Nova, a deal CME valued at $642 million. PPF would receive $529 million in cash and 3.5 million CME Class A shares, making it CME's second largest shareholder. CME also received an option to buy PPF's remaining 15% interest in TV Nova companies.

The U.S. Ambassador to the Czech Republic commented that "CME's acquisition of TV Nova is the largest U.S. direct investment in the history of the Czech Republic and is an acknowledgement of the renewed confidence of the investment community in the stability and opportunities in the country today."[2] Michael Garin, CEO of CME, succinctly described the deal as " . . . a very big day for CME."[3]

The ownership of the broadcast license for TV Nova was still an issue at the time of the acquisition. TV Nova's license was owned by CET 21. The deal gave CME control of PPF's wholly-owned subsidiary, Vilja, which held a 52% ownership interest in CET 21. In its regulatory filing, CME explained, "A minority interest exists in CET 21,

Professor Mihir A. Desai and Research Associate Kathleen Luchs prepared this case. This case was developed from published sources. HBS cases are developed solely as the basis for class discussion. Cases are not intended to serve as endorsements, sources of primary data, or illustrations of effective or ineffective management.

[1]Robert Anderson, "CME Agrees Dollars 642m Czech TV Station Deal," *Financial Times*, December 14, 2004 available from Factiva http://www.factiva.com (accessed Jan. 11, 2005).

[2]CME Press Release, Dec. 13, 2004 available at http://www.cetv-net.com.

[3]CME Conference Call, Dec. 13, 2004. Transcript available from Factiva http://www.factiva.com (accessed Jan. 11, 2005).

the ownership of which has not been finally resolved. The resolution of claims related to this minority interest will not reduce CME's indirect ownership interest in CET 21 or alter its control position of the TV Nova Group."[4] According to CME, its initial "attributable economic interest" in TV Nova would be 56%, but the company declined to comment on the minority interest in CET 21 before its 10-K filing.

The case concerning ownership stakes in CET 21 had been before the Czech courts for several years. In December 2003, the Prague Municipal Court ruled that Vladimir Zelezny should be listed in the registry of companies as a 61% owner of CET 21. While this decision had subsequently been overturned, Zelezny remained listed as owner of CET 21. A few days after CME announced its acquisition of TV Nova, the case concerning ownership stakes in CET 21 reached the Supreme Court in the Czech Republic. No decision was expected for at least six months.

CME asserted that its deal with PPF guaranteed its control over TV Nova and the station's license. Furthermore, CME was confident that changes in the Czech Republic—including its recent membership in the European Union—provided sufficient safeguards for its investment. Nonetheless, some analysts remained cautious. In commenting on the deal, Stephen Farley, of Farley Capital, noted, "So far we are agnostic on the Nova acquisition . . . Do we actually know who owns Nova or its licence company now?"[5]

---

[4]CME, December 16, 2004 8-K (Bermuda: CME, 2004), p. 3, available on CME website, http://www.cetv-net.com.

[5]"Czech Republic: Is it Safe?" *Economist Intelligence Unit*, Dec. 20, 2004 available from Factiva ⟨http://www.factiva.com⟩ (accessed Jan. 11, 2005).

REGULATORY REGIMES

In addition to legal rules that govern investor protections and business conditions, firms also must interact with conflicting and overlapping regulatory regimes. This module gives readers a chance to think like regulators—which can be very helpful in deciphering regulatory actions and, perhaps more importantly, in predicting their actions.

Regulatory bodies have tremendous influence in shaping markets, and different regulatory regimes around the world sometimes collide with each other, particularly in the area of antitrust. The first case in this module, Antitrust Regulations in a Global Setting: The EU Investigation of the GE–Honeywell Merger, illustrates just such a clash between antitrust regulators in different countries. The formation of the European Union created a consolidated economy comparable in size to the United States and a regulatory regime somewhat analogous to the federal government. Not surprisingly, Brussels and Washington have different rules, raising issues for those companies that operate in both the United States and the EU. Some of the most heated regulatory conflicts have arisen in the antitrust sphere where American giants such as Microsoft and General Electric have found themselves at odds with the European Commission.

Planning in the context of diverse regulatory regimes poses a special challenge for the multinational manager. What country's laws govern? Do multiple countries' laws govern? Are they consistent? Is there a risk of being punished by one country for something the other permits or even demands? It may also be difficult to predict which rules will ultimately take precedence—if any. Earlier modules and cases dealt with situations where managers looked abroad for opportunities. The cases in this module examine some of the constraints that managers may confront because of different or conflicting regulatory regimes abroad. Managers in multinational businesses therefore need to understand the kinds of regulatory issues that may affect their business or the international economy. The first case in this module focuses on enforcement and compliance, and the second case examines the appropriate design of regulatory systems in the first instance.

Antitrust Regulations in a Global Setting: The EU Investigation of the GE–Honeywell Merger investigates the potential merger between General Electric and Honeywell in 2001. The merger between the two American firms had already been approved in the United States, but also required the approval of the European Commission. The EU refused to approve the merger without significant concessions from GE, and the dispute highlighted the different approaches of the European and U.S. antitrust authorities. This case provides a perspective on the antitrust issues raised by the cross-border effects of even domestic mergers; it also explores why regulators in the United States and Europe came to different conclusions. What, if anything, was the impact of the U.S. decision on the EU decision? Should it have had an impact? A noteworthy aspect of the case is that the EU intervened in a deal between two U.S. multinationals. Doing business as a multinational means expanded business opportunities, but it also means expanded regulatory compliance obligations.

The second case, Redesigning Sovereign Debt Restructuring Mechanisms, asks whether the world needs a global bankruptcy regime to service government borrowers. Historically, sovereign debt crises have been handled by creditors in a fairly ad hoc manner. A potential solution is an international statutory debt-restructuring regime that is administered by a multilateral agency. This case examines three major debt crises and looks at the historical policies of the institutions involved and the possibilities for reform. For those who manage investments abroad, the first-order questions are: What will the recovery be on the bonds in a bankruptcy? Will a global bankruptcy regime make it easier or harder for governments to borrow in international markets? This case looks at one proposal for reforming the process by which sovereigns in default recover.

OVERVIEW OF THE CASES

Antitrust Regulations in a Global Setting: The EU Investigation of the GE–Honeywell Merger

On July 3, 2001, the European Commission blocked the proposed $45 billion merger between General Electric (GE) and Honeywell. The decision came two months after the U.S. Department of Justice announced its own decision not to challenge the proposed merger. Because of its outcome and the size of the thwarted deal, the decision of the European Union (EU) was highly publicized in business, legal, academic, and political circles. However, it was not the first time that a proposed merger between two American companies was blocked, let alone reviewed, by the European Commission. Between September 1990 and July 2002, the regulatory authorities of the European Commission received 2,055 notifications of proposed combinations. Approximately half of these notifications involved at least one non-European firm.

The GE–Honeywell case raises awareness of a more general phenomenon in business economics: the increasing importance of merger regulation in the global economy. As a result, business combinations are facing a much greater probability of regulatory intervention and, ultimately, prohibition. For the interested companies, the associated transaction and opportunity costs can be huge. It is therefore important for the corporate managers behind those deals to understand how and why international regulators make decisions about mergers. The crucial questions for the GE–Honeywell case are:

- Should European Competition Commissioner Mario Monti be worried about this merger?

- What are horizontal mergers? Vertical mergers? Conglomerate mergers? Are these different types of mergers equally problematic for consumer welfare?

- How would you evaluate the consequences of this merger? What is the relevant market?

- How would you argue/negotiate this case if you were GE CEO Jack Welch?

Redesigning Sovereign Debt Restructuring Mechanisms

Anne O. Krueger of the International Monetary Fund is proposing a new approach to sovereign defaults, the Sovereign Debt Restructuring Mechanism (SDRM). The SDRM would create a new international legal framework for sovereign defaults, similar to bankruptcy proceedings in the private sector. The SDRM would be overseen by a new judicial group within the IMF and implemented through international treaties. Krueger has to construct a convincing case that the SDRM would be more effective than alternative approaches to sovereign defaults. This case provides information on some major sovereign defaults (the crises in Latin America, Mexico, and Asia), and on the existing institutions and processes that creditors and debtors turn to in sovereign defaults. This case raises a question that is not usually contemplated in markets—what happens when countries go broke? To answer that general question, first consider these:

- Why do countries default on their debt?
- Why do so many countries default? What prevents more countries from defaulting on their debt?
- What problems prevent effective debt resolutions?
- Would the SDRM prevent those problems? Would it create any problems?

ADDITIONAL READING

Bulow, Jeremy. 2002. "First World Governments and Third World Debt." *Brookings Papers on Economic Activity* (1): 229–255.

Nalebuff, Barry J. 2001. "Bundling and the GE–Honeywell Merger." Yale School of Management, Working Paper Series ES, No. 22.

Patterson, Donna E., and Carl Shapiro. 2001, Fall. "Transatlantic Divergence in GE–Honeywell: Causes and Lessons." *Antitrust Magazine:* 1–19.

Roubini, Nouriel. 2002, April 4. "Do We Need a New International Bankruptcy Regime? Comments on Bulow, Sachs, and White." Draft, Brookings Panel on Economic Activity, Symposium: A Bankruptcy Court for Sovereign Debt, available at http://www.stern.nyu.edu/globalmacro.

Shleifer, Andrei. 2003. "Will the Sovereign Debt Market Survive?" *American Economic Review,* 93(2): 85–89.

White, Michelle J. 2002. "Sovereigns in Distress: Do They Need Bankruptcy?" *Brookings Papers on Economic Activity*, 1: 287–319.

24

Antitrust Regulations in a Global Setting: The EU Investigation of the GE–Honeywell Merger

As he prepared for his meeting with Jack Welch, CEO of General Electric Co. (GE), on June 13, 2001, the European Competition Commissioner Mario Monti puzzled over the conditional approval by the U.S. Department of Justice of GE's $45 billion acquisition of Honeywell. Monti's mandate was to protect free competition and prevent excessive concentrations of market power affecting consumers' interests in the Member States of the European Union. He and his colleagues had been formally reviewing the GE–Honeywell transaction for several months and had significant concerns over the anti-competitive effects the merger might entail. The forthcoming meeting with Welch would be their last opportunity to discuss face-to-face the structural and behavioral remedies that would be required for the proposed merger to gain the EU's approval. Still, GE had received a green light from Washington, subject only to minimal conditions. Monti found himself in the uncomfortable position of judging a merger between two American companies that had won U.S. regulatory approval, but might nonetheless run afoul of European rules.

Monti knew his final decision would have significant ramifications—it would highlight the harmony or disparities in different regulatory regimes and the institutions that enforce them around the world. It also might crystallize the differences in the way the U.S. and European antitrust authorities measured market power and the varying degrees to which giving corporations freedom to act as they see fit was balanced against

Professors Mihir A. Desai and Belen Villalonga and Research Associate Mark F. Veblen prepared this case. This case was developed from published sources. HBS cases are developed solely as the basis for class discussion. Cases are not intended to serve as endorsements, sources of primary data, or illustrations of effective or ineffective management.

the desire to protect consumer interests and competitive pricing. This was a particularly high-profile deal and so it would create a precedent that executives and regulators would remember.

But Monti had to put the political issues aside and consider the merger on its economic merits and make sure that GE received a fair hearing in the procedures established by the European Union under its Merger Control Regulation (the Merger Regulation). The rules, adopted as part of the economic and political integration of Europe, were designed to protect the interests of consumers of the EU Member States, and Monti had to consider the transaction in that light.

THE EUROPEAN UNION'S MERGER TASK FORCE

Monti headed the Competition Commission, which, through its Merger Task Force (MTF) was the department of the European Commission in charge of merger control. Exhibit 1 shows the organizational chart of the European Union's institutions. Since 1990, the Commission had the power to review mergers between companies of any nationality whose combined worldwide and European revenues were above the thresholds established in the Merger Regulation. The proposed GE–Honeywell merger easily exceeded those thresholds.

The merger review process began informally, as soon as the merger was publicly announced, with information gathering and pre-merger contacts with the parties and third parties, including customers and competitors. The formal review only began when the deal was officially notified to the Commission, and could consist of one or two formal investigative phases. Phase I gave the MTF between one month and six weeks to decide whether to clear the deal or to open a more detailed line of enquiry (Phase II).

Phase II, if entered, began with an in-depth investigation that could lead to a Statement of Objections issued by the MTF. In such case, the parties to the transaction were then allowed a written reply and an Oral Hearing where third parties including customers and competitors might also participate. The results were then discussed by an Advisory Committee where the 15 EU Member States were allowed to comment on the transaction. Four months after the Phase II review had begun, a final decision had to be reached to (i) approve the transaction, (ii) approve it subject to remedies, or (iii) prohibit it. Remedies encompassed all structural or behavioral corrective actions merging parties might undertake to resolve any anti-competitive issues raised in the Statement of Objections. Examples of structural remedies included divestitures of certain divisions of the merging companies to reduce competitive harm. Behavioral remedies could entail commitments by the parties not to engage in anti-competitive practices, or agreements by the parties to facilitate competition in the market by, for instance, granting competitors access to essential facilities or exclusive resources.

If the Commission found the transaction to be incompatible with the Common Market, the parties would have the right to appeal that decision to the Court of First Instance of the European Communities (typically a two- to three-year process).[1]

The Oral Hearings for the GE–Honeywell case were held on May 29. Phase II had begun on March 5, 2001, so the final decision was due by the beginning of July. Exhibit 2 shows a timeline of events associated with the GE–Honeywell proposed merger.

---

[1]This is procedurally different from the U.S. merger review process, where anti-trust authorities must obtain an order from an independent judicial authority *prior* to blocking a transaction.

EXHIBIT 1

INSTITUTIONAL ORGANIZATION CHART, EUROPEAN UNION

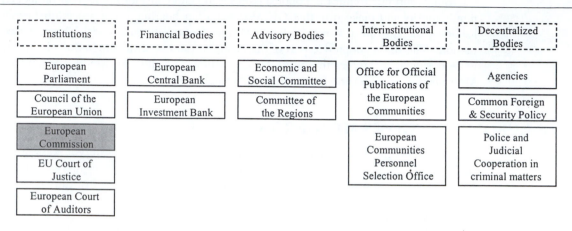

The Twenty Commissioners of the European Commission

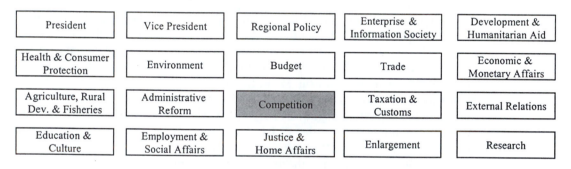

Structure of the Competition Commission

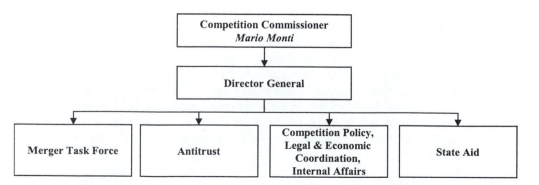

Source: Organization in force at the time of the GE–Honeywell case. Created by casewriter based on information from *Europa: The European Union On-Line* available at http://europa.eu.int/.

EXHIBIT 2

GE–HONEYWELL MERGER INVESTIGATION TIMELINE

Date	Event
October 20, 2000	• United Technologies' announces possible $40 bn bid for Honeywell
October 22, 2000	• GE announces intention to acquire Honeywell in tax-free merger valued at $45 bn
January 11, 2001	• Honeywell shareholders approve merger
December 2000	• Commencement of U.S. Dept. of Justice investigation
	• <u>Problems</u>: merger would (i) reduce competition in U.S. military helicopter engines and result in higher prices, lower quality, and reduced innovation for U.S. military, and reduce competition in heavy maintenance, repair, and overhaul services for certain Honeywell aircraft engines and auxiliary power units, (ii) higher prices, lower quality for business aircraft users
February 5, 2001	• Commencement of European Commission (EC) investigation
	• <u>Problem areas</u>: (i) horizontal overlaps (large regional jet engines) (ii) vertical effects (Honeywell components to competing engine suppliers, GECAS as the leading buyer and lessor of aircraft), and (iii) conglomerate effects (bundling of jet engines, avionics, and non-avionics, financial strength)
May 2, 2001	• GE and Honeywell agree to U.S. DOJ requirements to divest Honeywell's ($200m) helicopter engine business and authorize a new MRO service provider
May 8, 2001	• EC issues a 155-page Statement of Objections to the GE–Honeywell merger
May 29–30, 2001	• Oral Hearing takes place in Brussels
June 13, 2001	• Jack Welch and Mario Monti meet to negotiate in person

Source: Compiled by casewriter.

GENERAL ELECTRIC AND THE COMMERCIAL AIRCRAFT ENGINE MARKET

GE was a diversified technology, services and manufacturing company with revenues of $130 billion and profits of $13 billion in 2000. It operated in more than 100 countries and employed 313,000 people worldwide. The company's five primary operating units were Aircraft Engines, Appliances, GE Capital Services, NBC, and Power Systems. The products manufactured by GE included appliances for consumer and commercial purposes, power generation and distribution products, commercial and military jet engines, and engineered materials such as plastics and industrial diamonds. NBC provided media and broadcasting services. GE Capital offered a broad array of financial and other services, such as consumer, commercial, and industrial financing, real estate financing, asset management and leasing, and insurance/reinsurance.

Not only was GE the largest company in the world by market capitalization, but GE Capital, if independent, would also have been one of the top 20 Fortune 500 companies. Its revenue far exceeded that of GE's other reporting units (see Exhibit 3). GE

EXHIBIT 3

GE REPORTING SEGMENTS (BILLIONS OF DOLLARS)

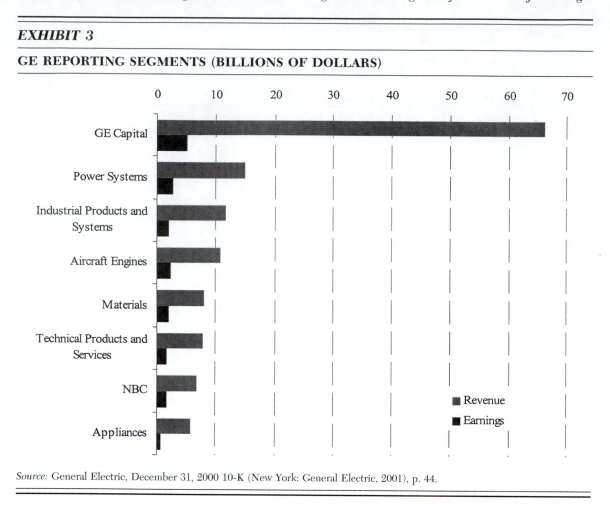

Source: General Electric, December 31, 2000 10-K (New York: General Electric, 2001), p. 44.

Capital frequently interacted with GE's industrial divisions, either by providing financing to GE's customers, or acting as a customer, purchasing GE products directly and then leasing them to third parties. One such example was the relationship between the Aircraft Engines division (GEAE) and GE Capital.

The Aircraft Engine division designed and manufactured engines for commercial and military applications. Buyers of large airplanes typically chose the airframe manufacturer and the engine manufacturer separately. Customers of GEAE included aircraft manufacturers, individual airlines, and leasing companies that purchased planes on a speculative basis and leased them on to airlines.

Aircraft Engine Market Segments

GE offered different engines for large commercial aircraft (made by Boeing and Airbus), regional aircraft (made by Embraer, Bombardier, Fairchild Dornier, and British Aerospace), and corporate jets (made by Cessna, Gulfstream, Raytheon, Bombardier, and Dassault). Each of these jet categories could be further subdivided into segments based on application (number of passengers and flight distance) and operating cost. Large commercial aircraft came in either wide- or narrow-body formats, both of which could be powered by engines made by GE, Rolls Royce, or Pratt & Whitney (a division of United Technologies). Market shares are reported in Exhibit 4. Large (70 to 90+ passengers) and small (30 to 50 passengers) regional jets serve different missions because the operating costs per seat-mile were such that a large jet could not economically be used for shorter or less densely traveled routes. GE, Rolls Royce, and Pratt & Whitney all offered engines for both large and small regional jets, and Honeywell sold engines for large regional jets. Similarly, the corporate jet market could be divided into light, medium, and heavy corporate jets based on plane size and distance traveled. All four engine manufactures were active in the medium-sized corporate jet market, but only Pratt & Whitney sold engines for light and heavy corporate jets. Exhibit 5 reports market shares for regional and corporate jet engines.

Most of the large commercial aircraft could be purchased with two or three different engine options. A few models, however, could only be purchased with one engine. This exclusivity typically resulted from the fact that the economics of a particular model could not justify multiple sources of engine supply (e.g. because of a low sales forecast for that particular model). Exclusivity could also arise contractually to compensate the engine manufacturer for providing financial assistance to the airframe manufacturer to fund research and development efforts during the design phase. Regional and corporate jets were generally sold with only one engine option, such that end customers chose among different airframe manufacturer/engine manufacturer bundles.

Maintenance, Repair, and Overhaul (MRO)

Jet engines required significant maintenance and repair and an associated stream of spare parts. Airlines and plane owners could maintain internal servicing operations, turn to independent MRO providers, or hire the original engine manufacturers to service engines. There were a significant number of MRO providers available in the market. The process of becoming certified to service engines was costly, as was the process to become a cer-

---

EXHIBIT 4

LARGE COMMERCIAL AIRCRAFT ENGINE MARKET SHARES

	GE/CFMI	P&W	RR
Narrow-body			
Engine installed base	51%	22%	27%
Engine order backlog	68%	13%	19%
Wide-body			
Engine installed base	54%	31%	15%
Engine order backlog	53%	28%	19%
Total			
Engine installed base	53%	27%	21%
Engine order backlog	65%	16%	19%

NOTES:

(1) Market shares for both installed base and order backlog are for aircraft still in production.

(2) GE and CFMI market shares have been aggregated; IAE's market share has been split evenly between P&W and RR.

Source: Commission of the European Communities Decision, 3 July 2001, Case No COMP/M.2220-General Electric/Honeywell.

EXHIBIT 5

REGIONAL AND CORPORATE JET ENGINE MARKET SHARES

	GE	HON	RR	P&W
Large regional jet aircraft				
Engine installed base	60–70%	30–40%	0%	0%
Engine order backlog	90–100%	0–10%	0%	0%
Corporate jets				
Engine installed base	0–10%	40–50%	30–40%	10–20%
Medium corporate jets				
Engine installed base	10–20%	60–70%	10–20%	0–10%

NOTE:

(1) Installed base market shares refer to aircraft still in production. Market shares for order backlog refer to jets not yet in service.

Source: Commission of the European Communities Decision, 3 July 2001, Case No COMP/M.2220-General Electric/Honeywell.

---

tified manufacturer of spare parts, because manufacturers had to reverse engineer parts unless they obtained licensing agreements from the original engine maker. In GE's engines, reverse engineering of their parts was virtually impossible because the technology embedded in the sophisticated engine core was a tightly guarded secret that the company did not share even with its joint venture partners. Spare parts constituted 70% of MRO expenditures, and 90–95% of spare parts were made by the original engine maker, for whom this was a significant source of aftermarket revenue. Over a 25-year life of an airplane, airlines paid around 200% of the price of the engine in MRO.

Airlines were increasingly outsourcing MRO through "fleet-hour-agreements" (also called "power-by-the-hour"). GE, for example, had recently begun offering bundled MRO services for a fixed price per engine flight hour. This freed airlines from devoting resources to training technicians, maintaining facilities, and buying spare parts. The trend in service contracts had altered GE's revenue mix from 57% original equipment sales and 43% after market revenue in 1990 to 33% / 67% in 2000, respectively. Cost savings associated with commonality of engine types within a fleet were substantial. Even line or support maintenance (which did not require removing the engine from the wing) was much less expensive. Training a technician on a new engine from a model family the technician already serviced cost roughly between $1,000 and $5,000. If the engine was from the same manufacturer but a different model family, the training costs jumped to $5,000 to $10,000 per technician. For engines from another manufacturer this ramped up to $20,000.

GE Capital

As one of the world's largest financial institutions, GE Capital put a strong balance sheet behind GE's industrial businesses. GE was able to parlay its financial strength into operating advantages through a number of channels. First, it helped GEAE to sell engines at deep discounts, pushing the break-even point on investments farther into the future. Second, it could provide direct financial support, on behalf of GE, to airframe manufacturers. Doing so during the design phase of a particular airframe might facilitate contractual exclusivity for GE to be the only engine certified for that airframe. Third, with the support of GE Capital, GE had for a number of years been acquiring independent MRO operations around the world, building a unique global network that could service not only GE-made engines but also those of GE's competitors.

GE Capital Aviation Services (GECAS)

GECAS was the single largest purchaser of new airplanes, accounting for approximately 10% of unit sales in the overall market. It also was one of the two leading aircraft leasing companies as it commanded 40% of the market for large commercial aircraft leases and was the only company active in leasing large regional jets. Its fleet was the largest, with over 1,000 planes. As the ultimate buyer of aircrafts, GECAS selected only GE-made engines for the planes it purchased, unless none was available.

HONEYWELL AND THE AVIONICS AND NON-AVIONICS MARKETS

Honeywell International, Inc. was a diversified technology and manufacturing company with annual sales of $25 billion in 2000. Its operations were spread around the world, with 120,000 employees in nearly 100 countries. Honeywell's primary product areas were avionics products and services; control technologies for buildings, homes and industry; automotive products; power generation systems; specialty chemicals; fibers; plastics; and electronic and advanced materials. The U.S. government, due mostly to its military purchases, accounted for $2.2 billion, or 10%, of 2000 sales. Aerospace products accounted for 40% of sales and nearly 60% of profits in 2000 (see Exhibit 6). Honeywell merged with AlliedSignal in 1999 and became the largest worldwide supplier of non-engine aerospace equipment, ahead of BF Goodrich, Hamilton Sundstrand (acquired by United Technologies in 1999), and Rockwell Collins (a subsidiary of Rockwell International that was soon to be spun off).

Avionics and Non-avionics Products

Avionics equipment served to control and navigate an airplane as well as to provide communications and weather condition determination functions. Such equipment accounted for approximately 5% of the purchase price of an airplane. Avionics and instrumentation for regional and corporate jets were increasingly purchased as an integrated cockpit configured to provide full flight capabilities, whereas the avionics products installed in large commercial jets could be purchased "à la carte." Within the market for large commercial jets—Boeing and Airbus planes—the market was further segmented by demand characteristic of products: (i) buyer furnished equipment (BFE) was multi-sourced by airframe makers and selected and purchased by end customers (airlines); (ii) standard seller furnished equipment (SFE-standard) was chosen by the airframe manufacture with only that option available to plane purchasers, and (iii) option seller furnished equipment (SFE-option) was chosen by airlines among two options pre-selected by the airframe makers. Examples of BFE included two-way voice and data transmission equipment, satellite communications equipment, weather radar systems, global positioning systems, cockpit data recorders, airborne collision avoidance systems (ACAS) and traffic alert and collision avoidance systems (TCAS).[2] Examples of SFE included flight management and autopilot systems.

[2]One of Honeywell's significant competitors for ACAS and TCAS equipment was L3, which acquired that business from Honeywell as a condition for the approval of the Honeywell/AlliedSignal merger.

EXHIBIT 6

HONEYWELL REPORTING SEGMENTS (BILLIONS OF DOLLARS)

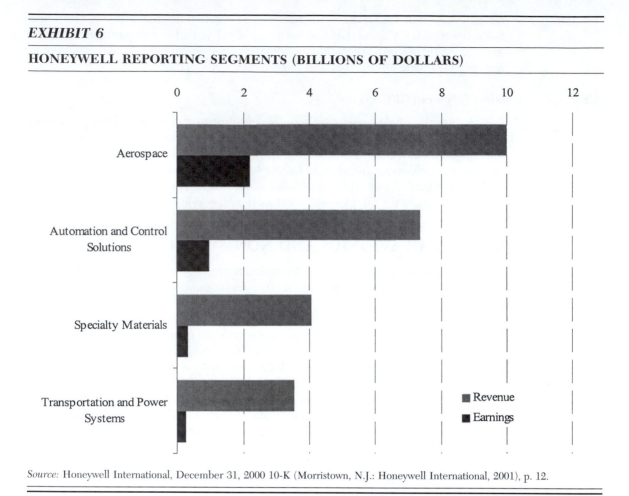

Source: Honeywell International, December 31, 2000 10-K (Morristown, N.J.: Honeywell International, 2001), p. 12.

Non-avionics products included auxiliary power units (small onboard gas turbine engines providing electricity for airflow for the cabin, inter alia), cabin climate control systems, landing gear, wheels, brakes and lighting. The market for non-avionics products mirrored that for avionics products in terms of the large vs. regional/corporate jet and BFE vs. SFE distinctions. Non-avionics products accounted for 3–5% of the purchase price of an airplane.

Honeywell, Rockwell Collins, Thales, and Hamilton Sunstrand accounted for 85% of avionics and non-avionics sales worldwide, and 95% of avionics sales (see Exhibit 7 for a summary of Honeywell's and its competitors' market shares by product). Honeywell was the only manufacturer with an integrated product offering capable of supplying the complete set of avionics products necessary for an aircraft. Although interoperability with competitors' complementary products is not necessary, a key advantage of providing a single integrated set for a plane is the weight savings that result from standardization. Bundling could occur when the manufacturer first approved equipment for an airframe, when an airline selected its BFE, when modifications or upgrades were being performed, and collaterally when warranties and volume discounts were structured. Market estimates suggested that approximately 20–30% of Honeywell's sales of such products were in "multi-product bids" whereby Honeywell bid for a series of pieces

EXHIBIT 7

HONEYWELL AVIONICS AND NON-AVIONICS PRODUCTS AND MARKET SHARES

Product	Description		Honeywell	Rockwell Collins	Thales	Litton	Universal Avionics	Trimble Avionics	L3	Teledyne	Smiths	Others
BFE Products												
Weather radar	Displays rainfall, turbulence and, in certain models, wind shear	Large Commercial	40–50%	50–60%	0%							
		Regional/Corp.	50–60%	30–40%	10–20%							
Communication/ navigation (Comm/Nav)	Transmits and receives pilot voice and other communications to/from ground or air operation centers	Large Commercial	30–40%	50–60%	10–20%							
		Regional/Corp.	40–50%	50–60%	10–20%							
Satellite communication (SatComm)	Sends and receives data and voice telephone to the ground via satellite	Large Commercial	50–60%	40–50%	0%							0%
		Regional/Corp.	60–70%	20–30%	0–10%							0–10%
Multi-mode receiver (MMR)	Provides precision approach guidance to airports with and without global positioning systems	With GPS										
		Large Commercial	20–30%	50–60%	30–40%							0%
		Regional/Corp.	30–40%	40–50%	0%							30–40%
		Without GPS										
		Large Commercial	40–50%	0%	0%	50–60%	0%	0%				
		Regional/Corp.	30–40%	20–30%	0%	0%	30–40%	0–10%				
Records	Records flight data and cockpit voice information	Large Commercial	40–50%						30–40%			10–20%
		Regional/Corp.	20–30%						40–50%			40–50%
Comm. mgmt & comm. addressing and reporting	Manages two-way text and data communication link between aircraft and ground control centers	Large Commercial	50–60%	40–50%						0–10%		
		Regional/Corp.	60–70%	40–50%						0%		

(Continued)

447

EXHIBIT 7 (*Continued*)

HONEYWELL AVIONICS AND NON-AVIONICS PRODUCTS AND MARKET SHARES

Product	Description		Honeywell	Rockwell Collins	Thales	Litton	Universal Avionics	Trimble Avionics	L3	Teledyne	Smiths	Others
Collision avoidance system	Helps prevent collisions by identifying and displaying the location of surrounding aircraft	Large Commercial	40–50%	20–30%					30–40%			
		Regional/Corp.	50–60%	10–20%					30–40%			
Terrain avoidance warning system	Provides flight crew with a map-like display of nearby terrain		Nearly 100%									
Inertial reference/ attitude-heading reference systems	Airframe motion sensors and navigation sensors used by other navigation onboard systems	Large Commercial	80–90%		°	10–20%						
		Regional/Corp.	80–90%	°		10–20%						
SFE Products												
Flight management system	Helps flight crews compute the most efficient flight profile and automatically navigates the aircraft	Large Commercial	60–70%	0%	Entering		0%	0%			30–40%	
		Regional/Corp.	30–40%	10–20%	0%		40–50%	0–10%			0%	

(*Continued*)

EXHIBIT 7 (Continued)

HONEYWELL AVIONICS AND NON-AVIONICS PRODUCTS AND MARKET SHARES

Product	Description		Honeywell	Rockwell Collins	Thales	Litton	Universal Avionics	Trimble Avionics	L3	Teledyne	Smiths	Others
Flight controls	Autopilot systems	Large Commercial	30–40%	20–30%	40–50%							0%
		Regional/Corp.	30–40%	40–50%	0–10%							20–30%
Air data computers	Gauge "true" airspeed, altitude, and vertical speed	Large Commercial	90–100%	0%								0–10%
		Regional/Corp.	20–30%	20–30%								50–60%
Displays	Electronic instrument systems	Large Commercial	30–40%	20–30%	40–50%							0%
		Regional	50–60%	30–40%	0–10%							0–10%
Air data inertial reference unit	Combines the functions of the air data computer and the inertial reference system		80–90%			10–20%						

NOTES:

[a] Thales and Rockwell have strong positions for attitude heading reference systems, which can be a cheaper alterative to inertial reference systems.

Source: Commission of the European Communities Decision, 3 July 2001, Case No COMP/M.2220-General Electric/Honeywell.

of equipment for an airframe, but did not offer the manufacturer the option of accepting an incomplete subset of those products.

Honeywell held a particularly strong position in the market for engine starters, where it commanded a 50–60% market share, and Hamilton Sunstrand held the remainder. Because of the sophisticated technological requirements of these crucial engine components, this market segment faced high barriers to entry. Hamilton Sunstrand's starters were only installed in Pratt & Whitney engines.

MRO

Servicing avionics and non-avionics resembled the MRO market for engines. Honeywell was the only provider of "nose-to-tail" integrated solutions capable of servicing all avionics and non-avionics products. Like GE, it offered maintenance cost-per-hour contracts to its customers. Due to rapid technological development, avionics products tended to be replaced rather than repaired. Original equipment suppliers typically serviced only their own equipment and not that of their competitors.

THE PROPOSED GE–HONEYWELL MERGER

On October 22, 2000, General Electric agreed to a $45 billion acquisition of Honeywell and Jack Welch accordingly delayed his retirement to oversee the transaction. This deal derailed the merger plans of United Technologies, which had announced two days earlier that it was contemplating a $40 billion bid for Honeywell. Speaking for management, Honeywell CEO Michael Bonsignore summarized the gains to Honeywell shareholders:

> This transaction preserves and strengthens the Honeywell brand worldwide while providing superior value to our shareowners, customers and employees. . . . Honeywell's rich global heritage of technology and innovation will be substantially enhanced as part of GE.[3]

The deal offered significant financial benefits to GE, which expected the transaction to result in double-digit earnings per share growth in the first year following the deal (excluding one-time charges). The following commentary by Credit Suisse First Boston was typical of the reactions of the equity research community immediately following the merger announcement:

> We believe GE's decision to trump United Technologies' merger discussions with Honeywell at the 11th hour is both offensive and defensive. Offensive because we believe GE has always admired the technological components of Honeywell's products and services. And defensive because GE could not let [United Technologies] establish itself as complete "nose-to-tail" equipment and service provider to commercial and military aerospace customers.
>
> GE has been the leader in migrating from being a jet engine manufacturer to becoming a higher value added service provider but we believe United Technologies was in the process of challenging that position. We felt [United Technologies] had the opportunity to capitalize on its acquisition of Sundstrand last year and offer its customers a more integrated package of systems and services for the complete airplane. The potential addition of Honeywell's suite of avionics products and landing gear systems would have given [United

---

[3]Brad Foss, "GE to acquire Honeywell for $45 billion in stock; Welch to remain chairman through 2001," *Associated Press Newswires*, Oct. 22, 2000 available from Factiva, ⟨http://www.factiva.com⟩.

Technologies] an almost complete set of products for commercial and military jets and left GE focused solely on manufacturing and servicing jet engines. The risk was that customers would move their business to a full solutions provider. With the acquisition of Honeywell, GE not only gains valuable real estate on the airplane but fends off the charge from United Technologies.[4]

In a joint press release announcing the deal, GE and Honeywell acknowledged that "[o]verlap in some areas is expected to raise antitrust concerns among U.S. and European regulators, who could require the combined company to divest some of its businesses as a condition of approval."[5] Analysts differed on how significant these antitrust considerations would be—some suggesting that there was little cause for concern for GE. Ultimately, U.S. antitrust authorities did approve the deal, conditional on a single divestiture—Honeywell's helicopter engine business—to avoid lessening competition in the production of U.S. military helicopter engines. Also required was the creation of a new independent MRO service provider for certain models of Honeywell aircraft engines and auxiliary power units. In Europe, however, difficulties arose with the regulators.

THE MERGER TASK FORCE'S ANALYSIS OF THE TRANSACTION

The MTF assessed the competitive effects of a merger by determining whether the proposed combination of businesses would create or strengthen a "dominant position" that would significantly impede effective competition in any of the markets affected by it. According to European case law, dominance is defined as

> a position of economic strength enjoyed by an undertaking which enables it to prevent effective competition being maintained in the relevant market by giving it the power to behave to an appreciable extent independently of its competitors, customers, and ultimately of consumers.[6]

The analysis of dominance is a process resulting from the combination of various economic (commercial and financial) and legal factors characterizing the industry and the competitors concerned in a given transaction. Prior to ruling on the possible dominance of the merged entity, the relevant markets, both geographically and in terms of the product concerned, have to be defined. The actual competitive assessment can then take place on the previously defined relevant markets. This assessment will typically include: (i) the calculation of the merging parties' market shares, especially in relation to their immediate competitors (traditionally referred to as "horizontal effects" of the concentration); (ii) the analysis of their possible position as a significant supplier or customer of their competitors (traditionally referred to as "vertical effects"); and (iii) the evaluation of their combined presence in neighboring or complementary product markets, especially when the merging parties share the same customer base, or the impact of their financial strength (traditionally referred to as "conglomerate effects"). These effects are then measured against the possibility for the current (or any potential) com-

---

[4]Michael T. Regan and Avram M. Fisher, Credit Suisse First Boston Equity Research, "GE: Agreement Reached with HON," Morning Call: Oct. 23, 2000.

[5]Brad Foss, "GE to acquire Honeywell for $45 billion in stock; Welch to remain chairman through 2001," *Associated Press Newswires*, Oct. 22, 2000 available from Factiva, ⟨http://www.factiva.com⟩.

[6]*United Brands Company and United Brands Continentaal BV v. Commission of the European Communities.* European Court of Justice Case 27/76, 14 February 1978, [1978]ECR 207 at 286.

petitors to constrain the merged entity and the ability of customers to bargain against its dominant position.

From the perspective of the European Union, the main product markets that would be affected by the combination of the GE and Honeywell businesses were part of the aerospace industry. Outside this industry, only the market for small marine gas turbines was deemed to be affected.[7]

Defining the relevant market for a competition analysis was often a hotly contested issue—and one that had proven to be determinative in prior rulings. In aerospace, the market was usually defined in terms of the installed base (of engines or avionics products), plus firm orders not yet delivered. In the GE–Honeywell case, the main point of contention was whether the "installed base" should refer only to aircraft that were still being produced or also include planes that had gone out of production. GE and Honeywell ("the parties") argued for the inclusion of airplanes that were no longer in production because of the revenue streams these provided to them and to their competitors. The MTF, however, considered aircraft no longer in production to be a smaller (and declining) source of revenue for engine suppliers than aircraft still in production and therefore not the appropriate proxy with which to measure the competitors' market power, and decided not to include the former in the installed base. The next step in defining the relevant market was determining the geographic scope and product range for every segment of the market. In aerospace, every product segment was considered to be a worldwide market for the purpose of computing market shares. Product market segmentation followed the delineations above: (i) large commercial jets, large and small regional jets, and heavy, medium, and light corporate jets for aircraft engines and MRO services; and (ii) each component type for avionics and non-avionics products. The parties disagreed with some of these delineations, arguing for broader definitions in certain markets and for narrower definitions in others.

The parties also disagreed with one aspect of the calculation of market shares beyond those related to market definition: the MTF's treatment of joint ventures. Such treatment was particularly relevant to the large commercial engine market since GE, Rolls Royce, and Pratt & Whitney had all entered joint ventures with other suppliers and, in some cases, with each other. GE and SNECMA of France were 50/50 partners in the CFMI joint venture, and Pratt & Whitney and Rolls Royce were each 32% partners in International Aero Engines (IAE).[8] Whenever a joint venture of firms competed with the independent market players in that market, the MTF, in line with its practice, attributed the market share of the entire joint venture to the partner(s) that was an independent player in the market. Thus, all of CFMI's market share was attributed to GE, and all of IAE's market share was attributed to Pratt & Whitney and Rolls Royce in equal proportions.

Market share estimates provided the main quantitative basis for determining whether the parties were or would become dominant players in any of these market segments as a result of horizontal integration. The MTF complemented the assessment by analyzing whether competitors might be disadvantaged, marginalized or even forced to exit the market in the long run as a result of the merged entity's vertical integration

---

[7]The small marine gas turbine market was a niche market that accounted for less than 10% of the small gas turbine (up to 10 MW) volume. The remaining 90% of the small gas turbine market was accounted for by industrial turbines. Honeywell had an approximate market share between 40% and 50%, followed by GE with a 25%–30% share. The bulk of the demand for small marine gas turbines was for units below 5 MW. Honeywell had a 70%–80% share of that niche, and GE a 10%–20% share.

[8]The other partners in IAE were MTU and Japanese Aero Engines Corp.

(for instance into GECAS) and of the transfer of specific GE features to Honeywell's products, such as its unparalleled financial strength.

The MTF's concerns about vertical and conglomerate effects (also called "portfolio effects") were fueled in this case by the objections raised by GE and Honeywell's competitors. United Technologies had expressed concerns that, as a result of the merger, GECAS would extend its GE-only procurement policy to the markets in which Honeywell competed, at the expense of its Hamilton Sunstrand unit. This argument was consistent with the MTF's own view that GE's vertical integration into aircraft purchasing, financing, and leasing through GECAS had contributed to its own dominance in engines, by serving as a launch customer and by causing airlines to standardize fleets around GE-powered aircraft. Rolls Royce, in turn, being an engine-only manufacturer (unlike United Technologies), was a key proponent of the dangers of allowing the merged entity to sell engines and avionics in bundles that other firms would not be able to replicate. Either type of effect, and of course both together, would place competitors at a disadvantage, and had the potential to lead to market foreclosure and to the subsequent elimination of competition in those arenas.

The MTF's analysis indicated that the merger of GE and Honeywell would create or strengthen a dominant position in several markets, for one or more of the reasons outlined above. It was thus clear to Monti that, for the transaction to gain his approval, the parties would have to agree to undertake a set of remedies far more comprehensive than those the U.S. Department of Justice had required. Monti needed to develop a clear stance on what the minimum requirements should be to prepare for the meeting with Welch on the proposed merger.

Redesigning Sovereign Debt Restructuring Mechanisms

Preparing for the International Monetary Fund (IMF) board meeting in spring 2003, Anne O. Krueger, First Deputy Managing Director of the IMF, carefully constructed her arguments. Priority one on the Board's agenda was reforming the international financial architecture. Krueger was proposing the establishment of a new statutory regime, commonly referred to as the Sovereign Debt Restructuring Mechanism (SDRM). Krueger's plan called for the creation of a legal framework that would be universal to all debt restructuring processes and the establishment of an organization to oversee adherence to the statutes; these changes would be enacted through ratification of an international treaty.

Reform of debt restructuring mechanisms had been on economists' and policymakers' minds since the late 1990s, when country after country faced major financial crises and defaults. Debtor countries found themselves in deep recessions, while having to cope with fiscal and monetary stresses such as extreme exchange rate fluctuations. The diverse methods sovereigns used to restructure their debt commitments added to the unpredictability of their precarious financial circumstances. With Argentina's 2002 default (the world's largest at USD 95 billion), bilateral and multilateral organizations that traditionally came to sovereign debtors' aid were forced to reexamine their past "bail-out" methods. These organizations had limited funds that had to cover all cases of sovereign defaults, so with a forecasted increase in the rate of sovereign defaults worldwide, the common practice of assembling large rescue loans packages per default episode would be unsustainable. There needed to be a mechanism that could help curb dangerous economic situations before they deepened into full-blown crises as well as allow a greater degree of burden sharing between official organizations, sovereign debtors, and creditors. As a result, reform debates dominated high-level economic policy debates. While there was general agreement on the need for reform, dif-

Professor Mihir A. Desai and Research Associates Christine B. Pham, Julia Stevens and Kathleen Luchs prepared this case. This case was developed from published sources. HBS cases are developed solely as the basis for class discussion. Cases are not intended to serve as endorsements, sources of primary data, or illustrations of effective or ineffective management.

ferent groups had had different views on how much change was needed and how to go about that change.

In constructing her proposal and arguments, there were various issues that Krueger had to revisit. First, she had to position the SDRM within the existing institutional framework of the IMF and the World Bank, which played significant roles in sovereign debt restructuring. Second, the SDRM needed to address challenges presented in past financial crises, such as those in Latin America (1982), Mexico (1994), and Asia (1997). Third, she had to tackle fully the advantages and disadvantages of her plan compared to alternative plans which were being championed by other groups. Two key questions at the board meeting would be whether Krueger's plan could solve the problems in the system, and whether its implementation was feasible.

KRUEGER'S ROLE

Krueger had served as the First Deputy Managing Director of the International Monetary Fund since September 2001. (See Exhibit 1 for details of Krueger's career.) The Managing Director, Horst Kohler, made the five-year appointment, which required approval from the IMF Board of Governors. As First Deputy Managing Director, Krueger had a wide range of responsibilities at the Fund, including chairing meetings of the Executive Board in Kohler's absence, carrying out country-specific functions, and managing internal IMF operations.

Krueger's deep experience with the international economy placed her in an ideal position to propose a new sovereign debt restructuring mechanism to the IMF board.

EXHIBIT 1

BIOGRAPHY OF ANNE O. KRUEGER

Anne O. Krueger has been the First Deputy Managing Director of the International Monetary Fund since September 1, 2001.

Before coming to the Fund, Ms. Krueger was the Herald L. and Caroline L. Ritch Professor in Humanities and Sciences in the Department of Economics at Stanford University. She was also the founding Director of Stanford's Center for Research on Economic Development and Policy Reform; and a Senior Fellow of the Hoover Institution. Ms. Krueger had previously taught at the University of Minnesota and Duke University and, from 1982 to 1986, was the World Bank's Vice President for Economics and Research. She received her undergraduate degree from Oberlin College and her Ph.D. in economics from the University of Wisconsin.

Ms. Krueger is a Distinguished Fellow and past President of the American Economic Association, a member of the National Academy of Sciences, and a Research Associate of the National Bureau of Economic Research. A recipient of a number of economic prizes and awards, she has published extensively on policy reform in developing countries, the role of multilateral institutions in the international economy, and the political economy of trade policy. Recent books edited by Ms. Krueger include Reforming India's Economic, Financial and Fiscal Policies (2003: with Sajjid Z. Chinoy); Latin American Macroeconomic Reform: The Second Stage (2003: with Jose Antonio Gonzales, Vittorio Corbo and Aaron Tornell); Economic Policy Reform and the Indian Economy (2003); A new approach to sovereign debt restructuring (2002); Economic Policy Reform: The Second Stage (2000), and The WTO as an International Organization (2000).

Source: Anne Krueger biography available from the website of the International Monetary Fund, ⟨http://www.imf.org/external/np/omd/bios/ak.htm⟩.

She held a PhD in economics, had taught extensively at Duke and Stanford, and had served as director of Stanford's Center for Research on Economic Development and Policy Reform. A Hoover Senior Fellow and research associate for the National Bureau of Economic Research, Krueger focused her research on policy reform in developing countries and the role of multilateral institutions in the international economy.

As Chief Economist and Vice President of Economics and Research at the World Bank in the 1980s, Krueger was intimately involved with sovereign debt issues. Because she joined the organization in 1982, just as the Latin American debt crisis was erupting, she played a pivotal role in the Bank's emergency response to the region. With her emphasis on a sound microeconomic environment for development, she helped set the tone for the Bank's contributions in Latin America and its management of the crisis.

Now, Krueger was advocating a fundamental change in the way sovereigns managed debt crises. The aim of a reformed restructuring process would be to encourage orderly and timely restructuring before a sovereign defaulted on its debt, and to create an established structure by which both debtors and creditors could restructure, minimize losses, and emerge with sustainable provisions for future debt service. According to Krueger, the bottom line was "that far-reaching developments in capital markets over the last two or three decades have not been matched by the development" of a response system that can handle the changes.[1] Krueger hoped that the SDRM would be the complete and appropriate response system that could both absorb the changes of today as well as prepare the system for the developments of the future.

A HISTORICAL VIEW: PIVOTAL DEFAULTS IN RECENT TIMES

Financial crises in the 19th and early 20th centuries were caused by factors such as natural disasters, wars, revolutions, and external economic shocks. By the 21st century, the main drivers of crisis cycles were weak banking systems, excessive capital market liberalization with inadequate regulatory mechanisms, and investor speculation and panic. Unlike the universal pegged exchange rate regime of the 1950s and 1960s, sovereign governments freely chose their exchange rate arrangements, depending on the policies they wanted to pursue at home. Maintaining the balance of payments in this heterogeneous environment proved difficult for many countries and has led to acute international crises. Described below are three severe cases: the Latin American debt crisis of 1982, the Mexican peso crisis of 1994, and the Asian financial crisis of 1997.

Latin American Debt Crisis (1982)[2]

In the early 1970s, debt in Latin American countries amounted to $28 billion, approximately 20% of the region's GDP. By 1982, the debt stock had reached $294 billion, 40% of the region's GDP, driven by soaring oil prices, high government expenditure, short-term loans, and widening trade deficits. (See Exhibit 2 for a Latin American debt table.)

---

[1]Anne O. Krueger, "New Approaches to Sovereign Debt Restructuring: An Update on Our Thinking," Speech at the Conference on Sovereign Debt Workouts: Hopes and Hazards, Institute for International Economics, Washington, D.C., April 1, 2002 available at ⟨http://www.imf.org/external/np/speeches/2002/040102.htm⟩.

[2]Drawn from Guillen R. Arturo and Ross Gandy, "Crisis, the Burden of Foreign Debt, and Structural Dependence," *Latin American Perspectives*, 16(1), 1989: 31–51; Robert A. Pastor, ed., *Latin American Debt Crisis: Adjusting to the Past or Planning for the Future* (Boulder: Lynne Reinner Publishers, 1987); and Jeffrey Sachs, "Managing the LDC Debt Crisis," *Brookings Papers on Economic Activity*, 1986 (2): 397–431.

EXHIBIT 2

DEBT TABLE FOR LATIN AMERICAN[a] DEBT CRISIS (1982)[b]

	1978	1979	1980	1981	1982	1983	1984	1985
Current Account Balance (US$)	−11.9	−16.1	−25.6	−37.1	−35.8	−4.0	2.6	−0.2
International reserves (RES) (US$)	33.8	47.6	47.1	41.9	32.3	32.2	41.6	43.6
Debt outstanding (LDOD), total long-term (US$)	112.8	132.2	150.6	182.5	209.1	254.7	275.1	285.3
Private sector LDOD (US$)	33.8	39.4	45.0	61.1	63.9	75.8	71.8	58.7
Public sector LDOD (US$)	79.0	92.8	105.7	121.4	145.1	178.9	203.3	226.7
Short-term debt outstanding (DOD, US$)	28.6	40.6	62.6	77.5	83.7	55.3	44.2	37.2
Short-term debt/Total debt (EDT) (%)	25.1	26.1	30.7	29.9	29.0	19.9	16.3	14.0
Aggregate net resource flows (US$)	22.5	25.3	24.4	41.7	33.3	17.9	14.9	11.5
Private net resource flows (US$)	20.9	24.1	22.1	39.1	30.0	15.1	11.2	7.8
Foreign direct investment, net inflows (US$)	3.5	4.5	5.1	7.4	6.1	4.9	4.0	5.6
Portfolio equity flows (US$)	0.0	0.0	0.0	0.1	0.0	0.0	0.0	0.0
Official net resource flows (US$)	1.6	1.1	2.3	2.6	3.3	2.8	3.7	3.7
Multilateral debt/Total debt (EDT) (%)	6.7	6.0	6.0	6.0	6.1	6.4	6.6	8.4
Reserves (RES)/Total debt (EDT) (%)	29.3	38.7	36.3	26.3	20.1	15.7	15.0	16.3
Total debt (EDT)/GNI (%)	39.6	38.0	36.3	37.3	47.7	58.3	64.3	68.6
Total debt (EDT)/Exports of goods and services (XGS) (%)	210.1	211.9	202.4	234.3	297.6	331.3	320.0	341.4
Debt service (TDS)/Exports of goods and services (XGS) (%)	37.5	37.6	39.3	46.7	51.9	46.1	42.6	40.9
Interest (INT)/Exports of goods and services (XGS) (%)	12.7	13.3	20.7	26.3	33.3	31.9	29.1	29.9

(Continued)

457

EXHIBIT 2 *(Continued)*

DEBT TABLE FOR LATIN AMERICAN[a] DEBT CRISIS (1982)[b]

	1978	1979	1980	1981	1982	1983	1984	1985
Net flows on debt, total (NFL, US$)	22.3	32.5	41.0	48.8	34.1	−4.5	3.9	0.9
Net flows on debt, total long-term (NFL, US$)	19.0	20.7	19.2	34.1	27.0	12.8	10.7	5.6
PPG, total public and publicly guaranteed (NFL, US$)	15.8	16.4	13.3	18.7	23.1	14.6	12.5	7.5
PPG, official creditors (NFL, US$)	1.5	1.0	2.2	2.5	3.1	2.6	3.5	3.4
PPG, bilateral (NFL, US$)	0.7	−0.1	0.8	1.0	0.7	1.2	0.6	0.7
PPG, multilateral (NFL, US$)	0.8	1.1	1.4	1.5	2.4	1.5	3.0	2.7
PPG, private creditors (NFL, US$)	14.4	15.4	11.1	16.2	20.0	11.9	9.0	4.1
PPG, bonds (NFL, US$)	2.3	0.6	0.7	1.4	4.0	−0.7	−1.0	−0.9
PPG, commercial banks (NFL, US$)	10.8	14.0	9.7	14.1	13.9	11.1	9.4	4.4
PNG, total private nonguaranteed (NFL, US$)	3.1	4.2	5.9	15.3	3.9	−1.8	−1.8	−1.9
PNG, bonds (NFL, US$)	0.0	0.0	0.0	0.0	0.0	0.0	0.0	0.0
PNG, commercial banks (NFL, US$)	3.1	4.2	5.9	15.3	3.9	−1.8	−1.8	−1.9
Short-term debt net flows (NFL, US$)	4.0	12.0	22.0	14.9	6.1	−22.5	−9.2	−6.1
Commitments, official creditors (COM, US$)	4.1	4.5	6.3	7.6	9.3	7.8	6.6	6.6
Commitments, private creditors (COM, US$)	25.3	30.4	21.9	31.4	33.3	19.2	15.5	11.1

[a]Data included for seven Latin American countries: Argentina, Brazil, Chile, Colombia, Mexico, Peru, and Venezuela.
[b]All currency units in US$ billions.

Source: World Bank Global Development Finance Database 2002.

While non-oil-producing countries were suffering from the OPEC price hikes in the late 1970s, oil trade boosted Mexico's economy and led to increased government spending. At the same time, Mexico's trade deficit widened. While Mexican oil exports had grown at an impressive rate, trade liberalization policies and reduced import controls caused imports to grow at a much faster rate than did Mexican exports. Appreciating exchange rates in the late 1970s and early 1980s made Mexican goods less competitive on the world market and further deteriorated the level of non-oil exports. To finance the deficit and increased government spending, both the public and private sectors recruited foreign investment. By 1981, over 50% of Mexican loans were short-term loans subject to interest rate changes. The result for Mexico was a heavy debt burden whose growth was accelerated by short-term contracts and soaring interest rates.

Other Latin American countries were non-oil producers and hard hit by the oil shocks. Many of the region's economies went into recession because of the large capital outflow to OPEC countries. Latin American countries took new loans to finance oil consumption. This increased borrowing was accompanied by two trends: movement away from government bonds toward commercial bank bonds, and deregulation and privatization. In the 1950s and 1960s, over half of Latin American loans came in the form of bonds from OECD governments. These loans had more restrictions, but also longer maturities and low interest rates. Commercial bank bonds, on the other hand, had fewer restrictions, but came with shorter maturities and higher interest rates. By 1982, government loans had dropped to 12% of all loans. Commercial bank debt rose from $19 billion in 1970 to almost $250 billion in 1983, with growth averaging 20.4% a year.

The actual crisis started in Mexico and rapidly spread to countries throughout South America, climaxing at the beginning of 1983. In February 1982, precipitated by a rapid decline in oil prices and $20 billion in private sector capital outflow, Mexico's peso depreciated 80%, leading to very high unemployment and inflation. After six months of attempting to defend the peso, the country almost exhausted its foreign reserve; the reserve-to-total-debt ratio dropped from a steady 6%–7% through 1981 to 2% in 1982. International commercial banks, Mexico's main source of capital, halted all loans to the country. At that point, the Mexican government had no choice but to announce its inability to service the $69 billion debt it had accumulated.

Mexico's announcement brought international capital flows into other Latin American countries to a standstill. As capital markets began to question the entire region's ability to service its debts, financing for these countries became almost non-existent overnight. Since most Latin American debt was composed of short-term loans, billions of dollars, which would have previously been refinanced, all came due at once. In addition, the short-term nature of these loans meant that their refinancing was subject to fluctuating interest rates. Between 1977 and 1981, world interest rates tripled, leading to exponential growth in Latin America's debt burden. Consequently, by 1982, it was close to impossible for Latin American countries to pay back the billions they owed without additional funding.

Aftermath

In the aftermath of the crisis, the Mexican and other Latin American governments adopted tight fiscal and monetary policies and nationalized the masses of debt accumulated by the private sector. The IMF stepped in to coordinate debt renegotiations and supplied over $9 billion in emergency loans between 1982 and 1985. Through this funding, most countries were able to continue servicing their debt and the region was able to go from a trade deficit of $2 billion in 1981 to a trade surplus of $31 billion by 1983.

Though debt service continued steadily, by 1985 Latin American economies had still not recovered. In response, different plans emerged from the U.S. to help ease the crisis, ranging from a request that commercial banks and multilateral institutions lend more to the most indebted countries to proposals for debt forgiveness. In 1989, after repeated rounds of rescheduling and negotiations, U.S. Treasury Secretary Brady presented his plan. The Brady Plan had two basic tenets: 1) commercial banks would negotiate debt relief with debtor nations in exchange for bonds or other tradable instruments whose characteristics could increase the likelihood of repayment, or at least be attractive enough for resale in secondary financial markets; and 2) debt relief would be accompanied by some form of economic policy reform and should be underwritten by official creditors.

The Latin American debt crisis was not fully resolved until interest rates declined globally in the early 1990s. This shift substantially decreased the size of debt-servicing payments, both foreign and domestic, and also led to a marked increase in investor confidence worldwide. The region recovered from the crisis in the early 1990s, but not before experiencing an economic recession, a sharp decline in real living standards, and a negative per capita GDP growth.

Mexican Peso Crisis (1994)

In the early 1990s, Mexico was considered one of the most promising emerging markets. The country had recovered from its 1982 debt crisis and had attracted over 70 billion of investor dollars by 1994. Mexico's implementation of the Brady Plan in 1990 to restructure Mexico's debt increased investor confidence, as did the country's set of economic reform policies, which eliminated capital controls, opened the economy to international competition, and privatized state owned enterprises.

Investor optimism in Mexico continued until late November 1994, bolstered by assurances from Mexican officials that Mexico would support its pegged exchange rate to avoid devaluation. However, Mexican reserves had fallen to $11 billion, and the country still had $30 billion in debt outstanding; with such an imbalance, the government could no longer hold the pegged rate. On December 20th, 1994, the Mexican government devalued the peso 15%, creating widespread investor panic. In one day, the Banco de Mexico lost $4 billion, a record amount for capital outflow for a country. (See Exhibit 3 for a debt table for the Mexican crisis.)

Central to Mexico's crisis were two types of government-issued bonds: peso-denominated Cetes, and dollar-denominated Tesobonos. Cetes were redeemed within 28 to 91 days and were particularly attractive to foreign investors because of their high rates of return—up to 16.5 % in April 1994—and low apparent risk, assuming no change in the exchange rate policy. As the government struggled to keep up with the Cetes' high interest payments, officials introduced Tesobonos, U.S. dollar-linked securities that paid out 6 to 8 percentage points less than the rate on Cetes. Tesobonos became favored by investors because of their guarantee against exchange rate depreciation, a risk when investing in emerging markets.

In December of 1993, 6% of government debt was in Tesobonos; a year later, Tesobonos accounted for 87% of government debt. The devaluation of the peso in December 1994 increased the burden of Mexico's dollar-denominated debt. By the end of 1994, Mexico's dollar-denominated debt had increased to $29 billion and its reserves fallen to $11 billion. These numbers made it clear that Mexico was headed toward a default on its loans.

After the Mexican crisis, investors became skeptical of emerging markets in general, and began to withdraw their support. This so-called "Tequila Effect" resulted in investor

EXHIBIT 3

DEBT TABLE FOR MEXICAN PESO CRISIS (1994)[a]

	1990	1991	1992	1993	1994	1995	1996	1997
Current account balance (US$)	−7.5	−14.9	−24.4	−23.4	−29.7	−1.6	−2.5	−7.7
International reserves (RES) (US$)	10.2	18.1	19.2	25.3	6.4	17.0	19.5	28.9
Total amount of debt rescheduled (US$)	36.9	1.2	0.3	0.0	0.0	0.0	0.0	0.0
Total change in debt stocks (DOD, US$)	10.6	9.6	−1.8	19.4	8.1	26.8	−9.1	−8.8
Debt outstanding (LDOD), total long-term (US$)	81.8	85.4	81.8	90.7	96.6	113.5	114.4	111.8
Private sector LDOD (US$)	6.2	8.0	11.2	16.0	17.6	18.8	20.7	27.6
Public sector LDOD (US$)	75.6	77.4	70.7	74.7	79.1	94.7	93.6	84.2
Short-term debt outstanding (DOD, US$)	16.1	21.9	24.5	36.3	39.3	37.3	29.8	27.9
Short-term debt/Total debt (EDT) (%)	15.0	19.0	22.0	28.0	28.0	22.0	19.0	19.0
Aggregate net resource flows (US$)	13.8	15.4	9.3	17.7	19.8	25.6	16.6	16.4
Private net resource flows (US$)	9.6	14.1	8.6	17.7	20.4	15.2	24.2	21.0
Foreign direct investment, net inflows (US$)	2.5	4.7	4.4	4.4	11.0	9.5	9.2	12.8
Portfolio equity flows (US$)	2.0	6.3	4.8	10.7	4.1	0.5	2.8	3.2
Official net resource flows (US$)	4.2	1.4	0.6	0.1	−0.5	10.4	−7.6	−4.5
Multilateral debt/Total debt (EDT) (%)	14.0	14.0	14.0	12.0	12.0	11.0	11.0	11.0
Reserves (RES)/Total debt (EDT) (%)	10.0	16.0	17.0	19.0	5.0	10.0	12.0	19.0
Total debt (EDT)/GNI (%)	41.0	37.0	32.0	34.0	34.0	61.0	49.0	38.0

(Continued)

461

EXHIBIT 3 *(Continued)*

DEBT TABLE FOR MEXICAN PESO CRISIS (1994)[a]

	1990	1991	1992	1993	1994	1995	1996	1997
Total debt (EDT)/Exports of goods and services (XGS) (%)	191.0	198.0	183.0	195.0	179.0	172.0	137.0	114.0
Debt service (TDS)/Exports of goods and services (XGS) (%)	21.0	24.0	34.0	36.0	26.0	27.0	35.0	32.0
Interest (INT)/Exports of goods and services (XGS) (%)	13.0	14.0	12.0	12.0	12.0	11.0	10.0	9.0
Net flows on debt, total (NFL, US$)	17.6	10.3	2.2	13.1	6.6	25.6	−4.9	−5.1
Net flows on debt, total long-term (NFL, US$)	9.2	4.3	0.1	2.6	4.7	15.5	4.6	0.4
PPG, total public and publicly guaranteed (NFL, US$)	7.4	2.5	−3.0	2.5	2.1	14.3	2.6	−6.7
PPG, official creditors (NFL, US$)	4.2	1.3	0.6	0.0	−0.6	10.4	−7.6	−4.6
PPG, bilateral (NFL, US$)	1.6	0.4	0.1	−0.2	−0.4	9.4	−8.0	−4.5
PPG, multilateral (NFL, US$)	2.6	0.9	0.5	0.2	−0.1	1.0	0.4	−0.1
PPG, private creditors (NFL, US$)	3.2	1.2	−3.6	2.5	2.7	3.9	10.2	−2.1
PPG, bonds (NFL, US$)	0.5	1.4	−3.4	3.1	4.0	3.5	10.3	−1.3
PPG, commercial banks (NFL, US$)	2.4	0.1	0.3	−0.1	−0.2	0.1	0.1	−0.4
PNG, total private nonguaranteed (NFL, US$)	1.9	1.8	3.1	0.0	2.6	1.2	2.0	7.0
PNG, bonds (NFL, US$)	0.2	0.6	2.6	5.8	3.6	0.2	1.1	1.7
PNG, commercial banks (NFL, US$)	1.7	1.2	0.4	−5.8	−1.0	1.0	0.9	5.3
Short-term debt net flows (NFL, US$)	7.4	5.8	2.7	11.7	3.1	−2.0	−7.5	−2.0
Commitments, official creditors (COM, US$)	5.9	5.2	3.3	2.0	3.5	15.2	0.9	1.9
Commitments, private creditors (COM, US$)	6.6	4.5	4.3	6.8	7.3	9.4	22.9	13.4

[a]All currency units in US$ billions.

Source: World Bank, *Global Development Finance Database 2002.*

panics in Argentina, Brazil, and the Philippines in 1995. All the countries that succumbed to these waves of panic were vulnerable due to their weak banking systems, large appreciations in their real exchange rates, and low levels of foreign exchange reserves.

Aftermath

On January 2, 1995, the United States, other major governments, and a few large private banks committed an $18 billion line of credit to Mexico. However, this amount, added to what was left in Mexico's reserves, could barely cover half of the country's financial obligations. To avoid a "systemic global financial debacle," the Clinton administration put together a direct loan package that included $20 billion from the U.S., $18 billion from the IMF, and $13 billion from the Bank for International Settlements, totaling over $50 billion.

The large loan packages paid virtually all outstanding Tesobonos. By the beginning of 1996, the crisis had smoothed out and growth had returned to the region. By mid-1996, the economy recovered, with inflation levels the lowest they had been since the crisis, a 4.5% growth rate and 4.1% unemployment. By the beginning of 1997, investors were once again bullish about Mexico and capital inflows had increased.

Asian Financial Crisis (1997)[3]

Rooted in the private sector, the Asian financial crisis started in June 1997 and caught the international market by surprise with its reach and severity. Like Latin American in 1982 and Mexico in 1994, the Asian financial debacle was a twin crisis, one that encompassed both currency upheavals and serious banking sector problems. Investors became wary of the region's ability to pay its debts in March 1997 when the Thai real estate bubble burst and debtors began missing loan payments. This set off a massive speculative attack on the baht. The crisis quickly spread to the Philippines, Malaysia, Indonesia, and Korea and, by October of that year, currencies in these countries had depreciated by an average of 40%. The initial currency crisis deepened into a simultaneous debt crisis when currency devaluations sharply increased real debt burdens. Many Asian banks and firms had taken on large amounts of foreign-denominated debt so devaluations in local currencies effectively made service of foreign debt much more expensive. (See Exhibit 4 for a debt table for the Asian crisis.)

Few investors anticipated such a crisis because Asia had had a long track record of economic success, with good fundamentals and a surplus in fiscal balances. In fact, the region enjoyed an enormous inflow of foreign capital up until the outbreak of the crisis, with $106.6 billion in external financing in 1996 and $40.5 billion in private flows. However, by 1997, the entire landscape had changed, with only $28.8 billion in external financing and $1.1 billion in private capital flowing into the region. The decline in external financing within a period of six months was equal to approximately 10% of the combined GDP of the five hardest hit countries. Looking back, analysts have attributed the crisis to an overvaluation of local currencies pegged to the dollar, excessive economic growth targets and correspondingly poor government policies, and investor panic and herd behavior.

[3]Drawn from: Nouriel Roubini, "An Introduction to Open Economy Macroeconomics, Currency Crises and the Asian Crisis", ⟨http://pages.stern.nyu.edu/~nroubini/NOTES/⟩; Steven Radelet and Jeffrey Sachs, "The East Asian Financial Crisis: Diagnosis, Remedies, Prospects," *Brookings Papers on Economic Activity*, 1998(1): 1-74; and Suk H. Kim and Magfuzul Haque, "The Asian Financial Crisis of 1997: Causes and Policy Responses," *Multinational Business Review* (Spring 2000).

EXHIBIT 4

DEBT TABLE FOR ASIAN FINANCIAL CRISIS (1997)[b]

	1994	1995	1996	1997	1998	1999	2000	2001
Current account balance (US$)	−22.2	−39.1	−53.8	−26.4	69.8	63.2	46.4	26.2
International reserves (RES) (US$)	102.8	117.1	131.8	95.0	142.3	182.2	203.1	210.4
Total amount of debt rescheduled (US$)	0.0	0.0	0.0	0.0	25.6	5.1	2.3	2.8
Total change in debt stocks (DOD, US$)	64.4	66.9	55.0	38.5	10.2	−12.9	−28.9	−35.4
Debt outstanding (LDOD), total long-term (US$)	222.3	252.5	271.4	307.4	361.7	361.6	334.0	314.9
Private sector LDOD (US$)	79.9	105.3	129.0	152.7	178.6	158.2	139.8	129.6
Public sector LDOD (US$)	142.4	147.1	142.4	154.7	183.2	203.4	194.2	185.3
Short-term debt outstanding (DOD, US$)	92.2	129.2	165.6	151.2	93.6	89.9	88.6	81.3
Short-term debt/Total debt (EDT) (%)	28.4	30.8	34.4	31.0	19.2	17.8	18.0	18.4
Aggregate net resource flows (US$)	44.7	46.1	64.2	50.0	23.6	14.9	16.3	4.6
Private net resource flows (US$)	42.3	44.9	65.3	38.6	13.5	4.7	12.2	1.8
Foreign direct investment, net inflows (US$)	10.2	13.8	17.5	17.8	16.8	17.3	13.1	6.1
Portfolio equity flows (US$)	13.3	10.0	11.8	−6.8	−0.3	12.9	10.9	10.1
Official net resource flows (US$)	2.3	1.2	−1.2	11.4	10.1	10.2	4.2	2.8
Multilateral debt/Total debt (EDT) (%)	10.8	9.8	8.4	7.8	9.0	9.4	9.4	9.8
Reserves (RES)/Total debt (EDT) (%)	39.8	36.0	35.4	23.4	33.0	42.6	47.4	52.8
Total debt (EDT)/GNI (%)	46.0	46.6	46.4	55.4	87.8	70.8	62.8	61.2

(Continued)

EXHIBIT 4   (Continued)

DEBT TABLE FOR ASIAN[a] FINANCIAL CRISIS (1997)[b]

	1994	1995	1996	1997	1998	1999	2000	2001
Total debt (EDT)/Exports of goods and services (XGS) (%)	122.4	114.6	117.0	114.8	132.4	123.4	97.2	103.0
Debt service (TDS)/Exports of goods and services (XGS) (%)	15.8	14.6	16.2	14.0	16.2	19.2	13.8	17.6
Interest (INT)/Exports of goods and services (XGS) (%)	6.0	6.0	5.8	5.6	6.4	6.0	5.4	5.0
Net flows on debt, total (NFL, US$)	47.6	58.3	70.4	41.5	−11.9	−29.4	−9.6	−27.8
Net flows on debt, total long-term (NFL, US$)	20.5	21.6	34.4	38.5	6.5	−15.9	−8.3	−12.0
PPG, total public and publicly guaranteed (NFL, US$)	4.4	5.7	4.9	22.5	18.0	−3.1	−7.4	−1.6
PPG, official creditors (NFL, US$)	1.7	0.6	−1.7	10.9	9.6	9.5	3.6	2.3
PPG, bilateral (NFL, US$)	2.2	0.6	−0.2	5.5	2.5	6.8	3.4	2.5
PPG, multilateral (NFL, US$)	−0.5	0.0	−1.5	5.4	7.1	2.7	0.1	−0.2
PPG, private creditors (NFL, US$)	2.7	5.1	6.6	11.6	8.5	−12.6	−11.0	−3.9
PPG, bonds (NFL, US$)	3.0	6.4	8.8	9.3	3.7	2.6	1.2	−0.6
PPG, commercial banks (NFL, US$)	−0.2	0.3	−2.1	1.4	4.9	−14.7	−12.2	−3.1
PNG, total private nonguaranteed (NFL, US$)	16.1	15.9	29.5	16.0	−11.5	−12.8	−0.9	−10.4
PNG, bonds (NFL, US$)	12.7	8.8	16.1	11.1	−3.4	−2.2	−0.9	0.4
PNG, commercial banks (NFL, US$)	3.4	7.2	13.4	5.0	−8.1	−10.6	0.0	−10.8
Short-term debt net flows (NFL, US$)	27.3	37.1	36.3	−14.3	−30.7	−5.1	−2.5	−7.5
Commitments, official creditors (COM, US$)	11.4	11.4	8.5	18.1	19.7	23.5	4.7	7.6
Commitments, private creditors (COM, US$)	13.0	14.1	16.2	16.6	12.3	13.1	9.7	8.2

[a]Data included for five Asian countries: Indonesia, Korea, Malaysia, Philippines, and Thailand.
[b]All currency units in US$ billions.

Source: World Bank, Global Development Finance Database 2002.

The Asian financial crisis caused currency values and stock prices in Asia to plunge between 40% to 80%, forced numerous bank closures and company bankruptcies, reached countries as far off as Brazil and, in total, pushed one third of the world into recession during 1998.

Aftermath

Before the crisis, capital flowing into Asia from official creditors such as the IMF and World Bank was negligible. After the crisis broke out, official monies jumped significantly to help contain the situation. Toward the end of 1997, the IMF had signed three emergency lending agreements for an unprecedented sum of international financial support to the countries hardest hit by the crisis: Thailand with $17 billion, Indonesia with $35 billion, and Korea with $57 billion. These loan packages came with stringent requirements, but the IMF-enforced policies failed to restore investor confidence in Asian markets or stabilize exchange rates. Currencies continued to fall until December 1997, when the IMF modified its policies and applied an approach based on debt restructuring and negotiation with private creditors.

The U.S. tried a new method with Korea. It obliged foreign commercial banks to roll over Korea's debt instead of waiting for market confidence to be restored before the country could access the capital markets again. Korea and its creditors initially announced a standstill on debt servicing then, in January of 1998, formally agreed to a complete rollover of all short-term debt due in the first quarter of that year. The framework, based on U.S. Chapter 11 bankruptcy procedures, presented a way to solve sovereign debt crises that relied on private sector funds rather than on bailout loans from the IMF.

Private capital from debt restructuring arrangements and public funds and policy guidance from IMF consultants enabled the affected countries to reschedule short-term foreign debt and reduce their reliance on foreign capital. They also reformed their banking systems so that their capital adequacy ratio was in line with the standard set by the Bank for International Settlements. Finally, they instituted reforms in the corporate sector, eliminating excess capacity and strengthening corporate governance.

Recent Developments

In 2001 and 2002, sovereign financial crises were still at the forefront of the international economic consciousness. According to Standard and Poor's, the rate of default by sovereign governments was on the rise, although at 13.4%, it was only one third of what it was at its peak of 31% in the 1980s. (See Exhibits 5, 6, and 7 for rates of sovereign debt defaults.) In 2002, over 27 countries defaulted on their loans, cumulating in a value of almost $133 billion in unpaid debts. (See Exhibits 8, 9, and 10 for the number of sovereign debt defaults and the amount of debt.) The existing approaches to sovereign debt restructuring came under increasing scrutiny with each new crisis.

EXISTING FRAMEWORK FOR SOVEREIGN DEBT RESTRUCTURING

The special characteristics of sovereign debt made the problem of debt restructuring complex. Sovereign debtors enjoyed considerable immunity compared to individual or corporate debtors. Creditors had a very limited ability to seize assets in a sovereign default. Furthermore, unlike corporate bankruptcy proceedings, creditors could not demand a 'change in management.' Counterbalancing the very real power of sovereigns was creditors' ability to refuse future loans, or demand high risk premiums. Sovereigns

EXHIBIT 5

SOVEREIGN DEFAULT RATES

Year	Number of Issuers	All Issuers in Default[a]	New Issuers in Default[a]	All Foreign Currency Debt[a,b]	Foreign Currency Bonds[a]	Local Currency[a]
1975	164	2.4	1.2	1.2	0.6	1.2
1976	165	2.4	0.6	2.4	0.6	0.6
1977	166	2.4	0.0	1.8	0.6	0.6
1978	169	4.7	2.3	4.1	0.6	0.6
1979	173	6.4	2.3	5.8	0.6	1.2
1980	174	6.3	1.7	5.7	0.6	0.6
1981	176	10.2	6.3	9.1	0.0	1.1
1982	176	15.9	5.7	15.3	0.0	1.7
1983	177	24.9	10.2	23.7	0.0	1.1
1984	178	25.3	1.1	23.6	0.6	1.7
1985	178	24.7	2.8	24.2	0.6	1.1
1986	179	28.5	5.6	27.9	0.6	1.7
1987	179	30.7	3.3	29.1	1.1	2.2
1988	179	30.2	1.7	29.6	1.1	1.1
1989	179	30.2	1.7	29.1	2.2	1.7
1990	178	30.9	2.2	29.8	1.1	2.8
1991	198	27.3	3.0	26.8	1.0	1.5
1992	198	29.3	3.5	28.8	2.0	1.5
1993	200	27.5	1.0	27	1.5	2.0
1994	201	25.4	0.5	24.9	1.5	2.0
1995	201	23.4	1.5	21.9	1.5	3.0
1996	201	22.4	1.0	20.4	1.5	3.5
1997	201	17.9	1.0	15.9	1.5	3.0
1998	201	17.4	2.5	14.9	2.5	4.0
1999	201	15.4	1.5	13.9	2.5	3.5
2000	201	14.9	2.0	12.9	2.5	2.5
2001	201	13.4	0.5	12.4	1.5	1.5
2002	202	13.9	3.0	13.4	2.0	2.0

[a]% of all sovereign issuers.

[b]Bank debt and bonds.

Source: Standard & Poor's, "Sovereign Defaults: Moving Higher Again in 2003?" *RatingsDirect*, 24 September 2002 reproduced with permission of Standard & Poor's, a division of The McGraw-Hill Companies, Inc.

had a powerful incentive to meet their debt obligations so that they could maintain access to international capital markets.

The existing framework for sovereign debt restructuring included international financial institutions such as the IMF and World Bank, but there was no standard approach to resolving a sovereign debt crisis. When a financial crisis did occur, sovereigns

EXHIBIT 6

RATES OF SOVEREIGN DEFAULTS (1824–2002)

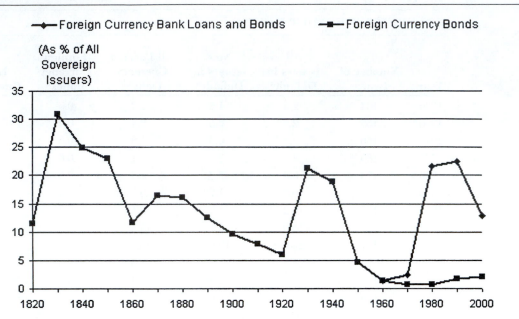

Source: Standard & Poor's, "Sovereign Defaults: Moving Higher Again in 2003?" *RatingsDirect*, 24 September 2002 reproduced with permission of Standard & Poor's, a division of The McGraw-Hill Companies, Inc.

EXHIBIT 7

RATE OF SOVEREIGN DEFAULTS (1975–2002)

Source: Standard & Poor's, "Sovereign Defaults: Moving Higher Again in 2003?" *RatingsDirect*, 24 September 2002 reproduced with permission of Standard & Poor's, a division of The McGraw-Hill Companies, Inc.

EXHIBIT 8

NUMBER OF COUNTRIES WITH SOVEREIGN DEBT DEFAULTS BY YEAR

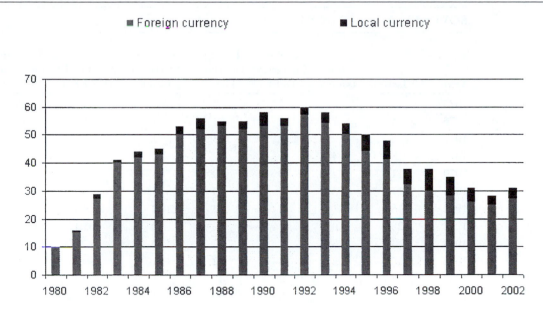

Source: Standard & Poor's, "Sovereign Defaults: Moving Higher Again in 2003?" *RatingsDirect,* 24 September 2002 reproduced with permission of Standard & Poor's, a division of The McGraw-Hill Companies, Inc.

EXHIBIT 9

AMOUNT OF SOVEREIGN DEBT IN DEFAULT (1980–2002)

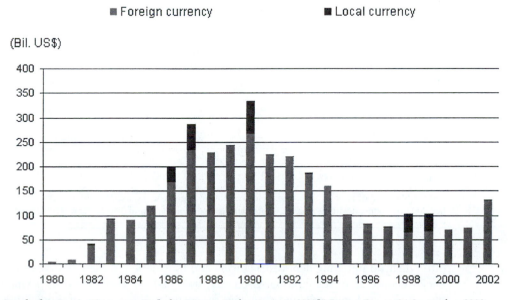

Source: Standard & Poor's, "Sovereign Defaults: Moving Higher Again in 2003?" *RatingsDirect,* 24 September 2002 reproduced with permission of Standard & Poor's, a division of The McGraw-Hill Companies, Inc.

EXHIBIT 10

SOVEREIGN DEBT IN DEFAULT

Year	All Issuers	New Issuers	Local Currency Debt	Foreign Currency Debt[a]	Foreign Currency Bonds	Total Debt (Bil US$)	Avg. Debt per Issuer (Bil. US$)
1975	4	2	2	2	1	2.4	0.8
1976	4	1	1	4	1	1.5	0.5
1977	4	0	1	3	1	1.6	0.5
1978	8	4	1	7	1	4.5	0.6
1979	11	4	2	10	1	6.9	0.7
1980	11	3	1	10	1	5.1	0.5
1981	18	11	2	16	0	9.4	0.5
1982	28	10	3	27	0	41.1	1.4
1983	44	18	2	42	0	93.0	2.1
1984	45	2	3	42	1	90.7	2.0
1985	44	5	2	43	1	120.5	2.7
1986	51	10	3	50	1	198.8	3.8
1987	55	6	4	52	2	287.6	5.1
1988	54	3	2	53	2	228.3	4.2
1989	54	3	3	52	4	243.7	4.4
1990	55	4	5	53	2	334.6	5.8
1991	54	6	3	53	2	225.2	4.0
1992	58	7	3	57	4	219.8	3.7
1993	55	2	4	54	3	187.2	3.2
1994	51	1	4	50	3	160.4	3.0
1995	47	3	6	44	3	100.5	2.0
1996	45	2	7	41	3	82.2	1.7
1997	36	2	6	32	3	75.6	2.0
1998	35	5	8	30	5	102.6	2.7
1999	31	3	7	28	5	103.2	2.9
2000	30	4	5	26	5	70.6	2.3
2001	27	1	3	25	3	74.2	2.7
2002[b]	28	6	4	27	4	132.6	4.3

[a]Bank debt and bonds.

[b]Through third quarter 2002.

Source: Standard & Poor's, "Sovereign Defaults: Moving Higher Again in 2003?" *RatingsDirect,* 24 September 2002 reproduced with permission of Standard & Poor's, a division of The McGraw-Hill Companies, Inc.

often delayed initiating debt restructuring and thus depleted their reserves and experienced economic destabilization. Creditors, who had no assurance of repayment, employed various legal and other strategies to maximize the amount of money they could recover, and their actions frequently exacerbated the crisis. Orderly and efficient sovereign debt restructuring was the exception rather than the rule.

Institutions[4]

In 1944, in the aftermath of the Great Depression and two world wars, economists from the United States and the United Kingdom initiated a meeting to create an international institution that would guide a new economic world order. In 1944, representatives from 44 countries gathered in Bretton Woods, New Jersey to establish the International Monetary Fund (IMF) and the International Bank for Reconstruction and Development (IBRD), the precursor of the modern-day World Bank Group.

International Monetary Fund

Starting with 44 members in 1944, the IMF had grown to 182 member countries by 2000. The IMF was owned by member governments and represented by a Board of Governors. (See Exhibit 11 for an organization chart for the IMF.) Governors for each country were ministers of finance (the Governor for the U.S. was the Secretary of the Treasury), and their votes were set in accordance with their country's GDP and financial contribution. This allocation system meant that the U.S. and other wealthy nations had a much higher representation in these institutions than in organizations such as the U.N., where each country had equal representation. Recommendations for IMF action were made by the Interim Committee, a group of 24 Governors that met twice a year and reported to the membership. Day-to-day operations were executed by a panel of 25 Executive Directors (the Executive Board), composed of 20 elected Governors and five Governors from the IMF's five largest shareholders.

The IMF, as the "overseer of the code of conduct" in international economic relations, provided a "good housekeeping seal of approval" on sovereign borrowers, signaling credit-worthy investments for private lenders. It acted as a negotiator and coordinator of creditors and debtors in debt crises and solved collective action problems by arranging concerted lending. A country in a balance of payment predicament or on the verge of imminent debt default could request IMF funding. The country could also take out IMF loans in set amounts, determined by its level of contribution to the organization. However, if its loans exceeded this proportional amount, the IMF could impose more stringent conditions on the recipient country. The IMF also provided emergency assistance and liquidity to emerging countries in financial crisis, as well as advice and technical assistance on policy reform to correct structural imbalances.

World Bank

Like the IMF, the World Bank secured funding through member countries' contributions and voting was proportional to GDP. Each member country was represented by its own Governor, which all together formed the Board of Governors. (See Exhibit 12 for an organization chart for the World Bank.) A group of Executive Directors, composed of select country representatives, managed the organization. Five distinct institutions, described in Exhibit 13, composed the World Bank Group. Together, these institutions coordinated their efforts to reduce poverty and improve standards of living world-wide.

---

[4]Drawn from Michael D. Bordo and Harold James, "The International Monetary Fund: Its Present Role in Historical Perspective", NBER Working Paper No. 7724, June 2000 and Anne O. Krueger, "Whither the World Bank and the IMF?" NBER Working Paper No. 6327, December 1997.

EXHIBIT 11

ORGANIZATION CHART OF THE INTERNATIONAL MONETARY FUND
(APRIL 30, 2001)

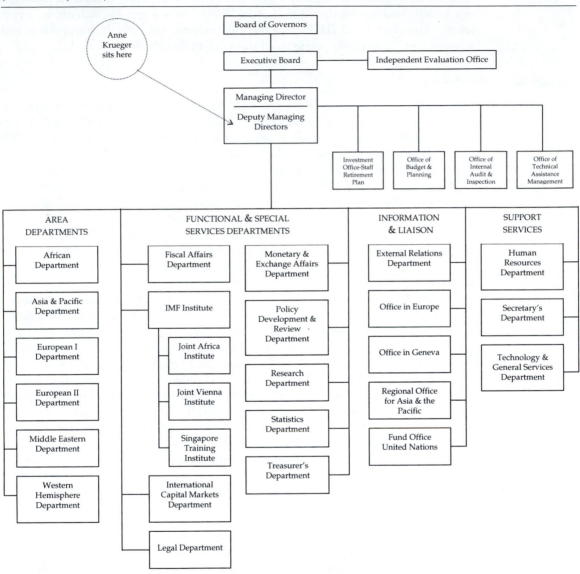

Source: IMF Web site at http://www.imf.org/external/np/obp/orgcht.htm.

The organization most relevant to the sovereign debt restructuring debate was the International Centre for Settlement of Investment Disputes (ICSID). ICSID was created in 1966 to help mediate investment disputes between sovereign debtors and private foreign investors. It was hoped that this more streamlined resolution process would help increase the flow of international investment.

EXHIBIT 12

ORGANIZATION CHART OF THE WORLD BANK

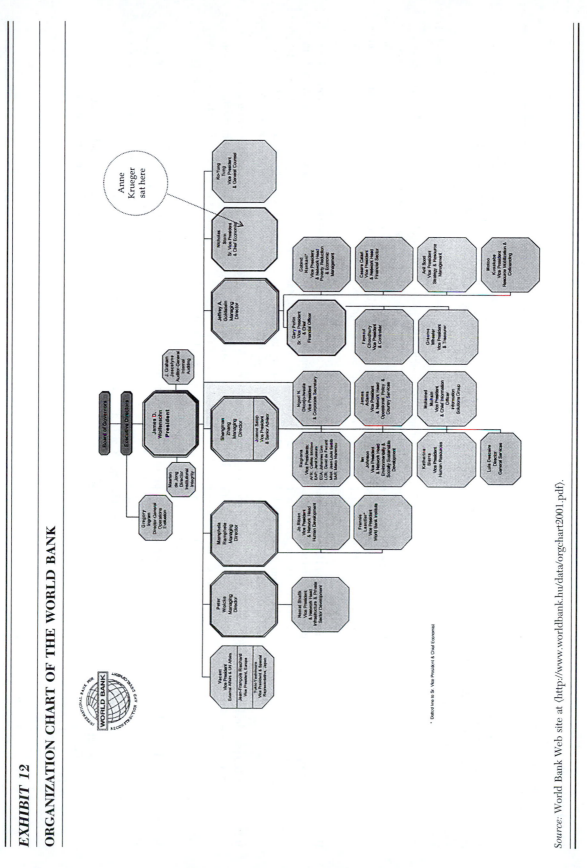

Source: World Bank Web site at ⟨http://www.worldbank.hu/data/orgchart2001.pdf⟩.

473

EXHIBIT 13

THE WORLD BANK GROUP

The World Bank Group

The World Bank Group consists of five closely associated institutions, all owned by member countries that carry ultimate decision-making power. Each institution plays a distinct role in the mission to fight poverty and improve living standards for people in the developing world.
The term "World Bank Group" encompasses all five institutions.
The term "World Bank" refers specifically to two of the five, IBRD and IDA.

IBRD	The International Bank for Reconstruction and Development	IBRD aims to reduce poverty in middle-income and creditworthy poorer countries by promoting sustainable development, through loans, guarantees, and nonlending—including analytical and advisory—services. IBRD does not maximize profit but has earned a net income each year since 1948. Its profits fund several developmental activities and ensure financial strength, which enables low-cost borrowings in capital markets, and good terms for borrowing clients. Owned by member countries, IBRD links voting power to members' capital subscriptions—in turn based on a country's relative economic strength.
IDA	The International Development Association	Contributions to IDA enable the World Bank to provide $6–7 billion per year in interest-free credits to the world's 78 poorest countries, home to 2.4 billion people. This support is vital because these countries have little or no capacity to borrow on market terms. In most of these countries incomes average under just $500 a year per person, and many people survive on much less. IDA helps provide access to better basic services (such as education, health care, and clean water and sanitation) and supports reforms and investments aimed at productivity growth and employment creation.
IFC	The International Finance Corporation	IFC's mandate is to further economic development through the private sector. Working with business partners, it invests in sustainable private enterprises in developing countries and provides long-term loans, guarantees, and risk management and advisory services to its clients. IFC invests in projects in regions and sectors underserved by private investment and finds new ways to develop promising opportunities in markets deemed too risky by commercial investors in the absence of IFC participation.
MIGA	The Multilateral Investment Agency	MIGA helps encourage foreign investment in developing countries by providing guarantees to foreign investors against losses caused by noncommercial risks, such as expropriation, currency inconvertibility and transfer restrictions, and war and civil disturbances. Furthermore, MIGA provides technical assistance to help countries disseminate information on investment opportunities. The agency also offers investment dispute mediation on request.
ICSID	The International Centre for Settlement of Investment Disputes	ICSID helps to encourage foreign investment by providing international facilities for conciliation and arbitration of investment disputes, in this way helping to foster an atmosphere of mutual confidence between states and foreign investors. Many international agreements concerning investment refer to ICSID's arbitration facilities. ICSID also has research and publishing activities in the areas of arbitration law and foreign investment law.

Source: World Bank Web site, "About Us" section at ⟨http://www.worldbank.org/⟩.

EXHIBIT 14

PARIS CLUB RESCHEDULINGS

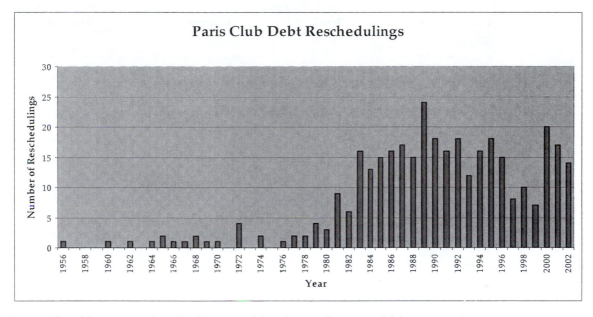

Source: Adapted by casewriter from data from Paris Club Web site at ⟨http://www.clubdeparis.org/en/presentation/presentation.php⟩. accessed: January 21, 2003.

Paris Club[5]

In seeking debt restructurings, countries sometimes turned to the Paris Club, an informal group of official creditors that negotiated over 360 debt rescheduling agreements for 78 debtor countries between 1956 and 2002. (See Exhibits 14 and 15 for details on Paris Club debt reschedulings.) The first Paris Club meeting occurred in 1956 when Argentina and its creditors agreed to meet in Paris to reach a debt rescheduling agreement. The term "Paris Club" was coined and simply referred to the meeting of debtor and creditors in Paris. Since then, the Paris Club evolved into an entity with more structure, while still retaining its ad-hoc, flexible nature. (See Exhibit 16 for details on the different types of Paris Club restructuring treatments.) There were 19 permanent members, who were large creditor governments. A handful of other governments participated in select negotiations due to their involvement with the debt negotiations. Only the countries who were in debt or who had debt owed to them participated in any given meeting. The Paris Club negotiated only for sovereign creditors, regardless of whether the debtors were from the public or private sectors. However, for cases involving commercial bank debt restructuring, the Paris Club had a sister organization, the London Club, which negotiated on behalf of private creditors. (See Exhibit 17 for a comparison of the Paris Club and London Club.)

[5]Drawn from the Paris Club website, ⟨www.clubdeparis.org⟩ and Alexis Rieffel, "The Role of the Paris Club in Managing Debt Problems," Princeton University International Finance Section's Essays in International Finance, No. 161 (Princeton, NJ: Princeton University, 1985).

EXHIBIT 15

PARIS CLUB DEBTOR COUNTRIES

By # of Paris Club Reschedulings		By Country	
Countries	# of Paris Club Reschedulings	Countries	# of Paris Club Reschedulings
Angola	1	Albania	3
Croatia	1	Algeria	2
Djibouti	1	Angola	1
El Salvador	1	Argentina	8
Gambia	1	Benin	5
Georgia	1	Bolivia	8
Guatemala	1	Bosnia	2
Haiti	1	Brazil	6
Kirgyzstan	1	Bulgaria	3
Sao Tome	1	Burkina Faso	5
Ukraine	1	Cambodia	3
Viet Nam	1	Cameroon	6
Yugoslavia	1	Central African Republic	7
Algeria	2	Chad	4
Bosnia	2	Chile	5
Dominican Republic	2	Congo	4
Egypt	2	Costa Rica	5
Kenya	2	Cote D'lvoire	9
Macedonia	2	Croatia	1
Panama	2	Djibouti	1
Romania	2	Dominican Republic	2
Rwanda	2	Ecuador	7
Somalia	2	Egypt	2
Trinidad	2	El Salvador	1
Albania	3	Equatorial Guinea	4
Bulgaria	3	Ethiopia	4
Cambodia	3	Ex-Yugoslavia	4
Ghana	3	Gabon	7
Mexico	3	Gambia	1
Turkey	3	Georgia	1
Yemen	3	Ghana	3
Chad	4	Guatemala	1
Congo	4	Guinea	6
Equatorial Guinea	4	Guinea-Bissau	4
Ethiopia	4	Guyana	5
Ex-Yugoslavia	4	Haiti	1
Guinea-Bissau	4	Honduras	4
Honduras	4	Indonesia	7
Liberia	4	Jamaica	7
Malawi	4	Jordan	6

(Continued)

EXHIBIT 15   (Continued)

PARIS CLUB DEBTOR COUNTRIES

By # of Paris Club Reschedulings		By Country	
Countries	# of Paris Club Reschedulings	Countries	# of Paris Club Reschedulings
Nicaragua	4	Kenya	2
Nigeria	4	Kirgyzstan	1
Sudan	4	Liberia	4
Benin	5	Macedonia	2
Burkina Faso	5	Madagascar	11
Chile	5	Malawi	4
Costa Rica	5	Mali	5
Guyana	5	Mauritania	8
Mali	5	Mexico	3
Philippines	5	Morocco	6
Russian Federation	5	Mozambique	8
Brazil	6	Nicaragua	4
Cameroon	6	Niger	10
Guinea	6	Nigeria	4
Jordan	6	Pakistan	6
Morocco	6	Panama	2
Pakistan	6	Peru	8
Poland	6	Philippines	5
Central African Republic	7	Poland	6
Ecuador	7	Republic of Congo	10
Gabon	7	Romania	2
Indonesia	7	Russian Federation	5
Jamaica	7	Rwanda	2
Tanzania	7	Sao Tome	1
Argentina	8	Senegal	13
Bolivia	8	Sierra Leone	9
Mauritania	8	Somalia	2
Mozambique	8	Sudan	4
Peru	8	Tanzania	7
Uganda	8	Togo	10
Zambia	8	Trinidad	2
Cote D'lvoire	9	Turkey	3
Sierra Leone	9	Uganda	8
Republic of Congo	10	Ukraine	1
Niger	10	Viet Nam	1
Togo	10	Yemen	3
Madagascar	11	Yugoslavia	1
Senegal	13	Zambia	8

Source: Adapted by casewriter from data from Paris Club Web site at ⟨http://www.clubdeparis.org/en/presentation/presentation.php⟩, accessed: January 21, 2003.

EXHIBIT 16

PARIS CLUB RESTRUCTURING TREATMENTS IN ORDER OF CONCESSIONALITY

Name	Who is it meant for?	Eligibility	Debt Reduction	non-ODA	non-ODA repayment	ODA	ODA repayment	Debt Swaps
Classic	standard middle-income countries	Any country that has an appropriate conditionality program with the IMF that shows need for debt relief i)	0%	rescheduled at standard market interest rates	case-by-case	rescheduled at standard market interest rates	case-by-case	no
Houston	highly indebted lower-middle income countries	GDP per capita less than USD 2995; ii) debt to GDP higher than 50%, debt to exports higher than 275%, scheduled debt service over exports higher than 30%; iii) stock of official bilateral debt of at least 150% of private debt	0%	rescheduled at standard market interest rates payments increasing year by year	15 years with 2–3 years grace and progressive as the original concessional interest rate	rescheduled at an interest rate at least as favourable of 10-year grace	up to 20 years with a maximum	bilateral an voluntary
Naples	highly indebted poor countries	i) GDP per capita less than USD 755; ii) have high level of indebtedness; iii) can only be eligible for World Bank IDA financing. "IDA-only" countries are considered as having few prospects of regaining market access rapidly, because of their low creditworthiness.	67%	"debt reduction option" (DR)—67% of the claims treated are cancelled, the outstanding part being rescheduled at the appropriate market rate; "debt service reduction option" (DSR)—the claims treated at a reduced interest rate	DR option—23 years repayment period with a 6-year grace and progressive payments; DSR option—33 years repayment period with progressive payments	rescheduled at an interest rate at least as favourable as the original concessional interest rate	40 years with 16-year grace and progressive repayment	bilateral and voluntary

(Continued)

EXHIBIT 16 *(Continued)*

PARIS CLUB RESTRUCTURING TREATMENTS IN ORDER OF CONCESSIONALITY

Name	Who is it meant for?	Eligibility	Debt Reduction	Debt Reduction non-ODA	non-ODA repayment	ODA	ODA repayment	Debt Swaps
Cologne	highly impoverished poor countries (HIPCs)	i) have a sound track record with the Paris Club and continuing strong economic adjustment; ii) have been declared eligible to the enhanced HIPC Initiative by the boards of the IMF and the World Bank. This includes low-income countries, who, even with full use of traditional rescheduling debt reduction mechanisms, cannot attain sustainable external debt levels without outside assistance	90% or more if necessary	"debt reduction option" (DR)—90 % or more of the claims treated are cancelled, the outstanding part being rescheduled at the appropriate market rate	23 years repayment period with a 6-year grace and progressive payments	rescheduled at an interest rate at least as favourable as the original concessional interest rate	41 years with 16-year grace and progressive repayment	bilateral and voluntary

Source: Adapted by casewriter from data from Paris Club Web site at ⟨http://www.clubdeparis.org/en/presentation/presentation.php⟩. accessed January 21, 2003.

EXHIBIT 17

PARIS CLUB VS. LONDON CLUB

Club	Creditors	Debtors
Paris	sovereign	public or private
London	private	public or private

Source: Created by casewriter based on information in Alexis Rieffel, "The Role of the Paris Club in Managing Debt Problems," Princeton University International Finance Section's Essays in International Finance, No. 161 (Princeton, NJ: Princeton University, 1985), p. 2.

Paris Club negotiations began when the French Treasury received a formal request from the debtor government to meet with the debtor and its creditors. To qualify for such a meeting, the debtor nation had to prove that it was facing imminent default. Second, the country was required to put an IMF conditionality program in place. Creditor and debtor countries then met in Paris to deliberate, and negotiations resulted in a non-legally binding document, detailing terms that the participating countries had to make official with formal bilateral agreements. Paris Club principles held that the debtor country could not grant another creditor restructuring terms that were more favorable for the debtor than the consensus reached in the Paris Club.

The hallmarks of the Paris Club were its efficiency and adaptability, but the club still faced important challenges. One was the phenomenon of "serial rescheduling," where a country came back year after year to reschedule its debts. Another problem was when a sovereign debtor unilaterally decided to impose terms from Paris Club negotiations on its private creditors, without going through either the London Club or other comparable negotiations. Due to the ad hoc nature of the Paris Club, creditors and international officials lacked enforcement mechanisms to keep countries in check.

The Process of Sovereign Debt Restructuring

The procedures for debt restructuring were highly variable since each default had its own set of circumstances and involved different groups of players. When sovereigns found themselves with balance of payment issues, they approached the IMF for emergency funding. The IMF assessed the country's financial status and determined whether or not it faced imminent default. If the IMF found that the country was indeed in an unsustainable debt situation, it began assembling a loan package for the debtor sovereign. The amount of the loan depended on the debtor's financial health (or lack thereof) and the conditionality plan that the IMF and the sovereign jointly developed. The plan usually called for policy changes such as tighter capital controls, reduced government spending, and exchange rate devaluations, so that the debtor would not continue down an unsustainable path.

After the IMF's official declaration that the sovereign was in trouble, the sovereign began the process of contacting its creditors and negotiating for debt reductions and restructuring. Paths diverged greatly at this point in the process, with some sovereigns using Paris and London Club procedures as vehicles for negotiations. Others requested officials from multilateral institutions such as the IMF and ICSID to arbitrate talks or involved steering committees or different representative bodies to help resolve problems and assess offers. During this negotiation period, sovereigns could unilaterally impose a suspension of debt service to keep creditors and capital invested in the process, but this happened only occasionally.

The negotiation period could be as short as one day (as has been the case for some Paris Club negotiations) or stretch over the course of a few months, depending on how smoothly the talks went. Once everyone agreed to a new set of terms, the IMF reviewed and approved the restructuring plan to ensure that the sovereign's obligations were in line with the conditionality program with regard to sustainability and competent debt service in the future.

A variety of obstacles could hold up the restructuring including creditor disagreement and litigation. A significant development in the mid-1990s was the emergence of "vulture creditors." These were investors who purchased indebted countries' bonds at discounted rates from less patient investors, and then relied on litigation to recover the full repayment amount. In 1983, Peru defaulted on $4.4 billion in debt, and restructuring had stretched into the mid-1990s. In 1995, before the restructuring was complete, Elliott Associates, a hedge fund, bought $55 million of the debt for $11.4 million. Holding up restructuring negotiations, Elliott Associates brought Peru to court in an attempt to recover payment in full. The courts ruled in favor of Elliott Associates and ordered Peru to pay the firm $58 million. While most other commercial creditors were taking a 45% discount on their payment terms, Elliott Associates received a 300% return on its investment, after subtracting litigation expenses.[6]

REFORM OPTIONS

The frequency of sovereign defaults and the subsequent painful restructurings gave rise to an active debate about what types of mechanisms should be used going forward. The goal was to create mechanisms that would lead to earlier restructurings (ideally before a sovereign defaulted on its loans), faster resolutions (therefore minimizing losses for both creditors and debtor), and increased health for the overall international economy.

There were three main reform options, with increasing degrees of legal intervention. The first option depended on market-based mechanisms—improving the processes that were already in place. The second option depended on contractual mechanisms—changing the process by incorporating legal clauses into bond contracts and other debt agreements. The third option was based on statutory mechanisms—changing the process by establishing an entirely new legal structure to govern sovereign debt restructuring.

Market-Driven Mechanisms for Debt Restructuring[7]

Supporters of the status quo argued that the existing market-driven mechanisms already provided an adequate framework for restructuring sovereign debt. Market-driven debt

[6]The ruling depended on a new interpretation of a standard "pari passu" sovereign bond clause. Pari passu stated that all debts held by a debtor had to be ranked equally. The conventional interpretation of the clause was that it provided a protective device for a sovereign's existing creditors: pari passu prevented a debtor nation from giving priority to the claim of a new creditor over the claims of its current creditors. Elliott Associates, however, argued for a novel interpretation of the clause. They contended that Peru had violated pari passu when it paid one group of creditors (those who had agreed to the new restructuring terms) before another (Elliott Associates, who had held out for the original contract terms).

[7]Drawn from Nouriel Roubini, "Do we need a new international bankruptcy regime? Comments on Bulow, Sachs, and White," Draft, Brookings Panel on Economic Activity, Symposium: A Bankruptcy Court for Sovereign Debt, April 4, 2002 available at ⟨http://www.stern.nyu.edu/globalmacro⟩.

restructurings had been successful in countries such as Ukraine, Pakistan, Ecuador, and Russia. In these cases, unilateral exchange offerings, or the replacement of existing bonds with new bonds and terms, had been accepted by very large and heterogeneous groups of creditors. Getting all creditors to agree to restructuring proposals was challenging, but not impossible, especially with the appropriate use of "carrots", or inducements to creditors to agree to settlement, and "sticks", such as the threat to default. Advocates of market-driven mechanisms held that the current system offered flexibility in the negotiation process and permitted the development of new, creative approaches to sovereign debt restructurings. For example, Glenn Hubbard, chairman of the Council of Economic Advisors, proposed that markets could come up with their own forums of negotiation in the form of a private bankruptcy court.[8]

The status quo market-based regime had the advantage of being the only universally recognized model that was already in place. Supporters of this option argued that working for reform and innovation within the existing framework could be more productive than trying to implement controversial new approaches that were as yet unproven.

Contractual Mechanisms for Debt Restructuring[9]

Proponents of contractual mechanisms argued that many of the current problems in debt restructurings could be resolved by including collective action clauses (CACs) in bond and loan contracts. A majority action clause in loan contracts bound all creditors to the decision of a super majority (usually 60%–75%). Such clauses ensured that when a majority of creditors agreed to restructuring proposals, the negotiations could not be blocked by a dissenting minority holding out for better terms. Other types of collective action clauses included engagement clauses, which detailed the process for debtors and creditors coming together to initiate restructuring, and initiation clauses, which defined what should happen in the period after the debtor requested restructuring procedures up to the time when creditors selected a representative to start negotiations.

John B. Taylor of the U.S. Treasury argued that the universal inclusion of CACs in debt contracts would address the current problems of sovereign debt restructuring while retaining the market-based regime. In April 2002, at an Institute for International Economics conference, Taylor commented: "both the contracts and the workout process described by the contracts [were] determined by the borrowers and lenders on their own terms." Sovereign defaults would be dealt with on a case-by-case basis and inconsistencies handled in an arbitration process defined in the contracts.

To create incentives for widespread adoption of these clauses, Taylor suggested that either the official sector could require the clauses to be used by any country that had or was seeking an IMF program, or the IMF could create financial incentives by lowering charges and interest rates for borrowing countries that included these clauses in their debt arrangements. There remained the problem of current debt contracts that did not include CACs. While creditors and debtors could be offered incentives to alter existing contracts to include CACs, they did not have to agree to do so. According to

---

[8]R. Glenn Hubbard, "Enhancing Sovereign Debt Restructuring," Conference on the Sovereign Debt Restructuring Mechanism, International Monetary Fund, Washington, D. C., January 22, 2003 available at ⟨http://www.whitehouse.gov/cea.infenhancingsovereigndebt_jan22_2003.pdf⟩.

[9]Drawn from John B. Taylor (Undersecretary of Treasury for International Affairs), "Sovereign Debt Restructuring: A U.S. Perspective," Conference on Sovereign Debt Workouts: Hopes and Hazards? Institute for International Economics, Washington, D.C., 2 April 2002 available at ⟨http://www.ustreas.gov/press/releases/po2056.htm⟩ accessed 27 Jan 2003.

U.S. Treasury estimates, if existing debt was swapped into bonds containing the clauses and all future contracts included them, the vast majority of bond contracts would be covered within a decade. As CACs had not yet been widely adopted in sovereign debt issues, it was not known how the clauses would be interpreted in different legal jurisdictions.

Statutory Mechanisms for Debt Restructuring[10]

Supporters of a new statutory regime argued that neither existing market-based mechanisms nor contractual mechanisms could fully address the problems that arose when a nation's debt burden became unsustainable. Reliance on market-based mechanisms too often resulted in delayed settlements and unnecessary hardships for both creditors and sovereign debtors. Contractual mechanisms, such as CACS, had long been an option but were not widely used in sovereign debt issues. Even if CACs were included in all bond contracts, the agreements applied only to a specific contract. Most restructurings involved many different bond issues and also bank creditors, and there was the potential for collective action problems across different bond issues.

The sovereign debt restructuring mechanism proposed by Ann Krueger would be a new international legal framework, designed to replicate the features of domestic bankruptcy proceedings in private sector insolvencies for sovereign debtors. There were four key elements in Krueger's plan. The first was the majority restructuring which would allow a "qualified majority" of creditors to bind the minority creditors to a restructuring agreement. The second element was a stay on creditor enforcement, which would prohibit creditors from litigating in the period after a sovereign suspended payments but before a restructuring agreement had been reached. The third element was the protection of creditor interests during suspension of payments and a stay on creditor action. A debtor sovereign would be prohibited from making any payments to "nonpriority creditors" and required to implement an IMF-sponsored or other similar program that ensured the sovereign was pursuing policies that preserved asset values. The final element was a provision for priority financing, which would encourage the lending of new money to debtor sovereigns by private creditors during the stay.

The SDRM addressed many of the same problems as the contractual mechanisms described above, in particular the disruptions and delays that occurred when a minority of creditors refused to agree to terms acceptable to a majority of creditors, causing a delay in restructuring settlements. The specific terms of the collective active clauses in bond agreements, however, were up to creditors and debtors, whereas the SDRM would provide a universal approach to restructuring when sovereign debts became unsustainable.

The proposed statutory regime would be implemented only at the request of the debtor sovereign. After the IMF had made the determination that the sovereign's debt situation was unsustainable, and an IMF conditionality program had been put in place, the sovereign would begin negotiations with its creditors. If the sovereign needed to implement or extend a stay on creditor enforcement, it had to request approval from a majority of creditors. Once satisfactory restructuring terms were reached, the creditor body would approve the plan by majority vote, and the program would be binding on

[10]Based on Anne O. Krueger, "New Approaches to Sovereign Debt Restructuring: An Update on Our Thinking," Speech at the Conference on Sovereign Debt Workouts: Hopes and Hazards, Institute for International Economics, Washington, D.C., April 1, 2002 available at ⟨http://www.imf.org/external/np/speeches/2002/040102.htm⟩.

all bondholders. As the sovereign reinitiated debt service, interim creditors were paid first under the priority financing provision.

Krueger's SDRM would be implemented through universal treaty obligations, most likely through an amendment of the IMF Articles. Such an amendment would achieve "universality in the absence of unanimity"—that is, the decision could be passed and made binding on the entire IMF membership with acceptance by three-fifths of the members, weighted by vote. The amendment would establish a separate judicial organ within the IMF that was completely independent from the influence of the IMF and not subject to IMF review. This judicial organ would oversee the sovereign debt restructuring process to make sure that the SDRM provisions were not abused.

KRUEGER'S CHALLENGE

The International Monetary Finance Committee asked the Fund, and specifically Anne Krueger, to formulate a concrete SDRM proposal by the spring 2003 board meetings. Krueger was determined to present a convincing case for the SDRM. She had to establish that the SDRM had significant advantages over other approaches and reform proposals, and that the establishment of a universal process for sovereign debt restructuring would create important benefits for creditors, debtors, and the international economy. Krueger began reviewing her draft proposal to ensure it met these objectives.

Index